Donated to

Fond du Lac Public Library

Gifts of the

Fox Valley Genealogical Society

LANDHOLDERS

of

NORTHEASTERN NEW YORK

1739-1802

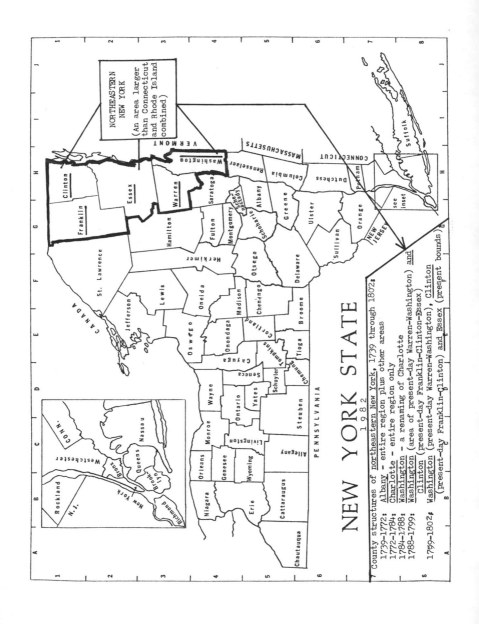

NEW YORK STATE
1982

County structures of northeastern New York, 1739 through 1802:

1739-1772: Albany - entire region plus other areas
1772-1784: Charlotte - entire region only
1784-1788: Washington - a renaming of Charlotte
1788-1799: Washington (area of present-day Warren-Washington) and
           Clinton (present-day Franklin-Clinton-Essex)
1799-1802: Washington (present-day Warren-Washington), Clinton
           (present-day Franklin-Clinton) and Essex (present bounds)

NORTHEASTERN NEW YORK

(An area larger
than Connecticut
and Rhode Island
combined)

LANDHOLDERS

of

NORTHEASTERN NEW YORK

1739-1802

Fred Q. Bowman

Baltimore
GENEALOGICAL PUBLISHING CO., INC.
1987

NOTE

This directory consists of two parts. The first part, pages 3-12, identifies approximately 600 original grantees whose land awards, 1739 through 1775, lay within northeastern New York. The second part, pages 13-209, identifies approximately 9000 persons whose land transactions were completed between 1764 and 1802 within this same region. Northeastern New York as here defined includes all the lands within the present counties of Clinton, Essex, Franklin, Warren, and Washington.

Appendix A, pages 211-13, serves three purposes. It furnishes the dates of organization of all the towns formed in northeastern New York prior to 1803. It indicates the population of the towns of this region as of 1790 and 1800 and it lists by counties the numbers of deeds and mortgage agreements filed in this region from 1772 through 1802 inclusive.

Appendix B discusses the incompleteness in deed filings in northeastern New York within the time period of concern. It provides a list of approximately 250 landholders whose names do not appear elsewhere in the book.

A map opposite the title page delineates the present and early-day counties of northeastern New York. A map on page 4 identifies by name of owner the principal land grants of this region immediately prior to 1779. Additionally, it locates scattered townships, these latter being predecessors of towns in parts of New York. A map on page 210 outlines the thirteen northeastern New York towns formed prior to mid-year 1788.

Part 2, the major segment of this report, reflects the fact that at contract time relatively large numbers of participants lived in northeastern New York. However, residence towns are identified in all the settled regions of early-day New York as well as in ten additional states, the Northwest Territory, Upper and Lower Canada, England, Ireland, Scotland, France, and Germany. Hundreds of family relationships are defined or implied. Frequently, occupations of participants are posted. Occasionally, probate matters are highlighted. Source citations are given for all transactions reported.

1

PART 1
ORIGINAL LANDHOLDERS, 1739-1775

In each of the entries of this section the posting sequence is this: date of award, name of grant, present town of grant's location, acreage, and grantees' names. The symbol X identifies the principal grantee. Name and place indexes are furnished for this section.

> (Source of data: <u>List of Patents of Lands & c To Be Sold in January, 1822, for Arrears of Quit Rent</u>, State Comptroller's Office, undated)

PRINCIPAL LANDHOLDERS OF NORTHEASTERN NEW YORK ABOUT 1775
(present-day Westport southward)

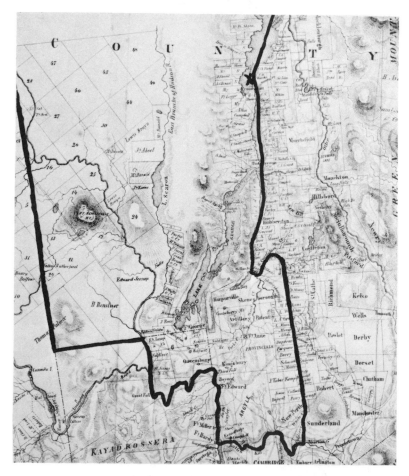

This is a segment of a province-wide map commissioned by Loyalist governor
William Tryon and published in London in 1779. A copy of this map is filed
inside the back cover of the octavo edition of E. B. O'Callaghan's Documentary
History of the State of New York, Volume 1 (Weed Parsons, Albany, 1849).

ORIGINAL LANDHOLDERS, 1739-1775

Present-day Washington County (entries 1 through 39)

1. 6/15/1739 Walloomsack Patent; town of White Creek (also a portion of Hoosick,
   Rensselaer County and a segment in Vermont); 12,000 acres.

   X Collins, Edward   Stuyvesant, Gerardus
     DeLancey, James   Van Rensselaer, Stephen
     Morris, Frederick   Williams, Charles

2. 7/18/1740 John Schuyler's Patent; towns of Argyle and Greenwich; 12,000 acres.

     Bayard, Samuel   X Schuyler, John
     Bayard, Stephen   Schuyler, Philip
     Livingston, John   Stevenson, James

3. 7/1/1743 Stephen Bayard's Patent; town of Argyle, 1300 acres
     Bayard, Stephen

4. 7/23/1761 Cambridge Patent (also known as Sawyer Patent); town of Cambridge
   (major segments in Schaghticoke and Pittstown, Rensselaer County);
   61,000 acres.

     Barber, David   Phelps, Ichabod
     Barber, Stephen   Phelps, Nathaniel
     Beach, Azariah   Pipon, Silas
     Beach, Benjamin   Porter, Increase
     Bleecker, John R.   Post, Israel
     Clinton, George   Post Jazaniah (sic)
     Duwey, Ebenezer   Post, Jedediah
     Filer, Samuel   Post, John
     Gelliet, John   Post, Jordan
     Gilbert, Samuel   Pratt, Elisha
     Gilbert, Samuel, Junr.   Pumroy, Benjamin
     Gilbert, Thomas   Pumroy, Eleazer
     Hosford, Obadiah   Russ, John
     House, Eliphalet   Sawyer, Edward
     Hutchinson, Jonathan   X Sawyer, Isaac
     Ingham, Daniel   Sawyer, John
     Jones, Ezekiel   Sawyer, Thomas
     Jones, Joel   Sumner, Clement
     Jones, Samuel   Sumner, William
     Lansing, Abraham Jacob   Tillotson, Daniel
     Lansingh, Francis   Trumble, Benjamin
     Lansingh, Jacob Abraham   Vandenburgh, Abraham
     Lansingh, Johannes Jacob   Vander Heyden, Derick
     Lothrop, Elijah   Vander Heyden, Jacob
     Marselius, Peter   Wells, Edmund
     Merrill, Gad   Wells, Joseph
     Merrill, John   Wells, Thomas
     Palmer, Stephen   Winne, Levinius
     Peters, John   Winterton, William
     Phelps, Alexander   Wright, Ephraim
     Phelps, David

5. 11/21/1761 Van Corlaer Patent; town of White Creek; 5000 acres.
     Lake, James   Lake, Thomas
     Lake, John   X Van Corlaer, Arent
     Lake, Nicholas, Junr.

6. 5/11/1762 Ryer Schermerhorn Patent (also known as Anaquasankcook Patent);
   "bounded west by Cambridge Patent"; 10,000 acres.

     Lynsen, Joseph   Schermerhorn, Jacob
     Quackenboss, Johannes   X Schermerhorn, Ryer
     Quackenboss, Nicholas   Schermerhorn, William
     Quackenboss, Peter   Smith, John
     Schermerhorn, Freeman   Smith, Thomas

5

7. 5/18/1762 Kingsbury Patent; town of Kingsbury; 10,000 acres.

Bostwick, Daniel	Prindle, John
X Bradshaw, James	Silye, Benjamin
Brownson, Samuel	Silye, Ebenezer
Camp, Israel	Star, Comfort
Canfield, Samuel	Taylor, Daniel
Hitchcock, Isaac	Taylor, Nathanial
Hitchcock, John	Thatcher, Partridge
Hitchcock, Jonathan	Warner, John
Noble, Gideon	Wildman, Benjamin
Noble, Thomas	Wright, Abel
Northrop, Amos	Wright, Kent
Porter, Preserved	

8. 3/13/1764 Argyle Patent (also known as Scotch Patent); town of Argyle; 47,450 acres. This patent granted "in trust for certain persons".

Campbell, Archibald	X Reid, Duncan
Gillaspie, Neil	Shaw, Neil
McNachten, Alexander	

9. 5/2/1764 Provincial Patent (also known as Cockroft Patent); town of Hartford; 26,000 acres.

Bloomer, Joshua	Ellsworth, Verdine
Brewerton, George, the elder	Glazier, Beamsly
Brewerton, George, the younger	Johnson, David, surgeon
Bull, Joseph	Jones, Thomas, surgeon
Byrne, Barnaby	Le Roux, Charles
X Cockroft, William	MacGinnis, Robert
Corsa, Isaac	Middleton, Peter
Corsa, Teunis	Ogden, Jonathan
Dawson, Henry	Rea, Richard
De Forest, Abraham	Snethew, Baruch
Duane, Cornelius	Thody, Michael
Dubois, Peter	Van Zandt, Tobias
Dunbar, George	White, Alexander

10. 5/3/1764 John Taber Kempe's Patent; town of Hebron; 10,200 acres.

Bard, John	Kissam, Benjamin
Cook, Abraham	Lintot, Bernard
Emott, James	Renaudet, Adrian
Frost, Thomas	Rutgers, Adrian
Hicks, Whitehead	Scott, John Morian
Jones, Samuel	Sharpe, Richard
Kempe, Elizabeth	Webb, William
X Kempe, John Taber	Woods, John
Kempe, Philadelphia	

11. 8/23/1764 Duperoon Patent; town of Granville; 2000 acres.

Duperoon, Philip

12. 8/23/1764 Munro Patent; town of Hebron; 2000 acres.

Munro, Harry

13. 8/23/1764 George Schneider Patent; town of Hebron; 2000 acres.

Schneider, George

14. 9/5/1764 De Conti Patent; town of Hebron (also a segment in Vermont); 2000 acres.

De Conti, Peter

15. 10/12/1764 De Forest Patent; town of Hebron; 5000 acres.

Concklin, Thomas	Hun, William
X De Forest, Isaac	Wool, Jeremiah
Hess, Johannes	

16. 10/24/1764 Artillery Patent; town of Fort Ann?; 24,000 acres.

Broune, Joseph	Davies, Thomas
Brown, Henry	Ford, William
Bruce, Archibald	Forman, William
Bruce, William	Godwin, John
Davies, David	Godwin, William

6

```
                    Grant, William              Sidwell, Thomas
                    Kennedy, John               Standish, David
                    Lawson, Francis             Stephens, Francis
                    Marshall, Walter          X Walton, Joseph
                    Mitchelson, Walter          Williamson, John
                    Oram, Samuel                Wilson, John
                    Pearce, Thomas Dean         Wilson, William
```

17. 4/26/1765 Faesch Patent; town of Hebron; 3000 acres.
              Faesch, George

18. 5/3/1765   McCulloch Patent; town of Hebron; 2000 acres.
              McCulloch, Nathaniel

19. 5/10/1765 McCloud Patent; southeastern part of town of Hebron; 200 acres.
              McCloud, Norman

20. 5/10/1765 Reid Patent; town of Hebron (also a segment in Vermont); 200 acres.
              Reid, John

21. 7/12/1765 Robert Munro's Patent; town of Granville; 200 acres.
              Munro, Robert

22. 7/16/1765 Sapeteen Patent; town of Granville; 50 acres.
              Sapeteen, Charles

23. 10/11/1765 James Grant Patent; town of White Creek; 4000 acres.
              Campbell, Archibald   X Grant, James

24. 10/14/1765 Sheriff Patent; town of Hebron; 3000 acres.
              Sheriff, William

25. 10/28/1765 Ecuyer Patent; town of Hampton (also a segment in Vermont);
              "subdivided together as one patent" with Mooney Patent; 3000 acres.
              Ecuyer, Simeon

26. 10/28/1765 Mooney Patent; town of Hampton (also a segment in Vermont);
              "Subdivided together as one patent" with Ecuyer Patent; 2000 acres.
              Mooney, David

27. 10/31/1765 Embury Patent; town of White Creek (also a segment in Vermont);
              8000 acres.
```
                    Cowen, Moses                Wilson, George
                    Embury, Peter               Wilson, James
                  X Embury, Philip              Wilson, John
                    Proctor, Thomas     .       Wilson, Samuel
```

28. 5/7/1767   Sutherland Patent; town of Hebron; 50 acres
              Sutherland, John

29. 2/27/1770 Reade Patent; town of Cambridge; 800 acres.
              Reade, Joseph, Junr.   Van Antwerp, Wilhelmus

30. 4/4/1770   Clark Patent; town of Hebron; 200 acres.
              Clark, John

31. 6/28/1770 Crabtree Patent; town of Salem; 200 acres.
              Crabtree, John

32. 6/28/1770 Law Patent; town of Fort Ann; 50 acres.
              Law, Michael

33. 6/28/1770 McCabe Patent; town of Salem; 100 acres.
```
                    Eaton, Thomas               Ramsay, Charles
                    Hickler, Philip             Swift, John
                  X McCabe, Ross
```

34. 6/28/1770 McFarlan Patent; town of Salem; 100 acres.
              Foy, John   X McFarlan, Archibald

35. 6/28/1770 Rogers Patent; town of Salem; 100 acres.
              Howell, Crismus   X Rogers, Edward

36. 4/17/1771 Lawrence Patent; Westfield-Fort Ann area; two tracts: 1000 acres
              in Washington County and 2000 acres in Warren County.
              Boel, Henry   Tuttle, Stephen
              X Lawrence, John

7

37. 4/1/1772 Hugh Scott's Patent; town of Putnam; 700 acres.
          Barron, William   Meachan, William
          Bickerton, Solomon   Miller, John
          Bridgman, John   Mitchell, William
          Bruckley, John   Monson, William
          Dougherty, John   X Scott, Hugh
          Hodge, John   Tool, William
          McCaber, John   White, Philip

38. 6/9/1774 Foster Patent; town of Salem; 50 acres.
          Foster, Manuel

39. 6/9/1774 Ryles Patent; town of Salem; 50 acres.
          Ryles, Jonathan.

Present-day Warren County (entries 40 through 71)

40. 5/20/1762 Queensbury Patent; town of Queensbury; 23,000 acres.
          Agard, Joshua   Pain, Ezekiel
          Buck, John   Preston, David
          Commins, Daniel   Preston, Ebenezer
          Elliot, Benjamin   Prindle, Aaron
          Graves, Jedediah   X Prindle, Daniel
          Hungerford, Samuel   Seeley, Benjamin
          Hungerford, Thomas   Seeley, John
          Leach, Amos   Tryon, Daniel
          Marsh, Elihu   Wanser, Abraham
          Marsh, Elihu, Junr.   Wanser, Anthony
          Northrop, Thomas   Weeks, Jonathan
          Page, John

41. 5/20/1768 Ebenezer Jessup's Patent; town of Luzerne; 7550 acres.
          Beeckman, Johannes   Johnson, William
          Bishop, Samuel   Jones, Jonathan
          Bleecker, Rutger   Knapp, Timothy
          Hall, Jacob   Matson, Isaac
          Hunter, David   Meyer, Jonas
        X Jessup, Ebenezer   Miller, Dederick
          Jessup, Edward   Murray, James
          Jessup, Joseph, Junr.

42. 5/21/1768 Ebenezer Jessup's Patent; town of Luzerne; 4100 acres.
          Beeckman, Johannes   Johnson, William
          Bleecker, Rutger   Jones, Jonathan
          Dole, James   Knapp, Timothy
          Hall, Jacob   Meyer, Jonas
          Hunter, David   Miller, Dederick
        X Jessup, Ebenezer   Murray, James
          Jessup, Edward   Woort, Cornelius Van Sante
          Jessup, Joseph, Junr.

43. 4/18/1769 McClay Patent; town of Warrensburgh; 200 acres.
          McClay, David

44. 9/27/1769 Ford Patent; town of Bolton; 1600 acres. Combined with Robinson Pat.
          Barnes, Hugh   Hughs, Peter
          Browall, Henry   Killing, John
          Dougherty, Jeremiah   Oates, Edmund
        X Ford, Thomas   Totten, William

45. 9/27/1769 Robinson Patent; town of Bolton; 750 acres. Combined with Ford Pat.
          Aggation, John   Howard, John
          Barnes, Joseph   Mitting, Thomas
          Bears, James   Penny, William
          Broddie, Robert   Prusk, John
          Carr, Thomas   Richardson, Joseph
          Elliott, Hamilton   X Robinson, George
          Frazier, Thomas   Russet, James
          Hooper, John

46. 7/4/1770   Deverick Patent; town of Queensbury; 50 acres.
                Deverick, Nicholas

47. 7/4/1770   Fairlie Patent; town of Queensbury; 200 acres.
                Fairlie, Joseph

48. 7/4/1770   Lowne, Patent; town of Queensbury; 50 acres.
                Lowne, Thomas

49. 7/4/1770   McGowan Patent; "Long Island in Lake George"; 100 acres.
                X McGowan, James   Underwood, George

50. 7/4/1770   Sarson Patent; town of Queensbury; 600 acres.
                Hasborne, Thomas   X Sarson, Paul
                Roach, Price

51. 7/4/1770   Stinson Patent; town of Queensbury; 200 acres
                Stinson, John

52. 3/8/1771   Porter Patent (also known as Non-Commissioned Officers' Patent);
                town of Bolton; 5600 acres.
                Bevan, John   Holland, George
                Boles, John   Kane, John
                Cahoon, Robert   Killpatrick, John
                Clarkson, William   Lewis, John
                Conway, John   Lindale, William
                Crawley, John   Littlewood, John
                Dennison, John   Lomex, Daniel
                Figg, Daniel   Lurkin, John
                Gibson, Barne   Miller, John
                Gillespie, Thomas   X Porter, Thomas
                Graham, Patrick   Proctor, Jonathan
                Hales, George   Reen, John
                Hales, John   Taylor, John
                Haswell, Edward   Thornbury, John

53. 3/28/1771   Garland Patent; town of Bolton; 1000 acres.
                Arnold, Matthew   Pennell, August
                Euler, George   Penter, Frederick
                Fink, Alexander   Rabb, John
                X Garland, Peter   Ridenbugh (sic), Jacob
                Halling, John   Rockstear, Paul
                Hoffman, Valentine   Ruger, Frederick
                Human, John   Thomas, James
                Lood, Casper   Weaver, Daniel
                Lynch, Joseph   Widdershine, Daniel
                Meaton, John   Zimmerman, Henry

54. 3/28/1771   McDonald Patent; town of Bolton; 1600 acres.
                Clark, Alexander   Nowland, William
                X McDonald, Neil   Ritchie, Thomas
                Malco, Frederick   Roost, Leonard
                Mickljohn, Walter   Rose, James

55. 4/5/1771   Mitchell Patent; towns of Bolton and Caldwell; 800 acres.
                Combined with David Smith's Patent below.
                Barron, Andrew   Mahan, Peter
                Braman, Patrick   Manone, Jacob
                Coyce, Jeremiah   X Mitchell, Hill
                Farlow, Charles   Scott, John
                Finney, John   Simon, John
                Ford, Samuel   Wells, William
                Gibson, James   Yeoman, Joseph
                Hitchcock, William   Young, Moses

56. 4/5/1771   David Smith's Patent; towns of Bolton and Caldwell; 2600 acres.
                Combined with Mitchell Patent above.
                Barron, Barnost   McConehy, John
                Bradshaw, James   Moore, Charles
                Crooks, John   Owen, Henry
                Harris, Gerreych   Ray, William

X Smith, David   Tyser, John
  Smith, Edward   Weathers, Richard
  Trestall, Andrew

57. 4/17/1771 Lawrence Patent; 2000 acres in Warren County (town not specified)
and 1000 acres in Washington County's Fort Ann area.
  Boel, Henry   Tuttle, Stephen
X Lawrence, John

58. 5/24/1771 Friend Patent; town of Hague; 200 acres.
  Friend, William

59. 5/24/1771 James Scott's Patent; town of Hague; 100 acres.
  Jackson, Hugh   X Scott, James

60. 4/10/1772 Edward Jessup's Patent; town of Luzerne; 2000 acres.
  Jessup, Ebenezer   X Jessup, Edward

61. 8/4/1774 Dodd Patent, town of Caldwell; 200 acres.
  Dodd, Morris

62. 8/4/1774 McKenzie Patent; town of Caldwell; 200 acres.
  McKenzie, Hector

63. 8/8/1774 Armstrong Patent; town of Caldwell; 200 acres.
  Armstrong, John

64. 8/8/1774 Kelly Patent; town of Caldwell; 50 acres.
  Kelly, Richard

65. 9/10/1774 Hyde Township Patent; town of Thurman; 40,000 acres.

Andrews, Gideon	X Jessup, Edward
Austin, Thomas	Jessup, Joseph, Junr.
Blakeney, Nicholas	Nafe, Jacob, Junr.
Blacklock, John	Nafe, Johannes
Brownson, Samuel	Newstead, John
Butler, John	Peterson, John
Crane, Joseph	Rogers, John
Crosby, William	Sym, Peter
Davids, John I.	Tillman, John
Davis, John	Van Bracklin, Garret
Egberts, Thomas	Van Bracklin, Guysbert
Fairchild, Jesse	Veder, Abraham
Fonda, Adam	Veder, Volckert
Fonda, Douwe	Vrooman, Hendrick
Fonda, Jelles	Vrooman, Hendrick, Junr.
Fonda, John	Vrooman, John Hendrick
Gardinier, Jacob	Wemp, Barent B.
Hansen, Hendrick	Wemp, Hendrick
Hansen, Peter	Wood, Timothy
Jessup, Ebenezer	Wright, Job

66. 10/4/1774 Dartmouth Patent; town of Stony Creek (?) and a segment in
Saratoga County; 47,000 acres.

Abeel, David	Gardner, Jacob
Abeel, Gerrit	Gillilan, John
Abeel, James	Hansen, Peter N.
Abeel, John	Hansen, Richard
Artin, Robert .	Keen, John
Bancker, Evert, Junr.	Kelly, John
Bennet, James	Lansing, Jacob
Bleecker, Rutger	Lansing, Jacob Gerrit
Bowles, John	Lee, John
Byvanck, Evert	Moran, James
Campbell, Archibald	Neilson, John
Cojemans, Samuel S.	Phillips, Thomas
Crossley, William	Phillipse, David
Delamater, John	Phillipse, Volckert
Fonda, John	Reeves, John
Fonda, Yelles	Roberts, Samuel
Gardiner, John	Shaver, Jacob

Stoutenburgh, Peter	X Van Rensselaer, Jeremiah
Sym, Peter	Van Rensselaer, Philip
Tuttle, Stephen	Van Veghten, Anthony
Van Brakelin, Nicholas	Voorhees, John, Junr.
Van Deusen, Matthew	Wood, Timothy
Van Orden, Andrew	Yates, Robert
Van Rensselaer, Henry K.	

67. 1/4/1775   Robertson Patent; town of Luzerne; 200 acres.
                Robertson, Joseph

68. 3/6/1775   Balfour Patent; town of Thurman (?) and a segment in Montgomery
                County; 5000 acres
                Balfour, Henry

69. 3/6/1775   Rutherford Patent; town of Johnsburg (?); 5000 acres.
                Rutherford, Walter

70. 3/25/1775 Goldthwaite Patent; town of Luzerne; 2000 acres.
                Goldthwaite, Joseph

71. 4/10/1775 Ross Patent; town of Luzerne; 2000 acres.
                Ross, James.

Present-day Essex County (entries 72 through 82)

72. 8/7/1764   Robert Grant's Patent; "bounded N. by Allen Campbell, S. by
                Donald Campbell, and E. by Lake Champlain."; 3000 acres.
                Grant, Robert

73. 8/7/1764   McIntosh Patent; town of Ticonderoga; 3000 acres.
                McIntosh, Alexander

74. 4/13/1765 Conolly Patent; town of Willsborough; 2000 acres.
                Conolly, James

75. 4/15/1765 Warton Patent; town of Willsborough; 3000 acres.
                Warton, John

76. 4/16/1765 Ross Patent; town of Willsborough; 2000 acres.
                Ross, James

77. 5/7/1765   Friswell Patent; two tracts: southeast corner of town of Platts-
                burgh (2000 acres) and a segment (1000 acres) in Essex County,
                town not specified.
                Friswell, John

78. 6/6/1765   Montresor Patent; "situate between Peru Bay and Lake Champlain,
                and extending southerly."; 3000 acres.
                Mee, Francis   Wallace, Robert
                X Montresor, John

79. 7/5/1765   Porter Patent; town of Moriah; 200 acres.
                Porter, Benjamin

80. 3/26/1771 Benzell Patent; two tracts: 1025 acres "on the neck of land on
                which Crownpoint stands" and a segment (210 acres) in Vermont.
                X Benzell, Adolphus   Benzell, Anna Ulrica

81. 1/25/1773 Gulse Patent; town of Schroon; 800 acres.
                Duncan, James   McWilliams, Thomas
                X Gulse, William   Stewart, Lodowick

82. 1/25/1773 Shonard Patent; town of Schroon; 200 acres.
                Barber, Edward   Putman, James
                Morrison, Samuel   X Shonard, Frederick.

Present-day Clinton County (entries 83 through 86)

83. 5/7/1765   Friswell Patent; two tracts: southeast corner of town of Platts-
                burgh (2000 acres) and a segment (1000 acres) in Essex County,
                town not specified.
                Friswell, John

84. 5/7/1765   Stewart Patent, northeast corner of town of Peru; 2000 acres.
               Stewart, Peter

85. 3/27/1769 Beekman Patent; town of Plattsburgh; 30,000 acres.

Bancker, Richard
Beeckman, Abraham
Beeckman, James
Beeckman, Mary
Beeckman, William
Beeckman, William, Junr.
Child, Francis
Cobham, James
Delanoy, Abraham
Delanoy, Abraham, Junr.
Ditmars, Johannes
Feris, William
Goelet, Peter
Hammersly, Thomas
Jones, Benjamin
Jones, Elias
Kettletas, Garrit
Kip, John I.
Marschalk, Andrew
Marschalk, Francis
Miller, Eleazer, Junr.
Rutgers, Robert
Suydam, Hendrick
Suydam, Jacobus
Sydell, John
Vanderveer, Cornelius
Vanderveer, Jacobus
Van Dyck, Rudolphus
Voorhees, Adrian
Vredenburgh, John

86. 7/11/1769 Dean Patent; two tracts: town of Chazy (13,410 acres) and a
               segment (16,590 acres) "called Grand Island" in Vermont.

Boyd, Robert
Campbell, William
Carpender, John
Codwise, Christopher
Dean, Elizabeth, Senr.
Dean, Elkanah
Dean, Elkanah, Junr.
Dean, Mary, Senr.
Dean, Nesbitt
Dean, Richard
Dean, William
Duyckinck, Christopher
Forbes, Alex
Everitt, Thomas
Hargrave, Robert
Hay, A. Hawkes
Holland, Thomas
Horsefield, Israel
Joyce, Edward
Keffler, Francis
Rhodes, Thomas
Slack, Richard
Smith, Samuel
Stakes, Benjamin
Stewart, Thomas
Stewart, William
Stocker, James
Strong, Gabriel
Van Dam Nicholas
Waldron, Samuel.

The postings in this section reflect all the transactions of all the grantees, grantors, mortgagees, and mortgagors whose land records were _filed_, 1772 through 1802, in the deed and mortgage books of the northeastern counties of Washington, Clinton, and Essex. Franklin and Warren, as shown on the map facing the title page, today lie in the region of concern. However, since both were formed after 1802, their names are not mentioned in this report.

Frequently in the eighteenth century many years elapsed between the date of a land contract's signing and the date of its filing. Therefore, it is not incongruous to note in Part 2 that many of the documents bear dates within the time span 1764 through 1771 despite the fact that none of these records was filed until after 12 March 1772, the formation date of Washington County.

Concerning the numbered entries in this section the left-margin dates are those of contract signings. _Gee_, _gor_, _mee_, and _mor_ symbolize _grantee_, _grantor_, _mortgagee_, and _mortgagor_ respectively. These postings define the contract roles of the persons whose names immediately follow them. Postings immediately succeeding the columnized names are the residence places of these persons. The underlined expressions indicate land locations.

Key entries, those which contain the land locations and which identify _all_ the transaction participants by name or number, are pre-signalled through the underlining of their left-margin entry numbers. These specialized entries through end-codings (example, D:12) specify the volume and page of the source book. _Gor_-headed entries are drawn from deed books; _mor_-headed from mortgage books. The counties where the books are filed are those noted in the underlined land-location postings. The Charlotte and Albany County lands of reference are filed in Washington County.

Two or more related entries must be reviewed before any land transaction becomes clear. Once the reader has selected an entry, regardless its nature, he is automatically led to its related posting(s). For example, if one starts with the entry for Albert Baker, Jr. which reads

350. 4/29/95 gee Baker, Albert, Junr.; Kingsbury, WAS. See 2348.

he is led to

2348. 4/29/95 gor Everson, Jacob (w. Margaret); Clinton, DUT; _Argyle, WAS_; co-gees 350, 362, 363. (B-2:517)

which in turn refers him to

362. 4/29/95 gee Baker, Caleb; Kingsbury, WAS. See 2348.

and to

363. 4/29/95 gee Baker, Charles; Kingsbury, WAS. See 2348.

From the above four entries one concludes that 29 April 1795 Jacob Everson and his wife Margaret, both of Clinton, Dutchess County, sell a land parcel in Argyle, Washington County, to Albert (Junior), Caleb, and Charles Baker, all three of Kingsbury, Washington County.

It is immaterial whether the reader starts his review with entry number 350, 362, 363, or 2348. Inevitably, the same four elements will be drawn together.

The entry items form a directory of all participants in all land sales and mortgage agreements of record within the time period of concern. For that reason one finds, pertaining to the above transaction, this additional entry:

2349. 4/29/95 gor Everson, Margaret. See 2348.

In the entries of Part 2 persons' names are generally spelled in the form first found on the documents of reference. These symbols and abbreviations are here used:

CHA	- Charlotte County, NY	ESS	- Essex County, NY
CLI	- Clinton County, NY	WAS	- Washington County, NY
Dist.	- District, a subdivision of a county		
Pat.	- a land patent.		

All places in New York, where possible, are posted as town and county (with state deleted) as indicated in "a" below. All out-of-state locations are posted as in "b".

    a) Washington, DUT (town of Washington, Dutchess County, New York)

    b) Poultney, RUT, VT (town of Poultney, Rutland County, Vermont).

Present-day town locations of some of Part 2's outmoded place-names (example, Walloomsack Patent) may be determined through reference to the place index of Part 1.

> Note: Sequentially through time local regions in New York have been defined as patents or manors, precincts, districts, townships, and finally towns. In northeastern New York the first town was formed in 1785 and the thirteenth mid-year 1788. By the end of 1802 the number of such units had increased to twenty-five.

> Cautions: In New York prior to 1772 all records of transactions concerning any lands north of Kingston were indiscriminately filed in Albany. Those relatively few pertaining to northeastern New York, difficult to cull from the massive set, have not been here pursued.

> With few exceptions the data posted in this section have been drawn from the opening lines of the 3550 records reviewed. The detailed land descriptions, found mid-section on most documents, occasionally contain genealogically-significant material. These mid-sections have not been here reviewed.

14

1. 5/1/96   gee Abbot, Adna; Cambridge, WAS. See 8866.
2. 5/1/96   mor Abbot, Adna (w. Anna); Cambridge, WAS; <u>Cambridge Pat., WAS</u>;
                   mee 8867.   (B:82)
3. 1/14/01 gee Abbot, Adnah; Cambridge, WAS. See 672.
4. 5/1/96   mor Abbot, Anna. See 2.
5. 1/14/01 mor Abbott, Adna; Cambridge, WAS; <u>Cambridge, WAS</u>; mee 673. (C:5)
6. 12/19/95 gee Abeel, Christopher, saddler; ---, SAR; See 3673.
7. 12/19/95 mor Abeel, Christopher, saddler; ---, SAR; <u>Saratoga Pat., WAS</u>
                   co-mor 14; mee 3674.   (B:16)
8. 4/19/99 gee Abeel, Christopher, saddler; ---, SAR. See 3667.
9. 5/17/87 mor Abeel, Gertrude. See 11.
10. 5/16/87 mor Abeel, James, merchant; City of N.Y.; <u>"east side of the north
                   branch of hudson's river"</u>; WAS; mee 3569 (mee is executor
                   of the estate of Thomas Harris, dec'd.).   (A:78)
11. 5/17/87 mor Abeel, James (w. Gertrude); ---, ---; <u>Abeel Pat., WAS</u>;
                   mee 1166.   (A:46)
12. 12/25/95 mor Abeel, James; Saratoga, SAR; <u>Saratoga Pat., WAS</u>; mee 2675.
                   Two contracts this date involving these persons. (B:9, C:3)
13. 12/19/95 gee Abeel, William, farmer; ---, WAS. See 3673.
14. 12/19/95 mor Abeel, William, farmer; ---, WAS. See 7.
15. 4/19/99 gee Abeel, William, farmer; ---, WAS. See 3667.
16. 9/11/98 gee Abel, Azel ("alias Simpson Goodspeede"); Orwell, RUT, VT.
                   See 2433.
17. 6/22/01 gee Abel, Azel; Elizabethtown, ESS. See 6417.
18. 5/1/73   mor Abiel, James; New Perth, CHA; <u>New Perth, CHA</u>; mee 1426. (A:8)
19. 6/5/92   --- Ackerson, Johannes. See 8001.
20. 5/11/97 mee Ackley, George; Whitehall, WAS. See 5211.
21. 1/2/02   mee Ackley, Joseph, joiner; Granville, WAS. See 5651.
22. 7/20/87 gee Adams, Andrew; ---, ---. See 100.
23. 1/19/90 mor Adams, Benjamin; Hampton, WAS; <u>---, WAS</u>; mee 6033. (A:186)
24. 4/13/91 gor Adams, Daniel (w. Deborah); Cambridge, WAS; <u>Cambridge, WAS</u>;
                   gee 8058.   (E:362)
25. 4/13/91 gor Adams, Deborah. See 24.
26. 2/26/98 mor Adams, Elijah, farmer; Troy, REN; <u>James Caldwell Pat., WAS</u>;
                   mee 2298.   (C:2)
27. 5/4/97   gee Adams, Elijah, Junr.; ---, REN. See 4066.
28. 1/4/00   gee Adams, Ezekiel, yeoman; Cambridge, WAS. See 4393.
29. 5/4/97   gee Adams, Jacob; ---, REN. See 4066.
30. 7/1/85   gee Adams, Joel; ---, ---. See 7055.
31. 7/11/86 gee Adams, Joel; ---, ---. See 7055.
32. 6/2/87   gee Adams, Joel; ---, ---. See 7055.
33. 12/7/87 mor Adams, Joel, Junr.; Whitehall, WAS; <u>Whitehall, WAS</u>; mee 8564.
34. 2/8/85   gee Adams, John, gentleman; ---, ---. See 5887.   (A:171)
35. 3/15/99 --- Adams, John, dec'd. See 6910.
36. 5/26/01 --- Adams, John, dec'd. See 5570.
37. 9/20/00 gor Adams, Lucretia. See 39.
38. 7/10/90 mor Adams, Parker; Hebron, WAS; <u>Hebron, WAS</u>; mee 1072. (A:231)
39. 9/20/00 mor Adams, Pliny (w. Lucretia); Hampton, WAS; <u>Granville, WAS</u>;
                   gee 989.   (E:46)
40. 8/7/00   gee Adams, Plyni (sic); Hampton, WAS. See 2248.
41. 3/19/99 mor Addams, Elijah; ---, ---; <u>John Houghton's Pat., ESS</u>; mee 2297.
                                                                      (A:1)
42. 2/24/98 mor Addams, Ephraim; Plymouth, WIN, VT; <u>Platt Rogers Pat., CLI</u>;
                   mee 5402.   (A:281)
43. 10/15/90 mee Addams, John; ---, ORA. See 6286.
44. 7/5/91   gor Addams, John; Plattsburgh, CLI; <u>Judd Pat., CLI</u>; gee 2285.
                                                                      (A:526)
45. 7/5/91   mee Addams, John; Plattsburgh, CLI. See 8131.
46. 7/6/91   gor Addams, John; Plattsburgh, CLI; <u>James Judd Pat., ESS</u>;
                   gees (two independent contracts) 8130 (A:21) and 8132 (A:40).
47. 7/6/91   mee Addams, John; Plattsburgh, CLI. See 2286, 2632, 4543, 8133.

48. 2/11/92 gor Addams, John; Plattsburgh, CLI; <u>James Judd Pat., CLI</u>;
 co-gees 3245, 3250. (A:310)
49. 2/11/92 mee Addams, John, yeoman; Plattsburgh, CLI. See 1999, 2466, 3249,
 6652.
50. 3/5/98 mee Addams, John; Plattsburgh, CLI. See 8343.
51. 5/24/02 --- Addams, John; Plattsburgh, CLI. See 6243.
<u>52.</u> 1/29/93 gor Addams, John, Esq., "high sheriff of Clinton County"; ---, ---;
 lands of Simon Metcalf, CLI (a forfeiture); gee 950. (A:289)
53. 11/19/96 mee Addams, John, Esq.; Plattsburgh, CLI. See 1254.
54. 5/1/94 mee Addams, Jonas; ---, ---. See 7867.
<u>55.</u> 5/27/00 gor Addams, Jonas; ---, ---; <u>Plattsburgh, CLI</u>; co-gors 6242, 507;
 gee 382 (Addams and co-gor 6242 are "acting executors of
 the estate of Simon R. Reeve late of the County of Hunterdon
 (NJ), deceased") (B:269)
56. 7/7/99 gee Adgate, Asa; ---, ESS. See 57.
<u>57.</u> 7/7/99 gor Adgate, Mathew; Canaan, COL; <u>"southerly end of an Island in</u>
 <u>the River Sable", ESS</u>; gee 56. (A:2)
58. 11/20/00 mee Adgate, Matthew; ---, ---. See 4098.
59. 7/1/00 mor Agarel, Caleb; ---, ---. See 60.
<u>60.</u> 7/1/00 mor Agarel, John; ---, ---; <u>---, ESS</u>; co-mor 59; mee 5572. (A:32)
61. 7/1/00 mor Agarel, John; ---, ---. See 191.
62. 8/29/00 gee Agarel, John; Jay, ESS. See 193.
<u>63.</u> 8/29/00 gor Agarel, John; Jay, ESS; <u>land earlier granted in trust for</u>
 Nathaniel Mallory, ESS; gee 192. (A:4)
64. 1/15/01 mor Agarel, John; ---, ---; <u>Jay, ESS</u>; mee 2313. (A:66)
65. 1/20/84 gee Aiken, Abraham; Dover, DUT. See 2790.
66. 4/14/88 gee Aikens, Stephan; ---, DUT. See 5923.
67. 1/1/00 gee Aingle, Ferdinand; ---, WAS. See 4920.
<u>68.</u> 1/2/00 mor Aingle, Ferdinand; Argyle, WAS; <u>Argyle, WAS</u>; co-mors 1277,
 7269; mee 4921. (C:4)
69. 11/30/96 mee Aken, Jonathan; ---, DUT. See 7969.
70. 12/29/91 gee Akens(?), Edward; ---, ---. See 4878.
71. 7/22/97 mee Akin, John; Pawling, DUT. See 8807.
72. 6/3/97 mee Akin, Jonathan; ---, DUT. See 7347.
73. 7/3/97 mee Akin, Jonathan; ---, DUT. See 2077.
74. 7/4/97 mee Akin, Jonathan; ---, DUT. See 703, 2071, 6228, 6235, 7413
 (five independent contracts).
75. 7/5/97 mee Akin, Jonathan; ---, DUT. See 7575.
76. 7/6/97 mee Akin, Jonathan; ---, DUT. See 3234, 7980 (two independent
 contracts).
'. 7/7/97 mee Akin, Jonathan; ---, DUT. See 5226.
78. 7/8/97 mee Akin, Jonathan; ---, DUT. See 2925, 5493 (two independent
 contracts).
79. 7/21/97 mee Akin, Jonathan; ---, DUT. See 8413.
80. 7/5/98 mee Akin, Jonathan; ---, DUT. See 7396.
<u>81.</u> 6/23/90 mor Akin, Stephen, cooper; Pawling, DUT; <u>Skeen Pat., CLI</u>; co-mees
 7585, 7586, 7588. (A:61)
<u>82.</u> 11/15/91 gor Akin, Stephen; Pawling, DUT; <u>Zephaniah Platt's Pat.(?), CLI</u>;
 gee 3216. (B:250)
<u>83.</u> 7/8/00 mor Albro, Andrews (w. Rebecca), yeoman; Hebron, WAS; <u>Hebron, WAS</u>;
 mee 2899. (C:4)
84. 7/8/00 mor Albro, Rebecca. See 83.
85. 6/1/91 gee Alden, Elijah; Willsborough, CLI. See 6450.
86. 1/7/83 gee Alexander, James; New Perth, CHA. See 4778.
87. 1/27/83 gee Alexander, James; New Perth, CHA. See 3322.
<u>88.</u> 11/10/83 gor Allaz, James, Esq., goldsmith, "formerly a Captain in the 60th
 Regiment of Infantry"; City of N.Y.; <u>Provincial Pat., CHA</u>;
 gee 4788. (A:87)
<u>89.</u> 11/13/83 gor Allaz, James, Esq.; City of N.Y.; <u>Provincial Pat., CHA</u>; gee
 4791. (A:91)
90. 10/11/92 gee Allen, Abraham; Plattsburgh, CLI. See 6255.
<u>91.</u> 10/12/92 mor Allen, Abraham, farmer; Plattsburgh, CLI; <u>Plattsburgh, CLI</u>;
 co-mees 511, 6257. (A:85)
92. 5/20/97 gee Allen, Abram, physician; Salem, WAS. See 1816.
93. 9/25/99 gee Allen, Clark, farmer; Salem, WAS. See 3365.
<u>94.</u> 7/3/01 gor Allen, Clark, innkeeper; Hartford, WAS; <u>Hartford, WAS</u>; co-gees
 3084, 3099. (E:410)

16

<u>95.</u>	12/1/96	mor	Allen, Dan; Manchester, ---, VT; <u>Willsborough, CLI</u>; mee 2788.
			(A:231)
<u>96.</u>	9/12/97	gor	Allen, Dan; Willsborough, CLI; <u>Willsborough, CLI</u>; gee 3247.
			(B:103)
<u>97.</u>	6/22/93	gor	Allen, David, farmer; Cambridge, WAS; <u>Cambridge Pat.</u>, WAS;
			gee 7713. (B-2:508)
98.	11/7/87	gor	Allen, Deborah. See 126.
99.	7/20/87	gee	Allen, Ebenezer, Major; ---, ---. See 2235.
<u>100.</u>	7/20/87	gor	Allen, Ebenezer, Major; ---, ---; <u>Little Pat.</u>, WAS (forfeited
			estate of --- "Skeen"); co-gor 2240; co-gees 22, 1548,
			1801, 1803, 2533, 2838, 2840, 3158, 3794, 3806. (A:55)
101.	12/29/91	gee	Allen Ebenezer; ---, ---. See 4878.
102.	4/9/96	gee	Allen, Elijah; Plattsburgh, CLI. See 5112.
<u>103.</u>	4/9/96	mor	Allen, Elijah; Plattsburgh, CLI; <u>Champlain, CLI</u>; mee 5113.
			(A:181)
104.	4/18/96	mee	Allen, Elijah; Plattsburgh, CLI. See 5274.
<u>105.</u>	10/14/90	mor	Allen, Isaac; Plattsburgh, CLI; <u>Plattsburgh, CLI</u>; co-mor 123.
			mee 6263. (A:57)
106.	10/12/92	gee	Allen, Isaac; Plattsburgh, CLI. See 6256.
107.	7/4/88	gee	Allen, Jabez; ---, CHI, VT. See 1977.
<u>108.</u>	9/16/91	mor	Allen, Jabez; Plattsburgh, CLI; <u>Zephaniah Platt's Pat.</u>, CLI;
			co-mees 509, 6254. (A:64)
<u>109.</u>	9/7/99	mor	Allen, James L.; Washington, DUT; <u>Chateaugay, CLI</u>; mee 320.
			(A:416)
<u>110.</u>	3/1/98	mor	Allen, John; ---, CLI; <u>Old Military Township #7 (Chateaugay)</u>,
			CLI; mee 5693. Three contracts this date involving these
			two persons. (A:261), (A:263), (A:264)
<u>111.</u>	9/6/86	gee	Allen Jonas, yeoman; Plattsburgh, WAS. See 5896.
<u>112.</u>	9/7/86	mor	Allen, Jonas, yeoman; Plattsburgh, WAS; <u>Plattsburgh, WAS</u>;
			mee 5835. (A:10)
113.	7/8/89	gee	Allen, Jonathan, cordwainer; Cambridge Dist., ALB. See 7578.
<u>114.</u>	10/24/94	mor	Allen, Jonathan; Willsborough, CLI; <u>Willsborough, CLI</u>;
			mee 2073. (A:142)
115.	5/10/94	gee	Allen, Joseph; Cambridge, WAS. See 138.
<u>116.</u>	7/17/01	mor	Allen, Lamberton, Junr.; Champlain, CLI; <u>Champlain, CLI</u>;
			mee 810. (B:39)
117.	12/5/84	gee	Allen, Obediah; Hoosick, ALB. See 8002.
<u>118.</u>	12/9/85	gor	Allen, Obediah (w. Pheebe); Cambridge Dist.; WAS; <u>---, WAS</u>;
			gee 1983. (C-2:50)
<u>119.</u>	3/9/86	mor	Allen, Palonerly(?); ---, ---; <u>Skenesborough, WAS</u>; mee 3196.
			(Deed Book B-1:239)
120.	12/9/85	gor	Allen, Pheebe. See 118.
121.	6/28/92	gee	Allen, Philemon; Salem, WAS. See 2344.
122.	10/14/90	gee	Allen, Reuben; Plattsburgh, CLI. See 6262.
123.	10/14/90	mor	Allen, Reuben; Plattsburgh, CLI. See 105.
124.	10/29/93	mee	Allen, Reuben; Plattsburgh, CLI. See 3360.
<u>125.</u>	3/13/89	gor	Allen, Stephen; ---, WAS; <u>Kingsbury, WAS</u>; gee 6907. (B-2:151)
<u>126.</u>	11/7/87	gor	Allen, Thomas (w. Deborah), yeoman; Plattsburgh, WAS;
			<u>Plattsburgh, WAS</u>; gee 5675. (A:237)
<u>127.</u>	10/5/91	mor	Allen, Thomas, farmer; Plattsburgh, CLI; <u>Plattsburgh, CLI</u>;
			mee 5845. (A:69)
<u>128.</u>	7/6/99	gor	Allen, Thomas; Plattsburgh, CLI; <u>Plattsburgh, CLI</u>; gee 7984.
			(B:326)
129.	10/12/89	gee	Allen, Zebulon; Shaftsbury, ---, VT. See 3442.
<u>130.</u>	4/2/90	gor	Allen, Zebulon; Bennington, ---, VT; <u>Cambridge Dist., WAS</u>;
			gee 2044. (D:9)
<u>131.</u>	1/22/98	gor	Allen, Zebulon; Cambridge, WAS; <u>Walloomsack Pat., WAS</u>;
			gee 2045. (D:1)
132.	9/12/97	gor	Allin, Margaret. See 133.
<u>133.</u>	9/12/97	gor	Allin, Simeon (w. Margaret); Argyle, WAS; <u>Argyle, WAS</u>;
			gee 416. (E:318)
134.	5/10/94	gor	Almy, Abigail. See 138.
135.	7/10/99	gor	Almy, Abigail. See 139.
136.	10/20/00	gor	Almy, Abigail. See 140.
137.	7/9/93	gee	Almy, Joseph; ---, ---, MA. See 3646.
<u>138.</u>	5/10/94	gor	Almy, Joseph (w. Abigail); Cambridge, WAS; <u>Cambridge, WAS</u>;
			gee 115. (D:159)

17

<u>139.</u>	7/10/99	gor	Almy, Joseph (w. Abigail); Cambridge, WAS; <u>Cambridge, WAS</u>; gee 2183. (E:195)
<u>140.</u>	10/20/00	gor	Almy, Joseph (w. Abigail); Cambridge, WAS; <u>Cambridge, WAS</u>; gee 6743. (E:197)
141.	4/30/00	gee	Alvord, John, yeoman; New Haven, ---, VT. See 3070.
142.	7/4/01	mee	Alvord, John; "late of the town of Monkton ... Vermont but now of the town of Chateaugay", CLI. See 3071.
143.	1/16/97	gee	Ames, Nathaniel; Shaftsbury, ---, VT. See 8006.
<u>144.</u>	1/18/02	mor	Ames, Royel; Cambridge, WAS; <u>Hebron, WAS</u>; mee 6100. (D:130)
145.	2/10/95	gee	Anderson, John; Hoosick, REN. See 147.
146.	2/10/95	gee	Anderson, Thomas; ---, REN. See 4917.
<u>147.</u>	2/10/95	gor	Anderson, Thomas; Hoosick, REN; <u>"Voloomsack" Pat., WAS</u>; gee 145. (C-2:38)
<u>148.</u>	9/3/92	mor	Andrew, William; ---, WAS; <u>Westfield, WAS</u>; co-mors 1335, 7237; mee 7234. (A:378)
<u>149.</u>	5/29/01	mor	Andrews, Benjamin; ---, ---; <u>Elizabethtown, ESS</u>; mee 5768. (A:62)
<u>150.</u>	10/19/01	mor	Andrews, Benjamin; ---, ---; <u>Elizabethtown, ESS</u>; co-mees 6400, 6423. (A:98)
151.	7/1/85	gee	Andrews, Christopher; ---, ---. See 7055.
<u>152.</u>	12/6/87	mor	Andrews, Christopher; Whitehall, WAS; <u>Whitehall, WAS</u>; mee 8563. (A:170)
<u>153.</u>	7/11/87	mor	Andrus, Titus; Brandon, RUT, VT; <u>Plattsburgh, WAS</u>; mee 6433. (A:24)
<u>154.</u>	2/13/94	mor	Anson, Silas, farmer; Washington, DUT; <u>Peru, CLI</u>; mee 5527 (A:152)
155.	12/3/89	gee	Anspach, Peter, "copartner under the firm of Anspach and Rogers"; City of N.Y. See 4053.
<u>156.</u>	8/17/95	gor	Anthony, Stephen, gentleman; Salem, WAS; <u>Argyle, WAS</u>; gee 3895. (B-2:460)
<u>157.</u>	4/1/88	gor	Antill, Edward, Esq.; ---, ---; <u>"on the little river Chazy" (Canadian Refugees' Pat.), CLI</u>; gee 1825. (A:202)
<u>158.</u>	7/1/88	mor	Antle(?), Edward, Esq. ("a Canadian refugee"); ---, ---; <u>1000-acre tract on Lake Champlain, WAS</u>(sic); co-mees 981, 3013, 3014. (A:83)
<u>159.</u>	9/13/02	mor	Aplin, Isaac; Granville, WAS; <u>Granville, WAS</u>; mee 713. (E:25)
<u>160.</u>	7/14/73	mee	Apthorp, Charles Ward, the Honorable; City of N.Y. See 3797.
161.	1/15/75	mee	Apthorp, Charles Ward; City of N.Y. See 243.
162.	12/15/98	gee	Arakuente, Thomas, trader; "Village of St. Regis, Lower, Canada". See 2990.
<u>163.</u>	12/29/98	gor	Arakuente, Thomas, trader; Caughnawaga, Lower Canada; <u>"hunting grounds of the Indians of St. Regis", CLI</u>; gee 6373. (B:169)
164.	1/15/02	gee	Archabald, Janes(sic); Easton, WAS. See 8645.
165.	11/1/91	gee	Archabald, John, yeoman; Salem, WAS. See 4338.
166.	8/18/92	gee	Archer, John, farmer; ---, CLI. See 2134.
167.	10/28/97	gee	Archer, Joseph, yeoman; Cambridge Dist., WAS. See 6912.
<u>168.</u>	11/3/91	mor	Archibald, John; Salem, WAS; <u>Salem, WAS</u>; mee 4339. (A:302)
169.	12/3/84	gee	Archy, James; Cambdon(?), WAS. See 2122.
170.	6/1/98	mor	Armitage, John, farmer; Cambridge, WAS. See 204.
171.	5/22/01	gee	Armstrong, Alexander, yeoman; Hebron, WAS. See 5294.
172.	7/1/00	mor	Armstrong, Ebenezer; ---, ---. See 8194.
173.	7/1/85	gee	Armstrong, James; New Perth, WAS. See 8285.
174.	6/15/95	gor	Armstrong, James F. (w. Susan); Trenton, ---, NJ. See 7129.
175.	6/2/69	gee	Armstrong, Robert; White Creek, ALB. See 2025.
<u>176.</u>	7/29/74	gor	Armstrong, Robert, freeholder; New Perth, CHA; <u>---, CHA</u>; co-gors 450, 6538; gee 8355. (B-1:170)
177.	6/15/95	gor	Armstrong, Susan. See 174.
178.	6/20/96	gee	Armstrong, William; Salem, WAS. See 5147.
<u>179.</u>	6/21-96	mor	Armstrong, William, farmer; Salem, WAS; <u>Argyle, WAS</u>; mee 5148. (B:104)
180.	4/13/97	gee	Arnold, Elisha; Danby, RUT, VT. See 8497.
<u>181.</u>	4/13/97	mor	Arnold, Elisha; Danby, RUT, VT; <u>Peru, CLI</u>; mee 8498. Two contracts this date involving these two persons. (A:218), (A:219)
182.	1/2/98	gee	Arnold, Elisha, merchant; Peru, CLI. See 8499.

18

183. 1/3/98 mor Arnold, Elisha; Peru, CLI; Peru, CLI; mee 8500. (A:255)
184. 2/2/99 mee Arnold, Elisha; Peru, CLI. See 4829.
185. 5/15/01 mee Arnold, Elisha; Peru, CLI. See 190.
186. 12/24/01 mee Arnold, Elisha; ---, ---. See 8203.
187. 8/10/02 mor Arnold, Hiram (w. Sena); ---, ---; Hartford, WAS; mee 938
       (mee is administrator of the estate of "Cornelius V.
       Brewerton late of Salem, deceased")   (E:9)
188. 5/15/01 --- Arnold, Isaac. See 190.
189. 3/7/00 mor Arnold, Joseph; Peru, CLI; Peru, CLI; mee 5372. (A:414)
190. 5/15/01 mor Arnold, Joseph, "son of Isaac Arnold"; Peru, CLI; Peru, CLI;
       mee 185.   (B:33)
191. 7/1/00 mor Arnold, Levi; ---, ---; ---, ESS; co-mor 61; mee 5572. (A:22)
192. 8/29/00 gee Arnold, Levi; Jay, ESS. See 63.
193. 8/29/00 gor Arnold, Levi; Jay, ESS; "part of Lot 1 earlier granted in
       trust for Nathaniel Mallory", ESS; gee 62.   (A:3)
194. 8/10/02 mor Arnold, Sena. See 187.
195. 9/23/96 mor Arnold, Shubal; Granville, WAS; ---, WAS; mee 3767. (B:114)
196. 9/3/98 gee Arnold, Stukeley; Peru, CLI. See 5873.
197. 9/4/98 mor Arnold, Stukely, farmer; Peru, CLI; Peru, CLI; mee 5874.
                                                     (A:334)
198. 4/13/97 mor Arnot, George, farmer; ---, ULS; Cambridge, WAS; mee 401.
                                                     (B:155)
199. 8/10/90 gee Arthur, Joshua, farmer; ---, SUF. See 7662.
200. 8/11/90 mor Arthur, Joshua, farmer; ---, SUF. See 202.
201. 8/10/90 gee Arthur, Reuben, farmer; ---, SUF. See 7662.
202. 8/11/90 mor Arthur, Reuben, farmer; ---, SUF; Zephaniah Platt's Pat., CLI;
       co-mor 200; mee 7663.   (A:50)
203. 6/22/91 gor Ashton, James; ---, ---. See 8450.
204. 6/1/98 mor Ashton, Thomas, farmer; Cambridge, WAS; Cambridge, WAS;
       co-mor 170; mee 7626.   (C:3)
205. 6/4/92 mor Assline, Prisk; Champlain, CLI; Mark Graves' Pat., CLI;
       mee 5367. See surname Pryx in Appendix B.   (A:80)
206. 1/20/97 gee Aston, James, farmer; Cambridge, WAS. See 6167.
207. 11/2/86 gee Atwater, Benjamin; Granville, WAS. See 753.
208. 11/2/86 gee Atwater, Jesse; Granville, WAS. See 753.
209. 2/25/01 gor Atwater, Jessee (w. Rachel); Granville, WAS; Granville, WAS;
       gee 606.   (F:70)
210. 5/1/86 mor Atwater, John; ---, ---; Skenesborough, WAS; mee 4457.
                                               (Deed Book B-1:246)
211. 2/25/01 gor Atwater, Rachel. See 209.
212. 9/5/81 gee Atwater, Jesse; ---, CHA. See 8543.
213. 4/26/00 mor Atwood, Jacob; Shoreham, ---, VT; Plattsburgh, CLI; mee 3239.
                                                     (A:430)
214. 3/9/86 mor Atwood, Samuel; ---, ---; Skenesborough, WAS; mee 3196.
                                               (Deed Book B-1:233)
215. 1/29/93 --- Atwood, Thomas B. See 950.
216. 9/1/02 mor Austin, Daniel; Hartford, WAS. See 8124.
217. 1/25/97 mor Austin, David, farmer; Hartford, WAS; Hartford, WAS;
       mee 1478.   (B:237)
218. 3/9/98 mor Austin, David (w. Hannah); Hartford, WAS; Hartford, WAS;
       mee 1488.   (B:238)
219. 6/25/98 mee Austin, David; Hartford, WAS. See 4840.
220. 11/24/00 mor Austin, David; Hartford, WAS. See 1297.
221. 6/19/01 mee Austin, David; Hartford, WAS. See 232.
222. 6/23/98 mee Austin, David, Esq.; Hartford, WAS. See 229a and 366
       (Austin involved in two contracts this date).
223. 12/25/98 mor Austin, David, Esq. (w. Hannah); Hartford, WAS; Hartford, WAS;
       mee 1497.   (C:1)
224. 4/13/01 mor Austin, Edward; Granville, WAS; Granville, WAS; mee 7589.
                                                     (D:44)
225. 3/9/98 mor Austin, Hannah. See 218.
226. 12/25/98 mor Austin, Hannah. See 223.
227. 6/19/01 mor Austin, Hannah. See 232.
228. 8/23/94 gee Austin, Isaac; Stephentown, REN. See 6690.
229. 11/21/01 gor Austin, James (w. Ruth); Easton, WAS; Easton, WAS; gee 1310.
                                                     (F:232)

19

229a. 6/23/98 mor Austin, Pasquay (w. Penelope), farmer; Hartford, WAS;
                  Hartford, WAS; mee 222.   (B:236)
230. 6/25/98 mee Austin, Pasquay. See 4840.
230a. 6/23/98 mor Austin, Penelope. See 229a.
231. 2/2/93 gee Austin, Phineas; Cambridge, WAS. See 2057.
232. 6/19/01 mor Austin, Rehoboam (w. Hannah); Argyle, WAS; Argyle, WAS;
                  mee 221.   (D:86)
233. 11/21/01 gor Austin, Ruth. See 229.
234. 11/30/96 mor Austline, Prisque, Junr.; Champlain, CLI; Champlain, CLI;
                  mee 5081. See surname Pryx in Appendix B. (A:212)
235. 4/8/96 gor Averil, Nathan (w. Rosanna); Plattsburgh, CLI; Plattsburgh,
                  CLI; gee 3105.   (A:426)
236. 4/8/96 gor Averil, Rosanna. See 235.
237. 8/17/85 mor Averill, Daniel; ---, ---; Plattsburgh, WAS; co-mors 238, 240;
                  mee 5890.   (Deed Book B-1:242)
238. 8/17/85 mor Averill, Daniel, Junr. See 237.
239. 6/7/02 mor Averill, Jesse; Granville, WAS; Granville, WAS; mee 4159.
                                      (D:191)
240. 8/17/85 mor Averill, Nathan; ---, ---. See 237.
241. 10/15/90 mor Averill, Nathan; Plattsburgh, CLI; Plattsburgh, CLI;
                  mee 6264.   (A:55)
242. 4/10/94 gee Averill, Nathan; Plattsburgh, CLI. See 7761.
243. 1/15/75 mor Avery, Samuel, gentleman; Norwich, ---, CT; land "mouth of
                  Otter Creek (probably in present-day Vermont) where it
                  emptieth into Lake Champlain"; mee 161.   (A:22)
244. 10/13/90 gee Avrill, Nathan; Plattsburgh, CLI. See 6261.
245. 8/24/96 mor Babcock, Isaac, farmer; Salem, WAS; Salem, WAS; mee 8535.
                                      (B:100)
246. 12/31/99 gee Babcock, Jesse, yeoman; Cambridge, WAS. See 248.
247. 2/17/00 gor Babcock, Jesse (w. Mary); Cambridge, WAS; Cambridge, WAS;
                  gee 252.   (E:89)
248. 12/31/99 gor Babcock, John (w. Rebeckah), yeoman; Cambridge, WAS, Cambridge,
                  WAS; co-gees 246, 251.   (E:87)
249. 2/17/00 gor Babcock, Mary. See 247.
250. 12/31/99 gor Babcock, Rebeckah. See 248.
251. 12/31/99 gee Babcock, Worden, yeoman; Cambridge, WAS. See 248.
252. 2/17/00 gee Babcock, Worden; Cambridge, WAS. See 247.
253. 4/14/01 gee Backes, Peter; Hebron, WAS. See 2900. Two contracts this
                  date involving these two persons.
254. 12/9/96 gee Backus, Ebenezer; Granville, WAS. See 6656.
255. 9/20/91 mor Badlam, William; Plattsburgh, CLI; ---, WAS; mee 6632. (A:65)
256. 10/12/92 mor Badlam, William; ---, CLI; Plattsburgh, CLI; co-mees 511,
                  6257.   (A:84)
257. 6/8/98 mor Bailey, Catherine. See 263.
258. 8/24/99 gor Bailey, Catherine. See 279.
259. 1/2/96 gee Bailey, James, merchant; City of N.Y. See 5822.
260. 2/4/96 --- Bailey, James; City of N.Y. See 5857.
261. 2/24/96 mor Bailey, James; City of N.Y. See 8754.
262. 4/9/96 gee Bailey, James, merchant; City of N.Y. See 608.
263. 6/8/98 mor Bailey, James (w. Catherine), merchant; City of N.Y. See 312.
264. 3/31/97 gee Bailey, James, merchant; City of N.Y. See 3882.
265. 6/24/97 --- Bailey, James, merchant; City of N.Y. See 6848.
266. 7/3/97 gee Bailey, James, merchant; City of N.Y. See 3910.
267. 10/26/97 gee Bailey, James, merchant; City of N.Y. See 5824.
268. 10/26/97 gor Bailey, James, merchant; City of N.Y. See 334 and 5825.
269. 11/22/97 --- Bailey, James; City of N.Y.; Old Military Township #7
                  (Chateaugay), CLI. This person appoints William Bailey
                  of Plattsburgh as his attorney to sell the above lands.
                                      (B:114)
270. 6/4/98 gee Bailey, James, merchant; City of N.Y. See 7569.
271. 6/22/98 gor Bailey, James; City of N.Y. See 5696.
272. 7/3/98 mee Bailey, James; City of N.Y. See 3107.
273. 8/7/98 mee Bailey, James; City of N.Y. See 6357.
274. 10/5/98 mee Bailey, James; City of N.Y. See 7685.
275. 10/18/98 mee Bailey, James; City of N.Y. See 3455.
276. 10/19/98 mee Bailey, James; City of N.Y. See 3456 and 3457.

277.	3/18/99	mee	Bailey, James, merchant; City of N.Y. See 6290.
278.	6/21/99	mee	Bailey, James; City of N.Y. See 2967.
279.	8/24/99	gor	Bailey, James (w. Catherine), merchant; City of N.Y.; Chateaugay and Clinton, CLI; gee 337. (B:244)
280.	8/27/99	gee	Bailey, James, merchant; City of N.Y. See 338.
281.	9/23/00	mee	Bailey, James; City of N.Y. See 5573.
282.	4/14/01	mee	Bailey, James, merchant; City of N.Y. See 3810.
283.	5/1/01	mee	Bailey, James, merchant; City of N.Y. See 294.
284.	5/19/01	mee	Bailey, James, merchant; City of N.Y. See 923.
285.	9/21/01	mee	Bailey, James, merchant; City of N.Y. See 455.
286.	3/10/02	mee	Bailey, James, merchant; City of N.Y. See 6238.
287.	2/4/96	---	Bailey, John; ---, DUT. See 5857.
288.	2/24/96	mor	Bailey, John; ---, DUT. See 8754.
289.	3/16/96	mor	Bailey, John; ---, DUT; Old Military Township #6 (Clinton), CLI; co-mors 2199, 3370, 7114, 7173, 7562, 7565, 8075, 8100; mee 4803. (A:183)
290.	3/16/96	---	Bailey, John; ---, DUT. See 2201, 3652, 7113, 7172, 7561, 7564, 8074, 8099. These nine persons jointly appoint Charles Platt of Poughkeepsie (DUT) to be their attorney to sell their lands in Clinton County. (A:438)
291.	6/22/98	gor	Bailey, John; ---, DUT. See 5696, 5697, 5698.
292.	6/5/01	mor	Bailey, John; Plattsburgh, CLI; Plattsburgh, CLI; mee 3885. (B:30)
292a.	2/2/02	mee	Bailey, John; Plattsburgh, CLI. See 3773.
293.	4/6/96	gor	Bailey, John, Esq.; ---, DUT; ---, WAS; gee 5689. (A:430)
294.	5/1/01	mor	Bailey, John, Esq.; Plattsburgh, CLI; Chateaugay, CLI; co-mees 283, 326. (B:32)
295.	8/27/99	gor	Bailey, Phebe. See 338.
296.	9/22/00	mor	Bailey, Phebe. See 340.
297.	12/17/00	gor	Bailey, Phebe. See 323.
298.	12/5/97	mee	Bailey, Theodorus; Poughkeepsie, DUT. See 7119.
299.	12/5/97	mee	Bailey, Theodorus, Esq.; Poughkeepsie, DUT. See 7120.
300.	2/4/91	gee	Bailey, William; Poughkeepsie, DUT. See 813.
301.	1/2/96	gee	Bailey, William, merchant; City of N.Y. See 5822.
302.	2/4/96	---	Bailey, William; City of N.Y. See 5857.
303.	2/24/96	mor	Bailey, William; City of N.Y. See 8754.
304.	4/9/96	gee	Bailey, William, merchant; City of N.Y. See 608.
305.	3/31/97	gee	Bailey, William, merchant; City of N.Y. See 3882.
306.	4/29/97	---	Bailey, William; City of N.Y. See 4020.
307.	7/3/97	gee	Bailey, William, merchant; Plattsburgh, CLI. See 3910.
308.	10/26/97	gee	Bailey, William; ---, ---. See 334.
309.	10/26/97	gor	Bailey, William; Plattsburgh, CLI. See 5825.
310.	11/22/97	---	Bailey, William; Plattsburgh, CLI. See 269.
311.	6/4/98	gee	Bailey, William; ---, CLI. See 7569.
312.	6/8/98	mor	Bailey, William, merchant; ---, CLI; ---, CLI; co-mors 257, 263; mee 7571. (A:304)
313.	6/22/98	gor	Bailey, William; City of N.Y. See 5696.
314.	7/3/98	mee	Bailey, William; Plattsburgh, CLI. See 3107.
315.	8/7/98	mee	Bailey, William; Plattsburgh, CLI. See 6357.
316.	10/5/98	mee	Bailey, William; Plattsburgh, CLI. See 7685.
317.	10/18/98	mee	Bailey, William; Plattsburgh, CLI. See 3455.
318.	10/19/98	mee	Bailey, William; Plattsburgh, CLI. See 3456 and 3457.
319.	6/21/99	mee	Bailey, William; Plattsburgh, CLI. See 2967.
320.	9/7/99	mee	Bailey, William; Plattsburgh, CLI. See 109.
321.	12/13/99	mee	Bailey, William; Plattsburgh, CLI. See 3139.
322.	9/23/00	mee	Bailey, William; Plattsburgh, CLI. See 5573.
323.	12/17/00	gor	Bailey, William (w. Phebe); Plattsburgh, CLI; Plattsburgh, CLI; gee 5787. (B:287)
324.	3/6/01	mee	Bailey, William; Plattsburgh, CLI. See 8246.
325.	4/14/01	mee	Bailey, William; Chateaugay, CLI. See 3810.
326.	5/1/01	mee	Bailey, William; Plattsburgh, CLI. See 294.
327.	11/25/01	mee	Bailey, William; Plattsburgh, CLI. See 5421.
328.	2/2/02	mee	Bailey, William; Plattsburgh, CLI. See 3104.
329.	6/8/02	mee	Bailey, William; Chateaugay, CLI. See 2463.
330.	7/27/02	mee	Bailey, William; Chateaugay, CLI. See 6288.
331.	9/25/02	mee	Bailey, William; Chateaugay, CLI. See 1534.

332. 6/24/97 --- Bailey, William, Esq.; Plattsburgh, CLI. See 6848.
333. 10/26/97 gee Bailey, William, Esq.; Plattsburgh, CLI. See 5824.
334. 10/26/97 gor Bailey, William, Esq.; Plattsburgh, CLI; Old Military Township
        #6 (Clinton), CLI; co-gors 268, 6850, 8081; gee 308.
                                                          (B:89)
335. 11/24/97 --- Bailey, William, Esq.; Plattsburgh, CLI. See 6851.
336. 3/18/99 mee Bailey, William, Esq.; Plattsburgh, CLI. See 6290.
337. 8/24/99 gee Bailey, William, Esq.; Plattsburgh, CLI. See 279.
338. 8/27/99 gor Bailey, William, Esq. (w. Phebe); Plattsburgh, CLI;
        Chateaugay, CLI; gee 280.   (B:235)
339. 10/31/99 --- Bailey, William, Esq.; Plattsburgh, CLI. See 812.
340. 9/22/00 mor Bailey, William, Esq. (w. Phebe); Plattsburgh, CLI;
        Plattsburgh, CLI; mee 3886.   (B:3)
341. 4/7/02 --- Bailey, William, Esq.; ---, CLI. See 1640.
342. 10/18/94 gee Bain, Casparus, yeoman; ---, WAS. See 1717.
343. 10/30/01 gee Bain, Casparus; ---, ---. See 4572.
344. 10/18/94 gee Bain, Hugh, yeoman; ---, WAS. See 1717.
345. 10/18/94 gee Bain, Philip, yeoman; ---, WAS. See 1717.
346. 10/18/94 gee Bain, William, yeoman; ---, WAS. See 1717.
347. 2/15/98 mor Baker, Abigail. See 364.
348. 6/23/98 mor Baker, Abigail. See 366.
349. 4/15/75 gor Baker, Albeart; Kingsbury, CHA; Kingsbury, CHA; gee 2583.
                                                          (A:18)
350. 4/29/95 gee Baker, Albert, Junr.; Kingsbury, WAS. See 2348.
351. 6/27/98 mor Baker, Anna. See 371.
352. 7/13/84 gee Baker, Benjamin; Granville, WAS. See 8515.
353. 4/3/00 mee Baker, Benjamin; ---, ---. See 1344.
354. 10/31/00 mee Baker, Benjamin; ---, ---. See 6229.
355. 11/7/00 mee Baker, Benjamin; ---, ---. See 3141.
356. 1/16/01 mee Baker, Benjamin; ---, ---. See 1923.
357. 3/13/02 mor Baker, Benjamin; Granville, WAS; Granville, WAS; mee 4154.
                                                          (D:153)
358. 5/2/97 mor Baker, Benjamin W., farmer; Champlain, CLI; Champlain, CLI;
        mee 2491.   (A:227)
359. 11/15/97 gee Baker, Benjamin W.; Champlain, CLI. See 5115.
360. 11/16/97 mor Baker, Benjamin W.; Champlain, CLI; Champlain, CLI; mee 5153.
                                                          (A:238)
361. 3/10/99 mee Baker, Benjamin W.; Champlain, CLI. See 6343.
361a. 3/10/99 mee Baker, Benjamin W.; Champlain, CLI. See 6355.
362. 4/29/95 gee Baker, Caleb; Kingsbury, WAS. See 2348.
363. 4/29/95 gee Baker, Charles; Kingsbury, WAS. See 2348.
364. 2/15/98 mor Baker, David (w. Abigail), farmer; Hartford, WAS; Hartford,
        WAS; mee 1486.   (C:13)
365. 6/7/98 mee Baker, David, yeoman; Hartford, WAS. See 7856.
366. 6/23/98 mor Baker, David (w. Abigail), weaver; Hartford, WAS; Hartford,
        WAS; mee 222.   (C:16)
367. 6/26/98 mee Baker, David; ---, ---. See 2709.
368. 6/27/98 mee Baker, David; Hartford, WAS. See 371.
369. 6/27/98 mee Baker, David; Hartford, WAS. See 4873.
370. 6/1/99 mor Baker, Elizabeth. See 379.
371. 6/27/98 mor Baker, George (w. Anna), yeoman; Hartford, WAS; Hartford,
        WAS; mee 368.   (C:17)
372. 11/14/93 gee Baker, John, yeoman; Cambridge, WAS. See 1762.
373. 5/9/95 gee Baker, John, yeoman; Cambridge, WAS. See 3113.
374. 9/11/95 gee Baker, John, yeoman; Cambridge Dist., WAS. See 3145a.
375. 5/1/00 mor Baker, John, farmer; Chester, WAS; Chester, WAS; mee 7772.
                                                          (D:197)
376. 5/27/00 gee Baker, John; Kingsbury, WAS. See 7196.
377. 8/27/01 gor Baker, Reuben; Plattsburgh, CLI; Plattsburgh, CLI; gee 5791.
                                                          (B:315)
378. 7/10/92 mor Baker, Solomon, farmer; Granville, WAS; land "east side of
        Wood Creek", WAS; mee 395.   (A:332)
379. 6/1/99 mor Baker, Stephen (w. Elizabeth); Queensbury, WAS; Queensbury,
        WAS; mee 7550.   (C:56)
380. 12/10/99 mor Baker, Stephen; Queensbury, WAS; Queensbury, WAS; mee 5666
                                                          (C:59)

22

381. 7/1/00   mor Baker, Stephen; ---, ---; ---, ESS; co-mor 7525; mee 5572.
                                                                    (A:31)
382. 5/27/00 gee Balch, Ebenezer, farmer; Plattsburgh, CLI. See 55.
383. 9/16/02 gee Balch, Timothy; Williamstown, BER, MA. See 5886.
384. 12/13/98 mor Baldwin, Amos; Queensbury, WAS; Queensbury, WAS; mee 887.
                                                                    (C:23)
385. 5/9/96   mee Baldwin, David; Southeast, DUT. See 1107.
386. 5/1/00   mor Baldwin, Hezekiah, Junr., farmer; Chester, WAS; Chester, WAS;
                    mee 7772. Three contracts this date involving these two
                    persons.   (D:210), (D:210a), (D:211)
387. 9/7/69   gor Ballard, Daniel; ---, ---. See 7955.
388. 4/20/73 gor Ballard, Daniel; ---, ---. See 7957.
389. 6/23/95 gee Ballard, John Murray; Fair Haven, WAS (sic). See 6068.
390. 6/23/95 mor Ballard, John Murray; Whitehall, WAS; Whitehall, WAS;
                    mee 6069.   (A:556)
391. 6/23/97 gee Banker, John; Plattsburgh, CLI. See 1634.
392. 6/23/97 gor Banker, John; Plattsburgh, CLI. See 8341.
393. 6/23/97 mor Banker, John; Plattsburgh, CLI. See 8342.
394. 10/2/00 mor Banker, Oliver; ---, ---; Willsborough, ESS; mee 1965. (A:15)
395. 7/10/92 mee Banta, Jacob, farmer; City of N.Y. See 378.
396. 11/11/73 mee Banyar, Goldsbrow, Esq.; City of N.Y. See 7988.
397. 4/26/94 mee Banyar, Goldsbrow, Esq.; Albany, ALB. See 8855.
398. 1/14/95 gor Banyar, Goldsbrow, Esq.; Albany, ALB; Cambridge, WAS;
                    gee 2033.   (B-2:511)
399. 11/11/96 gor Banyar, Goldsbrow, gentleman; Albany, ALB; Isaac Sawyer's
                    Pat., WAS; gee 4668.   (C-2:108)
400. 11/12/96 mee Banyar, Goldsbrow, gentleman; Albany, ALB. See 4669.
401. 4/13/97 mee Banyar, Goldsbrow, Esq.; Albany, ALB. See 198.
402. 3/1/76   mor Banyar, William, gentleman; City of N.Y.; Social Borough, CHA;
                    mee 4096.   (A:27)
403. 6/29/98 gee Barber, Alpheus; Argyle, WAS. See 413.
404. 4/26/98 gee Barber, Amasa; Argyle, WAS. See 412.
405. 12/6/00 gor Barber, Amasa (w. Elizabeth); Argyle, WAS; Argyle, WAS;
                    gee 4923.   (E:234)
406. 1/24/01 mee Barber, Amasa; Argyle, WAS. See 415.
407. 4/2/94   mor Barber, Benjah; Newport, ---, RI; Easton, WAS; mee 4052.
                                                                    (A:502)
408. 1/15/02 gor Barber, Benjamin (w. Lydia); Plattsburgh, CLI; Granville, WAS;
                    gee 7913.   (F:118)
409. 6/2/93   mor Barber, Daniel, yeoman; Cambridge, WAS; Cambridge, WAS;
                    mee 7360.   (A:476)
410. 5/2/96   gee Barber, Daniel; Argyle, WAS. See 2100a.
411. 5/2/96   mor Barber, Daniel, gentleman; Argyle, WAS; Argyle, WAS;
                    co-mees 1290, 2101, 2216, 5584.   (C:64)
412. 4/26/98 gor Barber, Daniel (w. Susanna), Argyle, WAS; Argyle, WAS;
                    gee 404.   (E:228)
413. 6/29/98 gor Barber, Daniel (w. Susannah), farmer; Argyle, WAS; Argyle,
                    WAS; gee 403.   (E:230)
414. 12/6/00 gor Barber, Daniel (w. Susanah); Argyle, WAS; Argyle, WAS;
                    gee 4923.   (E:231)
415. 1/24/01 mor Barber, Daniel, yeoman; Argyle, WAS; Argyle, WAS; mee 406.
                                                                    (D:27)
416. 9/12/97 gee Barber, Daniel, Senior; Argyle, WAS. See 133.
417. 8/14/92 gee Barber, David, farmer; Westfield, WAS. See 4449.
418. 9/16/95 gor Barber, David; Hartford, WAS; Hartford, WAS; gee 1001.
                                                                    (B-2:549)
419. 12/6/00 gor Barber, Elizabeth. See 405.
420. 2/2/90   gee Barber, George, farmer; Cambridge, ALB. See 7273.
421. 6/17/94 gee Barber, George, farmer; Cambridge, WAS. See 6711.
422. 6/23/96 gee Barber, George, yeoman; Cambridge, WAS. See 8589.
423. 2/25/96 gee Barber, James; Cambridge, WAS. See 7131.
424. 1/15/02 gor Barber, Lydia. See 408.
425. 4/9/96   gee Barber, Smith, farmer; Argyle, WAS. See 3681.
426. 4/9/96   mor Barber, Smith; Argyle, WAS; Saratoga Pat., WAS; mee 3682.
                                                                    (B:35)
427. 4/23/96 gee Barber, Smith, farmer; Argyle, WAS. See 3686.

428. 4/23/96 mor Barber, Smith, farmer; Argyle, WAS; Saratoga Pat., WAS;
mee 3687. (B:138)
429. 6/15/99 gee Barber, Smith, farmer; Argyle, WAS. See 2106.
430. 12/6/00 gor Barber, Susanah. See 414.
431. 4/26/98 gor Barber, Susanna. See 412.
432. 6/29/98 gor Barber, Susanna. See 413.
433. 3/18/00 gee Barber, William; Middle Hero, CHI, VT. See 5151.
434. 3/18/00 mor Barber, William; Middle Hero, CHI, VT; Champlain, CLI;
mee 5090 (A:424)
435. 5/1/00 mor Bard, Elisha, farmer; Chester, WAS; Chester, WAS; mee 7772.
(D:220)
436. 2/20/93 gee Barker, James; ---, ---. See 4975.
437. 5/20/95 gor Barker, James (w. Mary); Cambridge, WAS; Cambridge, WAS;
gee 5243. (B-2:399)
438. 3/2/99 gee Barker, James; Westfield, WAS. See 1120.
439. 2/7/90 mor Barker, John; Dartmouth, BRI, MA; Van Curlaer Pat., WAS;
mee 4773. (A:320)
440. 7/3/99 mee Barker, John; Cambridge, WAS. See 1358.
441. 5/20/95 gor Barker, Mary. See 437.
442. 7/6/88 mor Barnes, James; Granville, WAS; Granville, WAS; mee 2381.
(A:118)
443. 12/14/93 gor Barnes, James, yeoman; Granville, WAS; Granville, WAS;
gee 2058. (B-2:133)
444. 7/6/88 gee Barnes, Robert, yeoman; Granville, WAS. See 2378.
445. 4/2/02 mor Barnes, William; Granville, WAS; Granville, WAS; mee 4155.
(D:154)
446. 7/2/92 gee Barns, Gamaliel, farmer; Westfield, WAS. See 4447.
447. 7/17/92 mor Barns, Gemaliel; Westfield, WAS; Westfield, WAS; co-mees
4442, 6579. (A:350)
448. 7/6/88 gee Barns, James, Junr., yeoman; Granville, WAS. See 2378.
449. 7/6/88 mor Barns, James, Junr.; Granville, WAS; ---, WAS; mee 2379.
(A:102)
450. 7/29/74 gor Barns, John, freeholder; New Perth; CHA. See 176.
451. 5/1/79 gor Barns, John, Capt.; New Perth, CHA; New Perth, CHA; gee 1320.
(B-1:22)
452. 12/22/75 gee Barns, John, Junr.; ---, ---. See 1341.
453. 7/6/88 mor Barns, Robert; Granville, WAS; Granville, WAS; mee 2379.
(A:106)
454. 7/10/90 mor Barnum, Israel; Hebron, WAS; Hebron, WAS; mee 1072. (A:243)
455. 9/21/01 mor Barnum, Jahiel; Chateaugay, CLI; Chateaugay, CLI; mee 285.
(B:49)
456. 9/17/01 gee Barr, Samuel; Pawlet, RUT, VT. See 3374.
457. 9/17/01 mor Barr, Samuel; Pawlet, RUT, VT; Salem, WAS; mee 3375. (D:87)
458. 2/20/01 mor Barrell, Colburn (w. Esther); ---, WAS; Hartford, WAS;
mee 937. (D:20b)
459. 2/20/01 mor Barrell, Esther. See 458.
460. 2/20/01 gee Barret, Colbun; ---, WAS. See 936.
461. 2/27/99 mor Barrows, Amos; Granville, WAS; Granville, WAS; mee 4135.
(C:56)
462. 5/28/85 mor Bartholemew, Lemme; Skenesborough, WAS; Skenes Little Pat.,
WAS; mee 8549. (Deed Book B-1:161)
463. 5/30/85 gee Bartholemew, Lemme; ---, ---. See 7055.
464. 7/1/90 mor Bartlet, Aaron; Salem, WAS; personal property?; "co-mees"
486, 490 (co-mees are parents of Aaron). (A:303)
465. 9/21/97 gor Bartlet, Aaron; Egremont, BER, MA (Aaron is "a child of
Moses Bartlet, deceased"); Salem, WAS; gee 478. (D:236)
466. 2/18/94 mor Bartlet, Bartholemew, yeoman; Salem, WAS; Salem, WAS;
mee 1457. (B:22)
467. 11/1/96 gor Bartlet, Bartholemew; Salem, WAS ("a child of Moses Bartlet,
deceased"); Salem, WAS; gee 476. (D:242)
468. 7/4/96 mor Bartlet, Henry; Fairfield, WAS; Fairfield, WAS; mee 2859.
(B:215)
469. 4/5/94 gor Bartlet, John, yeoman; Salem, WAS (" a child of Moses
Bartlet, deceased"); Salem, WAS; gee 471. (D:243)
470. 4/5/94 --- Bartlet, Moses, dec'd; Salem, WAS. See 469.

471. 4/5/94 gee Bartlet, Moses (Junr.?); Salem, WAS. See 469.
472. 5/20/95 gee Bartlet, Moses (Junr.?). See 6333.
473. 2/12/96 --- Bartlet, Moses, yeoman, dec'd.; "late of Salem". See 4172.
474. 2/12/96 gee Bartlet, Moses (Junr.?); Salem, WAS. See 4172.
475. 11/1/96 --- Bartlet, Moses, dec'd.; Salem, WAS. See 467.
476. 11/1/96 gee Bartlet, Moses (Junr.?); Salem, WAS. See 467.
477. 9/21/97 --- Bartlet, Moses, dec'd.; Salem, WAS. See 465.
478. 9/21/97 gee Bartlet, Moses (Junr.?); Salem, WAS. See 465.
479. 2/26/98 --- Bartlet, Moses, dec'd.; Salem, WAS. See 484.
480. 2/26/98 gee Bartlet, Moses (Junr.?); Salem, WAS. See 484.
481. 5/20/95 --- Bartlet, Mosses, dec'd.; Salem, WAS. See 6333.
482. 3/24/79 gee Bartlet, Mosses; ---, HAM, MA. See 3558.
483. 5/25/96 mor Bartlet, Thomas, house carpenter; Salem, WAS; Salem, WAS;
               mee 2129.   (C:25)
484. 2/26/98 gor Bartlet, Thomas; Cambridge, WAS ("a child of Moses Bartlet,
               dec'd."); Salem, WAS; gee 480.   (D:240)
485. 4/6/98 mor Bartlet, Thomas, farmer; Cambridge, WAS; Ryer Schermerhorn's
               Pat., WAS; mee 6143.   (C:18)
486. 7/1/90 mee Bartlett, Joseph (w. Sarah); Salem, WAS. See 464.
487. 12/10/91 mee Bartlett, Joseph; Salem, WAS. See 8832.
488. 12/13/91 gor Bartlett, Joseph; Salem, WAS; Salem, WAS; gee 8833. Two
               contracts this date involving these two persons.
                                         (B-2:9), (B-2:225)
489. 11/30/95 gee Bartlett, Moses; Salem, WAS. See 3501.
490. 7/1/90 mee Bartlett, Sarah. See 486.
491. 11/20/94 gor Barton, Lewis, physician; ---, DUT; Westfield, WAS; co-gees
               826, 7210.   (C-2:10)
492. 11/15/00 mor Bartow, Elijah; Queensbury, WAS; Queensbury, WAS; mee 8349.
                                         (D:18b)
493. 12/18/95 mor Basset, John, farmer; Easton, WAS; Saratoga Pat., WAS;
               mee 3672.   (B:5)
494. 2/20/01 mor Bassett, Abigail. See 495.
495. 2/20/01 mor Bassett, Ebenezer (w. Abigail); Easton, WAS; Saratoga Pat.,
               WAS; co-mees 778, 798, 7676.   (D:20b)
496. 12/18/95 mor Bassett, John, farmer; Easton, WAS; Saratoga Pat., WAS;
               mee 3672.   (B:8)
497. 1/16/00 gee Bassey, Philip; Westfield, WAS. See 4182.
498. 4/6/01 gee Bates, David; Willsborough, ESS. See 4741.
499. 2/26/96 mor Bates, Edward, innholder; Salem, WAS; Salem, WAS; mee 2128.
                                         (C:52)
500. 1/13/02 mee Battey, Benjamin; Easton, WAS. See 6011.
501. 10/23/89 gor Battey, James, farmer; ---, WAS; Argyle, WAS; gee 1407.
                                         (A:452)
502. 3/20/82 gor Battey, Thomas, Senr. farmer; New Perth, CHA; New Perth, CHA;
               gee 1432.   (B-1:62)
503. 9/1/72 gee Batty, David; White Creek, CHA. See 739.
504. 12/9/83 gee Baty, John; New Perth, CHA. See 1393.
505. 10/24/93 mee Bayard, Nicholas, gentleman; Montreal, Lower Canada. See
               7887.
506. 10/24/93 mee Bayard, Rebecca; ---, WES. See 7887.
507. 5/27/00 gor Bayard, Rebecca, spinster; ---, WES. See 55.
508. 8/5/91 --- Bayard, Samuel, gentleman; ---, WES; ---, CLI. See 6266.
                                         (A:200)
509. 9/16/91 mee Bayard, Samuel; ---, ---. See 108.
510. 10/11/92 gor Bayard, Samuel; ---, WES. See 6255. (two contracts)
511. 10/12/92 mee Bayard, Samuel; ---, WES. See 91, 256, 2068. (three contracts)
512. 8/17/01 mee Beach, David; Plattsburgh, CLI. See 3285.
513. 4/10/92 gor Beach, Mary. See 515.
514. 5/1/93 gor Beach, Mary. See 516.
515. 4/10/92 gor Beach, Thomas (w. Mary); Cambridge, WAS; Cambridge, WAS;
               gee 8402.   (A:356)
516. 5/1/93 gor Beach, Thomas (w. Mary); Cambridge, WAS; Cambridge, WAS;
               gee 1084.   (F:16)
517. 4/23/87 gee Beadle, Daniel; Saratoga, ALB. See 3632.
518. 9/7/87? mor Beadle, Daniel; Kingsbury, WAS; Kingsbury, WAS; mee 3631.
                                         (A:72)

25

519. 5/4/92 gor Beadle, Daniel; Easton, WAS; <u>Kingsbury, WAS</u>; gee 522.
(B-2:25)
520. 7/16/00 gee Beadle, Daniel, yeoman; Easton, WAS. See 4950.
521. 7/9/01 gee Beadle, Daniel, yeoman; Easton, WAS. See 8267.
522. 5/4/92 gee Beadle, David; Kingsbury, WAS. See 519.
<u>523.</u> 8/6/92 gor Beadle, David, yeoman; Kingsbury, WAS; <u>Kingsbury, WAS</u>;
gee 3977. (B-2:26)
<u>524.</u> 3/29/94 gor Beadle, David; Kingsbury, WAS; <u>Kingsbury, WAS</u>; gee 3978.
(B-2:347)
525. 9/8/00 mee Beadle, Michael; Easton, WAS. See 657.
526. 3/26/02 mee Beadle, Michael, yeoman; Easton, WAS. See 1920.
527. 7/1/02 mee Beadle, Michael; Easton, WAS. See 535.
<u>528.</u> 6/23/89 gor Beadle, Thomas; Easton Dist., WAS; <u>Cambridge Dist., WAS</u>;
gee 2748. (E:26)
<u>529.</u> 10/27/92 mor Beadlestone, Henry; ---, WAS; <u>Harris Pat., WAS</u>; mee 7235.
(A:388)
530. 10/9/95 gee Beak(?), Jonathan; Cambridge, WAS. See 7031.
531. 6/15/97 gee Beaman, Abraham; Peru, CLI. See 6319.
532. 12/22/95 mee Beard, Amos; Granville, WAS. See 2060.
<u>533.</u> 12/22/95 mor Beard, Amos; Granville, WAS; <u>Granville, WAS</u>; mee 4128. (B:1)
<u>534.</u> 4/5/00 mor Beard, Amos; Granville, WAS; <u>Granville, WAS</u>; mee 4139. (C:62)
<u>535.</u> 7/1/02 mor Beard, David; Easton, WAS; <u>Easton, WAS</u>; mee 527. (E:8)
536. 9/2/94 mee Beard, Waterman, yeoman; Easton, WAS. See 7076.
<u>537.</u> 9/6/96 gor Beardsley, Amanuel; Peru, CLI; <u>Peru, CLI</u>; co-gees 6897,
8704. (A:509)
<u>538.</u> 10/3/92 mor Beardsley, Emanuel; Willsborough, CLI; <u>Willsborough, CLI</u>;
mee 5848. (A:83)
<u>539.</u> 10/4/92 mor Beardsley, Emanuel; Plattsburgh, CLI; <u>---, CLI</u>; mee 5729.
(A:94)
540. 5/13/01 gee Beardsley, Ichiel, Junr.; Peru, CLI. See 6416.
541. 6/5/97 gee Beardsley, Jehiel, Junr.; Peru, CLI. See 543.
542. 9/4/01 gee Beardsley, Jehiel, Junr.; Peru, CLI. See 5885.
<u>543.</u> 6/5/97 gor Beardsley, Jehiel, Senr., gentleman; Peru, CLI; <u>Platt Rogers'</u>
<u>Pat., CLI</u>; co-gees 541, 546 (co-grantees are <u>brothers</u>).
(B:277)
544. 10/6/91 gee Beardsley, Johiel; Middletown, RUT, VT. See 5727.
545. 6/27/92 gee Beardsley, Johiel; Plattsburgh, CLI. See 7743.
546. 6/5/97 gee Beardsley, John; Peru, CLI. See 541.
547. 5/13/01 gee Beardsley, John; Peru, CLI. See 6416.
548. 9/4/01 gee Beardsley, John; Peru, CLI. See 5885.
549. 4/15/65 gee Beatey, James, farmer; ---, ORA. See 4396.
550. 12/14/92 mee Beatey, John; ---, ---. See 852.
551. 4/1/70 gee Beatey, Thomas, Senr.; ---, ALB. See 1420.
<u>552.</u> 10/27/89 mor Beattey, James, farmer; ---, WAS; <u>Argyle, WAS</u>; co-mees 2144,
2145, 2146. (A:180)
<u>553.</u> 9/21/01 mor Beaty, John; ---, WAS; <u>Granville, WAS</u>; mee 1694. (D:92)
<u>554.</u> 8/15/00 mor Beaumont, Dan; Kinderhook, COL. See 555.
<u>555.</u> 8/15/00 mor Beaumont, William, Esq.; Champlain, CLI; <u>Champlain, CLI</u>;
co-mor 554; mee 5095. (B:6)
556. 7/7/02 gee Beaumont, William; ---, ---. See 7869.
<u>557.</u> 12/15/88 mor Beck, Joseph (w. Margaret), haymaker; City of N.Y.;
<u>Queensbury, WAS</u>; mee 585. (A:321)
558. 12/15/88 mor Beck, Margaret. See 557.
559. 11/24/01 gor Becker, Hannah. See 571.
560. 4/26/68 gee Becker, Johannes, yeoman; Niscothaw (sic), ALB. See 6730.
561. 2/5/96 gee Becker, John; Thurman, WAS. See 7767.
<u>562.</u> 11/15/96 gor Becker, John D., merchant; Salem, WAS; <u>Salem, WAS</u>; gee 1813.
(C-2:149)
<u>563.</u> 11/21/96 mor Becker, John D., gentleman; Salem, WAS; <u>Salem, WAS</u>; mee
8536. (B:132)
<u>564.</u> 4/21/97 mor Becker, John D., merchant; Salem, WAS; <u>Salem, WAS</u>; mee 3209.
(B:192)
565. 11/12/01 mee Becker, John P., yeoman; Argyle, WAS. See 8345.
566. 2/20/96 gor Becker, Lenah. See 568.
567. 2/19/96 mee Becker, Martinus; Cambridge, WAS. See 7506.
<u>568.</u> 2/20/96 gor Becker, Martinus (w. Lenah); Cambridge, WAS; <u>Hoosick Pat.,</u>
<u>WAS</u>; gee 7507 (B-2:521)

26

569.	9/29/85	gee	Becker, Metinus; Cambridge, ALB. See 6727
570.	4/15/96	mor	Becker, Peter, farmer; Easton, WAS; Saratoga Pat., WAS; mee 3684. (B:25)
571.	11/24/01	gor	Becker, Peter (w. Hannah); Easton, WAS; Argyle, WAS; gee 8346. (F:147)
572.	4/26/68	gee	Becker, Peter, Junr., yeoman; Schoharie, ALB. See 6730.
573.	12/3/01	mor	Beckwith, Grant; Plattsburgh, CLI. See 1241.
574.	12/23/01	mor	Beckwith, Robins; Plattsburgh, CLI; Plattsburgh, CLI; mee 5950. (B:52)
575.	12/23/99	gee	Bedell, Richard; Westfield, WAS. See 5393.
576.	6/4/01	mor	Beebe, David; Peru, CLI; Peru, CLI; mee 628. (B:30)
577.	2/10/98	mor	Beebe, Hopson; Ballstown, SAR; Granville, WAS; mee 2969. (B:239)
578.	3/14/00	mor	Beebe, Samuel; Granville, WAS; Granville, WAS; mee 4137. (C:61)
579.	4/29/91	mee	Beekman, Abraham K.; ---, ---. See 5981.
580.	10/1/91	mee	Beekman, Abraham K.; City of N.Y. See 3727.
581.	5/1/93	gor	Beekman, Abraham K., gentleman; City of N.Y.; Beekman's Pat., CLI; gee 4266. (A:323)
582.	5/1/93	mee	Beekman, Abraham K.; City of N.Y. See 4267.
583.	12/4/80	gor	Beekman, Gerard G., Esq.; Flushing, Long Island, NY; Westfield, CHA; gee 5003. (A:441)
584.	10/15/89	mee	Beekman, James, merchant; City of N.Y. See 1343, 5079, 8199 (three contracts).
585.	12/15/88	mee	Beekman, James I., gentleman; City of N.Y. See 557.
586.	10/15/95	mee	Beekman, James I., gentleman; City of N.Y. See 3259.
587.	10/12/99	gee	Beekman, John, druggist; City of N.Y. See 2886.
588.	2/1/94	mee	Beekman, John Ia. (w. Maria); ---, ---. See 1038.
589.	8/25/00	gor	Beekman, Maggy; City of N.Y.; Beekmantown, CLI; gee 1957 (grantee is god-daughter of Maggy). (B:366)
590.	2/1/94	mee	Beekman, Maria. See 588.
591.	5/2/91	mee	Beekman, William; City of N.Y. See 5189.
592.	10/15/89	mee	Beekman, William, Esq.; City of N.Y. See 595 and 8264 (two contracts).
593.	1/15/90	mee	Beekman, William, Esq.; City of N.Y. See 8265.
594.	6/4/88	mor	Beeman, Abraham; Plattsburgh, CLI; Plattsburgh, CLI; mee 5839. (A:16)
595.	10/15/89	mor	Beeman, Abraham; Plattsburgh, CLI; Beekman, CLI; co-mor 5272; mee 592. (A:43)
596.	3/31/97	gee	Beeman, Abraham, merchant; Peru, CLI. See 3588.
597.	8/20/85	mor	Beeman, Samuel, yeoman; Plattsburgh, WAS; Plattsburgh, WAS; mee 5834. (A:1)
598.	8/30/93	gee	Beeman, Samuel, merchant; Hampton, WAS. See 5957.
599.	9/1/01	mor	Belding, Samuel, blacksmith; ---, ---, VT; Champlain, CLI; mee 1024. (B:42)
600.	8/13/97	mee	Bell, Elizabeth; Cambridge, WAS. See 6595.
601.	6/22/91	gor	Bell, Isaac; ---, ---. See 8450.
602.	5/22/00	gor	Bell, Isabel. See 605.
603.	7/3/92	gee	Bell, James, farmer; Salem, WAS. See 8575.
604.	2/7/97	mor	Bell, James, gentleman; ---, CLI; Canadian & Nova Scotia Refugees' Pat., CLI; mee 2867. (A:285)
605.	5/22/00	gor	Bell, James (w. Isabel); Salem, WAS; Salem, WAS; gee 7726. (E:236)
606.	2/25/01	gee	Bell, James; Salem, WAS. See 209.
607.	11/1/79	gee	Bell, William; New Perth, CHA. See 1429.
608.	4/9/96	gor	Bell, William, merchant; City of N.Y. "land (set) apart for the military", CLI; co-gees 262, 304, 3881. (A:475)
609.	12/2/89	gor	Bellanger, Julian, "late a soldier in the Regiment of Moses Hazen, Esq."; ---, ---.; Champlain, CLI; gee 5141. (A:512)
610.	11/10/95	gor	Bellows, Deliverance. See 613.
611.	9/2/90	mor	Bellows, Thomas; Salem, WAS; Shereiff's Pat. (Hebron), WAS; mee 6980. (A:247)
612.	9/2/90	gee	Bellows, Thomas, Esq.; Hebron, WAS. See 6987 and 6999 (two contracts).

27

613. 11/10/95 gor Bellows, Thomas, Esq. (w. Deliverance); Hebron, WAS; Hebron, WAS; gee 685.   (B-2:489)

614. 4/12/94 gor Beman, Abraham; Hampton, WAS; Hampton, WAS; gee 3840.
                                                                  (C-2:186)

615. 4/1/97 mor Beman, Abraham, merchant; Peru, CLI; Peru, CLI; mee 5868.
                                                                  (A:222)

616. 6/15/97 mor Beman, Abraham; Peru, CLI; Peru, CLI; co-mor 8216; mee 6320.
                                                                  (A:224)

617. 7/31/99 mor Beman, Abraham; Peru, CLI; Peru, CLI; mee 626.   (A:397)
618. 3/4/01 gor Beman, Mary. See 627.
619. 3/1/96 mor Beman, Nathan; Plattsburgh, CLI; Plattsburgh, CLI; mee
                  5859.   (A:203)

620. 3/29/96 gee Beman, Nathan; Plattsburgh, CLI. See 625.
621. 3/2/98 mor Beman, Nathan, farmer; Plattsburgh, CLI; Old Military Town-
                  ship #7 (Chateaugay), CLI; co-mees 6854, 8086. (A:268)

622. 12/26/01 mee Beman, Nathan; Chateaugay, CLI. See 7405.
623. 8/20/85 gee Beman, Samuel, yeoman; Plattsburgh, CLI. See 5891.
624. 8/1/93 mor Beman, Samuel (w. Silence), merchant; Hampton, WAS;
                  Hampton, WAS; mee 5956.   (A:505)

625. 3/29/96 gor Beman, Samuel; Plattsburgh, CLI; Plattsburgh, CLI; gee 620.
                                                                  (A:408)

626. 7/31/99 mee Beman, Samuel; Hampton, WAS. See 617.
627. 3/4/01 gor Beman, Samuel (w. Mary); Hampton, WAS; Hampton, WAS; gee
                  1194.   (E:311)

628. 6/4/01 mee Beman, Samuel; Chateaugay, CLI. See 576.
629. 8/1/93 mor Beman, Silence. See 624.
630. 6/1/91 gee Benedict, Elijah; Willsborough, CLI. See 6450.
631. 9/1/95 gee Benedict, Elijah; Willsborough, CLI. See 5155.
632. 9/1/95 gor Benedict, Elijah; Willsborough, CLI; Willsborough, CLI;
                  gee 5154.   (A:482)

633. 3/16/87 gee Benedict, Nehemiah; Norwalk, FAI, CT. See 5914.
634. 10/23/95 mor Benedict, Reuben; ---, CLI; Peru, CLI; mee 6404. (A:188)
635. 3/16/87 gor Benedict, Thomas, 4th; Norwalk, FAI, CT. See 5836.
636. 6/9/97 gor Benedict, Thomas, 4th; Norwalk, ---, CT; Plattsburgh, CLI;
                  gee 3589.   (B:64)

637. 6/10/97 mee Benedict, Thomas, 4th; Norwalk, FAI, CT. See 3590.
638. 1/10/85 gee Benet, Phinehas; White Creek; WAS. See 8391.
639. 1/19/96 gee Beninger, Abraham; grocer; City of N.Y. See 651.
640. 5/1/84 gee Benn, Casparus; ---, ---. See 3927.
641. 5/1/84 gee Benn, Hugh; ---, ---. See 3927.
642. 5/1/84 gee Benn, James; ---, ---. See 3927.
643. 5/1/84 gee Benn, John; ---, ---. See 3927.
644. 5/1/84 gee Benn, Philip; ---, ---. See 3927.
645. 5/1/84 gee Benn, William; ---, ---. See 3927.
646. 4/15/82 gee Bennet, Phineas; White Creek, CHA. See 8387.
647. 10/2/86 gor Bennet, Phineas, carpenter; Salem, WAS; Salem, WAS; co-gees
                  1382, 1385, 1387, 2204.   (A:315)

648. 4/2/95 mee Bennet, Roger; Kingsbury, WAS. See 6694.
649. 12/23/84 gee Benning, Abraham; Hampton, WAS. See 8281.
650. 11/20/86 gee Benninger, Isaac, merchant; Salem, WAS. See 2844.
651. 1/19/96 gor Benninger, Isaac, merchant; Salem, WAS; Jessup's Pat., WAS;
                  gee 639.   (B-2:514)

652. 7/7/91 gee Benson, Bildad, farmer; Easton, WAS. See 779.
653. 7/7/91 mor Benson, Bildad, farmer; Easton, WAS. See 7487.
654. 3/1/90 gor Benson, Egbert, Esq.; City of N.Y. See 3448.
655. 3/12/91 gor Benson, Egbert, Esq.; ---, ---. See 3445.
656. 5/18/92 gor Benson, Egbert, Esq.; ---, ---. See 3446.
657. 9/8/00 mor Benson, Jacob, farmer; Easton, WAS; Saratoga Pat., WAS;
                  mee 525.   (C:65)

658. 1/13/02 mee Benson, Jacob; Easton, WAS. See 6011.
659. 6/11/93 mor Benson, Job, Junr., farmer; ---, WAS; Easton, WAS; mee 7206.
                                                                  (A:421)

660. 6/8/93 gee Benson, Jobe, Junr., farmer; ---, WAS. See 2608.
661. 4/6/97 gee Bentley, James; Kingsbury, WAS. See 7020.
662. 10/1/01 mor Bentley, Joseph; Queensbury, WAS; Queensbury, WAS; mee 3282.
                                                                  (D:101)

28

663. 4/6/97   gee   Bentley, Layton; Kingsbury, WAS. See 7020.
664. 10/13/96 mor   Bentley, Richard, carpenter; Granville, WAS; Granville, WAS;
                     mee 3771.   (B:120)
665. 10/10/96 gor   Bently, Abigail. See 667.
666. 1/23/94 gee   Bently, Benjamin; Kingsbury, WAS. See 2291.
667. 10/10/96 gor   Bently, Thomas (w. Abigail), yeoman; Argyle, WAS; Saratoga
                     Pat., WAS; gee 6057.   (D:442)
668. 5/5/96   ---   Benzell, Adolphus. See 7322.
669. 2/5/96   mor   Berry, Richard, farmer; Easton, WAS; Saratoga Pat., WAS;
                     mee 3676.   (B:28)
670. 3/22/99 gor   Berry, Richard (w. Thankful); ---, ---. See 1043.
671. 3/22/99 gor   Berry, Thankful. See 670.
672. 1/14/01 gor   Besse, Joseph (w. Salley); Cambridge, WAS; Cambridge, WAS;
                     gee 3.   (E:93)
673. 1/14/01 mee   Besse, Joseph; Cambridge, WAS. See 5.
674. 11/2/01 gor   Besse, Peter (w. Sarah), yeoman; Cambridge, WAS; Cambridge,
                     WAS; gee 3164.   (F:212)
675. 1/14/01 gor   Besse, Salley. See 672.
676. 11/2/01 gor   Besse, Sarah. See 674.
677. 7/23/99 mor   Betts, Betsey. See 679.
678. 10/10/95 mor   Betts, Jonathan; Cambridge, WAS; Cambridge, WAS; mee 7032.
                                                                    (C:19)
679. 7/23/99 mor   Betts, Jonathan (w. Betsey), farmer; Cambridge, WAS; Cambridge,
                     WAS; mee 5034.   (C:59)
680. 5/20/00 mor   Betty, Benjamin (w. Penelopy), farmer; Easton, WAS; Saratoga
                     Pat., WAS; co-mees 777, 797, 7675.   (C:62)
681. 5/20/00 mor   Betty, Penelopy. See 680.
682. 6/6/89   mor   Beveridge, Andrew; Hobron, WAS; Hebron, WAS; co-mees:
                     "Executors of the estate of John Morin Scott, Esq.,
                     deceased"(6750, 6813, 4617, 4634 - posted in the order
                     shown).   (A:178)
683. 4/25/95 gor   Bewell, Daniel; Hampton, WAS; Hampton, WAS; co-gor 684;
                     gee 7254.   (D:390)
684. 4/25/95 gor   Bewell, Preserve; Hampton, WAS. See 683.
685. 11/10/95 gee   Beymer, David, cordwainer; Hebron, WAS. See 613.
686. 8/31/93 mor   Bibbins, Deborah. See 687.
687. 8/31/93 mor   Bibbins, Samuel (w. Deborah), farmer; Hampton, WAS; Hampton,
                     WAS; mee 5958.   (A:437)
688. 5/16/01 mor   Bidwell, Phineas, farmer; Chateaugay, CLI; Chateaugay, CLI;
                     co-mees 6865, 8097.   (B:38)
689. 10/6/85 gee   Biggelo, Hopstil; ---, ---. See 7055.
690. 10/6/85 gee   Biggelo, Samuel; ---, ---. See 7055.
691. 11/9/91 gee   Billings, Elijah; Cambridge, WAS. See 3218.
692. 11/9/91 mor   Billings, Elijah; Cambridge, WAS; Cambridge, WAS; mee 3219.
                                                                    (A:326)
693. 2/25/95 gor   Billings, Elijah (w. Rebeckah); Cambridge, WAS; Cambridge,
                     WAS; co-gees 3373, 3394.   (B-2:362)
694. 2/25/95 gor   Billings, Rebeckah. See 693.
695. 10/14/96 gor   Bininger, Abraham, yeoman; Salem, WAS; West Salem, WAS;
                     gee 7908.   (D:57)
696. 11/3/02 gor   Bininger, Abraham, farmer; Salem, WAS; Salem, WAS; gee 698.
                                                                    (F:285)
697. 2/26/96 mor   Bininger, Isaac, merchant; Salem, WAS; Salem, WAS; mee 2128.
                                                                    (C:24)
698. 11/3/02 gee   Bininger, Isaac, farmer; Salem, WAS. See 696.
699. 8/13/02 gor   Binnegar, Abraham (w. Catherine), merchant; City of N.Y.;
                     Jessup's Pat., WAS (land "originally sold by attainder
                     of Edward and Ebenezer Jessup formerly of the City of
                     Albany to George Gillmore formerly of Cambridge deceased");
                     co-gees 2841, 4072.   (F:259)
700. 8/13/02 gor   Binnegar, Catherine. See 699.
701. 4/11/96 gor   Birge, Elijah; Cambridge Dist.; WAS; Cambridge, WAS;
                     gee 4217   (D:86)
702. 4/11/96 mee   Birge, Elijah; Cambridge, WAS. See 4218.
703. 7/4/97   mor   Bishop, Abraham, farmer; Granville, WAS; Granville, WAS;
                     co-mees 74, 2935, 2948.   (B:202)

704. 12/21/97 mee Bishop, Abram; Granville, WAS. See 5212.
705. 6/4/98   mee Bishop, Isaac; Granville, WAS. See 8612.
706. 6/16/00 gee Bishop, Isaac; Granville, WAS. See 6047.
707. 9/21/01 mor Bishop, Isaac; ---, WAS; Granville, WAS; mee 1694. (D:146)
708. 10/6/01 gor Bishop, Isaac; Granville, WAS; Granville, WAS; gee 7739.
                                                              (F:88)
709. 12/17/01 mee Bishop, Isaac; Granville, WAS. See 2019.
710. 2/4/02   mee Bishop, Isaac, merchant; Granville, WAS. See 3814.
711. 2/19/02 mee Bishop, Isaac; Granville, WAS. See 1687.
712. 4/16/02 mee Bishop, Isaac, merchant; Granville, WAS. See 7094.
713. 9/13/02 mee Bishop, Isaac; Granville, WAS. See 159.
714. 10/19/02 mee Bishop, Isaac; Granville, WAS. See 8024.
715. 7/13/92 mor Bishop, John C., merchant; Granville, WAS. See 3402.
716. 12/29/94 gor Bishop, John C., merchant; Granville, WAS. See 1850.
717. 12/11/97 gee Bishop, John C.; ---, ---. See 1851.
718. 6/2/98   gor Bishop, John C.; Granville, WAS; Granville, WAS; co-gors
                        1852, 3403; gee 4026.   (D:38)
719. 6/4/98   mee Bishop, John C.; Granville, WAS. See 8612.
720. 2/10/00 mee Bishop, John C.; Granville, WAS. See 6322.
721. 6/23/01 mee Bishop, John C.; Granville, WAS. See 3436.
722. 9/21/01 mor Bishop, John C.; ---, WAS; Granville, WAS; mee 1693. (D:145)
723. 9/28/01 mee Bishop, John C.; Granville, WAS. See 4854.
724. 11/26/01 mee Bishop, John C.; Granville, WAS. See 4100.
725. 12/24/01 mee Bishop, John C.; Granville, WAS. See 3020.
726. 4/10/02 mee Bishop, John C.; Granville, WAS. See 6010.
727. 5/28/99 gor Bishop, Peter, Esq.; Northeast, DUT; Argyle, WAS; co-gors
                        3462, 3464; gee 4547.   (E:54)
728. 2/22/02 gee Bishop, Samuel; Monkton, ADD, VT. See 2010.
729. 7/6/88   mor Bishop, Theophelis; Granville, WAS; Granville, WAS; mee 2379.
                                                              (A:113)
730. 3/16/89 mor Bishop, Theophilus; Granville, WAS; Granville, WAS; mee 830.
                                                              (A:159)
731. 3/12/99 mor Blackman, Charity. See 733.
732. 9/5/00   mor Blackman, Elijah (w. Thankful), tanner; Cambridge, WAS;
                        Cambridge Pat., WAS; mee 4039.   (C:64)
733. 3/12/99 mor Blackman, Jedediah (w. Charity), farmer; Hampton, WAS;
                        Hampton, WAS; mee 5970.   (C:53)
734. 9/5/00   mor Blackman, Thankful. See 732.
735. 2/24/01 gor Blackslee, David (w. Sarah); Granville, WAS; Granville, WAS;
                        gee 2112.   (E:249)
736. 2/24/01 gor Blackslee, Sarah. See 735.
737. 11/19/87 gor Blackwell, Joseph (w. Mary); City of N.Y.; Kingsbury, WAS;
                        gee 7015.   (B-2:22)
738. 11/19/87 gor Blackwell, Mary. See 737.
739. 9/1/72   gor Blair, John; Western(Warren), WOR, MA; Turner's Pat., CHA;
                        gee 503.   (B-1:46)
740. 7/7/86   gee Blair, John; ---, ---. See 2618.
741. 12/5/89 gee Blair, John; Cambridge Dist., WAS. See 747.
742. 12/5/89 --- Blair, John, dec'd.; Cambridge Dist.; WAS. See 747.
743. 2/13/90 gor Blair, John; Cambridge, ALB; Cambridge, WAS (sic); gee 746.
                                                              (B-2:382)
744. 2/26/00 mor Blair, John; Cambridge, WAS, Cambridge, WAS; mee 2843.
                                                              (C:60)
745. 12/5/89 gor Blair, Robert; Cambridge Dist, WAS. See 747.
746. 2/13/90 gee Blair, Robert; Cambridge, WAS. See 743.
747. 12/5/89 gor Blair, Sarah ("widow of John Blair of Cambridge District")
                        ---, ---; ---, WAS; co-gors: Elizabeth Gilmore, David and
                        Susannah French, Jonathan and Jane French, Solomon and
                        Dinah King, John and Isabella McCullock, David and Sarah
                        Harkness, Robert Blair (co-gors are all "children" of
                        John Blair, dec'd); gee 741.   (A:259)
748. 5/2/96   mor Blake, James, farmer; Cambridge, WAS; Cambridge and Argyle(?),
                        WAS; co-mees 1290, 2101, 2216, 5584. (C:58)
749. 8/27/92 mor Blake, John, merchant; Albany, ALB; Canadian and Nova Scotia
                        Pat., CLI; mee 4806.   (A:127)
750. 7/22/97 mee Blakeley, David, merchant; Albany, ALB. See 2603.

30

751. 9/5/81 gee Blakslee, David; ---, CHA. See 8543.
752. 11/19/81 gee Blakslee, David, Capt.; ---, CHA. See 8544.
753. 11/2/86 gor Blakslee, David, Capt.; Granville, WAS; Granville, WAS;
    co-gees 207, 208.   (C-1:24)
754. 5/10/93 mor Blanchard, Abner, blacksmith; Whitehall, WAS; Whitehall, WAS;
    mee 8579.   (A:412)
755. 9/6/93 gee Blanchard, Anthony I., attorney; Salem, WAS. See 3326.
756. 11/6/93 gee Blanchard, Anthony I., attorney; Salem, WAS. See 3527.
757. 8/24/94 mee Blanchard, Anthony I, Esq., attorney; ---, ---. See 2917.
758. 11/7/95 gee Blanchard, Anthony J., attorney; Salem, WAS. See 8587.
759. 6/20/01 mee Blanchard, Anthony T.; ---, ---. See 2505.
760. 10/2/02 mee Blanchard, Anthony T.; ---, ---. See 3707, 5431 (two contracts).
761. 6/4/85 mor Blanchard, Azariel; Skenesborough, WAS; Skenesborough, WAS;
    mee 8551.   (Deed Book B-1:169)
762. 7/1/85 gee Blanchard, Azariel; ---, ---. See 7055.
763. 11/16/99 gee Blasdel, Thomas, farmer; Kingsbury, WAS. See 7151.
764. 2/19/96 --- Blaz, Christian. See 765.
765. 2/19/96 gor Blaz, Daniell; "late from Canada, brother and heair at law
    to Christian Blaz late a soldier ... who served in the
    New York line receipt of 20 pounds from Robert Smith of
    Watervliet..." (Gives to R.S. all the claim that is due
    to Christian in U.S. or state-granted bounty lands, CLI);
    gee 7247.   (A:444)
766. 4/25/95 gee Bleau, Peter, laborer; Champlain, CLI. See 1990.
767. 8/6/92 gor Blecker, John N. (w. Margaret), merchant; Albany, ALB; Easton,
    WAS; gee 4922.   (A:518)
768. 8/6/92 gor Blecker, Margaret. See 767.
769. 9/30/90 --- Bleecker, Barent, merchant; Albany, ALB. See 2872.
770. 1/2/98 mee Bleecker, Barent, merchant; Albany, ALB. See 6645 and 6646.
771. 10/27/98 gee Bleecker, Barent, merchant; Albany, ALB. See 4533.
772. 5/30/99 mee Bleecker, Barent; ---, ALB. See 1970.
773. 2/14/00 mee Bleecker, Barent; Albany, ALB. See 2197 and 2198.
774. 11/1/00 mee Bleecker, Barent; Albany, ALB. See 5199.
775. 10/18/02 --- Bleecker, Barent, merchant; Albany, ALB. See 3136.
776. 7/6/99 mee Bleecker, Henry, merchant; Albany, ALB. See 8483.
777. 5/20/00 mee Bleecker, Henry, merchant; Albany, ALB. See 680 and 8484.
778. 2/20/01 mee Bleecker, Henry, merchant; Albany, ALB. See 495.
779. 7/7/91 gor Bleecker, Jacob, Junr., Esq.; Albany. ALB; Saratoga Pat., WAS;
    co-gees 652, 6383, 6385, 7486.   (F:150)
780. 7/7/91 mee Bleecker, Jacob, Junr., Esq.; Albany, ALB. See 7487.
781. 9/1/95 gor Bleecker, Jacob, gentleman; Albany, ALB; Argyle and Easton,
    WAS; co-gor 795; gee 7790.   (F:68)
782. 1/2/98 mee Bleecker, John; ---, SAR. See 6645 and 6646.
783. 10/27/98 gee Bleecker, John; Stillwater, SAR. See 4533.
784. 2/14/00 mee Bleecker, John; ---, SAR. See 2197 and 2198.
785. 11/1/00 mee Bleecker, John; ---, SAR. See 5199.
786. 7/1/94 mee Bleecker, John N., Esq.; Albany, ALB. See 3055.
787. 1/2/98 mee Bleecker, John R., merchant; Albany, ALB. See 6645.
788. 5/30/99 mee Bleecker, John R.; ---, ALB. See 1970.
789. 10/18/02 --- Bleecker, John R., merchant; Albany, ALB. See 3136.
790. 9/30/90 --- Bleecker, John R., Junr., merchant; Albany, ALB. See 2872.
791. 1/2/98 mee Bleecker, John R., Junr.; Albany, ALB. See 6646.
792. 10/27/98 gee Bleecker, John R., Junr., merchant; Albany, ALB. See 4533.
793. 2/14/00 mee Bleecker, John R., Junr.; Albany, ALB. See 2197 and 2198.
794. 11/1/00 mee Bleecker, John R., Junr.; Albany, ALB. See 5199.
795. 9/1/95 gor Bleecker, John T., merchant; Albany, ALB. See 781.
796. 7/6/99 mee Bleecker, Nicholas, merchant; Albany, ALB. See 8483.
797. 5/20/00 mee Bleecker, Nicholas, merchant; Albany, ALB. See 680 and 8484.
798. 2/20/01 mee Bleecker, Nicholas, merchant; Albany, ALB. See 495.
799. 10/4/92 gor Bleeker, Esther. See 800.
800. 10/4/92 gor Bleeker, John (w. Esther); City of N.Y.; Cambridge, WAS;
    co-gees 2756, 6017.   (B-2:14)
801. 4/7/98 mee Blo, Peter; Champlain, CLI. See 4029.
802. 7/30/01 mee Bloodgood, Francis, Esq.; Albany, ALB. See 7303.
803. 5/1/99 gor Bloodgood, James; Albany, ALB; Fairfield, WAS; gee 6587.
                                                         (D:408)

31

804. 9/17/99 mee Bloodgood, James; Albany, ALB. See 7199.
805. 4/29/95 mor Blow, Peter, laborer; Champlain, CLI; Champlain, CLI;
            mee 6414.   (A:156)
806. 7/11/91 gor Boardman, John; Troy, REN; Cambridge Dist., WAS; gee 3577.
                                                              (A:222)
807. 7/13/91 gor Boardman, John; Troy, REN; Cambridge, WAS; gee 3578. (A:224)
808. 5/6/01 mee Bogart, Cornelius I.; City of N.Y. See 2170.
809. 5/27/01 mee Bogart, Cornelius I., attorney; City of N.Y. See 2001.
810. 7/17/01 mee Bogart, Cornelius I., attorney; City of N.Y. See 116.
811. 1/5/88 mee Bogart, Cornelius I., Esq.; City of N.Y. See 3845.
812. 10/31/99 --- Bogert, Cornelius I., attorney; City of N.Y.; Canadian and
                 Nova Scotia Refugees' Pat., CLI (Bogert appoints William
                 Bailey, Esq., of Plattsburgh to serve as his attorney in
                 the sale of the above lands)   (A:213)
813. 2/4/91 gor Boileau, Pierre, Lieutenant; ---, CLI; Canadian and Nova
                 Scotia Refugees' Pat., CLI; gee 300.   (A:493)
814. 9/7/69 gor Bolton, Hugh; ---, ---. See 7955.
815. 4/20/73 gor Bolton, Hugh; ---, ---. See 7957.
816. 9/7/69 gor Bolton, Mathew; ---, ---. See 7955.
817. 4/20/73 gor Bolton, Mathew; ---, ---. See 7957.
818. 6/15/99 mor Bond, Sally. See 822.
819. 10/11/84 gee Bond, William, farmer; ---, ALB. See 8252.
820. 10/12/84 mor Bond, William, farmer; ---, ALB; "Township of Hyde", WAS;
            mee 8253.   (A:492)
821. 5/7/95 mor Bond, William, farmer; Albany, ALB; Hyde (township), WAS;
            mee 8255.   (C:61)
822. 6/15/99 mor Bond, William (w. Sally); Kingsbury, WAS; Kingsbury, WAS;
            mee 8626.   (C:58)
823. 6/1/02 mee Bond, William, yeoman; Thurman, WAS. See 4524.
824. 2/9/95 mor Bondish, Gideon; ---, ---; Saratoga Pat., WAS; mee 3278.
                                                              (A:534)
825. 2/26/96 mor Bonny, Levi, farmer; Salem, WAS; Salem, WAS; mee 2128.
                                                              (C:26)
826. 11/20/94 gee Boochee, Jacob; ---, DUT. See 491.
827. 12/29/00 gor Borden, John; Willsborough, ESS; Willsborough, ESS; gee 7051.
                                                              (A:10)
828. 3/16/89 gor Borey, David, gentleman; Woolverhampton, Stafford (England);
                 Granville, WAS; gee 1308.   (C-1:78)
829. 3/16/89 gor Borry, David, gentleman; Woolverhampton, Stafford (England);
                 Granville, WAS; gee 7593.   (A:???)
830. 3/16/89 mee Borry, David; ---, ---. See 730, 1842, and 2337.
831. 3/22/89 mee Borry, David; ---, ---. See 4394.
832. 4/10/89 mee Borry, David; ---, ---. See 1299.
833. 4/16/89 mee Borry, David; ---, ---. See 1840.
834. 4/22/89 mee Borry, David; Wolverhampton, Stafford, England.   See 1303.
835. 4/22/89 mee Borry, David; ---, ---. See 3658, 5320, 8466.
836. 6/9/89 mee Borry, David; ---, ---. See 5560.
837. 3/16/89 mee Bory, David, Lt.; Wolverhampton, Safford, ---. See 1309,
                 7594.
838. 4/21/89 mee Bory, David; Wolverhampton, Safford, ---. See 5369.
839. 11/10/74 gee Bostwick, Adam, schoolmaster; Cambridge, WAS. See 1553.
840. 7/1/00 mor Bostwick, Ebenezer; ---, ---. See 8194.
841. 4/10/94 mor Bostwick, Medad; Fairfield, WAS; Jessup's Pat., WAS;
            mee 4270.   (A:487)
842. 1/7/00 mor Bosworth, Joshua C., farmer; Champlain, CLI; Canadian and
                 Nova Scotia Refugees' Pat., CLI; mee 5118.   (A:426)
843. 8/25/00 mee Bosworth, Roderick; Champlain, CLI. See 2338.
844. 10/24/92 gee Bothwell, Alexander, farmer; Salem, WAS. See 4451.
845. 12/11/95 gee Bothwell, James, yeoman; Salem, WAS. See 2454.
846. 11/5/88 gee Bott, William, innholder; Kingsbury, WAS. See 1889.
847. 2/10/89 mee Bott, William; Kingsbury, WAS. See 8697.
848. 3/2/89 mee Bott, William; Willsborough, CLI. See 3500.
849. 5/14/95 gor Bott, William, Esq.; Willsborough, CLI; Willsborough, CLI;
                 gee 8121. Two contracts this date involving these two
                 persons.   (A:534), (A:537)
850. 5/14/95 mee Bott, William, Esq.; Willsborough, CLI. See 8125.

851. 2/18/86 gor Bottom, Jabesh; ---, WAS; Granville, WAS; gee 6040. (B-1:229)
852. 12/14/92 mor Bough, James, merchant; Salem, WAS; Salem, WAS; co-mor 853;
                      mee 550.   (A:394)
853. 12/14/92 mor Bough, John, merchant; Salem, WAS. See 852.
854. 8/24/90 mor Bowen, O. Dan; Cambridge, WAS; Bean Pat., WAS; mee 6030.
                                                                      (A:291)
855. undated mee Bowerman(?), Jacob, merchant; City of N.Y. See 6420.
856. 8/26/70 mor Bowler, John; City of N.Y.; "west side of the Connecticut
                      River, GLO (in Vermont); mee 1555.   (A:58)
857. 7/20/71 mor Bowler, John; City of N.Y.; "west side of Connecticut
                      (River)", CUM (in Vermont); mee 1556.   (A:50)
858. 1/16/76 gor Bowles, Catharine. See 859.
859. 1/16/76 gor Bowles, John (w. Catharine); City of N.Y.; ---, CHA; gee 6138.
860. 6/12/86 --- Bowne, Daniel; ---, ---. See 2587. /   (A:175)
861. 5/21/84 gor Bowne, George; "late of the City of Burlington, now of the
                      City of Philadelphia, merchant, brother and heir of
                      Haydock Bowne, late of the City of New York, merchant,
                      deceased"; Queensbury, WAS; gee 6340. Two contracts
                      this date between this grantor and grantee. (C-2:267 & 326)
862. 5/21/84 --- Bowne, Haydock, dec'd. See 861.
863. 6/29/01 gee Bowne, Robert, merchant; City of N.Y. See 6048.
864. 12/12/01 gee Bowne, Robert, merchant; City of N.Y. See 6049.
865. 7/26/98 mee Bowne, Walter; City of N.Y. See 8699.
866. 12/2/99 mee Bowne, Walter, merchant; City of N.Y. See 1857.
867. 1/4/93 mor Bowsan, Jacob; Champlain, CLI; Mark Graves' Pat., CLI;
                      mee 3835.   (A:136)
868. 3/10/84 gor Boyd, Elenor. See 872.
869. 3/12/84 mee Boyd, Robert; Precinct of New Windsor, ULS. See 5514.
870. 7/12/80 gee Boyd, Robert, Esq.; New Windsor, ULS. See 5041.
871. 7/13/80 gee Boyd, Robert, Esq.; New Windsor, ULS. See 5042.
872. 3/10/84 gor Boyd, Robert, Esq. (w. Elenor); New Windsor Precinct, ULS;
                      Argyle, WAS; gee 5500.   (C-1:32)
873. 3/12/84 gee Boyd, Robert, Esq.; New Windsor Precinct, ULS. See 5501.
874. 5/21/99 mor Boyd, Rufus; ---, ---.; Bolton, WAS; mee 3439.   (C:57)
875. 1/15/02 mee Bozworth, Ichabod I.; Champlain, CLI. See 877.
876. 4/16/97 mor Bozworth, Joshua C.; Lebanon, WIN, CT; Champlain, CLI;
                      mee 5114.   (A:215)
877. 1/15/02 mor Bozworth, Joshua C.; Champlain, CLI; Champlain, CLI; mee 875.
                                                                      (B:66)
878. 10/26/01 gor Brace, Banister; Kingsbury, WAS; Queensbury, WAS; gee 1317.
                                                                      (F:110)
879. 10/26/01 mor Brace, Banister; Kingsbury, WAS; Queensbury, WAS; mee 1318.
                                                                      (D:141)
880. 2/16/02 gor Brace, Joanna. See 881.
881. 2/16/02 gor Brace, Levi (w. Joanna); Cambridge, WAS; Cambridge, WAS;
                      co-gees 8323, 8325.   (F:283)
882. 2/17/02 mee Brace, Levi, Junr.; Cambridge, WAS. See 8326.
883. 1/1/96 mee Brace, William; Cambridge Dist., WAS. See 3266.
884. 9/21/96 mor Brace, William; ---, ---.; Kingsbury, WAS; mee 7009. (B:240)
885. 10/24/96 mor Brace, William, yeoman; Cambridge, WAS; Hebron, WAS;
                      mee 8595.   (B:101)
886. 5/24/99 mor Brace, William, yeoman; Hebron, WAS; Kingsbury, WAS;
                      mee 4945.   (C:55)
887. 12/13/98 mee Bradley, Daniel; Queensbury, WAS. See 384.
888. 2/26/95 gee Bradley, Stephen; Westfield, WAS. See 7335.
889. 12/22/98 gor Bradley, Stephen; Wallingford, RUT, VT; Westfield, WAS;
                      gee 2008.   (D:358)
890. 6/5/71 gor Bradshaw, James; Kingsbury, ALB; Kingsbury, ALB; gee 8783.
                                                                      (B-2:243)
891. 12/19/82 gor Bradshaw, Thomas, Lieut.; Cambridge, ALB; Kingsbury, CHA;
                      gee 6925.   (C-1:43)
892. 4/30/98 mee Bradshaw, Thomas; Kingsbury, WAS. See 2501.
893. 7/3/02 mee Bradshaw, Thomas; Kingsbury, WAS. See 4940.
894. 12/24/99 gor Brag, Elizabeth. See 895.
895. 12/24/99 gor Brag, Peleg (w. Elizabeth), merchant; Argyle, WAS; Argyle,
                      WAS; gee 4522.   (D:337)

33

896. 12/24/99 mee Brag, Peleg; Argyle, WAS. See 4523.
897. 3/10/00 gor Bragg, Elizabeth. See 903.
898. 12/--/01 mor Bragg, Julius, blacksmith; Chateaugay, CLI; Chateaugay, CLI;
                   co-mees 6866, 8098.   (B:58)
899. 4/30/89 gee Bragg, Peleg; Schaghticook, ALB. See 6487.
900. 7/10/94 gee Bragg, Peleg, farmer; Argyle, WAS. See 4660.
901. 11/24/98 gee Bragg, Peleg, merchant; Argyle, WAS. See 2210.
902. 12/4/99 gee Bragg, Peleg; Argyle, WAS. See 8016.
903. 3/10/00 gor Bragg, Peleg (w. Elizabeth); Argyle, WAS; Argyle, WAS;
                   gee 3609.   (D:356)
904. 3/10/00 mee Bragg, Peleg, merchant; Argyle, WAS. See 3610.
905. 5/1/00   mor Braley, Roger, farmer; Chester, WAS; Chester, WAS; mee 7772.
                   Two contracts this date involving these two persons.
                                                     (D:202), (D:204)
906. 5/1/00   mor Braley, Solomon, farmer; Chester, WAS; Chester, WAS;
                   mee 7772.   (D:207)
907. 5/1/00   mor Braley, Stephen, farmer; Chester, WAS; Chester, WAS;
                   mee 7772. Two contracts this date involving these
                   two persons.   (D:202), (D:203)
908. 12/10/94 gor Brantingham, Hannah. See 909.
909. 12/10/94 gor Brantingham, Thomas H. (w. Hannah); ---, ---.; land "set
                   apart for Use of the Troops", CLI; gee 7920. (A:359)
910. 2/8/98   mor Brayton, David, farmer; Hartford, WAS; Hartford, WAS;
                   mee 1483.   (C:14)
911. 5/31/99 mor Brayton, David (w. Sarah), farmer, ---, WAS. See 918.
912. 2/8/98   mor Brayton, Henry; Hartford, WAS; Hartford, WAS; mee 1483.
                   Two contracts this date involving these two persons.
                                                     (B:244), (C:15)
913. 5/31/99 mor Brayton, Henry (w. Mahittible), farmer; ---, WAS. See 918.
914. 5/31/99 mor Brayton, Mahittible. See 913.
915. 5/31/99 mor Brayton, Phebe. See 918.
916. 5/31/99 mor Brayton, Sarah. See 911.
917. 2/8/98   mor Brayton, Thomas; Hartford, WAS; Hartford, WAS; mee 1483.
                                                                   (B:243)
918. 5/31/99 mor Brayton, Thomas (w. Phebe), farmer, ---, WAS; Provincial Pat.,
                   WAS; co-mors 911, 913, 914, 916; mee 933. (C:57)
919. 1/1/96   gee Breakenridge, Jonathan; ---, CHI, VT. See 5287.
920. 5/1/02   gor Breakenridge, Jonathan; Charlotte, CHI, VT; Willsborough, ESS;
                   gee 5288.   (A:50)
921. 12/3/02 mee Breakenridge, Jonathan; ---, ---. See 5598.
922. 2/20/97 mee Bredy, George, tailor; City of N.Y. See 3174.
923. 5/19/01 mor Brewer, Archabald; Chateaugay, CLI; Chateaugay, CLI; mee 284.
                                                                   (B:37)
924. 3/13/98 mee Brewer, George; ---, SAR. See 4022.
925. 6/30/98 gor Brewerton, Cornelius V.; ---, WAS; Hartford, WAS; gee 3957.
                                                               (C-2:329)
926. 8/10/02 --- Brewerton, Cornelius V., dec'd. See 187.
927. 8/10/02 --- Brewerton, Cornelius V., dec'd. See 4089.
928. 3/13/98 mee Brewerton, George; ---, SAR. See 6945.
929. 6/16/98 mee Brewerton, George, gentleman; ---, SAR. See 3420.
930. 9/26/00 mee Brewerton, George; City of N.Y. See 1151.
931. 3/20/98 gor Brewerton, Henry (w. Mary), attorney, City of N.Y.;
                   Provincial Pat., WAS; gee 3332.   (E:81)
932. 4/19/99 mee Brewerton, Henry, attorney; City of N.Y. See 3333.
933. 5/31/99 mee Brewerton, Henry, attorney; City of N.Y. See 918.
934. 6/--/98 mee Brewerton, James, gentleman; ---, SAR. See 6992.
935. 6/16/98 mee Brewerton, James; ---, SAR. See 6911.
936. 2/20/01 gor Brewerton, James; City of N.Y.; Hartford, WAS; gees (two
                   independent contracts) 460 (E:173) and 7328 (E:175).
937. 2/20/01 mee Brewerton, James, City of N.Y. See 458 and 7329.
938. 8/10/02 mee Brewerton, James; ---, ---. See 187 and 4089.
939. 3/20/98 gor Brewerton, Mary. See 931.
940. 12/1/98 gor Brewerton, William; ---, WAS; Hartford, WAS; gee 8716. (D:223)
941. 12/12/98 mee Brewerton, William; ---, WAS. See 4863.
942. 1/24/01 mor Brewerton, William; Hartford, WAS; Hartford, WAS; mee 4857.
                                                                   (D:18)

34

943. 2/4/97 gee Breymer, David, farmer; Hebron, WAS. See 8488.
944. 7/2/92 gee Bridge, George, farmer; Westfield, WAS. See 4446.
945. 3/12/93 gor Bridgen, Catherine. See 946.
946. 3/12/93 gor Bridgen, Thomas B., Esq. (w. Catherine); City of N.Y.;
　　　　　　　　　Granville, WAS; co-gees 1649, 2665, 5448, 5468, 5473,
　　　　　　　　　8728.　　　　　　　　　　　　　　　　　　　(B-2:44)
947. 5/30/93 mee Bridgen, Thomas B., Esq.; City of N.Y. See 5474.
948. 3/12/96 mor Bridgen, Thomas B., Esq.; City of N.Y.; Duerville, CLI;
　　　　　　　　　mee 7621.　　　　　　　　　　　　　　　　　(A:180)
949. 5/5/96 mor Bridgen, Thomas B., Esq.; City of N.Y.; Duerville, CLI;
　　　　　　　　　mee 1174.　　　　　　　　　　　　　　　　　(A:191)
950. 1/29/93 gee Bridgen, Thomas Bridgen, "lately called Thomas B. Atwood";
　　　　　　　　　City of N.Y. See 52.
951. 2/6/69 gor Bridges, Daniel; Greenwich, HAM, MA; Turner Pat., ALB;
　　　　　　　　　gee 4383.　　　　　　　　　　　　　　　　(B-1:113)
952. 11/9/02 mor Briggs, Abner, blacksmith; Easton, WAS; Easton, WAS;
　　　　　　　　　mee 8056.　　　　　　　　　　　　　　　　　(E:31)
953. 7/6/93 mor Briggs, David, hatter; Easton, WAS; Saratoga Pat., WAS;
　　　　　　　　　mee 6008.　　　　　　　　　　　　　　　　(A:429)
954. 1/18/00 mor Briggs, Elizabeth. See 961.
955. 12/10/92 mor Briggs, George, housewright; Easton, WAS; Easton, WAS;
　　　　　　　　　mee 3426.　　　　　　　　　　　　　　　　(A:410)
956. 5/10/92 gor Briggs, Grace. See 959.
957. 9/20/02 mee Briggs, Jabish, yeoman; Easton, WAS. See 1499.
958. 4/14/88 gee Briggs, Jeremiah; Westfield, WAS. See 5357.
959. 5/10/92 gor Briggs, Jeremiah (w. Grace); Westfield, WAS; Provincial Pat.,
　　　　　　　　　WAS; gee 3641.　　　　　　　　　　　　　　(D:247)
960. 3/10/00 gor Briggs, Sarah. See 962.
961. 1/18/00 mor Briggs, William (w. Elizabeth), yeoman; Cambridge, WAS;
　　　　　　　　　Cambridge, WAS; co-mees 3418, 3425.　　　　　(C:60)
962. 3/10/00 gor Briggs, William, (w. Sarah), yeoman; Hoosick, REN; Willson's
　　　　　　　　　Pat., WAS; gee 5203.　　　　　　　　　　　(E:219)
963. 5/12/98 gee Brigham, Wright, schoolmaster; Hartford, WAS. See 5384.
964. 7/1/94 gee Brigs, Jeremiah; Queensbury, WAS. See 3260.
965. 2/6/88 mor Brinckerhoff, Isaac (w. Sophia). See 6145.
966. 2/27/88 gor Brinckerhoff, Isaac. See 6124.
967. 9/22/96 mor Brinckerhoff, Isaac (w. Sophia), merchant; Hebron, WAS;
　　　　　　　　　Hebron, WAS; mee 6139.　　　　　　　　　　(B:89)
968. 5/25/98 mor Brinckerhoff, Isaac (w. Sophia), merchant; Hebron, WAS;
　　　　　　　　　Hebron, WAS; mee 8069.　　　　　　　　　　(C:54)
969. 2/6/88 mor Brinckerhoff, Sophia. See 965.
970. 2/27/88 gor Brinckerhoff, Sophia. See 6124.
971. 5/25/98 goo Brinckerhoff, Sophia. See 968.
972. 11/20/90 gor Brinckerhoof, Isaac (w. Sophia), merchant; Hebron, WAS.
　　　　　　　　　See 6146.
973. 11/20/90 gor Brinckerhoof, Sophia, "late Sophia Quackenboss". See 972.
974. 1/1/88 gor Brinkerhoff, Isaac; City of N.Y. See 6123.
975. 8/6/93 gor Brinkerhoff, Isaac; Hebron, WAS. See 6159.
976. 1/1/88 gor Brinkerhoff, Sophia, "the late Sophia Quackenbos". See 6123.
977. 9/1/98 gor Broadwell, Noah, blacksmith; Plattsburgh, CLI. See 5829.
978. 12/17/01 goo Broadwell, Noah; Plattsburgh, CLI. See 5794.
979. 12/17/01 mor Broadwell, Noah; Plattsburgh, CLI; Plattsburgh, CLI;
　　　　　　　　　gee 5793.　　　　　　　　　　　　　　　　(B:313)
980. 5/2/96 gee Broford, Robert; Argyle, WAS. See 2100b.
981. 7/1/88 mee Brooks, David; ---, ---. See 158.
982. 4/25/93 mor Brooks, Jabez; Charlotte, CHI, VT; Champlain, CLI; co-mor
　　　　　　　　　5661; mee 5109.　　　　　　　　　　　　　(A:108)
983. 2/8/98 mor Brooks, Miriam. See 985.
984. 4/1/02 gor Brooks, Miriam. See 986.
985. 2/8/98 mor Brooks, Silas (w. Miriam), farmer; Hartford, WAS; Hartford,
　　　　　　　　　WAS; mee 1483.　　　　　　　　　　　　　(C:13)
986. 4/1/02 gor Brooks, Silas (w. Miriam), farmer; Hartford, WAS; Champlain,
　　　　　　　　　CLI; gee 6663.　　　　　　　　　　　　　(B:332)
987. 4/26/86 gee Brooks, Uri; Salem, WAS. See 1820.
988. 2/9/93 gor Brooks, Uri, tanner; Salem, WAS; Salem, WAS; gee 1673.
　　　　　　　　　　　　　　　　　　　　　　　　　　　(B-2:108)

35

989.	9/20/00	gee	Broome, John, Esq., merchant; City of N.Y. See 39.
990.	11/27/95	mor	Brotherton, John, farmer; ---, SAR; Peru, CLI; mee 5740. (A:167)
991.	2/1/98	gee	Brown, Amasa, clergyman; Hartford, WAS. See 1474.
992.	2/8/98	mor	Brown, Amasa, clergyman; Hartford, WAS; Hartford, WAS; mee 1483. (C:14)
993.	3/25/99	mee	Brown, Amasa, clergyman; Hartford, WAS. See 1574.
994.	7/2/92	gee	Brown, Andrew, farmer; Westfield, WAS. See 4446.
995.	8/13/95	gor	Brown, Andrew, farmer; Hartford, WAS; Hartford, WAS; gee 5383. (C-2:138)
996.	11/17/64	gor	Brown, Archibald. See 4417.
997.	12/24/94	mee	Brown, Archibald; "Glascow ... Scotland, druggist". See 7608.
998.	12/25/92	gor	Brown, Asa; Queensbury, WAS; Queensbury, WAS; gee 5122. (B-2:68)
999.	6/22/98	gee	Brown, Benjamin L.; Hartford, WAS. See 5696.
1000.	6/23/98	mor	Brown, Benjamin L.; Hartford, WAS; Old Military Township #6 (Clinton), CLI; mee 5699 (A:315)
1001.	9/16/95	gee	Brown, Caleb; Hartford, WAS. See 418.
1002.	3/19/00	gee	Brown, Caleb, merchant; Hartford, WAS. See 1347.
1003.	2/8/98	mor	Brown, Daniel; Hartford, WAS; Hartford, WAS; mee 1483. (B:242)
1004.	2/22/98	mor	Brown, Daniel (w. Jennet), merchant; Hartford, WAS; Hartford, WAS; mee 5539. (C:239)
1005.	5/9/01	mee	Brown, Daniel; Hartford, WAS. See 8155.
1006.	5/30/01	mor	Brown, Daniel; Hartford, WAS; Hartford, WAS; co-mor 1817a; mee 4898. (D:55)
1007.	11/7/96	gor	Brown, Elizabeth. See 1029.
1008.	1/2/02	mor	Brown, Hannah. See 1010.
1009.	2/4/90	mor	Brown, Isaac; Argyle, WAS; personal property?; "mee" 4866. (A:210)
1010.	1/2/02	mor	Brown, James (w. Hannah), yeoman; Argyle, WAS; Hebron, WAS; mee 2672. (D:184)
1011.	2/22/98	mor	Brown, Jennet. See 1004.
1012.	7/6/88	gee	Brown, Jeremiah; Granville, WAS. See 2378.
1013.	7/6/88	mor	Brown, Jeremiah; ---, ---.; ---, WAS; mee 2380. (A:90)
1014.	2/27/90	gor	Brown, Jeremiah; Granville, WAS; Granville, WAS; gee 3985. (A:366)
1015.	10/8/88	gee	Brown, John, farmer; Ticonderoga, CLI. See 1934.
1016.	7/2/89	gor	Brown, John; Ticonderoga, CLI; ---, CLI (a 2-year lease?); co-gor 3396; co-gees 2211, 7644. (A:92)
1017.	4/18/91	gor	Brown, John, yeoman; Argyle, WAS; Argyle, WAS; gee 4716. (C-1:81)
1018.	11/10/95	gor	Brown, John, farmer; Wallkill, ULS; Argyle, WAS; gee 1374. (C-2:127)
1019.	7/7/98	gee	Brown, John; Pittstown, REN. See 2804.
1020.	4/8/99	gee	Brown, John; Argyle, WAS. See 4408.
1021.	4/2/90	---	Brown, Jonathan; Stamford, FAI, CT. See 1037.
1022.	10/27/94	---	Brown, Jonathan; Stamford, FAI, CT. See 1039.
1023.	8/31/96	mor	Brown, Jonathan; ---, REN; Canadian and Nova Scotia Refugees' Pat., CLI; mee 4862. (A:236)
1024.	9/1/01	mee	Brown, Jonathan; Pittstown, REN. See 599.
1025.	8/31/96	mor	Brown, Jonathan, Esq.; ---, REN; Moorfield, CLI; mee 4862. (A:237)
1026.	9/11/01	mee	Brown, Jonathan, Esq.; Pittstown, REN. See 1128.
1027.	11/3/96	mor	Brown, Oliver, farmer; Champlain, CLI; Canadian and Nova Scotia Refugees' Pat.; mee 7890. (A:204)
1028.	2/4/95	gee	Brown, Samuel; Salem, WAS. See 7333.
1029.	11/7/96	gor	Brown, Samuel (w. Elizabeth); Westfield, WAS; Westfield, WAS; gee 6655. (C-2:208)
1030.	6/30/97	gee	Brown, Samuel; Westfield, WAS. See 8475.
1031.	6/30/97	mor	Brown, Samuel; Westfield, WAS; Granville, WAS; mee 8472. (C:15)
1032.	3/18/01	gee	Brown, Samuel; Granville, WAS. See 1810.
1033.	4/29/85	gor	Brown, Solomon, Capt.; New Perth, CHA; New Perth, CHA; gee 8647. (A:163)
1034.	10/5/89	gor	Brown, Thomas; Granville, WAS; ---, WAS; gee 2247. (A:465)
1035.	7/28/92	gee	Brown, Thomas, yeoman; Granville, WAS. See 3410.

1036. 6/17/80 gee Brown, Valentine, yeoman; "Charlot Precinct", DUT. See 8696.
1037. 4/2/90 --- Brown, William, Balltown, ALB. Brown appoints "my trusty
friend Jonathan Brown of Stamford (CT) my Lawfull Attorney
... to sell, let or Lease fifty-four acres ... in Balltown
and to sell four hundred acres at Lake Champlain in the
County of Clinton..." (A:381)
1038. 2/1/94 mor Brown, William, farmer; Salem, WAS; Hebron, WAS; co-mor
2979; co-mees 588, 590, 2864, 2865, 2866, 7673, 7677,
8049, 8050. (A:510)
1039. 10/27/94 gor Brown, William, "late of Ballstown, County of Saratoga by
Jonathan Brown of Stamford", his attorney; Moore's Pat.,
CLI; gee 1168. (A:378)
1040. 10/28/94 gor Brown, William, "late of Ballstown", SAR; Moore's Pat, CLI;
gee 1169. (A:379)
1041. 3/22/99 gor Brownell, Experience. See 1043.
1042. 1/27/97 gee Brownell, Joshua; Cambridge, WAS. See 1714.
1043. 3/22/99 gor Brownell, Joshua (w. Experience), yeoman; Cambridge, WAS;
Saratoga Pat., WAS; co-gors 670, 671; gee 5636. (D:88)
1044. 12.20/99 gee Brownell, Joshua; Cambridge, WAS. See 8776.
1045. 12/23/00 gor Brownell, Joshua, yeoman; Cambridge, WAS; Easton, WAS;
gee 3891. (E:167)
1046. Data repositioned.
1047. 5/17/99 gee Brownson, John; North Hero, FRA, VT. See 5085.
1048. 5/18/99 mor Brownson, John; North Hero, FRA, VT; Champlain, CLI;
mee 4527. (A:387)
1049. 1/1/02 mor Brownson, John; Champlain, CLI; Canadian and Nova Scotia
Pat., CLI; mee 5037. (B:59)
1050. 6/5/92 gee Brownwell, Charles; ---, ---, RI. See 8001.
1051. 6/22/93 gor Bruce, Archibald; ---, ---. See 1053.
1052. 8/11/86 mee Bruce, Judith, widow; City of N.Y. See 8787.
1053. 6/22/93 gor Bruce, Judith, "widdow and executrix together with Archibald
Bruce and Isaac Low of the ... will ... of William Bruce,
late surgeon to his Britannic Majesty's Regiment of
artillery"; land "near Fort Ann", WAS; gee 8789. (B-2:179)
1054. 6/22/93 --- Bruce, William, dec'd. See 1053.
1055. 5/25/85 gee Brundige, Daniel, Lieut.; ---, ---. See 7055.
1056. 5/25/85 mor Brundridge, Daniel; Skenesborough, WAS; Skenesborough, WAS;
mee 8548. (Deed Book B-1:163)
1057. 3/2/97 mee Brunson, Isaac, merchant; City of N.Y. See 3754.
1058. 11/10/98 gor Brunson, Reuben (w. Sarah); Plattsburgh, CLI; Plattsburgh,
CLI; gee 8245. (B:180)
1059. 11/10/98 gor Brunson, Sarah. See 1058.
1060. 7/17/70 mor Brush, Crane; City of N.Y.; land "east side of Hudson's
River, ALB; mee 1554. (A:53)
1061. 1/4/96 mor Brydia, David; Plattsburgh, CLI; Plattsburgh, CLI; mee 5743.
(A:168)
1062. 11/12/90 mor Bryson, John; ---, WAS; Argyle, WAS; mee 4595. (A:258)
1063. 12/13/90 mee Bryson, John; Hebron, WAS. See 5505.
1064. 10/29/91 gor Bryson, John, miller; Argyle, WAS; Argyle, WAS; gee 3781.
(B-2:88)
1065. 6/7/93 gor Buchanan, Almy. See 1069.
1066. 7/15/91 gor Buchanan, Lille. See 1074.
1067. 6/7/93 gor Buchanan, Lillie. See 1076.
1068. 6/13/93 gor Buchanan, Lilly. See 1078.
1069. 6/7/93 gor Buchanan, Thomas (w. Almy); City of N.Y. See 6484.
1070. 10/2/95 mee Buchanan, Thomas, Mr., merchant; City of N.Y. See 4191.
1071. 7/10/90 gor Buchanan, Walter, merchant; City of N.Y.; Hebron, WAS;
gees (four independent contracts) 2565 (C-1:73),
5296 (A:323), 8683 (A:392), 8710 (C-1:97).
1072. 7/10/90 mee Buchanan, Walter, merchant; City of N.Y. See 38, 454, 1898,
2566, 2661, 2991, 5300, 6894, 7574, 8630, 8631, 8711, 8871.
1073. 12/28/90 mee Buchanan, Walter; City of N.Y. See 1868 and 6267.
1074. 7/15/91 gor Buchanan, Walter (w. Lille), merchant; City of N.Y.;
Grant Pat., WAS; co-gees 8293, 8573. (B:2:301)
1075. 8/13/92 mee Buchanan, Walter, merchant; City of N.Y. See 2567.
1076. 6/7/93 gor Buchanan, Walter (w. Lillie); City of N.Y. See 6484.

1077.	6/10/93	gee	Buchanan, Walter, merchant; City of N.Y. See 8259.
1078.	6/13/93	gor	Buchanan, Walter (W. Lilly), merchant; City of N.Y.;
			Argyle, WAS; gee 4495. (B-2:147)
1079.	6/14/93	mee	Buchanan, Walter, merchant; City of N.Y. See 4490.
1080.	6/24/67	gee	Buchannan, Thomas, merchant, City of N.Y. See 1202.
1081.	6/24/67	gee	Buchannan, Walter, merchant, City of N.Y. See 1202.
1082.	6/14/93	mee	Buchannan, Walter, merchant; City of N.Y. See 4489.
1083.	2/8/98	mor	Buck, Abigail, widow of John Buck, dec'd.; Hartford, WAS;
			Hartford, WAS; mee 1483. (C:13)
1084.	5/1/93	gee	Buck, Amos; Cambridge, WAS. See 516.
1085.	4/8/01	gor	Buck, Amos (w. Sarah), farmer; Cambridge, WAS; Cambridge,
			WAS; gee 3276. (E:224)
1086.	4/8/01	mee	Buck, Amos, farmer; Cambridge, WAS. See 3277.
1087.	10/18/96	mor	Buck, David; ---, WAS; Queensbury, WAS; co-mor 8365;
			mee 3965. (B:190)
1088.	6/6/96	gee	Buck, John; Hartford, WAS. See 1348.
1089.	2/8/98	---	Buck, John, dec'd. See 1083.
1090.	10/5/96	mee	Buck, John, Esq.; Granville, WAS. See 1614.
1091.	3/7/98	mor	Buck, Jonathan; Pleasant Valley (Crown Point), CLI;
			Pleasant Valley (Crown Point), CLI; mee 5871. (A:280)
1092.	4/8/01	gor	Buck, Sarah. See 1085.
1093.	10/10/95	mor	Buck, Solomon; Cambridge, WAS, Cambridge, WAS; mee 7032.
			(C:20)
1094.	12/21/98	gee	Buck, Solomon; Cambridge, WAS. See 5225.
1095.	2/5/99	gor	Buck, Solomon; Cambridge, WAS; Cambridge, WAS; gee 1390.
			(D:230)
1096.	5/6/00	gee	Buck, Solomon; Argyle, WAS. See 4548.
1097.	8/25/02	mor	Buckle, William; ---, ---; ---, ESS; mee 6501. (A:86)
1098.	12/30/94	gor	Buckman, Samuel H., shoemaker; Hartford, WAS; Hartford, WAS;
			gee 5953. (B-2:357)
1099.	12/10/91	mor	Budd, Jonathan, yeoman; Rye, WES; Argyle, WAS; mee 4584.
			(A:327)
1100.	6/26/00	gor	Budd, Jonathan; Argyle, WAS; Argyle, WAS; gee 2041. (E:8)
1101.	2/26/01	gor	Budd, Jonathan, yeoman; Argyle, WAS; Argyle, WAS; gee 3414.
			(E:306)
1102.	2/26/01	mee	Budd, Jonathan, yeoman, Argyle, WAS. See 3415.
1103.	3/26/01	gor	Budd, Jonathan, cordwainer; Argyle, WAS; Argyle, WAS;
			gee 2042. (E:304)
1104.	3/26/01	mee	Budd, Jonathan, cordwainer; Argyle, WAS. See 2043.
1105.	9/15/94	gee	Buell, Daniel; ---, ---. See 2012.
1106.	1/1/95	gor	Buell, Daniel; Hampton, WAS. See 1284, 8814, 8815.
1107.	5/9/96	mor	Bull, Daniel (w. Susannah); Southeast, DUT; Hartford, WAS;
			co-mees 385, 2450. (B:147)
1108.	9/20/97	mor	Bull, Daniel (w. Susannah); Hartford, WAS; Hartford, WAS;
			mee 5359. (B:219)
1109.	9/28/93	gee	Bull, Frederick; Hartford, HAR, CT. See 5009. (two contracts)
1110.	4/5/95	gor	Bull, Frederick; Hartford, HAR, CT; Jessup's Purchase, WAS;
			gee 1116. Two contracts this date involving these two
			persons. (C-2:242), (C-2:245)
1111.	7/3/92	gor	Bull, Joseph; Hartford, HAR, CT; Westfield, WAS; gee 3739.
			(D:75)
1112.	2/15/91	mor	Bull, Manning; Wstfield, WAS; Westfield, WAS; mee 1735.
			(A:282)
1113.	9/1/02	mee	Bull, Manning; Hartford, WAS. See 8124.
1114.	11/11/97	mor	Bull, Manning, Esq.; Hartford, WAS; Hartford, WAS; mee 1472.
			(B:231)
1115.	3/22/92	gor	Bull, Nathaniel, gentleman; Westfield, WAS; Westfield, WAS;
			gee 3331. (E:85)
1116.	4/5/95	gee	Bull, Samuel; Middletown, MID, CT See 1110. (two contracts)
1117.	5/9/96	mor	Bull, Susannah. See 1107.
1118.	9/20/97	mor	Bull, Susannah. See 1108.
1119.	1/2/02	mee	Bull, Wadsworth; Granville, WAS. See 5207.
1120.	3/2/99	gor	Bullock, William; Westfield, WAS; Westfield, WAS; gee 438.
			(E:242)
1121.	4/14/01	mor	Bullus, James; Champlain, CLI; Champlain, CLI; mee 5119.
			(B:22)

1122.	9/4/86	gee	Bump, Jacob. See 1734.
1123.	9/8/99	mor	Burdick, Ephraim; Easton, WAS; Saratoga Pat., WAS; mee 3695.
			(C:21)
1124.	8/28/93	gee	Burdick, George; Cambridge, WAS. See 1326.
1125.	4/1/95	gee	Burdick, George; Cambridge, WAS. See 8839.
1126.	8/2/02	gee	Burdick, Wait; Plattsburgh, CLI. See 6629.
1127.	3/27/01	mee	Burg, Elijah; Argyle, WAS. See 1503.
1128.	9/11/01	mor	Burnham, Ashbil; Kingsbury, WAS; Champlain, CLI; mee 1026.
			(B:77)
1129.	7/10/90	gee	Burnham, Josiah; ---, ALB. See 2862.
1130.	7/10/90	gee	Burnham, William; ---, ALB. See 2862.
1131.	4/26/94	gor	Burns, Jane, "widow and one of the heirs of Elizabeth McNeill, deceased"; ---, ---.; Argyle, WAS; gee 4734.
			(C-2:303)
1132.	8/1/98	mor	Burras, Jabez, gentleman; ---, WAS; Provincial Pat., WAS; co-mees 5328, 5340. Mortgagees are executors of the estate of John Leake, dec'd. (C:63)
1133.	10/22/00	gor	Burres, David (w. Nancy); Cambridge, WAS; Cambridge, WAS; gee 4268. (F:116)
1134.	10/22/00	gor	Burres, Nancy. See 1133.
1135.	12/30/85	gee	Burroughs, Benjamin; ---, ---. See 7055.
1136.	10/6/85	gee	Burroughs, James. See 7055.
1137.	12/15/84	gee	Burroughs, Jeremiah. See 7055.
1138.	7/1/86	gee	Burroughs, Jeremiah; Whitehall, WAS. See 8561.
1139.	9/1/86	mor	Burroughs, Jeremiah; White Creek, WAS; Whitehall, WAS; mee 8562. (Deed Book B-1:251)
1140.	10/7/94	gee	Burroughs, Jeremiah; ---, ---. See 8583.
1141.	10/6/85	gee	Burroughs, John; ---, ---. See 7055.
1142.	8/9/92	gor	Burroughs, John (w. Mary), yeoman; Whitehall, WAS; Whitehall, WAS; gee 2416. (B-2:394)
1143.	8/9/92	gor	Burroughs, Mary. See 1142.
1144.	12/15/84	gee	Burroughs, Matthew; ---, ---. See 7055.
1145.	12/17/98	gor	Burrows, Betsey. See 1150.
1146.	9/26/00	mor	Burrows, Betsey. See 1151.
1147.	1/26/02	mor	Burrows, Betsey. See 1152.
1148.	9/21/97	mee	Burrows, Jabez, saddler; Hartford, WAS. See 3321.
1149.	8/1/98	gee	Burrows, Jabez; ---, WAS. See 5327.
1150.	12/17/98	gor	Burrows, Jabez (w. Betsey); Hartford, WAS; Hartford, WAS; co-gees 1153, 1156. (D:28)
1151.	9/26/00	mor	Burrows, Jabez (w. Betsey); Hartford, WAS; Hartford, WAS; mee 930. (C:65)
1152.	1/26/02	mor	Burrows, Jabez, Esq. (w. Betsey); Hartford, WAS; Hartford, WAS; mee 5667. (D:147)
1153.	12/17/98	gee	Burrows, Roswell; Groton, NEW, CT. See 1150.
1154.	11/2/01	gor	Burrows, Roswell, yeoman; Groton, NEW, CT; Hartford, WAS; gee 1155. (E:446)
1155.	11/2/01	gee	Burrows, Silas, yeoman; Groton, NEW, CT. See 1154.
1156.	12/17/98	gee	Burrows, Silus, yeoman; Groton, NEW, CT. See 1150.
1157.	9/15/98	gee	Bushee, Samuel; Saratoga, SAR. See 3255.
1158.	9/25/99	mee	Bushee, Samuel; Kingsbury, WAS. See 1530.
1159.	5/5/01	mor	Butler, George W.; Cambridge, WAS; Cambridge, WAS; co-mees 1839, 2615, 3007, 6470, 6948, 7450. Co-mortgagees are all trustees of the Associate Congregation of Cambridge. (D:62b)
1160.	7/16/92	gee	Button, Gideon, yeoman; Hebron, WAS. See 5051.
1161.	5/3/97	mor	Button, Gideon, yeoman; Hebron, WAS; Hebron, WAS; co-mor 1164; mee 8598. (B:168)
1162.	9/5/00	mor	Button, Mary. See 1165.
1163.	7/16/62	gee	Button, Peter, yeoman; Hebron, WAS. See 5051.
1164.	5/3/97	mor	Button, Peter, yeoman; Hebron, WAS. See 1161.
1165.	9/5/00	mor	Button, Shubal (w. Mary), farmer; Cambridge, WAS; Cambridge, WAS; mee 4039. (C:63)
1166.	5/17/87	mee	Byvanck, Evert, merchant; City of N.Y. See 11.
1167.	2/16/99	mor	Cable, Apphia. See 1172.
1168.	10/27/94	gee	Cable, John, farmer; Ballstown, SAR. See 1039.
1169.	10/28/94	gee	Cable, John, farmer; Ballstown, SAR. See 1040.

1170. 5/28/00 mee Cable, John; Ballstown, SAR. See 8214.
1171. 7/3/95 gee Cable, Jonathan, yeoman; ---, WAS. See 6892.
1172. 2/16/99 mor Cable, Jonathan (w. Apphia); Hartford, WAS; Hartford, WAS;
                      mee 1498.   (C:37)
1173. 5/28/00 mee Cable, Lemuel; Milton, SAR. See 5593.
1174. 5/5/96 mee Cadiot, Jean, gentleman; City of N.Y. See 949.
1175. 5/2/96 gor Caldwell, Elizabeth. See 1187.
1176. 5/2/96 gor Caldwell, Elizabeth. See 1185 and 1187.
1177. 6/30/96 gor Caldwell, Elizabeth. See 1190.
1178. 2/11/01 gor Caldwell, Elizabeth. See 1192.
1179. 7/26/02 gor Caldwell, Elizabeth. See 1196.
1180. 5/23/87 gee Caldwell, James. See 6007.
1181. 12/20/87 mee Caldwell, James, merchant; Albany, ALB. See 1532.
1182. 9/21/93 mee Caldwell, James. merchant; Albany, ALB. See 6315.
                      (two contracts)
1183. 12/17/93 mee Caldwell, James; Albany, ALB. See 2726, 5414, 5415, 7919,
                      8321.
1184. 7/9/94 gee Caldwell, James, merchant; Albany, ALB. See 6518.
1185. 5/2/96 gor Caldwell, James (w. Elizabeth); Albany, ALB; David Campbell's
                      Pat., WAS; co-gor 8039; co-gees 1287, 2098, 2213, 5574.
                                                              (B-2:546)
1186. 5/2/96 gor Caldwell, James, gentleman; Albany, ALB; Donald Campbell's
                      Pat., WAS; co-gor 8034; gees (three independent contracts)
                      4918 (C-2:1), 7257 (C-2:95), 7356 (F:34).
1187. 5/2/96 gor Caldwell, James (w. Elizabeth), gentleman; Albany, ALB;
                      land "east side of Hudson River", WAS; co-gor 8039a;
                      gee 5660. Two contracts this date involving these
                      persons.   (C-2:253), (C-2:314)
1188. 5/2/96 mee Caldwell, James, ---, ---. See 2102.
1189. 5/2/96 mee Caldwell, James. merchant; Albany, ALB. See 6088 and 7357.
1190. 6/30/96 gor Caldwell, James (w. Elizabeth); Albany, ALB. See 8046.
1191. 6/27/97 gor Caldwell, James, gentleman; Albany, ALB. See 8041.
1192. 2/11/01 gor Caldwell, James (w. Elizabeth), merchant; Albany, ALB;
                      land "west side of Lake George, WAS; gee 7535. (E:149)
1193. 2/11/01 mee Caldwell, James, merchant; Albany, ALB. See 7536.
1194. 3/4/01 gee Caldwell, James; Albany, ALB. See 627.
1195. 7/24/02 mee Caldwell, James, merchant; Albany, ALB. See 7045.
1196. 7/26/02 mee Caldwell, James (w. Elizabeth); Albany, ALB. See 8207.
1197. -/-/95 gor Caldwell, Joseph, yeoman; Kingsbury, WAS; Kingsbury, WAS;
                      gee 4956.   (B-2:537)
1198. 5/20/97 gor Caldwell, Joseph, yeoman; Kingsbury, WAS; Kingsbury, WAS;
                      gee 1751.   (D:412)
1199. 3/9/98 mor Calkin, Aaron (w. Rachel); Hartford, WAS; Hartford, WAS;
                      mee 1488.   (B:248)
1200. 3/9/98 mor Calkin, Rachel. See 1199.
1201. 11/1/00 mor Callender, Nathaniel; Champlain, CLI; Champlain, CLI;
                      mee 1738.   (B:23)
1202. 6/24/67 gor Campbell, Angus, merchant; City of N.Y.; Argyle, WAS;
                      co-gees 1080, 1081, 1846, 4821, 6474, 6899. (A:128)
1203. 1/14/65 gee Campbell, Ann, wife of James Gillis, farmer, of Orange
                      County, N.Y. See 6217.
1204. 1/15/65 gee Campbell, Ann, wife of James Gillis of 1203 above. See 6219.
1205. 4/26/65 gor Campbell, Ann. See 2822.
1206. 1/2/76 gor Campbell, Ann. See 1223.
1207. 3/9/76 gee Campbell, Ann. See 1218.
1208. 7/10/87? mee Campbell, Ann; ---, ---. See 7656.
1209. 1/14/65 gor Campbell, Archibald, merchant; City of N.Y. See 6217.
1210. 1/15/65 gor Campbell, Archibald, merchant; City of N.Y. See 6219.
                      Six contracts this date involving these persons.
1211 through 1215 inclusive. Data repositioned.
1216. 3/21/65 gor Campbell, Archibald, merchant; City of N.Y. See 6232.
1217. 10/22/65 gor Campbell, Archibald, merchant; City of N.Y. See 6220.
1218. 3/9/76 gor Campbell, Archibald; Fort Edward, CHA (this contract
                      identifies terms of his will dated 1/2/76); Argyle, CHA;
                      co-gees Ann Campbell, his "loving wife", and Sarah
                      McNeil, his "aged mother".   (A:23)

1219.	7/20/92	gor	Campbell, Archibald; Albany, ALB; Westfield, WAS; gee 7018.
			(B-2:19)
1220.	4/30/93	gor	Campbell, Archibald, executor of the will of George Gunn, "late of Washington County, deceased"; Cambridge, WAS; Salem WAS; gee 6534. (B-2:42)
1221.	6/16/98	mee	Campbell, Archibald; ---, ---. See 4491.
1222.	1/2/76	mee	Campbell, Archibald, Esq.; ---, CHA. See 3019.
1223.	1/2/76	gor	Campbell, Archibald, Esq. (w. Ann); ---, CHA; Argyle, CHA; gee 3018. (A:21)
1224.	5/18/85	gor	Campbell, Catharine; Argyle, WAS; Argyle, WAS; gee 4228. (A:103)
1225.	9/12/64	gee	Campbell, Donald. See 1233.
1226.	10/28/01	mor	Campbell, Donald; Albany, ALB; Peru, CLI; mee 4224. (B:61)
1227.	7/22/86	mor	Campbell, Donald, Esq.; City of N.Y.; Grant Pat., WAS; mee 4823. (Deed Book B-1:247)
1228.	6/8/73	gor	Campbell, Duncan, Colonel; ---, DUT; McCulloch Pat., CHA; gee 3535 (B-1:69)
1229.	6/1/92	gor	Campbell, Duncan; Augusta, Lunenburgh Dist., Upper Canada; Argyle, WAS; gee 2207. (B-2:527)
1230.	5/13/96	gor	Campbell, Duncan, "late a Lieutenant ... in the New York Regiment commanded by Col. James Livingston", City of N.Y.; "bounty lands", CLI; co-gees 2311, 7249. (A:521)
1231.	3/7/85	---	Campbell, Elizabeth, dec'd. See 6721 and 6723.
1232.	5/7/85	---	Campbell, Elizabeth, dec'd. See 4000.
1233.	9/12/64	gor	Campbell, George; London, England; land "east side of the Hudson River, ALB; gee 1225. (A:273)
1234.	4/8/01	gor	Campbell, James, Esq.; Augusta, Granville Co., Upper Canada; Argyle, WAS; gee 5069. (E:325)
1235.	6/3/88	gor	Campbell, John; German Camp, COL; Argyle, WAS; co-gees 1739 and 7788. (B-2:30)
1236.	1/24/95	mee	Campbell, John; Albany, ALB. See 7194.
1237.	7/3/98	mor	Campbell, John; Chateaugay, CLI; Old Military Township #7 (Chateaugay), CLI; co-mees 5752, 5811, 8758. (A:329)
1238.	7/12/80	gor	Campbell, Mary, Junr. See 5041.
1239.	7/13/92	gor	Campbell, Robert, "late a Captain in his Britannic Majesty's Sixtieth Regiment of Foot but now of the County of Gloucester ... Great Britain"; Granville, WAS; gee 1968. (B-2:2)
1240.	3/18/89	gor	Campbell, Robert, Esq., Capt.; ---, ---.; Granville, WAS; gee 3724. (A:112)
1241.	12/3/01	mor	Cantfield, Salvinus; Plattsburgh, CLI; Plattsburgh, CLI; co-mor 573; mee 5949. (B:53)
1242.	5/14/95	mee	Cantine, Peter, Junr., Esq.; Redhook, DUT. See 1587.
1243.	5/28/98	mee	Cantine, Peter, Junr., Esq.; Red Hook, DUT. See 1588.
1244.	6/29/98	mee	Cantine, Peter, Junr., Esq.; Red Hook, DUT. See 2890.
1245.	4/29/83	gee	Carey, John; New Perth, CHA. See 3872.
1246.	12/10/89	gor	Carey, John, yeoman; Hebron, WAS; Hebron, WAS; gee 8198. (C-1:72)
1247.	11/1/00	mor	Carey, Moses (w. Sophronia), farmer; Argyle, WAS. See 5199.
1248.	11/1/00	mor	Carey, Sophronia. See 1247.
1249.	6/9/74	---	Cargill, Elizabeth. See 4796.
1250.	2/8/98	mor	Carington, Eli (w. Phoebe), farmer; Hartford, WAS; Hartford, WAS; mee 1483. (B:246)
1251.	2/8/98	mor	Carington, Phoebe. See 1250.
1252.	5/24/92	gee	Carlile, Samuel; Hebron. WAS. See 3869.
1253.	11/19/00	gor	Carly, Michael, yeoman; Champlain, CLI; Champlain, CLI; gee 2090. (B:253)
1254.	11/19/96	mor	Carman, Joseph, carpenter; Fishkill, DUT; Willsborough, CLI; mee 53. (A:206)
1255.	11/18/93	mee	Carpenter, Benjamin; ---, DUT. See 6517.
1256.	5/1/94	mee	Carpenter, Benjamin; ---, DUT. See 6526.
1257.	1/26/93	mor	Carpenter, Daniel I., carpenter; ---, DUT; Hutton's Bush, WAS; mee 3651. (A:402)
1258.	5/1/00	mor	Carpenter, Jesse, farmer; Chester, WAS; Chester, WAS; mee 7772. Two contracts this date involving these two persons. (D:224), (D:225)

1259. 5/1/00 mor Carpenter, Joseph, farmer; Chester, WAS; Chester, WAS;
mee 7772.   (D:225)
1260. 6/11/01 mor Carpenter, Moly. See 1261.
1261. 6/11/01 mor Carpenter, Rowland (w. Moly), farmer; Hebron, WAS; Hebron,
WAS; mee 5228.   (D:69)
1262. 12/25/95 gee Carpenter, William; Kingsbury, WAS. See 1566.
1263. 3/12/95 gee Carr, Daniel, yeoman; Granville, WAS. See 7595.
1264. 2/8/98 mor Carrington, Aaron, carpenter; Hartford, WAS; Hartford, WAS;
mee 1483   (B:245)
1265. 3/4/90 gee Carswell, Abner, yeoman; Salem, WAS. See 1270.
1266. 3/4/90 mor Carswell, Abner; Salem, WAS; Salem, WAS; mee 1271. (A:478)
1267. 6/10/96 mor Carswell, David (w. Martha); Salem, WAS; Salem, WAS;
mee 4915.   (B:44)
1268. 12/20/96 mee Carswell, David, yeoman; Salem, WAS. See 7720.
1269. 6/10/96 mor Carswell, Martha. See 1267.
1270. 3/4/90 gor Carswell, Nathaniel, yeoman; Salem, WAS; Salem, WAS;
gee 1265.   (B-2:234)
1271. 3/4/90 mee Carswell, Nathaniel, Mr.; Salem, WAS. See 1266.
1272. 9/6/99 gee Carter, Amasa, farmer; Argyle, WAS. See 6905.
1273. 5/3/80 gee Carter, Asa; farmer; ---, ALB. See 7648.
1274. 5/3/88 mor Carter, Asa; ---, ---. See 6361.
1275. 6/27/97 gor Carter, Asa; Argyle, WAS; Argyle, WAS; gee 6363. (C-2:165)
1276. 6/27/97 mor Carter, Asa; ---, ---; Argyle, WAS; mee 6364.   (B:187)
1277. 1/2/00 mor Carter, Asa; Argyle, WAS. See 68.
1278. 1/1/00 gee Carter, Asia; ---, WAS. See 4920.
1279. 8/19/96 gee Carter, Benjamin; Cambridge, WAS. See 8153.
1280. 10/30/86 gee Carver, Joseph; ---, ---, RI. See 8236.
1281. 1/23/97 mor Carver, Salmon, yeoman; Whitehall, WAS; Hampton, WAS;
mee 8300, 8314.   (C:73)
1282. 9/15/94 gee Carver, Solomon; ---, ---. See 2012.
1283. 1/1/95 gee Carver, Solomon; Whitehall, WAS. See 8815.
1284. 1/1/95 gor Carver, Solomon; Whitehall, WAS; ---, WAS; co-gors 1106,
8243; co-gees 1370, 5374, 8813.   (B-2:323)
1285. 1/1/95 gor Carver, Solomon; Whitehall, WAS. See 8814.
1286. 2/17/97 gee Cary, Moses; Argyle, WAS. See 2191.
1287. 5/2/96 gee Case, Elijah; ---, WAS. See 1185.
1288. 5/2/96 gor Case, Elijah (w. Silence), gentleman; Argyle, WAS. See 2099.
1289. 5/2/96 gor Case, Elijah (w. Silence), gentleman; Argyle, WAS. See 2100.
1289a. 5/2/96 gor Case, Elijah (w. Silence), gentleman; Argyle, WAS. See 2100a.
Seven contracts this date involving these persons.
1289b 5/2/96 gor Case, Elijah (w. Silence), gentleman; Argyle, WAS. See 2100b.
Two contracts this date involving these persons.
1289c 5/2/96 gor Case, Elijah (w. Silence), gentleman; Argyle, WAS. See 2100c.
1290. 5/2/96 mee Case, Elijah; Argyle, WAS. See 411, 748, 3303, 3312, 3893,
6372, 6512, 7597.
1291. 5/2/96 mor Case, Elijah; ---, WAS. See 2102. Three contracts this
date involving these two persons.
1292. 5/2/96 mor Case, Elijah; Argyle, WAS. See 8745.
1293. 5/3/96 mor Case, Elijah; Argyle, WAS. See 1416.
1294. 12/12/96 gor Case, Elijah (w. Silence); Argyle, WAS. See 2104.
1295. 5/2/99 mee Case, Elijah, gentleman; Argyle, WAS. See 1417.
1295a 6/15/99 gor Case, Elijah (w. Silence); Argyle, WAS. See 2106.
1296. 10/21/00 mee Case, Elijah; Argyle, WAS. See 3098.
1297. 11/24/00 mor Case, Elijah (w. Silience), farmer; Argyle, WAS; Hartford,
WAS; mee 220.   (C:75)
1298. 3/4/02 mee Case, Elijah; Hartford, WAS. See 1712.
1299. 4/10/89 mor Case, Philip; Hebron, WAS; Granville, WAS; mee 832. (A:175)
1300. 2/25/92 gor Case, Philip; Hebron, WAS; Granville, WAS; gee 2496.(A:430)
1301. 6/2/02 mee Case, Philip; Granville, WAS. See 2323.
1302. 12/28/01 mee Case, Phillip; Granville, WAS. See 5058.
1303. 4/22/89 mor Case, Reuben; Granville, WAS; Granville, WAS; mee 834.
(A:150)
1304. 5/2/96 gor Case, Silence. See 1288.
1304a. 5/2/96 gor Case, Silence. See 1289.
1304b. 5/2/96 gor Case, Silence. See 1289a. Seven contracts this date.
1304c. 5/2/96 gor Case, Silence. See 1289b. Two contracts this date.

1304d. 5/2/96   gor   Case, Silence. See 1289c.
1305. 12/12/96 gor   Case, Silence. See 1294.
1306. 6/15/99 gor   Case, Silence. See 1295a.
1307. 11/24/00 mor   Case, Silience. See 1297.
1308. 3/16/89 gee   Case, Timothy; Granville, WAS. See 828.
1309. 3/16/89 mor   Case, Timothy; Hebron, WAS; ---, WAS; mee 837.   (A:146)
1310. 11/21/01 gee   Casey, William, tanner; Easton, WAS. See 229.
1311. 6/1/86   mee   Casswell, Nathan; Queensbury, WAS. See 3592.
1312. 10/21/00 mee   Caswell, Abner; Salem, WAS. See 1818.
1313. 7/1/93   gee   Caswell, Alexander; Salem, WAS. See 8527.
1314. 7/11/92 gee   Caswell, David, yeoman; Hebron, WAS. See 3763.
1315. 6/4/98   mor   Caswell, David; Salem, WAS; Salem, WAS; mee 7697. (C:27)
1316. 10/10/91 gee   Caswell, Gilbert, yeoman; Elizabethtown, Lunenburg Dist.,
                          Province of Quebec. See 3734.
1317. 10/26/01 gee   Caswell, John; Queensbury, WAS. See 878.
1318. 10/26/01 mee   Caswell, John; Queensbury, WAS. See 879.
1319. 6/1/86   mee   Caswell, Nathan. See 3592.
1320. 5/1/79   gee   Caswell, Nathaniel; "Cold Rain", HAM, MA. See 451.
1321. 6/9/96   mor   Cathcart, Andrew, shopkeeper; "south side of Mohawk River,
                          MON; Granville, WAS; mee 3849.   (B:71)
1322. 10/4/97 mor   Cathcart, Silas; Easton, WAS; Saratoga Pat., WAS; mee 3690.
                                                                   (B:218)
1323. 6/20/01 gee   Center, John S.; Cambridge, WAS. See 4843.
1324. 9/16/01 mor   Center, John S. (w. Phebe); Cambridge, WAS; ---, WAS;
                          mee 8159.   (D:229)
1325. 4/16/91 gor   Center, John Shelden (w. Phebe); Cambridge, WAS; Cambridge
                          Pat., WAS; gee 8059.   (E:360)
1326. 8/28/93 gor   Center, John Shelden (w. Phebe); Cambridge, WAS; Cambridge
                          Pat., WAS; gee 1124.   (C-2:22)
1327. 4/16/91 gor   Center, Phebe. See 1325.
1328. 8/28/93 gor   Center, Phebe. See 1326.
1329. 9/16/01 gor   Center, Phebe. See 1324.
1330. 7/18/99 gor   Chace, Benjamin (w. Elizabeth), hatter; Hudson, COL; Old
                          Military Township #3 (Black Brook), CLI; gee 4554.
                                                                   (B:350)
1331. 10/3/99 mor   Chace, Caleb; Westfield, WAS; Bolton, WAS; mee 7223. (C:40)
1332. 5/2/97   gor   Chace, Daniel, yeoman; Argyle, WAS; Argyle, WAS; gee 1709.
                                                                   (F:240)
1333. 7/18/99 gor   Chace, Elizabeth. See 1330.
1334. 9/16/02 mor   Chace, Enock; Plattsburgh, CLI; Plattsburgh, CLI; mee 5490.
                                                                   (B:78)
1335. 9/3/92   mor   Chace, Joshua; ---, WAS. See 148.
1336. 7/4/00   mor   Chadwick, Eunice. See 1338.
1337. 6/20/01 gor   Chadwick, Eunice. See 1339.
1338. 7/4/00   mor   Chadwick, John (w. Eunice); Cambridge, WAS; land "north bank
                          of Hoosack River", WAS; co-mors 2474, 2478, 4838, 4842;
                          mee 8158.   (C:74)
1339. 6/20/01 gor   Chadwick, John (w. Eunice); Kingsbury, WAS. See 4843.
1340. 5/1/71   gee   Chalmers, John, farmer; ---, ---. See 1422.
1341. 12/22/75 mor   Chalmers, John; ---, ---; New Perth, WAS; gee 452. (B-2:268)
1342. 3/2/98   mor   Chamberlain, James K., farmer; ---, CLI; Old Military Town-
                          ship #7 (Chateaugay), CLI; co-mor 1342a; mees 6854, 8086.
                                                                   (A:269)
1342a. 3/2/98   mor   Chamberlain, Joseph, Junr. See 1342.
1343. 10/15/89 mor   Chamberlain, Joshua, yeoman; Beekman, CLI; Beekmantown, CLI;
                          mee 584.   (A:44)
1344. 4/3/00   mor   Chandler, Moses, tailor; Granville, WAS; Granville, WAS;
                          co-mees 353, 8172. Co-mortgagees are overseers of the
                          poor, town of Granville.   (D:31)
1345. 6/22/98 gee   Chapen, Gad; Hartford, WAS. See 5697.
1346. 6/23/98 mor   Chapen, Gad; Hartford, WAS; land "Old Military Township #7
                          (Chateaugay), CLI; mee 5699.   (A:318)
1347. 3/19/00 gor   Chapin, Gad, farmer; Hartford, WAS; Hartford, WAS; gee 1002.
                                                                   (E:268)
1348. 6/6/96   gor   Chapin, Luke; Hartford, WAS; Hartford, WAS; gee 1088.
                                                                   (C-2:116)

43

1349. 11/18/86 mor Chapman, Daniel, laborer; ---, DUT; <u>Plattsburgh, CLI</u>;
              mee 5900.   (A:7)
1350. 5/18/90 gor Chapman, Daniel, farmer; Plattsburgh, CLI; <u>Plattsburgh,</u>
              <u>CLI</u>; co-gees 7428, 7434.   (A:177)
1351. 1/1/01 gee Chapman, Ebenezer, farmer; Hebron, WAS. See 3952.
1352. 1/1/01 mor Chapman, Ebenezer (w. Ledia), farmer; Hebron, WAS; <u>Hebron,</u>
              <u>WAS</u>; mee 3858.   (C:76)
1353. 1/31/93 mee Chapman, Jabez, Esq.; East Haddam, ---, CT. See 8238.
1354. 1/1/01 mor Chapman, Ledia. See 1352.
1355. 8/1/97 mor Chapman, Samuel; Vergennes, ADD, VT; <u>Plattsburgh, CLI</u>;
              mee 5460.   (A:233)
1356. 11/3/01 mor Chase, Joshua; Queensbury, WAS; <u>Queensbury, WAS</u>; co-mor
              1357; co-mees 5391, 7538.   (D:115)
1357. 11/3/01 mor Chase, Mary; Queensbury, WAS. See 1356.
1358. 7/3/99 mor Chase, Samuel; Cambridge, WAS; <u>Cambridge, WAS</u>; mee 440.
                                                             (C:42)
1359. 12/8/98 mor Chatfield, Harry; Plattsburgh, CLI; <u>Plattsburgh, CLI</u>;
              mee 6358.   (A:403)
1360. 9/30/91 gor Cheney, Reuben, farmer; Salem, WAS; <u>Salem, WAS</u>;
              gee 4885.   (A:235)
1361. 7/21/92 gor Cheney, Reuben, yeoman; Salem, WAS; <u>Salem, WAS</u>;
              gee 1362.   (C-2:162)
1362. 7/21/92 gee Cheney, Willard, "son of Reuben Cheney", Salem, WAS.
              See 1361.
1363. 5/15/97 mor Cheney, Willard, yeoman; Salem, WAS; <u>Salem, WAS</u>;
              mee 5031.   (B:170)
1364. 7/8/85 mor Chenney, Reuben; New Perth, WAS; <u>New Perth, WAS</u>;
              co-mees 6240, 6669.   (B:182)
1365. 10/7/90 mor Cherry, James; Cambridge, ALB; <u>Argyle, WAS</u>; co-mees
              4619, 4636, 6752, 6826. Co-mees are executors of the
              estate of the Hon. John Morine Scott.   (A:252)
1366. 11/21/95 gee Childs, Joseph, mariner; Portsmouth, NEW, RI. See 2545.
1367. 1/24/92 mee Chinn, Edward; ---, ---. See 5564.
1368. 1/4/95 gor Christy, Elizabeth. See 1372.
1369. 9/15/94 gee Christy, Peter; ---, ---. See 2012.
1370. 1/1/95 gee Christy, Peter; Hampton, WAS. See 1284.
1371. 1/1/95 gee Christy, Peter; Hampton, WAS. See 8814, 8815.
1372. 1/4/95 gor Christy, Peter (w. Elizabeth); Hampton, WAS. See 8816.
1373. 1/5/95 gee Christy, Peter; Hampton, WAS. See 8817.
1374. 11/10/95 gee Christy, Peter; Argyle, WAS. See 1018.
1375. 6/19/01 mee Church, Bethiel; Salem, WAS. See 1379.
1376. 6/1/02 mor Church, Chester, yeoman; Argyle, WAS. See 4524.
1377. 10/12/96 mor Church, Daniel, farmer; Granville, WAS; <u>Granville, WAS</u>;
              mee 3770.   (B:128)
1378. 5/13/00 --- Church, Sarah. See 8457.
1379. 6/19/01 mor Church, Silas; Cambridge, WAS; <u>Cambridge, WAS</u>; mee 1375.
                                                             (D:63)
1380. 10/23/95 gee Church, William H., Junr.; Quashicook, WAS. See 6706.
1381. 3/10/98 mor Church, William H.; Cambridge, WAS; <u>"Church's Mills ...</u>
              <u>near ... Sodom", WAS</u>; mee 3963.   (C:33)
1382. 10/2/86 gee Clap, Isaac, yeoman; Salem, WAS. See 647.
1383. 1/2/91 gor Clap, Isaac, sawyer (or lawyer); Salem, WAS; <u>Salem, WAS</u>;
              co-gors 1386, 2205; gee 1389.   (A:317)
1384. 10/10/86 gee Clap, Isaac Lemuel, farmer; Salem, WAS. See 8388.
1385. 10/2/86 gee Clap, Lemuel, yeoman; Salem, WAS. See 647.
1386. 1/2/91 gor Clap, Lemuel, sawyer or lawyer; Salem, WAS. See 1383.
1387. 10/2/86 gee Clap, Stephen, yeoman; Salem, WAS. See 647.
1388. 10/10/86 gee Clap, Stephen, farmer; Salem, WAS. See 8388.
1389. 1/2/91 gee Clap, Stephen, Esq.; Salem, WAS. See 1383.
1390. 2/5/99 gee Clapp, Isaac; Salem, WAS. See 1095.
1391. 8/16/99 gor Clapp, Isaac, farmer; Salem, WAS; <u>Cambridge, WAS</u>; mee 4472.
                                                             (C:74)
1392. 12/14/90 gee Clapp, Stephen, Esq.; Salem, WAS. See 1580.
1393. 12/9/83 gor Clark, Benjamin; New Perth, CHA; <u>New Perth, CHA</u>;
              co-gees 504, 7731.   (B-1:140)
1394. 9/30/90 mor Clark, Ebenezer; Hebron, WAS; <u>Shereiff's Pat., WAS</u>;
              mee 6981.   (A:235)

44

1395.	5/9/95	gee	Clark, Ebenezer; Argyle, WAS. See 3628.
1396.	9/25/01	gee	Clark, Ebenezer. See 4571.
1397.	5/18/92	gee	Clark, Ebenezer, Esq.; ---, WAS. See 3446.
1398.	3/20/94	gor	Clark, Ebenezer, Esq.; Argyle, WAS; Argyle, WAS; gee 7704. (B-2:285)
1399.	7/16/94	mee	Clark, Ebenezer, Esq.; Argyle, WAS. See 3156.
1400.	11/6/98	gee	Clark, Ebenezer, Esq.; Hartford, WAS. See 7233.
1401.	?/27/99	gee	Clark, Ebenezer, Esq.; ---, WAS. See 4724.
1402.	5/14/99	mee	Clark, Ebenezer, Esq.; Argyle, WAS. See 7364.
1403.	1/26/91	gor	Clark, Elenor, "widow of Robert Clark of Salem", WAS; Salem, WAS; ---, WAS; co-gors 1404, 1405, 1412, 1443, 4504, 4507, 7457, 7466; gee 4514. (A:220)
1404.	1/26/91	gor	Clark, Elenor, the younger; Salem, WAS. See 1403.
1405.	1/26/91	gor	Clark, Elizabeth; Salem, WAS. See 1403.
1406.	9/24/93	gor	Clark, Elizabeth. See 1415.
1407.	10/23/89	gee	Clark, George, mariner; City of N.Y. See 501.
1408.	12/25/86	gee	Clark, James; Hebron, WAS. See 4653.
1409.	12/25/86	gee	Clark, John; Hebron, WAS. See 4653.
1410.	9/9/01	mor	Clark, John; Plattsburgh, CLI; Chateaugay, CLI; mee 5984. (B:74)
1411.	9/6/75	gee	Clark, Robert; New Perth, CHA. See 1428.
1412.	1/26/91	gor	Clark, Robert; Salem, WAS. See 1403.
1413.	1/26/91	---	Clark, Robert, dec'd. See 1403.
1414.	1/7/93	gor	Clark, Silas, saddler; Cambridge, WAS; Cambridge, WAS; gee 4525. (E:427)
1415.	9/24/93	gor	Clark, Silas (w. Elizabeth); Cambridge Dist., WAS; Cambridge Dist., WAS; gee 1586. (D:15)
1416.	5/3/96	mor	Clark, Silas; Argyle, WAS; Argyle, WAS; co-mees 1293, 2103, 2229, 5586. (C:39)
1417.	5/2/99	mor	Clark, Silas; Easton, WAS; Argyle, WAS; co-mees 1295, 2105, 2230, 5588. (C:39)
1418.	11/4/65	gor	Clark, Thomas, Dr.; New Perth, ALB; New Perth, ALB; gee 4307. (WAS Co. B-1:101)
1419.	5/1/66	gor	Clark, Thomas, physician; ---, ---; New Perth, ALB; gee 4308. (WAS Co. A:8)
1420.	4/1/70	gor	Clark, Thomas, Dr.; New Perth, ALB; Turner Pat., ALB; gee 551. (WAS Co. B-1:173)
1421.	5/1/70	mor	Clark, Thomas, Dr.; New Perth, ALB; Turner Pat., ALB; mee 4914. (WAS Co. A:24)
1422.	5/1/71	gor	Clark, Thomas, physician; ---, ---; Newport, ALB; gee 1340. (WAS Co. B-2:265)
1423.	5/1/71	gor	Clark, Thomas, physician; ---, ---; New Perth, ALB; gee 8614. (WAS Co. A:194)
1424.	9/12/--	gor	Clark, Thomas, Dr.; Albany, ALB; New Perth, CHA; gee 7512. (B-1:96)
1425.	11/1/72	gor	Clark, Thomas, physician; ---, ---; New Perth, CHA; gee 8639. (B-1:7)
1426.	5/1/73	mee	Clark, Thomas, Doctor; ---, ---. See 18.
1427.	11/16/73	gee	Clark, Thomas, Dr.; New Perth, CHA. See 2182.
1428.	9/6/75	gor	Clark, Thomas, Dr.; New Perth, CHA; Turner Pat., CHA; gee 1411. (C-1:13)
1429.	11/1/79	gor	Clark, Thomas, Dr.; New Perth, CHA; New Perth, CHA; gees (two independent contracts) 607 (B-1:1) and 6539 (B-1:3).
1430.	6/7/80	gor	Clark, Thomas, Dr.; New Perth, CHA; New Perth, CHA; cogees 3538, 3562. (B-1:63)
1431.	5/8/81	gor	Clark, Thomas, Dr.; New Perth, CHA; ---, CHA; gee 3131. (C-1:1)
1432.	3/20/82	gee	Clark, Thomas, Dr.; New Perth, CHA. See 502.
1433.	4/2/82	gor	Clark, Thomas, Dr.; New Perth, CHA; New Perth, CHA; gee 4925. (B-1:51)
1434.	2/13/83	gor	Clark, Thomas, Dr.; New Perth, CHA; New Perth, CHA; gee 6466. (A:78)
1435.	9/13/83	gor	Clark, Thomas. Dr.; Albany, ALB; New Perth, CHA; gee 3563. (B-1:122)
1436.	11/1/83	gor	Clark, Thomas, Dr., "late of New Perth ... now of Albany..."; New Perth, CHA; gee 2753. (A:29)

1437. 3/3/84 gor Clark, Thomas, Dr.; Albany, ALB; New Perth, CHA; land for
use by the Presbyterian Church minister, the Rev. James
Proudfoot; co-gees 3251, 3600, 7847 (co-gees are trustees
of the Presbyterian Church at New Perth).   (B-1:85)

1438. 6/5/84 gor Clark, Thomas, Dr.; Albany, ALB; Turner Pat., WAS; gee 6304.
(C-1:34)

1439. 3/3/85 gor Clark, Thomas, Dr.; Albany, ALB; New Perth, WAS; gee 3532.
(B-1:200)

1440. 6/10/85 gor Clark, Thomas, Dr.; Albany, ALB; ---, WAS; gee 1795.
(B-1:159)

1441. 7/11/87 gor Clark, Thomas, Dr.; Long Cane Settlement, ---, SC;
Salem, WAS; gee 1637.   (C-2:72)

1442. 7/29/87 gor Clark, Thomas, Dr.; New Perth, WAS; Black Creek Dist., WAS;
gee 7410.   (A:372)

1443. 1/26/91 gor Clark, Thomas; Salem, WAS. See 1403.

1444. 3/7/92 --- Clark, Thomas, Rev., dec'd, of New Perth (Salem), WAS;
(former owner of the land in the transaction of
Samuel Hopkins in 3565).

1445. 5/19/79 gor Clark, William, yeoman; Cambridge Dist., CHA; Cambridge
Dist., CHA; co-gor 1448; gee 1589.   (E:261)

1446. 6/30/92 gee Clark, William, farmer; Westfield, WAS. See 4445.

1447. 11/23/95 gor Clark, William, farmer; Saratoga, SAR; Hafford (sic), WAS;
gee 5194.   (B-2:492)

1448. 5/19/79 gor Clark, William, Junr., yeoman; Cambridge Dist., CHA.
See 1445.

1449. 10/7/99 mor Clarke, John; Plattsburgh, CLI; Plattsburgh, CLI;
mee 5758.   (A:433)

1450. 8/19/00 mee Clarke, John; Plattsburgh, CLI. See 6550.

1451. 7/24/87 gor Clarke, Thomas, Dr.; Long Cane Settlement, ABE, SC;
Thomas Clark's Pat., WAS; gee 3048.   (D:392)

1452. 2/13/97 gee Cleaveland, Asa, yeoman; Cambridge, WAS. See 8860.

1453. 7/8/97 gee Cleaveland, Benjamin, yeoman; Salem, WAS. See 1778.

1454. 7/4/99 mor Cleaveland, John; Fairfield, WAS; Ebenezer Jessup's Pat.,
WAS; co-mees 2459, 3118.   (C:126)

1455. 6/15/85 gee Clemens, Jonathan; East Bay, WAS. See 8233.

1456. 7/1/00 mor Clemons, David; ---, ---; ---, ESS; mee 5572.   (A:33)

1457. 2/18/94 mee Cleveland, Asa; Salem, WAS. See 466.

1458. 10/5/79 gee Cleveland, Benjamin, farmer; New Perth, CHA. See 1688.

1459. 6/5/00 gor Cleveland, Banjamin, yeoman; Salem, WAS; Salem, WAS;
gee 1467.   (E:270)

1460. 6/5/00 mor Cleveland, Benjamin, yeoman; Salem, WAS; Salem, WAS;
mee 1468. "It is mutually agreed between ... Benjamin
and Margaret his wife to live separate and apart from
each other on account of some unhappy differences ..."
(D:50b)

1461. 11/9/92 mor Cleveland, John, yeoman; Troy, REN. See 6282.

1462. 7/6/88 gee Cleveland, Jonas, yeoman; ---, WAS. See 2378.

1463. 7/6/88 mor Cleveland, Jonas; ---, ---; Granville, WAS; mee 2379.
(A:96)

1464. 6/5/00 --- Cleveland, Margaret. See 1460.

1465. 6/2/85 mor Cleveland, Moses; Windham (VT?); New Perth, WAS; mee 7103.
(A:60)

1466. 11/29/94 mor Cleveland, Oliver (w. Zuba); Fairhaven, RUT, VT; Hampton,
WAS; mee 5965.   (A:520)

1467. 6/5/00 gee Cleveland, Palmer, yeoman; Salem, WAS. See 1459.

1468. 6/5/00 gee Cleveland, Palmer, yeoman; Salem, WAS. See 1460.

1469. 10/7/01 gee Cleveland, Palmer; Salem, WAS. See 5291.

1470. 11/29/94 mee Cleveland, Zuba. See 1466.

1471. 6/15/02 mor Clintock, John; Whitehall, WAS; Whitehall, WAS; co-mees
1602, 1604, 1608, 1611. Co-mees are all heirs of Abel
Comstock, deceased.   (D:195)

1472. 11/11/97 mee Clinton, De Witt, Esq.; City of N.Y. See 1114.

1473. 1/24/98 gor Clinton, De Witt, Esq. (w. Maria); ---, ---; Hartford, WAS;
gee 3958.   (C-2:271)

1474. 2/1/98 gor Clinton, De Witt, Esq. (w. Maria); City of N.Y.; Hartford,
WAS; gee 991.   (F:270)

46

1475. 4/25/93 gor Clinton, George; ---, ---. See 7168.
1476. 9/16/99 gor Clinton, George; City of N.Y. See 7600.
1477. 6/23/98 mee Clinton, George, Esq.; City of N.Y. See 7121.
1478. 1/25/97 mee Clinton, Maria, wife of De Witt Clinton; ---, ---. See 217.
1479. 1/24/98 gor Clinton, Maria. See 1473.
1480. 1/25/98 mee Clinton, Maria, wife of De Witt Clinton. See 3959.
1481. 1/31/98 mee Clinton, Maria, wife of De Witt Clinton. See 7642.
1482. 2/1/98 gor Clinton, Maria. See 1474.
1483. 2/8/98 mee Clinton, Maria, wife of De Witt Clinton. See 910, 912
         (two contracts), 917, 985, 992, 1003, 1083, 1250, 1264,
         2558, 2881, 3366, 3657, 4106, 5478, 5538, 6482, 6688, 7037,
         7397, 7983, 8189. (twenty-three contracts this date).
1484. 2/10/98 mee Clinton, Maria, wife of De Witt Clinton. See 1752.
1485. 2/12/98 mee Clinton, Maria, wife of De Witt Clinton; City of N.Y.
         See 4899 and 7858.
1486. 2/15/98 mee Clinton, Maria, wife of De Witt Clinton. See 364.
1487. 2/20/98 mee Clinton, Maria, wife of De Witt Clinton. See 2035.
1488. 3/9/98 mee Clinton, Maria, wife of De Witt Clinton; City of N.Y.
         See 218, 1199, 1770, 4107, 4299, 7510, 8452. (six
         contracts this date).
1489. 3/14/98 mee Clinton, Maria, wife of De Witt Clinton. See 8022.
1490. 4/6/98 mee Clinton, Maria, wife of De Witt Clinton. See 5547.
1491. 6/1/98 mee Clinton, Maria, wife of De Witt Clinton. See 8636.
1492. 6/9/98 mee Clinton, Maria, wife of De Witt Clinton, Esq.; City of N.Y.
         See 3240 and 7682.
1493. 6/26/98 mee Clinton, Maria, wife of De Witt Clinton, Esq. See 3090, 7470.
1494. 11/3/98 mee Clinton, Maria, wife of De Witt Clinton. See 2993.
1495. 11/9/98 mee Clinton, Maria, wife of De Witt Clinton. See 6279.
1496. 12/12/98 mee Clinton, Maria, wife of De Witt Clinton. See 2002.
1497. 12/25/98 mee Clinton, Maria, City of N.Y. See 223, 3363.
1498. 2/16/99 mee Clinton, Maria, wife of De Witt Clinton. See 1172.
1499. 9/20/02 mor Closson, Abraham (w. Sarah), yeoman; Easton, WAS; Easton,
         WAS; mee 957.   (E:16)
1500. 9/20/02 mor Closson, Sarah. See 1499.
1501. 12/8/95 gee Clough, Amasa, yeoman; Hebron, WAS. See 1508.
1502. 12/12/95 gee Clough, Amasa, Mr.; Hebron, WAS. See 8682.
1503. 3/27/01 mor Clough, Elijah; Cambridge, WAS; Cambridge, WAS; mee 1127.
                                                            (D:59)
1504. 1/30/00 mor Clough, John (w. Mary), yeoman; Hebron, WAS; Hebron, WAS;
         mee 2898.   (C:42)
1505. 1/31/86 gor Clough, Jonathan; Black Creek Dist., WAS; Black Creek Dist.,
         WAS; gee 8662.   (A:344)
1506. 7/9/92 gee Clough, Jonathan; Hebron, WAS. See 4208.
1507. 1/10/86 gor Clough, Luther; Black Creek Dist., WAS; Black Creek Dist.,
         WAS; gee 8193.   (A:34)
1508. 12/8/95 gor Clough, Luther, yeoman; "late of the town of Hebron", WAS;
         Hebron, WAS; gee 1501.   (B-2:502)
1509. 1/30/00 mor Clough, Mary. See 1504.
1510. 6/7/86 gor Cochran, Gertrude. See 1513.
1511. 4/26/68 gor Cochran, Gertruy. See 1512.
1512. 4/26/68 gor Cochran, John (w. Gertruy), "Doctor of Physick"; ---, ---,
         East New Jersey. See 6730.
1513. 6/7/86 gor Cochran, John (w. Gertrude); City of N.Y.; Fort Edward, WAS;
         gee 7006.   (C-1:20)
1514. 1/9/94 mor Cochran, John, farmer; ---, CLI; Peru, CLI; mee 5275.
         Mortgagee is executor of the estate of Zacheus Newcomb
         "late of Clinton,... Dutchess County."   (A:132)
1515. 10/3/95 mor Cochran, John; Peru, CLI; Zephaniah Platt's Pat., CLI;
         mee 5276. Mortgagee is executor of the estate of
         Zacheus Newcomb, deceased.   (A:160)
1516. 7/1/00 mor Cochran, John; ---, ---; ---, ESS; mee 5572.   (A:51)
1517. 9/22/00 gee Cochran, John, yeoman; Cambridge, WAS. See 5601. (2 contracts)
1518. 9/7/93 gee Cochran, John, Esq.; Peru, CLI. See 5933.
1519. 9/20/93 gee Cochran, John, Esq.; Peru, CLI. See 8364.
1520. 9/27/94 mor Cochran, John, Esq.; Peru, CLI; Peru, CLI; mee 5854.
                                                            (A:144)

1521. 9/28/96 mor Cochran, John, Esq.; Peru, CLI; Zephaniah Platt's Pat., CLI;
          mee 5862.   (A:198)
1522. 6/3/02 gor Cochran, John, Junr.; Champlain, CLI; Jay, ESS; gee 3233.
                                                              (A:60)
1523. 10/25/98 mor Cochran, Mary. See 1529.
1524. 1/20/95 gee Cochran, Robert; Argyle, WAS. See 7019. Two contracts
          this date involving these two persons.
1525. 2/4/96 --- Cochran, Robert; ---, WAS. See 5857.
1526. 2/24/96 mor Cochran, Robert; ---, WAS. See 8754.
1527. 6/22/98 gor Cochran, Robert; ---, WAS. See 5696.
1528. 10/24/98 gee Cochran, Robert; Kingsbury, WAS. See 4531.
1529. 10/25/98 mor Cochran, Robert (w. Mary); Kingsbury, WAS; Argyle, WAS;
          mee 4532.   (C:32)
1530. 9/25/99 mor Cochran, Robert; Kingsbury, WAS; Kingsbury Pat., WAS;
          mee 1158.   (C:40)
1531. 2/13/87 gee Cochran, Robert, Esq.; Crown Point, WAS. See 5127.
1532. 12/20/87 mor Cochran, Robert, Esq.; Crown Point, WAS; Moorfield, WAS
          mee 1181.   (ESS Co. A:36)
1533. 3/4/96 gee Cochran, Robert, Esq.; Kingsbury, WAS. See 1937.
1534. 9/25/02 mor Cochran, Seth; Cambridge, FRA, VT; Old Military Township
          #7 (Chateaugay), CLI; mee 331.   (B:80)
1535. 7/26/98 mee Cock, Andrew; City of N.Y. See 8699.
1536. 7/26/98 mee Cock, Joshua; City of N.Y. See 8699.
1537. 7/26/98 mee Cock, Oliver; City of N.Y. See 8699.
1538. 5/12/00 gor Cockburn, Catharine. See 1540.
1539. 1/21/86 gor Cockburn, William; ---, ULS. See 4958.
1540. 5/12/00 gor Cockburn, William (w. Catharine), gentleman; Kingston, ULS;
          Granville, WAS; gee 3405.   (F:183)
1541. 5/13/00 mee Cockburn, William, gentleman; Kingston, ULS. See 2360,
          3076, 3077, 3574, 4787, 5330, 5447, 6471, 7962, 8457.
          (ten contracts)
1542. 5/5/91 gee Coe, William; ---, ORA. See 4085.
1543. 8/2/98 mee Coffin, Abigal. See 1546.
1544. 6/9/00 gor Coffin, Elizabeth. See 1547.
1545. 7/4/95 gee Coffin, Laban, "late of New Bedford", BRI, MA. See 8845.
1546. 8/2/98 mee Coffin, Ralph (w. Abigal); Westfield, WAS. See 2522.
1547. 6/9/00 gor Coffin, William (w. Elizabeth), farmer; Easton, WAS;
          Saratoga Pat., WAS; gee 8608.   (D:436)
1548. 7/20/87 gee Cogsal, John; ---, ---. See 100.
1549. 4/1/94 gor Colden, Alexander, "eldest son and heir of Richard Nicholls
          Colden, formerly of the City of New York Esquire deceased";
          gentleman; Lansingburgh, REN; Cambridge, WAS; gee 1559.
                                                             (B-2:408)
1550. 3/18/96 gor Colden, Alexander, gentleman; Lansingburgh, REN; Cambridge,
          WAS; co-gees 4033, 4045.   (C-2:232)
1551. 11/22/69 gor Colden, Alexander, Esq.; City of N.Y.; Cambridge, ALB;
          gee 8448.   (WAS Co. E:128)
1552. 11/24/69 gor Colden, Alexander, Esq.; City of N.Y.; Cambridge Dist.,
          ALB; gee 8449.   (WAS Co. E:131)
1553. 11/10/74 gor Colden, Alexander, Esq.; City of N.Y.; Cambridge, ALB;
          gee 839.   (WAS Co. E:20)
1554. 7/17/70 mee Colden, Cadwallader, Esq., dec'd, exec's. of. See 1060.
1555. 8/26/70 mee Colden, Cadwallader, Esq., dec'd, exec's. of. See 856.
1556. 7/20/71 mee Colden, Cadwallader, Esq., dec'd, exec's. of. See 857.
1557. 3/8/75 mee Colden, Cadwallader, Esq., dec'd, exec's. of. See 7519.
1558. 4/19/02 mor Colden, Cadwallader R., gentleman; City of N.Y.; Cambridge,
          WAS (several parcels); co-mees 2032, 7780, 7782. (D:170)
1559. 4/1/94 gee Colden, Henrietta Maria, widow of Richard N. Colden, deceased;
          Lansingburgh, REN. See 1549.
1560. 4/1/94 --- Colden, Richard N., dec'd. See 1559.
1561. 4/1/94 --- Colden, Richard Nicholls, dec'd. See 1549.
1562. 9/3/92 mor Cole, Amasa; ---, WAS. See 5485.
1563. 6/7/92 mor Cole, Benjamin, yeoman; Hebron, WAS. See 2703.
1564. 12/30/94 mor Cole, Benjamin, yeoman; Hebron, WAS; Hebron, WAS; mee 3951.
                                                              (B:93)
1565. 10/10/99 mor Cole, Charlotte. See 1569.

48

1566. 12/25/95 gor Cole, Freegift (w. Mary); Kingsbury, WAS; <u>Kingsbury, WAS</u>;
    gee 1262. (D:54)
1567. 4/7/96 mor Cole, Jeremiah, farmer; Easton, WAS; <u>Saratoga Pat., WAS</u>;
    mee 3677. (B:27)
1568. 10/16/94 gor Cole, John (w. Sarah), blacksmith; Hebron, WAS; <u>Hebron, WAS</u>;
    gee 8329. (E:382)
1569. 10/10/99 mor Cole, Levi (w. Charlotte), farmer; Cambridge, WAS;
    <u>Cambridge Pat., WAS</u>; mee 4040. (C:73)
1570. 3/25/99 mor Cole, Lois. See 1574.
1571. 12/25/95 gor Cole, Mary. See 1566.
1572. 10/21/01 mor Cole, Samuel; Kingsbury, WAS; <u>Kingsbury, WAS</u>; mee 1635.
    (D:137)
1573. 10/16/94 gor Cole, Sarah. See 1568.
1574. 3/25/99 mor Cole, Thomas (w. Lois), yeoman; Hartford, WAS; <u>Hartford, WAS</u>; mee 993. (C:76)
1575. 7/10/93 mee Cole, John B., merchant; City of N.Y. See 5343.
1576. 11/18/01 mor Colkins, Richard; Peru, CLI; <u>Peru, CLI</u>; mee 3447. (B:48)
1577. 12/31/96 mor Collins, Christopher; Manchester, ---, VT; <u>Willsborough, CLI</u>; mee 2789. (A:232)
1578. 12/29/91 --- Collins, Edward. See 4878.
1579. 6/30/02 gee Collins, Samuel; Cambridge, WAS. See 3057.
1580. 12/14/90 gor Collins, Thomas, innkeeper; Salem, WAS; <u>Salem, WAS</u>;
    gee 1392. (C-1:88)
1581. 4/8/96 mor Collins, Thomas; Salem, WAS; <u>Salem, WAS</u>; mee 7104. (B:20)
1582. 3/4/94 gor Collins, Wallsingham, gentleman; Easton, WAS; <u>Easton, WAS</u>;
    gee 3892. (B-2:185)
1583. 8/15/92 mor Collins, Walsingham, gentleman; Easton, WAS; <u>Easton, WAS</u>;
    mee 4805. (A:392)
1584. 10/28/94 gee Collins, Zerubabel, yeoman; Cambridge, WAS. See 2690.
1585. 4/12/96 mor Colt, Daniel; Lansingburgh, REN. See 5513.
1586. 9/24/93 gee Colter, George; Cambridge Dist, WAS. See 1415.
1587. 5/14/95 mor Colver, Charles; Canaan, COL; <u>Champlain, CLI</u>; mee 1242.
    (A:165)
1588. 5/28/98 mor Colver, Nathaniel, yeoman; Champlain, CLI; <u>Champlain, CLI</u>;
    mee 1243. (A:325)
1589. 5/19/79 gee Colvin, Benjamin, yeoman; Cambridge Dist., CHA. See 1445.
1590. 6/25/85 gee Colvin, Benjamin; Bennington, ALB (sic). See 7147.
1591. 8/5/86 gee Colvin, Benjamin; Bennington, ALB (sic). See 7148.
1592. 11/11/86 gor Colvin, Benjamin; Bennington, ALB (sic); <u>Kingsbury, WAS</u>;
    gee 3973. (C-1:52)
1593. 1/30/89 gor Colvin, Benjamin; Cambridge Dist., ALB; <u>Kingsbury, WAS</u>;
    gee 4912. (A:298)
1594. 5/23/01 mor Colvin, Benjamin; Cambridge, WAS; <u>Cambridge, WAS</u>; mee 8167.
    (D:67)
1595. 7/10/02 mor Colvin, Benjamin, Esq. (w. Mary); Cambridge, WAS;
    <u>Cambridge, WAS</u>; mee 5038. (E:5)
1596. 7/10/02 mor Colvin, Mary. See 1595.
1597. 10/7/94 gee Colvin, Oliver; ---, ---. See 8583.
1598. 9/19/98 mor Colvin, Oliver; Kingsbury, WAS; <u>Kingsbury, WAS</u>; mee 8792.
    (C:28)
1599. 7/3/02 mee Colvin, Oliver; Kingsbury, WAS. See 4940.
1600. 11/9/01 --- Comfort, David (w. Sarah); ---, MID, NJ. See 3412.
1601. 11/9/01 --- Comfort, Sarah. See 1600.
1602. 6/15/02 mee Comstock, Abel. See 1471.
1603. 6/15/02 mee Comstock, Abel, dec'd. See 1471.
1604. 6/15/02 mee Comstock, Clarifey; ---, ---. See 1471.
1605. 11/20/96 gee Comstock, Daniel, farmer; ---, WAS. See 5337.
1606. 3/7/89 gee Comstock, David; Granville, WAS. See 7468.
1607. 2/28/00 mee Comstock, David; ---, CAY. See 2402.
1608. 6/15/02 mee Comstock, David. See 1471.
1609. 5/2/96 gee Comstock, Jeremiah; Kingsbury, WAS. See 2914.
1610. 5/21/00 mee Comstock, Jeremiah; Kingsbury, WAS. See 5035.
1611. 6/15/02 mee Comstock, Phebe. See 1471.
1612. 7/1/00 mor Comstock, Zachariah; ---, ---; <u>---, ESS</u>; mee 5572. (A:20)
1613. 8/11/97 mor Cone, Polly. See 1615.
1614. 10/5/96 mor Cone, Timothy, physician; Granville, WAS; <u>Granville, WAS</u>;
    mee 1090. (B:99)

49

<u>1615.</u>	8/11/97	mor	Cone, Timothy (w. Polly), physician; Granville, WAS; Granville, WAS; mee 4130. (B:213)
<u>1616.</u>	7/31/92	mor	Congdon, John; Westfield, WAS; <u>Westfield, WAS</u>; co-mees 4444, 6581. (A:353)
1617.	5/18/99	mee	Conger, Azariah; Cambridge, WAS. See 4303.
1618.	11/23/02	mee	Conger, Azeriah; Cambridge, WAS. See 7044.
1619.	11/23/02	mee	Conger, Mary; Cambridge, WAS. See 7044. Mary <u>may</u> be wife of Azeriah in #1618.
<u>1620.</u>	6/8/97	gor	Conkey, Alexander; Pelham, HAM, MA; <u>Salem, WAS</u>; gee 7948. (D:380)
1621.	8/13/92	gee	Conkey, John; Salem, WAS. See 1626.
<u>1622.</u>	10/26/95	gor	Conkey, John, yeoman; Salem, WAS; <u>Salem, WAS</u>; gee 1628. (C-2:129)
1623.	9/7/69	gor	Conkey, Joshua; ---, ---. See 7955.
1624.	4/20/73	gor	Conkey, Joshua; ---, ---. See 7957.
1625.	12/29/91	gor	Conkey, Joshua; ---, ---. See 4878.
<u>1626.</u>	8/13/92	gor	Conkey, Joshua; Salem, WAS; <u>Salem, WAS</u>; gee 1621. (B-2:467)
1627.	2/2/93	gee	Conkey, Joshua; Salem, WAS. See 4402.
1628.	10/26/95	gee	Conkey, Joshua, Esq.; Salem, WAS. See 1622.
1629.	10/5/87	gee	Conkey, Silas, clothier; Argyle Dist., WAS. See 4879.
1630.	11/22/91	gee	Conkey, Silas; Argyle, WAS. See 4869.
1631.	9/7/69	gor	Conkey, William; ---, ---. See 7955.
1632.	4/20/73	gor	Conkey, William; ---, ---. See 7957.
1633.	6/23/97	gee	Conkling, Benjamin; Goshen OR A. See 8341.
<u>1634.</u>	6/23/97	gor	Conkling, Benjamin, yeoman; Goshen, OR A; <u>Plattsburgh, CLI</u>; co-gees 391, 8629. (B:105)
1634a.	6/23/97	mee	Conkling, Benjamin; Goshen, OR A. See 8342.
1635.	10/21/01	mee	Conkling, David; Kingsbury, WAS. See 1572.
<u>1636.</u>	6/7/93	gor	Connolly, John; Lasomption, Lower Canada; ---, CLI; gee 2811. (A:335)
1637.	7/11/87	gee	Conoway, William; Salem, WAS. See 1441.
<u>1638.</u>	3/8/88	gor	Conoway, William; Salem, WAS; <u>Salem, WAS</u>; gee 2717. (C-2:74)
1639.	7/16/01	mee	Constable, William; City of N.Y. See 5355.
<u>1640.</u>	4/7/02	---	Constable, William; City of N.Y.; ---, CLI. Constable appoints William Bailey, Esq., as his attorney for the sale of the above land. (B:374)
1641.	10/24/91	mee	Convers, Thomas, Esq.; Granville, WAS. See 8455.
1642.	6/25/96	gee	Converse, Isaac, yeoman; Westfield, WAS. See 8533.
<u>1643.</u>	6/25/96	mor	Converse, Isaac, yeoman; Westfield, WAS; <u>Westfield, WAS</u>; mee 8590. (B:65)
<u>1644.</u>	6/5/97	mor	Converse, William Royal; farmer; Champlain, CLI; <u>Champlain, CLI</u>; mee 2083. (A:357)
<u>1645.</u>	10/28/01	gor	Conway, John (w. Mary), yeoman; Hebron, WAS; <u>Hebron, WAS</u>; gee 6211. (F:161)
1646.	10/28/01	mee	Conway, John, yeoman; Hebron, WAS. See 6212.
1647.	10/28/01	gor	Conway, Mary. See 1645.
<u>1648.</u>	1/7/99	mor	Cook, Abel; Pattsburgh, CLI; <u>Old Military Township #7 (Chateaugay), CLI</u>; mee 4019. (A:418)
1649.	3/12/93	gee	Cook, Amasa, farmer; Granville, WAS. See 946.
1650.	5/30/93	mor	Cook, Amasa, farmer; ---, WAS. See 5474.
1651.	9/3/99	gor	Cook, Amasa; Granville, WAS. See 5470.
1652.	6/20/01	gor	Cook, Amasa; Granville, WAS. See 5476.
<u>1653.</u>	3/6/02	mor	Cook, Amasa; Granville, WAS; <u>Granville, WAS</u>; mee 4153. (D:155)
1654.	12/2/99	mee	Cook, Andrew, merchant; City of N.Y. See 1857.
1655.	5/1/82	gee	Cook, Asaph; Granville, CHA. See 8513.
1656.	7/2/92	gee	Cook, Charles, farmer; Westfield, WAS. See 4447.
<u>1657.</u>	7/18/92	mor	Cook, Charles; Westfield, WAS; <u>Westfield, WAS</u>; co-mees 4443, 6580. (A:351)
<u>1658.</u>	1/30/01	mor	Cook, Charles; Granville, WAS; <u>Granville, WAS</u>; mee 4142. (D:30)
<u>1659.</u>	5/29/97	mor	Cook, Edward (w. Margaret), carpenter; Cambridge, WAS; <u>Cambridge, WAS</u>; mee 1664. (B:176)
1660.	4/7/00	mor	Cook, Edward, farmer; Argyle, WAS. See 4384.

1661. 5/29/97 mor Cook, Margaret. See 1659.
1662. 1/3/93 mee Cook, Mary Ann, Mrs., "widdow ... of Thomas Cook"; ---, ---.
                  See 4658.
1663. 5/14/93 mee Cook, Mary Ann, widow of Thomas Cook of Cambridge, dec'd.
                  See 8641.
1664. 5/29/97 mee Cook, Mary Ann, widow of Thomas Cook; Cambridge, WAS.
                  See 1659.
1665. 12/2/99 mee Cook, Oliver, merchant; City of N.Y. See 1857.
1666. 4/19/96 gor Cook, Richard, farmer; Hartford, WAS; Hartford, WAS;
                  gee 2003.   (C-2:186)
1667. 1/11/97 mor Cook, Samuel, farmer; Thurman, WAS; ---, CLI; mee 5631.
                                                               (A:245)
1668. 12/1/85 gee Cook, Thomas, yeoman; Argyle, WAS. See 5254.
1669. 1/3/93 --- Cook, Thomas, dec'd.; ---, ---. See 1662.
1670. 5/14/93 --- Cook, Thomas, dec'd.; Cambridge, WAS. See 1663.
1671. 5/29/97 --- Cook, Thomas, dec'd. See 1664.
1672. 7/6/88 mor Cooley, Nathaniel; Granville, WAS; Granville, WAS; mee 2379.
                                                               (A:119)
1673. 2/9/93 gee Cooley, Seth, hatter; Salem, WAS. See 988.
1674. 2/6/01 gee Coolidge, Jonathan; Easton, WAS. See 2282.
1675. 11/5/94 gor Coon, Abraham; Kingsbury, WAS; Kingsbury, WAS; gee 7238.
                                                               (D:14)
1676. 5/5/94 gee Coon, Daniel, yeoman; Salem, WAS. See 2708.
1677. 6/8/95 gee Coon, Daniel, farmer; Salem, WAS. See 4952.
1678. 6/8/95 mor Coon, Daniel (w. Elizabeth), yeoman; Salem, WAS; Salem, WAS;
                  mee 4932.   (A:551)
1679. 6/10/96 mor Coon, Daniel, yeoman; Salem, WAS; Salem, WAS; mee 4347.
                                                               (B:43)
1680. 2/12/99 mor Coon, Daniel; Salem, WAS; Salem, WAS; mee 5000.   (C:35)
1681. 4/17/99 gor Coon, Daniel (w. Elizabeth), yeoman; Salem, WAS; Salem, WAS;
                  gee 4349.   (D:119)
1682. 7/20/01 mor Coon, Daniel; Salem, WAS; Salem, WAS; mee 4346.   (D:78)
1683. 6/8/95 gor Coon, Elizabeth. See 1678.
1684. 4/17/99 gor Coon, Elizabeth. See 1681.
1685. 5/10/97 gee Coonlee, James, yeoman; Argyle, WAS. See 2999.
1686. 7/9/92 gee Cooper, George; Salem, WAS. See 2718.
1687. 2/19/02 mor Cooper, Isaac; Granville, WAS; Granville, WAS; co-mor 1691;
                  mee 711.   (D:188)
1688. 10/5/79 gor Cooper, Joseph, blacksmith; New Perth, CHA; New Perth, CHA;
                  gee 1458.   (C-2:228)
1689. 1/6/85 gee Cooper, Joseph; White Creek, WAS. See 8517.
1690. 10/18/90 gor Cooper, Joseph, yeoman; Salem, WAS; Salem, WAS; co-gees
                  4325, 4327 (family relationship of co-gees, if any,
                  not stated).   (A:168)
1691. 2/19/02 mor Cooper, Samuel; Granville, WAS. See 1687.
1692. 9/21/01 mee Cooper, Thomas, "Master in Chancery of the State of New York".
                  See 5435.
1693. 9/21/01 mee Cooper, Thomas, "Master in Chancery for the State of New York";
                  City of N.Y. See 722, 3235, 3406, 3517, 5366, 7344, 8399.
                  (seven contracts).
1694. 9/21/01 mee Cooper, Thomas, "Master in Chancery for the State of New
                  York ... and trustee for the creditors of John Kelly
                  late of the City of New York ... deceased." See 553,
                  707, 2053, 3853, 7738, 8467, 8606. (seven contracts).
1695. 11/24/82 gee Cooper, William, yeoman; Cambridge, WAS. See 8338.
1696. 4/13/92 gee Cooper, William, farmer; ---, WAS. See 2355.
1697. 6/22/95 mor Corbin, Joseph; Williamstown, BER, MA; Champlain, CLI;
                  mee 3661.   (A:163)
1698. 5/27/91 gee Corbin, Royal; Champlain, CLI. See 2649, 3584 (two contracts).
1699. 10/18/93 gee Corbin, Royal; Champlain, CLI. See 5129.
1700. 5/16/96 mee Corbin, Royal, Esq.; Champlain, CLI. See 4948.
1701. 9/18/98 mee Corbin, Royal; Craftsborough, ---, VT. See 4949.
1702. 10/15/00 mee Corbin, William, merchant; Champlain, CLI. See 7753.
1703. 6/22/93 gee Corey, James, farmer; Willsborough, CLI. See 2813.
1704. 5/12/01 mor Corey, James; ---, ---; Willsborough, ESS; mee 6496. (A:68)
1705. 3/15/92 gor Corey, John; Galway, SAR; Cambridge, WAS; gee 3081. (C-2:134)

51

1706.   3/9/97   ---   Corey, John, dec'd. See 1707.
1707.   3/9/97   gor   Corey, Thankful, widow of John Corey of Galway, SAR, dec'd.;
                         Cambridge, WAS; gee 3082.   (C-2:135)
1708.   5/10/99 gor   Corey, Thankful, widow; Argyle, WAS; Argyle, WAS; gee 6298.
                                                                       (F:246)
1709.   5/2/97   gee   Corey, Thankfull; Argyle, WAS. See 1332.
1710.   3/4/02   mor   Cornel, Caran. See 1712.
1711.   3/4/02   mor   Cornel, James (w. Silvea); Argyle, WAS. See 1712.
1712.   3/4/02   mor   Cornel, Peledge (w. Caran); Hebron, WAS; Hartford, WAS;
                         co-mors 1711, 1713; mee 1298.   (D:160)
1713.   3/4/02   mor   Cornel, Silvea. See 1711.
1714.   1/27/97 gor   Cornel, Thomas; Easton, WAS; Saratoga Pat., WAS; gee 1042.
                                                                       (D:175)
1715.   6/20/98 gor   Cornell, Elizabeth. See 1720.
1716.   2/20/99 mor   Cornell, Elizabeth. See 1721.
1717.   10/18/94 gor   Cornell, Gilliam (w. Lydia), merchant; City of N.Y.;
                         Argyle, WAS; co-gees 342, 344, 345, 346. (C-2:143)
1718.   10/18/94 gor   Cornell, Lydia. See 1717.
1719.   6/1/98   mee   Cornell, Paul; Cambridge, WAS. See 2326.
1720.   6/20/98 gor   Cornell, Paul (w. Elizabeth); Cambridge, WAS; Cambridge,
                         WAS; co-gors 5535, 5537; gee 2332.   (D:349)
1721.   2/20/99 mor   Cornell, Paul (w. Elizabeth); Cambridge, WAS; Cambridge,
                         WAS; mee 2745.   (C: 38)
1722.   12/1/99 mee   Cornell, Paul; Cambridge, WAS. See 2333.
1723.   11/26/85 mee   Cornell, Thomas; Saratoga, ALB. See 3591.
1724.   8/28/94 gee   Cornell, Thomas; Easton, WAS. See 4486.
1725.   10/28/94 gee   Cornell, Zebulon, yeoman; Cambridge, WAS. See 2690.
1726.   7/16/98 mor   Cornwall, Edward; Fairfield, WAS; Edward Jessup's Pat., WAS;
                         mee 8042.   (C:30)
1727.   12/29/91 gee   Cornwall, Zebulon; ---, ---. See 4878.
1728.   11/18/02 mor   Cornwell, Esther. See 1729.
1729.   11/18/02 mor   Cornwell, John (w. Esther), farmer; Fairfield, WAS; land
                         "east side of the Hudson's river", WAS; mee 4035. (E:33)
                       Corrigo. See also Perrigo.
1730.   5/2/96   gor   Corrigo, Anna. See 1731.
1731.   5/2/96   gor   Corrigo, Robert, Junr., gentleman; Argyle, WAS. See 2100c.
1732.   10/15/95 mor   Corrington, Aaron, yeoman; ---, WAS. See 3259.
1733.   6/12/86 ---   Corsa, Isaac, gentleman; City of N.Y. See 2587.
1734.   9/4/86   gor   Corsa, Isaac; City of N.Y.; Granville, WAS; gee 1122. (A:56)
1735.   2/15/91 mee   Corsa, Mary; Newton, Province of Quebec, Canada. See 1112.
1736.   11/1/00 mor   Corse, Azariah, yeoman; Hebron, WAS; Hebron, WAS; mee 5236.
                                                                       (C:75)
1737.   3/21/01 gor   Corse, Azariah; Hebron, WAS; Hebron, WAS; co-gees 5237,
                         5238.   (F:273)
1738.   11/1/00 mee   Corss, Joseph; Champlain, CLI. See 1201.
1739.   6/3/88   gee   Cotterill, Nathan, yeoman; Argyle, WAS. See 1235.
1740.   4/8/99   mee   Cottrell, Nathan; Argyle, WAS. See 4927.
1741.   4/13/99 gee   Cottrell, Nathan, farmer; Argyle, WAS. See 3717.
1742.   5/31/02 gor   Cottrell, Nathan; Argyle, WAS; Kingsbury, WAS; gee 4939.
                                                                       (F:248)
1743.   1/19/96 gee   Coulter, Alexander; Hebron, WAS. See 8679.
1744.   5/7/88   gee   Cous, Peter; Redhook, DUT. See 3188.
1745.   6/2/00   gor   Couse, Elizabeth. See 1749.
1746.   4/2/87   gee   Couse, Hans Ties(?), ---, DUT. See 4245.
1747.   10/13/89 gee   Couse, Peter; Little Nine Partners, DUT. See 3921.
1748.   7/13/90 gee   Couse, Peter; Little Nine Partners, DUT. See 3941.
1749.   6/2/00   gor   Couse, Peter (w. Elizabeth), farmer; Little Nine Partners,
                         DUT; Argyle, WAS; gee 7447.   (E:10)
1750.   1/23/97 gee   Couse, Salmon, yeoman; Whitehall, WAS. See 8299.
1751.   5/20/97 gee   Covil, James; Kingsbury, WAS. See 1198.
1752.   2/10/98 mor   Covil, Jonathan (w. Mary), farmer; Hartford, WAS; Hartford,
                         WAS; mee 1484.   (C:27)
1753.   8/23/99 gor   Covil, Jonathan (w. Mary), farmer; Hartford, WAS; Hartford,
                         WAS; gee 5326.   (F:170)
1754.   4/2/00   mee   Covil, Jonathan, yeoman; Hartford, WAS. See 8186.
1755.   2/10/98 mor   Covil, Mary. See 1752.

1756. 8/23/99 gor Covil, Mary. See 1753.
1757. 5/20/00 mee Covill, James; Kingsbury, WAS. See 3509.
1758. 12/29/91 gee Covill, Micajah; ---, ---. See 4878.
1759. 5/11/74 gor Cowan, Ephraim, yeoman; Cambridge, ALB; Cambridge, ALB;
                     gee 3982.   (F:167)
1760. 2/21/93 gor Cowan, Ephraim, yeoman; Cambridge Dist., WAS; Cambridge
                     Dist., WAS; gee 6305.   (C-2:32)
1761. 11/12/98 mor Cowan, Ephraim (w. Sarah); Westfield, WAS; Westfield, WAS;
                     mee 8799.   (C:34)
1762. 11/14/93 gor Cowan, Moses, farmer; Cambridge, WAS; Cambridge, WAS;
                     gee 372.   (B-2:473)
1763. 3/29/00 mor Cowan, Nancy. See 1766.
1764. 4/18/83 gor Cowan, Patrick; Cambridge Dist., ALB; Cambridge Dist., ALB;
                     gee 7078.   (B-2:386)
1765. 11/12/98 mor Cowan, Sarah. See 1761.
1766. 3/29/00 mor Cowan, William (w. Nancy); Cambridge, WAS; Cambridge, WAS;
                     mee 2329.   (C:43)
1767. 7/2/92 gee Cowden, David; Cambridge, WAS. See 2842.
1768. 6/20/01 mee Cowden, James Simpson, Esq.; Cambridge, WAS. See 4302.
1769. 1/7/91 gee Cowen, Ephraim; ---, ALB. See 7367.
1770. 3/9/98 mor Cowen, Joseph (w. Phebe); Hartford, WAS; Hartford, WAS;
                     mee 1488.   (B:247)
1771. 12/5/93 mee Cowen, Mosses; Cambridge, WAS. See 7064.
1772. 3/9/98 mor Cowen, Phebe. See 1770.
1773. 10/20/86 gee Cowen, William; ---, WAS. See 5248.
1774. 4/20/01 mee Cowen, William; Cambridge, WAS. See 1804.
1775. 4/20/73 gor Craford, John; ---, ---. See 7957.
1776. 8/16/96 mor Cragin(?), Joseph; Salem, WAS; Hebron, WAS; mee 7089.
                                                                     (B:188)
1777. 10/28/94 gee Crags, Elihu, yeoman; Cambridge, WAS. See 2690.
1778. 7/8/97 gor Craig, Joseph; Salem, WAS; ---, WAS; gee 1453. (C-2:200)
1779. 4/1/96 mor Crandal, Abel; Cambridge, WAS; Cambridge, WAS; mee 5656.
                                                                     (C:29)
1780. 6/23/00 gor Crandal, Elizabeth. See 1783.
1781. 12/8/95 gee Crandal, Ezra, farmer; Easton, WAS. See 3670.
1782. 4/19/99 gee Crandal, Ezra, farmer; Easton, WAS. See 3667.
1783. 6/23/00 gor Crandal, Ezra (w. Elizabeth), yeoman; Easton, WAS; Easton,
                     WAS; gee 6289.   (D:447)
1784. 9/29/02 mor Crandall, Eber, Junr.; Canaan, COL; Argyle, WAS; mee 7722.
                                                                     (E:21)
1785. 12/8/95 mor Crandel, Ezra, farmer; Easton, WAS; Saratoga Pat., WAS;
                     mee 3671.   (B:14)
1786. 7/4/97 mor Crawford, James; Hebron, WAS; Argyle, WAS; mee 4188. (B:229)
1787. 11/29/00 gor Crawford, James (w. Martha); Cambridge, WAS; Cambridge, WAS;
                     gee 7986.   (F:135)
1788. 4/1/01 mor Crawford, James, farmer; Cambridge, WAS; ---, WAS;
                     co-mor 4686; mee 3859.   (D:25b)
1789. 8/24/01 gor Crawford, James, yeoman; Cambridge, WAS; Cambridge, WAS;
                     gee 4389.   (E:348)
1790. 9/7/69 gee Crawford, John; Pelham, HAM, MA. See 7955.
1791. 9/7/69 gor Crawford, John; ---, ---. See 7955.
1792. -/-/70 gor Crawford, John (w. Susannah); Pelham, ---, --; ---, ALB;
                     gee 6683.   (A:121)
1793. 11/29/00 gor Crawford, Martha. See 1787.
1794. -/-/70 gor Crawford, Susannah. See 1792.
1795. 6/10/85 gee Creighton, Robert; Black Creek, WAS. See 1440.
1796. 7/3/97 gee Crippen, Alice. See 1799.
1797. 9/6/90 gee Crippen, Alpheus; Granville, WAS. See 2245.
1798. 7/15/90 gee Crippen, Hose(?); Granville, WAS. See 2244.
1799. 7/3/97 mor Crippen, Joseph (w. Alice), farmer; Granville, WAS;
                     Granville, WAS; co-mees 2934, 2946. Co-mortgagees are
                     executors of the will of James Grant "late of the town
                     of Pawling (DUT) deceased."   (B:195)
1800. 2/3/02 gee Crippen, Nathan R.; Hillsdale, COL. See 2926.
1801. 7/20/87 gee Cristy, James; ---, ---. See 100.
1802. 4/20/96 gor Cristy, Petter, farmer; Hampton, WAS; Hampton, WAS;
                     gee 4509.   (F:95)

1803. 7/20/87 gee Cristy, William; ---, ---. See 100.
1804. 4/20/01 mor Crocker, Eleazer (w Susanna); Cambridge, WAS; Cambridge, WAS; mee 1774. (D:121)
1805. 5/4/82 gee Crocker, Ephraim, yeoman; ---, CHA. See 1807.
1806. 3/18/01 gor Crocker, Hannah. See 1810.
1807. 5/4/82 gee Crocker, Levi, yeoman; ---, ---. See 1805.
1808. 5/4/82 gor Crocker, Levi, gentleman; Becket, BER, MA; land "above Saraghtoga", CHA; co-gees 1805, 1807. (A:63)
1809. 6/2/73 gee Crocker, Levy, yeoman; Saratoga, ALB. See 4276.
1810. 3/18/01 gor Crocker, Peter (w. Hannah); Hebron, WAS; Hebron, WAS; gee 1032. (F:188)
1811. 4/20/01 mor Crocker, Susanna. See 1804.
1812. 11/20/90 gee Crooker, Seth; Wellington, TOL, CT. See 6146.
1813. 11/15/96 gee Crookshank, William, farmer; Salem, WAS. See 562.
1814. 4/11/00 gee Crookshanks, Nathaniel; ---, ---. See 8538.
1815. 11/15/96 gee Crookshanks, William; Salem, WAS. See 8596.
1816. 5/20/97 gor Crookshanks, William, merchant; Salem, WAS; Salem, WAS; gee 92. (C-2:330)
1817. 2/11/96 mee Crosbys, Cyrenius; Amenia, DUT. See 4508.
1817a. 5/30/01 mor Cross, Elihu; Shaftsbury, BEN, VT. See 1006.
1818. 10/21/00 mor Crosset, Jacob. yeoman; Salem, WAS; Salem, WAS; mee 1312. (C:77)
1819. 4/28/75 gor Crossett, James; New Perth, CHA; New Perth, CHA; gee 3537. (B-1:66)
1820. 4/26/86 gor Crossett, James; Salem, WAS; Salem, WAS; gee 987. (A:526)
1821. 5/29/90 gor Crossett, James; Salem, WAS. See 8568.
1822. 4/20/73 gor Crossett, William; ---, ---. See 7957.
1823. Data repositioned.
1824. 9/7/69 gor Crossett, William; ---, ---. See 7955.
1825. 4/1/88 gee Crossfield, Timothy; "of Lake Champlain", CLI. See 157.
1826. 4/9/00 mor Crothers, Robert (w. Sarah), farmer; Cambridge, WAS; Cambridge, WAS; co-mees 7751, 7752. (C:43)
1827. 4/9/00 mor Crothers, Sarah. See 1826.
1828. 10/12/96 mor Crouch, David; Granville, WAS; Granville, WAS; mee 3762. (B:122)
1829. 7/1/00 mor Crouch, Phineas; ---, ---; ---, ESS; mee 5572. (A:35)
1830. 11/23/70 gee Crozer, John; "Green Bush"; ALB. See 4781.
1831. 1/18/90 mor Crutenden(?), Timothy; Poultney, ---, VT; land west of Poultney town line?; WAS; mee 6031. (A:187)
1832. 11/30/84 gee Crysta, Peter, husbandman; ---, WAS. See 8232.
1833. 4/12/01 mor Culver, Anna. See 1835.
1834. 4/1/01 mee Culver, Bezaliel, yeoman; Cambridge, WAS. See 8398.
1835. 4/12/01 mor Culver, Bezaliel (w. Anna); Cambridge, WAS; Kingsbury, WAS; co-mees 8503, 8508. (D:156)
1836. 9/3/01 mor Culver, Mabel. See 1838.
1837. 9/3/01 mee Culver, Nathan, farmer; Cambridge, WAS. See 8393.
1838. 9/3/01 mor Culver, Nathan (w. Mabel), farmer; Cambridge, WAS; Cambridge, WAS; mee 6177. (D:89)
1839. 5/5/01 mee Cummings, Robert; Cambridge, WAS. See 1159.
1840. 4/16/89 mor Cummins, Abraham; Granville, WAS; Granville, WAS; mee 833. (A:166)
1841. 4/8/90 gor Cummins, Abraham (w. June); Granville, WAS; Granville, WAS; gee 3726. (C-1:64)
1842. 3/16/89 mor Cummins, Henry; Granville, WAS; Granville, WAS; mee 830. (A:156)
1843. 4/8/90 gor Cummins, June. See 1841.
1844. 8/11/01 gor Cummins, Nathan, yeoman; Champlain, CLI; Champlain, CLI; gee 6662. (B:335)
Curby. See also Kirby.
1845. 6/24/99 gee Curby, Elihu, blacksmith; Easton, WAS. See 5642.
1846. 6/24/67 gee Currie, Archibald, merchant; City of N.Y. See 1202.
1847. 6/7/93 gor Currie, Archibald (w. Catherine); City of N.Y. See 6484.
1848. 6/7/93 gor Currie, Catherine. See 1847.
1849. 9/27/94 gor Curtice, Daniel, yeoman; Granville, WAS; Robert Campbell's Pat., WAS; gee 3399. (D:376)

1850. 12/29/94 gor Curtice, Daniel; Granville, WAS; Granville, WAS; co-gors
      716, 3042, 3400, 4118; gee 4776.   (D:217)
1851. 12/11/97 gor Curtice, Daniel; Granville, WAS; Granville, WAS; co-gees
      717, 3401.   (D:375)
1852. 6/2/98 gor Curtice, Daniel; Granville, WAS. See 718.
1853. 12/30/83 gor Curtis, Daniel; Granville, WAS; Granville, WAS; gee 2029.
      (A:66)
1854. 7/13/92 mor Curtis, Damiel, farmer; Granville, WAS. See 3402.
1855. 11/15/98 mor Curtis, Daniel (w. Lucy), saddler and tanner; Granville,
      WAS; Granville, WAS; mee 3852.   (C:31)
1856. 10/8/96 mor Curtis, Daniel, Junr.; Granville, WAS; Granville, WAS;
      mee 4129.   (B:103)
1857. 12/2/99 mor Curtis, Enos (w. Mary), farmer; Queensbury, WAS;
      Queensbury, WAS; co-mees 866, 1654, 1665, 3100, 3967,
      3971, 5492, 5495.   (C:41)
1858. 4/25/93 mor Curtis, Larah, farmer; Charlotte, CHI, VT; Champlain, CLI;
      mee 5109.   (A:107)
1859. 11/15/98 mor Curtis, Lucy. See 1855.
1860. 12/2/99 mor Curtis, Mary. See 1857.
1861. 5/1/00 mor Curtis, Nathaniel, Junr., farmer; Chester, WAS; Chester, WAS;
      mee 7772.   (D:210)
1862. 5/1/00 mor Curtis, Philo, farmer; Chester, WAS; Chester, WAS; mee 7772.
      (D:200)
1863. 5/1/00 mor Curtis, Zacheus H., farmer; Chester, WAS; Chester, WAS;
      mee 7772. Two contracts this date involving these two
      persons.   (D:219), (D:220)
1864. 10/15/92 mor Cushman, Paul; ---, CLI; Plattsburgh, CLI; mee 5351. (A:89)
1865. 2/2/87 mor Cutler, Ephraim; ---, ---. See 2159.
1866. 10/12/99 mor Cutler, Isaac; Fairhaven, RUT, VT; Hampton, WAS; mee 3820.
      (C:41)
1867. 6/11/99 mee Cutter, Ephraim; Cambridge, WAS. See 6328.
1868. 12/28/90 mor Cutter, John; Hebron, WAS; Hebron, WAS; mee 1073. (A:269)
1869. 5/26/88 gor Cuyler, Charlotte, "formerly Charlotte Gilliland";
      Willsborough, CLI; Willsborough, CLI; co-gor 1882;
      gee 6510.   (A:67)
1870. 6/11/88 gor Cuyler, Charlotte. See 1883.
1871. 6/11/88 gor Cuyler, Charlotte; Willsborough, CLI; Willsborough, CLI;
      co-gor 1884; gee 7377.   (A:77)
1872. 9/28/88 gor Cuyler, Charlotte; Willsborough, CLI; Willsborough, CLI;
      co-gor 1885; gee 4278.   (A:87)
1873. 10/14/88 gor Cuyler, Charlotte. See 1886.
1874. 10/25/88 gor Cuyler, Charlotte. See 1887.
1875. 11/3/88 gor Cuyler, Charlotte. See 1888.
1876. 11/5/88 gor Cuyler, Charlotte. See 1889.
1877. 3/2/89 gor Cuyler, Charlotte. See 1890.
1878. 4/25/89 gor Cuyler, Charlotte. See 1891.
1879. 7/7/95 gor Cuyler, Charlotte. See 1892.
1880. 12/28/02 mor Cuyler, John C., merchant; Albany, ALB; Fairfield, WAS;
      mee 4034.   (E:40)
1881. 9/30/99 gee Cuyler, John T.; Albany. ALB See 2860.
1882. 5/26/88 gor Cuyler, Stephen; Willsborough, CLI. See 1869.
1883. 6/11/88 gor Cuyler, Stephen (w. Charlotte); Willsborough, CLI;
      Willsborough, CLI; gee 7377a.   (A:74)
1884. 6/11/88 gor Cuyler, Stephen; Willsborough, CLI. See 1871.
1885. 9/28/88 gor Cuyler, Stephen. See 1872.
1886. 10/14/88 gor Cuyler, Stephen (w. Charlotte), gentleman; Willsborough, CLI;
      Willsborough, CLI; gee 3497.   (A:59)
1887. 10/25/88 gor Cuyler, Stephen (w, Charlotte), gentleman; Willsborough, CLI;
      Willsborough, CLI; gee 3298.   (A:37)
1888. 11/3/88 gor Cuyler, Stephen (w. Charlotte), gentleman; Willsborough, CLI;
      Willsborough, CLI; gee 3498.   (A:57)
1889. 11/5/88 gor Cuyler, Stephen (w. Charlotte), gentleman; Willsborough, CLI;
      Willsborough, CLI; gee 846.   (A:52)
1890. 3/2/89 gor Cuyler, Stephen (w. Charlotte), gentleman; Willsborough, CLI;
      Willsborough, CLI; gee 3487.   (A:62)
1891. 4/25/89 gor Cuyler, Stephen (w. Charlotte), gentleman; Willsborough, CLI
      Willsborough, CLI; gee 3489.   (A:64)

1892.	7/7/95	gor	Cuyler, Stephen (w. Charlotte); ---, ---; Willsborough, CLI; gee 3470. (A:384)
1893.	9/3/92	mor	Dailey, David; Westfield, WAS; Westfield, WAS; mee 7234. (A:377)
1894.	2/21/01	mor	Daily, Jacob; Champlain, CLI; Canadian and Nova Scotia Refugees' Pat., CLI; mee 5098. (B:13)
1895.	3/28/01	mor	Daily, Jacob; Champlain, CLI; Champlain, CLI; mee 7761a. (B:22)
1896.	5/1/02	mor	Daley, William, farmer; Chester, WAS; Chester, WAS; mee 7775. (D:224)
1897.	2/3/95	gor	Daly, Jonathan, farmer; Willsborough, CLI; Willsborough, CLI; gee 2535. (A:35)
1898.	7/10/90	mor	Danah, Isaac; Hebron, WAS; Hebron, WAS; mee 1072. (A:253)
1899.	5/30/01	mor	Daniels, Ebenezer; ---, ---; Willsborough, ESS; mee 6497. (A:69)
1900.	6/26/97	mor	Daniels, John, farmer; Willsborough, CLI; Willsborough, CLI; mee 2802. (A:229)
1901.	9/27/98	mor	Daniels, John, yeoman; Bridport, ADD, VT; Willsborough, CLI; mee 2805. (A:351)
1902.	2/12/02	mor	Daniels, John; ---, ---; ---, ESS; mee 6499. (A:77)
1903.	7/7/91	gee	Darby, Benjamin, farmer; Hebron, WAS. See 7190.
1904.	8/24/90	gee	Darby, Jesse; Hebron, WAS. See 6998.
1905.	8/24/90	mor	Darby, Jesse; Hebron, WAS; Shereiff's Pat. (Hebron),WAS; mee 6978. (A:228)
1906.	7/7/91	gee	Darby, Samuel, farmer; Hebron, WAS. See 7190.
1907.	9/18/75	gee	Darlen, Garshum; ---, ---. See 3800.
1908.	8/15/93	mor	Darling, Jessup, farmer; Ridgefield, FAI, CT; Jessup's Pat., WAS; mee 7672. (A:426)
1909.	6/5/84	gee	Darrough, Jedediah, farmer; Black Creek Dist., WAS. See 4204.
1910.	6/1/92	gee	Darrow, Jadadiah; Hebron, WAS. See 8741.
1911.	5/13/85	gor	Darrow, Jedediah, farmer; Black Creek Dist., WAS; Black Creek Dist., WAS; gee 8386. (C-1:2)
1912.	2/16/97	mor	Darrow, Jonathan; ---, CLI; Champlain, CLI; mee 1940. (A:405)
1913.	12/11/99	mor	Darrow, Walter; Champlain, CLI; Champlain, CLI; mee 1944. (A:407)
1914.	9/15/68	gor	Davies, Thomas, "Capt. Lieutenant of ... Royal Regiment of Artillery"; ---, ---; Walton Pat., ALB; gee 8782. (B-2:176)
1915.	3/20/02	mor	Davis, James; ---, ---; Willsborough, ESS; mee 5777. (A:83)
1916.	10/3/96	mor	Davis, John; Willsborough, CLI; Willsborough, CLI; mee 5865. (A:201)
1917.	3/2/99	gee	Davis, John; Thurman, WAS. See 7770.
1918.	12/1/95	gee	Davis, Noah; Crown Point, CLI. See 6452.
1919.	1/7/95	mor	Davis, Peter, farmer; Easton, WAS; Saratoga Pat., WAS; mee 2264. (A:532)
1920.	3/26/02	mor	Davis, Peter, yeoman; Easton, WAS; Easton, WAS; mee 526. (D:228)
1921.	12/23/00	mor	Davis, Robert; ---, ---; Elizabethtown, ESS; mee 7522. (A:79)
1922.	10/12/96	mor	Day, Comfort; Granville, WAS; Granville, WAS; mee 3770. (B:125)
1923.	1/16/01	mor	Day, Elkanah; Granville, WAS; Granville, WAS; co-mees 356, 8175. Co-mortgagees are overseers of the poor, Granville. (D:33)
1924.	8/14/02	mor	Day, Elkanah; Granville, WAS; Granville, WAS; mee 4164. (E:14)
1925.	9/6/98	mor	Day, Elkany, blacksmith; Granville, WAS; Granville, WAS; mee 1986. (C:48)
1926.	3/21/94	gor	Day, Hannah. See 1928.
1927.	6/2/02	mor	Day, Lemuel; Granville, WAS. See 2323.
1928.	3/21/94	gor	Day, Nathan (w. Hannah); Granville, WAS; Granville, WAS; gee 7590. (B-2:191)
1929.	10/11/96	mor	Day, Noah, farmer; Granville, WAS; Granville, WAS; mee 3769. (B:124)

1930.	10/26/73	mee	Deal, Samuel, merchant; City of N.Y. See 3023.
1931.	7/14/01	mor	Dealey, William, yeoman; Argyle, WAS; <u>Argyle, WAS</u>;
			mee 7627. (D:149)
1932.	10/8/88	gor	Deall, Peter; ---, ---. See 1934.
1933.	7/5/93	gee	Deall, Peter, merchant; City of N.Y. See 6732.
1934.	10/8/88	gor	Deall, Samuel; ---, ---; <u>Ticonderoga, CLI</u>; co-gors 1932,
			5306, 5308; co-gees 1015, 3395. (A:89)
1935.	7/5/93	gee	Deall, Samuel, miller; Mill Neck, WES. See 6732.
1936.	7/5/93	---	Deall, Samuel, dec'd. See 6732.
1937.	3/4/96	gor	Deall, Samuel (w. Sarah), miller; Rye, WES; <u>Crown Point, CLI</u>;
			gee 1533. (A:421)
1938.	3/4/96	gor	Deall, Sarah. See 1937.
1939.	11/16/01	mor	Dean, Isaiah; ---, ---; <u>Queensbury, WAS</u>; mee 2471. (D:138)
1940.	2/16/97	mee	Dean, James; ---, HER. See 1912.
1941.	6/17/99	mee	Dean, James; Westmoreland, ONE. See 5316.
1942.	10/3/99	mee	Dean, James; Westmoreland, ONE. See 4030.
1943.	10/24/99	mee	Dean, James; Westmoreland, ONE. See 4031.
1944.	12/11/99	mee	Dean, James; Westmoreland, ONE. See 1913.
1945.	5/17/01	gee	Dean, Jonathan; Clinton, DUT. See 2494.
1946.	5/20/00	mor	Dean, Josiah (w. Tempe); Queensbury, WAS; <u>Queensbury, WAS</u>;
			mee 8823. (C:49)
1947.	5/20/00	mor	Dean, Tempe. See 1946.
1948.	2/16/84	mor	Deane, Mary. See 1949.
1949.	2/16/84	mor	Deane, Prichard (w. Mary), distiller; City of N.Y.; <u>land</u>
			<u>"west side of Lake Champlain"</u>, CHA; mee 3842.
			(Deed Book B-1:119)
1950.	12/24/95	mor	Deane, Solomon E., physician; Cambridge, WAS; <u>Cambridge,</u>
			<u>WAS</u>; mee 6332. (B:61)
1951.	4/10/99	mor	Deen, Esther. See 1953.
1952.	7/19/00	gor	Deen, James; Queensbury, WAS; <u>Queensbury, WAS</u>; gee 6342.
			(E:50)
1953.	4/10/99	mor	Deen, Joel (w. Esther); Queensbury, WAS; <u>Queensbury, WAS</u>;
			mee 8822. (C:46)
1954.	5/4/96	gee	Deen, Josiah; Queensbury, WAS. See 1956.
1955.	4/6/95	mor	Deen, Samuel; Queensbury, WAS; <u>Queensbury, WAS</u>; mee 8192.
			(A:541)
1956.	5/4/96	gor	Deen, Samuel; Queensbury, WAS; <u>Queensbury, WAS</u>; gee 1954.
			(D:435)
1957.	8/25/00	gee	De Labigarre, Maria; Rhinebeck, DUT. See 589.
1958.	12/19/01	mee	De Labigarre, Peter; Rhinebeck, DUT. See 8350.
1959.	2/4/94	mee	De Lancey, John; City of N.Y. See 8495.
1960.	7/1/85	---	Delancey, Oliver, Esq. See 8285.
1961.	1/24/86	---	De Lancey, Oliver, "late of the City of New York". See 8286.
1962.	2/6/86	gor	De Lancey, Oliver; City of N.Y. See 8287.
1963.	6/24/85	---	Delancey, Oliver, Esq. See 8284.
1964.	3/14/86	---	De Lancey, Oliver, Esq. See 8289.
1965.	10/2/00	mee	Delanie, John; ---, ---. See 394.
1966.	10/6/92	gor	Delavan, Nathaniel, farmer; ---, DUT; <u>Granville, WAS</u>;
			gee 3725. (B-2:5)
1967.	4/18/96	mor	Delavergne, James, farmer; Pittstown, REN; <u>Saratoga Pat.,</u>
			<u>WAS</u>; mee 3685. (B:33)
1968.	7/13/92	gee	Delivan, Nathaniel, farmer; ---, DUT. See 1239.
1969.	10/25/91	---	De Long, Francis. Husband of Margaret in #1971.
1970.	5/30/99	mor	De Long, Francis (w. Margarett); Argyle, WAS; <u>Argyle, WAS</u>;
			co-mees 772, 788, 2857. (C:47)
1971.	10/25/91	---	De Long, Margaret; Argyle, WAS. See 4201.
1972.	5/30/99	mor	De Long, Margarett. See 1970.
1973.	9/22/00	mee	Delord, Henry; Peru, CLI. See 6607.
1974.	7/7/02	gee	Delord, Henry; ---, ---. See 7869.
1975.	6/6/00	mee	Delord, Henry, Esq.; Peru, CLI. See 8332.
1976.	8/8/87	gee	Demaray, Samuel, farmer; ---, WAS. See 5919.
1977.	7/4/88	gor	Demaray, Samuel, farmer; Plattsburgh, CLI; <u>---, CLI</u>;
			gee 107. (A:18)
1978.	5/20/99	gee	Deming, Samuel; Cambridge, WAS. See 6312.
1979.	5/1/98	gor	Denning, William; ---, ---. See 7097.
1980.	7/4/92	gee	Dennis, Shaderick, farmer; ---, WAS. See 6117.

1981. 2/20/96 gee Dennis, Shadrach, carpenter; Cambridge, WAS. See 7579.
1982. 6/13/96 gee Dennis, Shadrach, farmer; Cambridge, WAS. See 5600.
1983. 12/9/85 gee Dennis, Shadrack; Cambridge Dist., WAS. See 118.
1984. 3/3/95 mee Denniston, Isaac; ---, ---. See 4424.
1985. 2/22/98 mor Denoyer(?), John, "yeoman or merchant"; Hartford, WAS;
                  Hartford, WAS; mee 5539.   (B:325)
1986. 9/6/88 mee Denslow, Rosebille, "tayloress"; Granville, WAS. See 1925.
1987. 12/30/93 gee de Peyster, Pierre; ---, ---. See 6714.
1988. 1/24/94 gee de Peyster, Pierre, "late of New York but now of London,
                  merchant". See 6715.
1989. 6/3/96 gee De Redder, Walter, farmer; Easton, WAS. See 4768.
1990. 4/25/95 gor Derevage, Francois (w. Rosanna), farmer; Champlain, CLI;
                  Canadian Refugees' Pat.(?), CLI; gee 766.   (A:376)
1991. 4/25/95 gor Derevage, Rosanna. See 1990.
1992. 6/5/95 gor De Ridder, Evert, farmer; Easton, WAS; Easton, WAS;
                  gee 8053.   (D:91)
1993. 6/26/76 gor De Ridder, Killyan, yeoman; Saratoga Pat., ALB; Saratoga
                  Pat., CHA; gee 8008, 8009.   (C-2:220)
1994. 11/4/00 gee de Rider, Simon; ---, ---. See 2557.
1995. 12/21/68 gee Desbrosses, Elias, merchant; City of N.Y. See 8418.
1996. 7/12/01 mor Deuel, Jonathan, farmer; Hebron, WAS; Hebron, WAS; mee 3860.
                                                              (D:75b)
1997. 6/6/92 gee Deury, Thaddeus; Westfield, WAS. See 5070.
1998. 4/17/92 gee Deury, Thomas; Westfield, WAS. See 3029.
1999. 2/11/92 mor Dewey, Elias, blacksmith; Plattsburgh, CLI; Judd Pat., CLI;
                  mee 49.   (A:90)
2000. 10/3/96 gor Dewey, Elias; Willsborough, CLI; James Judd's Pat., CLI;
                  gee 5863.   (B:132)
2001. 5/27/01 mor Dewey, Elias; Champlain, CLI; Champlain, CLI; mee 809.
                                                              (B:37)
2002. 12/12/98 mor Dewey, Eliazer (w. Freelove), farmer; Hartford, WAS;
                  Hartford, WAS; mee 1496.   (C:44)
2003. 4/19/96 gee Dewey, Ezekiel, blacksmith; Hartford, WAS. See 1666.
2004. 12/12/98 mor Dewey, Freelove. See 2002.
2005. 9/30/90 gee Dewey, Thaddeus, farmer; Westfield, WAS. See 2872.
2006. 9/30/99 mor Dewey, Thaddeus, farmer; Westfield, WAS; Westfield, WAS;
                  mee 2871.   (C:48)
2007. 12/5/99 mee Dewey, Thaddeus; Westfield, WAS. See 8702.
2008. 12/22/98 gee Dewey, Thomas; Westfield, WAS. See 889.
2009. 9/3/00 mee Dewey, Thomas; Westfield, WAS. See 7874.
2010. 2/22/02 gor De Wit, John; Clinton, DUT; Willsborough, ESS; gee 728.
                                                              (A:55)
2011. 6/24/94 mee De Witt, John, Esq.; ---, DUT. See 5285.
2012. 9/15/94 gor De Witt, Simeon, Surveyor General of the State of New York;
                  ---, ---; Skene's Little Pat., WAS; co-gees 1105, 1282,
                  1369, 5373, 8241, 8812.   (B-2:317)
2013. 10/25/94 gee Dexter, Amos; Willsborough, CLI. See 2014.
2014. 10/25/94 gor Dexter, Elijah; Willsborough, CLI; Willsborough, CLI;
                  gee 2013.   (A:382?)
2015. 10/17/89 mor Dexter, Elijah, Junr.; Willsborough, CLI; Willsborough, CLI;
                  mee 6442.   (A:30)
2016. 10/14/89 gee Dexter, Elisha, Junr.; Willsborough, CLI. See 6439.
2017. 7/1/00 mor Dexter, Joseph; ---, ---; ---, ESS; mee 5572. (A:24)
2018. 10/17/89 mor Dexter, Thomas; Willsborough, CLI; Willsborough, CLI;
                  mee 6442.   (A:25)
2019. 12/17/01 mor Dibble, Cornish; Granville, WAS; Granville, WAS; co-mees
                  709, 7741.   (D:125)
2020. 7/1/00 mor Dibble, Levi; ---, ---; ---, ESS; co-mor 6300; mee 5572.
                                                              (A:21)
2021. 8/20/86 gee Dick, John; Hebron, WAS. See 7464.
2022. 6/18/91 gee Dick, John; Hebron, WAS; Hebron, WAS; gee 3719. (A:209)
2023. 2/10/80 gor Dick, Margaret; Pelham, HAM, MA; White Creek, CHA;
                  gee 5569.   (B-1:20)
2024. 5/18/89 gor Dick, Margaret, executor of the estate of Thomas Dick,
                  late of Pelham, deceased; Pelham, HAM, MA; ---, WAS;
                  gee 4513.   (A:219)

2025. 6/2/69 gor Dick, Thomas; Pelham, ---, --; White Creek, ALB; gee 175.
(B-2:113)
2026. 6/2/69 gor Dick, Thomas; Pelham, HAM, --; ---, ALB; gee 5258. (E:158)
2027. 6/30/84 gor Dick, Thomas; Pelham, HAM, MA; New Perth, WAS; gee 2982.
(B-1:103)
2028. 5/18/89 --- Dick, Thomas, dec'd, "late of Pelham", HAM, MA. See 2024.
2029. 12/30/83 gee Dickerson, Nathan; Glastonbury, HAR, CT. See 1853.
2030. 9/24/96 gee Dickinson, Benjamin; Queensbury, WAS. See 2448.
2031. 1/22/01 gor Dickinson, Benjamin, merchant; City of N.Y.; ---, WAS;
gee 5632. (F:103)
2032. 4/19/02 mee Dickinson, John D.; Troy, REN. See 1558.
2033. 1/14/95 gee Dickson, David, farmer; Cambridge, WAS. See 398.
2034. 4/20/95 gor Dickson, David (w. Sarah), farmer; Cambridge, WAS;
Cambridge, WAS; gee 7446. (B-2:516)
2035. 2/20/98 mor Dickson, Joseph (w. Nabby), farmer; Hartford, WAS;
Hartford, WAS; mee 1487. (B:249)
2036. 2/20/98 mor Dickson, Nabby. See 2035.
2037. 4/20/95 gor Dickson, Sarah. See 2034.
2038. 1/30/93 gee Dillingham, Joshua, blacksmith; Hanover, PLY, MA. See 5019.
2039. 7/6/88 mor Dillingham, William; Granville, WAS; Granville, WAS;
mee 2380. (A:136)
2040. 5/11/01 gee Dings, Adam A., yeoman; Livingston, COL. See 8443.
2041. 6/26/00 gee Dings, Jacob, yeoman; Argyle, WAS. See 1100.
2042. 3/26/01 gee Dings, Jacob, farmer; Argyle, WAS. See 1103.
2043. 3/26/01 mor Dings, Jacob, farmer; Argyle, WAS; Argyle, WAS; mee 1104.
(D:48b)
2044. 4/2/90 gee Divinell, Allen; Cambridge, WAS. See 130.
2045. 1/22/98 gee Divinell(?), Ebenezer; Cambridge, WAS. See 131.
2046. 3/1/98 gee Dixon, Hannah, daughter of Moses Dixon; Peru, CLI. See 2050.
2047. 6/11/88 gee Dixon, Moses, farmer; Plattsburgh, CLI. See 5925.
2048. 7/3/93 mor Dixon, Moses; Provincial Pat., WAS; Provincial Pat., WAS;
mee 5335. (A:491)
2049. 4/13/96 gor Dixon, Moses; Peru, CLI; Peru, CLI; gee 2051. Grantee is
a son of the grantor. (B:126)
2050. 3/1/98 gor Dixon, Moses; Peru, CLI; Peru, CLI; gee 2046. Grantee is
a daughter of the grantor. (B:129)
2051. 4/13/96 gee Dixon, Solomon, a son of Moses Dixon; Peru, CLI. See 2049.
2052. 5/29/90 gee Doan, David; Granville, WAS. See 7658.
2053. 9/21/01 mor Doane, David; ---, WAS; Granville, WAS; mee 1694. (D:145)
2054. 1/24/92 mor Doane, John; Cambridge, WAS; Walloomsack Pat., WAS;
mee 5541. (A:319)
2055. 5/1/02 mor Dobbin, David; Argyle, WAS; Argyle, WAS; mee 4079. (D:230)
2056. 2/2/93 gor Dobson, Margaret. See 2057.
2057. 2/2/93 gor Dobson, Thomas (w. Margaret); City of N.Y.; Queensbury,
WAS; gee 231. (B-2:251)
2058. 12/14/93 gee Dodge, Asahel, yeoman; Granville, WAS. See 443.
2059. 10/12/96 mor Dodge, Asahel; Granville, WAS; Granville, WAS; mee 3770.
(B:106)
2060. 12/22/95 mor Dodge, Jordan; Granville, WAS; Granville, WAS; mee 532.
(B:2)
2061. 11/17/95 mor Doe, Reuben; Burlington, ---, VT; Peru, CLI; mee 3587.
(A:235)
2062. 11/25/01 gor Dominick, Ann. See 2063.
2063. 11/25/01 gor Dominick, Francis (w. Ann), gentleman; City of N.Y.;
---, WAS; gee 4890. (F:254)
2064. 1/4/96 mor Donaghy, William, yeoman; ---, ---, VT; Willsborough, CLI;
mee 5743. (A:169)
2065. 3/5/92 gee Donaldson, James, yeoman; Cambridge, WAS. See 7836 and
7837 (two independent contracts).
2066. 11/2/96 mee Donaldson, James; Hebron, WAS. See 8703.
2067. 10/11/92 gee Dopp, Peter; Plattsburgh, CLI. See 6255.
2068. 10/12/92 mor Dopp, Peter; Plattsburgh, CLI; ---, CLI; co-mees 511, 6257.
(A:85)
2069. 6/22/91 gor Dorr, Jonathan; ---, ---. See 8450.
2070. 3/23/02 mee Doty, Chillus; Salem, WAS. See 2780.

2071.	7/4/97	mor	Doty, Isaac (w. Rachel), yeoman; Granville, WAS; Granville,
*2071a.			* WAS; co-mees 74, 2935, 2948. (B:206)
2072.	6/18/93	mor	Doty, Jonathan, farmer; Willsborough, CLI; Willsborough,
			CLI; co-mor 3986; mee 2812. (A:131)
2073.	10/24/94	mee	Doty, Jonathan; Willsborough, CLI. See 114.
2074.	7/4/97	mor	Doty, Rachel. See 2071.
2075.	7/3/97	mor	Doty, Sarah. See 2077.
2076.	7/4/99	mor	Doty, Shadrach; Whitehall, WAS; Whitehall, WAS; mee 4136.
			(C:47)
2077.	7/3/97	mor	Doty, Silas (w. Sarah), farmer; Granville, WAS; Granville,
			WAS; co-mees 73, 2934, 2946. (B:207)
2078.	5/10/80	gor	Doty, Theodore, Capt.; New Perth, CHA; New Perth, CHA;
			gee 7479. (B-1:117)
2079.	9/15/73	gor	Douglas, Benjamin; New Haven, NEW, CT; land "east side of
			Hudson's river", CHA; co-gees 5232, 5234. (C-2:123)
2080.	8/31/92	mee	Douglass, George, Junr., merchant; City of N.Y. See 4520.
2081.	2/23/01	mor	Douglass, George; whitehall, WAS; Whitehall, WAS; mee 8389.
			(D:24)
2082.	7/2/95	gee	Douglass, James; Kingsbury, WAS. See 5627.
2083.	6/5/97	mee	Douglass, John, farmer; Champlain, CLI. See 1644.
2084.	4/2/00	mor	Douglass, John; ---, ---; Willsborough, ESS; mee 8818. (A:9)
2085.	7/1/00	mor	Douglass, John; ---, ---; ---, ESS; mee 5572. (A:17)
2086.	4/30/01	gor	Douglass, John; Willsborough, ESS; Willsborough, ESS;
			gee 8819. (A:32)
2087.	7/14/01	mor	Douglass, John; ---, ---; Willsborough, ESS; co-mees
			4271, 6996. (A:71)
2088.	8/5/94	gor	Douglass, Martha. See 2092.
2089.	9/3/00	gee	Douglass, Nathaniel, Esq.; Champlain, CLI. See 5655.
2090.	11/19/00	gee	Douglass, Nathaniel, Junr., yeoman; Champlain, CLI. See 1253.
2091.	11/17/98	mor	Douglass, Peleg; Tinmouth, RUT, VT; Old Military Township
			#7 (Chateaugay), CLI; co-mees 6862, 8094. (A:371)
2092.	8/5/94	gor	Douglass, Wheeler (w. Martha); Lansingburgh, REN; land
			"west side of Lake George", WAS; gee 8038. (C-2:6)
2093.	6/23/92	gee	Douglass, William, Esq.; Stephentown, REN. See 4760.
2094.	7/15/91	mor	Doury, Pelatiah; ---, ---; Hebron, WAS; mee 6982. (A:300)
2095.	10/3/96	gee	Dow, Peter; Willsborough, CLI. See 5864.
2096.	10/3/96	mor	Dow, Peter; Willsborough, CLI; Willsborough, CLI; mee 5865.
			(A:200)
2097.	12/2/88	mor	Drake, William; Granville, WAS; Granville, WAS; mee 2380a.
			(A:134)
2098.	5/2/96	gee	Draper, John; ---, WAS. See 1185.
2099.	5/2/96	gor	Draper, John (w. Lidia), gentleman; Argyle, WAS; Argyle, WAS;
			co-gors 1288, 1304, 5580, 5582; co-gees 4012, 4013.
			(D:324)
2100.	5/2/96	gor	Draper, John (w. Lydia), gentleman; Argyle, WAS; Argyle, WAS;
			co-gors 1289, 1304a, 2214, 2221, 5580a, 5583; gee 2113.
			(C-2:165)
2100a.	5/2/96	gor	Draper, John (w. Lydia); Argyle, WAS; Argyle, WAS; co-gors
			1289a, 1304b, 2227, 2232, 5580b, 5583a; gees 410 (E:320),
			3092 (F:81), 3143 (F:47), 3143 (F:50), 4025 (F:60),
			4099 (F:57), 4989 (F:38), 5479 (F:52), 6297 (F:114),
			6639 (F:45), 7356 (F:31), 7363 (F:36); co-gees 6330
			and 6331 (F:27). (thirteen independent contracts)
2100b.	5/2/96	gor	Draper, John (w. Lidya), gentleman; Argyle, WAS; Donald
			Campbell's Pat., WAS; co-gors 1289b, 1304c, 2227a, 2232a,
			5581a, 5583b; gee 4990 (F:41); co-gees 980, 7026 (F:43).
			(two independent contracts)
2100c.	5/2/96	gor	Draper, John (w. Lydia), gentleman; Argyle, WAS; Argyle, WAS;
			co-gors 1289c, 1304d, 1730, 1731, 2215, 2221a; gee 3701.
			(C-2:155)
2101.	5/2/96	mee	Draper, John; Argyle, WAS. See 411, 748, 3303, 3312, 3893,
			6372, 6512, 7597, 8745. (nine independent contracts)
2102.	5/2/96	mor	Draper, John; ---, WAS; Donald Campbell's Pat., WAS;
			co-mors 1291, 2218, 2276, 5585; mees 1188 (B:66), 2294
			(B:55), 8045 (B:50). (three contracts)
2103.	5/3/96	mee	Draper, John; Argyle, WAS. See 1416.
*2071a.	8/2/98	mee	Doty, Jacob; City of N.Y. See 2522.

2104. 12/12/96 gor Draper, John (w. Lydia); Argyle, WAS; Argyle, WAS; co-gors
                   1294, 1305, 2219, 2222, 5580c, 5587; gee 3306. (C-2:212)
2105. 5/2/99 mee Draper, John, gentleman; Argyle, WAS. See 1417.
2106. 6/15/99 gor Draper, John (w. Lydia); Argyle, WAS; Argyle, WAS; co-gors
                   1295a, 2220, 5589; gee 429.   (F:55)
2107. 5/2/96 gor Draper, Lidia. See 2099.
2107a. 5/2/96 gor Draper, Lydia. See 2100. (two contracts)
2107b. 5/2/96 gor Draper, Lydia. See 2100a (six contracts)
2107c. 5/2/96 gor Draper, Lydia. See 2100b.(two contracts)
2108. 12/12/96 gor Draper, Lydia. See 2104.
2109. 6/15/99 gor Draper, Lydia. See 2106.
2110. 3/20/84 gee Draper, Nathaniel; Granville, CHA. See 2894.
2111. 10/28/84 gee Draper, Nathaniel, farmer; Granville, WAS. See 3357.
2112. 2/24/01 gee Draper, Nathaniel; Granville, WAS. See 735.
2113. 5/2/96 gee Drinkwater, Amos; ---, REN. See 2100.
2114. 10/8/97 gor Drinkwater, Amos (w. Lucy); Hoosick, REN; Argyle, WAS;
                   co-gees 2117, 2119.   (E:342)
2115. 10/8/97 gor Drinkwater, Lucy. See 2114.
2116. 10/28/97 gor Drinkwater, Olive. See 2120.
2117. 10/8/97 gee Drinkwater, Ollive. See 2119.
2118. 10/28/97 gee Drinkwater, Ollive. See 2120. (two contracts)
2119. 10/8/97 gee Drinkwater, Samuel (w. Ollive). See 2117.
2120. 10/28/97 gor Drinkwater, Samuel (w. Olive), farmer; Hoosick, REN;
                   Argyle, WAS; gee 5498. Three contracts this date
                   involving these persons. (C-2:273), (C-2:312), (E-44)
2121. 4/3/92 mee Duane, James, "trustee for the creditors of Peter Du Bois,
                   late of the City of New York ...". See 8574.
2122. 12/3/84 gor Duane, James, Esq., the Hon.; City of N.Y.; "West Cambdon",
                   WAS; gee 169.   (A:458)
2123. 12/23/84 gor Duane, James, Esq. See 8281.
2124. 5/10/91 gor Duane, James, Esq., "trustee of the estate of David Shaw,
                   merchant, late of the City of New York ..."; City of N.Y.;
                   Kingsbury, WAS; gee 3163.   (C-1:106)
2125. 3/30/92 gor Duane, James, Esq., "sole trustee for the creditors of Peter
                   Du Bois, late of the City of New York, deceased"; City of
                   New York; Turner's Pat., WAS; gee 8524.   (B-2:127)
2126. 4/16/92 gee Duane, James, Esq.; City of N.Y. See 4826.
2127. 2/25/96 mee Duane, James, Esq.; Duanesburgh, ALB. See 8829.
2128. 2/26/96 mee Duane, James, Esq.; Duanesburgh, ALB. See 499, 697, 825,
                   2458, 3168, 4911, 5511, 5515, 7256, 7373, 7716, 8200
                   (two contracts), 8221.
2129. 5/25/96 mee Duane, James, Esq.; ---, ALB. See 483.
2130. 9/29/96 mee Duane, James, Esq. See 5568.
2131. 4/15/01 gor Duane, James C.; ---, ---. See 2132.
2132. 4/15/01 gor Duane, Maria; ---, ---; Kingsbury, WAS; co-gors 2131, 5321;
                   gee 6839.   (F:165)
2133. 8/18/92 gor Dubay, Elizabeth. See 2134.
2134. 8/18/92 gor Dubay, John, "late a soldier in the regiment commanded by
                   Moses Hazen" (w. Elizabeth); ---, ---; Canadian and Nova
                   Scotia Refugees' Pat., CLI; gee 166. (A:489)
2135. 9/14/67 gor Dubois, Catharine. See 2136.
2136. 9/14/67 gor Dubois, Peter (w. Catharine), merchant; City of N.Y.;
                   Turner's Pat., ALB; gee 4825.   (B-2:121)
2137. 3/30/92 --- Dubois, Peter. See 2125.
2138. 4/3/92 --- Du Bois, Peter. See 2121.
2139. 7/12/01 gee Duel, Jonathan, farmer; Hebron, WAS. See 3953.
2140. 2/14/69 gee Duer, Henrietta, spinster; Fulham, Middlesex, --. See 2141.
2141. 2/14/69 gor Duer, William, Esq., "late of the City of New York but now
                   of Fulham, County of Middlesex ..."; Schuyler Pat., WAS;
                   gee 2140.   (A:519)
2142. 9/7/74 mor Duer, William, Esq.; ---, CHA; land "east side of Hudsons
                   River above Saragthoga", CHA; mee 8260.   (A:15)
2143. 12/29/91 gor Duer, William, Esq.; City of N.Y.; land "in diverse parts
                   and parcels in the State of New York"; gee 4249. (A:261)
2144. 10/27/89 mee Duffie, James; ---, ---. See 552.
2145. 10/27/89 mee Duffie, John; City of N.Y. See 552.

61

2146. 10/27/89 mee Duffie, Mary; City of N.Y. See 552.
2147. 2/19/87 gor Duncan, George; Cambridge, Dist., ALB; Salem, WAS;
            gee 5173.   (A:144)
2148. 4/3/88 gor Duncan, George; Salem, WAS; Salem, WAS; gee 2489. (A:96)
2149. 4/14/88 gor Duncan, George; Salem, WAS; Salem, WAS; gee 2490. (A:95)
2150. 6/8/02 mee Dunfee, Cornelius; Salem, WAS. See 4655.
2151. 1/13/96 mee Dunham, Charles; Plattsburgh, CLI. See 5011.
2152. 9/27/96 mor Dunham, Charles; Plattsburgh, CLI; Plattsburgh, CLI;
            mee 5861.   (A:194)
2153. 7/15/00 mee Dunham, Charles; Plattsburgh, CLI. See 5985.
2154. 7/15/01 gee Dunham, Charles; Plattsburgh, CLI. See 5986.
2155. 6/2/94 mor Dunham, Jonathan, cordwainer; Cambridge, WAS; Cambridge, WAS;
            mee 8856.   (A:504)
2156. 7/19/88 gee Dunham, Joseph W.; Argyle, WAS. See 3172.
2157. 11/27/90 gor Dunham, Joseph W., farmer; Argyle, WAS; Westfield Dist., WAS;
            gee 4180.   (B-2:77)
2158. 10/17/94 gor Dunham, Joseph W.; Argyle, WAS; Westfield, WAS; gee 8181.
                                                              (B-2:529)
2159. 2/2/87 mor Dunham, Richardson; ---, ---; Salem, WAS; co-mor 1865;
            mee 5030.   (A:45)
2160. 10/29/98 mor Dunham, Silvenus, farmer; Easton, WAS; land "east side of
            the Hudson River", WAS; co-mees 5007, 5008.   (C:45)
2161. 5/29/97 gor Dunlap, Catherine. See 2163.
2162. 6/22/91 gee Dunlap, John, "minister of the gospel"; Cambridge, WAS.
            See 8450.
2163. 5/29/97 gor Dunlap, John (w. Catherine), "minister of the gospel";
            Cambridge, WAS; Cambridge, WAS; gee 2270.   (D:83)
2164. 5/29/97 mee Dunlap, John, the Rev.; Cambridge, WAS. See 2271, 7647.
            (two contracts)
2165. 12/8/89 gee Dunn, George, farmer; ---, ULS. See 3443.
2166. 3/12/91 gee Dunn, George; Argyle, WAS. See 3445.
2167. 8/4/95 gee Dunn, Stephen; Queensbury, WAS. See 5210.
2168. 1/14/98 gee Dunn, Stephen; ---, ---; Kingsbury, WAS; gee 8369. (D:420)
2169. 1/17/98 mee Dunn, Stephen; ---, ---. See 8370.
2170. 5/6/01 mor Dunning, Eli, "late of Castleton in ... Vermont but at present
            of the town of Champlain ..."; Champlain, CLI; mee 808.
                                                              (B:26)
2171. 11/8/99 mee Dunton, Amasa; Cambridge, WAS. See 2369.
2172. 10/27/00 mor Dunton, Josiah, blacksmith; Cambridge, WAS; "Fly Kill", WAS;
            mee 4069.   (C:49)
2173. 2/15/02 mor Dunton, Josiah, yeoman; Cambridge, WAS; Cambridge, WAS;
            mee 4071.   (D:141)
2174. 9/1/95 gee Dunton, Thomas; Cambridge, WAS. See 5411.
2175. 6/19/90 gee Durand, Francis, merchant; City of N.Y. See 4122.
2176. 3/6/95 mee Durand, Francis; ---, SOM, NJ. See 6626.
2177. 10/13/90 gee Durand, Francis Marinus, merchant; Plattsburgh, CLI. See 6261.
2178. 6/11/88 gee Durand, Marinus Francis, merchant; "of New York". See 2531.
2179. 10/14/90 mor Durand, Marinus, Francis, merchant; ---, CLI; Plattsburgh,
            CLI; mee 6263.   (A:53)
2180. 8/26/84 gee Durfee, Lemuel; Cambridge Dist., ALB. See 8713.
2181. 11/16/73 gor Durham, Anne. See 2182.
2182. 11/16/73 gor Durham, John (w. Anne); Elizabethtown, ESS, NJ; ---, CHA;
            gee 1427.   (B:4)
2183. 7/10/99 gee Durham, Joseph; Cambridge, WAS. See 139.
2184. 7/30/93 mor Durham, Mary. See 2185.
2185. 7/30/93 mor Durham, Uzziel (w. Mary), farmer; Cambridge, WAS; Cambridge,
            WAS; mee 8027.   (A:423)
2186. 2/14/00 mor Durkee, Christeen. See 2198.
2187. 2/14/00 mor Durkee, Elisabeth. See 2192.
2188. 2/17/97 mor Durkee, Elizabeth. See 2191.
2189. 2/14/00 mor Durkee, Eva. See 2197.
2190. 10/25/91 --- Durkee, Eve; Argyle, WAS. See 4201.
2191. 2/17/97 gor Durkee, James (w. Elizabeth), yeoman; Argyle, WAS; Argyle,
            WAS; gee 1286.   (E:455)
2192. 2/14/00 mor Durkee, James (w. Elisabeth); Argyle, WAS. See 2198.
2193. 1/6/90 gee Durkee, James, Junior; ---, WAS. See 2243.

2194. 2/14/00 mor Durkee, Lydias (w. Mercy); Argyle, WAS. See 2198.
2195. 2/14/00 mor Durkee, Mercy. See 2194.
2196. 10/25/91 --- Durkee, Nathan. Husband of Eve Durkee, #2190.
2197. 2/14/00 mor Durkee, Nathan (w. Eva); Argyle, WAS; Argyle, WAS; co-mors
           5174, 5175; co-mees 773, 784, 793, 5557.   (D:12)
2198. 2/14/00 mor Durkee, Solomon (w. Christeen); Argyle, WAS; Argyle, WAS;
           co-mors 2187, 2192, 2194, 2195, 6013, 6014; co-mees
           773, 784, 793, 5558.   (D:131)
2199. 3/16/96 mor Dustan, Peter; City of N.Y. See 289.
2200. 6/22/98 gor Dusten, Peter; ---. See 5697, 5698. (two contracts)
2201. 3/16/96 --- Duston, Peter; City of N.Y. See 290.
2202. 10/9/75 mor Dutcher, Moses; Kingsbury, CHA; Kingsbury, CHA; mee 2584.
                                                    (A:26)
2203. 7/1/84 gee Dutcher, Moses; ---, ---. See 6605.
2204. 10/2/86 gee Dwella, Abner, yeoman; Salem, WAS. See 647.
2205. 1/2/91 gor Dwella, Abner, sawyer or lawyer; Salem, WAS. See 1383.
2206. 10/10/86 gee Dwelly, Abner; Salem, WAS. See 8388.
2207. 6/1/92 gee Dwelly, Abner, Esq.; Salem, WAS. See 1229.
2208. 4/2/96 mee Dyer, Charles; Shaftsbury, BEN, VT. See 4845.
2209. 11/24/98 gor Dyer, Esther. See 2210.
2210. 11/24/98 gor Dyer, Ezra (w. Esther), farmer; Argyle, WAS; Argyle, WAS;
           gee 901.   (D:274)
2211. 7/2/89 gee Eager, James; ---, CLI. See 1016.
2212. 1/24/94 gee Eagleston, Andrew, yeoman; Hebron, WAS. See 6133.
2213. 5/2/96 gee Eagleston, Asa; ---, WAS. See 1185.
2214. 5/2/96 gor Eagleston, Asa (w. Joanna), gentleman; Argyle, WAS. See 2100.
2215. 5/2/96 gor Eagleston, Asa (w. Joanna), gentleman; Argyle, WAS. See 2100c.
2216. 5/2/96 mee Eagleston, Asa; Argyle, WAS. See 411, 748, 3303, 3312.
2217. 5/2/96 mee Eagleston, Asa, gentleman, Argyle, WAS. See 6372, 7597.
2218. 5/2/96 mor Eagleston, Asa; ---, WAS. See 2102. (two contracts)
2219. 12/12/96 gor Eagleston, Asa (w. Joanna); Argyle, WAS. See 2104.
2220. 6/15/99 gor Eagleston, Asa (w. Joanna); Argyle, WAS. See 2106.
2221. 5/2/96 gor Eagleston, Joanna. See 2214.
2221a. 5/2/96 gor Eagleston, Joanna. See 2215.
2222. 12/12/96 gor Eagleston, Joanna. See 2219.
2222a. 6/15/99 gor Eagleston, Joanna. See 2220.
2223. 8/24/89 mor Eaglestone, Abraham, tradesman; Willsborough, CLI. See 2225.
2224. 4/23/02 gee Eaglestone, John; Hebron, WAS. See 3434.
2225. 8/24/89 mor Eaglestone, Judah, tradesman; Willsborough, CLI; Willsborough,
           CLI; co-mors 2223, 2226; mee 2807a.   (A:99)
2226. 8/24/89 mor Eaglestone, Richard, tradesman; Willsborough, CLI. See 2225.
2227. 5/2/96 gor Eagleton, Asa (w. Joanna); Argyle, WAS. See 2100a.
           (seven contracts)
2227a. 5/2/96 gor Eagleton, Asa (w. Joanna), gentleman; Argyle, WAS. See 2100b.
           (two contracts)
2228. 5/2/96 mee Eagleton, Asa; Argyle, WAS. See 3893, 6512, 8745.
           (three contracts)
2229. 5/3/96 mee Eagleton, Asa; Argyle, WAS. See 1416.
2230. 5/2/99 mee Eagleton, Asa, gentleman; Argyle, WAS. See 1417.
2231. 5/2/96 mor Eagleton, Isaac, farmer; Argyle, WAS. See 3893.
2232. 5/2/96 gor Eagleton, Joanna. See 2227. (seven contracts)
2232a. 5/2/96 gor Eagleton, Joanna. See 2227a. (two contracts)
2233. 5/28/85 gee Earl, Daniel; ---, ---. See 7055.
2234. 12/30/85 gee Earl, Daniel; ---, ---. See 7055.
2235. 7/20/87 gor Earl, Daniel, Junr.; ---, ---; Skene's Pat., WAS; co-gees
           99, 2239.   (B-2:189)
2236. 8/29/88 gor Earl, Daniel, Junr.; Whitehall, WAS; Kingsbury, WAS;
           gee 7016.   (B-2:20)
2237. 8/18/90 gor Earl, Daniel, Junr.; Whitehall, WAS; Whitehall, WAS;
           gee 3777.   (A:173)
2238. 3/13/93 gor Earl, Daniel, Junr.; Whitehall, WAS; Col. Josiah Throop's
           Grant, CLI; gee 5342.   (A:345)
2239. 7/20/87 gee Earl, Jonas; ---, ---. See 2235.
2240. 7/20/87 gor Earl, Jonas; ---, ---. See 100.
2241. 7/5/88 gor Earl, Jonas; Cambridge, ALB; Westfield, WAS; co-gees 3028,
           4865, 6308, 6310.   (A:148)

63

2242. 5/30/85 gee Earl, Robert; ---, ---. See 7055.
2243. 1/6/90 gor Earl, Willoughby; "Kingdom of Great Britain"; land "near Fort Edward", WAS; gee 2193. (A:296)
2244. 7/15/90 gor Earll, Daniel, Junr.; Whitehall, WAS; Granville, WAS; gee 1798. (A:248)
2245. 9/6/90 gor Earll, Daniel, Junr.; Whitehall, WAS; Granville, WAS; gees 1797 (A:182) and 2968 (A:180). (two contracts)
2246. 10/14/93 gor Earll, Daniel, Junr.; Whitehall, WAS; Earll Pat., CLI; gee 5344. (A:344)
2247. 10/5/89 gee Earll, Jonas; Cambridge, WAS. See 1034.
2248. 8/7/00 gor Earll, Jonas; Granville, WAS; Granville, WAS; gee 40. (E:48)
2249. 1/25/02 mor Earll, Nathaniel; Whitehall, WAS; Whitehall, WAS; mee 8541. (D:151)
2250. 5/20/90 gor Earll, Robert, yeoman; Whitehall, WAS; Whitehall, WAS; gees 5245 (A:161), 8061 (A:161). (two contracts)
2251. 6/16/88 gee Eastman, Joseph; New Milford, FAI, CT. See 3636.
2252. 6/15/98 gor Easton, Elizabeth. See 2253. (two contracts)
2253. 6/15/98 gor Easton, Joshua (w. Elizabeth); Cambridge, WAS; Cambridge, WAS; gees 4284 (D:78) and 4288 (D:77). (two contracts)
2254. 9/22/96 mor Eaten, John, "the third"; Granville, WAS; Granville, WAS; mee 3766. (B:107)
2255. 9/22/96 mor Eaten, Joshua, farmer; Granville, WAS; Granville, WAS; co-mor 2256; mee 3766. (B:123)
2256. 9/22/96 mor Eaten, Joshua, "the second"; Granville, WAS. See 2255.
2257. 5/1/00 mor Eaton, Joshua, farmer; Chester, WAS; Chester, WAS; mee 7772. (D:208)
2258. 5/1/02 mor Eaton, Joshua, farmer; Granville, WAS; Chester, WAS; mee 7775. (D:227)
2259. 2/24/02 mor Eaton, Noah; Champlain, CLI; Champlain, CLI; mee 2854. (B:64)
2260. 7/7/86 gee Eddie, James; ---, ---. See 2618.
2261. 9/23/96 mor Eddy, Abiel, farmer; Granville, WAS; Granville, WAS; mee 3761. (B:108)
2262. 4/27/98 mor Eddy, Amos; Cambridge, WAS; Cambridge, WAS; co-mor 7095; mee 8249. (B:253)
2263. 5/21/93 gor Eddy, Ezekiah; Argyle, WAS; Argyle, WAS; co-gees 4887, 7646. (B-2:43)
2264. 1/7/95 mee Eddy, Henry, farmer; Easton, WAS. See 1919.
2265. 12/1/97 mee Eddy, John; ---, ---. See 4721.
2266. 12/29/96 mor Edgar, David, yeoman; Salem, WAS; Salem, WAS; mee 6677. (B:140)
2267. 9/7/69 gor Edgar, William; ---, ---. See 7955.
2268. 4/20/73 gor Edgar, William; ---, ---. See 7957.
2269. 4/28/91 gee Edie, James; Cambridge, SAR. See 7296.
2270. 5/29/97 gee Edie, James, farmer; Cambridge, WAS. See 2163.
2271. 5/29/97 mor Edie, James (w. Jean), farmer; Cambridge, WAS; Cambridge, WAS; mee 2164. (B:177)
2272. 5/29/97 mor Edie, Jean. See 2271.
2273. 2/9/96 mor Edmiston, Robert; Argyle, WAS; Argyle, WAS; co-mees 4647, 6763, 6822, 8119. Co-mortgagees are all "executors of the late John Morin Scott, Esq., deceased". (B:95)
2274. 6/30/98 gee Eegelton, John, Esq.; Hebron, WAS. See 6184.
2275. 11/10/94 gee Egleston, Asa, mason; Argyle, WAS. See 3011.
2276. 5/2/96 mor Egleston, Asa; ---, WAS. See 2102.
2277. 3/1/93 gee Egleston, Giles; Argyle, WAS. See 4478.
2278. 5/5/94 gee Egleston, Giles; Argyle, WAS. See 8319.
2279. 8/16/98 mor Egleston, Joseph; ---, CLI; Old Military Township #7 (Chateaugay), CLI; co-mor 2280; co-mees 6860, 8092. (B:1)
2280. 8/16/98 mor Egleston, Moses; ---, CLI. See 2279.
2281. 2/6/01 gor Egleston, Rebecka. See 2282.
2282. 2/6/01 gor Egleston, Samuel (w. Rebecka); Argyle, WAS; Easton, WAS; gee 1674. (E:144)
2283. 5/21/91 gee Eights(?), Abraham, sailmaker; Albany, ALB. See 8395.
2284. 5/2/-- gor Eldredg, James (w. Sarah); Willsborough, CLI; Judd Pat, CLI; gee 2289. (A:522)
2285. 7/5/91 gee Eldredg, James, yeoman; Willsborough, CLI. See 44.

2286. 7/6/91   mor Eldredg, James; Willsborough, CLI; <u>Judd Pat., CLI</u>; mee 47.
                                                                           (A:70)
2287. 5/2/--   gor Eldredg, Sarah. See 2284.
2288. 10/17/00 mor Eldredg, Stephen; ---, ---. See 4544.
2289. 5/2/--   gee Eldredg, William; Willsborough, CLI. See 2284.
2290. 1/14/95 gor Eldridge, William C.; Cambridge, WAS; <u>Cambridge, WAS</u>;
                        gee 3748.   (C-2:348)
2291. 1/23/94 gor Eliot, Benjamin (son of John Eliot), yeoman; Kingsbury, WAS;
                        ---, WAS; gee 666.   (C-2:40)
2292. 1/23/94 --- Eliot, John. See 2291.
2293. 3/23/96 gor Ellice, Alexander; "at present at Albany", ALB; <u>Zephaniah</u>
                        <u>Platt's Pat., CLI</u>; gee 2964.   (B:69)
2294. 5/2/96   mee Ellice, Alexander, merchant; London, England. See 2102.
2295. 5/2/96   mee Ellice, Alexander, merchant; "late of the City of London",
                        England. See 2965.
2296. 1/23/97 mee Ellice, Alexander, merchant; London, England. See 3837.
2297. 3/19/99 mee Ellice, Alexander; ---, ---. See 41.
2298. 12/27/98 mee Ellice, Alexander, Esq.; London, England. See 26.
2299. 4/3/01   mee Ellice, Alexander, Esq.; London, England. See 2704, 3513,
                        8223, 8224.
2300. 7/5/93   mor Ellice, Lyman, merchant; Pittstown, REN; <u>---, WAS</u>; co-mor
                        2301; mee 7718.   (A:432)
2301. 7/5/93   mor Ellice, Marvil, merchant; Pittstown, REN. See 2300.
2302. 1/--/96 gee Elliot, Joseph. See 7617.
2303. 1/5/96   gee Elliot, Joseph; Argyle, WAS. See 8007.
2304. 4/6/93   gee Elliott, Benjamin, "well-beloved son" of John Elliott;
                        ---, WAS. See 2305.
2305. 4/6/93   gor Elliott, John, yeoman; Kingsbury, WAS; <u>Kingsbury, WAS</u>;
                        gee 2304.   (B-2:69)
2306. 5/1/00   mor Ellis, Ezekiel, farmer; Chester, WAS; <u>Chester, WAS</u>;
                        mee 7772.   (D:207)
2307. 2/4/94   gee Ellis, Lyman; Pittstown, REN. See 4421.
2308. 2/21/94 mor Ellis, Lyman; Pittstown, REN; <u>John Delancey Pat., CLI</u>;
                        co-mor 2310; mee 4422.   (A:139)
2309. 2/4/94   gee Ellis, Marvel; Pittstown, REN. See 2307.
2310. 2/21/94 gee Ellis, Marvel; Pittstown, REN. See 2308.
2311. 5/13/96 gee Ellis, Marvill; Troy, REN. See 1230.
2312. 4/8/90   mee Ellison, Thomas; City of N.Y. See 7587.
2313. 1/15/01 mee Ellmore, Asa; ---, ---. See 64.
2314. 1/12/98 mee Elmes, Thomas, merchant; City of N.Y. See 5059.
2315. 12/23/01 gee Elmes, Thomas, merchant; City of N.Y. See 5506.
2316. 9/23/00 gor Elmore, Asa; Jay, ESS; <u>Peru, CLI</u>; gee 8438.   (B:343)
2317. 9/24/00 mee Elmore, Asa; Jay, ESS. See 8439.
2318. 8/8/87   gee Elmore, John, farmer; ---, WAS. See 5920.
2319. 10/12/90 mor Elmore, John; Plattsburgh, CLI. See 2322.
2320. 8/8/87   gee Elmore, Lot, farmer; ---, WAS. See 5920.
2321. 8/6/88   gee Elmore, Lot, farmer; Plattsburgh, CLI. See 4881.
2322. 10/12/90 mor Elmore, Lot; Plattsburgh, CLI; <u>Plattsburgh, CLI</u>; co-mor
                        2319; mee 5844.   (A:51)
2323. 6/2/02   mor Elsworth, John; Granville, WAS; <u>Granville, WAS</u>; co-mor
                        1927; mee 1301.   (D:183)
2324. 9/2/01   --- Embury, John, dec'd. See 2833.
2325. 6/1/98   mor Empey, Elisabeth. See 2326.
2326. 6/1/98   mor Empey, Thomas (w. Elisabeth); Cambridge, WAS; <u>Cambridge, WAS</u>;
                        co-mees 1719, 5534.   (C:66)
2327. 6/6/99   gee Empey, Thomas; Cambridge, WAS. See 5657.
2328. 2/21/00 mee Empey, Thomas; Cambridge, WAS. See 6460.
2329. 3/29/00 mee Empey, Thomas; Cambridge, WAS. See 1766.
2330. 6/12/00 mee Empey, Thomas; Cambridge, WAS. See 6339.
2331. 12/1/99 gee Emphey, Elisabeth. See 2333.
2332. 6/20/98 gee Emphey, Thomas; Cambridge, WAS. See 1720.
2333. 12/1/99 mor Emphey, Thomas (w. Elisabeth); Cambridge, WAS; <u>Cambridge,</u>
                        <u>WAS</u>; co-mees 1722, 5536.   (C:67)
2334. 11/25/91 mor Empy, Anthony; Cambridge, WAS; personal loan?; co-mor 2335;
                        mee 4556.   (A:305)
2335. 11/25/91 mor Empy, Thomas; Cambridge, WAS. See 2334.

<table>
<tr><td>2336.</td><td>10/7/95</td><td>mor</td><td>English, Luke, farmer; Easton, WAS; <u>Easton, WAS</u>; mee 7212.
(A:610)</td></tr>
<tr><td>2337.</td><td>3/16/89</td><td>mor</td><td>Enny(?), Thomas; Granville, WAS; <u>Granville, WAS</u>; mee 830.
(A:161)</td></tr>
<tr><td>2338.</td><td>8/25/00</td><td>mor</td><td>Enos, James; Brandon, RUT, VT; <u>Champlain, CLI</u>; mee 843.
(B:9)</td></tr>
<tr><td>2339.</td><td>1/13/01</td><td>mor</td><td>Ensign, Amos; Granville, WAS; <u>Granville, WAS</u>; mee 4141.
(D:29)</td></tr>
<tr><td>2340.</td><td>7/5/91</td><td>gee</td><td>Ensign, Ezekel; Stillwater, SAR. See 8031.</td></tr>
<tr><td>2341.</td><td>9/20/84</td><td>gee</td><td>Estee, Asa; Brookfield, ---, MA. See 4061.</td></tr>
<tr><td>2342.</td><td>1/25/91</td><td>gor</td><td>Estee, Asa; Salem, WAS; <u>Salem, WAS</u>; gee 2343.   (C-1:95)</td></tr>
<tr><td>2343.</td><td>1/25/91</td><td>gee</td><td>Estee, Stephen; Salem, WAS. See 2342.</td></tr>
<tr><td>2344.</td><td>6/28/92</td><td>gor</td><td>Estee, Stephen; Salem, WAS; <u>Salem, WAS</u>; gees 121 (C-1:93)
and 6563 (C-1:94). (two independent contracts)</td></tr>
<tr><td>2345.</td><td>7/1/00</td><td>mor</td><td>Esters, Stephen; ---, ---; <u>---, ESS</u>; mee 5572.   (A:57)</td></tr>
<tr><td>2346.</td><td>7/9/95</td><td>gee</td><td>Everest, Sylvia; Plattsburgh, CLI. See 5736.</td></tr>
<tr><td>2347.</td><td>8/8/87</td><td>gee</td><td>Everitt, Edward; Washington, DUT. See 5919.</td></tr>
<tr><td>2348.</td><td>4/29/95</td><td>gor</td><td>Everson, Jacob (w. Margaret); Clinton, DUT; <u>Argyle, WAS</u>;
co-gees 350, 362, 363.   (B-2:517)</td></tr>
<tr><td>2349.</td><td>4/29/95</td><td>gor</td><td>Everson, Margaret. See 2348.</td></tr>
<tr><td>2349a.</td><td>6/6/89</td><td>mee</td><td>Executors of the estate of John Morin Scott, dec'd.
See 682.</td></tr>
<tr><td>2350.</td><td>11/29/91</td><td>mee</td><td>Executors of the estate of John Morin Scott, Esq., dec'd.
(executors not named). See 6191 and 6192 (two contracts).</td></tr>
<tr><td>2351.</td><td>12/13/96</td><td>gor</td><td>"Executors of the late John Morin Scott, Esq., deceased"
(executors not named); ---, ---; <u>Hebron, WAS</u>; gee 2904.
(D:212)</td></tr>
<tr><td>2352.</td><td>2/13/98</td><td>mor</td><td>Fabun, James; ---, WAS; <u>Westfield, WAS</u>; mee 7236. (B:260)</td></tr>
<tr><td>2353.</td><td>3/13/91</td><td>gee</td><td>Fairchild, Aaron; ---, ULS. See 4360.</td></tr>
<tr><td>2354.</td><td>8/3/75</td><td>gee</td><td>Fairchild, Benjamin; ---, CHA. See 3733.</td></tr>
<tr><td>2355.</td><td>4/13/92</td><td>gor</td><td>Fairchild, Benjamin (w. Milison), farmer; ---, WAS;
"Mountford Patent", WAS; gee 1696.   (C-1:87)</td></tr>
<tr><td>2356.</td><td>5/17/96</td><td>mor</td><td>Fairchild, Jesse, Esq.; Arlington, BEN, VT; <u>Cambridge, WAS</u>;
mee 3305.   (B:46)</td></tr>
<tr><td>2357.</td><td>5/13/00</td><td>mor</td><td>Fairchild, Lucy. See 2360.</td></tr>
<tr><td>2358.</td><td>4/13/92</td><td>gor</td><td>Fairchild, Milison. See 2355.</td></tr>
<tr><td>2359.</td><td>5/25/01</td><td>mor</td><td>Fairchild, Peter; Whitehall, WAS; <u>Whitehall, WAS</u>; mee 8390.
(D:59b)</td></tr>
<tr><td>2360.</td><td>5/13/00</td><td>mor</td><td>Fairchild, Senton (w. Lucy), farmer; Granville, WAS;
<u>Granville, WAS</u>; mee 1541.   (C:92)</td></tr>
<tr><td>2361.</td><td>5/29/00</td><td>mor</td><td>Fairman, Frederick; Chateaugay, CLI; <u>Chateaugay, CLI</u>;
mee 5943.   (A:440)</td></tr>
<tr><td>2362.</td><td>5/2/96</td><td>gee</td><td>Falkner, John, blacksmith; Salem, WAS. See 4332.</td></tr>
<tr><td>2363.</td><td>7/27/97</td><td>gor</td><td>Falshaw, John (w. Mary), farmer; Granville, WAS; <u>Granville,</u>
WAS; gee 8476.   (D:219)</td></tr>
<tr><td>2364.</td><td>7/27/97</td><td>gor</td><td>Falshaw, Mary. See 2363.</td></tr>
<tr><td>2365.</td><td>11/17/85</td><td>gee</td><td>Fansworth, Ebenezer; ---, ---. See 7055.</td></tr>
<tr><td>2366.</td><td>4/15/91</td><td>gor</td><td>Fansworth, Ebenezer, yeoman; Kingsbury, WAS; <u>Artillery Pat.</u>,
WAS; gee 2368.   (A:515)</td></tr>
<tr><td>2367.</td><td>7/1/91</td><td>gor</td><td>Fansworth, Ebenezer, yeoman; Kingsbury, WAS; <u>Westfield, WAS</u>;
gee 2761.   (A:516)</td></tr>
<tr><td>2368.</td><td>4/15/91</td><td>gee</td><td>Fansworth, Josiah, yeoman; Westfield, WAS. See 2366.</td></tr>
<tr><td>2369.</td><td>11/8/99</td><td>mor</td><td>Farley, John; Cambridge, WAS; <u>Cambridge, WAS</u>; mee 2171.
(C:94)</td></tr>
<tr><td>2370.</td><td>6/11/94</td><td>gor</td><td>Farnsworth, Joseph; Kingsbury, WAS; <u>Artillery, Pat.</u>,
Westfield, WAS; gee 2762.   (B-2:484)</td></tr>
<tr><td>2371.</td><td>9/27/91</td><td>mee</td><td>Farnsworth, Joseph Dean; Plattsburgh, CLI. See 5928.</td></tr>
<tr><td>2372.</td><td>12/22/77</td><td>mee</td><td>Farquhar, James, merchant; City of N,Y. See 6095.</td></tr>
<tr><td>2373.</td><td>5/11/87</td><td>mee</td><td>Farquhar, James; ---, ---. See 3388.</td></tr>
<tr><td>2374.</td><td>4/22/88</td><td>gor</td><td>Farquhar, James, merchant; City of N.Y.; <u>Granville, WAS</u>;
gee 3037.   (A:150)</td></tr>
<tr><td>2375.</td><td>4/22/88</td><td>mee</td><td>Farquhar, James; ---, ---. See 3038.</td></tr>
<tr><td>2376.</td><td>7/1/88</td><td>---</td><td>Farquhar, James. See 2382.</td></tr>
<tr><td>2377.</td><td>7/6/88</td><td>gor</td><td>Farquhar, James; City of N.Y.; <u>Cockport Pat., WAS</u>; gee 4112.
(A:375)</td></tr>
</table>

2378. 7/6/88 gor Farquhar, James, merchant; City of N.Y.; Granville, WAS;
gees 444 (A:332), 448 (A:330), 1012 (A:364), 1462 (A:335),
2972 (A:357), 3408 (A:327), 4062 (A:346), 7591 (A:406),
8468 (A:337). (nine independent contracts)
2379. 7/6/88 mee Farquhar, James; ---, ---. See 449, 453, 729, 1463, 1672,
2773, 2971, 4063, 4113, 5319, 7592, 8361, 8465, 8469.
2380. 7/6/88 mee Farquhar, James; City of N.Y. See 1013, 2039, 3409, 3755,
3791, 6933, 7863.
2380a. 12/2/88 mee Farquhar, James, merchant; City of N.Y. See 2097.
2380b. 7/13/92 mee Farquhar, James, merchant; City of N.Y. See 3402.
2381. 7/6/88 mee Farquhar, James, Esq., merchant; City of N.Y. See 442,
3073, 8464.
2382. 7/1/88 gor Farquhar, William, merchant, "by his attorney James Farquhar
of the City of New York by his substitute Alexander
Webster of Hebron ..., Esq."; ---, ---; Granville, WAS;
gee 7864. (D:398)
2383. 9/18/97 mor Farr, Lent; Westfield, WAS; Westfield, WAS; mee 3170.
(B:225)
2384. 12/5/99 mor Farr, Reuben; Westfield, WAS. See 8702.
2385. 12/3/94 mor Fasket, John (w. Zilpha), farmer; Hampton, WAS; Hampton, WAS;
mee 5967. (A:525)
2386. 12/3/94 mor Fasket, Zilpha. See 2385.
2387. 10/10/92 gor Faulkner, Anna. See 2391.
2388. 11/1/92 gor Faulkner, Catharine. See 2392.
2389. 3/3/94 gor Faulkner, Catharine. See 2395.
2390. 1/19/99 gor Faulkner, Catherine. See 2399.
2391. 10/10/92 gor Faulkner, John (w. Anna); Cambridge, WAS; Cambridge, WAS;
gee 6617. (B-2:51)
2392. 11/1/92 gor Faulkner, John (w. Catharine); Cambridge, WAS; Cambridge,
WAS; gee 5575. (B-2:366)
2393. 4/6/93 gor Faulkner, John, yeoman; Cambridge, WAS; Cambridge, WAS;
co-gees 5404, 5408. (B-2:53)
2394. 6/22/93 mor Faulkner, John, yeoman; Cambridge, WAS; Cambridge, WAS;
mee 2677. (A:417)
2395. 3/3/94 gor Faulkner, John (w. Catharine); Cambridge, WAS; Cambridge,
WAS; gee 5576. (B-2:369)
2396. 7/15/93 mor Faulkner, John, Junr., blacksmith; Cambridge, WAS;
Cambridge, WAS; mee 8580. (A:450)
2397. 5/1/98 mor Faulkner, John, Junr.; Salem, WAS; Salem, WAS; mee 7696.
(C:84)
2398. 8/20/98 mor Faulkner, John, Junr.; Salem, WAS; Salem, WAS; mee 5033.
(C:88)
2399. 1/19/99 gor Faulkner, John, Junr. (w. Catherine); Salem, WAS;
Salem, WAS; gee 4210. (D:423)
2400. 4/6/93 mee Faulkner, John, Senr.; Cambridge, WAS. See 5409.
2401. 2/28/00 mor Felch, Eunice. See 2402.
2402. 2/28/00 mor Felch, John, Junr. (w. Eunice); Granville, WAS; Granville,
WAS; mee 1607. (C:91)
2403. 4/26/96 mor Felshaw, John (w. Mary), gentleman; "late of Kilingly",
WIN, CT; Granville, WAS; mee 8473. (B:88)
2404. 4/26/96 mor Felshaw, Mary. See 2403.
2405. 3/2/02 mor Felt, Aaron; ---, ---; Elizabethtown, ESS; mee 3861. (A:80)
2406. 3/6/02 gee Felt, Aaron, farmer; Elizabethtown, ESS. See 3862.
2407. 3/6/02 mor Felt, Aaron; ---, ---; Elizabethtown, ESS; mee 3231. (A:82)
2408. 6/1/02 gor Felt, Aaron, mine owner; Elizabethtown, ESS; Elizabethtown,
ESS; co-gees 3232, 6566. (A:58)
2409. 12/24/94 mor Ferguson, John; Cambridge, WAS; Argyle, WAS; mee 7608.
(A:543)
2410. 6/1/96 mor Ferguson, John, yeoman; "now of Cambridge", WAS;
Argyle, WAS; mee 4587. (B:58)
2411. 7/27/96 mee Ferguson, John, yeoman; Cambridge, WAS. See 5412.
2412. 12/15/96 gor Ferguson, John; Cambridge, WAS; Argyle, WAS; gee 2484.
(D:141)
2413. 12/15/96 mee Ferguson, John; Cambridge, WAS. See 2485.
2414. 11/24/97 mee Ferguson, Samuel, farmer; Cambridge, WAS. See 5413.
2415. 2/11/96 gor Ferrand, William, yeoman; Dunham, Montreal Dist., Lower
Canada; Champlain, CLI; gee 5132. (B:24)

67

2416. 8/9/92 gee Ferren, John, yeoman; Whitehall, WAS. See 1142.
2417. 5/20/89 gor Ferriol, Alexander, "late in the Army of the United
States ... and a refugee from Canada"; ---, ---;
Champlain, CLI; gee 6522.   (B:264)
2418. 5/30/89 gor Ferriol, Alexander, "late in the Army of the Unites
states ... and a refugee from Canada"; ---, ---;
Champlain, CLI; gee 6523.   (B:262)
2419. 1/9/96 gor Ferriole, Joseph, farmer; Crown Point, CLI; Canadian and
Nova Scotia Refugees' Pat., CLI; co-gees 3836, 4004.
                                                 (A:410)
2420. 7/7/91 gor Ferris, Isaac (w. Sarah), carpenter; Plattsburgh, CLI;
Plattsburgh, CLI; gee 6631.   (A:247)
2421. 7/29/86 gee Ferris, Jacob, carpenter; Plattsburgh, WAS. See 5895.
2422. 3/30/87 gor Ferris, Jacob (w. Sarah); ---, ---; ---, CLI; gee 5149.
                                                 (B:34)
2423. 11/25/87 gor Ferris, Jacob; Plattsburgh, WAS ---, CLI; gee 5150.
                                                 (B:29)
2424. 9/26/92 gor Ferris, Jacob; Plattsburgh, CLI; land "south side of the
River Saranac", CLI; gee 6624.   (A:270)
2425. 10/16/92 gee Ferris, Jacob; Plattsburgh, CLI. See 5803.
2426. 10/16/92 gor Ferris, Jacob (w. Sarah); Plattsburgh, CLI; Plattsburgh,
CLI; gee 5816.   (A:277)
2427. 3/21/94 mor Ferris, Jacob, carpenter; Plattsburgh, CLI; Plattsburgh,
CLI; mee 5110.   (A:117)
2428. 9/17/94 gor Ferris, Jacob (w. Sarah), carpenter; Plattsburgh, CLI;
Plattsburgh, CLI; gee 7830.   (A:499)
2429. 6/18/89 gor Ferris, Jacob, Esq.; Plattsburgh, CLI; Plattsburgh, CLI;
gee 6630.   (A:82)
2430. 3/12/98 mor Ferris, James; Queensbury, WAS; Queensbury, WAS; mee 5634.
                                                 (C:84)
2431. 9/27/86 mor Ferris, Lewis, carpenter; Plattsburgh, WAS; Plattsburgh,
WAS; mee 5898.   (Clinton Co. A:2)
2432. 6/16/00 mor Ferris, Morris, farmer; Queensbury, WAS; Queensbury, WAS;
mee 8801.   (C:187)
2433. 9/11/98 gor Ferris, Noah; Elizabethtown, CLI; Elizabethtown, CLI;
gee 16.   (B:184)
2434. 11/1/93 gee Ferris, Reed, farmer; Pawling, DUT. See 2439.
2435. 3/30/87 gor Ferris, Sarah. See 2422.
2436. 7/7/91 gor Ferris, Sarah. See 2420.
2437. 10/16/92 gor Ferris, Sarah. See 2426.
2438. 9/17/94 gor Ferris, Sarah. See 2428.
2439. 11/1/93 gor Ferris, Warren, miller; Queensbury, WAS; Queensbury, WAS;
gee 2434.   (B-2:375)
2440. 8/29/97 gor Ferriss, Kezia. See 2449.
2441. 11/1/93 gee Ferriss, Moriss; Pawling, DUT. See 2447.
2442. 5/26/98 gee Ferriss, Nathan; Peru, CLI. See 3060.
2443. 5/28/98 mor Ferriss, Nathan; Peru, CLI; Peru, CLI; mee 3061. (A:299)
2444. 11/1/93 gor Ferriss, Salle. See 2447.
2445. 9/24/96 gor Ferriss, Salle. See 2448.
2446. 10/2/92 gor Ferriss, Warren, farmer; Queensbury, WAS; Queensbury, WAS;
gee 5630.   (F:101)
2447. 11/1/93 gor Ferriss, Warren (w. Salle), miller; Queensbury, WAS;
Queensbury, WAS; gee 2441.   (D:413)
2448. 9/24/96 gor Ferriss, Warren, Esq. (w. Salle); Queensbury, WAS;
---, WAS; gee 2030.   (C-2:216)
2449. 8/29/97 gor Ferriss, Warren, Esq. (w. Kezia); Queensbury, WAS;
Queensbury, WAS; gee 5633.   (F:99)
2450. 5/9/96 mee Field, Joseph C.; Southeast, DUT. See 1107.
2451. 3/19/95 mee Filford, George, Junr.; Hebron, WAS. See 6537.
2452. 12/11/95 gor Fillmore, Abigail. See 2454.
2453. 12/18/98 mor Fillmore, Earl; Franklin, NEW, CT; Champlain; CLI;
mee 5084.   (A:401)
2454. 12/11/95 gor Fillmore, Eliphalet (w. Abigail); Granville, WAS;
Granville, WAS; gee 845.   (B-2:505)
2455. 12/3/88 mor Finch, Isaac; Washington Precinct; DUT; Zephaniah Platt's
Pat., CLI; mee 5781.   (A:20)

2456. 5/1/00 mor Finch, James; ---, ---; ---, WSS; mee 5571. (A:60)
2457. 7/19/91 mor Finch, John; Washington, DUT; ---, CLI; mee 5726. (A:67)
2458. 2/26/96 mor Finch, Joshua, farmer; Salem, WAS; Salem, WAS; mee 2128. (C:90)
2459. 7/4/99 mee Finlasson, Matthew; Lansingburgh, REN. See 1454.
2460. 9/21/01 mor Finn, William; Argyle, WAS; Argyle, WAS; mee 5361. (D:112)
2461. 3/3/98 mor Finney, Heman; Pleasant Valley, CLI; Pleasant Valley, CLI; mee 5870. (Pleasant Valley in Crown Point) (A:273)
2462. 3/3/98 mor Finney, Joel; Pleasant Valley (Crown Point), CLI; Pleasant Valley, CLI; mee 5941. (A:275)
2463. 6/8/02 mor Finney, Rufus, farmer; New Haven, ---, VT; Old Military Township #7 (Chateaugay), CLI; mee 329. (B:80)
2464. 1/5/02 mor Finton, Erastus, farmer; Cambridge, WAS. See 3523.
2465. 7/28/89 mor Fish, Abner; Willsborough, CLI; Willsborough, CLI; mee 3492. (A:39)
2466. 2/11/92 mor Fish, Abner, yeoman; Willsborough, CLI; Judd Pat., CLI; co-mor 2468; mee 49. (A:92)
2467. 5/1/02 mor Fish, Benjamin farmer; Chester, WAS; Chester, WAS; mee 7775. (D:204)
2468. 2/11/92 mor Fish, Ebenezer, yeoman; Willsborough, CLI. See 2466.
2469. 5/28/01 gor Fish, John; Saratoga, SAR; Easton, WAS; gee 6564. (E:328)
2470. 7/4/01 mee Fish, John, yeoman; Saratoga, SAR. See 6568.
2471. 11/16/01 mee Fish, John; ---, ---. See 1939.
2472. 2/6/02 gor Fish, John; Saratoga, SAR; Easton, WAS; gee 6565. (F:199)
2473. 1/12/73 gor Fisher, Donald, tailor; City of N.Y.; land "east side of Hudson's River, CHA; gee 4395. (E:244)
2474. 7/4/00 mor Fisher, Elizabeth. See 2478.
2475. 6/20/01 gor Fisher, Elizabeth. See 2479.
2476. 11/3/99 mee Fisher, Henry; Albany, ALB. See 3016.
2477. 6/27/96 mor Fisher, John (w. Ruth); Cambridge, WAS; "Williams Patent", WAS; gee 4557. (D:103)
2478. 7/4/00 mor Fisher, John W. (w. Elizabeth); Cambridge, WAS. See 1338.
2479. 6/20/01 gor Fisher, John W. (w. Elizabeth); Cambridge, WAS. See 4843.
2480. 6/27/96 gor Fisher, Ruth. See 2477.
2481. 9/8/95 mor Fitch, Abigail. See 2483.
2482. 9/5/95 gee Fitch, Asa; Salem, WAS. See 4886.
2483. 9/8/95 mor Fitch, Asa (w. Abigail), physician; Salem WAS; Salem, WAS; mee 4867. (A:602)
2484. 12/15/96 gee Fitch, Asa; Salem, WAS. See 2412.
2485. 12/15/96 mor Fitch, Asa; Salem, WAS; Argyle, WAS; mee 2413. (B:143)
2486. 1/21/97 mee Fitch, Asa; Salem, WAS. See 4905.
2487. 6/1/99 gee Fitch, Asa, physician; Salem, WAS. See 2510.
2488. 10/27/00 mee Fitch, Asa, Esq.; Salem, WAS. See 2530.
2489. 4/3/88 gee Fitch, Benjamin; Salem, WAS. See 2148.
2490. 4/14/88 gee Fitch, Benjamin; Salem, WAS. See 2149.
2491. 5/2/97 mee Fitch, Chauncey, Esq.; Plattsburgh, CLI. See 358.
2492. 7/4/99 gor Fitch, Chauncey, Esq., sheriff of Clinton County; ---, ---; Zephaniah Platt's Pat., CLI; gee 5177. (B:197)
2493. 4/8/00 gor Fitch, Chauncey, Esq., sheriff of Clinton County; ---, ---; Plattsburgh, CLI; gee 6673. (B:360)
2494. 5/17/01 gor Fitch, Chauncey, Esq., "late sheriff of the County of Clinton; ---, ---; Old Military Township #3 (Black Brook), CLI; gee 1945. (B:281)
2495. --/--/85 gee Fitch, Elisha; White Creek, WAS. See 3818.
2496. 2/25/92 gee Fitch, Elisha; Duanesburgh, ALB. See 1300.
2497. 8/19/96 mor Fitch, Elisha (w. Elizabeth); Salem, WAS; Salem, WAS. mee 8592. (B:83)
2498. 8/19/96 mor Fitch, Elizabeth. See 2497.
2499. 11/18/99 gor Fitch, Elizabeth. See 2502.
2500. 9/6/97 mee Fitch, Joseph; Kingsbury, WAS. See 5057.
2501. 4/30/98 mor Fitch, Joseph; Kingsbury, WAS; Kingsbury, WAS; mee 892. (C:87)
2502. 11/18/99 gor Fitch, Joseph (w. Elizabeth); Kingsbury, WAS; Kingsbury, WAS; gee 8808. (D:421)
2503. 4/8/93 gee Fitch, Nathaniel; Willsborough, CLI. See 3224.
2504. 1/4/98 gor Fitch, Nathaniel; Willsborough, CLI; Willsborough, CLI; gee 3226. (A:38)

69

2505. 6/20/01 mor Fitch, Nathaniel; ---, ---; ---, ESS; mee 759. (A:64)
2506. 12/6/91 gor Fitch, Pelatiah; Salem, WAS; Salem, WAS; gee 7841. (A:412)
2507. 9/30/90 gee Fitch, Pelatiah, Esq.; Salem, WAS. See 4335.
2508. 1/21/97 mor Fitch, William; Salem, WAS. See 4905.
2509. 12/8/98 mor Fitch, William, yeoman; Argyle, WAS; Salem, WAS; mee 4348.
                                                              (C:89)
2510. 6/1/99 gor Fitch, William, yeoman; Argyle, WAS; Salem, WAS; gee 2487.
                                                              (D:139)
2511. 9/26/00 mee Fitz Simmons, Felix; Saratoga, SAR. See 7779.
2512. 5/22/90 mor Flaack, James; Hebron, WAS; Hebron, WAS; mee 7275. (A:250)
2513. 6/22/92 gee Flaak, James, trustee of the First Presbyterian Congregation;
                 Hebron, WAS. See 4207.
2514. 6/15/92 gee Flaak, James, Junr., yeoman; Hebron, WAS. See 6756.
2515. 6/26/94 gor Flack, James, Junr., farmer; Hebron, WAS; Hebron, WAS;
                 gee 6544.   (B-2:199)
2516. 2/9/99 mee Flack, James, "Second"; Hebron, WAS. See 3705.
2517. 6/15/89 gee Fleck, James; Hebron, WAS. See 6751.
2518. 5/3/90 gee Fleck, James; Hebron, WAS. See 8275.
2519. 3/2/01 gee Fletcher, Solomon, farmer; Argyle, WAS. See 4685.
2520. 3/15/84 gee Flint, Asa; Cambridge, ALB. See 7352.
2521. 12/1/85 gor Flint, Asa, yeoman; Kingsbury, WAS; Kingsbury, WAS;
                 gee 3635.   (A:37)
2522. 8/2/98 mor Folger, Elisha (w. Hephzibah); Queensbury, WAS; Westfield,
                 WAS; co-mors 1543, 1546; co-mees 2071a, 2586a, 3277a, 3280a.
2523. 11/5/98 mee Folger, Elisha; Queensbury, WAS. See 6649 and 7900. /// (C:86)
2524. 5/21/01 mee Folger, Elisha, merchant; Queensbury, WAS. See 5664.
2525. 8/2/98 mor Folger, Hephzibah. See 2522.
2526. 9/6/94 gor Folsom, Elizabeth; ---, ---. See 2529.
2527. 3/24/91 gee Folsom, John, merchant; Argyle, WAS. See 4767.
2528. 5/21/91 gee Folsom, John; Argyle, WAS. See 8395.
2529. 9/6/94 gor Folsom, John, merchant; Argyle, WAS; Argyle, WAS; co-gor
                 2526; gee 7839.   (B-2:403)
2530. 10/27/00 mor Folsom, John, Esq.; Argyle, WAS; Argyle, WAS; mee 2488.
                                                              (C:93)
2531. 6/11/88 gor Fontfreyde, John, merchant; Cumberland Head (Plattsburgh),
                 CLI; Plattsburgh, CLI; gee 2178.   (A:226)
2532. 4/9/94 mee Fontfreyde, John; Plattsburgh, CLI. See 8773.
2533. 7/20/87 gee Foot, William; ---, ---. See 100.
2534. 9/1/98 gee Foquit, John Lewis; Plattsburgh, CLI. See 5829.
2535. 2/3/95 gee Forbes, Asa; Willsborough, CLI. See 1897.
2536. 3/17/97 gee Forbes, Asa; Willsborough, CLI. See 6490.
2537. 9/20/00 mor Forbes, Asa; ---, ---; Willsborough, ESS; mee 5881. (A:41)
2538. 12/19/00 gor Forbes, Asa; Willsborough, ESS; Willsborough, ESS; gee 3393.
                                                              (A:25)
2539. 2/23/01 mor Forbes, Asa; ---, ---; Willsborough, ESS; mee 6495. (A:49)
2540. 10/7/00 gor Forbes, Elisha (w. Lucy), forge master; Sandy Hill, WAS;
                 Kingsbury, WAS; gee 8375.   (E:41)
2541. 10/7/00 gor Forbes, Lucy. See 2540.
2542. 2/15/01 mor Force, Joseph; Queensbury, WAS; Queensbury, WAS; mee 5445.
                                                              (D:136)
2543. 3/10/91 gee Force, Timothy; Whitehall, WAS. See 7499.
2544. 11/21/95 gor Ford, Adria. See 2545.
2545. 11/21/95 gor Ford, Thomas (w. Adria); Cambridge, WAS; Cambridge, WAS;
                 gee 1366.   (B-2:509)
2546. 9/27/94 gee Forster, Jonathan, farmer; Argyle, WAS. See 8019.
2547. 6/15/95 gee Forster, Jonathan, farmer; Argyle, WAS. See 7129.
2548. 9/2/95 gor Forster, Jonathan (w. Sarah), farmer; Argyle, WAS;
                 Saratoga Pat., WAS; gee 6394.   (C-2:132)
2549. 10/27/98 gor Forster, Jonathan (w. Sarah), farmer; Argyle, WAS;
                 Saratoga Pat., WAS; gee 7454.   (D:58)
2550. 12/5/86 gor Forster, Patience. See 2553.
2551. 9/2/95 gor Forster, Sarah. See 2548.
2552. 10/27/98 gor Forster, Sarah. See 2549.
2553. 12/5/86 gor Forster, William (w. Patience), yeoman; Saratoga, ALB;
                 Saratoga Pat., WAS; gee 7453.   (D:61)
2554. 7/15/02 mor Fort, Abraham I.; Cambridge, WAS; Hoosick Pat., WAS
                 mee 7231.   (E:20)

2555. 2/5/98 gee Fort, John I.; ---, ---, NY. See 7152.
2556. 2/5/98 mee Fort, John I.; ---, REN. See 7153.
2557. 11/4/00 gor Fort, John I.; ---, ---; Saratoga Pat., WAS; co-gor 8013;
gee 1994.   (E:59)
2558. 2/8/98 mor Fosdick, William, shoemaker; Hartford, WAS; Hartford, WAS;
mee 1483.   (B:257)
2559. 4/28/00 gee Foster, Allen; Argyle, WAS. See 2564.
2560. 4/30/88 gee Foster, James; Hebron, WAS. See 4627.
2561. 9/7/92 gee Foster, Jonathan, farmer; Argyle, WAS. See 8030.
2562. 9/28/92 mor Foster, Jonathan (w. Sarah); Argyle, WAS; Saratoga Pat.,
WAS; mee 8029.   (A:383)
2563. 9/27/94 gor Foster, Jonathan (w. Sarah), farmer; Argyle, WAS; Saratoga
Pat., WAS; gee 8018.   (B-2:315)
2564. 4/28/00 gor Foster, Jonathan (w. Sarah); Argyle, WAS; Argyle, WAS;
gee 2559.   (F:13)
2565. 7/10/90 gee Foster, Richard; Hebron, WAS. See 1071.
2566. 7/10/90 gee Foster, Richard; Hebron, WAS; Hebron, WAS; mee 1072. (A:238)
2567. 8/13/92 mor Foster, Richard, yeoman; Hebron, WAS; Hebron, WAS; mee 1075.
(A:376)
2568. 6/29/00 gor Foster, Richard; Hebron, WAS; ---, WAS; gee 2570. (E:147)
2569. 6/30/00 mor Foster, Richard, yeoman; Hebron, WAS; Hebron, WAS;
mee 8734.   (C:93)
2570. 6/29/00 gee Foster, Samuel. See 2568.
2571. 6/30/00 mor Foster, Samuel, yeoman; Hebron, WAS; Hebron, WAS; mee 8734.
(C:92)
2572. 9/28/92 mor Foster, Sarah. See 2562.
2573. 9/27/94 gor Foster, Sarah. See 2563.
2574. 4/28/00 gor Foster, Sarah. See 2564.
2575. 5/6/94 mor Fowler, Abner; Corinth, ORA, VT; Willsborough, CLI;
mee 3225.   (A:179)
2576. 3/10/97 gor Fowler, Abner; Willsborough, CLI; Willsborough, CLI;
gee 2577.   (A:51)
2577. 3/10/97 gee Fowler, John; Willsborough, CLI. See 2576.
2578. 7/2/99 mor Fowler, John; ---, ---; Willsborough, ESS; mee 6494. (A:42)
2579. 11/12/99 mor Fowler, Joseph; ---, ---; Jay, ESS; mee 3229.   (A:4)
2580. 5/1/02 mor Fox, Jehiel, farmer; Chester, WAS; Chester, WAS; mee 7775.
Two contracts this date involving these persons. (D:205)
2581. 3/12/98 mor Fox, Thomas; Champlain, CLI; Champlain, CLI; mee 5116.
(A:292)
2582. 9/24/71 gor Franklin, Henry (w. Mary), merchant; City of N.Y.;
Kingsbury, ALB; gee 3615.   (A:11)
2583. 4/15/75 gee Franklin, Henry; City of N.Y. See 349.
2584. 10/9/75 mee Franklin, Henry, merchant; City of N.Y. See 2202.
2585. 7/1/84 --- Franklin, Henry, dec'd., "late of the City of New York".
See 6605.
*2586a 2586. 6/12/86 --- Franklin, John; ---, ---. See 2587.
2587. 6/12/86 --- *Franklin, Maria, an "infant"; ---, --- (estate papers filed
in Deed Book A:204). Walter Franklin "late of the City
of New York, merchant, deceased", in his will, appoints as
Maria's guardians John and Samuel Franklin and Daniel Bowne.
This date, on request of these men, the court appoints
as their and Maria's attorney "their loving friend Isaac
Corsa, gentleman," of the City of New York. (Reference is
made to Walter's lands in the Provincial Patent, WAS.)
2588. 9/24/71 gor Franklin, Mary. See 2582.
2589. 6/12/86 --- Franklin, Samuel; ---. ---. See 2587.
2590. 11/23/01 gor Franklin, Samuel, merchant; City of N.Y.; Small's Pat, ESS;
gee 7192.   (A:67)
2591. 8/6/93 mee Franklin, Thomas, gentleman; Philadelphia, PA. See 6608.
2592. 6/12/86 --- Franklin, Walter, dec'd. See 2587.
2593. 3/20/87 gee Fraser, Alexander, "timber merchant of Chambly in the
Province of Caneday now residing in the County of
Addison", VT. See 6489.
2594. 5/10/93 mor Fraser, Alexander, gentleman; Willsborough, CLI;
Willsborough, CLI; mee 5731.   (A:129)
2595. 7/3/99 gee Fraser, Sarah; Willsborough, ESS. See 6508.
*2586a. 8/2/98 mee Franklin, John, Junr.; City of N.Y. See 2522.

2596. 7/18/99 gee Fraser, Sarah; Willsborough, ESS. See 5757.
2597. 1/15/65 gee Frasier, William, ship carpenter; City of N.Y. See 6219.
2598. 11/10/89 mee Frasier, William; City of N.Y. See 4766.
2599. 12/9/89 gee Frazier, Alexander, gentleman; ---, CLI. See 5106.
2600. 11/7/89 gor Frazier, Ruth. See 2601.
2601. 11/7/89 gor Frazier, William (w. Ruth), carpenter; City of N.Y.;
                          Argyle, WAS; gee 4765.   (C-2:25)
2602. 5/16/97 gor Freeman, Andrew; Salem, WAS; Cambridge, WAS; gee 6619.
                                                                   (C-2:323)
2603. 7/22/97 mor Freeman, Andrew, gentleman; Salem, WAS; Salem, WAS;
                          mee 750.   (B:210)
2604. 8/30/94 mor Freeman, Chester; Argyle, WAS; Schuyler's Pat. and Argyle,
                          WAS; mee 6012.   (A:500)
2605. 10/28/96 gee Freeman, Elijah; Easton, WAS. See 3353.
2606. 7/5/99 gee Freeman, Elijah; Easton, WAS. See 3355.
2607. 11/2/99 mee Freeman, Melancthon; Piscatequa, MID, NJ. See 4663.
2608. 6/8/93 gor Freeman, Stephen, farmer; ---, WAS; Saratoga Pat., WAS;
                          gee 660.   (E:295)
2609. 1/25/99 gee Freeman, Stephen; Easton, WAS. See 3004.
2609a. 12/20/99 gor Freeman, Stephen; Easton, WAS. See 8776.
2610. 3/14/87 gee Frelich, George; ---, ---. See 5911.
2611. 7/7/86 gee French, David; ---, ---. See 2618.
2612. 12/5/89 gor French, David; ---, WAS. Husband of Susannah French in 2626.
2613. 3/20/92 gor French, David, yeoman; Cambridge, WAS; Cambridge, WAS;
                          gee 3272.   (E:394)
2614. 9/14/99 gee French, David; Cambridge, WAS. See 6371.
2615. 5/5/01 mee French, David; Cambridge, WAS. See 1159.
2616. 12/5/89 gor French, Jane; Cambridge Dist., WAS. See 747.
2617. 3/5/99 gor French, Jane. See 2622.
2618. 7/7/86 gor French, Jonathan, gentleman; Cambridge Dist., WAS;
                          Cambridge Dist., WAS; co-gees 740, 2260, 2611, 4361,
                          5029, 7311, 7903 (Co-grantees are trustees of the
                          Associate Congregation of Cambridge).   (B-2:424)
2619. 12/5/89 gor French, Jonathan. Husband of Jane French in 2616.
2620. 11/7/95 mee French, Jonathan; Cambridge Dist., WAS. See 4305.
2621. 3/5/99 gee French, Jonathan; Cambridge, WAS. See 6174 and 6176.
2622. 3/5/99 gor French, Jonathan (w. Jane); Cambridge, WAS; Cambridge, WAS;
                          gee 6175.   (E:387)
2623. 1/18/90 --- French, Peter P.; Hampton, WAS. This person requested
                          registration of the mortgage executed by Caleb Warren
                          as reflected in entry 8211.
2624. 10/7/94 gee French, Peter P.; ---, ---. See 8583.
2625. 10/25/94 mor French, Peter P., gentleman; ---, WAS; Hampton, WAS;
                          mee 5960.   (A:507)
2626. 12/5/89 gor French, Susannah; Cambridge Dist., WAS. See 747.
2627. 7/1/00 mor Frisby, Simeon; ---, ---; ---, ESS; mee 5572.   (A:25)
2628. 7/31/00 mor Frost, David; Rutland, RUT, VT. See 5094.
2629. 10/5/85 gee Fuller, Aaron; ---, ---. See 7055.
2630. 10/7/85 mor Fuller, Aaron; Skenesborough, WAS; Skenesborough, WAS;
                          mee 8558.   (Deed Book B-1:220)
2631. 8/11/96 gor Fuller, Betsey. See 2636.
2632. 7/6/91 mor Fuller, Daniel; Willsborough, CLI; Judd Pat., CLI; mee 47.
                                                                     (A:71)
2633. 2/13/00 gor Fuller, Daniel (w. Sarah); Willsborough, ESS; James Judd's
                          Pat., ESS; gee 7683.   (A:42)
2634. 2/13/02 mor Fuller, Daniel; ---, ---; James Judd's Pat., ESS; co-mees
                          6401, 6425.   (A:97)
2635. 5/1/00 mor Fuller, Darius, farmer; Chester, WAS; Chester, WAS;
                          mee 7772.   (D:223)
2636. 8/11/96 gor Fuller, Ebenezer (w. Betsey), yeoman; Queensbury, WAS;
                          Queensbury, WAS; gee 6341.   (C-2:249)
2637. 10/6/85 gee Fuller, Ephraim; ---, ---. See 7055.
2638. 10/6/85 gee Fuller, Henry; ---, ---. See 7055.
2639. 10/7/85 mor Fuller, Henry; Skenesborough, WAS; Skenesborough, WAS;
                          mee 8558.   (Deed Book B-1:222)
2640. 9/30/96 gee Fuller, Henry; Westfield, WAS. See 2763.

2641. 4/9/88   mor Fuller, John; ---, HAM, MA; <u>Whitehall, WAS</u>; mee 3199. (A:365)
2642. 4/29/88 gee Fuller, John; ---, HAM, MA. See 3200.
2643. 10/5/85 gee Fuller, Mathew; ---, ---. See 7055.
2644. 6/26/99 mor Fuller, Matthew; Queensbury, WAS; <u>Queensbury, WAS</u>;
                    mee 5388. Mortgagee is "surviving partner of Platt
                    Smith and David Osborn, Junr.".   (D:64)
2645. 10/6/85 gee Fuller, Robert; ---, ---. See 7055.
2646. 2/13/00 gor Fuller, Sarah. See 2633.
2647. 7/2/94   gee Fullerton, Alexander, yeoman; Hebron, WAS. See 6759.
2648. 7/2/94   mor Fullerton, Alexander, yeoman; Hebron, WAS; <u>Hebron, WAS</u>;
                    co-mees 4644, 6760, 6809. Co-mortgagees are all executors
                    of the estate of John Morin Scott, Esq., dec'd. (C:91)
2649. 5/27/91 gor Fulmer, Christian; "Germain Town" (perhaps German Flats), HER;
                    <u>Mark Graves' Pat., CLI</u>; co-gees 1698, 5128.   (B:12)
2650. 8/20/94 gee Furgeson, Samuel, farmer; Cambridge, WAS. See 7301.
2651. 8/20/94 gee Furguson, Samuel, farmer; Cambridge, WAS. See 7300.
2652. 9/4/97   mee Furman, Gabriel; City of N.Y. See 6627.
2653. 9/1/98   gor Gage, Hannah. See 2654.
2654. 9/1/98   gor Gage, Isaac (w. Hannah); Ferrisburg, ADD, VT; <u>Plattsburgh,</u>
                    <u>CLI</u>; gee 3065.   (B:186)
2655. 12/1/98 gor Gaine, Cornelia. See 2657.
2656. 1/11/94 mee Gaine, Hugh; ---, ---. See 6515.
2657. 12/1/98 gor Gaine, Hugh (w. Cornelia), bookseller; City of N.Y.;
                    <u>Artillery Pat., WAS</u>; gee 8793.   (D:416)
2658. 10/15/98 mee Gainer, Edward; Cambridge, WAS. See 4694.
2659. 1/12/98 gee Galbreath, David, merchant; City of N.Y. See 5059.
2660. 12/23/01 gee Galbreath, David, merchant; London, England; See 5506.
2661. 7/10/90 mor Gallop, Joseph; Hebron, WAS; <u>Hebron, WAS</u>; mee 1072. (A:244)
2662. 5/6/94   gor Gallop, Joseph; Hebron, WAS; <u>Hebron, WAS</u>; gee 5304. (B-2:462)
2663. 6/4/94   --- Galloway, John, dec'd., farmer; Cambridge, WAS. See 3699.
2664. 5/31/94 gee Galloway, Mary, widow; Cambridge, WAS. See 7299.
2665. 3/12/93 gee Galpin, Joseph, farmer; Granville, WAS. See 946.
2666. 5/30/93 gor Galpin, Joseph, farmer. See 5474.
2667. 2/16/92 mor Galt, Alexander; ---, ---; Salem, WAS; mee 4737. (A:319)
2668. 11/16/99 gee Galt, Luther, blacksmith; Hebron, WAS. See 6106.
2669. 8/4/73   mor Gamal, Alexander; ---, De Forest Pat., CHA; co-mees
                    7144, 7264, 7278. Co-mortgagees are all executors of the
                    estate of William Smith, Esq., dec'd.   (A:6)
2670. 1/1/85   gee Gambell, Alexander; Black Creek, WAS. See 6667.
2671. 6/18/96 gee Gamble, James; Hebron, WAS. See 6764.
2672. 1/2/02   mee Gamble, James, yeoman; Hebron, WAS. See 1010.
2673. 6/11/93 mee Gansevoort, Harme, Mr.; Albany, ALB. See 6618.
2674. 12/13/91 mee Gansevoort, Leonard, merchant; Albany, ALB. See 3639.
2675. 12/30/91 mee Gansevoort, Leonard, merchant; Albany, ALB. See 5590.
2676. 11/6/92 mee Gansevoort, Leonard; Albany, ALB. See 5065.
2677. 6/22/93 mee Gansevoort, Leonard, merchant; Albany, ALB. See 2394.
2678. 6/26/01 mee Gansevoort, Leonard, Esq.; Bethlehem, ALB. See 8141.
2679. 12/30/94 mor Gardaner, Samuel, yeoman; Hebron, WAS; <u>Hebron, WAS</u>;
                    mee 3857.   (B:92)
2680. 12/13/89 gor Gardenier, Derick, gentleman; ---, COL; <u>Willsborough, CLI</u>;
                    gee 3482.   (A:206)
2681. 4/1/94   mor Gardineer, Ishmael (w. Susannah); Cambridge, WAS; <u>Hoosick</u>
                    <u>Pat. and Cambridge Pat., WAS</u>; co-mors 2682, 2683;
                    mee 7361.   (A:494)
2682. 4/1/94   mor Gardineer, Joshua (w. Lydia); Cambridge, WAS. See 2681.
2683. 4/1/94   mor Gardineer, Lydia. See 2682.
2684. 4/1/94   mor Gardineer, Susannah. See 2681.
2685. 6/3/94   gor Gardiner, Ishmael (w. Susannah); Cambridge, WAS; <u>Argyle,</u>
                    <u>WAS</u>; co-gors 2686, 2687; gee 6066.   (B-2:379)
2686. 6/3/94   gor Gardiner, Joshua (w. Lydia); Cambridge, WAS. See 2685.
2687. 6/3/94   gor Gardiner, Lydia. See 2686.
2688. 6/3/94   gor Gardiner, Susannah. See 2685.
2689. 10/28/94 gor Gardinier, Christian. See 1584.
2690. 10/28/94 gor Gardinier, Samuel (w. Christian), yeoman; Cambridge, WAS;
                    <u>Cambridge, WAS</u>; co-gees 1584, 1725, 1777. (B-2:287)

2691. 1/30/99 gor Gardner, Abijah; Cornwall, Starmont "County"(?), Upper Canada;
 Willsborough, CLI; gee 6283.   (A:1)
2692. 5/15/92 gee Gardner, Ishmael, yeoman; Argyle, WAS. See 4585.
2693. 4/1/94 gee Gardner, Ishmael; Cambridge, WAS. See 7369.
2694. 12/7/99 gor Gardner, Ishmael(w. Susannah); Cambridge, WAS; Cambridge,
 WAS; gee 2697.   (D:364)
2695. 5/15/92 gee Gardner, Joshua, yeoman; Argyle, WAS. See 4585.
2696. 4/1/94 gee Gardner, Joshua; Cambridge, WAS. See 7369.
2697. 12/7/99 gee Gardner, Joshua; Cambridge, WAS. See 2694.
2698. 12/7/99 gor Gardner, Susannah. See 2694.
2699. 4/2/95 gor Gardnier, Ishmael (w. Susannah); Cambridge, WAS; Argyle, WAS;
 co-gors 2700, 2701; gee 6067.   (B-2:377)
2700. 4/2/95 gor Gardnier, Joshua (w. Lydia); Cambridge, WAS. See 2699.
2701. 4/2/95 gor Gardnier, Lidia. See 2700.
2702. 4/2/95 gor Gardnier, Susannah. See 2699.
2703. 6/7/92 mor Gardnor, Samuel, yeoman; Hebron, WAS; Hebron, WAS; co-mor
 1563; mee 6990.   (A:375)
2704. 4/3/01 mor Garfield, Nathaniel, farmer; Bolton, WAS; ---, WAS;
 mee 2299.   (D:163)
2705. 8/6/01 mor Garlick, Richard; Plattsburgh, CLI; Plattsburgh, CLI;
 mee 5771.   (B:57)
2706. 10/29/93 mor Garlick, Samuel; Lanesborough, BER, MA. See 3360.
2707. 10/16/89 mor Garner, Abijah; Willsborough, CLI; Willsborough, CLI;
 mee 6440.   (A:28)
2708. 5/5/94 gor Gates, Joshua; Westfield, WAS; Salem Dist., WAS; gee 1676.
                                                       (D:64)
2709. 6/26/98 mor Gates, Levi, Junr. (w. Nancy); Hartford, WAS; Hartford, WAS;
 mee 367.   (B:262)
2710. 6/26/98 mor Gates, Nancy. See 2709.
2711. --/--/87 gee Gault, Alexander; ---, ---. See 7055.
2712. 12/8/89 mor Gault, Alexander (w. Maby); Salem, WAS; Salem, WAS;
 mee 4736.   (A:182)
2713. 3/6/90 gor Gault, Alexander (w. Mely), yeoman; Salem, WAS; Salem, WAS;
 gee 4742.   (A:268)
2714. 3/5/92 gor Gault, Alexander (w. Mely); Salem, WAS; Salem, WAS;
 co-gees 3559, 3564.   (A:266)
2715. 7/1/86 gor Gault, James, farmer; Salem, WAS; Turner Pat., WAS;
 gee 2716.   (C-1:30)
2716. 7/1/86 gee Gault, John; Salem, WAS. See 2715.
2717. 3/8/88 gee Gault, John Fenton; Salem, WAS. See 1638.
2718. 7/9/92 gor Gault, John Fenton; Salem, WAS; Salem, WAS; gee 1686. (A:374)
2719. 12/8/89 mor Gault, Maby. See 2712.
2720. 3/6/90 gor Gault, Mely. See 2713.
2721. 3/5/92 gor Gault, Mely. See 2714.
2722. 11/3/97 mor Gaylord, Enos, farmer; ---, HAR, CT; ---, CLI; co-mor 8501;
 mee 5691.   (A:241)
2723. 7/13/99 gor Gear, Jacob (w. Tamison), yeoman; Argyle, WAS; Argyle, WAS;
 gee 7659.   (D:345)
2724. 7/13/99 gor Gear, Tamison. See 2723.
2725. 12/6/97 mor Gebhard, Philip; Claverack, COL; Saratoga Pat, WAS;
 mee 8057.   (B:264)
2726. 12/17/93 mor Geer, Jacob, yeoman; ---, WAS; Argyle, WAS; co-mees 1183,
 8037.   (A:461)
2727. 11/18/83 gee Geers, Lemuel; Black Creek Dist., CHA. See 4314.
2728. 1/2/88 mor Geers, Lemuel; Hebron, WAS; Hebron, WAS; mee 8565. (A:69)
2729. 2/15/91 gor Gelston, John; City of N.Y.; Hebron, WAS; co-gors 2730,
 6691, 7723; gee 4470.   (A:237)
2730. 2/15/91 gor Gelston, Mary; City of N.Y. See 2729.
2731. 6/28/74 gor George, James, yeoman; ---, ALB; De Forest Pat., CHA;
 co-gors 2905, 8676; gee 4309.   (B-1:98)
2732. 7/4/92 gee Getty, Adam; Hebron, WAS. See 3566.
2733. 12/10/81 gee Getty, David, yeoman; ---, CHA. See 2735.
2734. 3/11/00 mee Getty, Ebenezer, yeoman; Hebron, WAS. See 6099.
2735. 12/10/81 gor Getty, Robert, Senr., yeoman; ---, ---; ---, CHA; gee 2733.
                                                      (B-1:95)

74

2736. 12/23/00 mor Gibbs, John; ---, ---; Elizabethtown, ESS; mee 7522. (A:44)
2737. 8/10/00 mor Gibbs, Jonas; ---, ---; Elizabethtown, ESS; mee 5879. (A:13)
2738. 9/30/90 mor Gibbs, Samuel Atwood; Hebron, WAS; Hebron, WAS; mee 6981.
                                                              (A:219)
2739. 1/18/02 mor Gibson, Abraham, yeoman; Cambridge, WAS; Hebron, WAS;
                        mee 4518.   (D:130)
2740. 4/25/96 gee Gibson, Colin; Cambridge, WAS. See 3274.
2741. 10/6/90 mor Gibson, William, yeoman; Hebron, WAS; De Forest Tract, WAS;
                        mee 7276.   (A:264)
2742. 10/26/90 gee Gibson, William, yeoman; Hebron, WAS. See 8291.
2743. 3/1/93 gee Gifford, Caleb; ---, ---. See 3380.
2744. 10/1/94 gee Gifford, Caleb; Cambridge, WAS. See 3378.
2745. 2/20/99 mee Gifford, Caleb; Cambridge, WAS. See 1721.
2746. 2/23/01 gor Gifford, Caleb (w. Ellefal); Cambridge, WAS; Cambridge, WAS;
                        gee 2750.   (E:419)
2747. 2/23/01 gor Gifford, Ellefal. See 2746.
2748. 6/23/89 gee Gifford, Hercules; Cambridge Dist., WAS. See 528.
2749. 8/12/00 gor Gifford, Hercules, yeoman, gentleman; Cambridge, WAS;
                        Cambridge, WAS; gee 2751.   (E:28)
2750. 2/23/01 gee Gifford, Joseph; Dartmouth, BRI, MA. See 2746.
2751. 8/12/00 gee Gifford, Mahaliel; Cambridge, WAS. See 2749.
2752. 4/18/96 mor Gifford, Peleg, yeoman; Cambridge, WAS; Saratoga Pat., WAS;
                        mee 3685.   (B:31)
2753. 11/1/83 gee Gilbert, Jedediah, carpenter; New Perth, CHA. See 1436.
2754. 10/19/01 mor Gilbert, John, farmer; Argyle, WAS; Argyle, WAS; mee 4590.
                                                              (D:109)
2755. 2/23/95 gor Gilbert, Jonah (w. Rachel); Cambridge, WAS; John Bleecker
                        Pat., WAS; gee 3091.   (C-2:5)
2756. 10/4/92 gee Gilbert, Josiah; Cambridge, WAS. See 800.
2757. 10/27/92 gor Gilbert, Josiah (w. Rachel); Cambridge, WAS; ---, WAS;
                        gee 6018)   (F:21)
2758. 10/27/92 gor Gilbert, Rachel. See 2757.
2759. 2/23/95 gor Gilbert, Rachel. See 2755.
2760. 2/10/02 mor Gilbert, Solomon; ---, ---; Willsborough, ESS; mee 6916.
                                                              (A:78)
2761. 7/1/91 gee Gilbert, Thomas, yeoman; Westfield, WAS. See 2367.
2762. 6/11/94 gee Gilbert, Thomas; Westfield, WAS. See 2370.
2763. 9/30/96 gor Gilbert, Thomas; Westfield, WAS; Westfield, WAS; gee 2640.
                                                              (C-2:246)
2764. 3/28/92 gor Gilchrist, Adam, gentleman; City of N.Y.; ---, WAS;
                        gee 8788.   (B-2:236)
2765. 7/15/99 gor Gilchrist, Adam (w. Hester), merchant; Charleston, ---, SC.
                        See 2771.
2766. 1/15/65 gee Gilchrist, Duncan, farmer; ---, ULS. See 6219.
2767. 4/18/75 gor Gilchrist, Duncan, Senr., farmer; Argyle, CHA; Argyle, CHA;
                        gee 4582.   (A:511)
2768. 7/15/99 gor Gilchrist, Elizabeth. See 2771.
2769. 7/15/99 gor Gilchrist, Hester. See 2765.
2770. 11/29/99 mor Gilchrist, Mary. See 2772.
2771. 7/15/99 gor Gilchrist, Robert (w. Elizabeth), gentleman; Westchester,
                        WES; Artillery Pat., WAS; co-gors 2765, 2769; gee 8794.
                                                              (D:194)
2772. 11/29/99 mor Gilchrist, Thomas (w. Mary), blacksmith; Hebron, WAS;
                        Hebron, WAS; mee 8110.   (C:105)
2773. 7/6/88 mor Gilder, David; Granville, WAS; Granville, WAS; mee 2379.
                                                              (A:104)
2774. 1/14/65 gor Gillaspie, Neal, farmer; ---, ULS. See 6217.
2775. Data repositioned.
2776. 1/15/65 gor Gillaspie, Neal, farmer; ---, ULS. See 6219. Six
                        contracts this date involving these persons.
2777. 3/21/65 gor Gillaspie, Neal, farmer; ---, ULS. See 6232.
2778. 10/22/65 gor Gillaspie, Neal, farmer; ---, ULS. See 6220.
2779. 1/15/65 gee Gillaspie, Neal, Junr., farmer; ---, ULS. See 6219.
2780. 3/23/02 mor Gillet, Daniel Ordway; Cambridge, WAS; Salem, WAS;
                        mee 2070.   (D:168)
2781. 5/31/92 gee Gillet, Samuel; ---, WAS. See 8237.

2782. 11/17/84 gee Gilliland, Anne, Miss. See 2786.
2783. 2/21/86 gee Gilliland, Charlotte, spinster, "one of the daughters and
                children of ... William Gilliland"; Willsborough, WAS.
                See 2794.
2784. 5/29/87 gee Gilliland, Charlotte, spinster, "of Willsborough but at
                present in the City of Albany", ALB. See 2796.
2785. 1/20/84 gor Gilliland, William; Albany, ALB; Willsborough, CHA;
                gee 6940.   (A:85)
2786. 11/17/84 gor Gilliland, William; ---, ---; "Janesborough", WAS;
                gee 6893. This land granted in trust for "Miss Anne
                Gilliland, daughter of William Gilliland and grand-
                daughter of Thomas Shadforth".   (A:192)
2787. 2/21/86 --- Gilliland, William. See 2783.
2788. 12/1/96 mee Gilliland, William; Troy, REN. See 95.
2789. 12/31/96 mee Gilliland, William; Troy, REN. See 1577.
2790. 1/20/84 gor Gilliland, William, Esq.; Albany, ALB; Willsborough, CHA;
                gee 65.   (A:96)
2791. 5/2/84 gor Gilliland, William, Esq.; Albany, ALB; Willsborough, WAS;
                gee 3496.   (A:124)
2792. 9/23/84 gor Gilliland, William, Esq.; Willsborough, WAS; Willsborough,
                WAS; gee 3389.   (A:109)
2793. 9/28/84 gor Gilliland, William, Esq.; Willsborough, WAS; Willsborough,
                WAS; gee 7381.   (A:35)
2794. 2/21/86 gor Gilliland, William, Esq.; "Clinton at Cape Elizabeth in
                Willsborough", WAS; land "in said Clinton", WAS;
                gee 2783.   (A:39)
2795. 3/14/87 gor Gilliland, William, Esq.; Willsborough, WAS; Willsborough,
                WAS; gee 7376.   (A:75)
2796. 5/29/87 gor Gilliland, William, Esq.; "of Willsborough but at present
                in the City of New York"; Friswell Pat., WAS;
                gee 2784.   (A:41)
2797. 5/21/95 mee Gilliland, William, Esq.; Troy, REN. See 5424.
2798. 9/30/96 gor Gilliland, William, Esq.; Troy, REN; Canadian Refugees'
                Bounty Land (originally granted to Glaud Monty, Junr.),
                CLI; gee 5138.   (B:26)
2799. 12/31/96 mee Gilliland, William, Esq.; Troy, REN. See 4254.
2800. 2/23/97 gor Gilliland, William, Esq.; Troy, REN; Willsborough, CLI;
                gee 4797.   (B:95)
2801. 2/23/97 mee Gilliland, William, Esq.; Troy, REN. See 4357.
2802. 6/26/97 mee Gilliland, William, Esq.; Troy, REN. See 1900.
2803. 10/21/97 mee Gilliland, William, Esq.; Troy, REN. See 7496.
2804. 7/7/98 gor Gilliland, William, Esq.; Troy, REN; Plattsburgh, CLI;
                gee 1019.   (B:156)
2805. 9/27/98 mee Gilliland, William, Esq.; Troy, REN. See 1901.
2806. 4/27/99 gor Gilliland, William, Esq.; Willsborough, ESS; Willsborough,
                ESS; gee 7379.   (A:22)
2807. 12/1/88 gor Gilliland, William, Junr.; Willsborough, CLI; Willsborough,
                CLI; gee 7378.   (A:72)
2807a. 8/24/89 mee Gilliland, William, Junr.; Willsborough, CLI. See 2225
2808. 6/30/92 gor Gilliland, William, Junr.; Troy, REN; Willsborough, CLI;
                gee 3477.   (B:77)
2809. 12/31/92 gor Gilliland, William, Junr., gentleman; Troy, REN; land on
                "west shore of the River Boquet", CLI (1000 acres);
                gee 8352.   (A:506)
2810. 2/6/93 mee Gilliland, William, Junr.; Willsborough, CLI. See 4301.
2811. 6/7/93 gee Gilliland, William, Junr., gentleman; Troy, REN. See 1636.
2812. 6/18/93 mee Gilliland, William, Junr.; Troy, REN. See 2072.
2813. 6/22/93 gor Gilliland, William, Junr.; Troy, REN; Willsborough, CLI;
                gee 1703.   (A:374)
2814. 6/24/93 gor Gilliland, William, Junr., gentleman; Troy, REN;
                Willsborough, CLI; gee 7387.   (A:370)
2815. 8/27/94 gor Gilliland, William, Junr., gentleman; Troy, REN; ---, CLI;
                gee 7628.   (A:8)
2816. Data repositioned.

2817. 7/16/94 gee Gilliland, William, Junr., Esq.; Troy, REN. See 8706.
2818. 9/29/98 mee Gilliland, William, Junr., Esq.; Troy, REN. See 3248.
2819. 3/18/89 gor Gillis, Alexander; Argyle, WAS; Salem, WAS; gee 3964. (A:230)
2820. 2/5/90 gee Gillis, Alexander; Argyle, WAS. See 2828.
2821. 12/10/99 mor Gillis, Alexander (w. Cathren), yeoman; Argyle, WAS;
        Argyle, WAS; mee 8114.   (C:105)
2822. 4/26/65 gor Gillis, Ann, "formerly Ann Campbell". See 2826.
2823. 12/10/99 mor Gillis, Cathren. See 2821.
2824. 12/26/99 mor Gillis, Ealoner. See 2829.
2825. 1/14/65 --- Gillis, James. See 1203.
2826. 4/26/65 gor Gillis, James (w. Ann), farmer; Cakeat, ORA; Argyle, ALB;
        gee 4577.   (A:488)
2827. 5/4/67 gor Gillis, James; Argyle, ALB; Argyle, ALB; gee 3944.
                                                            (B-1:192)
2828. 2/5/90 gor Gillis, James; Argyle, WAS; Argyle, WAS; gee 2820. (A:154)
2829. 12/26/99 gor Gillis, James, Junr. (w. Ealoner); Argyle, WAS; Argyle, WAS;
        gee 4515.   (F:19)
2830. 9/2/01 gor Gillis, Margaret. See 2833.
2831. 8/13/02 gor Gillis, Mary. See 2835.
2832. 7/12/00 mor Gillis, Robert, yeoman; Hebron, WAS; Argyle, WAS; mee 4561.
                                                            (D:120)
2833. 9/2/01 gor Gillis, Robert (w. Margaret, "formerly Margaret Hamilton
        and the daughter of John Embury, deceased"), yeoman;
        Argyle, WAS; Cambridge, WAS; gee 8190.   (E:365)
2834. 2/27/86 gee Gillis, Samuel; yeoman; New Perth Dist., WAS. See 7455.
2835. 8/13/02 gor Gillis, Samuel (w. Mary), yeoman; Salem, WAS; Salem, WAS;
        gee 6411.   (F:256)
2836. 8/13/02 mee Gillis, Samuel; Salem, WAS. See 6412.
2837. 1/15/65 --- Gillis, James. See 1204.
2838. 7/20/87 gee Gillmore, David; ---, ---. See 100.
2839. 8/13/02 --- Gillmore, George, dec'd. See 699.
2840. 7/20/87 gee Gillmore, James; ---, ---. See 100.
2841. 8/13/02 gee Gillmore, James, yeoman; Cambridge, WAS. See 699.
2842. 7/2/92 gor Gillmore, William; Cambridge, WAS; Isaac Sawyer's Pat., WAS;
        gee 1767.   (E:24)
2843. 2/26/00 mee Gillmore, William; Cambridge, WAS. See 744.
2844. 11/20/86 gor Gilmore, Elizabeth, "administrator" of the estate of George
        Gilmore, dec'd.; Cambridge Dist., ALB; Jessup's Pat., WAS;
        gee 650.   (B-2:513)
2845. 12/5/89 gor Gilmore, Elizabeth; Cambridge Dist., WAS. See 747.
2846. 1/11/86 gor Gilmore, George, Capt.; Cambridge Dist., WAS; land "east
        side of Hudson's River", WAS; gee 4269. (A:207)
2847. 11/20/86 --- Gilmore, George, dec'd. See 2844.
2848. 9/6/90 gee Gilmore, William; Cambridge, ALB. See 7353.
2849. 9/25/90 gee Gilmore, William; Cambridge, ALB. See 8841.
2850. 10/1/90 gee Gilmore, William, yeoman; Cambridge, WAS. See 7295.
2851. 12/17/93 gee Gilmore, William; Cambridge, WAS. See 3815.
2852. 7/1/85 gee Glason, Jason; ---, ---. See 7055.
2853. 7/1/85 mor Glason, Jason; ---, ---; Skenesborough, WAS; mee 8555.
                                                (Deed Book B-1:225)
2854. 2/24/02 mee Glason, Samuel; East Sudbury, MID, MA. See 2259.
2855. 5/8/93 gee Glen, Cornelius; Argyle, WAS. See 6757.
2856. 5/8/93 mor Glen, Cornelius, yeoman; Argyle, WAS. See 7620.
2857. 5/30/99 mee Glen, Cornelius; ---, ALB. See 1970.
2858. 9/30/99 gor Glen, Frances. See 2860.
2859. 7/4/96 mee Glen, Jacob; Schenectady, ALB. See 468.
2860. 9/30/99 gor Glen, Jacob (w. Frances); Schenectady, ---; Fairfield, WAS;
        gee 1881.   (D:185)
2861. 10/19/02 mor Glen, Jacob; Schenectady, ALB; Fairfield and Queensbury,
        WAS; mee 5241.   (E:24)
2862. 7/10/90 gor Glen, Jacob, Esq.; Glens Falls, ALB; ---, WAS; gees
        1129 (A:183) and 1130 (A:185).(two contracts)
2863. 8/24/92 mee Glen, Jacob, Esq.; Glens Falls, SAR. See 3508 and 6036.
2864. 2/1/94 mee Glen, Jacob S.; ---, ---. See 1038.
2865. 2/1/94 mee Glen, John S.; ---, ---. See 1038.
2866. 2/1/94 mee Glen, Sarah; ---, ---. See 1038.

77

2867. 2/7/97 mee Glenny, James; ---, CLI. See 604.
2868. 5/5/96 gee Goddard, Moses, yeoman; "late of Vermont". See 7326.
2869. 5/5/96 gee Goddard, Moses; ---, ---. See 7326.
2870. 9/30/90 --- Godwin, John, Col., dec'd. See 2872.
2871. 9/30/99 mee Godwin, William, Lt. Col., "Royal Artillery, Kingdom of
        Great Britain". See 2006.
2872. 9/30/90 gor Godwin, William, Esq.; "Colonel in one of his brittanic
        majesty's regiments ... and nephew and heir at law of Col.
        John Godwin heretofore of the same Regiment, deceased";
        Abbots Bromley, Stafford, England; Westfield, WAS;
        gee 2005. This deed signed by Wm. Godwin's attornies
        Barent Bleecker and John R. Bleecker, Junr., both of
        Albany, ALB. (E:416)
2873. 10/14/98 gor Goff, Abner (w. Ruth), yeoman; Hebron, WAS; Hebron, WAS;
        gee 2902. (D:206)
2874. 10/14/98 gor Goff, Ruth. See 2873.
2875. 11/3/01 mor Gofft, Christopher; ---, ---; Jay, ESS; mee 5653. (A:84)
2876. 9/23/96 mor Gold, Ebenezer; Granville, WAS; Granville, WAS; mee 3767.
        (B:130)
2877. 9/22/96 mor Gold, Salmon, farmer; Granville, WAS; ---, WAS; mee 3766.
        (B:112)
2878. 5/8/88 gor Golden, Elias (w. Margaret); Cambridge Dist., ALB;
        Cambridge Dist., ALB; gee 3201. (D:163)
2879. 5/8/88 gor Golden, Margaret. See 2878.
2880. 8/18/83 gee Goodale, Ezekiel, yeoman; Black Creek, CHA. See 3222.
2881. 2/8/98 mor Gooding, Matthew (w. Mercy); Hartford, WAS; Hartford, WAS;
        mee 1483. (B:261)
2882. 2/8/98 mor Gooding, Mercy. See 2881.
2883. 9/11/98 --- Goodspeede, Simpson. See 16.
2884. 5/11/90 mee Goodwin, John, druggist; City of N.Y. See 6075.
2885. 8/8/96 gee Goodwin, John, druggist; City of N.Y. See 7640.
2886. 10/12/99 gor Goodwin, John, druggist; City of N.Y.; Whitehall, WAS;
        gee 587. (D:321)
2887. 12/14/75 gee Gordin, Robert; Skenesborough, CHA. See 3484.
2888. 4/18/87 gor Gordon, Robert; Parish of St. Rose, Quebec, Canada;
        Artillery Pat., WAS; gee 4193. (A:100)
2889. 4/11/97 mor Gorham, Anthony; Champlain, CLI; Champlain, CLI; mee 7693.
        (A:223)
2890. 6/29/98 mor Gorham, Anthony; Champlain, CLI; Champlain, CLI;
        mee 1244. (A:327)
2891. 6/12/90 gor Gorline, Lewis, "late a Lieutenant in the Regiment of
        Infantry whereof Moses Hazen, Esq., was Commanding Officer.";
        "Canadian Refugees' land granted in 1784 by Gov. George
        Clinton, Esq."; gee 8180. (A:139)
2892. 5/30/89 gor Gosselin, Clement, "late in the Army of the United States
        ... and a Refugee from Canada"; Champlain, CLI; gee 6523.
        (B:274)
2893. 9/5/81 gee Gould, Jabez; ---, CHA. See 8543.
2894. 3/20/84 gor Gould, Jabez; Granville, CHA; Granville, CHA; gee 2110.
        (E:252)
2895. 2/4/99 mee Gould, Thomas, merchant; Albany, ALB. See 5144.
2896. 3/16/99 mee Gourlay, Thomas; Hebron, WAS. See 3644.
2897. 8/31/99 mee Gourlay, Thomas, merchant; Hebron, WAS. See 6105.
2898. 1/30/00 mee Gourlay, Thomas, merchant; Hebron, WAS. See 1504.
2899. 7/8/00 mee Gourlay, Thomas; Hebron, WAS. See 83.
2900. 4/14/01 gor Gourlay, Thomas; Hebron, WAS; Hebron, WAS; gee 253. Two
        contracts this date involving these two persons.
        (E:378), (E:380)
2901. 12/13/96 gee Gourlay, Thomas, merchant; Hebron, WAS. See 4936.
2902. 10/14/98 gee Gourley, Thomas, merchant; Hebron, WAS. See 2873.
2903. 5/18/99 gee Gourley, Thomas, merchant; Hebron, WAS. See 7463.
2904. 12/13/96 gee Gourly, Thomas; Hebron, WAS. See 2351.
2905. 6/28/74 gee Gowen, Moses; ---, ALB. See 2731.
2906. 6/27/98 gor Gragg, Adams (w. Janey), farmer; Argyle, WAS; Argyle, WAS;
        gee 8810. (F:29)
2907. 6/27/98 gor Gragg, Janey. See 2906.

2908.	12/19/93	mor	Graham, Agnes. See 2921.
2909.	8/20/93	gee	Graham, David, farmer; Westfield, WAS. See 7073.
2910.	9/8/00	gee	Graham, David; Hartford, WAS. See 4783.
2911.	1/21/88	gor	Graham, Duncan, farmer; Poughkeepsie Precinct, DUT; Argyle, WAS; gee 4712. (D:33)
2912.	1/23/88	mee	Graham, Duncan; Poughkeepsie, DUT. See 4713.
2913.	3/3/94	mee	Graham, Elizabeth; City of N.Y. See 3437.
2914.	5/2/96	gor	Graham, Elizabeth; City of N.Y.; Kingsbury Pat., WAS; gee 1609. (D:291)
2915.	7/15/73	mee	Graham, Ennis, tailor; City of N.Y. See 3798.
2916.	4/3/94	mee	Graham, James; Salem, WAS. See 3054.
2917.	8/24/94	mor	Graham, James, farmer; Salem, WAS; Salem, WAS; mee 757. (A:499)
2918.	10/30/94	gor	Graham, James, farmer; Salem, WAS; Salem, WAS; gee 7449. (F:226)
2919.	5/7/84	gee	Graham, John, yeoman; New Perth, CHA. See 4505.
2920.	8/20/93	gee	Graham, John, farmer; Westfield, WAS. See 7073.
2921.	12/19/93	mor	Graham, John (w. Agnes), farmer; Cambridge, WAS; Cambridge, WAS; mee 6169. (A:472)
2922.	9/8/00	gee	Graham, John; Hartford, WAS. See 4783.
2923.	2/3/02	gor	Graham, Lucina. See 2926.
2924.	11/12/98	mor	Graham, Rebeckah. See 2929.
2925.	7/8/97	mor	Graham, Roswell (w. Susena), farmer; Granville, WAS; Granville, WAS; co-mees 78, 2939, 2955. (B:203)
2926.	2/3/02	gor	Graham, Roswell (w. Lucina); Granville, WAS; Granville, WAS; gee 1800. (F:268)
2927.	7/8/97	mor	Graham, Susena. See 2925.
2928.	6/9/74	gor	Graham, William, "eldest son of Elizabeth Mac Alpine"; ---, ORA. See 4796.
2929.	11/12/98	mor	Graham, Winthrop (w. Rebeckah); Westfield, WAS; Westfield, WAS; mee 8799. (C:103)
2930.	3/3/00	gor	Graham, Winthrop, farmer; Westfield, WAS; Westfield, WAS; gee 5994. (D:396)
2931.	9/6/89	gee	Graham, Wintrup; Westfield, WAS. See 7008.
2932.	11/30/96	mee	Grant, Christy; ---, DUT. See 7969.
2933.	6/3/97	mee	Grant, Christy; ---, DUT. See 7347.
2934.	7/3/97	mee	Grant, Christy; ---, DUT. See 1799 and 2077.
2935.	7/4/97	mee	Grant, Christy; ---, DUT. See 703, 2071, 6228, 6235, 7413.
2936.	7/5/97	mee	Grant, Christy; ---, DUT. See 7575.
2937.	7/6/97	mee	Grant, Christy; ---, DUT. See 3234 and 7980.
2938.	7/7/97	mee	Grant, Christy; ---, DUT. See 5226.
2939.	7/8/97	mee	Grant, Christy; ---, DUT. See 2925 and 5493.
2940.	7/21/97	mee	Grant, Christy; ---, DUT. See 8413.
2941.	7/5/98	mee	Grant, Christy; ---, DUT. See 7396.
2942.	11/30/96	mee	Grant, James; ---, DUT. See 7969.
2943.	11/30/96	---	Grant, James, dec'd. See 7969.
2944.	6/3/97	mee	Grant, James; ---, DUT. See 7347.
2945.	6/3/97	---	Grant, James, dec'd.; Pawling, DUT. See 7347.
2946.	7/3/97	mee	Grant, James; ---, DUT. See 1799 and 2077.
2947.	7/3/97	---	Grant, James, dec'd.; Pawling, DUT. See 1799.
2948.	7/4/97	mee	Grant, James; ---, DUT. See 703, 2071, 6228, 6235, 7413.
2949.	7/4/97	---	Grant, James, dec'd.; Pawling, DUT. See 7413.
2950.	7/5/97	mee	Grant, James; ---, DUT. See 7575.
2951.	7/5/97	---	Grant, James, dec'd.; Pawling, DUT. See 7575.
2952.	7/6/97	---	Grant, James; ---, DUT. See 3234, 7980.
2953.	7/6/97	---	Grant, James, dec'd.; Pawling, DUT. See 7980.
2954.	7/7/97	mee	Grant, James; ---, DUT. See 5226.
2955.	7/8/97	mee	Grant, James; ---, DUT. See 2925 and 5493.
2956.	7/8/97	---	Grant, James, dec'd.; Pawling, DUT. See 5493.
2957.	7/21/97	mee	Grant, James; ---, DUT. See 8413.
2958.	7/21/97	---	Grant, James, dec'd.; ---, ---. See 8413.
2959.	7/5/98	mee	Grant, James. See 7396.
2960.	7/5/98	---	Grant, James, dec'd.; Pawling, DUT. See 7396.
2961.	8/14/92	gee	Graton, James, farmer; Westfield, WAS. See 4450.
2962.	5/1/00	mor	Graves, Ansel, farmer; Chester, WAS; Chester, WAS; mee 7772. (D:201)

2963. 10/11/91 mor Graves, Benjamin; Plattsburgh, CLI; Plattsburgh, CLI;
                       mee 5679.   (A:83)
2964. 3/23/96 gee Graves, Benjamin; ---, CLI. See 2293.
2965. 5/2/96 mor Graves, Benjamin; Plattsburgh, CLI; Peru, CLI; mee 2295.
                                                                    (A:216)
2966. 4/19/97 gor Graves, Benjamin; Plattsburgh, CLI; Zephaniah Platt's Pat.,
                       CLI; co-gees 5748, 8756.   (B:67)
2967. 6/21/99 mor Graves, Benjamin; Plattsburgh, CLI; Old Military Township
                       #7 (Chateaugay), CLI; co-mees 278, 319.   (A:417)
2968. 9/6/90 gee Graves, David; Granville, WAS. See 2245.
2969. 2/10/98 mee Graves, David; Granville, WAS. See 577.
2970. 7/1/00 mor Graves, Jonathan; ---, ---; ---, ESS; mee 5572. (A:28)
2971. 7/6/88 mor Graves, Lebbeus; Granville, WAS; Granville, WAS; mee 2379.
2972. 7/6/88 gee Graves, Libeus, yeoman; Granville, WAS. See 2378. /(A:121)
2973. 5/1/00 mor Graves, Noahdiah, farmer; Chester, WAS; Chester, WAS;
                       mee 7772.   (D:199)
2974. 9/7/69 gor Gray, Adam Clark; ---, ---. See 7955.
2975. 4/20/73 gor Gray, Adam Clark; ---, ---. See 7957.
2976. 4/26/99 mor Gray, Daniel C.; Hebron, WAS; Hebron, WAS; mee 8602. (C:104)
2977. 6/7/90 gee Gray, David, farmer; ---, WAS. See 4719.
2978. 12/20/96 mor Gray, Elihu; Hebron, WAS. See 7720.
2979. 2/1/94 mor Gray, Isaac, farmer; Salem, WAS. See 1038.
2980. 8/28/69 gee Gray, John; White Creek, ALB. See 3637.
2981. 8/14/87 gor Gray, John; Salem, WAS; Salem, WAS; gee 2989.   (A:472)
2982. 6/30/84 gee Gray, John, Junr.; New Perth, WAS. See 2027.
2983. 8/16/94 gee Gray, John, Junr., yeoman; Salem, WAS. See 8581.
2984. 9/10/96 gor Gray, John, Junr. (w. Margaret); Salem, WAS; Salem, WAS;
                       gee 6621.   (C-2:76)
2985. 9/10/96 mee Gray, John, Junr.; ---, ---. See 6622.
2986. 5/10/00 gor Gray, John, Junr., farmer; Salem, WAS; Salem, WAS;
                       gee 3151.   (E:375)
2987. 9/10/96 gor Gray, Margaret. See 2984.
2988. 12/20/96 mor Gray, Martha; Hebron, WAS. See 7720.
2989. 8/14/87 gee Gray, Nathaniel, yeoman; Salem, WAS. See 2981.
2990. 12/15/98 gor Gray, William, trader; Village of St. Regis, Lower Canada;
                       ---, CLI; gee 162.   (B:173)
2991. 7/10/90 mor Green, Abner; Hebron, WAS; Hebron, WAS; mee 1072. (A:255)
2992. 9/2/01 gor Green, Anna. See 2998.
2993. 11/3/98 mor Green, Artemos (w. Easter), farmer; Hartford, WAS;
                       Hartford, WAS; mee 1494.   (C:102)
2994. 4/11/95 gee Green, Caleb, "the son of Rufus Green"; ---, ---. See 5735.
2995. 11/3/98 mor Green, Easter. See 2993.
2996. 9/20/93 mor Green, Henry; Peru, CLI; Zephaniah Platt's Pat., CLI;
                       mee 5852.   (A:111)
2997. 9/15/00 mor Green, Hezekiah, yeoman; Hebron, WAS; Hebron, WAS;
                       mee 6208.   (C:106)
2998. 9/2/01 gor Green, James (w. Anna), physician; Argyle, WAS; Cambridge,
                       WAS; gee 8190.   (E:369)
2999. 5/10/97 gor Green, John (w. Mary), yeoman; Argyle, WAS; Argyle, WAS
                       gee 1685.   (D:202)
3000. 5/14/99 mee Green, John, farmer; Cambridge, WAS. See 8644.
3001. 1/25/99 gor Green, Lydia. See 3004.
3002. 5/10/97 gor Green, Mary. See 2999.
3003. 6/19/98 gee Green, Richard; Easton, WAS. See 8775.
3004. 1/25/99 gor Green, Richard (w. Lydia); Easton, WAS; Saratoga Pat., WAS;
                       gee 2609.   (D:48)
3005. 4/11/95 --- Green, Rufus. See 2994.
3006. 9/4/96 gee Green, Samuel; Cambridge, WAS. See 7133.
3007. 5/5/01 mee Green, Samuel; Cambridge, WAS. See 1159.
3008. 10/14/95 mee Green, Solomon; Kingsbury, WAS. See 6869.
3009. 11/1/94 mee Gregory, Elijah; Hebron, WAS. See 4184.
3010. 11/30/90 gee Gregory, Thomas; Lanesborough, ---, MA. See 6409.
3011. 11/10/94 gor Gregory, Thomas, yeoman; Hebron, WAS; Hebron, WAS;
                       gee 2275.   (B-2:422)
3012. 3/30/95 gor Gregory, Thomas; Argyle, WAS; Argyle, WAS; gee 7261.
                                                                    (C-2:96)

3013. 7/1/88   mee Grier, James; ---, ---, See 158.
3014. 7/1/88   mee Grier, John; ---, ---. See 158.
3015. 11/3/99 mor Griffeth, Asenath. See 3016.
3016. 11/3/99 mor Griffeth, David (w. Asenath); Whitehall, WAS; Whitehall, WAS;
                      mee 2476.   (C:106)
3017. 5/16/01 mor Griffeth, Thomas; Whitehall, WAS; Whitehall, WAS; mee 4145.
                                                                  (D:47)
3018. 1/2/76   gee Griffin, Benjamin; ---, CHA. See 1223.
3019. 1/2/76   mor Griffin, Benjamin; ---, CHA; Argyle, CHA; mee 1222. (A:30)
3020. 12/24/01 mor Griffin, Jacob; Cambridge, WAS; Granville, WAS; mee 725.
                                                                  (D:187)
3021. 9/28/01 mor Griffin, Jonathan; Queensbury, WAS; Queensbury, WAS;
                      co-mees 5354, 7901.   (D:98)
3022. 5/2/01   gee Griffith, Micah, Junr.; Whitehall, WAS. See 8540.
3023. 10/26/73 mor Griffiths, John, Esq.; Kingsbury, CHA; Kingsbury, CHA;
                      mee 1930.   (A:12)
3024. 10/6/85 gee Griffiths, Micah; ---, ---. See 7055.
3025. 10/6/85 gee Griffiths, Thomas; ---, ---. See 7055.
3026. 5/22/98 mor Griswold, Ephraim; Westfield, WAS; Westfield, WAS;
                      mee 8798.   (B:263)
3027. 9/4/02   mor Griswold, Stephen; ---, ---; Elizabethtown, ESS; mee 5520.
                                                                  (A:87)
3028. 7/5/88   gee Griswould, John; Westfield, WAS. See 2241.
3029. 4/17/92 gor Griswould, John; Westfield, WAS; Westfield, WAS; gee 1998.
                                                                  (A:471)
3030. 5/19/96 gee Groesbeck, Alada. See 3032.
3031. 4/3/97   gor Groesbeck, Alada, See 3033.
3032. 5/19/96 gee Groesbeck, William (w. Alada); Cambridge, WAS. See 8142.
3033. 4/3/97   gor Groesbeck, William (w. Alada); ---, REN; Cambridge, WAS;
                      gee 8143.   (C-2:339)
3034. 9/20/73 gee Groome, Francis, shopkeeper; City of N.Y. See 7885.
3035. 10/20/85 gee Groome, Francis; City of N.Y. See 4244.
3036. 4/24/88 gee Grover, Abigail. See 3039.
3037. 4/22/88 gee Grover, John, Capt.; Granville, WAS. See 2374.
3038. 4/22/88 mor Grover, John; Granville, WAS; Granville, WAS; mee 2375.
                                                                  (A:115)
3039. 4/24/88 gor Grover, John, Capt. (w. Abigail); Granville, WAS; Granville,
                      WAS; gee 3723.   (A:152)
3040. 4/27/87 mor Grover, John, Junr.; Granville, WAS; Granville, WAS;
                      mee 8622.   (A:63)
3041. 7/13/92 mor Grover, Joseph, farmer; Granville, WAS. See 3402.
3042. 12/29/94 gor Grover, Joseph; Granville, WAS. See 1850.
3043. 12/11/90 gee Gummers, Asa; ---, ---. See 7459.
3044. 12/13/90 mor Gummers, Asa; Hebron, WAS. See 5505.
3045. 3/23/98 --- Gumstock, ---, widow. See 7961.
3046. 3/23/98 --- Gumstock, Abel, dec'd. See 7961.
3047. 4/30/93 --- Gunn, George, dec'd. See 1220.
3048. 7/24/87 gee Guthrie, George; Hebron, WAS. See 1451.
3049. 7/2/92   gor Guthrie, George, yeoman; Hebron, WAS; Hebron, WAS;
                      gee 5068.   (A:352)
3050. 5/1/00   mee Cuthric, George, yeoman; Hebron, WAS. See 8669.
3051. 4/3/94   mor Guthrie, Martha. See 3054.
3052. 1/22/02 mor Guthrie, Samuel, Senr. (w. Sarah); ---, ---; Hebron, WAS;
                      mee 6101.   (D:185)
3053. 1/22/02 mor Guthrie, Sarah. See 3052.
3054. 4/3/94   mor Guthrie, William (w. Martha); Salem, WAS; Salem, WAS;
                      mee 2916.   (A:488)
3055. 7/1/94   mor Guy, Henry, merchant; Argyle, WAS; Saratoga Pat., WAS;
                      mee 786.   (A:498)
3056. 12/9/01 mor Guy, Henry; Argyle, WAS; Argyle, WAS; mee 7654. (D:129)
3057. 6/30/02 gor Guy, Henry (w. Hepzibah); Argyle, WAS; Argyle, WAS;
                      gee 1579.   (F:281)
3058. 6/30/02 gor Guy, Hepzibah. See 3057.
3059. 3/7/99   gee Hadock, Henry, merchant; City of N.Y. See 6284.
3060. 5/26/98 gor Haff, John; Peru, CLI; Peru, CLI; gee 2442.   (B:136)
3061. 5/28/98 mee Haff, John; Peru, CLI. See 2443.

81

3062. 12/26/91 gee Haffner, John; Saratoga, SAR. See 7710.
3063. 9/15/00 gee Haggert, Andrew; Argyle, WAS. See 4373.
3064. 11/1/98 mor Haight, Aaron; Queensbury, WAS; Queensbury, WAS; mee 5392.
(C:119)
3065. 9/1/98 gee Haight, Henry; Willsborough, CLI. See 2654.
3066. 2/4/00 gor Haight, Henry; Willsborough, CLI; Plattsburgh, CLI; gee
7985. (B:328)
3067. 8/7/98 mor Haight, Samuel; ---, CLI; Old Military Township #7
(Chateaugay), CLI; co-mees 6858, 8090. (A:337)
3068. 8/15/98 gee Haight, Samuel, farmer; ---, CLI. See 6859.
3069. 8/16/98 mor Haight, Samuel; ---, CLI; Old Military Township #7
(Chateaugay), CLI; co-mees 6860, 8092. (A:339)
3070. 4/30/00 gor Haight, Samuel, farmer; Chateaugay, CLI; Old Military
Township #7 (Chateaugay), CLI; gee 141. (B:259)
3071. 7/4/01 mor Haight, Samuel, farmer; Chateaugay, CLI; Chateaugay, CLI;
mee 142. (B:35)
3072. 6/11/73 mee Hake, Samuel; City of N.Y. See 7336.
3073. 7/6/88 mor Hale, Jacob; Granville, WAS; Granville, WAS; mee 2381.
(A:101)
3074. 5/13/00 mor Hale, Lydia. See 3076.
3075. 5/13/00 mor Hale, Nancy. See 3077.
3076. 5/13/00 mor Hale, Reuben (w. Lydia); Granville, WAS; Granville, WAS;
mee 1541. (C:130)
3077. 5/13/00 mor Hale, Samuel (w, Nancy), farmer; Granville, WAS; Granville,
WAS; mee 1541. (C:130)
3078. 7/28/00 gee Hale, William; Rutland, RUT, VT. See 6553.
3079. 7/29/00 mor Hale, William; Rutland, RUT, VT; Champlain, CLI; mee 6554.
(B:8)
3080. 10/26/91 gee Hall, Burges; Cambridge, WAS. See 7355.
3081. 3/15/92 gee Hall, Burgess; Cambridge, WAS. See 1705.
3082. 3/9/97 gee Hall, Burgess; Cambridge, WAS. See 1707.
3083. 6/26/98 mor Hall, Diadema. See 3090.
3084. 7/3/01 gee Hall, Ezra; Plattsburgh, CLI. See 94.
3085. 5/14/01 mor Hall, Ira; Granville, WAS; Granville, WAS; mee 4144. (D:45)
3086. 1/26/01 gor Hall, John (w. Mary); Argyle, WAS; Argyle, WAS; gee 4173.
(E:95)
3087. 1/26/01 mee Hall, John; Argyle, WAS. See 4174.
3088. 5/15/01 mor Hall, John (w. Mary), yeoman; Hebron, WAS; Hebron, WAS;
mee 3120. (D:43)
3089. 7/10/84 gor Hall, Jonathan; ---, ---; Black Creek Dist., CHA; gee 4784.
(A:115)
3090. 6/26/98 mor Hall, Jonathan (w. Diadema), farmer; Hartford, WAS;
Hartford, WAS; mee 1493. (B:267)
3091. 2/23/95 gee Hall, Joseph; Cambridge, WAS. See 2755.
3092. 5/2/96 gee Hall, Liman; Cambridge, WAS. See 2100a.
3093. 1/26/01 gor Hall, Mary. See 3086.
3094. 5/15/01 mor Hall, Mary. See 3088.
3095. 12/18/99 mor Hall, Sarah. See 3097.
3096. 12/18/96 gee Hall, Thomas, yeoman; Hebron, WAS. See 6810.
3097. 12/18/99 mor Hall, Thomas (w. Sarah), yeoman; Hebron, WAS; Hebron, WAS;
mee 8115. (C:128)
3098. 10/21/00 mor Hall, Thomas, farmer; Pittstown, REN; Argyle, WAS;
mee 1296. (C:132)
3099. 7/3/01 gee Hall, Thomas; Plattsburgh, CLI. See 94.
3100. 12/2/99 mee Hallet, Richard S., merchant; City of N.Y. See 1857.
3101. 1/9/93 gor Hallett, Jonah, gentleman; New Town, Quebec, Canada;
---, WAS; gee 8578. (B-2:40)
3102. 7/26/98 mee Hallett, Richard S.; City of N.Y. See 8699.
3103. 9/26/94 gee Hally, Nicholas, farmer; Willsborough, CLI. See 3469.
3104. 2/2/02 mor Halsey, Epinetus; Plattsburgh, CLI; Plattsburgh, CLI;
co-mees 328, 5796. (B:64)
3105. 4/8/96 gee Halsey, Frederick; Plattsburgh, CLI. See 235.
3106. 1/16/97 gor Halsey, Frederick, "minister of the gospel"; Plattsburgh,
CLI. See 8772.
3107. 7/3/98 mor Halstead, James; Chateaugay, CLI; Old Military Township #7
(Chateaugay), CLI; co-mees 272, 314. (A:308)

3108. 6/2/00 mor Halstead, John; ---, ---; Elizabethtown, ESS; mee 5764.
                                                                    (A:12)
3109. 5/13/01 gor Halstead, John; Ferrisburgh, ADD, VT. See 6416.
3110. 6/22/01 gor Halstead, John; Elizabethtown, ESS. See 6417.
3111. 5/13/01 gor Halstead, Phebe; Ferrisburgh, ADD, VT. See 6416.
3112. 6/22/01 gor Halstead, Phebe; Elizabethtown, ESS. See 6417.
3113. 5/9/95 gor Hamilton, George (w. Margaret D.), gentleman; Cambridge,
                   WAS; Cambridge, WAS; gee 373.   (B-2:475)
3114. 9/7/85 gor Hamilton, James, Senr.; ---, ALB; ---, WAS; gee 4772.
                                                          (C-1:49)
3115. 12/16/73 gor Hamilton, John, farmer; ---, CHA. See 8684.
3116. 3/30/74 gor Hamilton, John, farmer; ---, CHA. See 8685.
3117. 10/26/92 gee Hamilton, John; Hebron, WAS. See 8649.
3118. 7/4/99 mee Hamilton, John; Lansingburgh, REN. See 1454.
3119. 8/1/99 mor Hamilton, John; Champlain, CLI; Champlain, CLI; mee 5087.
                                                        (A:399)
3120. 5/15/01 mee Hamilton, John, Esq.; Hebron, WAS. See 3088.
3121. 6/1/92 gee Hamilton, Joseph; Hebron, WAS. See 8741.
3122. 7/2/92 gor Hamilton, Joseph, farmer; Hebron, WAS; Hebron, WAS;
                   co-gor 7681; gee 7975.   (A:448)
3123. 10/19/01 mee Hamilton, Joseph, yeoman; Hebron, WAS. See 5620.
3124. 5/19/98 gor Hamilton, Margaret, "widow, and one of the daughters of
                   Elizabeth McNeil"; ---, ---; Argyle, WAS; gee 4588.
                                                   (C-2:300)
3125. 9/2/01 --- Hamilton, Margaret. See 2833.
3126. 5/9/95 gor Hamilton, Margaret D. See 3113.
3127. 1/28/93 gor Hamilton, Richard; Salem, WAS. See 4769.
3128. 4/12/96 mor Hamilton, Richard; Lansingburgh, REN. See 5513.
3129. 9/7/69 gor Hamilton, Robert; ---, ---. See 7955.
3130. 4/20/73 gor Hamilton, Robert; ---, ---. See 7957.
3131. 5/8/81 gee Hamilton, William; Black Creek Dist., CHA. See 1431.
3132. 9/4/96 gee Hammand, William; Cambridge, WAS. See 7133.
3133. 5/6/90 mee Hammersley, Andrew; City of N.Y. See 4688.
3134. 2/6/98 gor Hammond, Dorithy. See 3135.
3135. 2/6/98 gor Hammond, William (w. Dorithy), yeoman; Cambridge, WAS;
                   Cambridge Pat., WAS; gee 4667.   (D:298)
3136. 10/18/02 --- Hamtramck, John F., "Colonel of the First United States
                   Regiment, and now residing at Detroit in the County of
                   Wayne, in the territory of the Northwest United States."
                   This person appoints Barent Bleecker and John R. Bleecker,
                   merchants, of Albany (ALB) as attorneys for the sale of
                   his lands in Clinton County.   (B:376)
3137. 11/6/98 mor Hanchet, Oliver, farmer; Chateaugay, CLI; Old Military
                   Township #6 (Clinton), CLI; mee 4021.   (A:382)
3138. 2/2/00 mor Hanchett, Oliver; Chateaugay, CLI; Old Military Township
                   #6 (Clinton), CLI; mee 6628.   (A:409)
3139. 12/13/99 mor Handley, Nicholas, physician; Plattsburgh, CLI; Plattsburgh,
                   CLI; mee 321.   (A:419)
3140. 7/23/96 mor Haner, Jacob, farmer; Easton, WAS; Saratoga Pat., WAS;
                   mee 3689.   (B:137)
3141. 11/7/00 mor Hanford, Shubal, yeoman; Granville, WAS; Granville, WAS;
                   co-mees 355, 8174. Co-mortgagees are overseers of the
                   poor, Granville.   (D:33b)
3142. 5/23/01 mor Hanks, Enoch; Argyle, WAS. See 3144. Two contracts this
                   date involving these persons.
3143. 5/2/96 gee Hanks, Isaac; Argyle, WAS. See 2100a. Two contracts this
                   date involving these persons.
3144. 5/23/01 mor Hanks, Isaac; Argyle, WAS; Argyle, WAS; co-mor 3142; mees
                   4549 (D:51) and 5224 (D:53). (two contracts)
3145. 1/1/87 gee Hanna, Nathaniel, yeoman; "now of the District of Cambridge,
                   late from Ireland." See 8661.
3145a. 9/11/95 gor Hanna, Nathaniel, yeoman; Cambridge Dist., WAS; Cambridge
                   Dist., WAS; gee 374.   (B-2:471)
3146. 10/25/91 --- Hannegan, Elizabeth; Argyle, WAS. See 4201.
3147. 10/25/91 --- Hannegan, John. Husband of Elizabeth Hannegan in 3146.
3148. 4/5/99 mor Hard, Philo; Arlington, BEN, VT; Cambridge, WAS; mee 8837.
                                                     (C:124)

3149. 12/5/89 gor Harkness, David. Husband of Sarah Harkness in 3152.
3150. 7/16/94 mor Harkness, Isabella. See 3156.
3151. 5/10/00 gee Harkness, James, farmer; Salem, WAS. See 2986.
3152. 12/5/89 gor Harkness, Sarah; Pelham, ---, MA. See 747.
3153. 9/10/90 gee Harkness, William, merchant; ---, WAS. See 6214.
<u>3154.</u> 9/10/90 mor Harkness, William, merchant; ---, WAS; <u>Salem, WAS;</u>
            mee 6215.   (A:260)
3155. 6/6/94 gee Harkness, William, Esq.; Salem, WAS. See 6542 and 6543.
<u>3156.</u> 7/16/94 mor Harkness, William, Esq. (w. Isabella); Salem, WAS; <u>Salem,</u>
            <u>WAS;</u> mee 1399.   (A:495)
3157. 10/12/84 gee Harlow, Isaac; East Bay, WAS. See 8231.
3158. 7/20/87 gee Harlow, Isaac; ---, ---. See 100.
3159. 9/17/88 gee Harlow, Isaac; Whitehall, WAS. See 8240.
<u>3160.</u> 11/3/96 mor Harlow, Isaac, Major; Whitehall, WAS; <u>Whitehall, WAS;</u>
            co-mees 8298, 8312.   (B:102)
3161. 11/19/83 gee Harnden, Samuel; ---, CHA. See 8545.
<u>3162.</u> 7/24/92 mor Harndon, Samuel; Granville, WAS; <u>Granville, WAS;</u> mee 8526.
                                                   (A:344)
3163. 5/10/91 gee Harper, John, farmer; Kingsbury, WAS. See 2124.
3164. 11/2/01 gee Harrington, Henry, yeoman; Cambridge, WAS. See 674.
<u>3165.</u> 11/20/95 mor Harrington, Preserved; Easton, WAS; <u>Easton, WAS;</u> mee 4239.
                                                   (B:270)
3166. 12/28/96 mor Harrington, Richard, farmer; Easton, WAS. See 3665.
3167. 2/26/96 mor Harris, Ebenezer, joiner; Salem, WAS. See 3168.
<u>3168.</u> 2/26/96 mor Harris, Edward, Esq.; Salem, WAS; <u>Salem, WAS;</u> co-mor 3167;
            mee 2128.   (C:125)
<u>3169.</u> 4/5/02 mor Harris, James, farmer; Lansingburgh, REN; <u>Hebron, WAS;</u>
            mee 3863.   (D:152)
3170. 9/18/97 mee Harris, Joshua; Kingsbury, WAS. See 2383.
3171. 11/12/00 mee Harris, Joshua, farmer; Kingsbury, WAS. See 5396 and 8262.
<u>3172.</u> 7/19/88 gor Harris, Moses, cooper; Queensbury Dist., WAS; <u>land "east</u>
            <u>side of Hudson's River", WAS;</u> gee 2156.   (A:169)
<u>3173.</u> 10/14/89 gor Harris, Moses; Queensbury, WAS; <u>---, WAS;</u> gee 5394. (A:469)
<u>3174.</u> 2/20/97 mor Harris, Moses, yeoman; ---, WAS; <u>---, WAS;</u> mee 922. (B:185)
3175. 5/25/85 gee Harris, Moses, Junr.; ---, ---. See 7055.
<u>3176.</u> 7/15/86 mor Harris, Moses, Junr.; ---, ---; <u>Argyle(?), WAS;</u> mee 4081.
                                                   (A:34)
<u>3177.</u> 11/3/88 gor Harris, Moses, Junr., cooper; ---, WAS; <u>Westfield Dist., WAS;</u>
            gee 4974.   (B-2:37)
<u>3178.</u> 2/5/89 mor Harris, Moses, Junr.; ---, ---; <u>Westfield, WAS;</u> mee 8566.
                                                   (A:173)
<u>3179.</u> 12/15/89 gor Harris, Moses, Junr.; Queensbury Dist., WAS; <u>---, WAS;</u>
            gee 5646.   (A:468)
<u>3180.</u> 10/5/90 gor Harris, Moses, Junr.; ---, WAS; <u>---, WAS;</u> gee 7201.
                                                 (B-2:330)
<u>3181.</u> 10/25/90 gor Harris, Moses, Junr.; ---, WAS; <u>---, WAS;</u> gee 7202.
                                                 (B-2:332)
<u>3182.</u> 9/1/92 gor Harris, Moses, Junr., farmer; Westfield, WAS; <u>---, WAS;</u>
            co-gees 7200, 7204.   (B-2:335)
<u>3183.</u> 7/27/93 gor Harris, Moses, Junr., yeoman; Westfield, WAS; <u>Westfield,</u>
            <u>WAS;</u> gee 7207.   (B-2:337)
3184. 5/16/87 --- Harris, Thomas, dec'd.; ---, ---. See 10.
<u>3185.</u> 2/10/72 mor Harris, Timothy; Kingsbury, ALB; <u>Kingsbury, ALB;</u> mee 3617.
                                                   (A:10)
<u>3186.</u> 5/6/01 gor Harris, William; Queensbury, WAS; <u>Westfield, WAS;</u> gee 3518.
                                                 (E:314)
3187. 10/21/96 mee Harrison, Mary, widow; City of N.Y. See 8594.
<u>3188.</u> 5/7/88 gor Harrison, Richard, Esq.; City of N.Y.; <u>Argyle, ALB</u> (sic);
            gee 1744.   (A:67)
3189. 6/29/90 mee Harrison, Richard, Esq.; City of N.Y. See 8658.
3190. 10/30/01 gee Harsha, John; ---, ---. See 4572.
3191. 5/30/85 gee Hart, Henry; ---, ---. See 7055.
3192. 1/3/86 mee Hart, Henry; ---, ---. See 7921.
<u>3193.</u> 2/23/86 gor Hart, Henry, merchant; ---, WAS; <u>---, WAS;</u> gees 7331 (A:203),
            7922 (C-2:175). (two contracts)

84

3194. 3/1/86   mee Hart, Henry; ---, ---. See 3990 and 7332.
3195. 3/6/86   mee Hart, Henry; ---, ---. See 7862.
3196. 3/9/86   mee Hart, Henry. See 119, 214, and 8376.
3197. 7/6/86   gor Hart, Henry; Kingsbury, WAS; Kingsbury, WAS; gee 8518a.
                                                              (A:99)
3198. 7/6/86   mor Hart, Henry; Kingsbury, WAS; Kingsbury, WAS; mee 8559.
                                                        (Deed Book B-1:249)
3199. 4/9/88   mee Hart, Henry; Kingsbury, WAS. See 2641.
3200. 4/29/88 gor Hart, Henry; Kingsbury, WAS; Whitehall, WAS; gee 2642.
                                                              (A:97)
3201. 5/8/88   gee Hart, Peleg; Tiverton, ---, RI. See 2878.
3202. 12/18/95 gor Hartwicke, John Burke, farmer; Plattsburgh, CLI; Champlain,
                        CLI; gee 5742.   (A:393)
3203. 2/8/96   gee Harvey, Benjamin; Hebron, WAS. See 4185.
3204. 1/1/01   --- Harvey, James. See 3952.
3205. 7/12/01 --- Harvey, James. See 3953.
3206. 5/26/02 --- Harvey, James, merchant; Salem, WAS. See 3864.
3207. --/--/87 gee Harvey, Moses; ---, ---. See 7055.
3208. 11/15/96 mee Harvey, Thomas, grocer; City of N.Y. See 5064.
3209. 4/21/97 mee Harvey, Thomas, gracer; City of N.Y. See 564.
3210. 4/25/93 gor Hasbrook, Isaac; ---, ---. See 7168.
3211. 9/10/93 mee Hasbrouck, Isaac; ---, ---. See 3906.
3212. 10/16/90 mor Haskins, Eliphalet; Plattsburgh, CLI; Plattsburgh, CLI;
                        mee 6265.   (A:58)
3213. 5/1/02   mor Haskins, Joseph, farmer; Chester, WAS; Chester, WAS;
                        mee 7775.   (D:205)
3214. 2/27/98 mor Haskins, Lemuel, farmer; ---, CLI; Old Military Township
                        #7 (Chateaugay), CLI; mee 5692.   (A:258)
3215. 12/22/98 mor Haskins, Lemuel, farmer; Chateaugay, CLI; Old Military
                        Township #7 (Chateaugay), CLI; co-mees 6863, 8095.
                                                              (A:360)
3216. 11/15/91 gee Hasstun, Jeremiah; Beekmantown, CLI. See 82.
3217. 11/8/91 gee Hastings, James; Cambridge, WAS. See 6707.
3218. 11/9/91 gor Hastings, James, yeoman; Cambridge, WAS; Cambridge, WAS;
                        gee 691.   (B-2; 361)
3219. 11/9/91 mee Hastings, James, yeoman; Cambridge, WAS. See 692.
3220. 11/9/91 mor Hastings, James; Cambridge, Dist., WAS; Anguasancook Pat.,
                        WAS; mee 6708.   (A:314)
3221. 1/28/83 gee Hatch, Benjamin; Kingsbury Dist., CHA. See 5356.
3222. 8/18/83 gor Hatch, Benjamin, yeoman; Great Barrington, BER, MA.
                        Provincial Pat., CHA; gee 2880.   (B-1:125)
3223. 6/1/91   gee Hatch, Charles; Willsborough, CLI. See 6450.
3224. 4/8/93   gor Hatch, Charles; Willsborough, CLI; Willsborough, CLI;
                        gee 2503.   (A:487)
3225. 5/6/94   mee Hatch, Charles; Willsborough, CLI. See 2575.
3226. 1/4/98   gee Hatch, Charles; Willsborough, CLI. See 2504.
3227. 11/21/98 mor Hatch, Charles; Willsborough, CLI; Willsborough, CLI;
                        mee 6492.   (A:374)
3228. 6/7/99   mee Hatch, Charles; ---, ---. See 5454 and 8227.
3229. 11/12/99 mee Hatch, Charles; ---, ---. See 2579.
3230. 8/28/00 mee Hatch, Charles; ---, ---. See 4211.
3231. 3/6/02   mee Hatch, Charles; ---, ---. See 2407.
3232. 6/1/02   gee Hatch, Charles, farmer; Willsborough, ESS. See 2408.
3233. 6/3/02   gee Hatch, Charles; Willsborough, ESS. See 1522.
3234. 7/6/97   mor Hatch, Henry (w. Rhody), farmer; Granville, WAS; Granville,
                        WAS; co-mees 76, 2937, 2952.   (B:204)
3235. 9/21/01 mor Hatch, Lewis (w. Mary); ---, WAS; Granville, WAS; mee 1693.
                                                              (D:96)
3236. 9/21/01 mor Hatch, Mary. See 3235.
3237. 7/6/97   mor Hatch, Rhody. See 3234.
3238. 6/7/98   --- Hatfield, Moses; Goshen ORA; Plattsburgh, CLI. This person
                        appoints Nathaniel Platt of Plattsburgh to act as his
                        attorney to sell the above lands.   (B:219)
3239. 4/26/00 mee Hatfield, Moses; Goshen, ORA. See 213.
3240. 6/9/98   mor Hathaway, Abial (w. Elizabeth), farmer; Hartford, WAS;
                        Hartford, WAS; mee 1492.   (B:266)

85

3241. 6/9/98   mor Hathaway, Elizabeth. See 3240.
3242. 1/7/99   gor Hatheway, Abial (w. Elizabeth); ---, WAS; Hartford, WAS;
                       gee 7680.   (E:451)
3243. 1/7/99   gor Hatheway, Elizabeth. See 3242.
3244. 9/7/98   mor Haven, Samuel; Willsborough, CLI; Willsborough, CLI;
                       mee 6491.   (A:375)
3245. 2/11/92   gee Havens, Cornelius, Junr. See 48.
3246. 2/11/92   mor Havens, Cornelius, Junr. See 3249.
3247. 9/12/97   gee Havens, Cornelius, Junr.; ---, ---. See 96.
3248. 9/29/98   mor Havens, Cornelius, Junr.; ---, ---; Willsborough, CLI;
                       mee 2818.   (A:353)
3249. 2/11/92   mor Havens, Samuel, yeoman; Willsborough, CLI; Judd Pat., CLI;
                       co-mor 3246; mee 49.   (A:91)
3250. 2/11/92   gee Havens, Samuel; Willsborough, CLI. See 48.
3251. 3/3/84   gee Hawha(?), John. See 1437.
3252. 10/20/98 mor Hawkes, Azur; ---, CLI; Old Military Township #7
                       (Chateaugay), CLI; co-mees 6861, 8093.   (A:369)
3253. 6/4/76   gee Hawkins, Joseph, gunsmith; Kingsbury, WAS. See 3616.
3254. 5/11/98   mor Hawkins, Joseph; Kingsbury, WAS; Kingsbury, WAS; mee 8797.
                                                                      (B:269)
3255. 9/15/98   gor Hawkins, Joseph (w. Rachel); Kingsbury, WAS; Kingsbury,
                       WAS; gee 1157.   (C-2:327)
3256. 9/15/98   gor Hawkins, Rachel. See 3255.
3257. 10/3/96   gee Hawkins, Thomas; Brookfield, CLI. See 7746.
3258. 10/3/96   mor Hawkins, Thomas; Willsborough, CLI; Willsborough, CLI;
                       mee 7747.   (A:200)
3259. 10/15/95 mor Hawley, Ichabod, yeoman; ---, WAS; Provincial Pat., WAS;
                       co-mors 1732, 3780, 4993; mee 586.   (A:606)
3260. 7/1/94   gor Hawley, Zadock; Ernesttown, Dist. of Midland, Upper Canada;
                       Queensbury, WAS; gee 964.   (B-2:343)
3261. 5/20/85   mee Hawshurst, William, merchant; City of N.Y. See 7324.
3262. 5/6/96   gor Hay, Catharine. See 3275.
3263. 10/12/90 gee Hay, James, merchant; Cambridge, WAS. See 8852.
3264. 11/29/92 mor Hay, James; Cambridge, WAS; Cambridge, WAS; mee 8854. (A:395)
3265. 1/1/96   gor Hay, James (w. Mary); Cambridge Dist., WAS; Cambridge Dist.,
                       WAS; gee 3273.   (E:391)
3266. 1/1/96   mor Hay, James, yeoman; Cambridge Dist., WAS; Cambridge Dist.,
                       WAS; mee 883.   (B:42)
3267. 8/10/01   mee Hay, James, farmer; Cambridge, WAS. See 6314.
3268. 10/15/91 gee Hay, John, farmer; Easton, WAS. See 4237.
3269. 11/16/01 mor Hay, John, farmer; Argyle, WAS; Argyle, WAS; mee 4593.
                                                                      (D:117)
3270. 1/1/96   gor Hay, Mary. See 3265.
3271. 1/29/87   mor Hay, Udney, Esq.; ---, ---; land "west side of Lake George",
                       WAS; mee 3740.   (A:39)
3272. 3/20/92   gee Hay, William, merchant; Cambridge, WAS. See 2613.
3273. 1/1/96   gee Hay, William, merchant; Cambridge Dist., WAS. See 3265.
3274. 4/25/96   gor Hay, William; Cambridge, WAS; Cambridge, WAS; gee 2740.
                                                                      (C-2:344)
3275. 5/6/96   gor Hay, William (w. Catharine), merchant; Cambridge, WAS;
                       Cambridge, WAS; gee 8359.   (C-2:236)
3276. 4/8/01   gee Hay, William, merchant; Cambridge, WAS. See 1085.
3277. 4/8/01   mor Hay, William, merchant; Cambridge, WAS; Cambridge, WAS;
*3277a.   *   mee 1086.   (D:32)
3278. 2/9/95   mee Haydock, Henry, merchant; City of N.Y. See 824.
3279. 6/16/00   gor Haydock, Henry, "who was called Henry Haydock Junior in the
                       life time of his father", merchant; City of N.Y. See 6047.
**3280a 3280. 6/16/00 ---, Haydock, Henry, Junr. See 3279.
        3281. 5/10/97 mee** Haydock, John W.; City of N.Y. See 6350.
        3282. 10/1/01 mee   Haydock, Joseph; City of N.Y. See 662, 3720, 3721, 5124,
                              5363, 6658.
3283. 7/13/01   gor Hayes, Jonathan (w. Unice); Granville, WAS; Granville, WAS;
                       gee 4807.   (E:331)
3284. 7/13/01   mee Hayes, Jonathan, yeoman; Granville, WAS. See 4808.
3285. 8/17/01   mor Hayes, Jonathan; Granville, WAS; Plattsburgh, CLI; mee 512.
* 3277a. 8/2/98   mee Haydock, Eben; City of N.Y. See 2522. /// (B:40)
**3280a. 8/2/98   mee Haydock, James; City of N.Y. See 2522.

86

3286. 7/13/01 gor Hayes, Unice. See 3283.
3287. 1/11/94 mor Haynes, Jonathan; Cambridge, WAS; Hoosick Pat., WAS;
                  mee 7707.   (A:497)
3288. 8/1/01 gor Hayward, Rachel. See 3289.
3289. 8/1/01 gor Hayward, Samuel (w. Rachel), blacksmith; Cambridge, WAS;
                  Cambridge, WAS; gee 6395.   (F:218)
3290. 2/18/01 mor Hayworth, George; Peru, CLI; Peru, CLI; mee 5883. (B:12)
3291. 12/8/89 gor Hazard, Ebenezer, gentleman; ---, ---. See 3443.
3292. 3/1/90 gor Hazard, Ebenezer, Esq.; City of N.Y. See 3448.
3293. 2/6/88 mee Hazard, John, mariner; City of N.Y. See 6145.
3294. 4/5/92 --- Hazen, ---, Colonel. See 4016.
3295. 12/18/98 mor Hazen, Levi; South Hero, CHI, VT; Champlain, CLI; mee 5084.
                                                                  (A:402)
3296. 8/18/92 --- Hazen, Moses (regimental commander, Rev. War); ---, ---.
                  See 2134.
3297. 6/12/90 --- Hazen, Moses, Esq.; ---, ---. See 2891.
3298. 10/25/88 gee Heath, Jesse, merchant; Willsborough, CLI. See 1887.
3299. 5/3/94 mor Heath, Jesse, yeoman; Willsborough, CLI; Willsborough, CLI;
                  mee 5067.   (A:133)
3300. 12/6/00 gee Heath, Joseph, yeoman; Hartford, WAS. See 6947.
3301. 4/6/83 gor Heath, Joseph, Junr.; Cambridge, WAS; Cambridge, WAS;
                  gee 8201.   (D:313)
3302. 1/31/93 gor Heath, Joseph, Junr. (w. Mahitable); Cambridge, WAS;
                  Cambridge, WAS; gee 8403.   (C-2:171)
3303. 5/2/96 mor Heath, Joseph, Junr.; Argyle, WAS; Argyle, WAS; co-mees
                  1290, 2101, 2216, 5584.   (B:182)
3304. 5/14/96 mee Heath, Joseph, Junr., yeoman; Cambridge, WAS. See 5378.
3305. 5/17/96 mee Heath, Joseph, Junr., gentleman; Cambridge, WAS. See 2356.
3306. 12/12/96 gee Heath, Joseph, Junr., farmer; Argyle, WAS. See 2104.
3307. 6/27/97 gee Heath, Joseph, Junr., farmer; Argyle, WAS. See 8041.
3308. 8/26/97 gor Heath, Joseph, Junr. (w. Mabel), farmer; Argyle, WAS;
                  Cambridge, WAS; gee 7046. Two contracts this date
                  involving these three persons. (C-2:251), (C-2:287)
3309. 8/26/97 gor Heath, Mabel. See 3308. (two contracts)
3310. 1/31/93 gor Heath, Mahitable. See 3302.
3311. 6/29/92 gor Heath, Winslow, farmer; Cambridge, WAS; Cambridge, Pat.,
                  WAS; gee 8525.   (E:275)
3312. 5/2/96 mor Heath, Winslow, farmer; Cambridge, WAS; Argyle, WAS;
                  co-mees 1290, 2101, 2216, 5584.   (C:126)
3313. 7/2/92 gee Hefford, Webster; Salem, WAS. See 4065.
3314. 3/6/98 mee Height, Joshua; Queensbury, WAS. See 5663.
3315. 7/1/00 mor Heincock, Uriah; ---, ---; ---, ESS; mee 5572. (A:16)
3316. 9/6/93 gor Henderson, Abigail. See 3326.
3317. 11/6/93 gor Henderson, Abigail. See 3327.
3318. 10/20/86 mee Henderson, David; Kingsbury, WAS. See 4693.
3319. 11/27/87 mee Henderson, David; Kingsbury, WAS. See 3334.
3320. 12/15/94 mee Henderson, David; Hartford, WAS. See 5516.
3321. 9/21/97 mor Henderson, David, yeoman; Hartford, WAS; Hartford, WAS;
                  mee 1148.   (B:217)
3322. 1/27/83 gor Henderson, James; New Perth, CHA; New Perth, CHA; gee 87.
                                                                  (B-1:78)
3323. 3/7/85 mee Henderson, James; ---, ---. See 3336.
3324. 3/14/86 gee Henderson, James; Salem, WAS. See 8289.
3325. 12/15/91 gee Henderson, James; Westfield, WAS. See 7452.
3326. 9/6/93 gor Henderson, James (w. Abigail), farmer; Salem, WAS; Salem,
                  WAS; gee 755.   (B-2:281)
3327. 11/6/93 gor Henderson, James (w. Abigail); Salem, WAS; Salem, WAS;
                  gee 756.   (B-2:283)
3328. 3/20/92 gee Henderson, James, Junr.; Salem, WAS. See 3330.
3329. 1/23/94 gor Henderson, James, Junr.; Salem, WAS; Salem, WAS; gee 4432.
                                                                  (B-2:130)
3330. 3/20/92 gor Henderson, James. Senr.; Salem, WAS; Salem, WAS; gee 3328.
                                                                  (A:264)
3331. 3/22/92 gee Henderson, John, yeoman; Westfield, WAS. See 1115.
3332. 3/20/98 gee Henderson, John, farmer; ---, WAS. See 931.
3333. 4/19/99 mor Henderson, John, farmer; Hartford, WAS; Provincial Pat., WAS;
                  mee 932.   (C:123)

87

3334. 11/27/87 mor Henderson, Sarah; Salem, WAS; a reference to personal
                     property?; mee 3319.   (A:68)
3335. 3/7/85 gee Henderson, William, yeoman; New Perth, WAS. See 8569.
3336. 3/7/85 mor Henderson, William; ---, ---; New Perth Dist., WAS;
                     mee 3323.   (A:75)
3337. 7/1/85 gee Henman(?), Lewis; ---, ---. See 7055.
3338. 5/12/01 --- Henry, Enoch F.; ---, ---. See 3341.
3339. 5/19/95 mee Henry, Robert R., merchant; Albany, ALB. See 8129.
3340. 12/13/96 mee Henry, Robert R., merchant; Albany, ALB. See 3529.
3341. 5/12/01 gee Henry, Sawtell T., "son of Enoch F. Henry"; Willsborough,
                     ESS. See 3476.
3342. 7/1/85 gee Herington, Peter; ---, ---. See 7055.
3343. 9/5/81 gee Hernden, Samuel; Granville, CHA. See 8543.
3344. 9/5/81 gee Herndon, Jonathan; Granville, CHA. See 8543.
3345. 2/14/00 gee Herring, Abraham, merchant. See 6323.
3346. 10/28/96 gor Herrington, Amasa; Easton, WAS. See 3353.
3347. 2/12/98 mor Herrington, Charles, Easton, WAS; Easton, WAS; co-mees
                     3356, 3666.   (C:128)
3348. 10/28/96 gor Herrington, Eleazer; Easton, WAS. See 3353.
3349. 9/5/81 gee Herrington, James; ---, CHA. See 8543.
3350. 7/2/85 mor Herrington, James; Skenesborough, WAS; Skenesborough, WAS;
                     mee 8556.   (Deed Book B-1:222)
3351. 10/28/96 gor Herrington, Nicholas; Easton, WAS. See 3353.
3352. 11/17/97 mor Herrington, Nicholas; Easton, WAS. See 3354.
3353. 10/28/96 gor Herrington, Preserved, Junr; Easton, WAS; Saratoga Pat.,
                     WAS; co-gors 3346, 3348, 3351; gee 2605.   (D:180)
3354. 11/17/97 mor Herrington, Preserved, Junr.; Easton, WAS; Saratoga Pat.,
                     WAS; co-mor 3352; mee 7218.   (B:251)
3355. 7/5/99 gor Herrington, Preserved, Senr.; Easton, WAS; Easton, WAS;
                     gee 2606.   (D:197)
3356. 2/12/98 mee Herrington, Richard; Easton, WAS. See 3347.
3357. 10/28/84 gor Herrinton, James, farmer; Granville, WAS; Granville, WAS;
                     gee 2111.   (E:251)
3358. 12/16/99 gor Herroun, John; Cambridge, WAS; Cambridge, WAS; gee 3359.
                                                                       (E:260)
3359. 12/16/99 gee Herroun, Oliver; Cambridge, WAS. See 3358.
3360. 10/29/93 mor Hewett, Elijah, Junr.; Lanesborough, BER, MA; Plattsburgh,
                     CLI; co-mor 2706; mee 124.   (A:113)
3361. 2/3/98 mee Hewett, John; Willsborough, CLI. See 3362.
3362. 2/3/98 mor Hewett, William; Willsborough, CLI; Willsb.,CLI; mee 3361.(A:333)
3363. 12/25/98 mor Hewitt, Ephraim (w. Lovicy), farmer; Hartford, WAS;
                     Hartford, WAS; mee 1497.   (C:120)
3364. 1/17/99 mor Hewitt, Ephraim (w. Lovicy), farmer; Hartford, WAS;
                     Hartford, WAS; mee 4900.   (C:121)
3365. 9/25/99 gor Hewitt, Ephraim (w. Lovisa), farmer; Hartford, WAS;
                     Hartford, WAS; gee 93.   (E:406)
3366. 2/8/98 mor Hewitt, George, shoemaker; Hartford, WAS; Hartford, WAS;
                     mee 1483.   (B:265)
3367. 12/25/98 mor Hewitt, Lovicy. See 3363.
3368. 1/17/99 mor Hewitt, Lovicy. See 3364.
3369. 9/25/99 gor Hewitt, Lovisa. See 3365.
3370. 3/16/96 mor Heyer, Isaac; City of N.Y. See 289.
3371. 6/22/98 gor Heyer, Isaac; City of N.Y. See 5697, 5698. (two contracts)
3372. 9/17/01 gor Heyford, Philotha. See 3374.
3373. 2/25/95 gee Heyford, Webster; Cambridge, WAS. See 693.
3374. 9/17/01 gor Heyford, Webster (w. Philotha); Salem, WAS; Salem, WAS;
                     gee 456.   (E:371)
3375. 9/17/01 mee Heyford, Webster; Salem, WAS. See 457.
3376. 11/14/94 gee Hibbard, Elijah; Granville, WAS. See 4105.
3377. 3/1/93 gor Hicks, Elizabeth. See 3380.
3378. 10/1/94 gor Hicks, John (w. Mary); Cambridge, WAS; Cambridge Pat., WAS;
                     gee 2744.   (B-2:400)
3379. 10/1/94 gor Hicks, Mary. See 3378.
3380. 3/1/93 gor Hicks, Pardon (w. Elizabeth); Cambridge, WAS; Cambridge Pat.,
                     WAS; co-gors 4835, 4836; gee 2743.   (B-2:395)

3381. 9/18/98 mor Hicks, Samuel, saddler; Bennington, BEN, VT; Champlain, CLI;
mee 5146. (A:388)
3382. 6/7/02 gor Hicks, Samuel, Esq.; Champlain, CLI; ---, CLI; gee 6664.
(B:330)
3383. 5/23/98 gee Hiern, Roger Alden, gentleman; ---, CLI. See 7629.
3384. 5/23/98 mor Hiern, Roger Alden, gentleman; ---, CLI. See 6507.
3385. 3/17/01 mee Hiern, Roger Alden; ---, ---. See 5387.
3386. 7/4/82 gor Higbe, Nehemiah; Granville, CHA; Granville, CHA; gee 6094.
(B-1:60)
3387. 7/4/82 gor Higbee, Nehemiah; Granville, CHA; Granville, CHA; gee 4056.
(B-1:53)
3388. 5/11/87 mor Higby, Nehemiah; ---, ---; land along "Pollet River on east
Creek", WAS; mee 2373. (A:41)
3389. 9/23/84 gee Higgins, Elisha, yeoman; Willsborough, WAS. See 2792.
3390. 4/16/99 gor Higgins, Elisha; Willsborough, ESS; Willsborough, ESS;
gee 3392. (A:29)
3391. 3/23/01 gor Higgins, Isaac; Willsborough, ESS; Willsborough, ESS;
gee 6509. (A:36)
3392. 4/16/99 gee Higgins, Israel; Willsborough, ESS. See 3390.
3393. 12/19/00 gee Higgins, Josiah; Willsborough, ESS. See 2538.
3394. 2/25/95 gee Higgins, William; Cambridge, WAS. See 693.
3395. 10/8/88 gee Higginson, Joseph, farmer; Ticonderoga, CLI. See 1934.
3596. 7/2/89 gor Higginson, Joseph; Ticonderoga, CLI. See 1016.
3397. 7/27/90 gee Hill, Alexander; Cambridge, WAS. See 7294.
3398. 1/29/95 gor Hill, Alexander, yeoman; Cambridge, WAS; Cambridge, WAS;
gees 3413 (D:73) and 3423 (D:70). (two contracts)
3399. 9/27/94 gee Hill, Benaiah; Granville, WAS. See 1849.
3400. 12/29/94 gor Hill, Benaiah; Granville, WAS. See 1850.
3401. 12/11/97 gee Hill, Benaiah; ---, ---. See 1851.
3402. 7/13/92 mor Hill, Benajah, farmer; Granville, WAS; ---, WAS; co-mors
715, 1854, 3041, 4103; mee 2380b. (A:336)
3403. 6/2/98 gor Hill, Benajah; Granville, WAS. See 718.
3404. 2/15/02 gee Hill, Benajah; Granville, WAS. See 6959.
3405. 5/12/00 gee Hill, Benijah, yeoman; Granville, WAS. See 1540.
3406. 9/21/01 mor Hill, Caleb (w. Cinthy); ---, ---; Granville, WAS;
mee 1693. (D:98)
3407. 9/21/01 mor Hill, Cinthy. See 3406.
3408. 7/6/88 gee Hill, Daniel, yeoman; Granville, WAS. See 2378.
3409. 7/6/88 mor Hill, Daniel; ---, ---; Granville, WAS; mee 2380. (A:86)
3410. 7/28/92 gor Hill, Daniel (w. Lowis), yeoman; Hebron, WAS; Granville,
WAS; gees 1035 (C-2:42) and 3792 (C-2:43). (two contracts)
3411. 2/26/00 mee Hill, Isabella; ---, ORA. See 7886.
3412. 11/9/01 --- Hill, Isabella; ---, ORA; ---, ESS and ---, CLI; co-persons
1600, 1601, 3961, 7896. These five persons are "heirs
at law" to the estate of George Trimble, Esq., late of the
County of Clinton (NY), dec'd. No land sale or mortgage
agreement noted here. (B:339)
3413. 1/29/95 gee Hill, James, yeoman; Cambridge, WAS. See 3398.
3414. 2/26/01 gee Hill, John, yeoman; Cambridge, WAS. See 1101.
3415. 2/26/01 mor Hill, John, yeoman; Cambridge, WAS; Argyle, WAS; mee 1102.
(D:49b)
3416. 7/28/92 gor Hill, Lowis. See 3410. Two contracts this date involving
these persons.
3417. 4/16/95 gee Hill, Margaret, "daughter of John and Elizabeth McCool;
wife of William Hill of Cambridge". See 4413.
3418. 1/18/00 mee Hill, Margaret. See 3425. Two contracts this date
involving these persons.
3419. 6/16/98 mor Hill, Susanna. See 3420.
3420. 6/16/98 mor Hill, Thomas (w. Susanna); Hartford, WAS; Hartford, WAS;
mee 929. (C:241)
3421. 10/10/98 gor Hill, Thomas; Hartford, WAS; Hartford, WAS; gee 4896.
(D:18)
3422. 10/12/98 gee Hill, Thomas. See 4897.
3423. 1/29/95 gee Hill, William, yeoman; Cambridge, WAS. See 3398.
3424. 4/16/95 --- Hill, William; Cambridge, WAS. See 3417.
3425. 1/18/00 mee Hill, William (w. Margaret), yeoman; Cambridge, WAS.
See 961 and 6582.

89

3426.　12/10/92　mee　Hillman, Benjamin; Cambridge, WAS.　See 955.
3427.　3/31/94　gee　Hillyard, Joshua; Plattsburgh, CLI.　See 3746.
3428.　4/19/94　mor　Hilton(?), William, Junr., laborer; ---, WAS; Whitehall,
　　　　　　　　　　　　WAS; mee 6673.　　　　　　　　　　　　　　　　(A:475)
3429.　4/14/75　mor　Hindman, Samuel; New Perth, CHA; Kemp Pat.(?), CHA;
　　　　　　　　　　　　mee 6771.　　　　　　　　　　　　　　　　　　(A:23)
3430.　1/15/98　mor　Hingham, Benjamin; ---, ---; Willsborough, CLI; mee 7854.
　　　　　　　　　　　　　　　　　　　　　　　　　　　　(Essex Co. A:3)
3431.　2/7/95　gee　Hiscock, Amos; Westfield, WAS.　See 7334.
3432.　3/5/96　gor　Hiscock, Amos (w. Polly); Westfield, WAS; Westfield, WAS;
　　　　　　　　　　　　gee 6654.　　　　　　　　　　　　　　　　　(C-2:215)
3433.　3/5/96　gor　Hiscock, Polly.　See 3432.
3434.　4/23/02　gor　Hiscox, Ann.　See 3435.
3435.　4/23/02　gor　Hiscox, Simeon Wells (w. Ann); Argyle, WAS; Hebron, WAS;
　　　　　　　　　　　　gee 2224.　　　　　　　　　　　　　　　　　(F:202)
3436.　6/23/01　mor　Hitchcock, Ebenezer; Granville, WAS; Granville, WAS;
　　　　　　　　　　　　mee 721.　　　　　　　　　　　　　　　　　　(D:186)
3437.　3/3/94　mor　Hitchcock, Isaac; ---, WAS; Kingsbury Pat., WAS; mee 2913.
　　　　　　　　　　　　　　　　　　　　　　　　　　　　　　(A:464)
3438.　10/7/95　gor　Hitchcock, Zina, physician; ---, WAS; Hitchcock Pat., WAS;
　　　　　　　　　　　　gee 7211.　　　　　　　　　　　　　　　　　(C-2:12)
3439.　5/21/99　mee　Hitchcock, Zina; ---, ---.　See 874.
3440.　5/21/99　mee　Hitchcock, Zina, physician; Kingsbury, WAS.　See 5658, 7246.
3441.　10/28/85　gee　Hoag, Elijah, yeoman; Walloomsack, ALB.　See 7660.
3442.　10/12/89　gor　Hoag, Elijah; Cambridge, ALB; Walloomsack Pat., WAS;
　　　　　　　　　　　　gee 129.　　　　　　　　　　　　　　　　　(C-2:350)
3443.　12/8/89　gor　Hobart, John Moss, gentleman; ---, ---; Argyle, WAS;
　　　　　　　　　　　　co-gors 3291, 4583, 5798 (grantors are all executors
　　　　　　　　　　　　of the estate of Alexander McDougall, dec'd.); gee 2165,
　　　　　　　　　　　　　　　　　　　　　　　　　　　　(C-2:126)
3444.　8/4/02　mee　Hobart, John Moss; Westchester, WES.　See 5302.
3445.　3/12/91　gor　Hobart, JohnMoss, Esq.; ---, ---; Argyle, WAS;
　　　　　　　　　　　　co-gors 655, 4596, 5800 (grantors are all executors of
　　　　　　　　　　　　the estate of Alexander McDougall, dec'd.); gee 2166.
　　　　　　　　　　　　　　　　　　　　　　　　　　　　(C-2:124)
3446.　5/18/92　gor　Hobart, John Moss, Esq.; ---, ---; Argyle, WAS; co-gors
　　　　　　　　　　　　656, 4597, 5801 (grantors are all executors of the
　　　　　　　　　　　　estate of Alexander McDougall, Esq., "late of the City
　　　　　　　　　　　　of New York, Deceased"); gee 1397.　　　(B-2:187)
3447.　11/18/01　mee　Hobart, John Sloss (sic); Westchester, WES.　See 1576.
3448.　3/1/90　gor　Hobart, John Sloss (sic), Esq; City of N.Y.; Argyle, WAS;
　　　　　　　　　　　　co-gors 654, 3292, 4594, 5799 (grantors are all executors
　　　　　　　　　　　　of the estate of Alexander McDougall, dec'd., of the
　　　　　　　　　　　　City of New York); gee 6675.　This transaction recorded
　　　　　　　　　　　　in A:157.　A parallel transaction, dated 9/29/90, is
　　　　　　　　　　　　recorded in A:164.
3449.　8/4/01　---　Hobart, John Sloss (sic), Esq. (w. Mary); Westchester, WES;
　　　　　　　　　　　　Zephaniah Platt Pat., CLI.　The above two persons appoint
　　　　　　　　　　　　Eleazer Miller, Esq., as their attorney for the sale of the
　　　　　　　　　　　　above lands.　　　　　　　　　　　　　　(B:284)
3450.　8/4/01　---　Hobart, Mary.　See 3449.
3451.　5/23/97　mor　Hochstrasser, Paul I.; ---, WAS; Hoosick Pat., WAS;
　　　　　　　　　　　　mee 8157.　　　　　　　　　　　　　　　　　(B:173)
3452.　8/16/86　gee　Hockings, John; ---, WAS.　See 8560.
3453.　12/29/91　gee　Hodges, Abraham; ---, ---.　See 4878.
3454.　10/31/92　gor　Hodges, Bathsheba.　See 3458.
3455.　10/18/98　mor　Hodges, Cornelius; ---, CLI; Old Military Township #7
　　　　　　　　　　　　(Chateaugay), CLI; co-mees 275, 317.　　(A:365)
3456.　10/19/98　mor　Hodges, Ezekiel; ---, CLI; Old Military Township #7
　　　　　　　　　　　　(Chateaugay), CLI; co-mees 276, 318.　　(A:367)
3457.　10/19/98　mor　Hodges, Josiah; ---, CLI; Old Military Township #7
　　　　　　　　　　　　(Chateaugay), CLI; co-mees 276, 318.　　(A:380)
3458.　10/31/92　gor　Hodges, Samuel (w. Bathsheba), yeoman; Hoosick, REN;
　　　　　　　　　　　　Van Curler Purchase, WAS; gee 5023.　　(D:292)
3459.　5/21/95　mor　Hoff, John (w. Rebecca); Peru, CLI; Zephaniah Platt's Pat.,
　　　　　　　　　　　　CLI; co-mees 7990, 7991, 7992.　　　　(A:157)

3460. 5/21/95 mor Hoff, Rebecca. See 3459.
3461. 1/17/97 mor Hoffman, Elias; Clinton, DUT. See 7994.
3462. 5/28/99 gor Hoffman, Henry; Livingston, COL. See 727.
3463. 10/24/93 mee Hoffman, Martin, farmer; ---, DUT. See 7887.
3464. 5/28/99 gor Hoffman, Matthias; Livingston, COL. See 727.
3465. 8/11/97 gee Hoffnagel, James, "a minor"; Willsborough, CLI. See 6929.
3466. 9/21/84 gee Hoffnagel, John, yeoman; Willsborough, WAS. See 3485.
3467. 3/28/91 gee Hoffnagel, John; Willsborough, CLI. See 3483 and 3488.
3468. 8/16/91 gor Hoffnagel, John, gentleman; Willsborough, CLI; Willsborough,
                  CLI; gee 5159.   (A:209)
3469. 9/26/94 gor Hoffnagel, John, merchant; Willsborough, CLI; Willsborough,
                  CLI; gee 3103.   (B:52)
3470. 7/7/95 gee Hoffnagel, John; ---, ---. See 1892.
3471. 9/3/95 gor Hoffnagel, John (w. Lois), farmer; Willsborough, CLI;
                  ---, CLI; gee 3622.   (B:48)
3472. 12/28/95 gor Hoffnagel, John (w. Lois); Willsborough, CLI; Willsborough,
                  CLI; gee 3494.   (B:46)
3473. 8/10/97 gor Hoffnagel, John; Willsborough, CLI; Willsborough, CLI;
                  gee 6928.   (A:13)
3474. 7/17/98 gor Hoffnagel, John, gentleman; Willsborough, CLI; Willsborough,
                  CLI; gee 6930.   (A:14)
3475. 2/20/99 gor Hoffnagel, John (w. Lois); Willsborough, CLI; Kingsbury,
                  WAS; gee 3980.   (D:316)
3476. 5/12/01 gor Hoffnagel, John; Willsborough, ESS; Willsborough, ESS;
                  gee 3341.   (A:57)
3477. 6/30/92 gee Hoffnagel, John, Junr., gentleman, Willsborough, CLI.
                  See 2808.
3478. 9/3/95 gor Hoffnagel, Lois. See 3471.
3479. 12/28/95 gor Hoffnagel, Lois. See 3472.
3480. 2/20/99 gor Hoffnagel, Lois. See 3475.
3481. 7/27/89 gor Hoffnagel, Melcheor; Willsborough, CLI; Willsborough, CLI;
                  gee 6698.   (A:94)
3482. 12/13/89 gee Hoffnagel, Melcheor, gentleman; Willsborough, CLI. See 2680.
3483. 3/28/91 gor Hoffnagel, Melcheor, gentleman; Willsborough, CLI;
                  Willsborough, CLI; gee 3467.   (A:184)
3484. 12/14/75 gor Hoffnagel, Melcher; Kingsbury, CHA; Artillery Pat., CHA;
                  gee 2887.   (A:28)
3485. 9/21/84 gor Hoffnagel, Melcher, merchant; Willsborough, WAS;
                  Willsborough, WAS; gee 3466.   (A:79)
3486. 12/21/84 mor Hoffnagel, Melcher, merchant; Willsborough, WAS; ---, WAS;
                  mee 5152.   (A:81)
3487. 3/2/89 gee Hoffnagel, Melcher, yeoman; Willsborough, CLI. See 1890.
3488. 3/28/91 gor Hoffnagel, Melchior; ---, ---; personal property?; gee
                  3467.   (A:186)
3489. 4/25/89 gee Hoffnagel, Melchor; Willsborough, CLI. See 1891.
3490. 7/27/89 mee Hoffnagel, Melchor; Willsborough, CLI. See 6699.
3491. 7/28/89 gor Hoffnagel, Melchor; Willsborough, CLI; Willsborough, CLI;
                  gee 3735.   (A:126)
3492. 7/28/89 mee Hoffnagel, Melchor; Willsborough, CLI. See 2465, 6651.
3493. 11/6/89 gee Hoffnagel, Melchor; Willsborough, CLI. See 6443.
3494. 12/28/95 gee Hoffnagel, Melchor, yeoman, gentleman; Willsborough, CLI.
                  See 3472.
3495. 6/13/74 gee Hoffnagel, Michael; ---, CHA. See 5439.
3496. 5/2/84 gee Hoffnagel, Michael, gentleman; Albany, ALB. See 2791.
3497. 10/14/88 gee Hoffnagel, Michael; Willsborough, CLI. See 1886.
3498. 11/3/88 gee Hoffnagel, Michael, gentleman; Willsborough, CLI. See 1888.
3499. 11/10/96 gee Hoffnagel, William; ---, ---. See 8271.
3500. 3/2/89 gor Hoffnagle, Melcheor, gentleman; Willsborough, CLI;
                  Willsborough, CLI; gee 848.   (A:54)
3501. 11/30/95 gor Holbrook, John; Salem, WAS; Salem, WAS; gee 489. (D:234)
3502. 1/1/96 gee Holcomb, Benjamin; Crown Point Dist., CLI. See 6453.
3503. 6/30/98 gee Holcomb, Levi; Westfield, WAS. See 8182.
3504. 7/22/92 mor Holcomb, Noah, yeoman; Hebron, WAS; Hebron, WAS; mee 6989.
                                                               (A:374)
3505. 11/6/93 gor Holcomb, Noah, yeoman; Hebron, WAS; Hebron, WAS; gee 8381.
                                                               (B-2:116)

91

3506. 11/16/93 gee Holcomb, Noah; Hebron, WAS. See 3856.
3507. 11/16/93 mor Holcomb, Noah; Hebron, WAS; Hebron, WAS; mee 3950. (A:441)
3508. 8/24/92 mor Holdridge, Thomas, farmer; ---, WAS; Glen Pat., WAS;
             mee 2863.   (A:361)
3509. 5/20/00 mor Holdridge, Thomas; Queensbury, WAS; Kingsbury, WAS;
             mee 1757.   (C:131)
3510. 6/24/99 mor Hollamback, William; Orwell, RUT, VT; Champlain, CLI;
             mee 5086.   (A:398)
3511. 10/20/00 mor Hollister, William; Granville, WAS; Granville, WAS;
             mee 4140.   (D:28)
3512. 8/24/90 mor Holly, Robert; Hebron, WAS; Sherieff's Pat. (Hebron), WAS;
             mee 6978.   (A:222)
3513. 4/3/01 mor Holman, John, farmer; Bolton, WAS; Bolton, WAS; mee 2299.
                                                                (D:81b)
3514. 6/4/98 mee Holmes, Jacob; Granville, WAS. See 8612.
3515. 3/20/99 gor Holmes, Jacob (w. Mary); Granville, WAS; Hartford, WAS;
             gee 5325.   (F:173)
3516. 2/28/01 mee Holmes, Jacob; Granville, WAS. See 8454.
3517. 9/21/01 mor Holmes, Jacob (w. Mary); ---, WAS; Granville, WAS; mee 1693.
                                                                (D:92)
3518. 5/6/01 gee Holmes, John; Westfield, WAS. See 3186.
3519. 6/2/01 mor Holmes, John, farmer; Westfield, WAS; Westfield, WAS;
             mee 8160.   (D:61)
3520. 3/20/99 gor Holmes, Mary. See 3515.
3521. 9/21/01 mor Holmes, Mary. See 3517.
3522. 11/20/90 mor Holmes, Moses; Willington, TOL, CT. See 6146.
3523. 1/5/02 mor Holt, Andrew, farmer; Cambridge, WAS; Cambridge, WAS;
             co-mor 2464; mee 5348.   (D:159)
3524. 5/1/00 mor Holt, Elisha, farmer; Chester, WAS; Chester, WAS;
             mee 7772. Two contracts this date involving these
             persons.   (D:216), (D:217)
3525. 4/10/92 gee Honeywood, John, attorney; Salem, WAS. See 4311.
3526. 6/6/99 --- Honeywood, St. John, Esq., dec'd. See 8461.
3527. 6/6/99 mee Honeywood, Sally; ---, ---. See 8461.
3528. 5/6/75 gee Hoofnagl, Michael, yeoman; ---, CHA. See 5440.
3529. 12/13/96 mor Hooker, Levi; Kingsbury, WAS; Kingsbury, WAS; co-mees
             3340, 8128.   (B:133)
3530. 7/5/92 mor Hooker, William; Hampton, WAS; Hampton, WAS; mee 8576.
                                                                (A:334)
3531. 2/11/96 --- Hopkens, Isaac, dec'd. See 1817.
3532. 3/3/85 gee Hopkens, Robert; New Perth, WAS. See 1439.
3533. 7/7/98 gor Hopkins, Abigail. See 3542.
3534. 5/2/98 gee Hopkins, Daniel, blacksmith; Rupert, BEN, VT. See 8708.
3535. 6/8/73 gee Hopkins, David, farmer; ---, CHA. See 1228.
3536. 12/16/73 gee Hopkins, David, farmer; ---, CHA. See 8684.
3537. 4/28/75 gee Hopkins, David; New Perth, CHA, "late of Road Island".
             See 1819.
3538. 6/7/80 gee Hopkins, David; New Perth, CHA. See 1430.
3539. 11/21/82 gor Hopkins, David; ---, ---. Hopkins is commissioner of
             forfeiture along with Alexander Webster, Esq., in 8280.
3540. 5/3/97 mor Hopkins, David, yeoman; Hebron, WAS; Hebron, WAS;
             co-mor 3554; mee 8598.   (B:160)
3541. 10/7/97 gee Hopkins, David, yeoman; Hebron, WAS. See 8599.
3542. 7/7/98 gor Hopkins, David (w. Abigail), yeoman; Hebron, WAS; Hebron,
             WAS; co-gors 3551, 3555; gee 6003.   (D:192)
3543. 6/11/01 mor Hopkins, David (w. Hannah), farmer; Hebron, WAS; Hebron,
             WAS; mee 5228.   (D:68)
3544. 4/20/79 gor Hopkins, David, Esq.; New Perth, CHA; Black Creek Dist,
             CHA; gee 3561.   (B-1:70)
3545. 9/8/81 gor Hopkins, David, Esq., commissioner of forfeitures; ---,
             ---. See 8278.
3546. 12/28/81 gor Hopkins, David, Esq., commissioner of forfeitures; ---,
             ---. See 8279.
3547. 5/3/91 mor Hopkins, David, Esq.; Hebron, WAS; Hebron, WAS; co-mees
             4620, 4637, 6753, 6827. Co-mortgagees are all "executors"
             of the estate of John Morine Scott, dec'd.   (A:286)

3548. 12/22/91 mor Hopkins, David, Esq.; Hebron, WAS; <u>Hebron, WAS</u>; mee 6801.
The person named as mortgagee is deceased. The executors
of his estate, not named, serve in his stead. (A:308)
3549. 3/7/92 gor Hopkins, Elizabeth. See 3565.
3550. 3/7/92 gor Hopkins, Griziel. See 3560.
3551. 7/7/98 gor Hopkins, Hannah. See 3555.
3552. 6/11/01 mor Hopkins, Hannah. See 3543.
<u>3553.</u> 2/16/89 gor Hopkins, Isaac; Hampton, WAS; <u>Hampton, WAS</u>; gee 4506.
(B-2:407)
3554. 5/3/97 mor Hopkins, Isaac, yeoman; Hebron, WAS. See 3540.
3554a. 10/7/97 gee Hopkins, Isaac; ---, ---. See 8599.
3555. 7/7/98 gor Hopkins, Isaac (w. Hannah), yeoman; Hebron, WAS. See 3542.
3556. 4/16/00 gee Hopkins, Joel, blacksmith; Hebron, WAS. See 6005.
<u>3557.</u> 10/30/72 gor Hopkins, Robert; New Perth, CHA; <u>Turner Pat., CHA</u>; gee 7826.
(B-1:142)
<u>3558.</u> 3/24/79 gor Hopkins, Robert; ---, CHA; <u>New Perth Dist., CHA</u>; gee 482.
(C-1:15)
3559. 3/5/92 gee Hopkins, Robert; Sandgate, BEN, VT. See 2714.
3560. 3/7/92 gee Hopkins, Robert (w. Griziel); Sandgate, BEN, VT. See 3565.
3561. 4/20/79 gee Hopkins, Samuel, cooper; New Perth, CHA. See 3544.
3562. 6/7/80 gee Hopkins, Samuel; New Perth, CHA. See 1430.
3563. 9/13/83 gee Hopkins, Samuel; New Perth, CHA. See 1435.
3564. 3/5/92 gee Hopkins, Samuel; Rupert, BEN, VT. See 2714.
<u>3565.</u> 3/7/92 gor Hopkins, Samuel (w. Elizabeth), yeoman; Rupert, BEN, VT;
<u>---</u>, WAS; co-gors 3550, 3560; gee 4744. See also #1444.
(A:269)
<u>3566.</u> 7/4/92 gor Hopkins, Samuel; Rupert, BEN, VT; <u>Hebron, WAS</u>; gee 2732.
(A:416)
<u>3567.</u> 5/27/99 mor Hopkins, Silvanus; Salem, WAS; <u>Salem, WAS</u>; mee 4067.
(C:125)
3568. 10/7/00 gee Hopkins, Thomas; Argyle, WAS. See 5613.
3569. 5/16/87 gee Hopkins, William, merchant; London, England. See 10.
3570. 7/25/87 gee Hopper, Lambert, farmer; Plattsburgh, WAS. See 5917.
3571. 3/5/98 mee Hoskins, Samuel, farmer; Westfield, WAS. See 8477.
<u>3572.</u> 12/14/80 mor Hotchkess, Jeremiah, yeoman; Hebron, CHA; <u>Hebron, CHA</u>;
oo-mcos 4612, 4629, 6745, 6811. Mortgagees are all
executors of the estate of John Morin Scott, Esq., dec'd.
(A:371)
3573. 5/13/00 mor Hough, Hannah. See 3574.
<u>3574.</u> 5/13/00 mor Hough, Samuel (w. Hannah); Granville, WAS; <u>Granville, WAS</u>;
mee 1541. (C:129)
3575. 2/26/96 mor Hough, Sarah. See 3579.
3576. 4/1/96 gor Hough, Sarah. See 3580.
3577. 7/11/91 gee Hough, William, blacksmith; Cambridge Dist., WAS. See 806.
3578. 7/13/91 gee Hough, William; Cambridge, WAS. See 807.
<u>3579.</u> 2/26/96 mor Hough, William (w. Sarah), farmer; Cambridge, WAS; <u>---</u>, WAS;
mee 8846. (B:24)
<u>3580.</u> 4/1/96 gor Hough, William (w. Sarah); Cambridge, WAS; <u>Cambridge, WAS</u>;
gee 8847. (B-2:539)
<u>3581.</u> 6/26/97 gor Hough, William, Senr.; Cambridge, WAS; <u>---</u>, WAS; gee 8505.
(D:362)
<u>3582.</u> 12/31/99 mor Hough, William, Senr.; Cambridge, WAS; <u>Thurman, WAS</u>;
mee 7774. (C:131)
<u>3583.</u> 4/24/99 mor Houlden, Joseph; Thurman, WAS; <u>Thurman Pat., WAS</u>; mee 7771.
(C:122)
<u>3584.</u> 5/27/91 gor Houseman, George; German Flatts, HER; <u>Mark Graves' Pat., CLI</u>;
co-gees 1698, 5128. (B:10)
3585. 2/16/96 gee Houseworth, Jacob, yeoman; Cambridge, WAS. See 6134.
<u>3586.</u> 10/15/92 mor How, John; Plattsburgh, CLI; <u>Zephaniah Platt's Pat., CLI</u>;
co-mees 5730, 5851. (A:94)
3587. 11/17/95 mee How, John; Peru, CLI. See 2061.
<u>3588.</u> 3/31/97 gor How, John, farmer; Peru, CLI; <u>Peru, CLI</u>; gee 596. (B:134)
3589. 6/9/97 gee Howard, Charles; Plattsburgh, CLI. See 636.
<u>3590.</u> 6/10/97 mor Howard, Charles; Plattsburgh, CLI; <u>Plattsburgh, CLI</u>; mee
637. (A:220)

3591. 11/26/85 mor Howard, Daniel, yeoman; ---, RUT, VT; Queensbury, WAS;
co-mor 3595; mee 1723.   (Deed Book B-1:252)
3592. 6/1/86 mor Howard, Daniel; ---, ---; Queensbury, WAS; co-mor 3596;
mees 1311 (Deed Book B-1:240) and 1319 (Deed Book B-1:241)
(two contracts).
3393. 3/1/98 mor Howard, Elisha; Plattsburgh, CLI; Old Military Township #7
(Chateaugay), CLI; mee 5693.   (A:260)
3594. 8/8/98 mor Howard, Elisha J.; Peru, CLI; Old Military Township #7
(Chateaugay), CLI; mee 5702.   (A:320)
3595. 11/26/85 mor Howard, Stephen, yeoman; Queensbury, WAS. See 3591.
3596. 6/1/86 mor Howard, Stephen; ---, ---. See 3592. Two contracts this
date involving these persons.
3597. 9/2/93 mor Howe, Chloe. See 3599.
3598. 8/26/93 gor Howe, John; Peru, CLI; Peru, CLI; gee 6318.   (B:56)
3599. 9/2/93 mor Howe, John (w. Chloe), merchant; Hampton, WAS; Hampton, WAS;
mee 5959.   (A:439)
3600. 3/3/84 gee Hoy(?), Richard. See 1437.
3601. 5/1/98 gee Hoy, William, Junr.; Salem, WAS. See 3602.
3602. 5/1/98 gor Hoy, William, Senr., reed maker; Salem, WAS; Salem, WAS;
gee 3601.   (C-2:276)
3603. 12/15/94 mor Hubbard, Gideon; Argyle, WAS; Saratoga Pat., WAS; mee 3638.
(A:529)
3604. 3/28/95 gor Hubbard, Israel; Cambridge, WAS; Cambridge, WAS; gee 3647.
(B-2:371)
3605. 8/15/98 mor Hubbard, Israel; Quashewke, WAS; Quashewke, WAS; mee 6710.
(C:127)
3606. 3/3/93 gee Hubbard, John, yeoman; Salem, WAS. See 5561.
3607. 7/1/85 gee Hubbart, Samuel; ---, ---. See 7055.
3608. 12/15/95 gee Hudson, Nathaniel; Lee, BER, MA. See 8400.
3609. 3/10/00 gee Huestis, Joseph; Argyle, WAS. See 903.
3610. 3/10/00 mor Huestis, Joseph, carpenter; Argyle, WAS, Argyle, WAS;
mee 904.   (C:129)
3611. 7/18/98 gee Huffnagel, Charles, "son of John Huffnagel of Willsborough",
CLI. See 6931.
3612. 7/18/98 --- Huffnagel, John. See 3611.
3613. 7/18/98 --- Huffnagel, John, Willsborough, CLI. See 3614.
3614. 7/18/98 --- Huffnagel, Lois, "wife of John Huffnagel of Willsborough",
CLI. See 6931.
3615. 9/24/71 gee Huffnagel, Michael, yeoman; Kingsbury, ALB. See 2582.
3616. 6/4/76 gor Huffnagel, Michael, yeoman; Kingsbury, CHA; ---, CHA;
gee 3253.   (C-2:290)
3617. 2/10/72 mee Huffnagle, Michael; ---, ---. See 3185.
3618. 3/25/72 gee Huffnagle, Michael; Kingsbury, ALB (sic). See 4565.
3619. 3/9/98 gee Huggin, William; Granville, WAS. See 8414.
3620. 6/22/95 gee Huggins, William; Granville, WAS. See 8412.
3621. 10/15/01 mor Hughs, Davis, yeoman; Pittstown, REN; Argyle, WAS; mee 5519.
(D:148)
3622. 9/3/95 gee Huit, John; Willsborough, CLI. See 3471.
3623. 2/15/96 gee Hulet, Nehemiah; Sandgate, BEN, VT. See 7343.
3624. 6/2/92 gor Hull, Daniel; Queensbury, WAS; Queensbury, WAS; gee 5549.
(B-2:79)
3625. 2/9/95 gor Humphrey, James (w. Margaret); Edwardsburgh, "County of
Grainwell", Upper Canada; Argyle, WAS; gee 3627. (D:311)
3626. 2/9/95 gor Humphrey, Margaret. See 3625.
3627. 2/9/95 gee Humphrey, Samuel; Argyle, WAS. See 3625.
3628. 5/9/95 gor Humphrey, Samuel, carpenter; Argyle, WAS; Argyle, WAS;
gee 1395.   (C-2:23)
3629. 5/12/83 gee Humstead, Jedediah, yeoman; Shaftsbury, BEN, VT. See 8229.
3630. 8/28/86 gor Hunsdon, Allan; Salem, WAS; Kingsbury, WAS; gee 3634.
(C-1:37)
3631. 9/7/87? mee Hunsdon, Allan; ---, ---. See 518.
3632. 4/23/87 gor Hunsdon, Allen; Salem, WAS; Kingsbury, WAS; gee 517. (A:64)
3633. 12/17/93 gor Hunsdon, Allen; Salem, WAS; Salem, WAS; gee 4503. (B-2:119)
3634. 8/28/86 gee Hunsdon, John; Kingsbury, WAS. See 3630.
3635. 12/1/85 gee Hunt, Edmond; Kingsbury, WAS. See 2521.
3636. 6/16/88 gor Hunt, Edmund, yeoman; Kingsbury, WAS; Kingsbury, WAS;
gee 2251.   (A:76)

3637. 8/28/69 gor Hunt, Ephraim; Greenwich, HAM, MA; Turner Pat., ALB;
               gee 2980.   (B-1:106)
3638. 12/15/94 mee Hunt, Jonathan, merchant; Troy, REN. See 3603.
3639. 12/13/91 mor Hunter(?), John, yeoman; Cambridge, WAS; Cambridge Pat.,
               WAS; mee 2674.   (A:407)
3640. 2/26/00 mee Hunter, Samuel; ---, ORA. See 7886.
3641. 5/10/92 gee Huntley, Andrew; Westfield, WAS. See 959.
3642. 11/1/86 gee Huntly, Andrew; Manchester, BEN, VT. See 3802.
3643. 9/8/01 mor Huper, Moses; New Chester; GRA, NH; Peru, CLI; mee 5773.
                                                                (B:55)
3644. 3/16/99 mor Hurd, David, yeoman; Hebron, WAS; Hebron, WAS; mee 2896.
                                                                (C:127)
3645. 7/9/93 gor Hussey, Lydia. See 3646.
3646. 7/9/93 gor Hussey, Sylvanus (w. Lydia); ---, ---, NY; land "east side
               of Hudson's River", WAS; gee 137.   (D:157)
3647. 3/28/95 gee Huston, Thomas; Cambridge, WAS. See 3604.
3648. 5/8/89 mor Hutcheson, Charles, Capt.; Hebron, WAS; Hebron, WAS; co-mees
               4616, 4633, 6749, 6812. Co-mortgagees are all executors
               of the estate of "the Hon. John Morin Scott, deceased".
                                                                (A:177)
3649. 12/12/91 mor Hutchun, William, yeoman; Hebron, WAS; Hebron, WAS; mee 7465.
                                                                (A:306)
3650. 2/16/92 mee Hutton, William; Hutton's Bush, WAS. See 4326.
3651. 1/26/93 mee Hutton, William; Hutton's Bush, WAS. See 1257.
3652. 3/16/96 --- Hyer, Isaac; City of N.Y. See 290.
3653. 10/13/94 gee Ingalls, Charles, gentleman; Salem, WAS. See 8582.
3654. 10/22/94 gee Ingalls, Charles, gentleman; Salem, WAS. See 8584.
3655. 9/4/97 mee Ingalls, Charles, gentleman; Salem, WAS. See 6842.
3656. 10/22/94 gee Ingals, Charles; Salem, WAS. See 8530.
3657. 2/8/98 mor Ingalsby, Aaron (w. Polly), farmer; Hartford, WAS;
               Hartford, WAS; mee 1483.   (B:271)
3658. 4/22/89 mor Ingersoll, Francis; Granville, WAS; Granville, WAS; mee 835.
                                                                (A:154)
3659. 3/20/93 mee Ingles, George; New Windsor, ULS. See 8656.
3660. 9/30/93 mee Ingles, George; New Windsor, ULS. See 4889.
3661. 6/22/95 mee Inglis, George; New Windsor, ULS. See 1697.
3662. 9/12/98 mor Inglish, Luke, farmer; Easton, WAS; Easton, WAS; mee 7221.
                                                                (B:272)
3663. 7/12/93 gee Ingols, Charles, gentleman; Salem, WAS. See 6368.
3664. 5/3/97 mor Ingraham, Amos, yeoman; Hebron, WAS; Hebron, WAS; mee 8598.
                                                                (B:165)
3665. 12/28/96 mor Inman, Abraham, farmer; Easton, WAS; Easton, WAS; co-mor
               3166; mee 4853.   (C:132)
3666. 2/12/98 mee Inman, Abraham; Easton, WAS. See 3347.
3667. 4/19/99 gor Inman, Sarah, wife of William Inman; ---, ONE; Saratoga
               Pat., WAS; co-gees 8 and 15 (D:260) and gee 1782 (D:446).
               (two contracts)
3668. 11/13/95 mee Inman, William, gentleman; Whitestown, HER. See 5637.
3669. 11/28/95 mee Inman, William, gentleman; Whitestown, HER. See 7787.
3670. 12/8/95 gor Inman, William, gentleman; Whitestown, HER; Saratoga Pat.,
               WAS; gee 1781.   (D:443)
3671. 12/8/95 mee Inman, William, gentleman; Whitestown, HER. See 1785.
3672. 12/18/95 mee Inman, William, gentleman; Whitestown, HER. See 493,
               496, 5329.
3673. 12/19/95 gor Inman, William, gentleman; Whitestown, HER; Saratoga Pat.,
               WAS; co-gees 6, 13.   (D:257)
3674. 12/19/95 mee Inman, William, gentleman; Whitestown, HER. See 7.
3675. 12/25/95 mee Inman, William, gentleman; Whitestown, HER. See 12.
               Two contracts this date involving these persons.
3676. 2/5/96 mee Inman, William; Whitestown, HER. See 669.
3677. 4/7/96 mee Inman, William, gentleman; ---, HER. See 1567.
3678. 4/7/96 mee Inman, William, gentleman; Whitestown, HER. See 8482.
3679. 4/8/96 gor Inman, William, gentleman; Whitestown, HER; Saratoga Pat,
               WAS; gee 3871.   (C-2:341)
3680. 4/8/96 mee Inman, William, gentleman; Whitestown, HER. See 3991.

3681. 4/9/96 gor Inman, William, gentleman; Whitestown, HER; Saratoga Pat., WAS; gee 425. (C-2:180)
3682. 4/9/96 mee Inman, William, gentleman; Whitestown, HER. See 426.
3683. 4/11/96 mee Inman, William, gentleman; Whitestown, HER. See 8453.
3684. 4/15/96 mee Inman, William, gentleman; Whitestown, HER. See 570.
3685. 4/18/96 mee Inman, William, gentleman; Whitestown, HER. See 1967 and 2752.
3686. 4/23/96 gor Inman, William, gentleman; Whitestown, HER.; Saratoga Pat., WAS; gee 427. (C-2:188)
3687. 4/23/96 mee Inman, William, gentleman; Whitestown, HER. See 428.
3688. 6/24/96 mee Inman, William, gentleman; Whitestown, HER. See 4861.
3689. 7/23/96 mee Inman, William, gentleman; Whitestown, HER. See 3140.
3690. 10/4/97 mee Inman, William; Whitestown, HER. See 1322.
3691. 4/19/99 --- Inman, William. See 3667. (two contracts)
3692. 4/19/99 gor Inman, William; Whitestown, ONE; Saratoga Pat., WAS; gee 3888. (D:118)
3693. 8/14/99 gee Inman, William, gentleman; Whitestown, ONE. See 5706.
3694. 8/14/99 gor Inman, William; Whitestown, ONE; Saratoga Pat., WAS; gee 5705. (D:183)
3695. 9/8/99 mee Inman, William; Whitestown, ONE. See 1123.
3696. 1/24/00 mor Irish, George; Peru, CLI; Peru, CLI; mee 5760. (A:413)
3697. 11/10/01 mor Irish, Jesse; Peru, CLI; Peru, CLI; mee 5774. (B:58)
3698. 2/9/92 gor Irvin, Daniel; Baskerville, ---, NJ?; land "east side of Hudson's River", WAS; gee 7085. (A:350)
3699. 6/4/94 gor Irvine, James (w. Mary), merchant; Cambridge, WAS; Cambridge, WAS; gee 7025. Mary, "previous to her intermarriage,(was) the widow ... of John Galloway of Cambridge, farmer". (F:83)
3700. 6/4/94 gor Irvine, Mary. See 3699.
3701. 5/2/96 gee Jackaways, George; Argyle, WAS. See 2100c.
3702. 2/9/99 mor Jackson, Mary. See 3705.
3703. 12/2/99 mor Jackson, Mary. See 3706.
3704. 5/28/92 gee Jackson, Nathan; Hebron, WAS. See 6754.
3705. 2/9/99 mor Jackson, Nathan (w. Mary), yeoman; Hebron, WAS; Hebron, WAS; mee 2516. (C:133)
3706. 12/2/99 mor Jackson, Nathan (w. Mary); Hebron, WAS; Hebron, WAS; mee 8112. (C:134)
3707. 10/2/02 mor Jackson, Samuel; ---, ---; Chesterfield, ESS; mee 760. (A:90)
3708. 1/12/97 gee Jackway, Hosea, yeoman; Whitehall, WAS. See 7911.
3709. 1/12/97 gee Jackway, Samuel, yeoman; Whitehall, WAS. See 7911.
3710. 1/14/97 mor Jackways, Samuel, yeoman; Whitehall, WAS; Whitehall, WAS; mee 7912. (B:143)
3711. 6/10/01 gee Jakway, George, farmer; Argyle, WAS. See 5565.
3712. 7/9/98 mor James, Elijah; South Hero, ---, VT; Old Military Township #7 (Chateaugay), CLI; mee 5700. (A:323)
3713. 7/28/87 gee Jameson, Neil, Junr., gentleman; City of N.Y. See 6336.
3714. 11/30/92 gor Jamieson, Neil, Junr., gentleman; "late of the City of New York". See 4419.
3715. 7/9/98 mor Janes, Elijah; South Hero, ---, VT; Old Military Township #7 (Chateaugay), CLI; mee 5700. (B:61)
3716. 4/9/99 mee Janes, Elijah; Lansingburgh, REN. See 4938.
3717. 4/13/99 gor Janes, Elijah; Lansingburgh, REN; Cambridge, WAS; co-gees 1741, 7784, 7785. (D:93)
3718. 6/16/00 --- Jenk, Joseph; ---, ---. See 6047.
3719. 6/18/91 gee Jenkins, George, Senr.; Hebron, WAS. See 2022.
3720. 10/1/01 mor Jenkins, Palmer; Queensbury, WAS; Queensbury, WAS; mee 3282. (D:102)
3721. 10/1/01 mor Jenkins, Simeon; Queensbury, WAS; Queensbury, WAS; co-mor 3722; mee 3282. (D:103)
3722. 10/1/01 mor Jenkins, Thomas; Queensbury, WAS. See 3721.
3723. 4/24/88 gee Jenks, Joseph; New Canaan, COL. See 3039.
3724. 3/18/89 gee Jenks, Joseph, merchant; New Canaan, COL. See 1240.
3725. 10/6/92 gee Jenks, Joseph, merchant; ---, COL. See 1966.
3726. 4/8/90 gee Jenner, Joseph, yeoman; Cambridge Dist., WAS. See 1841.
3727. 10/1/91 mor Jersey, John; Plattsburgh, CLI; Beekman's Pat., CLI; mee 580. (A:75)

3728. 8/3/75 gor Jessup, Abigail. See 3733.
3729. 12/30/85 --- Jessup, Ebenezer; ---, --- (forfeiture of his lands in
Washington County). See 3731.
3730. 8/13/02 --- Jessup, Ebenezer. See 699.
3731. 12/30/85 --- Jessup, Edward; ---, --- (forfeiture of his lands in
Washington County); gee 3920 and others.   (A:553)
3732. 8/13/02 --- Jessup, Edward; ---, ---. See 699.
3733. 8/3/75 gor Jessup, Edward, Esq. (w. Abigail); "Colony of Rensselaer";
"Mountford" Pat., CHA; gee 2354.   (C-1:86)
3734. 10/10/91 gor Jessup, Joseph, gentleman; Elizabethtown, Lunenburg Dist.,
Quebec, Canada; Jessup's Lower Pat., WAS; gee 1316.
(C-1:85)
3735. 7/28/89 gee Jewett, William; Willsborough, CLI. See 3491.
3736. 7/17/98 gor Jewett, William; Willsborough, CLI; Willsborough, CLI;
gee 5461.   (B:143)
3737. 11/23/01 mee Jewett, William; ---, ---. See 8123.
3738. 11/23/01 gor Jewitt, William; Stafford, ---, VT; Willsborough, ESS;
gee 8122.   (A:44)
3739. 7/3/92 gee Jillson, George; Westfield, WAS. See 1111.
Joans. See also Jones.
3740. 1/29/87 mee Joans, John; ---, ---. See 3271.
3741. 11/18/00 mee Johnson, Anna; Cambridge, WAS. See 7552.
3742. 10/22/79 gor Johnson, Barent, Esq.; Gravesend, KIN; Cuyler and Leakes
Pat., ALB (sic); gee 3756.   (A:459)
3743. 3/2/97 mor Johnson, Catherine. See 3754.
3744. 5/4/84? gor Johnson, Daniel; ---, ---; Argyle, WAS; co-gees 3945 and
7551.   (B-1:197)
3745. 5/26/91 mee Johnson, Eden; Plattsburgh, CLI. See 5724.
3746. 3/31/94 gor Johnson, Eden, yeoman; Plattsburgh, CLI; Plattsburgh, CLI;
gee 3427.   (A:342)
3747. 5/27/91 mor Johnson, Edin; Plattsburgh, CLI; Plattsburgh, CLI;
mee 5725.   (A:63)
3748. 1/14/95 gee Johnson, Elisha, Esq.; Willington, TOL, CT. See 2290.
3749. 5/25/85 gee Johnson, Esbon; ---, ---. See 7055.
3750. 5/28/85 mor Johnson, Esborn(?); Skenesborough, WAS; Skenesborough, WAS;
mee 8549.   (Deed Book B-1:166)
3751. 7/20/87 gee Johnson, Gurdin; Granville, WAS. See 7371.
3752. 8/8/87 mor Johnson, Gurdin; Granville, WAS; Granville, WAS; co-mees
4906, 4907, 4910.   (A:48)
3753. 11/1/86 gee Johnson, Gurdun; Granville, WAS. See 7372.
3754. 3/2/97 mor Johnson, Horace (w. Catherine), merchant; City of N.Y.;
"Canadian and Nova Scotia Pat. #4" (Saranac), CLI;
mee 1057.   (A:242)
3755. 7/6/88 mor Johnson, Israel; Granville, WAS; Granville, WAS; mee 2380.
(A:93)
3756. 10/22/79 gee Johnson, Jaques; Flushing, QUE. See 3742.
3757. 11/18/00 mee Johnson, Jaques; Cambridge, WAS. See 7552.
3758. 6/17/95 gor Johnson, John; Charles Town, ---, SC; Granville, WAS;
gee 4991.   (B-2:446)
3759. 6/17/95 mee Johnson, John; Charlstown, ---, SC. See 4992.
3760. 9/22/96 mee Johnson, John; Charles Town, ---, SC. See 5654.
3761. 9/23/96 mee Johnson, John; Charles Town, ---, SC. See 2261.
3762. 10/12/96 mee Johnson, John; Charles Town, ---, SC. See 1828.
3763. 7/11/92 gor Johnson, John, Esq.; ---, ---, SC; Hebron, WAS; gee 1314.
(A:414)
3764. 9/21/96 mee Johnson, John, Esq.; Charles Town, ---, SC. See 5434.
3765. 9/22/96 gor Johnson, John, Esq.; Charlestown, ---, SC; Granville, WAS;
gee 6834.   (E:254)
3766. 9/22/96 mee Johnson, John, Esq.; Charles Town, ---, SC. See 2254,
2255, 2877, 3790, 8165, 8611.
3767. 9/23/96 mee Johnson, John, Esq.; Charles Town, ---, SC. See 195, 2876,
6835.
3768. 10/1/96 mee Johnson, John, Esq.; Charles Town, ---, SC. See 7351.
3769. 10/11/96 mee Johnson, John, Esq.; Charles Town, ---, SC. See 1929,
7038, 8456.

97

3770. 10/12/96 mee Johnson, John, Esq.; Charles Town, ---, SC. See 1377, 1922,
                2059.
3771. 10/13/96 mee Johnson, John, Esq.; Charles Town, ---, SC. See 664.
3772. 3/16/98 mor Johnson, Stephen; ---, CLI; Old Military Township #7
                (Chateaugay), CLI; mee 5694.   (A:256)
3773. 2/2/02 mor Johnson, Stephen; Chateaugay, CLI; Old Military Township
                #7 (Chateaugay), CLI; mee 292a.   (B:65)
3774. 9/7/69 gor Johnson, Thomas; ---, ---. See 7955.
3775. 4/20/70 gor Johnson, Thomas, farmer; White Creek, ALB; Turner Pat., ALB;
                gee 4319.   (A:6)
3776. 4/20/73 gor Johnson, Thomas; ---, ---. See 7957.
3777. 8/18/90 gee Johnson, Timothy; Whitehall, WAS. See 2237.
3778. 5/12/02 gor Johnson, Timothy, yeoman; Granville, WAS; Granville, WAS;
                co-gors 4813, 6393; gee 4902.   (F:193)
3779. 10/12/93 mor Johnston, Abigail. See 3787.
3780. 10/15/95 mor Johnston, David, yeoman; ---, WAS. See 3259.
3781. 10/29/91 gee Johnston, John, farmer; Cambridge, WAS. See 1064.
3782. 7/4/92 mor Johnston, John, carpenter; Argyle, WAS; Argyle, WAS;
                mee 8296.   (A:380)
3783. 11/27/94 mor Johnston, John, carpenter; Argyle, WAS; Argyle, WAS;
                mee 4931.   (A:512)
3784. 4/14/01 mee Johnston, Stephen; Hartford, WAS. See 4272.
3785. 4/20/76 gor Johnston, Thomas; New Perth, CHA; Turner Pat., CHA;
                gee 6680.   (B-1:88)
3786. 10/12/93 gee Johnston, Timothy; Granville, WAS. See 4789.
3787. 10/12/93 mor Johnston, Timothy (w. Abigail); Granville, WAS; Granville,
                WAS; co-mors 4815, 6392; co-mees 4793, 4794. (A:431)
                Jones. See also Joans.
3788. 4/4/92 gee Jones, Abijah; Kingsbury, WAS. See 7010.
3789. 6/7/99 gor Jones, Allice. See 3795.
3790. 9/22/96 mor Jones, Christopher P., clothier; Granville, WAS; Granville,
                WAS; mee 3766.   (B:131)
3791. 7/6/88 mor Jones, Comfort; Ganville, WAS; Granville, WAS; mee 2380.
                                    (A:94)
3792. 7/28/92 gee Jones, Comfort; Granville, WAS. See 3410.
3793. 6/5/87 gee Jones, Cornelius; ---, ---. See 7055.
3794. 7/20/87 gee Jones, Cornelius; ---, ---. See 100.
3795. 6/7/99 gor Jones, Cornelius (w. Allice), minister of the gospel;
                Whitehall, WAS; Whitehall, WAS; gee 7052.   (D:149)
3796. 7/13/73 mor Jones, Daniel, farmer; Queensbury, ALB (sic); Kingsbury, CHA;
                co-mees 7142, 7270, 7289. Co-mortgagees are all executors
                of the estate of William Smith, Esq., dec'd. (A:3)
3797. 7/14/73 mor Jones, Daniel; Queensbury, CHA; Kingsbury, CHA; mee 160.
                                   (A:20)
3798. 7/15/73 mor Jones, Daniel, yeoman; Queensbury, CHA; Kingsbury, CHA;
                mee 2915.   (A:2)
3799. 11/26/73 gor Jones, Daniel, yeoman; Queensbury, ALB (sic); Kingsbury, CHA;
                gee 3805.   (A:24)
3800. 9/18/75 gor Jones, Daniel (w. Sarah); ---, CHA; Jessup Pat., CHA;
                gee 1907.   (A:74)
3801. 11/26/73 gee Jones, Deborah. See 3805.
3802. 11/1/86 gor Jones, Ezra; Westfield, WAS; Westfield, WAS; gee 3642.
                                  (A:123)
3803. 7/1/85 gee Jones, Isaac; ---, ---. See 7055.
3804. 4/1/02 mor Jones, Isaac; ---, ---; Willsborough, ESS; mee 6500. (A:85)
3805. 11/26/73 gee Jones, John (w. Deborah), yeoman; Queensbury "alias Kianderossa",
                ALB (sic). See 3799.
3806. 7/20/87 gee Jones, Oliver; ---, ---. See 100.
3807. 6/21/97 gor Jones, Oliver, yeoman; Whitehall, WAS; Whitehall, WAS;
                gee 8719.   (C-2:196)
3808. 6/22/97 mee Jones, Oliver, yeoman; Whitehall, WAS. See 8720.
3809. 2/4/02 mor Jones, Polly. See 3814.
3810. 4/14/01 mor Jones, Rufus; New Haven, ADD, VT; Chateaugay, CLI; co-mees
                282, 325.   (B:49)
3811. 9/18/75 gor Jones, Sarah. See 3800.
3812. 1/23/96 mee Jones, Thomas, physician; City of N.Y. See 6609.

3813. 11/19/96 mee Jones, Thomas, physician; City of N.Y. See 4895.
3814. 2/4/02   mor Jones, Thomas (w. Polly); Granville, WAS; Granville, WAS;
                      mee 710.   (D:190)
3815. 12/17/93 gor Joslin, Benjamin (w. Sarah); Cambridge, WAS; land "east
                      of the Hudson's River", WAS; gee 2851.   (B-2:439)
3816. 12/17/93 gor Joslin, Sarah. See 3815.
3817. 8/20/96   gee Judson, Nathaniel; Southeast, DUT. See 5458.
3818. --/--/85 gor Kanady, Alexander; White Creek, WAS; Black Creek Dist., WAS;
                      gee 2495.   (C-1:38)
3819. 4/18/01   mee Kane, John, merchant; City of N.Y. See 7494.
3820. 10/12/99 mee Karner, Derrick; Underhill, CHI, VT. See 1866.
3821. 5/1/02   mor Kay, William; Argyle, WAS; Argyle, WAS; mee 4079. (D:229)
3822. 12/12/98 mor Keating, Jane. See 3823. (two contracts)
3823. 12/12/98 mor Keating, John (w. Jane), merchant; Lansingburgh, REN. See
                      7390 and 7391. (two contracts)
3824. 11/4/86   mee Keeline, Daniel; City of N.Y. See 4352.
3825. 10/1/01   gee Keeling, Adam, merchant; Troy, REN. See 4148.
3826. 10/13/01 mor Keeling, Adam; Troy, REN; Granville, WAS; co-mor 6209;
                      mee 4150.   (D:123)
3827. 5/30/01   mor Keese, Parmelia. See 3833.
3828. 1/24/92   mor Keese, Richard, "farmer, of Lake Champlain"; Zephaniah
                      Platt's Pat., CLI; mee 7610.   (A:118)
3829. 4/11/98   mor Keese, Richard; Peru, CLI; Old Military Township #7
                      (Chateaugay), CLI; mee 5809.   (A:294)
3830. 2/8/92   gee Keese, William, yeoman; Plattsburgh, CLI. See 5929.
3831. 2/9/92   mor Keese, William, yeoman; Washington, DUT; Plattsburgh, CLI;
                      mee 5846.   (A:76)
3832. 4/11/98   mor Keese, William; Peru, CLI; Old Military Township #7
                      (Chatraugay), CLI; mee 5809.   (A:297)
3833. 5/30/01   mor Keese, William (w. Parmelia), farmer; Peru, CLI; Old Military
                      Township #7 (Chateaugay), CLI; co-mees 4120, 4121. (B:69)
3834. 12/10/98 gor Keet, John, yeoman; Cambridge, WAS; Cambridge, WAS; gee
                      7393.   (D:101)
3835. 1/4/93   mee Kellogg, Eliphalet, Esq.; Ballston, SAR. See 867.
3836. 1/9/96   gee Kellogg, Isaac, farmer; Crown Point, CLI. See 2419.
3837. 1/23/97   mor Kellogg, Isaac; Ticonderoga, CLI; James Caldwell Pat., CLI;
                      mee 2296   (A:211)
3838. 1/17/90   mor Kellogg, Jason; Hampton, WAS; ---, WAS; mee 6084. (A:205)
3839. 1/18/90   gee Kellogg, Jason; Hampton, WAS. See 6034.
3840. 4/12/94   gee Kellogg, Jason; Hampton, WAS. See 614.
3841. 2/22/98   mor Kellogg, William; Pleasant Valley (Crown Point), CLI;
                      Pleasant Valley, CLI; mee 7748.   (A:277)
3842. 2/16/84   mee Kelly, John; City of N.Y. See 1949.
3843. 1/21/86   mee Kelly, John; City of N.Y. See 4958.
3844. 9/21/86   gor Kelly, John; City of N.Y.; land "west side of Lake Champlain",
                      WAS; gee 3954.   (A:69)
3845. 1/5/88   mor Kelly, John; ---, ---; land "east side of the waters running
                      from Wood Creek into Lake Champlain", WAS; mee 811.
                                                                  (A:74)
3846. 10/16/92 gee Kelly, John; Plattsburgh, CLI. See 5930.
3847. 1/16/96   gor Kelly, John, gentleman; City of N.Y.; Granville, WAS; gee 6325.
                      Grantee is "wife of Bille Richardson".   (D:449)
3848. 5/25/96   mee Kelly, John, gentleman; City of N.Y. See 7721.
3849. 6/9/96   mee Kelly, John, gentleman; City of N.Y. See 1321.
3850. 3/2/98   mee Kelly, John, gentleman; City of N.Y. See 4117.
3851. 9/1/98   mee Kelly, John, gentleman; City of N.Y. See 7979.
3852. 11/15/98 mee Kelly, John, gentleman; City of N.Y. See 1855.
3853. 9/21/01   --- Kelly, John, "late of the City of New York, deceased".
                      See 1694.
3854. 1/6/88   mor Kelly, John, Esq.; City of N.Y.; land "near Lake St. Catharine,
                      WAS; mee 4959.   (A:81)
3855. 4/5/92   gor Kelly, John, Esq.; City of N.Y.; Simon Metcalf Tract, CLI;
                      gee 5971.   (B:120)
3856. 11/16/93 gor Kemble, Peter, merchant; City of N.Y.; Hebron, WAS; gee 3506.
                                                                  (B-2:248)
3857. 12/30/94 mee Kemble, Peter, merchant; City of N.Y. See 2679.

3858.	1/1/01	mee	Kemble, Peter, merchant; City of N.Y. See 1352.
3859.	4/1/01	mee	Kemble, Peter, merchant; City of N.Y. See 1788.
3860.	7/12/01	mee	Kemble,Peter, merchant; City of N.Y. See 1996.
3861.	3/2/02	mee	Kemble, Peter; ---, ---. See 2405.
3862.	3/6/02	gor	Kemble, Peter, merchant; City of N.Y. Elizabethtown, ESS; gee 2406. (A:46)
3863.	4/5/02	mee	Kemble, Peter, merchant; City of N.Y. See 3169.
3864.	5/26/02	gor	Kemble, Peter, merchant; City of N.Y. (Kemble sells through his attorney, James Harvey, merchant, of Salem, WAS); Hebron, WAS; gee 4955. (F:197)
3865.	10/23/73	mee	Kemp, John Tabor; City of N.Y. See 4313.
3866.	9/8/81	---	Kemp, John Tabor, Esq.; ---, ---. See 8278.
3867.	10/5/85	---	Kemp, John Tabor; ---, ---; Skenesborough(?), WAS (forfeiture of Kemp's lands); gee 5044. (A:545)
3868.	9/7/74	mee	Kempe, John Tabor, Esq.; City of N.Y. See 8272.
3869.	5/24/92	gor	Keneady, Alexander; Salem, WAS; Hebron, WAS; gee 1252. (A:345)
3870.	12/16/83	gor	Keneday, Alexander; New Perth, CHA; New Perth, CHA; gee 4477. (B-1:132)
3871.	4/8/96	gee	Kenion, Nathaniel, farmer; Easton, WAS. See 3679.
3872.	4/29/83	gor	Kenneady, Alexander; New Perth, CHA; Black Creek Dist., CHA; gee 1245. (C-2:222)
3873.	4/29/94	mor	Kennedy, Alexander; Argyle, WAS; Argyle, WAS; mee 4675. (C:150)
3874.	5/1/99	mor	Kennedy, Jannet. See 3875.
3875.	5/11/99	mor	Kennedy, Neil (w. Jannet), yeoman; Argyle, WAS; Argyle, WAS; mee 6060. (C:152)
3876.	3/31/97	gor	Kent, Elizabeth. See 3882.
3877.	4/25/93	gor	Kent, James; ---, ---. See 7168.
3878.	9/10/93	mee	Kent, James; ---, ---. See 3906.
3879.	2/4/96	---	Kent, James; City of N.Y. See 5857.
3880.	2/24/96	mor	Kent, James; City of N.Y. See 8754.
3881.	4/9/96	gee	Kent, James, attorney; City of N.Y. See 608.
3882.	3/31/97	gor	Kent, James (w. Elizabeth), attorney; City of N.Y.; Old Military Township #6 (Clinton), CLI; co-gees 264, 305. (B:123)
3883.	5/1/97	mee	Kent, James, attorney; City of N.Y. See 7176.
3884.	6/22/98	gor	Kent, James; City of N.Y. See 5696.
3885.	6/5/01	mee	Kent, James; Albany, ALB. See 292.
3886.	9/22/00	mee	Kent, James, Esq.; Albany, ALB. See 340.
3887.	12/6/99	mor	Kent, John; Plattsburgh, CLI; Plattsburgh, CLI; mee 5876. (A:431)
3888.	4/19/99	gee	Kenyion, Nathaniel, farmer; Easton, WAS. See 3692.
3889.	9/5/00	mor	Kenyon, David (w. Mary), farmer; Argyle, WAS; Cambridge Pat., WAS; mee 4039. (C:153)
3890.	9/5/00	mor	Kenyon, Mary. See 3889.
3891.	12/23/00	gee	Kenyon, Nathaniel, yeoman; Easton, WAS. See 1045.
3892.	3/4/94	gee	Kenyon, Phineas; ---, WAS, RI See 1582.
3893.	5/2/96	mor	Kenyon, Phinehas, farmer; Argyle, WAS; Argyle, WAS; co-mor 2231; co-mees 1290, 2101, 2228, 5584. (C:152)
3894.	8/29/96	gee	Kenyon, Thurston; Easton, WAS. See 7768.
3895.	8/17/95	gee	Kenyon, William, Senr., farmer; Argyle, WAS. See 156.
3896.	4/12/96	---	Ker, George; ---, ---. See 5512.
3896a.	4/12/96	---	Ker, George; ---, ---. See 3898.
3897.	4/12/96	mee	Ker, Mary; City of N.Y. See 5512.
3898.	4/12/96	mee	Ker, Mary (wife of George Ker); City of N.Y. See 5513.
3899.	8/5/99	mor	Kesley, Robert; ---, ---; Elizabethtown, ESS; mee 5166. (A:2)
3900.	11/9/01	mee	Ketchum, Daniel; Granville, WAS. See 6202.
3901.	8/24/98	mor	Ketchum, George; Chateaugay, CLI; Old Military Township #7 (Chateaugay), CLI; mee 5703. (A:342)
3902.	11/14/97	gor	Ketchum, Hezekiah (w. Mary), merchant; Waterford, SAR; ---, CLI; co-gees 5688, 5826, 5940, 7177. (B:107)
3903.	8/23/92	gee	Ketchum, Joseph, merchant; Plattsburgh, CLI. See 7881.
3904.	4/25/93	gee	Ketchum, Joseph; ---, ---. See 7168.
3905.	8/24/93	mor	Ketchum, Joseph, merchant; Plattsburgh, CLI; ---, CLI; mee 7871. (A:114)

3906.	9/10/93	mor	Ketchum, Joseph (w. Phebe), merchant; Plattsburgh, CLI; Plattsburgh, CLI; co-mees 3211, 3878, 7169. Co-mortgagees are the "surviving executors" of the estate of Israel Smith late of Poughkeepsie in Dutchess County, deceased. (A:111)
3907.	11/14/97	gor	Ketchum, Mary. See 3902.
3908.	9/10/93	mor	Ketchum, Phebe. See 3906.
3909.	3/14/97	mor	Ketchum, Phebe, innkeeper; Plattsburgh, CLI; Plattsburgh, CLI; mee 7187. (A:288)
3910.	7/3/97	gor	Ketchum, Phebe, innkeeper; Plattsburgh, CLI; Plattsburgh, CLI; co-gees 266, 307. (B:286)
3911.	2/10/97	gee	Ketchum, Phoebe. See 7175.
3912.	6/25/96	mor	Kibbe, Mosses, yeoman; Westfield, WAS; Westfield, WAS; mee 8534. (B:63)
3913.	9/7/69	gor	Kid, Charles; ---, ---. See 7955.
3914.	4/20/73	gor	Kid, Charles; ---, ---. See 7957.
3915.	3/2/86	gee	Kilborn, Elisha, Junr.; Castleton, RUT, VT. See 8235.
3916.	5/19/98	gee	Killmer, Simon A., blacksmith; Argyle, WAS. See 6883.
3917.	7/28/98	gor	Killmore, Adam, (w. Catherine), farmer; Argyle, WAS; Argyle, WAS; gee 7141. (D:200)
3918.	6/1/98	mor	Killmore, Anganitchie. See 3931.
3919.	7/28/98	gor	Killmore, Catherine. See 3917.
3920.	12/30/85	gee	Killmore, George; ---, ---. See 3731.
3921.	10/13/89	gor	Killmore, George; Argyle, WAS; Argyle, WAS; gee 1747. (A:126)
3922.	8/3/90	mor	Killmore, George; Argyle, WAS; Argyle, WAS; mee 8522. (A:283)
3923.	1/10/92	gor	Killmore, George; Argyle, WAS; Argyle, WAS; gee 7024. (A:245)
3924.	8/17/92	gor	Killmore, George; Argyle, WAS; Argyle, WAS; gee 3926. (C-2:206)
3925.	8/8/99	gor	Killmore, George (w. Mary), yeoman; Argyle, WAS; Argyle, WAS; gee 8429. (D:278)
3926.	8/17/92	gee	Killmore, Henry; Argyle, WAS. See 3924.
3927.	5/1/84	gor	Killmore, Jerry, yeoman; Argyle, WAS; Argyle, WAS; co-gees 640, 641, 642, 643, 644, 645. Co-grantees are all children of "the late James Benn of the Manor of Livingston". (B-1:210)
3928.	8/8/99	gor	Killmore, Mary. See 3925.
3929.	5/4/97	gee	Killmore, Simeon; ---, ---. See 7810.
3930.	7/6/89	gee	Killmorem Simon, Senr., farmer; Argyle, WAS. See 3940.
3931.	6/1/98	mor	Killmore, Simon A. (w. Anganitchie), blacksmith; Argyle, WAS; Argyle, WAS; mee 6884. (C:149)
3932.	12/22/02	mor	Killmore, Simon A., blacksmith; Argyle, WAS; Argyle, WAS; mee 6887. (E:37)
3933.	12/1/00	mor	Kilmer, Adam (w. Catharine); Argyle, WAS; ---, WAS; co-mor 3936; mee 5552. (D:10)
3934.	12/1/00	mor	Kilmer, Catharine. See 3933.
3935.	2/10/84	gee	Kilmer, George; Argyle, CHA. See 7539.
3936.	12/1/00	mor	Kilmer, John; Argyle, WAS. See 3933.
3937.	2/20/89	gee	Kilmore, Adam, Junr., farmer; Argyle, WAS. See 3939.
3938.	8/10/84	gor	Kilmore, George; Argyle, WAS; Argyle, WAS; gee 7546. (B-1:195)
3939.	2/20/89	gor	Kilmore, George, farmer; Argyle, WAS; Argyle, WAS; gee 3937. (C-1:68)
3940.	7/6/89	gor	Kilmore, George, farmer; Argyle, WAS; Argyle, WAS; gee 3930. (A:307)
3941.	7/13/90	gor	Kilmore, George; Argyle, WAS; Argyle, WAS; gee 1748. (A:223)
3942.	1/1/94	gor	Kilmore, Hanah. See 3949.
3943.	5/3/97	gor	Kilmore, Hanah. See 3947.
3944.	5/4/67	gee	Kilmore, Jerrey; Livingston Manor, ALB. See 2827.
3945.	5/4/84?	gee	Kilmore, Jerry; ---, ---. See 3744.
3946.	10/17/97	mor	Kilmore, Nicholas, yeoman; Argyle, WAS; Argyle, WAS; mee 6678. (B:230)
3947.	5/3/97	gor	Kilmore, Simeon (w. Hanah). See 7807.
3948.	5/4/97	mee	Kilmore, Simeon; ---, ---. See 8248.
3949.	1/1/94	gor	Kilmore, Simon (w. Hanah); Argyle, WAS; Argyle, WAS; co-gees 8427, 8440. (B-2:154)
3950.	11/16/93	mee	Kimble, Peter, merchant; City of N.Y. See 3507.
3951.	12/30/94	mee	Kimble, Peter, merchant; City of N.Y. See 1564.

3952. 1/1/01 gor Kimble, Peter, merchant; City of N.Y.; Hebron, WAS (land is sold by Kimble's attorney, James Harvey, merchant, of Salem, WAS); gee 1351. (E:283)
3953. 7/12/01 gor Kimble, Peter, merchant; City of N.Y.; Hebron, WAS (land is sold by Kimble's attorney, James Harvey, merchant, of Salem, WAS); gee 2139. (E:448)
3954. 9/21/86 gee Kimble, Peter, Esq.; City of N.Y. See 3844.
3955. 4/22/84 gee Kimmis, John; Anguasanhook, ALB. See 6713.
3956. 4/13/93 gee Kincaid, John, merchant; Westfield, WAS. See 6195.
3957. 6/30/98 gee Kincaid, John; ---, WAS. See 925.
3958. 1/24/98 gee Kincaid, John, Esq., merchant; Hartford, WAS. See 1473.
3959. 1/25/98 mor Kincaid, John, Esq.; Hartford, WAS; Hartford, WAS; mee 1480. (C:151)
3960. 2/26/00 mee King, Andrew; ---, ORA. See 7886.
3961. 11/9/01 --- King, Andrew; ---, ORA. See 3412.
3962. 12/5/89 gor King, Dinah; Cambridge Dist., WAS. See 747 and 3974.
3963. 3/10/98 mee King, Hezekiah; Cambridge, WAS. See 1381.
3964. 3/18/89 gee King, James; Salem, WAS. See 2819.
3965. 10/18/96 mee King, John; ---, SAR. See 1087.
3966. 7/26/98 mee King, John; City of N.Y. See 8699.
3967. 12/2/99 mee King, John, merchant; City of N.Y. See 1857.
3968. 12/12/01 gee King, John; Granville, WAS. See 7641.
3969. 12/12/01 mor King, John; Granville, WAS; Granville, WAS; mee 7740. (D:135)
3970. 7/26/98 mee King, Reay; Philadelphia, ---, PA. See 8699.
3971. 12/2/99 mee King, Reay, merchant; City of Philadelphia, PA. See 1857.
3972. 5/4/95 gee King, Samuel, farmer; Argyle, WAS. See 8020.
3973. 11/11/86 gee King, Solomon; Kingsbury, WAS. See 1592.
3974. 12/5/89 gor King, Solomon. Husband of Dinah King in 3962.
3975. 5/16/91 gor King, Solomon, Capt.; Cambridge, WAS; Cambridge, WAS; gee 5607. (D:44)
3976. 5/17/91 gor King, Solomon, Capt.; Cambridge, WAS; Cambridge, WAS; gee 5608. (D:41)
3977. 8/6/92 gee King, Solomon; Kingsbury, WAS. See 523.
3978. 3/29/94 gee King, Solomon; Kingsbury, WAS. See 524.
3979. 5/13/96 mor King, Solomon, Colonel; Cambridge, WAS; Cambridge, WAS; co-mees 6674 and 8859. (B:38)
3980. 2/20/99 gee King, Solomon; Kingsbury, WAS. See 3475.
3981. 2/5/95 gee King, Solomon, Esq.; Cambridge, WAS. See 4380.
3982. 5/11/74 gee King, William, yeoman; Amenia, DUT. See 1759.
3983. 3/9/02 mor Kingsbury, Anne. See 3984.
3984. 3/9/02 mor Kingsbury, Charles (w. Anne); Danby, RUT, VT; Cambridge, WAS; mee 8506. (D:231)
3985. 2/27/90 gee Kingsbury, Ebenezer; ---, ---. See 1014.
3986. 6/18/93 mor Kingsbury, Uriah, farmer; Willsborough, CLI. See 2072.
3987. 12/1/97 gee Kingsley, James, blacksmith; Westfield, WAS. See 3989.
3988. 6/8/91 gee Kingsley, John, Junr.; Whitehall, WAS. See 8572.
3989. 12/1/97 gor Kingsley, John, Junr.; Westfield, WAS; Whitehall, WAS; co-gees 3987, 5567. (C-2:284)
3990. 3/1/86 mor Kingsley, Zephaniah; ---, ---; Artillery Pat., WAS; mee 3194. (Deed Book B-1:232)
3991. 4/8/96 mor Kinion, Nathaniel, farmer; Easton, WAS; Saratoga Pat., WAS; mee 3680. (B:34)
3992. 5/19/98 --- Kinlock, William; "late of Boston". See 6882.
3993. 3/23/89 gee Kinne, Denison; Westfield, WAS. See 4429.
3994. 10/16/90 mor Kinyon, Christopher; Plattsburgh, CLI; Plattsburgh, CLI; mee 6265. (A:60)
3995. 10/31/99 gee Kinyon, Nathaniel, yeoman; Easton, WAS. See 8054.
3996. 5/4/95 gee Kinyon, Robert, farmer; Argyle, WAS. See 8020.
3997. 12/15/97 gee Kinyon, Robert; Argyle, WAS. See 8621.
3998. 10/21/01 gee Kinyon, Robert, farmer; Argyle, WAS. See 4731.
3999. 12/15/97 gee Kinyon, Robert, Junr.; Argyle, WAS. See 8621.
4000. 5/7/85 gor Kip, Leonard, merchant; City of N.Y. (Kip is executor of the will of Elizabeth Campbell, dec'd.); Argyle, WAS; gee 6718. (B-1:206)
Kirby. See also Curby.
4001. 7/18/99 mee Kirby, Edmund, merchant; City of N.Y. See 4493.

4002. 6/24/99 gee Kirby, Elihu. See 1845.
4003. 3/27/02 mee Kirby, Elihu, blacksmith; Cambridge, WAS. See 8394.
4004. 1/9/96 gee Kirby, John, farmer; Crown Point, CLI. See 2419.
4005. 7/4/96 mor Kirtland, John (w. Lucy); ---, WAS; personal loan?;
             mee 7625.   (B:77)
4006. 7/4/96 mor Kirtland, Lucy. See 4005.
4007. 11/4/91 gee Knapp, Obadiah, blacksmith; Canaan, COL. See 4970.
4008. 7/8/02 mor Kneeland, Ichabod; Granville, WAS; Granville, WAS; mee 4161.
                                                                (E:7)
4009. 11/26/94 gee Knickerbacker, John, Esq.; Schaghticoke, REN. See 7946.
4010. 7/4/96 gor Knute, Frederick (w. Maria), farmer; Watervliet, ALB;
             Easton, WAS; gee 6941.   (C-2:286)
4011. 7/4/96 gor Knute, Maria. See 4010.
4012. 5/2/96 gee Kynon, Robert; Argyle, WAS. See 2099.
4013. 5/2/96 gee Kynon, Robert, Junr.; Argyle, WAS. See 2099.
4014. 5/13/89 gor Labombard, Joseph, "a refugee from Canada"; Champlain, CLI;
             gee 5105.   (A:511)
4015. 3/8/97 gor La Bonte, John Batest, "late a Captain in the Volunteer
             Refugees from Canada now (of) the Parish of St. Tour,
             Montreal Dist., Lower Canada"; Champlain, CLI; gee 5139.
                                                                (B:93)
4016. 4/5/92 gor Lacost, Francis, "late a soldier in Col. Hazen's Regiment
             of Canada Refugees serving in the Continental Army
             during the late War"; Warwick, ORA; Bounty Lands, CLI;
             gee 7733.   (A:516)
4017. 3/15/97 gee Laforgue, Martial, merchant, "late of Montreal but now of
             ... Champlain", CLI. See 7840.
4018. 4/15/96 mee Lake, Abraham; Hoosick, REN. See 7906.
4019. 1/7/99 mee Lamb, John; City of N.Y. See 1648.
4020. 4/29/97 --- Lamb, John, Esq.; City of N.Y.; Old Military Township #7
             (Chateaugay), CLI. Lamb appoints William Bailey,
             merchant, "at present of the City of New York" to be his
             attorney to sell the above lands.   (B:116)
4021. 11/6/98 mee Lamb, John, Esq.; City of N.Y. See 3137.
4022. 3/13/98 mor Lamb, Martin (w. Olive); ---, WAS; Hartford, WAS; mee 924.
                                                                (B:287)
4023. 3/13/98 mor Lamb, Olive. See 4022.
4024. 1/12/80 gor Lamon, Francis; White Creek, CHA; White Creek, CHA; gee 4469.
                                                              (B-1:44)
4025. 5/2/96 gee Lamphear, Amos; Argyle, WAS. See 2100a.
4026. 6/2/98 gee Lamson, Oliver; Granville, WAS. See 718.
4027. 1/4/00 mor Lane, Ama. See 4028.
4028. 1/4/00 mor Lane, Asa (w. Ama), farmer; Argyle, WAS; Argyle, WAS;
             mee 6061.   (C:164)
4029. 4/7/98 mor Lane, Joseph, blacksmith; Champlain, CLI; ---, CLI;
             co-mor 4032; mee 801.   (A:287)
4030. 10/3/99 mor Lane, Joseph; Champlain, CLI; Champlain, CLI; mee 1942.
                                                              (A:405)
4031. 10/24/99 mor Lane, Joseph; Champlain, CLI; Champlain, CLI; mee 1943.
                                                              (A:406)
4032. 4/7/98 mor Lane, Witt, blacksmith; Champlain, CLI. See 4029.
4033. 3/18/96 gee Lansing, Abraham, merchant; Albany, ALB. See 1550.
4034. 12/28/02 mee Lansing, Abraham A.; Albany. ALB. See 1880.
4035. 11/18/02 mee Lansing, Abraham H., farmer; Watervliet, ALB. See 1729.
4036. 6/13/94 gor Lansing, Cornelius; Troy, REN. See 4042.
4037. 8/17/99 mee Lansing, Gerrit G., merchant; Easton, WAS. See 6428.
4038. 1/30/00 mee Lansing, Gerrit G., merchant; Argyle, WAS. See 8733.
4039. 9/5/00 mee Lansing, Gerrit G., merchant; Argyle, WAS. See 732, 1165,
             3889.
4040. 10/10/99 mee Lansing, Gerrit T., merchant; Argyle, WAS. See 1569.
4041. 6/13/94 --- Lansing, Jacob, dec'd. See 4042.
4042. 6/13/94 gor Lansing, Jacob A.; Troy, REN; Cambridge Pat., WAS;
             co-gors 4036, 4043 (grantors are all heirs at law of
             Abraham Jacob Lansing, deceased," of Troy); gee 8857.
                                                              (E:212)
4043. 6/13/94 gor Lansing, Levinus; Troy, REN. See 4042.

<u>4044.</u> 2/12/76 gor Lansingh, Abraham Jacob, gentleman; Lansingburgh, ALB;
                                  Cambridge Pat., WAS; gee 8322.   (D:352)
4045. 3/18/96 gee Lansingh, Gerrit, merchant; Easton, WAS. See 1550.
4046. 1/21/92 mee Lansings, Cornelius; ---, REN. See 4761 and 4762.
4047. 7/6/96 gee Lant, Casparus; Claverack, COL. See 4487.
4048. 12/16/99 mee Lant, Casparus; Argyle, WAS. See 7622.
4049. 7/6/96 gee Lant, William; Claverack, COL. See 4487.
4050. 12/16/99 mee Lant, William; Argyle, WAS. See 7622.
4051. 2/2/99 mee Lapham, Nathan; Danby, RUT, VT. See 4829.
4052. 4/2/94 mee Lapham, Thomas; Easton, WAS. See 407.
<u>4053.</u> 12/3/89 gor La Pierre, Thomas, "a Canadian refugee"; ---, ---; <u>Canadian</u>
                                <u>and Nova Scotia Refugees' Pat.</u>, CLI; co-gees 155, 6402.
                                                          (A:264)
<u>4054.</u> 11/21/99 mor Latee, Moses; ---, ---; <u>Crown Point, ESS</u>; mee 5875. (A:7)
<u>4055.</u> 9/8/01 gee Latham, Hubbard; Southampton, SUF. See 7002.
4056. 7/4/82 gee Lathrop, Ebenezer; Lebanon, WIN, CT. See 3387.
4057. 10/7/99 mee Lathrop, Samuel; Cambridge, WAS. See 7440.
<u>4058.</u> 9/19/86 gor Laurant, Joseph, "a Canadian refugee"; ---, ---; <u>Canadian</u>
                                <u>and Nova Scotia Refugees' Pat.</u>, CLI; gee 7643. (B:204)
4059. 11/28/93 mor Law, Abigail. See 4074.
4060. 12/9/99 gor Law. Abigail. See 4075.
<u>4061.</u> 9/20/84 gor Law, John; New Perth, WAS; <u>New Perth, WAS</u>; gee 2341. (C-1:14)
<u>4062.</u> 7/6/88 gee Law, John, yeoman; Granville, WAS. See 2378.
<u>4063.</u> 7/6/88 mor Law, John; Granville, WAS; <u>Granville, WAS</u>; mee 2379. (A:128)
<u>4064.</u> 8/9/91 gor Law, John, carpenter; Granville, WAS; <u>Granville, WAS</u>;
                                gee 8178.   (C-2:318)
<u>4065.</u> 7/2/92 gor Law, John; Salem, WAS; <u>Salem, WAS</u>; gee 3313.   (A:426)
<u>4066.</u> 5/4/97 gor Law, John; Salem, WAS; <u>land "joining McDonald's Bay in Lake</u>
                                <u>George", WAS</u>; co-gees 27, 29.   (C-2:183)
4067. 5/27/99 mee Law, John; Salem, WAS. See 3567.
4068. 12/9/99 gee Law, John, yeoman; Cambridge, WAS. See 4075.
4069. 10/27/00 mee Law, John; Cambridge, WAS. See 2172.
<u>4070.</u> 1/7/01 mor Law, John (w. Mary); Cambridge, WAS; <u>Anguasanhook(?), WAS</u>;
                                mee 6168.   (D:1)
4071. 2/15/02 mee Law, John, yeoman; Cambridge, WAS. See 2173.
4072. 8/13/02 gee Law, John, Esq.; Salem, WAS. See 699.
4073. 1/7/01 mor Law, Mary. See 4070.
<u>4074.</u> 11/28/93 mor Law, Robert (w. Abigail), farmer; Cambridge, WAS; <u>Cambridge,</u>
                                <u>WAS</u>; mee 6166.   (A:470)
<u>4075.</u> 12/9/99 gor Law, Robert (w. Abigail), yeoman; Cambridge, WAS; <u>Cambridge,</u>
                                <u>WAS</u>; gee 4068.   (E:1)
<u>4076.</u> 12/28/92 gor Lawrance, John, Esq.; City of N.Y.; <u>Granville, WAS</u>; gee 8577.
                                                    (B-2:38)
4077. 4/25/96 mee Lawrence, Catharine, widow; City of N.Y. See 5529.
4078. 5/27/00 mee Lawrence, Catharine; City of N.Y. See 6387.
4079. 5/1/02 mee Lawrence, Catharine; City of N.Y. See 2055, 3821, 4538.
4080. 1/22/96 mee Lawrence, Effingham, gentleman; ---, Quebec, Canada.
                                See 6612.
4081. 7/15/86 mee Lawrence, John, Esq.; City of N.Y. See 3176.
<u>4082.</u> 5/9/99 gor Lawrence, John, Esq.; City of N.Y.; <u>Argyle, WAS</u>; gee 7634.
                                                   (D:112)
4083. 2/8/85 gee Lawrence, Jonathan, gentleman; ---, ---. See 5887.
<u>4084.</u> 3/14/87 gee Lawrence, Jonathan; ---, ---. See 5911.
<u>4085.</u> 5/5/91 gor Lawrence, Jonathan, merchant; City of N.Y.; <u>Cumberland Head,</u>
                                <u>(Plattsburgh), CLI</u>; gee 1542.   (A:245)
4086. 1/1/97 mee Lawrence, Jonathan; City of N.Y. See 7993.
<u>4087.</u> 2/6/97 gor Lawrence, Jonathan, Esq.; City of N.Y.; <u>Plattsburgh, CLI</u>;
                                gee 7185.   (A:545)
4088. 8/10/02 mor Leach, Betsey. See 4089.
<u>4089.</u> 8/10/02 mor Leach, Oliver (w. Betsey); Hartford, WAS; <u>Hartford, WAS</u>;
                                mee 938. Mortgagee is the administrator of the estate
                                of Cornelius V. Brewerton "late of Salem".   (E:11)
4090. 7/3/93 --- Leak, John, dec'd. See 5335.
4091. 6/10/84 mee Leake, John; ---, ---. See 6335.
4092. 7/29/91 mee Leake, John, gentleman; City of N.Y. See 4104.
4093. 4/30/93 --- Leake, John, gentleman, dec'd.; City of N.Y. See 5334.

4094. 11/20/96 --- Leake, John, dec'd. See 5337.
4095. 8/1/98 --- Leake, John, dec'd. See 1132 and 5327.
4096. 3/1/76 mee Leake, John, Esq.; City of N.Y. See 402.
4097. 6/8/84 gor Leake, John, Esq.; City of N.Y.; Skenesborough, WAS;
          gee 6334.   (B-2:207)
4098. 11/20/00 mor Leavitt, Asaph; ---, ---; Willsborough, ESS; mee 58. (A:39)
4099. 5/2/96 gee Ledsen, William; Argyle, WAS. See 2100a.
4100. 11/26/01 mor Lee, Anson; Granville, WAS; Granville, WAS; mee 724. (D:188)
4101. 4/13/01 mor Lee, Ezra; Granville, WAS; Granville, WAS; mee 4143. (D:46)
4102. 4/9/98 mor Lee, Jonathan, farmer; Westfield, WAS; Westfield, WAS;
          mee 8791.   (B:288)
4103. 7/13/92 mor Lee, Ladoik, farmer; Granville, WAS. See 3402.
4104. 7/29/91 mor Lee, Nathan (w. Sarah), yeoman; Westfield, WAS; Provincial
          Pat., WAS; co-mors 7859, 7860; mee 4092.   (A:307)
4105. 11/14/94 gor Lee, Nathan, farmer; Granville, WAS; Granville, WAS;
          gee 3376.   (B-2:494)
4106. 2/8/98 mor Lee, Nathan, farmer; Hartford, WAS; Hartford, WAS;
          mee 1483.   (B:283)
4107. 3/9/98 mor Lee, Nathan (w. Sarah), farmer; Hartford, WAS; Hartford,
          WAS; mee 1488.   (B:285)
4108. 3/1/98 mor Lee, Noah, farmer; ---, CLI; Old Military Township #7
          (Chateaugay), CLI; co-mees 6853, 8084.   (A:283)
4109. 2/27/96 mor Lee, Robert P.; City of N.Y.; Old Military Township #7
          (Chateaugay), CLI; co-mor 5542; mee 4802.   (A:185)
4110. 7/29/91 mor Lee, Sarah. See 4104.
4111. 3/9/98 mor Lee, Sarah. See 4107.
4112. 7/6/88 gee Lee, William, yeoman; Granville, WAS. See 2377.
4113. 7/6/88 mor Lee, William; Granville, WAS; Granville, WAS; mee 2379.
                                                         (A:123)
4114. 9/10/92 gor Lee, William, gentleman; Granville, WAS; Granville, WAS;
          gee 7340.   (B-2:232)
4115. 7/3/93 gor Lee, William; Granville, WAS; Granville, WAS; gee 7341.
                                                         (B-2:228)
4116. 10/21/93 gor Lee, William; Granville, WAS; Granville, WAS; gee 7342.
                                                         (B-2:230)
4117. 3/2/98 mor Lee, William; Granville, WAS; Granville, WAS; mee 3850.
                                                         (B:286)
4118. 12/29/94 gor Lee, Zadock; Granville, WAS. See 1850.
4119. 5/1/02 mor Leggett, Charles, farmer; Chester, WAS; Chester, WAS;
          mee 7775.   (D:227)
4120. 5/30/01 mee Leggett, Joseph, merchant; City of N.Y. See 3833.
4121. 5/30/01 mee Leggett, Thomas, merchant; City of N.Y. See 3833.
4122. 6/19/90 gor Leglise, Dominique, gentleman; New Rochelle, WES; ---, CLI;
          gee 2175.   (A:136)
4123. 2/20/96 gor Leister, John, "late a soldier in the army of the United
          States in the --- New York Regiment commanded by Col.
          James Livingston"; ---, ---; sells for $50 "land (in
          Clinton County) that is or may be granted to me by the
          Congress (of the U.S.), the Legislature of the State
          (of N.Y.), or other ways as bounty or gratuity lands
          for my services in the Army"; gee 7248.   (A:443)
4124. 7/26/91 mee Leonard, Enoch; Albany, ALB. See 4609.
4125. 10/1/01 gor Leonard, Mary. See 4148.
4126. 1/11/94 mee Leonard, Timothy; Granville, WAS. See 8407.
4127. 10/7/94 gee Leonard, Timothy; ---, ---. See 8583.
4128. 12/22/95 mee Leonard, Timothy; Granville, WAS. See 533.
4129. 10/8/96 mee Leonard, Timothy; Granville, WAS. See 1856.
4130. 8/11/97 mee Leonard, Timothy, merchant, Granville, WAS. See 1615.
4131. 3/23/98 mee Leonard, Timothy; ---, ---. See 7961.
4132. 8/21/98 mee Leonard, Timothy; Granville, WAS. See 8409.
4133. 9/4/98 mee Leonard, Timothy; Granville, WAS. See 7853.
4134. 1/12/99 mee Leonard, Timothy; Granville, WAS. See 5450.
4135. 2/27/99 mee Leonard, Timothy; Granville, WAS. See 461.
4136. 7/4/99 gee Leonard, Timothy; Granville, WAS. See 2076.
4137. 3/14/00 mee Leonard, Timothy; Granville, WAS. See 578.
4138. 3/15/00 mee Leonard, Timothy; Granville, WAS. See 5390.

4139.	4/5/00	mee	Leonard, Timothy; Granville, WAS. See 534.
4140.	10/20/00	mee	Leonard, Timothy; Granville, WAS. See 3511.
4141.	1/13/01	mee	Leonard, Timothy; Granville, WAS. See 2339.
4142.	1/30/01	mee	Leonard, Timothy; Granville, WAS. See 1658.
4143.	4/13/01	mee	Leonard, Timothy; Granville, WAS. See 4101.
4144.	5/14/01	mee	Leonard, Timothy; Granville, WAS. See 3085.
4145.	5/16/01	mee	Leonard, Timothy; Granville, WAS. See 3017.
4146.	5/30/01	mee	Leonard, Timothy; Granville, WAS. See 5453.
4147.	8/5/01	mee	Leonard, Timothy; Granville, WAS. See 7963.
4148.	10/1/01	gor	Leonard, Timothy (w. Mary); Granville, WAS; Granville, WAS;
			co-gees 3825, 6210. (F:228)
4149.	10/7/01	---	Leonard, Timothy. See 5291.
4150.	10/13/01	mee	Leonard, Timothy; Granville, WAS. See 3826.
4151.	1/22/02	mee	Leonard, Timothy; Granville, WAS. See 7914.
4152.	2/15/02	mee	Leonard, Timothy; Granville, WAS. See 5472.
4153.	3/6/02	mee	Leonard, Timothy; Granville, WAS. See 1653.
4154.	3/13/02	mee	Leonard, Timothy; Granville, WAS. See 357.
4155.	4/2/02	mee	Leonard, Timothy; Granville, WAS. See 445.
4156.	5/15/02	mee	Leonard, Timothy; Granville, WAS. See 6473 and 8458.
4157.	5/17/02	mee	Leonard, Timothy; Granville, WAS. See 5446.
4158.	6/5/02	mee	Leonard, Timothy; Granville, WAS. See 5477.
4159.	6/7/02	mee	Leonard, Timothy; Granville, WAS. See 239 and 5324.
4160.	6/15/02	mee	Leonard, Timothy; Granville, WAS. See 4390.
4161.	7/8/02	mee	Leonard, Timothy; Granville, WAS. See 4008.
4162.	7/21/02	mee	Leonard, Timothy; Granville, WAS. See 6640.
4163.	7/24/02	mee	Leonard, Timothy; Granville, WAS. See 5643.
4164.	8/14/02	mee	Leonard, Timothy; Granville, WAS. See 1924.
4165.	2/25/97	mee	Leonard, Timothy, Esq.; Granville, WAS. See 8408.
4166.	4/13/02	mee	Le Roux, Charles, gentleman; City of N.Y. See 7637.
4167.	4/26/02	mee	Le Roux, Charles, gentleman; City of N.Y. See 7471.
4168.	12/4/93	mee	Le Roy, Jacob, merchant; City of N.Y. See 7346.
4169.	2/3/95	mee	Le Roy, Jacob, merchant; City of N.Y. See 4846.
4170.	12/4/93	mee	Le Roy, Robert, merchant; City of N.Y. See 7346.
4171.	2/3/95	mee	Le Roy, Robert, merchant; City of N.Y. See 4846.
4172.	2/12/96	gor	Lettebrand, Hartman, tailor; Clermont, COL (Lettebrand is
			"lawful heir to the estate of Moses Bartlet, deceased")
			Salem, WAS; gee 474. (D:232)
4173.	1/26/01	gee	Leverse, Isaac; Easton, WAS. See 3086.
4174.	1/26/01	mor	Leverse, Isaac (w. Jenny); Easton, WAS; Argyle, WAS;
			mee 3087. (D:8)
4175.	1/26/01	mor	Leverse, Jenny. See 4174.
4176.	1/24/92	mee	Levingston, Cathrine; ---, ---. See 5564.
4177.	1/24/92	mee	Levingston, James; ---, ---. See 5564.
4178.	1/24/92	---	Levingston, John, dec'd.; ---, SAR. See 5564.
4179.	1/21/92	mee	Levinius, Jacob A.; ---, REN. See 4761, 4762.
4180.	11/27/90	gee	Lewis, Henry, farmer; "late of Danby", RUT, VT. See 2157.
4181.	8/6/98	gee	Lewis, Henry; Westfield, WAS. See 8183.
4182.	1/16/00	gor	Lewis, Henry; Westfield, WAS; Westfield, WAS; gee 497.(F:108)
4183.	4/10/90	gee	Lewis, Morgan; ---, DUT. See 6731.
4184.	11/1/94	mor	Lewis, Nathan, mason; Hebron, WAS; Hebron, WAS; mee 3009.
			(A:531)
4185.	2/8/96	gor	Lewis, Nathen; Hebron, WAS; Hebron, WAS; gee 3203. (B-2:510)
4186.	3/22/90	gee	Lewis, Robert, Senr.; Albany, ALB. See 5993.
4187.	5/20/95	mor	Lewis, William, farmer; Christie's Manor, Lower Canada.
			See 5353.
4188.	7/4/97	mee	Liddle, John; Hebron, WAS. See 1786.
4189.	4/8/00	mor	Liddle, John (w. Rachel), yeoman; Argyle, WAS; Argyle, WAS;
			mee 6062. (D:4)
4190.	10/2/95	mor	Liddle, Margaret. See 4191.
4191.	10/2/95	mor	Liddle, Mark(?) (w. Margaret); Argyle, WAS; Argyle, WAS;
			mee 1070. (A:605)
4192.	4/8/00	mor	Liddle, Rachel. See 4189.
4193.	4/18/87	gee	Linda, George Andrew; ---, WAS. See 2888.
4194.	7/1/02	mee	Linda, George Andrew; Whitehall, WAS. See 7444.
4195.	10/25/91	---	Lindsay, Agnes, widow; Argyle, WAS. See 4201.
4196.	10/25/91	---	Lindsay, Allen; Argyle, WAS. See 4201.

4197. 9/15/90 mor Lindsay, Daniel, yeoman; Argyle, WAS; Argyle, WAS; mee 4743.
(A:366)
4198. 10/25/91 --- Lindsay, Daniel; Argyle, WAS. See 4201.
4199. 10/1/93 gor Lindsay, Daniel (w. Nely), yeoman; Argyle, WAS; Argyle, WAS;
gee 4965. (B-2:392)
4200. 10/25/91 --- Lindsay, David; Argyle, WAS. See 4201.
4201. 10/25/91 --- Lindsay, Duncan, dec'd. (Lindsay died intestate at Argyle,
WAS). In this agreement Lindsay's sons John, David,
Daniel, and Allen agree to support their widowed mother
Agnes and to make equitable distribution of their father's
estate among their sisters: Margaret De Long, Elisabeth
Hannegan, Eve Durkee, Mary Peterson, and Ann Peterson.
(A:254)
4202. 10/1/93 gor Lindsay, Nely. See 4199.
4203. 12/23/85 gor Lindsey, Duncan, farmer; Argyle, WAS; Argyle, WAS; gee 5610.
(A:299)
4204. 6/5/84 gor Lintot, Bernard, gentleman; "late of Branford", CT.;
Black Creek Dist., WAS; gee 1909. (B-1:138)
4205. 10/3/94 gor Lintott, Bernard; ---, ---, GA; Hebron, WAS; co-gor 4206;
gee 8382. (B-2:498)
4206. 10/3/94 gor Lintott, William; ---, ---, GA. See 4205.
4207. 6/22/92 gor Litle, Isaac; Hebron, WAS; Hebron, WAS; co-gees 2513, 4331,
6076. Grantees are all trustees of the Presbyterian
Congregation of Hebron. (A:311)
4208. 7/9/92 gor Litle, Isaac, gentleman; Hebron, WAS; Hebron, WAS; gee 1506.
(A:466)
4209. 2/1/97 gor Litle, Isaac, Major; Hebron, WAS; Hebron, WAS; gee 8635.
(C-2:195)
4210. 1/19/99 gee Little, Andrew; Salem, WAS. See 2399.
4211. 8/28/00 mor Little, Thomas; ---, ---; Willsborough, ESS; mee 3230. (A:72)
4212. 12/1/00 mee Littlefield, Saunders, yeoman; Kingsbury, WAS. See 7527.
4213. 6/23/96 gor Livingston, Abraham (w. Maria), gentleman; Stillwater, SAR;
Canadian and Nova Scotia Refugees' Pat., CLI; gee 8493.
(B:190)
4214. 4/11/96 mor Livingston, Agness. See 4218.
4215. 4/2/91 mor Livingston, Alexander; Argyle, WAS; Argyle, WAS; mee 6888.
(A:279)
4216. 4/23/91 gee Livingston, Alexander, farmer; Argyle, WAS. See 4220.
4217. 4/11/96 gee Livingston, Alexander; Cambridge Dist., WAS. See 701.
4218. 4/11/96 mor Livingston, Alexander (w. Agness); Cambridge, WAS;
Cambridge Pat., WAS; mee 702. (C:162)
4219. 4/4/99 mor Livingston, Alexander; Cambridge, WAS; Cambridge, WAS;
mee 8537. (C:163)
4220. 4/23/91 gor Livingston, Archibald, weaver; Argyle, WAS; Argyle, WAS;
co-gees 4216, 4241. (A:206)
4221. 10/13/00 gee Livingston, Benjamin, merchant; Argyle, WAS. See 8670.
4222. 10/13/00 mor Livingston, Benjamin (w. Hannah), merchant; Argyle, WAS;
Argyle, WAS; mee 8671. (C:166)
4223. 1/24/00 gor Livingston, Benjamine, yeoman; Hebron, WAS; Hebron, WAS;
gee 4333. (E:207)
4224. 10/28/01 mee Livingston, Brockholst, Esq.; City of N.Y. See 1226.
4225. 4/28/02 mee Livingston, Brockholst, Esq.; City of N.Y. See 4235.
4226. 4/28/02 mor Livingston, Catharine. See 4235.
4227. 6/15/95 gor Livingston, Catherine, widow; City of N.Y. ("executor of the
estate of William Smith Livingston, attorney, late of the
same place, deceased"). See 7129.
4228. 5/18/85 gee Livingston, Daniel; ---, ALB. See 1224.
4229. 6/15/95 --- Livingston, Elizabeth, dec'd. See 7129.
4230. 10/13/00 mor Livingston, Hannah. See 4222.
4231. 1/22/96 mee Livingston, Henry Alexander; City of N.Y. See 6611.
4232. 2/20/96 --- Livingston, James, Col. See 4123.
4233. 5/13/96 --- Livingston, James, Col. See 1230.
4234. 3/15/97 --- Livingston, James; ---, ---. See 7840.
4235. 4/28/02 mor Livingston, John (w. Catharine), gentleman; Manor of Livingston,
COL; Canadian and Nova Scotia Refugees' Pat., CLI; mee 4225.
(B:84)

4236. 11/14/88 gor Livingston, Margaret, Lady; Clermont, COL; Saratoga Dist.,
ALB (sic); gee 6638.   (Washington Co. D:46)
4237. 10/15/91 gor Livingston, Margaret; Clermont, COL; Saratoga Pat., WAS;
gee 3268.   (B-2:84)
4238. 6/15/95 gor Livingston, Margaret, widow; Livingston Manor, COL. See 7129.
4239. 11/20/95 mee Livingston, Margaret; Clermont, COL. See 3165.
4240. 6/15/95 gor Livingston, Maturin, attorney; City of N.Y. See 7129.
4241. 4/23/91 gee Livingston, Moses, farmer; Argyle, WAS. See 4220.
4242. 6/15/95 gor Livingston, Peter R., attorney; City of N.Y. See 7129.
4243. 9/20/73 gee Livingston, Peter Van Brugh, merchant; City of N.Y.
See 7885.
4244. 10/20/85 gor Livingston, Peter Van Brugh; City of N.Y.; land "east side
of ... Wood Creek, CHA (sic); gee 3035.   (C-1:3)
4245. 4/2/87 gor Livingston, Peter Van Brugh; City of N.Y.; Indian Purchase,
WAS; gee 1746.   (C-2:2)
4246. 10/24/93 mee Livingston, Philip I., Esq.; ---, WES. See 7887.
4247. 6/15/95 gor Livingston, Robert James; Paris, France. See 7129.
4248. 10/21/96 mee Livingston, Susannah, widow: Elizabethtown, ---, NJ.
See 8594.
4249. 12/29/91 gee Livingston, Walter. See 2143.
4250. 6/15/95 --- Livingston, William, Smith, attorney, dec'd. See 4227.
4251. 2/28/98 mor Lobdell, Silvanus; Pleasant Valley (Crown Point), CLI;
Pleasant Valley, CLI; mee 7750.   (A:278)
4252. 4/1/95 gee Lockwood, Ezekiel; Peru, CLI. See 5733.
4253. 7/1/00 mor Lockwood, Ezekiel; ---, ---; ---, ESS; mee 5572. Two
contracts this date involving these persons. (A:54), (A:55)
4254. 12/31/96 mor Loggan, Robert, Junr.; ---, ---, VT; ---, CLI; mee 2799.
(A:233)
4255. 9/17/96 gee Long, Abner; Hebron, WAS. See 6957.
4256. 7/1/85 gee Long, David, Dr.; ---, ---. See 7055.
4257. 10/7/94 gee Long, David; ---, ---. See 8583.
4258. 5/25/96 mor Long, David; Hebron, WAS; Hebron, WAS; mee 5998. (B:73)
4259. 7/21/97 mor Long, David, physician; Hebron, WAS; Hebron, WAS; mee 5999.
(B:193)
4260. 4/19/00 gor Long, David (w. Margaret); Hebron, WAS; Lintott's Pat., WAS;
gee 8168.   (D:414)
4261. 6/10/69 gee Long, Edward; White Creek, ALB. See 7645.
4262. 4/2/88 gor Long, Edward (w. Sarah); Salem, WAS; Salem, WAS; gee 6533.
(A:71)
4263. 4/19/00 gor Long, Margaret. See 4260.
4264. 4/2/88 gor Long, Sarah. See 4262.
4265. 12/17/94 gor Long, William; ---, ONT; Salem, WAS; gee 8531. (B-2:533)
4266. 5/1/93 gee Long, Zachariah; Plattsburgh, CLI. See 581.
4267. 5/1/93 mor Long, Zachariah, farmer; Plattsburgh, CLI; Plattsburgh, CLI;
mee 582.   (A:102)
4268. 10/22/00 gee Look, Nathan; Cambridge, WAS. See 1133.
4269. 1/11/86 gee Loop, Hendrick, Ensign; Cambridge Dist, WAS. See 2846.
4270. 4/10/94 mee Loop, Hendrick; Fairfield, WAS. See 841.
4271. 7/14/01 mee Lord, Benjamin A.; ---, ---. See 2087.
4272. 4/14/01 mor Lothrop, Philander, merchant; Hartford, WAS; Hartford, WAS;
mee 3784.   (D:35)
4273. 9/20/92 gor Lott, Jeremus, Esq. (w. Lammetje); ---, KIN; Palmer's Purchase,
WAS and MON; gee 5954.   (C-2:223)
4274. 9/20/92 gor Lott, Lammetje. See 4273.
4275. 10/6/01 mor Lovely, Valentine; Hinesburg, CHI, VT; Peru, CLI; mee 5774.
(B:42)
4276. 6/2/73 gor Low, Isaac, merchant; City of N.Y.; land "above Saratoga",
ALB (sic); gee 1809.   (A:61)
4277. 6/22/93 gor Low, Isaac; ---, ---. See 1053.
4278. 9/28/88 gor Low, Wilson; Willsborough, CLI. See 1872.
4279. 12/22/90 gor Lowry, Catharine. See 4280.
4280. 12/22/90 gor Lowry, James (w. Catharine); ---, ---; ---, WAS; gee 5242.
(A:190)
4281. 9/19/99 gee Lucas, David; ---, ---, Vt. See 7424.
4282. 9/19/99 mor Lucas, David (w. Elizabeth); ---, ---, VT; Cambridge, WAS;
mee 7425.   (C:165)

4283. 9/19/99 mor Lucas, Elizabeth. See 4282.
4284. 6/15/98 gee Lucas, Francis; Cambridge, WAS. See 2253.
4285. 9/7/69 gor Lucas, James, dec'd.; ---, ---. See 7955.
4286. 4/20/73 gor Lucas, James, dec'd.; ---, ---. See 7957.
4287. 9/7/69 gor Lucas, John; ---, ---. See 7955.
4288. 6/15/98 gee Lucas, Joseph; Cambridge, WAS. See 2253.
4289. 9/7/69 gor Lucas, Martha, "sister of James Lucas, deceased". See 7955.
4290. 4/20/73 gor Lucas, Martha, "only sister of James Lucas"; ---, ---.
                 See 7957.
4291. 5/24/02 gor Luce, Eley M. (w. Thankful); Argyle, WAS; Argyle, WAS;
                 gee 4723.   (F:238)
4292. 11/24/91 mor Luce, John; Easton, WAS; Saratoga Pat., WAS; mee 8000. (A:352)
4293. 5/24/02 gor Luce, Thankful. See 4291.
4294. 4/20/73 gor Lucere, John; ---, ---. See 7957.
4295. 4/27/92 mor Lucke, John, Junr., laborer; ---, CLI; Champlain, CLI;
                 mee 6413.   (A:155)
4296. 1/1/96 gee Luis, Nathan; Crown Point Dist., CLI. See 6454.
4297. 5/26/85 mee Lush, Stephen; ---, ---. See 7375.
4298. 11/24/85 mee Lush, Stephen, Esq.; Albany, ALB. See 4684.
4299. 3/9/98 mor Lyman, Benjamin (w. Polly), farmer; Hartford, WAS; Hartford,
                 WAS; mee 1488.   (B:284)
4300. 3/9/98 mor Lyman, Polly. See 4299.
4301. 2/6/93 mor Lynde, Jonathan, merchant; Willsborough, CLI; Willsborough,
                 CLI; mee 2810.   (A:100)
4302. 6/20/01 mor Lyon, Dan (w. Mabel), yeoman; Cambridge, WAS; Cambridge,
                 WAS; mee 1768.   (D:122)
4303. 5/18/99 mor Lyon, Jonathan; Cambridge, WAS; Cambridge, WAS; mee 1617.
                                                                (D:57)
4304. 6/20/01 mor Lyon, Mabel. See 4302.
4305. 11/7/95 mor Lyon, Mathew, schoolmaster; Cambridge Dist., WAS; Cambridge
                 Dist., WAS; mee 2620.   (A:612)
4306. 2/9/93 gee Lytall, William, yeoman; Hebron, WAS. See 6131.
4307. 11/4/65 gee Lytle, Andrew, blacksmith; New Perth, ALB. See 1418.
4308. 5/1/66 gee Lytle, Andrew; ---, ---. See 1419.
4309. 6/28/74 gcc Lytle, Andrew; New Perth, CHA. See 2731.
4310. 9/12/74 gee Lytle, Andrew; ---, ---. See 7271.
4311. 4/10/92 gor Lytle, Andrew, yeoman; Salem, WAS; Salem, WAS; gee 3525.
                                                                (D:138)
4312. 12/8/86 gor Lytle, Andrew, Senr., blacksmith; Salem, WAS; Hebron, WAS;
                 gees 4320 and 4328 (two contracts). (B-2:478), (E:203)
4313. 10/23/73 mor Lytle, Isaac; New Perth, CHA; Kemp Pat., CHA; mee 3865.
                                                                (A:4)
4314. 11/18/83 gor Lytle, Isaac; Black Creek Dist., CHA; Black Creek Dist.,
                 CHA; gee 2727.   (B-1:83)
4315. 7/1/85 gee Lytle, Isaac; ---, ---. See 7055.
4316. --/--/87 gee Lytle, Isaac; ---, ---. See 7055.
4317. 3/6/87 gee Lytle, Isaac; ---, ---. See 7055.
4318. 6/24/88 mee Lytle, Isaac; ---, ---. See 7666.
4319. 4/20/70 gee Lytle, James, farmer; White Creek, ALB. See 3775.
4320. 12/8/86 gee Lytle, James; Hebron, WAS. See 4312.
4321. 5/31/96 gor Lytle, James, yeoman; ---, WAS. See 6890.
4322. 11/3/97 gee Lytle, James, farmer; Argyle, WAS. See 5612.
4323. 9/25/01 gee Lytle, James. See 4571.
4324. 5/2/96 gor Lytle, Jannit. See 4332.
4325. 10/18/90 gee Lytle, Martha; Salem, WAS. See 1690.
4326. 2/16/92 mor Lytle, Robert; Hebron, WAS; Hutton's Bush, WAS; mee 3650.
                                                                (C:165)
4327. 10/18/90 gee Lytle, Samuel; Salem, WAS. See 1690.
4328. 12/8/86 gee Lytle, William; Hebron, WAS. See 4312.
4329. 4/1/90 mor Lytle, William; Hebron, WAS; Hebron, WAS; mee 7274. (A:284)
4330. 4/21/91 gee Lytle, William, yeoman; Hebron, WAS. See 8292.
4331. 6/22/92 gee Lytle, William, trustee of the First Presbyterian Congregation,
                 Hebron, WAS. See 4207.
4332. 5/2/96 gor Lytle, William (w. Jannit); Salem, WAS; Salem, WAS; gee 2362.
                                                                (B-2:551)
4333. 1/24/00 gee Lytle, William, yeoman; Hebron, WAS. See 4223.

4334. 3/6/01 mee Lytle, William; Salem, WAS. See 7514.
4335. 9/30/90 gor McAdam, Ann, "widow of William McAdam late of New York";
  City of N.Y.; Turner Pat., WAS; gee 2507.   (A:246)
4336. 10/11/91 gor McAdam, Ann, "widow ... of William McAdam, Esq. ... of
  the City of New York, deceased"; ---, ---; Salem, WAS;
  gee 7475.   (A:239)
4337. 10/12/91 mee McAdam, Ann, "widow of William McAdam, merchant, City of
  New York, deceased"; ---, ---. See 7476.
4338. 11/1/91 gor McAdam, Ann,"widow and executor of the estate of William
  McAdam, merchant, ..."; City of N.Y.; Salem, WAS; gee 165.
                                                     (A:233)
4339. 11/3/91 mee McAdam, Ann, Mrs., "widow of William McAdam ..."; City of N.Y.
  See 168.
4340. 9/30/90 --- McAdam, William, dec'd. See 4335.
4341. 10/12/91 --- McAdam, William, dec'd. See 4337.
4342. 11/1/91 --- McAdam, William, dec'd. See 4338.
4343. 11/3/91 --- McAdam, William, dec'd. See 4339.
4344. 10/11/91 gor McAdam, William, Esq., dec'd. See 4336.
4345. 6/22/64 gor McAllister, Charles; Little Britain, ULS; Argyle, WAS;
  gee 4575.   (A:481)
4346. 7/20/01 mee McAllister, John; Salem, WAS. See 1682.
4347. 6/10/96 mee McAllister, John, Esq.; Salem, WAS. See 1679.
4348. 12/8/98 mee McAllister, John, Esq.; Salem, WAS. See 2509.
4349. 4/17/99 gee McAllister, John, Esq.; Salem, WAS. See 1681.
4350. 11/20/00 gor McAlpin, John, schoolmaster; Northeast, DUT; Argyle, WAS;
  gee 8430.   (E:180)
4351. 11/20/00 gor McAlpine, John; Northeast, DUT; Argyle, WAS; gee 8442.
                                                     (E:177)
4352. 11/4/86 mor McAlpine, Robert; City of N.Y.; Scotch Pat., WAS; mee 3824.
                                                     (A:49)
4353. 1/21/01 gor McArthur, Duncan, farmer; Argyle, WAS; Argyle, WAS; gee 4475.
                                                     (E:437)
4354. 6/7/64 gor McArthur, John, "son of Neil McArthur, deceased"; Claverack,
  ALB; Argyle, ALB; gee 4574   (Washington Co. C-2:268)
4355. 6/7/64 --- McArthur, Neil, dec'd. See 4354.
4356. 2/28/01 mee McArthur, William; Plattsburgh, CLI. See 7526.
4357. 2/23/97 mor McAulay, William; Willsborough, CLI; Willsborough, CLI;
  mee 2801.   (A:228)
4358. 10/7/95 gee McAulay, William, Esq.; Cambridge, WAS. See 4521.
4359. 10/7/94 gee McAuley, Hugh; ---, ---. See 8583.
4360. 3/13/91 gor McAuley, John; Newburgh, ULS; Willsborough, CLI; gee 2353.
                                                     (A:198)
4361. 7/7/86 gee McAuley, William; ---, ---. See 2618.
4362. 7/10/99 mee McAuley, William; Cambridge, WAS. See 5991.
4363. 5/1/00 mor McBride, Daniel, farmer; Chester, WAS; Chester, WAS;
  mee 7772.   (D:221)
4364. 7/6/95 gee McCallister, John, Esq.; Salem, WAS. See 4926.
4365. 4/25/71 gor McCarter, Ann. See 4552.
4366. 9/15/00 gor McCarter, Jean. See 4369.
4367. 8/7/01 gor McCarter, John, Junr., farmer; Salem, WAS. See 4368.
4368. 8/7/01 gor McCarter, John, Senr., farmer; Salem, WAS; Salem, WAS;
  co-gors 4367, 4372; gee 4370.   (F:277)
4369. 9/15/00 gor McCarter, Robert (w. Jean); Argyle, WAS. See 4373.
4370. 8/7/01 gee McCarter, Robert; Hebron, WAS. See 4368.
4371. 9/15/00 gor McCarter, Rose. See 4373.
4372. 8/7/01 gor McCarter, Samuel, farmer; Salem, WAS. See 4368.
4373. 9/15/00 gor McCarter, William (w. Rose); Argyle, WAS; Argyle, WAS;
  co-gors 4366, 4369; gee 3063.   (E:68)
4374. 12/25/97 gee McCaslin, John O., farmer; Salem, WAS. See 4817.
4375. 4/25/71 gor McCay, Alexander. See 4550.
4376. 3/15/86 mor McClallan, Robert; ---, ---; Kemp Pat., WAS; co-mor 4376a;
  mee 8273.   (A:37)
4376a. 3/15/86 mor McClallan, William; ---, ---. See 4376.
4377. 4/13/72 gee McClaughry, Andrew; Springtown, ALB. See 4379.
4378. 2/15/95 gor McClaughry, Ann. See 4380.
4379. 4/13/72 gor McClaughry, Matthew; New Perth, ALB; New Perth, ALB;
  gee 4377.   (A:132)

110

4380. 2/5/95 gor McClaughry, Richard (w. Ann), yeoman; Kortright, OTS;
Cambridge, WAS; co-gees 3981, 8830.   (B-2:465)
4381. 11/12/96 gee McClean, John, farmer; Cambridge, WAS. See 6142.
4382. 3/15/99 mee McClean, John; Cambridge, WAS. See 6910.
4383. 2/6/69 gee McCleary, Daniel; White Creek, ALB. See 951.
4384. 4/7/00 mor McCleery, John, farmer; Argyle, WAS; Argyle, WAS; co-mor
1660; mee 6616.   (C:204)
4385. 3/11/96 gor McCleland, John, farmer; Cambridge, WAS; Cambridge, WAS;
gee 6377.   (D:55)
4386. 6/15/92 gee McClellan, James, yeoman; Hebron, WAS. See 6737.
4387. 12/23/91 mor McClellan, Robert; Hebron, WAS; Hebron, WAS; mee 8295. (A:367)
4388. 12/23/91 mor McClellan, William, farmer; Hebron, WAS; Hebron, WAS;
mee 8295.   (A:368)
4389. 8/24/01 gee McClellan, William; Hebron, WAS. See 1789.
4390. 6/15/02 mor McClintock, John (w. Rebecah); Whitehall, WAS; Whitehall,
WAS; mee 4160.   (D:191)
4391. 6/15/02 mor McClintock, Rebecah. See 4390.
4392. 6/22/91 gor McClung, John; ---, ---. See 8450.
4393. 1/4/00 gor McClung, Thomas, "Student of Physick"; Pittstown, REN;
Cambridge, WAS; gee 28.   (D:281)
4394. 3/22/89 mor McClure, Thomas; ---, ---; Borry Tract, WAS; mee 831. (A:148)
4395. 1/12/73 gee McCole, Duncan; ---, CHA. See 2473.
4396. 4/15/65 gor McColeman, John, farmer; ---, ULS; Argyle, WAS; gee 549.
(A:146)
4397. 1/8/93 gor McColester, Hamilton; Salem, WAS; Westfield, WAS; gee 6653.
(C-2:231)
4398. 9/10/83 gor McCollister, Hamilton; White Creek, CHA; Turner Pat., CHA;
gee 6681.   (B-2:241)
4399. 5/25/85 gee McCollister, Hamilton; ---, ---. See 7055.
4400. 3/23/89 gor McCollister, Hamilton; Salem, WAS. See 4429.
4401. 12/29/91 gor McCollister, Hamilton; ---, ---. See 4878.
4402. 2/2/93 gor McCollister, Hamilton; Salem, WAS; Salem, WAS; gee 1627.
(C-2:121)
4403. 11/16/85 gor McCollister, Hamilton, Esq., sheriff of Washington County;
---, ---; Artillery Pat., WAS (sheriff's sale); gees
7694 (C-2:179) and 8786 (B-2:263). (two contracts)
4404. 9/7/69 gor McCollom, Daniel; ---, ---. See 7955.
4405. 4/20/73 gor McCollom, Daniel; ---, ---. See 7957.
4406. 9/5/01 gee McCollum, Daniel, cordwainer; Argyle, WAS. See 4407.
4407. 9/5/01 gor McCollum, John, yeoman; Argyle, WAS; Argyle, WAS; gee 4406.
(F:230)
4408. 4/8/99 gor McConnelly, Duncan (w. Marcy); Argyle, WAS; Argyle, WAS;
gee 1020.   (E:279)
4409. 4/8/99 gor McConnelly, Marcy. See 4408.
4410. 9/2/00 mee McConnely, Duncan, tailor; Argyle, WAS. See 8380.
4411. 5/23/98 mee McCook, John; Cambridge, WAS. See 5596.
4412. 4/16/95 gor McCool, Elizabeth. See 4413.
4413. 4/16/95 gor McCool, John (w. Elizabeth); Cambridge, WAS; Cambridge, WAS;
gee 3417.   (C-2:152)
4414. 5/24/98 gor McCool, John; Cambridge, WAS; Cambridge, WAS; gee 5597.
(C-2:315)
4415. 1/4/94 gor McCoole, Elizabeth. See 4416.
4416. 1/4/94 gor McCoole, John (w. Elizabeth); Cambridge, WAS; land "east of
Hudsons River, WAS; gee 6917.   (B-2:183)
4417. 11/17/64 gor McCore, Archibald, "commonly called ... Archibald Brown";
Cakeat, ORA; Argyle, ALB; gee 4576.   (A:484)
4418. 1/24/89 --- McCormick, Daniel; City of N.Y. See 7293.
4419. 11/30/92 gor McCormick, Daniel, merchant; City of N.Y.; ---, WAS, with
a segment in VT; co-gor 3714; gee 5955.   (C-2:45)
4420. 3/22/88 gee McCormick, Daniel, Esq.; City of N.Y. See 6337.
4421. 2/4/94 gor McCormick, Daniel, Esq.; City of N.Y.; Delancey Pat., CLI;
co-gees 2307, 2309.   (A:460)
4422. 2/21/94 mee McCormick, Daniel, Esq.; City of N.Y. See 2308.
4423. 11/5/93 mee McCoy, William, farmer; Salem, WAS. See 4542.
4424. 3/3/95 mor McCoy, William, farmer; Salem, WAS; Argyle, WAS; mee 1984.
(A:559)

4425. 5/4/95 mee McCoy, William; Salem, WAS. See 6620.
4426. 5/1/82 gor McCracken, Joseph; New Perth, CHA. See 8513.
4427. 11/19/83 gor McCracken, Joseph, Colonel; ---, CHA. See 8546.
4428. 8/16/86 gor McCracken, Joseph, Colonel; ---, WAS. See 8560.
4429. 3/23/89 gor McCracken, Joseph; Salem, WAS; Westfield, WAS; co-gor 4400;
             gee 3993.   (A:107)
4430. 10/31/98 mee McCracken, Joseph; Salem, WAS. See 8712.
4431. 6/9/83 gor McCracken, Joseph, Esq.; ---, ---; White Creek, CHA;
             gee 6573.   (B-1:188)
4432. 1/23/94 gee McCracken, Joseph, Esq.; Salem, WAS. See 3329.
4433. 11/29/91 gee McCracken, Samuel, Junr.; Westfield, WAS. See 8690.
4434. 9/5/81 gor McCraken, ---, Major; ---, ---. See 8543.
4435. 5/17/99 mor McCraken, Hannah. See 4453.
4436. 9/5/81 gor McCraken, Joseph, Major; ---, ---. See 8543. (Eight contracts)
4437. 11/19/81 gor McCraken, Joseph, Colonel; ---, CHA. See 8544.
4438. 11/19/83 gor McCraken, Joseph; ---, CHA. See 8545.
4439. 6/1/84 gor McCraken, Joseph; White Creek, WAS. See 8514.
4440. 7/13/84 gor McCraken, Joseph; White Creek, WAS. See 8515.
4441. 5/26/85 gee McCraken, Joseph; ---, ---. See 7055.
4442. 7/17/92 mee McCraken, Joseph; ---, ---. See 447.
4443. 7/18/92 mee McCraken, Joseph; ---, ---. See 1657.
4444. 7/31/92 mee McCraken, Joseph; ---, ---. See 1616.
4445. 6/30/92 gor McCraken, Joseph, Esq.; Salem, WAS; Westfield, WAS;
             co-gor 6575; gee 1446.   (A:434)
4446. 7/2/92 gor McCraken, Joseph, Esq.; Salem, WAS; Westfield, WAS;
             gees 944 (A:386), 994 (A:384), 6480 (A:425), 7472 (A:383).
             (four contracts)
4447. 7/2/92 gor McCraken, Joseph, Esq.; Salem, WAS; Westfield, WAS;
             co-gor 6576; gees 446 (A:418) and 1656 (A:420).
             (two contracts)
4448. 7/3/92 gor McCraken, Joseph, Esq.; Salem, WAS; Westfield, WAS;
             co-gor 6577; gee 6025.   (A:427)
4449. 8/14/92 gor McCraken, Joseph, Esq.; Salem, WAS; Westfield, WAS;
             gee 417.   (A:462)
4450. 8/14/92 gor McCraken, Joseph, Esq.; Salem, WAS; Westfield, WAS;
             co-gor 6578; gee 2961.   (A:464)
4451. 10/24/92 gor McCraken, Samuel, cordwainer; Westfield, WAS; Salem, WAS;
             gee 844.   (F:216)
4452. 2/7/95 gee McCraken, Samuel; Westfield, WAS. See 7334.
4453. 5/17/99 mor McCraken, William (w. Hannah); Hebron, WAS; Hebron, WAS;
             mee 8680.   (C:201)
4454. 4/20/73 gee McCray, Elisabeth. See 7957.
4455. 4/20/73 gee McCray, Martha. See 7957.
4456. 4/20/73 gee McCray, Thomas. See 7957.
4457. 5/1/86 mee McCrea, John; ---, ---. See 210.
4458. 7/12/85 gee McCreedy, Charles; Plattsburgh, WAS. See 5888.
4459. 10/16/90 mor McCreedy, Thomas; Plattsburgh, CLI; Plattsburgh, CLI;
             mee 6265.   (A:59)
4460. 6/29/92 gee McCreedy, Thomas; Plattsburgh, CLI. See 5680.
4461. 9/7/69 gor McCreelis, Hannah, "widow of John McCreelis, deceased".
             See 7955.
4462. 4/20/73 gor McCreelis, Hannah, widow of John McCreelis; ---, ---.
             See 7957.
4463. 9/7/69 --- McCreelis, John, dec'd.; ---, ---. See 7955.
4464. 4/20/73 --- McCreelis, John, dec'd.; ---, ---. See 7957.
4465. 12/5/89 gee McCullock, Isabella; Bennington, BEN, VT. See 747.
4466. 12/5/89 gor McCullock, John. Husband of Isabella McCullock in 4465.
4467. 10/24/85 gee McDonald, Alexander; New Perth, WAS. See 7480.
4468. 4/1/02 mor McDonald, Daniel (w. Margaret), farmer; Hebron, WAS;
             Hebron, WAS; mee 5229.   (E:36)
4469. 1/12/80 gee McDonald, John, farmer; White Creek, CHA. See 4024.
4470. 2/15/91 gee McDonald, John, farmer; Hebron, WAS. See 2729.
4471. 2/1/96 gee McDonald, John; Thurman, WAS. See 7766.
4472. 8/16/99 mee McDonald, John; Cambridge, WAS. See 1391.
4473. 5/5/01 mee McDonald, John; Cambridge, WAS. See 7529.
4474. 4/1/02 mor McDonald, Margaret. See 4468.

4475. 1/21/01 gee McDonald, William; Argyle, WAS. See 4353.
4476. 10/20/01 mor McDonald, William; Argyle, WAS; Argyle, WAS; mee 4591. (D:111)
4477. 12/16/83 gee McDonell, Alexander; New Perth, CHA. See 3870.
4478. 3/1/93 gor McDougall, Alexander (w. Amy), farmer; Argyle, WAS; ---, WAS; gee 2277. (B-2:98)
4479. 12/8/89 --- McDougall, Alexander, Esq.; late of the City of N.Y., dec'd., "formerly Major General in the Army of the United States ..." See 3443.
4480. 3/12/91 --- McDougall, Alexander, Esq.; late of the City of N.Y., dec'd. See 3445.
4481. 5/18/92 --- McDougall, Alexander, Esq., dec'd.; City of N.Y. See 3446.
4482. 3/6/93 gor McDougall, Alexander, Junr.; Argyle, WAS; Argyle, WAS; gee 5623. (B-2:96)
4483. 3/1/93 gor McDougall, Amy. See 4478.
4484. 4/25/98 gee McDougall, James; ---, WAS. See 4530.
4485. 11/23/92 gor McDowl, John, merchant; Albany, ALB; Easton, WAS; gee 7205. (B-2:339)
4486. 8/28/94 gor McDowl, John; Albany, ALB; Saratoga Pat., WAS; gee 1724. (D:401)
4487. 7/6/96 gor McDuffee, Mary; Poughkeepsie, DUT; Argyle, WAS; co-gor 7849; co-gees 4047, 4049. (C-2:147)
4488. 3/1/90 --- McDugall, Alexander, dec'd. See 3448.
4489. 6/14/93 mor MacEacherin, Angus, laborer; City of N.Y.; Argyle, WAS; mee 1082. (A:465)
4490. 6/14/93 mor McEachern, Angus, laborer; City of N.Y.; Argyle, WAS; mee 1079. (A:419)
4491. 6/16/98 mor McEachern, Angus, gentleman; Lansingburgh, REN; Argyle, WAS; mee 1221. (B:296)
4492. 5/21/99 mor McEachern, Angus; Troy, REN; Argyle, WAS; mee 8048. (C:202)
4493. 7/18/99 mor McEachern, Angus; Troy, REN; Argyle, WAS; co-mees 4001, 6006, 6045. (C:201)
4494. 4/12/92 gee McEachran, Neal, farmer; Argyle, WAS. See 8065.
4495. 6/13/93 gee McEachron, Angus, laborer; City of N.Y. See 1078.
4496. 5/5/01 mee McEachron, John; Argyle, WAS. See 7529.
4497. 10/27/92 mor McEachron, Neal, yeoman; Argyle, WAS; Argyle, WAS; mee 8066. (A:385)
4498. 2/1/96 gee McEwan, Duncan; Thurman, WAS. See 7766.
4499. 2/9/96 gee McFaden, John; Argyle, WAS. See 6821.
4500. 2/9/96 mor McFaden, John; Argyle, WAS; Argyle, WAS; co-mees 4647, 6763, 6822, 8106. Co-mortgagees are all "executors of the late John Morin Scott, Esq., deceased". (B:94)
4501. 7/5/97 mor McFarland, Andrew, yeoman; Hampton, WAS; Hampton, WAS; co-mees 8301, 8315. (D:164)
4502. 2/14/00 gee McFarland, Andrew, farmer; Hampton, WAS. See 4511.
4503. 12/17/93 gee McFarland, Daniel, shoemaker; Cambridge, WAS. See 3633.
4504. 1/26/91 gor McFarland, Janny; Salem, WAS. See 1403.
4505. 5/7/84 gor McFarland, John, yeoman; New Perth, CHA; New Perth, CHA; gee 2919. (C-1:27)
4506. 2/16/89 gee McFarland, John; ---, ---. See 3553.
4507. 1/26/91 gor McFarland, John (w. Janny); Salem, WAS. See 1403.
4508. 2/11/96 mor McFarland, John, farmer; Hampton, WAS; Skene's Pat., WAS; mee 1817. (B:25)
4509. 4/20/96 gee McFarland, John, farmer; Hampton, WAS. See 1802.
4510. 1/22/00 gor McFarland, John, farmer; Cambridge, WAS; Cambridge Pat., WAS; gee 6469. (D:339)
4511. 2/14/00 gor McFarland, John, farmer; Hampton, WAS; Hampton, WAS; gee 4502. (F:93)
4512. 7/29/77 gor McFarland, William; New Perth, WAS; New Perth, WAS; gee 4924. (A:451)
4513. 5/18/89 gee McFarland, William, yeoman; Salem, WAS. See 2024.
4514. 1/26/91 gee McFarland, William; Salem, WAS. See 1403.
4515. 12/26/99 gee McFarland, William; Salem, WAS. See 2829.
4516. 6/24/92 gor McFarlin, James, Junr.; Salem, WAS; Salem, WAS; gee 4942. (C-2:229)
4517. 6/1/85 gee McFarren, John; ---, ---. See 7055.
4518. 1/18/02 mee McGibon, John; Hebron, WAS. See 2739.

4519.	10/7/95	gor	McGill, Janet. See 4521.

4519. 10/7/95 gor McGill, Janet. See 4521.
4520. 8/31/92 mor McGill, John, merchant; Cambridge, WAS; Cambridge, WAS;
mee 2080. (A:364)
4521. 10/7/95 gor McGill, John (w. Janet), merchant; Cambridge, WAS;
Cambridge, WAS; gee 4358. (D:294)
4522. 12/24/99 gee McGill, John; Easton, WAS. See 895.
4523. 12/24/99 mor McGill, John, merchant; Easton, WAS; Argyle, WAS; mee 896.
(C:204)
4524. 6/1/02 mor McGill, John, yeoman; Easton, WAS; Thurman, WAS; co-mors
1376, 7786; mee 823. (E:27)
4525. 1/7/93 gee McGill, Patrick; Cambridge, WAS. See 1414.
4526. 8/31/73 mor McGlashan, Leonard; ---, ---; land "east side of waters
running from Wood Creek into Lake Champlain", CHA
(prob. in present-day VT); mee 6268. (A:7)
4527. 5/18/99 mee McGrant, John; Alburgh, FRA, VT. See 1048.
McGregor. See also MacGregor.
4528. 8/6/90 mee McGregor, Col (sic); City of N.Y. See 5429.
4529. 1/1/96 gor McGregor, Col, merchant; City of N.Y.; ---, CLI; gee 5806.
(A:399)
4530. 4/25/98 gor McGregor, Coll, merchant; City of N.Y.; Fort Edward Pat.,
WAS; gee 4484. (D:131)
4531. 10/24/98 gor McGregor, Coll, merchant; City of N.Y.; Argyle, WAS;
gee 1528. (D:24)
4532. 10/25/98 mee McGregor, Coll, merchant; City of N.Y. See 1529.
4533. 10/27/98 gor McGregor, Coll, gentleman; City of N.Y.; Argyle, WAS;
co-gees 771, 783, 792, 5556. (D:21)
4534. 7/19/99 gor McGregor, John, merchant; City of N.Y.; ---, WAS and a
segment in VT; gee 5972. (F:208)
4535. 4/27/92 mee McGregor, Robert, merchant; Cambridge, WAS. See 4774.
4536. 10/18/65 gor McGuire, John; City of N.Y. See 4758.
4537. 12/1/85 gee McIllvray, Donald, yeoman; Argyle, WAS. See 5254.
4538. 5/1/02 mor McInroy, John; Argyle, WAS; Argyle, WAS; mee 4079. (D:183)
4539. 11/5/93 mor McIntire, Anna. See 4542.
4540. 1/20/98 gor McIntire, Daniel; Livingston Manor, COL; Scotch Pat., WAS;
gee 4546. (D:317)
4541. 5/28/99 gor McIntire, Daniel I., farmer; Livingston, COL; Argyle, WAS;
gee 4547. (E:52)
4542. 11/5/93 mor McIntire, John (w. Anna), farmer; Salem, WAS; Salem, WAS;
mee 4423. (A:435)
4543. 7/6/91 mor McIntire, Joseph; Willsborough, CLI; Judd Pat., CLI;
mee 47. (A:72)
4544. 10/17/00 mor McIntire, Joseph; ---, ---; Willsborough, ESS; co-mor 2288;
mee 5882. (A:40)
4545. 2/13/02 mor McIntire, Joseph, Junr.; ---, ---; James Judd Pat., ESS;
co-mees 6401, 6425. (A:96)
4546. 1/20/98 gee McIntire, Peter; Argyle, WAS. See 4540.
4547. 5/28/99 gee McIntire, Peter; Argyle, WAS. See 727, 4541.
4548. 5/6/00 gor McIntosh, Elizabeth, "late and unmarried by the name of
Elizabeth Mount, daughter of James Mount late of Argyle
in the County of Washington, yeoman, deceased"; ---, ---;
Argyle, WAS; gee 1096. (E:75)
4549. 5/23/01 mee McIntosh, Elizabeth, "otherwise Elizabeth Mount"; ---, WAS.
See 3144.
4550. 4/25/71 gor McKay, Alexander, "now of the City of New York but formerly
of the County of Albany, merchant, ... called Alexander
McCay" (w. Ann); Argyle, ALB; gee 4580. (A:505)
4551. 4/26/71 gor McKay, Alexander (w. Ann), merchant; City of N.Y.; Argyle, ALB;
gee 4581. (A:508)
4552. 4/25/71 gor McKay, Ann, "otherwise called Ann McCarter". See 4550.
4553. 4/26/71 gor McKay, Ann. See 4551.
4554. 7/18/99 gee McKay, William, blacksmith; Hoosick, REN. See 1330.
4555. 11/21/91 gor McKee, Agness. See 4559.
4556. 11/25/91 mee McKee, James; Cambridge, WAS. See 2334.
4557. 6/27/96 gee McKee, James, yeoman; Cambridge, WAS. See 2477.
4558. 6/15/99 gee McKee, James, yeoman; Cambridge, WAS. See 7065.
4559. 11/21/91 gor McKee, William (w. Agness), farmer; Hebron, WAS; Hebron, WAS;
gee 6878. (A:242)

114

4560. 11/24/91 mee McKee, William; Hebron, WAS. See 6879.
4561. 7/12/00 mee McKee, William, yeoman; Argyle, WAS. See 2832.
4562. 9/25/01 gee McKee, William. See 4571.
4563. 3/25/72 gor McKenney, Amos. See 4565.
4564. 2/4/84 gor McKenney, Elinor; ---, ---. See 4567.
4565. 3/25/72 gor McKenney, James, yeoman; Kingsbury, ALB; Kingsbury, ALB;
                   co-gors 4563, 4566; gee 3618. (Washington Co. A:27)
4566. 3/25/72 gor McKenney, John; Kingsbury, ALB. See 4565.
4567. 2/4/84 gor McKenney, John; Kingsbury, CHA; Artillery Pat., CHA;
                   co-gors 4564, 4568; gee 7451.   (A:389)
4568. 2/4/84 gor McKenney, Lydia; ---, ---. See 4567.
4569. 9/25/01 gor McKesson, Alexander, farmer; ---, ADA, PA. See 4571.
4570. 10/30/01 gor McKesson, Alexander, farmer; ---, ADA, PA. See 4572.
4571. 9/25/01 gor McKesson, James, farmer; ---, ADA, PA; Duncan Reid Pat.,
                   WAS; co-gors 4569, 4599, 4601, 6271; co-gees 1396, 4323,
                   4562, 6064, 6329, 8431. Co-grantees are all trustees of
                   the First Presbyterian Congregation, Argyle, WAS.(E:429)
4572. 10/30/01 gor McKesson, James, farmer; ---, ADA, PA; Argyle, WAS; co-gors
                   4570, 4600, 4602, 6272, "by their attorney, John
                   McKesson of the City of New York"; co-gees 343, 3190,
                   4625, 6270, 6351, 6379. Co-grantees are all trustees of
                   the Associate Congregation, Argyle, WAS.   (F:72)
4573. 5/14/64 gee McKesson, John, attorney; City of N.Y. See 4729.
4574. 6/7/64 gee McKesson, John, attorney; City of N.Y. See 4354.
4575. 6/22/64 gee McKesson, John, attorney; City of N.Y. See 4345.
4576. 11/17/64 gee McKesson, John, attorney; City of N.Y. See 4417.
4577. 4/26/65 gee McKesson, John, attorney; City of N.Y. See 2826.
4578. 10/18/65 gee McKesson, John, attorney; City of N.Y. See 4758.
4579. 10/22/65 gee McKesson, John, attorney; City of N.Y. See 6220.
4580. 4/25/71 gee McKesson, John, attorney; City of N.Y. See 4550.
4581. 4/26/71 gee McKesson, John, attorney; City of N.Y. See 4551.
4582. 4/18/75 gee McKesson, John, attorney; City of N.Y. See 2767.
4583. 12/8/89 gor McKesson, John, gentleman; ---, ---. See 343.
4584. 12/10/91 mee McKesson, John, attorney; City of N.Y. See 1099.
4585. 5/15/92 gor McKesson, John, attorney; City of N.Y.; Argyle, WAS;
                   co-gees 2692, 2695.   (B-2:33)
4586. 4/22/94 gor McKesson, John, attorney; City of N.Y.; Argyle, WAS;
                   gee 7614.   (B-2:388)
4587. 6/1/96 mee McKesson, John; City of N.Y. See 2410.
4588. 5/19/98 gee McKesson, John, attorney; City of N.Y. See 3124.
4589. 10/6/01 mee McKesson, John, attorney; City of N.Y. See 4665.
4590. 10/19/01 mee McKesson, John, attorney; City of N.Y. See 2754.
4591. 10/20/01 mee McKesson, John, attorney; City of N.Y. See 4476, 6596, 7365.
4592. 10/30/01 --- McKesson, John; City of N.Y. See 4572.
4593. 11/16/01 mee McKesson, John, attorney; City of N.Y. See 3269, 7818.
4594. 3/1/90 gor McKesson, John, Esq.; City of N.Y. See 3448.
4595. 11/12/90 mee McKesson, John, Esq.; City of N.Y. See 1062.
4596. 3/12/91 gor McKesson, John, Esq.; ---, ---. See 3445.
4597. 5/18/92 gor McKesson, John, Esq.; ---, ---. See 3446.
4598. 4/24/94 mee McKesson, John, Esq.; City of N.Y. See 7633.
4599. 9/25/01 gor McKesson, Maria, singlewoman; City of N.Y. See 4571.
4600. 10/30/01 gor McKesson, Maria, singlewoman; City of N.Y. See 4572.
4601. 9/25/01 gor McKesson, William, farmer; ---, ADA, PA. See 4571.
4602. 10/30/01 gor McKesson, William, farmer; ---, ADA, PA. See 4572.
4603. 11/24/02 mor McKibben, Margaret. See 4604.
4604. 11/24/02 mor McKibben, Thomas (w. Margaret); Argyle, WAS; Argyle, WAS;
                   mee 6886.   (E:38)
4605. 7/22/91 mor McKinley, Elizabeth. See 4608.
4606. 3/1/87 gee McKinley, Samuel; ---, ---. See 7055.
4607. 1/5/88 mor McKinley, William; Whitehall, WAS; Whitehall, WAS; mee 8145.
                                                                 (A:75)
4608. 7/22/91 mor McKinley, William (w. Elizabeth); Whitehall, WAS; Whitehall,
                   WAS; mee 8146.   (A:311)
4609. 7/26/91 mor McKinly, Samuel; Whitehall, WAS; Whitehall, WAS; mee 4124.
                                                                 (A:290)
4610. 4/2/85 gor McKinney, John, yeoman; Kingsbury, WAS; Kingsbury, WAS;
                   co-gor 6054; gee 7467.   (B-1:186)

115

4611. 3/10/85 mee McKinnion, Neil; ---, ---. See 6704.
4612. 12/14/80 mee McKnight, Charles (w. Mary), physician; ---, ---. See 3572.
4613. 4/2/86 gor McKnight, Charles, physician; City of N.Y. See 6746.
4614. 6/7/86 mee McKnight, Charles; ---, ---. See 4953.
4615. 12/14/87 mee McKnight, Charles; ---, ---. See 7191.
4616. 5/8/89 mee McKnight, Charles, physician. See 3648.
4617. 6/6/89 mee McKnight, Charles, physician. See 682.
4618. 6/25/89 gor McKnight, Charles, physician. See 6751.
4619. 10/7/90 mee McKnight, Charles. See 1365.
4620. 5/3/91 mee McKnight, Charles (w. Mary), physician; ---, ---. See 3547.
4621. 5/28/92 --- McKnight, Charles, physician, dec'd.; City of N.Y. See 6754.
4622. 6/14/92 gor McKnight, Charles, physician, dec'd.; ---, ---. See 6755.
4623. 6/15/92 gor McKnight, Charles, physician, dec'd.; ---, ---. See 6737 and 6756.
4624. 2/18/02 --- McKnight, Charles, physician, dec'd. See 8117.
4625. 10/30/01 gee McKnight, David; ---, ---. See 4572.
4626. 5/4/76 gee McKnight, George; New Perth, CHA. See 8277.
4627. 4/30/88 gor McKnight, George, Lieut.; Hebron, WAS; Hebron, WAS; gee 2560. (A:388)
4628. 7/8/93 gee McKnight, John; Argyle, WAS. See 4697.
4629. 12/14/80 mee McKnight, Mary; ---, ---. See 4612.
4630. 4/2/86 gor McKnight, Mary, wife of Charles McKnight, physician; City of N.Y. See 6746.
4631. 6/7/86 mee McKnight, Mary; ---, ---. See 4953.
4632. 12/14/87 mee McKnight, Mary. See 7191.
4633. 5/8/89 mee McKnight, Mary. See 3648.
4634. 6/6/89 mee McKnight, Mary. See 682.
4635. 6/25/89 gor McKnight, Mary. See 6751.
4636. 10/7/90 mee McKnight, Mary. See 4619.
4637. 5/3/91 mee McKnight, Mary; ---, ---. See 4620.
4638. 5/28/92 gor McKnight, Mary, wife of Charles McKnight, dec'd.; City of N.Y. See 6754.
4639. 6/14/92 gor McKnight, Mary, widow of Charles McKnight, dec'd.; City of N.Y. See 6755.
4640. 6/15/92 gor McKnight, Mary, widow of Charles McKnight, dec'd.; ---, ---. See 6737 and 6756.
4641. 5/8/93 gor McKnight, Mary; City of N.Y. See 6757.
4642. 5/8/93 mee McKnight, Mary; ---, ---. See 7620.
4643. 7/2/94 gor McKnight, Mary; City of N.Y. See 6759.
4644. 7/2/94 mee McKnight, Mary; City of N.Y. See 2648.
4645. 2/9/96 gor McKnight, Mary; City of N.Y. See 6821.
4646. 2/9/96 mee McKnight, Mary; ---, ---. See 5619.
4647. 2/9/96 mee McKnight, Mary; City of N.Y. See 2273 and 4500.
4648. 6/18/96 gor McKnight, Mary; City of N.Y. See 6764.
4649. 7/8/97 mee McKnight, Mary; City of N.Y. See 8015.
4650. 11/28/98 mee McKnight, Mary; City of N.Y. See 8643.
4651. 12/1/99 --- McKnight, Mary, dec'd. See 8111.
4652. 2/18/02 --- McKnight, Mary, dec'd. See 8117.
4653. 12/25/86 gor McKnight, St. George; Hebron, WAS; Hebron, WAS; co-gees 1408 and 1409. (C-1:77)
4654. 4/8/88 gee McKraken, William; Salem, WAS. See 8480.
4655. 6/8/02 mor McLalin, James; Schaghticoke, REN; Salem, WAS; mee 2150. (E:20)
4656. 2/1/96 gee McLaren, John; Thurman, WAS. See 7766.
4657. 7/10/94 gor McLaughry, Thomas, yeoman; Kortright, OTS; Cambridge, WAS; gee 8858. (E:215)
4658. 1/3/93 mor McLean, Allan, farmer; Argyle, WAS; Argyle, WAS; mee 1662. (A:397)
4659. 4/15/88 gee McLean, Allen, farmer; Argyle, WAS. See 7649.
4660. 7/10/94 gor McLean, Allen (w. Christian); Argyle, WAS; Argyle, WAS; gee 900. (B-2:221)
4661. 5/19/96 gor McLean, Allen; Argyle, WAS; Argyle, WAS; gee 5049. (C-2:163)
4662. 6/15/96 mor McLean, Allen, yeoman; Argyle, WAS; Argyle, WAS; mee 4916. (B:60)
4663. 11/2/99 mor McLean, Andrew; Argyle, WAS; Cambridge, WAS; co-mor 4673; mee 2607. (C:203)
4664. 7/10/94 gor McLean, Christian. See 4660.

116

4665. 10/6/01 mor McLean, Donald, farmer; Argyle, WAS; Argyle, WAS;
        mee 4589.   (D:116)
4666. 6/13/94 gee McLean, Francis, yeoman; Cambridge, WAS. See 8340.
4667. 2/6/98 gee McLean, Francis, yeoman; Cambridge, WAS. See 3135.
4668. 11/11/96 gee McLean, John; Cambridge, WAS. See 399.
4669. 11/12/96 mor McLean, John, farmer; Cambridge, WAS; Sawyer Pat., WAS;
        mee 400. Two contracts this date involving these persons.
                                              (B:117), (B:118)
4670. 5/26/01 mee McLean, John; ---, ---. See 5570.
4671. 1/19/02 mee McLean, John; Cambridge, WAS. See 5314.
4672. 11/23/02 mee McLean, John, Esq.; Cambridge, WAS. See 7044.
4673. 11/2/99 mor McLean, Thomas; Argyle, WAS. See 4663.
4674. 6/13/91 gor McLeod, Norman; Lacheene, ---, Canada; Hebron, WAS;
        co-gees 8743 and 8744.   (B-2:75)
4675. 4/29/94 mee McMichel, John, cooper; Marbletown, ULS. See 3873.
4676. 1/27/97 gee McMillan, Andrew; Salem, WAS. See 4679.
4677. 1/28/97 mor McMillan, Andrew (w. Mary), yeoman; Salem, WAS; Salem, WAS;
        mee 4678.   (B:152)
4678. 1/28/97 mee McMillan, John, yeoman; Salem, WAS. See 4677.
4679. 1/27/97 gor McMillan, John, Senr. (w. Mary); Salem, WAS; Salem, WAS;
        gee 4676.   (C-2:159)
4680. 1/27/97 gor McMillan, Mary. See 4679.
4681. 1/28/97 mor McMillan, Mary. See 4677.
4682. 5/28/01 gor McMullan, John, Junr.; Cambridge, WAS; ---, WAS; gee 8604.
                                                          (E:278)
4683. 3/2/01 gor McMullen, Anna. See 4685.
4684. 11/24/85 mor McMullen, John; New Perth, WAS; New Perth, WAS; co-mees
        4298 and 7606.   (Deed Book B-1:199)
4685. 3/2/01 gor McMullen, John (w. Anna), farmer; Argyle, WAS; Argyle, WAS;
        gee 2519.   (E:210)
4686. 4/1/01 mor McMullin, John; Argyle, WAS. See 1788.
4687. 5/28/01 mor McMullin, John, Junr.; Cambridge, WAS; Cambridge Pat., WAS;
        mee 8605.   (D:54)
4688. 5/6/90 mor McMurry, Robert; Salem, WAS; Salem, WAS; mee 3133. (A:215)
4689. 1/14/65 gor McNachten, Alexander, farmer; ---, ORA. See 6217.
4690. 1/15/65 gor McNachten, Alexander, farmer; ---, ORA. See 6219. (six contracts)
4691. 3/21/65 gor McNachten, Alexander, farmer; ---, ORA. See 6232.
4692. 10/22/65 gor McNachten, Alexander, farmer; ---, ORA. See 6220.
4693. 10/20/86 mor McNall, Joseph; Kingsbury, WAS; personal property?; mee 3318.
                                      (Washington Co. Deed Book B-1:258)
4694. 10/15/98 mor McNamara, John (w. Lydia); Cambridge, WAS; Wilson's Pat., WAS;
        mee 2658.   (C:195)
4695. 10/15/98 mor McNamara, Lydia. See 4694.
4696. Data repositioned.
4697. 7/8/93 gor McNaughton, Alexander (w. Catharine); Argyle, WAS; Argyle, WAS;
        co-gor 4703; gee 4628.   (B-2:149)
4698. 12/30/93 gor McNaughton, Alexander (w. Catharine), farmer; Argyle, WAS;
        Argyle, WAS; co-gor 4704; gee 4816.   (B-2:142)
4699. 5/18/79 gor McNaughton, Alexander, Esq.; Argyle, WAS; Argyle, WAS;
        gee 6666.   (C-1:82)
4700. 8/6/92 gor McNaughton, Archibald, yeoman; Argyle, WAS; Argyle, WAS;
        gee 4718.   (A:475)
4701. 5/8/93 gee McNaughton, Archibald; Argyle, WAS. See 6757.
4702. 5/8/93 mor McNaughton, Archibald, yeoman; Argyle, WAS. See 7620.
4703. 7/8/93 gor McNaughton, Archibald; ---, ---. See 4697.
4704. 12/30/93 gor McNaughton, Archibald, farmer; Argyle, WAS. See 4698.
4705. 1/5/96 gor McNaughton, Archibald; Argyle, WAS. See 8007.
4706. 7/8/93 gor McNaughton, Catharine. See 4697.
4707. 12/30/93 gor McNaughton, Catharine. See 4698.
4708. 5/30/88 gee McNaughton, Daniel; "Rupert in the New State, Head of
        Indian River, North America". See 5040.
4709. 5/23/94 gor McNaughton, Daniel (w. Hannah), farmer; Pawlet, RUT, VT;
        Argyle, WAS; gee 4714.   (D:35)
4710. 5/30/88 gee McNaughton, Finlay; "Rupert in the New State, Head of
        Indian River, North America". See 5040.
4711. 5/23/94 gor McNaughton, Hannah. See 4709.

4712.	1/21/88	gee	McNaughton, Malcolm, farmer; Argyle, WAS. See 2911.
4713.	1/23/88	mor	McNaughton, Malcolm; ---, ---; Argyle, WAS; mee 2912. (A:70)
4714.	5/23/94	gee	McNaughton, Malcolm; farmer; Argyle, WAS. See 4709.
4715.	4/26/90	gee	McNaughton, Robert; Argyle, WAS. See 6671.
4716.	4/18/91	gee	McNaughton, Robert; ---, ---. See 1017.
4717.	6/18/92	gee	McNaughton, Robert; Argyle, WAS. See 6672.
4718.	8/6/92	gee	McNaughton, Robert, yeoman; Argyle, WAS. See 4700.
4719.	6/7/90	gor	McNeal, John, yeoman; ---, ALB; Salem, WAS; gee 2977. (A:202)
4720.	7/28/96	gee	McNeal, John, Argyle, WAS. See 6276.
4721.	12/1/97	mor	McNeal, Sarah; Argyle, WAS; Queensbury, WAS; co-mees 2265, and 5164. Co-mortgagees are "executor and executrix of the ... will ... of John Murray, deceased." (B:258)
4722.	9/22/97	gee	McNeil, Archibald; Argyle, WAS. See 4969.
4723.	5/24/02	gee	McNeil, Archibald; Argyle, WAS. See 4291.
4724.	2/27/99	gor	McNeil, Arthur; City of N.Y.; Argyle, WAS; co-gors 4728, and 4759; gee 1401. Co-gors 4728 and 4759 are children of Arthur above and of "Barbara McNeil, deceased, one of the daughters of Elizabeth McNeil, deceased." (D:252)
4725.	2/27/99	---	McNeil, Barbara, dec'd. See 4724.
4726.	5/19/98	---	McNeil, Elizabeth. See 3124.
4727.	2/27/99	---	McNeil, Elizabeth, dec'd. See 4724.
4728.	2/27/99	gor	McNeil, John; ---, ---. See 4724.
4729.	5/14/64	gor	McNeil, Margaret, spinster; Wallkill Precinct, ULS; Argyle, ALB; gee 4573. (A:479)
4730.	10/21/01	gor	McNeil, Margaret. See 4731.
4731.	10/21/01	gor	McNeil, Neil (w. Margaret), mill carpenter; Argyle, WAS; Argyle, WAS; gee 3998. (E:423)
4732.	3/9/76	gee	McNeil, Sarah. See 1218.
4733.	4/26/94	---	McNeill, Elizabeth, dec'd. See 1131.
4734.	4/26/94	gee	McNeill, John, attorney; City of N.Y. See 1131.
4735.	11/21/82	gee	McNeis, Alexander, Lieut., yeoman; ---, ---. See 8280.
4736.	12/8/89	mee	McNeish, James; Salem, WAS. See 2712.
4737.	2/16/92	mee	McNeiss, Alexander; Salem, WAS. See 2667.
4738.	6/26/93	mee	McNeiss, Alexander, yeoman; Salem, WAS. See 7049.
4739.	12/20/92	---	McNeiss, Elizabeth. See 7419.
4740.	6/20/90	gee	McNiel, John, farmer; Argyle, WAS. See 6227.
4741.	4/6/01	gor	McNight, Archibald; Charlotte, CHI, VT; Willsborough, ESS; gee 498. (A:31)
4742.	3/6/90	gee	McNish, Alexander; Salem, WAS. See 2713.
4743.	9/15/90	mee	McNish, Alexander; Salem, WAS. See 4197.
4744.	3/7/92	gee	McNish, Alexander. See 3565.
4745.	1/12/87	gor	McNitt, Alexander, gentleman; Salem Pat., WAS; Turner Pat., WAS; gee 4749. (A:65)
4746.	12/21/96	gor	McNitt, Alexander (w. Jane); Salem, WAS; Salem, WAS; co-gees 4747 and 4754. (D:431)
4747.	12/21/96	gee	McNitt, Alexander, Junr. See 4746.
4748.	5/30/97	gee	McNitt, Alexander, Junr., yeoman; Salem, WAS. See 5056.
4749.	1/12/87	gee	McNitt, Andrew, yeoman; Salem Pat., WAS. See 4745.
4750.	12/2/88	gor	McNitt, Andrew; Salem, WAS; Turner Pat., WAS; gee 7971. (A:102)
4751.	6/24/85	gee	McNitt, Daniel; New Perth, WAS. See 8284.
4752.	1/3/91	gee	McNitt, Daniel, farmer; Salem, WAS. See 7972.
4753.	2/25/95	gee	McNitt, Daniel; Salem, WAS. See 6137.
4754.	12/21/96	gee	McNitt, Daniel; Salem, WAS. See 4746.
4755.	4/12/97	gee	McNitt, Daniel, yeoman; Salem, WAS. See 8597.
4756.	12/21/96	gor	McNitt, Jane. See 4746.
4757.	10/18/65	---	McPhaden, John, dec'd. See 4758.
4758.	10/18/65	gor	McPhaden, Neil; City of N.Y.; Argyle, ALB; co-gors 4536, 4757, 5311; gee 4578. (A:486)
4759.	2/27/99	gor	McPherson, Mary McNeil; ---, ---. See 4724.
4760.	6/23/92	gor	McPherson, Murdock, Esq.; Champlain, CLI; Canadian and Nova Scotia Refugees' Pat., CLI; gee 2093. (A:214)
4761.	1/21/92	mor	McPhillip, James, yeoman; ---, WAS; Cambridge, WAS; co-mees 4046 and 4179. (A:315)
4762.	1/21/92	mor	McPhillip, John, Esq.; ---, WAS; Cambridge, WAS; co-mees 4046 and 4179. (A:315)

4763. 1/28/93 gor McQueen, Alexander; Salem, WAS. See 4769.
4764. 1/28/93 gee McQueen, Catherine; Salem, WAS. See 4769.
4765. 11/7/89 gee McQueen, John, yeoman; ---, WAS. See 2601.
4766. 11/10/89 mor McQueen, John, yeoman; Argyle, WAS; Argyle, WAS; mee 2598.
　　　　　　　　　　　　　　　　　　　　　　　　　　　　　　　　(A:183)
4767. 3/24/91 gor McQueen, John, miller; Argyle, WAS; Scotch Pat., WAS;
　　　　　　　　　gee 2527.　　　　　　　　　　　　　　(B-2:355)
4768. 6/3/96 gor McQueen, John (w. Priscilla), farmer; Milton, SAR; Argyle,
　　　　　　　　　WAS; gee 1989.　　　　　　　　　　　(C-2:27)
4769. 1/28/93 gor McQueen, John, Junr.; Salem, WAS; Salem, WAS; co-gors
　　　　　　　　　4763, 4764; gee 3127. Grantor 4764 is "widow of Peter
　　　　　　　　　McQueen, deceased".　　　　　　　　(B-2:16)
4769a. 1/28/93 --- McQueen, Peter, dec'd. See 4769.
4770. 6/3/96 gor McQueen, Priscilla. See 4768.
4771. 4/22/76 gee McQueen, Peter; ---, CHA. See 6665.
4772. 9/7/85 gee McQuen, Peter; ---, WAS. See 3114.
4773. 2/7/90 mee McVicar, Archibald; Cambridge, WAS. See 439.
4774. 4/27/92 mor McVicar, Archibald, farmer; Cambridge, WAS; Cambridge, WAS;
　　　　　　　　　mee 4535.　　　　　　　　　　　　　　(A:330)
4775. 5/8/86 gee McWhirter, Samuel, yeoman; Hebron, WAS. See 5350.
4776. 12/29/94 gee McWhorter, John, farmer; Granville, WAS. See 1850.
4777. 12/30/94 mor McWhorter, John, Esq.; Granville, WAS; Granville, WAS;
　　　　　　　　　mee 8586.　　　　　　　　　　　　　　(A:530)
4778. 1/7/83 gor McWhorter, Mathew; New Perth, CHA; New Perth, CHA; gee 86.
　　　　　　　　　　　　　　　　　　　　　　　　　　　　　　　　(B-1:76)
4779. 12/30/89 gor McWhorter, Mathew; Salem, WAS; Salem, WAS; gee 7043. (A:243)
4780. 7/3/92 gor McWhorter, Mathew; Salem, WAS; Salem, WAS; gee 8268. (A:419)
4781. 11/23/70 gor McWhorter, Matthew; White Creek, ALB; Turner Pat., ALB;
　　　　　　　　　gee 1830.　　　　　　　　　　　　　　(A:43)
4782. 3/13/95 mee McWhorter, Matthew; ---, ---. See 5952.
4783. 9/8/00 gor McWhorter, Matthew, Junr.; Salem, WAS; Hartford, WAS;
　　　　　　　　　co-gees 2910 and 2922.　　　　　　　(E:413)
4784. 7/10/84 gee McWhorter, Samuel; ---, ---. See 3089.
4785. 5/9/86 gor McWhorter, Samuel; Hebron Dist., WAS; Hebron Dist., WAS;
　　　　　　　　　gee 8722.　　　　　　　　　　　　　　(C-1:8)
4786. 5/13/00 mor McWithey, Abigail. See 4787.
4787. 5/13/00 mor McWithey, Silas (w. Abigail), farmer; Granville, WAS;
　　　　　　　　　Granville, WAS; mee 1541.　　　　　(C:204)
4788. 11/10/83 gee Mabbett, Joseph S., farmer; ---, DUT. See 88.
4789. 10/12/93 gor Mabbett, Joseph S. (w. Mary); ---, DUT; Granville, WAS;
　　　　　　　　　co-gors 4790, 4792; co-gees 3786, 4814, 6391. (F:189)
4790. 10/12/93 gor Mabbett, Mary. See 4789 and 4792.
4791. 11/13/83 gee Mabbett, Titus; ---, DUT. See 89.
4792. 10/12/93 gor Mabbett, Titus (w. Mary); ---, DUT. See 4789.
4793. 10/12/93 mee Mabbit, Joseph S.; Washington, DUT. See 3787.
4794. 10/12/93 mee Mabbit, Titus; Washington, DUT. See 3787.
4795. 2/21/00 mor Mabbitt, Israel; Washington, DUT; Walloomsack Pat., WAS;
　　　　　　　　　mee 7075.　　　　　　　　　　　　　　(C:203)
4796. 6/9/74 gor MacAlpine, Elizabeth, "formerly Elizabeth Cargill"; ---, ORA;
　　　　　　　　　Argyle, CHA; co-gor 2928; gee 7816.　　(A:140)
4797. 2/23/97 gee Macaulay, William, Esq.; Willsborough, CLI. See 2800.
4798. 10/8/89 gee Macauley, John; ---, DUT. See 7618.
　　　　　　　　　MacGregor. See also McGregor.
4799. 6/27/93 mee MacGregor, Cole, merchant; City of N.Y. See 8047.
4800. 1/2/96 mee MacGregor, Cole, merchant; City of N.Y. See 5807.
4801. 2/24/96 mee MacGregor, Cole, merchant; City of N.Y. See 8754.
4802. 2/27/96 mee MacGregor, Cole, merchant; City of N.Y. See 4109.
4803. 3/16/96 mee MacGregor, Cole, merchant; City of N.Y. See 289.
4804. 2/24/96 gor MacGregor, Cole, merchant; City of N.Y.; ---, CLI;
　　　　　　　　　co-gees 5746, 8753.　　　　　　　　(A:403)
4805. 8/15/92 mee Mackay, William, gentleman; Boston, ---, MA. See 1583.
4806. 8/27/92 mee Mackay, William, Esq.; ---, ---, MA. See 749.
4807. 7/13/01 gee Macomber, James; Taunton, BRI, MA. See 3283.
4808. 7/13/01 mor Macomber, James, yeoman; Taunton, BRI, MA; Granville, WAS;
　　　　　　　　　mee 3284.　　　　　　　　　　　　　　(D:74b)
4809. 4/29/96 gor Macumber, John; Washington, DUT; ---, CLI; gee 4810. (A:53)

119

4810. 4/29/96 gee Macumber, John, Junr.; ---, ALB. See 4809.
4811. 11/2/97 mor Magoon, Isaack; Ware, HAM, MA; Salem, WAS; mee 7101. (C:194)
4812. 10/12/93 mor Main, Constant. See 4815.
4813. 5/12/02 gor Main, Jeremiah, physician; Bridgewater, ONE. See 3778.
4814. 10/12/93 gee Main, Jeremiah, Junr.; Granville, WAS. See 4789.
4815. 10/12/93 mor Main, Jeremiah, Junr. (w. Constant), Granville, WAS.
               See 3787.
4816. 12/30/93 gee Mains, James; Argyle, WAS. See 4698.
4817. 12/25/97 gor Mairs, George, the Rev. (w. Sarah); Argyle, WAS; Argyle, WAS;
               gee 4374.   (C-2:226)
4818. 12/25/97 gor Mairs, Sarah. See 4817.
4819. 4/26/86 gor Malcom, Sarah. See 4822.
4820. 5/8/66 gee Malcom, William, merchant; City of N.Y. See 7553.
4821. 6/24/67 gee Malcom, William, merchant; City of N.Y. See 1202.
4822. 4/26/86 gor Malcom, William (w. Sarah); City of N.Y.; Argyle, WAS;
               gee 6274.   (A:134)
4823. 7/22/86 mee Malcom, William, Esq.; City of N.Y. See 1227.
4824. 6/15/95 gor Mallet, Jonathan (w. Mary); London, England. See 7129.
4825. 9/14/67 gee Mallet, Jonathan, Esq.; City of N.Y. See 2136.
4826. 4/16/92 gor Mallet, Jonathan, Esq.; "at present residing in England";
               ---, WAS; gee 2126.   (B-2:125)
4827. 6/15/95 gor Mallet, Mary. See 4824.
4828. 11/10/95 gor Mallory, Nathaniel; Mallory's Bush, CLI. See 5739.
4829. 2/2/99 mor Mallory, Nathaniel; Jay, CLI; Jay, CLI; co-mees 184, 4051,
               5301.   (A:377)
4830. 7/1/00 mor Mallory, Nathaniel; ---, ---; ---, ESS; co-mors 5423, 8217;
               mee 5572.   (A:37)
4831. 8/29/00 --- Mallory, Nathaniel. See 63 and 193.
4832. 1/2/65 gor Man, Isaac, merchant; City of N.Y.; land "county of Albany
               between Fort Edward and Lake George"; gee 7145. (C-2:335)-WAS Co.
4833. 12/21/68 --- Man, Isaac, "late of the City of New York, merchant, an
               insolvent debtor". See 8418.
4834. 5/24/94 mor Manchester, Elias; Cambridge Dist., WAS; Cambridge Dist,
               WAS; mee 6055.   (A:489)
4835. 3/1/93 gor Manchester, Hannah. See 4836.
4836. 3/1/93 gor Manchester, Stephen (w. Hannah); Cambridge, WAS. See 3380.
4837. 6/20/01 gor Mann, Abigail. See 4843.
4838. 7/4/00 mor Mann, Abizar. See 4842.
4839. 7/29/92 gee Mann, Hezekiah, carpenter; Westfield, WAS. See 4891.
4840. 6/25/98 mor Mann, Hezekiah (w. Molly); Hartford, WAS; Hartford, WAS;
               co-mees 219, 230.   (B:294)
4841. 6/25/98 mor Mann, Molly. See 4840.
4842. 7/4/00 mor Mann, Solomon (w. Abizar); Cambridge, WAS. See 1338.
4843. 6/20/01 gor Mann, Solomon (w. Abigail); Cambridge, WAS; ---, WAS;
               co-gors 1337, 1339, 2475, 2479; gee 1323.   (F:242)
4844. 6/2/87 gee Manvill, Daniel; ---, ---. See 7055.
4845. 4/2/96 mor Marcomber, Joshua; Cambridge, WAS; Hoosick Pat., WAS;
               mee 2208.   (B:295)
4846. 2/3/95 mor Mark, Jacob, merchant; City of N.Y.; Old Military Township
               #5 (Dannemora), CLI; co-mees 4169, 4171.   (A:146)
4847. 11/3/97 --- Mark, Jacob, merchant; City of N.Y.; Cumberland Head
               (Plattsburgh), CLI (72 farms). Mark, this date, appoints
               Lewis Ransom of Cumberland Head as his attorney to sell
               the above farms.   (B:210)
4848. 8/25/02 gor Marks, Stephen; Chateaugay, CLI; Old Military Township #6
               (Clinton), CLI; co-gees 5978, 5979.   (B:356)
4849. 4/10/00 mor Marnay, Louis, Junr.; Champlain, CLI; Champlain, CLI;
               mee 5093.   (A:423)
4850. 11/29/00 gor Marselus, Anna. See 4852.
4851. 11/29/00 mee Marselus, Guysbert; Albany, ALB. See 4964.
4852. 11/29/00 gor Marselus, Gysbert (w. Anna); City of N.Y.; Easton, WAS;
               gee 4963.   (E:63)
4853. 12/28/96 mee Marselus, Gysbert, Esq.; Albany, ALB. See 3665.
4854. 9/28/01 mor Marsh, Benjamin; Granville, WAS; Granville, WAS; mee 723.
                                                             (D:185)
4855. 9/7/69 gor Marsh, Jonathan; ---, ---. See 7955.

120

4856. 4/20/73 gor Marsh, Jonathan; ---, ---. See 7957.
4857. 1/24/01 mee Marshal, Josiah; Hartford, WAS. See 942.
4858. 2/6/94 gee Marshal, Thomas; Kingsbury, WAS. See 4860.
4859. 6/13/94 gee Marshall, Alexander, yeoman; Cambridge, WAS. See 8340.
4860. 2/6/94 gor Marshall, David, yeoman; Westfield, WAS; Westfield, WAS;
                gee 4858.   (B-2:141)
4861. 6/24/96 mor Marshall, Francis; Queensbury, WAS; Saratoga Pat., WAS;
                mee 3688.   (B:134)
4862. 8/31/96 mee Marshall, Francis, Esq.; Watervliet, ALB. See 1023 and
                1025. (two contracts)
4863. 12/12/98 mor Marshall, Josiah (w. Mary); ---, WAS; Hartford, WAS;
                mee 941.   (C:196)
4864. 12/12/98 mor Marshall, Mary. See 4863.
4865. 7/5/88 gee Marten, Kingsley; Westfield, WAS. See 2241.
4866. 2/4/90 mee Marten, Walter; Salem, WAS. See 1009.
4867. 9/8/95 mee Marten, Walter, Esq.; Salem, WAS. See 2483.
4868. 2/5/90 mee Martin, Aaron; Salem, WAS. See 7245.
4869. 11/22/91 gor Martin, Adam; Salem, WAS; Argyle, WAS; gee 1630. (A:370)
4870. 7/21/90 gor Martin, Adam, Esq.; Salem, WAS; Salem, WAS; gee 4883. (A:211)
4871. 9/1/90 gor Martin, Adam, Esq.; Salem, WAS; Salem, WAS; gee 4884. (A:210)
4872. 6/27/98 mor Martin, Anna. See 4873.
4873. 6/27/98 mor Martin, Daniel (w. Anna), yeoman; Hartford, WAS; Hartford,
                WAS; mee 369.   (B:293)
4874. 9/8/01 mor Martin, James; Alexandria, GRA, NH; Plattsburgh, CLI;
                mee 5772.   (B:56)
4875. 6/28/82 gor Martin, John, yeoman; "lately of New Perth", CHA; New Perth,
                CHA; gee 7584.   (B-1:128)
4876. 11/7/91 --- Martin, John Baptiste. See 6521.
4877. 12/30/85 gee Martin, Moses; ---, ---. See 7055.
4878. 12/29/91 gor Martin, Moses; ---, ---; twelve parcels of the Washington
                County lands in the Walloomsack Patent (lands originally
                granted to Edward Collins and others, 6/15/1739); co-gors
                1625, 4401; gees 70 (Lot 3), 101 (Lot 4), 1727 (Lot 10),
                1758 (Lot 1), 3453 (Lot 5), 5205 (Lot 9), 5206 (Lot 8),
                7315 (Lot 11), 7319 (Lot 7), 7399 (Lot 6), 7829 (Lot 12),
                8721 (Lot 2).   (A:249)
4879. 10/5/87 gor Martin, Moses, Esq.; Salem, WAS; Argyle, WAS; gee 1629. (A:214)
4880. 8/8/87 gee Martin, Richard, farmer; ---, WAS. See 5920.
4881. 8/6/88 gor Martin, Richard, farmer; Plattsburgh, CLI; ---, CLI;
                gee 2321.   (A:27)
4882. 9/5/95 gor Martin, Sarah. See 4886.
4883. 7/21/90 gee Martin, Walter, gentleman; Salem, WAS. See 4870.
4884. 9/1/90 gee Martin, Walter, gentleman; Salem, WAS. See 4871.
4885. 9/30/91 gee Martin, Walter, farmer; Salem, WAS. See 1360.
4886. 9/5/95 gor Martin, Walter, Esq. (w. Sarah); Salem, WAS; Salem, WAS;
                gee 2482.   (D:144)
4887. 5/21/93 gee Martin, William; Cambridge, WAS. See 2263.
4888. 5/9/01 mor Martin, William; Argyle, WAS; Argyle, WAS; mee 7817. (D:42b)
4889. 9/30/93 mor Marvin, Jared; Stillwater, SAR; Champlain, CLI; mee 3660.
                                                                 (A:115)
4890. 11/25/01 gee Mash, Amos, farmer; Pittstown, REN. See 2063.
4891. 7/29/92 gor Mason, Daniel, druggist; Westfield, WAS; Westfield, WAS;
                gee 4839.   (A:440)
4892. 8/7/92 mor Mason, Daniel, merchant; Westfield, WAS; Westfield, WAS;
                mee 5002.   (A:343)
4893. 10/7/94 gee Mason, Daniel; ---, ---. See 8583.
4894. 5/11/95 mee Mason, Daniel; Hartford, WAS. See 6481.
4895. 11/19/96 mor Mason, Daniel (w. Deborah); ---, WAS; Cockroft Pat., WAS;
                mee 3813.   (B:145)
4896. 10/10/98 gee Mason, Daniel; Hartford, WAS. See 3421.
4897. 10/12/98 gor Mason, Daniel; Hartford, WAS; ---, WAS; gee 3422. (D:20)
4898. 5/30/01 mee Mason, Daniel; Hartford, WAS. See 1006.
4899. 2/12/98 mor Mason, Daniel, Esq.; Hartford, WAS; Hartford, WAS;
                mee 1485.   (B:292)
4900. 1/17/99 mee Mason, Daniel, Esq.; Hartford, WAS. See 3364.
4901. 7/4/00 gor Mason, Daniel, Esq. (w. Debby); Hartford, WAS; Hartford, WAS;
                gee 7040.   (F:163)

4902.	5/12/02	gee	Mason, Daniel, Esq.; Hartford, WAS. See 3778.
4903.	7/4/00	gor	Mason, Debby. See 4901.
4904.	11/19/96	mor	Mason, Deborah. See 4895.
4905.	1/21/97	mor	Mason, Thaddeus; Salem, WAS; Argyle, WAS; co-mor 2508; mee 2486. (C:201)
4906.	8/8/87	mee	Masters, James Shelton; ---, ---. See 3752.
4907.	8/8/87	mee	Masters, Josiah; ---, ---. See 3752.
4908.	9/10/90	mee	Masters, Josiah; ---, ---. See 6216.
4909.	5/5/90	mee	Masters, Josiah, Esq.; ---, ALB. See 6213.
4910.	8/8/87	mee	Masters, Nicholas; ---, ---. See 3752.
4911.	2/26/96	mor	Matchet, William; Salem, WAS; Salem, WAS; mee 2128. (C:198)
4912.	1/30/89	mee	Mateson, William; Kingsbury, WAS. See 1593.
4913.	5/1/70	mee	Mather(?), Robert. See 4914.
4914.	5/1/70	mee	Mathes or Mather(?), Robert, farmer; New Perth, CHA. See 1421.
4915.	6/10/96	mee	Matheson, Daniel; Argyle, WAS. See 1267.
4916.	6/15/96	mee	Matheson, Daniel, yeoman; Argyle, WAS. See 4662.
4917.	2/10/95	gor	Mathews, David; Hoosick, REN; "Valamsack" Pat., WAS; gee 146. ("Valamsack" intended Walloomsack?) (C-2:39)
4918.	5/2/96	gee	Mathews, David; ---, REN. See 1186.
4919.	5/2/96	mor	Mathews, David, yeoman; ---, REN; Donald Campbell's Pat., WAS; mee 8045. (B:52)
4920.	1/1/00	gor	Mathews, David; ---, REN; Argyle, WAS; co-gees 67, 1278, 7268. (D:269)
4921.	1/2/00	mee	Mathews, David; ---, REN. See 68.
4922.	8/6/92	gee	Mathews, John, farmer; Shaftsbury, ---, VT. See 767.
4923.	12/6/00	gee	Mathews, Samuel; Argyle, WAS. See 405 and 414.
4924.	7/29/77	gee	Mathews, William; New Perth, CHA. See 4512.
4925.	4/2/82	gee	Mathews, William, carpenter; New Perth, CHA. See 1433.
4926.	7/6/95	gor	Mathison, Daniel, yeoman; "late of ... Salem", WAS; Salem, WAS; gee 4364. (B-2:456)
4927.	4/8/99	mor	Matteson, Atwood; Kingsbury, WAS; Kingsbury, WAS; co-mors 4929, 4934, 4937; mee 1740. (C:199)
4928.	4/9/99	mor	Matteson, Atwood; Kingsbury, WAS. See 4938.
4929.	4/8/99	mor	Matteson, Charles; Kingsbury, WAS. See 4927.
4930.	4/9/99	mor	Matteson, Charles; Kingsbury, WAS. See 4938.
4931.	11/27/94	mor	Matteson, Daniel; Salem, WAS. See 3783.
4932.	6/8/95	mee	Matteson, Daniel, yeoman; Salem, WAS. See 1678.
4933.	6/22/99	mee	Matteson, Daniel; Salem, WAS. See 6171.
4934.	4/8/99	mor	Matteson, Job; Kingsbury, WAS. See 4927.
4935.	4/9/99	mor	Matteson, Job; Kingsbury, WAS. See 4938.
4936.	12/13/96	gor	Matteson, Joseph, yeoman; Hebron, WAS; Hebron, WAS; gee 2901. (D:210)
4937.	4/8/99	mor	Matteson, William; Kingsbury, WAS. See 4927.
4938.	4/9/99	mor	Matteson, William; Kingsbury, WAS; Kingsbury, WAS; co-mors 4928, 4930, 4935; mee 3716. (C:200)
4939.	5/31/02	gee	Matteson, William; Kingsbury, WAS. See 1742.
4940.	7/3/02	mor	Matteson, William; Kingsbury, WAS; Kingsbury, WAS; co-mees 893, 1599. (E:4)
4941.	7/7/02	mor	Matteson, William; Kingsbury, WAS; Kingsbury, WAS; co-mees 7781, 7783. (E:2)
4942.	6/24/92	gee	Matthews, David; Salem, WAS. See 4516.
4943.	6/1/96	gee	Matthews, David; Salem, WAS. See 8532.
4944.	1/31/98	gee	Matthews, David; Hoosick, REN. See 6365.
4945.	5/24/99	mee	Matthews, David, gentleman; Hoosick, REN. See 886.
4946.	6/7/99	gor	Matthews, David, gentleman; Hoosick, REN; Argyle, WAS; gee 6903. (D:173)
4947.	6/7/99	mee	Matthews, David, gentleman; Hoosick, REN. See 6904.
4948.	5/16/96	mor	Matthews, John, weaver; Champlain, CLI; Champlain, CLI; co-mees 1700, 5136. (A:192)
4949.	9/18/98	mor	Matthews, John, weaver; Champlain, CLI; Champlain, CLI; co-mees 1701, 5133. (A:385)
4950.	7/16/00	gor	Matthews, John (w. Tryphena), farmer; Easton, WAS; Easton, WAS; gee 520. (E:79)
4951.	7/16/00	gor	Matthews, Tryphena. See 4950.
4952.	6/8/95	gor	Mattison, Daniel; Salem, WAS; Salem, WAS; gee 1677. (B-2:428)

4953. 6/7/86 mor Mattison, Henry; Hebron, WAS; Scott Pat., WAS; co-mees
4614, 4631, 6747, 6806. Co-mortgagees are executors of
the estate of John Morine Scott, dec'd.   (A:289)
4954. 11/13/97 gee Mattison, Henry, farmer; Hebron, WAS. See 6140.
4955. 5/26/02 gee Mattison, Henry, farmer; Hebron, WAS. See 3864.
4956. --/--/95 gee Mattison, William; Kingsbury, WAS. See 1197.
4957. 8/10/99 gor Mattocks, James; Kingsbury, WAS; Kingsbury, WAS; gee 8371.
(D:386)
4958. 1/21/86 gor Maunsell, John, Esq.; "County of New York"; land "west side
of ... Katharine Lake", WAS; co-gor 1539; gee 3843. (A:81)
4959. 1/6/88 mee Maunsell, John, Esq.; ---, ---. See 3854.
4960. 6/12/95 gor Maxwell, Collen, yeoman; Cambridge, WAS; Cambridge, WAS;
gee 5517.   (B-2:431)
4961. 6/12/95 mee Maxwell, Collen, yeoman; Cambridge, WAS. See 5518.
4962. 4/30/90 gor Maxwell, William, Esq.; City of N.Y.; Beekman Pat., CLI;
gee 7878.   (A:129)
4963. 11/29/00 gee May, Ellis; Easton, WAS. See 4852.
4964. 11/29/00 mor May, Ellis; Easton, WAS; Easton, WAS; mee 4851.   (D:19b)
4965. 10/1/93 gee Maycomber, George, yeoman; Cambridge, WAS. See 4199.
4966. 3/11/99 gee Mayhew, Wadsworth; Cambridge, WAS. See 7802.
4967. 10/10/01 mee Maynard, Gardner; Hartford, WAS. See 7077.
4968. 9/22/97 gor Mayne, Jean. See 4969.
4969. 9/22/97 gor Mayne, Joseph (w. Jean), farmer; Argyle, WAS; Argyle, WAS;
gee 4722.   (C-2:319)
4970. 11/4/91 gor Mead, Enos, yeoman; ---, SAR; "Summerset", WAS; gee 4007.
(D:198)
4971. 12/24/93 gor Mead, Enos, yeoman; ---, SAR; ---, WAS; gee 7209. (B-2:341)
4972. 5/1/00 mor Mead, Gidion, farmer; Chester, WAS; Chester, WAS; mee 7772.
(D:218)
4973. 5/1/00 mor Mead, Isaac, farmer; Chester, WAS; Chester, WAS; mee 7772.
(D:221)
4974. 11/3/88 gee Mead, Israel, farmer; Kingsbury, WAS. See 3177.
4975. 2/20/93 gor Mead, Job, Junr.; ---, ---; Cambridge Pat., WAS; co-gor
4977; gee 436.   (B-2:397)
4976. 5/1/00 mor Mead, Levi, farmer; Chester, WAS; Chester, WAS; mee 7772.
Two contracts this date involving these persons.
(D:213), (D:214)
4977. 2/20/93 gor Mead, Nathan; ---, ---. See 4975.
4978. 5/1/00 mor Mead, Nehemiah, Junr., farmer; Chester, WAS; Chester, WAS;
mee 7772. Two contracts this date involving these persons.
(D:201), (D:208)
4979. 5/1/00 mor Mead, Newcomb, farmer; Chester, WAS; Chester, WAS; mee 7772.
(D:222)
4980. 5/1/00 mor Mead, Noah, farmer; Chester, WAS; Chester, WAS; mee 7772.
(D:200)
4981. 5/1/00 mor Mead, William, farmer; Chester, WAS; Chester, WAS; mee 7775.
(D:197)
4982. 8/20/93 gor Means, James (w. Polly); Argyle, WAS. See 4983.
4983. 8/20/93 gor Means, John (w. Mary); Argyle, WAS; Argyle, WAS; co-gors
4982, 4985; gee 7838.   (B-2:491)
4984. 8/20/93 gor Means, Mary. See 4983.
4985. 8/20/93 gor Means, Polly. See 4982.
4986. 9/8/00 mor Meeker, Benjamin; ---, ---; Elizabethtown, ESS; mee 7520.
(A:48)
4987. 9/8/00 mor Meeker, Rufus; ---, ---; Elizabethtown, ESS; mee 7520.
(A:45)
4988. --/--/87 gee Melcher, Isaac; ---, ---. See 7055.
4989. 5/2/96 gee Menter, Reuben; Argyle, WAS. See 2100a.
4990. 5/2/96 gee Mentor, Elijah; Argyle, WAS. See 2100b.
4991. 6/17/95 gee Merchant, Hezekiah, yeoman; ---, ---, MA. See 3758.
4992. 6/17/95 mor Merchant, Hezekiah, yeoman; ---, ---, MA; Granville, WAS;
mee 3759.   (A:553)
4993. 10/15/95 mor Meretheu, Jeremiah, yeoman; ---, WAS. See 3259.
4994. 6/24/95 mor Meriam, Elizabeth. See 4998.
4995. 4/21/88 gee Meriam, Jonathan; Salem, WAS. See 7937.
4996. 9/14/89 gee Meriam, Jonathan; Salem, WAS. See 7933.

4997. 6/24/95 gee Meriam, Jonathan; Salem, WAS. See 7925.
4998. 6/24/95 mor Meriam, Jonathan (w. Elizabeth), yeoman; Salem, WAS; Salem,
                     WAS; mee 7926.   (A:557)
4999. 6/30/95 gee Meriam, Jonathan; Salem, WAS. See 7927.
5000. 2/12/99 mee Meriam, Jonathan; Salem, WAS. See 1680.
5001. 1/3/91   gee Meritt, Alexander, Capt.; Salem, WAS. See 7972.
5002. 8/7/92   mee Merrick, John, farmer; Westfield, WAS. See 4892.
5003. 12/4/80 gee Merrik, John, Esq.; ---, WAS. See 583.
5004. 3/13/01 mor Merrimon, George; Plattsburgh, CLI; Plattsburgh, CLI;
                     mee 5766.   (B:28)
5005. 8/15/98 mee Merrit, Daniel; Easton, WAS. See 8164.
5006. 8/15/98 mee Merrit, Isaac; Easton, WAS. See 8164.
5007. 10/29/98 mee Merritt, Daniel, merchant; Easton, WAS. See 2160.
5008. 10/29/98 mee Merritt, Isaac, merchant; Easton, WAS. See 2160.
5009. 9/28/93 gor Mersereau, Joshua; Union, TIO; Jessup's Purchase, WAS;
                     gee 1109. Two contracts this date involving these
                     persons.   (C-2:241), (C-2:244)
5010. 1/29/93 --- Metcalf, Simon. See 52.
5011. 1/13/96 mor Middleton, Hugh; Plattsburgh, CLI; Plattsburgh, CLI;
                     mee 2151.   (A:179)
5011a. 1/14/65 gor Middleton, Peter, physician; City of N.Y. See 6217.
5012. 1/15/65 gor Middleton, Peter, physician; City of N.Y. See 6219.
                     Six contracts this date involving these persons.
5013. 3/21/65 gor Middleton, Pater, physician; City of N.Y. See 6232.
5014. 10/22/65 gor Middleton, Peter, physician; City of N.Y. See 6220.
5015. 7/26/93 --- Middleton, Peter, physician, dec'd. See 6889.
5016. 7/3/95   --- Middleton, Peter, physician, dec'd.; City of N.Y. See 6892.
5017. 5/31/96 --- Middleton, Peter, physician, dec'd. See 6890.
5018. 11/23/97 --- Middleton, Peter, dec'd. See 6891.
5019. 1/30/93 gor Milk, John, farmer; ---, REN; Easton, WAS; gee 2038.
                                                                   (C-2:164)
5020. 8/15/93 mee Millar, John, farmer; Cambridge, WAS. See 8328.
5021. 5/8/02   gor Millard, Olive. See 5022.
5022. 5/8/02   gor Millard, Philo (w. Olive); Whitehall, WAS; Whitehall, WAS;
                     gee 7250.   (F:263)
5023. 10/31/92 gee Milleman, John; Hoosick, REN. See 3458.
5024. 5/21/00 mor Miller, Betsey. See 5035.
5025. 2/29/96 gee Miller, Burnet; Stanford, DUT. See 8755.
5026. 7/10/96 gee Miller, Burnet, Esq.; Stanford, DUT. See 8769.
5027. 7/15/91 mor Miller, Daniel, yeoman; Hebron, WAS; Hebron, WAS; mee 6983.
                                                                   (A:299)
5028. 8/4/01   --- Miller, Eleazer; ---, CLI. See 3449.
5029. 7/7/86   gee Miller, George; ---, ---. See 2618.
5030. 2/2/87   mee Miller, James; ---, ---. See 2159.
5031. 5/15/97 mee Miller, John, yeoman; Cambridge, WAS. See 1363.
5032. 11/8/97 mee Miller, John; Cambridge, WAS. See 5641.
5033. 8/20/98 mee Miller, John; Cambridge, WAS. See 2398.
5034. 7/23/99 mee Miller, John, farmer; Cambridge, WAS. See 679.
5035. 5/21/00 mor Miller, John (w. Betsey); Kingsbury, WAS; Kingsbury, WAS;
                     mee 1610.   (C:204)
5036. 12/23/01 mor Miller, John, farmer; Argyle, WAS; Argyle, WAS; co-mor
                     5039; mee 5553.   (D:134)
5037. 1/1/02   mee Miller, John; Plattsburgh, CLI. See 1049.
5038. 7/10/02 mee Miller, John, yeoman; Cambridge, WAS. See 1595.
5039. 12/23/01 mor Miller, Joseph, farmer; Argyle, WAS. See 5036.
5040. 5/30/88 gor Milligan, David, Esq., merchant; City of London, England;
                     land "at the head of Indian River", WAS; co-gees 4708,
                     4710.   (C-1:100)
5041. 7/12/80 gor Mills, David (w. Mary, "late Mary Campbell, Junior"),
                     cordwainer; Shawangunk Precinct, ULS; Argyle, WAS;
                     gee 870.   (B-1:151)
5042. 7/13/80 gor Mills, David (w. Mary), cordwainer; Shawangunk, ULS;
                     Argyle, CHA; gee 871.   (B-1:154)
5043. 11/12/89 gee Mills, George; Pawlet, RUT, VT. See 8261.
5044. 10/5/85 gee Mills, James; ---, ---. See 3867.
5045. 8/6/90   mor Mills, Jemmima. See 5046.
5046. 8/6/90   mor Mills, John (w. Jemmima); ---, WAS. See 5429.

5047. 7/12/80 gor Mills, Mary. See 5041.
5048. 7/13/80 gor Mills, Mary. See 5042.
5049. 5/19/96 gee Mills, Nicholas; Argyle, WAS. See 4661.
5050. 7/1/00 mor Mills, Timothy; ---, ---. See 7033.
5051. 7/16/92 gor Miner, Ezra, yeoman; Hebron, WAS; Hebron, WAS; co-gees
1160, 1163.   (C-2:248)
5052. 11/27/94 gor Miner, John; Queensbury, WAS; Queensbury, WAS; gee 8510.
(B-2:474)
5053. 8/24/90 mor Minor, Ezra; Corinth, WAS; Hebron, WAS; mee 6997. (A:272)
5054. 9/23/82 gee Mis(?), Josiah; Granville, WAS. See 5662.
5055. 5/1/02 mor Mitchel, David, farmer; Chester, WAS; Chester, WAS;
mee 7775.   (D:198)
5056. 5/30/97 gor Mitchel, Isaac, yeoman; Salem, WAS; Salem, WAS; gee 4748.
(D:429)
5057. 9/6/97 mor Mitchel, Isaac; Kingsbury, WAS; Kingsbury, WAS; mee 2500.
(B:191)
5058. 12/28/01 mor Mitchel, Thomas; Granville, WAS; Granville, WAS; mee 1302.
(D:128)
5059. 1/12/98 mor Mitchell, Andrew (w. Margaret), merchant; City of N.Y.;
Whitehall, WAS; co-mees 2314, 2659.   (B:291)
5060. 5/30/85 gee Mitchell, Ensign; ---, ---. See 7055.
5061. 6/1/85 mor Mitchell, Ensign; Skenesborough, WAS; Skenesborough, WAS;
mee 8550.   (Deed Book B-1:168)
5062. 12/24/98 mor Mitchell, Isaac; Kingsbury, WAS; Kingsbury, WAS; co-mees
7105, 7222. Co-mortgagees are executors "of the estate
of Platt Smith, late of Dutchess County, deceased." (C:197)
5063. 1/12/98 mor Mitchell, Margaret. See 5059.
5064. 11/15/96 mor Mitchell, William; Salem, WAS; Cambridge, WAS; mee 3208.
(B:119)
5065. 11/6/92 mor Mix, Samuel; Champlain, CLI; Champlain, CLI; co-mees 2676,
8051.   (A:97)
5066. 5/2/91 mor Mix, Stephen; Plattsburgh, CLI. See 5189.
5067. 5/3/94 mee Moffit, William; Grand Island, ---, VT. See 3299.
5068. 7/2/92 gee Molby, Jonathan; Salem, WAS. See 3049.
5069. 4/8/01 gee Montgomery, David, farmer; Argyle, WAS. See 1234.
5070. 6/6/92 gor Montresor, John, Esq.; "Kingdom of Great Britain"; ---, WAS;
gee 1997.   (A:473)
5071. 5/4/89 --- Monty, Amable. See 5072.
5072. 5/4/89 gor Monty, Francis, Junr.; Champlain, CLI; Champlain, CLI;
co-gor 5075("otherwise Amable Monty"); gee 5078.
Grantors are "sons of Francis Monty, Senior". (A:161)
5073. 5/4/89 --- Monty, Francis, Senr. See 5072.
5074. 9/30/96 --- Monty, Glaud, Junr.; ---, ---. See 2798.
5075. 5/4/89 gor Monty. Lenfant; Champlain, CLI. See 5072.
5076. 9/1/94 gee Monvill, Eliud; Whitehall, WAS. See 8695.
5077. 6/10/88 mor Mooers, Benjamin; ---, ---; Plattsburgh, CLI; mee 5839a. (A:12)
5078. 5/4/89 gee Mooers, Benjamin; Plattsburgh, CLI. Mooers is appointed
as their attorney by the grantors in 5072 in the sale
of their Clinton County lands.
5079. 10/15/89 mor Mooers, Benjamin; Beekman, CLI; Beekman, CLI; mee 584. (A:37)
5080. 11/8/96 gor Mooers, Benjamin, merchant; Plattsburgh, CLI; ---, CLI;
gee 5937.   (B:74)
5081. 11/30/96 mee Mooers, Benjamin; Plattsburgh, CLI. See 234.
5082. 6/6/98 mee Mooers, Benjamin; Plattsburgh, CLI. See 7422.
5083. 7/9/98 gee Mooers, Benjamin; Plattsburgh, CLI. See 5639.
5084. 12/18/98 mee Mooers, Benjamin; Plattsburgh, CLI. See 2453 and 3295.
(two contracts)
5085. 5/17/99 gor Mooers, Benjamin; Plattsburgh, CLI; Champlain, CLI;
gee 1047.   (B:189)
5086. 6/24/99 mee Mooers, Benjamin; Plattsburgh, CLI. See 3510.
5087. 8/1/99 mee Mooers, Benjamin; Plattsburgh, CLI. See 3119.
5088. 9/25/99 gor Mooers, Benjamin; Plattsburgh, CLI; Champlain, CLI;
gee 6659.   (B:334)
5089. 9/25/99 mee Mooers, Benjamin; Plattsburgh, CLI. See 6660.
5090. 3/18/00 mee Mooers, Benjamin; Plattsburgh, CLI. See 434.
5091. 4/7/00 mee Mooers, Benjamin; Plattsburgh, CLI. See 6234.

5092. 4/8/00 gor Mooers, Benjamin; Plattsburgh, CLI; Champlain, CLI; gee 7902. (B:224)
5093. 4/10/00 mee Mooers, Benjamin; Plattsburgh, CLI. See 4849.
5094. 7/31/00 gor Mooers, Benjamin; Plattsburgh, CLI; Canadian and Nova Scotia Refugees' Pat., CLI; gee 2628. (B:240)
5095. 8/15/00 mee Mooers, Benjamin; Plattsburgh, CLI. See 555.
5096. 2/17/01 mor Mooers, Benjamin; Plattsburgh, CLI; Cumberland Head (Plattsburgh), CLI; mee 7609. (B:13)
5097. 2/20/01 mee Mooers, Benjamin; Plattsburgh, CLI. See 7754.
5098. 2/21/01 mee Mooers, Benjamin; Plattsburgh, CLI. See 1894 and 5977. (two contracts)
5099. 4/14/01 mee Mooers, Benjamin; Plattsburgh, CLI. See 5230.
5100. 4/15/01 mee Mooers, Benjamin; Plattsburgh, CLI. See 6196.
5101. 6/29/01 mee Mooers, Benjamin; Plattsburgh, CLI. See 7678.
5102. 2/19/02 mee Mooers, Benjamin; Plattsburgh, CLI. See 8512.
5103. 4/5/02 mee Mooers, Benjamin; Plattsburgh, CLI. See 7420.
5104. 6/7/88 gee Mooers, Benjamin, Esq.; Plattsburgh, CLI. See 7433.
5105. 5/13/89 gee Mooers, Benjamin, Esq.; Plattsburgh, CLI. See 4014.
5106. 12/9/89 gor Mooers, Benjamin, Esq., Sheriff of Clinton County; ---, ---; ---, CLI; gee 2599. (A:181)
5107. 6/14/92 gee Mooers, Benjamin, Esq.; Plattsburgh, CLI. See 8120.
5108. 6/28/92 gee Mooers, Benjamin, Esq.; Plattsburgh, CLI. See 5665.
5109. 4/25/93 mee Mooers, Benjamin, Esq.; Plattsburgh, CLI. See 982 and 1858. (two contracts)
5110. 3/21/94 mee Mooers, Benjamin, Esq.; Plattsburgh, CLI. See 2427.
5111. 5/20/95 mee Mooers, Benjamin, Esq.; ---, ---. See 5353.
5112. 4/9/96 gor Mooers, Benjamin, Esq.; Plattsburgh, CLI; Canadian and Nova Scotia Refugees' Pat., CLI; gee 102. (A:428)
5113. 4/9/96 mee Mooers, Benjamin, Esq.; Plattsburgh, CLI. See 103.
5114. 4/16/97 mee Mooers, Benjamin, Esq.; Plattsburgh, CLI. See 876.
5115. 11/15/97 gor Mooers, Benjamin, Esq.; Plattsburgh, CLI; Champlain, CLI; gee 359. (B:98)
5116. 3/12/98 mee Mooers, Benjamin, Esq.; Plattsburgh, CLI. See 2581.
5117. 7/31/98 mee Mooers, Benjamin, Esq.; Plattsburgh, CLI. See 5462.
5118. 1/7/00 mee Mooers, Benjamin, Esq.; Plattsburgh, CLI. See 842.
5119. 4/14/01 mee Mooers, Benjamin, Esq.; Plattsburgh, CLI. See 1121.
5120. 10/3/96 gee Mooers, Jacob, Esq.; Plattsburgh, CLI. See 6504.
5121. 10/1/01 mor Moon, Benjamin; Queensbury, WAS. See 5124.
5122. 12/25/92 gee Moon, Robert; Queensbury, WAS. See 998.
5123. 10/1/01 mor Moon, Robert, Junr.; Queensbury, WAS. See 5124.
5124. 10/1/01 mor Moon, Solomon; Queensbury, WAS; Queensbury, WAS; co-mors 5121, 5123; mee 3282. (D:106)
5125. 5/2/93 gee Mooney, James; Cambridge, WAS. See 8843.
5126. 7/22/01 gee Mooney, James, yeoman; Cambridge, WAS. See 7134.
5127. 2/13/87 gor Moor, Pliny; Kinderhook Dist., COL; Moorfield Pat., WAS; gee 1531. (A:104)
5128. 5/27/91 gee Moor, Pliny; Champlain, CLI. See 2649 and 3584. (two contracts)
5129. 10/18/93 gor Moor, Pliny; Champlain, CLI; Mark Graves Pat., CLI; co-gor 1699; gee 7162. (B:231)
5130. 10/--/95 gee Moor, Pliny; Champlain, CLI. See 5156.
5131. 10/28/95 gee Moor, Pliny; Champlain, CLI. See 5157.
5132. 2/11/96 gee Moor, Pliny; Champlain, CLI. See 2415.
5133. 9/18/98 gee Moor, Pliny; Champlain, CLI. See 4949.
5134. 8/2/88 mee Moor, Pliny, Esq.; Kinderhook Dist., COL. See 5218.
5135. 7/20/93 mee Moor, Pliny, Esq.; ---, CLI. See 7974.
5136. 5/16/96 mee Moor, Pliny, Esq.; Champlain, CLI. See 4948.
5137. 8/20/96 gee Moor, Pliny, Esq.; Champlain, CLI. See 5459.
5138. 9/30/96 gee Moor, Pliny, Esq.; Champlain, CLI. See 2798.
5139. 3/8/97 gee Moor, Pliny, Esq.; Champlain, CLI. See 4015.
5140. 6/20/96 gor Moore, Ann. See 5147.
5141. 12/2/89 gee Moore, Benjamin; ---, ---. See 609.
5142. 12/19/89 gor Moore, Benjamin, Esq., sheriff of Clinton County; ---, ---; Willsborough, CLI; gee 5687. (A:133)
5143. 5/1/02 gee Moore, Bethsheba; Plattsburgh, CLI. See 7489.
5144. 2/4/99 mor Moore, Daniel, merchant; Albany, ALB; Benjamin Birdsalll Pat., CLI; mee 2895. (A:378)

5145. 4/12/00 gor Moore, Pliny; Champlain, CLI; Champlain, CLI; gee 6661.
(B:337)
5146. 9/18/98 mee Moore, Pliny, Esq.; Champlain, CLI. See 3381.
5147. 6/20/96 gor Moore, Thomas William (w. Ann); ---, ---; Argyle, WAS;
gee 178. (C-2:90)
5148. 6/21/96 mee Moore, Thomas William; ---, ---. See 179.
5149. 3/30/87 gee Moores, Benjamin; Point aux Roch, ---, --. See 2422.
5150. 11/25/87 gee Moores, Benjamin; Beekmantown; ---, NY. See 2423.
5151. 3/18/00 gor Moores, Benjamin; Plattsburgh, CLI; Champlain, CLI;
gee 433. (B:208)
5152. 12/21/84 mee Moorhous, John, yeoman; Willsborough, WAS. See 3486.
5153. 11/16/97 mee Moors, Benjamin, Esq.; Plattsburgh, CLI. See 360.
5154. 9/1/95 gee More, Josephes; Willsborough, CLI. See 632.
5155. 9/1/95 gor More, Josephus; Willsborough, CLI; Willsborough, CLI;
gee 631. (A:485)
5156. 10/--/95 gor Morehouse, David; Stillwater, SAR; Mark Graves' Pat., CLI;
gee 5130. (B:14)
5157. 10/28/95 gor Morehouse, David; Stillwater, SAR; Champlain, CLI; gee 5131.
(B:22)
5158. 8/16/91 --- Morehouse, John, Junr. See 5159.
5159. 8/16/91 gee Morehouse, Rosanah, "wife of John Morehouse Junior";
Willsborough, CLI. See 3468.
5160. 8/4/83 gee Morey, John, yeoman; New Perth, CHA. See 7929.
5161. 1/19/90 mor Morgan, Abraham; Hampton, WAS; Hampton, WAS; mee 6035.
(A:329)
5162. 1/19/90 mor Morgan, Abraham; Hampton, WAS; ---, WAS; mee 6087. (A:203)
5163. 11/22/94 mor Morgan, Abraham, farmer; Hampton, WAS; Hampton, WAS;
mee 5963. (A:527)
5164. 12/1/97 mee Morgan, Anstis; ---, ---. See 4721.
5165. 11/21/94 mor Morgan, David (w. Mary), farmer; Hampton, WAS; Hampton, WAS;
mee 5962. (A:515)
5166. 8/5/99 mee Morgan, James; ---, ---. See 3899.
5167. 9/5/96 mee Morgan, Jonas; ---, ---. See 5503.
5168. 6/27/00 mee Morgan, Jonas; ---, ---. See 7087.
5169. 1/18/90 mor Morgan, Joseph; Hampton, WAS; ---, WAS; mee 6086. (A:207)
5170. 11/21/94 mor Morgan, Mary. See 5165.
5171. 2/6/86 gee Morgan, Nathan; New Perth, WAS. See 8287.
5172. 2/16/87 gee Morgan, Nathan; Salem, WAS. See 7719.
5173. 2/19/87 gee Morgan, Nathan; Salem, WAS. See 2147.
5174. 2/14/00 mor Morgan, Pelatiah (w. Sarah); Argyle, WAS. See 2197.
5175. 2/14/00 mor Morgan, Sarah. See 5174.
5176. 2/22/94 gee Morhous, John, gentleman; Peru, CLI. See 5181.
5177. 7/4/99 gee Morhous, John, Junr.; Willsborough, CLI. See 2492.
5178. 2/13/00 mee Morhous, John, Junr., Esq.; ---, ---. See 8209.
5179. 4/28/92 gee Morhous, William, gentleman; Willsborough, CLI. See 7664.
5180. 4/28/92 mor Morhous, William; Willsborough, CLI; Zephaniah Platt's Pat.,
CLI; mee 7665. (A :82)
5181. 2/22/94 gor Morhous, William; Peru, CLI; Zephaniah Platt's Pat., CLI;
gee 5176. (B:154)
5182. 6/5/00 gor Morres, Charity. See 5183.
5183. 6/5/00 gor Morres, Robert (w. Charity); Shaftsbury, ---, VT; Cambridge,
WAS; gee 8060. (D:433)
5184. 1/19/90 mor Morris, James; Hampton, WAS; ---, WAS; mee 6087. (A:188)
5185. 11/21/94 mor Morris, Keziah. See 5192.
5186. 11/5/87 gor Morris, Lewis; Morrisania, WES; Argyle, WAS; gee 6695.
(C-1:99)
5187. 11/5/87 mee Morris, Lewis; Morrisania, ---. See 6689.
5188. 8/16/87 mor Morris, Robert; Plattsburgh, WAS; Plattsburgh, WAS; mee
5922. (A:8)
5189. 5/2/91 mor Morris, Robert, farmer; Plattsburgh, CLI; Beekmantown, CLI;
co-mor 5066; mee 591. (A:73)
5190. 1/18/90 gee Morris, Solomon; Hampton, WAS. See 6085.
5191. 11/21/94 gee Morris, Solomon; Hampton, WAS. See 5961.
5192. 11/21/94 mor Morris, Solomon (w. Keziah), farmer; Hampton, WAS; Hampton,
WAS; mee 5962. (A:523)
5193. 3/7/97 gee Morris, William, farmer; ---, WAS. See 5968.

127

5194. 11/23/95 gee Morrison, Joseph; Hartford, WAS. See 1447.
5195. 9/17/88 gee Morseilis, Guysbert, gentleman; A;bany, ALB. See 5196.
5196. 9/17/88 gor Morseilis, Margaret; Albany, ALB; Saratoga Pat., WAS;
                   gee 5195.   (B-2;312)
5197. 10/17/92 gor Mos(?), Thomas, carpenter; Plattsburgh, CLI. See 6633.
5198. 11/1/00 mor Moses, Catherine. See 5199.
5199. 11/1/00 mor Moses, Enam (w. Catherine), farmer; Argyle, WAS; Argyle, WAS;
                   co-mors 1247, 1248; co-mees 774, 785, 794, 5559. (D;133)
5200. 5/1/02 mor Mosher, David, farmer; Chester, WAS; Chester, WAS; mee 7775.
                                                                     (D;216)
5201. 7/3/97 gee Mosher, Elisha; Cambridge, WAS. See 8806.
5202. 5/1/00 mor Mosher, Isaac, farmer; Chester, WAS; Chester, WAS; mee
                   7772.   (D;215)
5203. 3/10/00 gee Mosher, Job, yeoman; Cambridge, WAS. See 962.
5204. 8/8/92 gor Mosher, Jonathan; ---, WAS; Westfield, WAS; gee 7203.
                                                                 (B-2;333)
5205. 12/29/91 gee Mosier, Allen; ---, ---. See 4878.
5206. 12/29/91 gee Mosier, Joseph; ---, ---. See 4878
5207. 1/2/02 mor Moss, Barnabas (w. Susannah); Granville, WAS; Granville, WAS;
                   co-mees 1119, 7067.   (D;126)
5208. 8/28/86 gee Moss, John; Kingsbury, WAS. See 7150.
5209. 7/21/92 gor Moss, John; Kingsbury, WAS; Kingsbury, WAS; gee 7556. (A;455)
5210. 8/4/95 gor Moss, John; Kingsbury, WAS; Kingsbury, WAS; gee 2167. (D;381)
5211. 5/11/97 mor Moss, John; Granville, WAS; Granville, WAS; mee 20. (B;180)
5212. 12/21/97 mor Moss, John; Granville, WAS; Granville, WAS; mee 704. (C;193)
5213. 3/24/91 gee Moss, John, Esq.; Kingsbury, WAS. See 7021.
5214. 10/8/99 gor Moss, John, Senr.; Kingsbury, WAS; Kingsbury, WAS; gee 8372.
                                                                 (D;384)
5215. 1/9/01 gee Moss, Joshua; Crown Point, ESS. See 7893.
5216. 1/9/01 gee Moss, Samuel; Crown Point, ESS. See 7893.
5217. 1/2/02 mor Moss, Susannah. See 5207.
5218. 8/2/88 mor Moss, Thomas, carpenter; Kings Dist., COL; Mark Graves Pat.,
                   CLI; mee 5134.   (A;17)
5219. 3/20/88 gee Mott, Ebenezer, farmer; ---, CLI. See 5838.
5220. 5/6/00 --- Mount, Elizabeth. See 4548.
5221. 5/23/01 --- Mount, Elizabeth. See 4549.
5222. 12/21/98 --- Mount, James, deceased. See 5225.
5223. 5/6/00 --- Mount, James, dec'd. See 4548.
5224. 5/23/01 mee Mount, Marcy. See 3144.
5225. 12/21/98 gor Mount, Mary, "daughter of James Mount late of Argyle ...
                   deceased"; Argyle, WAS; gee 1094.   (E;73)
5226. 7/7/97 mor Mourdock, Ely (w. Jemimah), farmer; Granville, WAS; Granville,
                   WAS; co-mees 77, 2938, 2954.   (B;207)
5227. 7/7/97 mor Mourdock, Jemimah. See 5226.
5228. 6/11/01 mee Munro, Peter Jay, Esq.; City of N.Y. See 1261, 3543, 7082,
                   8725.
5229. 4/1/02 mee Munro, Peter, Jay, Esq.; City of N.Y. See 4468, 6735.
5230. 4/14/01 mor Munsee, Peter; Champlain, CLI; Champlain, CLI; mee 5099. (B;24)
5231. 12/25/97 gor Munson, Esther. See 5235.
5232. 9/15/73 gee Munson, Hester. See 5234.
5233. 3/3/98 mor Munson, Jearard, Junr., farmer; ---, CLI; Old Military
                   Township #7 (Chateaugay), CLI; co-mees 6855, 8087. (A;271)
5234. 9/15/73 gee Munson, John (w. Hester); New Haven, "County of New Haven",
                   --. See 2079.
5235. 12/25/97 gor Munson, John (w. Esther); Hebron, WAS; Hebron, WAS; gee 5484.
                                                                 (C-2;266)
5236. 11/1/00 mee Munson, John, farmer; Hebron, WAS. See 1736.
5237. 3/21/01 gee Munson, John, 3rd; Hebron, WAS. See 1737.
5238. 3/21/01 gee Munson, Thomas; Hebron, WAS. See 1737.
5239. 2/5/96 gee Murch, William; Cambridge, WAS. See 7130.
5240. 2/23/01 mee Murdock, Eli, yeoman; Granville, WAS. See 6650.
5241. 10/19/02 mee Murdock, James, "messieurs, and company, merchants";
                   Schenectady, ALB. See 2861.
5242. 12/22/90 gee Murray and Sansom, merchants; City of N.Y. See 4280.
5243. 5/20/95 gee Murray, Isaac, yeoman; Cambridge, WAS. See 437.
5244. 12/1/97 --- Murray, John, dec'd. See 4721.

128

5245. 5/20/90 gee Murrey, Peter; Whitehall, WAS. See 2250.
5246. 12/1/99 --- Myer, Helena. See 8111.
5247. 2/18/02 --- Myer, Helena, dec'd. See 8117.
5248. 10/20/86 gor Myer, John R., merchant; City of N.Y.; <u>Argyle, WAS</u>; gee
1773.   (B-2:305)
5249. 12/1/85 gor Myers, Ann. See 5254.
5250. 2/9/96 gor Myers, Helena. See 6762.
5251. 2/9/96 mee Myers, Helena. See 6763. Three contracts this date
involving these persons.
5252. 6/18/96 --- Myers, Helena. See 6764.
5253. 12/18/96 gor Myers, Helena; ---, ---. See 6810.
5254. 12/1/85 gor Myers, John R., merchant; City of N.Y.; <u>Argyle, WAS</u>;
co-gees 1668, 4537.   (A:227)
5255. 3/9/90 mor Nadan, John; Westfield, WAS; <u>Provincial Pat., WAS</u>;
mee 5358.   (A:278)
5256. 12/30/94 gor Neilson, Susannah. See 5257.
5257. 12/30/94 gor Neilson, William, Esq. (w. Susannah), merchant; City of N.Y.;
<u>Cambridge, WAS</u>; gee 8844.   (D:169)
5258. 6/2/69 gee Nevins, John; White Creek, ALB. See 2026.
5259. 9/26/98 --- Newcomb, Christian, farmer; Poughkeepsie, DUT; <u>Plattsburgh
and Peru, CLI</u>; co-person 5281, Zacheus Newcomb. These
two persons, through the will of their father, Zacheus
Newcomb, Esq., dec'd,(along with their brothers Daniel,
Thomas, and John) are devised the above lands. Christian
and Zacheus, Junior,here appoint Kinner Newcomb of
Clinton County to be their attorney in the division and
sale of these lands.   (B:162)
5260. 9/26/98 --- Newcomb, Daniel. See 5259.
5261. 10/12/01 mor Newcomb, James; Chateaugay, CLI; <u>Chateaugay, CLI</u>; co-mor
5266; mee 8077. Six contracts this date involving these
persons.   (B:47 and others)
5262. 9/26/98 --- Newcomb, John. See 5259.
5263. 3/3/89 gee Newcomb, Kinner; Plattsburgh, CLI. See 5629.
5264. 11/3/89 gee Newcomb, Kinner, farmer; Plattsburgh, CLI. See 5783.
5265. 9/26/98 --- Newcomb, Kinner. See 5259.
5266. 10/12/01 mor Newcomb, Kinner; Chateaugay, CLI. See 5261.
5267. 4/23/01 mor Newcomb, Luther (w. Pamela); Whitehall, WAS; <u>Whitehall, WAS</u>;
mee 8148.   (D:167)
5268. 4/23/01 mor Newcomb, Pamela. See 5267.
5269. 8/14/87 gee Newcomb, Platt, "an infant"; Plattsburgh, WAS. See 5921.
5270. 1/7/89 gee Newcomb, Simon, farmer; Plattsburgh, CLI. See 7690.
5271. 1/7/89 mor Newcomb, Simon; Plattsburgh, CLI; <u>Plattsburgh, CLI</u>; mee
7691.   (A:19)
5272. 10/15/89 mor Newcomb, Simon; Plattsburgh, CLI. See 595.
5273. 4/17/90 mee Newcomb, Simon; Plattsburgh, CLI. See 7692.
5274. 4/18/96 mor Newcomb, Simon; Plattsburgh, CLI; <u>Plattsburgh, CLI</u>;
mee 104.   (A:189)
5275. 1/9/94 mee Newcomb, Thomas; ---, ---. See 1514.
5276. 10/3/95 mee Newcomb, Thomas; Clinton, DUT. See 1515.
5277. 9/26/98 --- Newcomb, Thomas; ---, ---. See 5259.
5278. 2/8/85 gee Newcomb, Zaccheus, gentleman; ---, ---. See 5887.
5279. 1/9/94 --- Newcomb, Zacheus, dec'd.; Clinton, DUT. See 1514.
5280 10/3/95 --- Newcomb, Zacheus, dec'd. See 1515.
5281. 9/26/98 --- Newcomb, Zacheus, Esq., dec'd. See 5259.
5282. 9/26/98 --- Newcomb, Zacheus (Junr), physician, Clinton, CLI. See 5259.
5283. 1/1/95 gee Newell, Ebenezer; Crown Point, CLI. See 5286.
5284. 11/9/96 gor Newell, Ebenezer; Elizabethtown, CLI; <u>Platt Rogers Pat., CLI</u>;
gee 8727.   (A:48)
5285. 6/24/94 mor Newell, Norman, yeoman; ---, ADD, VT; <u>Platt Rogers Pat., CLI</u>;
mee 2011.   (A:137)
5286. 1/1/95 gor Newell, Norman; Crown Point, CLI; <u>Platt Rogers Pat., CLI</u>;
gee 5283.   (B:80)
5287. 1/1/96 gor Newell, Norman; Crown Point Dist., CLI; <u>Platt Rogers Pat., CLI</u>;
gee 919.   (B:81)
5288. 5/1/02 gee Newell, Norman; Willsborough, ESS. See 920.
5289. 5/1/02 gor Newell, Norman; Willsborough, ESS; <u>Willsborough, ESS</u>;
gee 8731.   (A:52)

129

5290. 5/15/00 mor Newell, Samuel; Champlain, CLI; Champlain, CLI; mee 5878.
(A:432)
5291. 10/7/01 gor "New Loan Officers of the County of Washington" (Ebenezer
Russell and Timothy Leonard); ---, ---; Salem, WAS
(in Turner's Pat.); gee 1469.   (E:453)
5292. 5/9/01 mor Newton, Alpheus; Kingsbury, WAS. See 8155. (two contracts)
5293. 5/22/01 mor Newton, Henry; Shaftsbury, BEN, VT. See 5294.
5294. 5/22/01 mor Newton, Samuel; Shaftsbury, BEN, VT; Hebron, WAS; co-mor
5293; mee 171.   (D:77b)
5295. 7/1/00 mee New York State (sale of state-owned lands). See "People
of the State of New York" in 5572.
5296. 7/10/90 gee Nicholes, Timothy, yeoman; Hebron, WAS. See 1071.
5297. 12/15/97 gee Nicholes, Timothy, Junr.; Hebron, WAS. See 5298.
5298. 12/15/97 gor Nicholes, Timothy, Senr.; Hebron, WAS; Hebron, WAS;
gee 5297.   (F:1)
5299. 11/6/93 mor Nicholl, Samuel, yeoman; Smithtown, SUF; Plattsburgh, CLI;
mee 7882.   (A:137)
5300. 7/10/90 mor Nicholls, Timothy; Hebron, WAS; Hebron, WAS; mee 1072.
(A:240)
5301. 2/2/99 mee Nichols, Joshua; New Haven, ADD, VT. See 4829.
5302. 8/4/02 mor Nichols, Thomas, farmer; Peru, CLI; Peru, CLI; mee 3444.
(B:76)
5303. 3/1/94 mor Nichols, Timothy, yeoman; Hebron, WAS; Hebron, WAS;
mee 5594.   (A:467)
5304. 5/6/94 gee Nichols, Timothy, Junr.; Hebron, WAS. See 2662.
5305. 1/27/94 gee Nicholson, William; Cambridge, WAS. See 8642.
5306. 10/8/88 gor Nicoll, Jane. See 5308.
5307. 7/5/93 gee Nicoll, Jane, wife of John Nicoll, merchant, City of New
Haven, ---, --. See 6732.
5308. 10/8/88 gor Nicoll, John (w. Jane); ---, ---. See 1934.
5309. 1/5/93 --- Nicoll, John. See 5307.
5310. 6/28/02 mor Nims, Daniel, Junr.; Bolton, WAS; Bolton, WAS; mee 7229. (E:29)
5311. 10/18/65 gor Niven, Rachel, "widow of John McPhaden, deceased". See 4758.
5312. 1/--/91 gee Nixon, Thomas, merchant; City of N.Y. See 6514.
5313. 11/7/91 gee Nixon, Thomas; ---, ---. See 6521. (two contracts)
5314. 1/19/02 mor Nobles, Nathan; Cambridge, WAS; Cambridge, WAS; mee 4671.
(D:156)
5315. 7/1/85 gee Nolls, Elisha; ---, ---. See 7055.
5316. 6/17/99 mor North, Abijah; Shoreham, ADD, VT; Champlain, CLI; mee 1941.
(B:7)
5317. 10/7/89 mor North, Aron; New Briton, COL; Willsborough, CLI; mee 6438.
(A:26)
5318. 4/14/98 mor North, Charles; Plattsburgh, cLI; Old Military Township #7
(Chateaugay), CLI; mee 5695.   (A:289)
5319. 7/6/88 mor North, Thomas; Granville, WAS; Granville, WAS; mee 2379.
(A:99)
5320. 4/22/89 mor North, Thomas; ---, ---; Granville, WAS; mee 835. (A:152)
5321. 4/15/01 gor North, William; ---, ---. See 2132.
5322. 12/28/99 mor Northrup, Anna. See 5323.
5323. 12/28/99 mor Northrup, John H. (w. Anna), blacksmith; Hebron, WAS;
Hebron, WAS; mee 8116. Mortgagee is the "only
surviving executor of the estate of John Morin Scott,
Esq., deceased".   (C:215)
5324. 6/7/02 mor Northrup, Clark; Granville, WAS; Granville, WAS; mee 4159.
(D:193)
5325. 3/20/99 gee Norton, Aaron; Hartford, WAS. See 3515.
5326. 8/23/99 gee Norton, Aaron, merchant; Hartford, WAS. See 1753.
5327. 8/1/98 gor Norton, John L.; ---, ---; Provincial Pat., WAS; co-gor
5339; gee 1149. Grantors are executors of the estate
of "John Leake, late of the City of New York, gentleman,
deceased."   (C-2:324)
5328. 8/1/98 mee Norton, John L.; ---, ---. See 1132.
5329. 12/18/95 mor Norton, John, Junr., farmer; Easton, WAS; Saratoga Pat., WAS;
mee 3672.   (B:11)
5330. 5/13/00 mor Norton, Josiah (w. Margaret); Granville, WAS; Granville, WAS;
mee 1541.   (C:217)

130

5331. 6/20/01 gee Norton, Josiah; Granville, WAS. See 5476.
5332. 6/26/01 mor Norton, Josiah; Granville, WAS; Granville, WAS; mee 7737.
(D:76b)
5333. 5/13/00 mor Norton, Margaret. See 5330.
5334. 4/30/93 gor Norton, Martha, "sole acting executrix to the ... will ...
of John Leake, late of the Hermitage of the City of New
York"; Grant Pat., WAS; gee 8411.   (B-2:104)
5335. 7/3/93 mee Norton, Martha, "sole acting executrix of the ... will
of John Leak, late of the City of New York, deceased";
---, ---. See 2048.
5336. 1/7/96 mee Norton, Martha, gentlewoman; City of N.Y. See 8351.
5337. 11/20/96 gor Norton, Martha, "acting executor of the will of John Leake,
gentleman, late of the City of New York, deceased";
---, ---; Provincial Pat., WAS; gee 1605. (C-2:145)
5338. 8/7/01 gor Norton, Oliver (w. Susanah), physician; Argyle, WAS;
Argyle, WAS; gee 8344.   (F:144)
5339. 8/1/98 gor Norton, Robert B.; ---, ---. See 5327.
5340. 8/1/98 mee Norton, Robert B.; ---, ---. See 1132.
5341. 8/7/01 gor Norton, Susanah. See 5338.
5342. 3/13/93 gee Noyes, Asa; Whitehall, WAS. See 2238.
5343. 7/10/93 mor Noyes, Asa; Whitehall, WAS; land "east side of Wood Creek,"
WAS; co-mees 1575 and 7977.   (A:425)
5344. 10/14/93 gee Noyes, Asa; Whitehall, WAS. See 2246.
5345. 10/16/93 gor Noyes, Asa; Whitehall, WAS; Champlain, WAS; gee 6042. (A:503)
5346. 7/--/94 gor Noyes, Asa (w. Lurany); Whitehall, WAS; Earll's Pat., CLI;
gee 6043.   (A:347)
5347. 7/--/94 gor Noyes, Lurany. See 5346.
5348. 1/5/02 mee Nye, Timothy, farmer; Salem, WAS. See 3523.
5349. 9/20/90 mor Odal, Jonas, "late of Hebron", WAS; ---, WAS (a discharge
of mortgage record); mee 6039.   (A:217)
5350. 5/8/86 gor Odel, Jonas, farmer; Hebron, WAS; Kemp Pat., WAS; gee 4775.
(C-1:59)
5351. 1/16/87 gor Odel, Jonas; Hebron, WAS; Hebron, WAS; gee 8478. (C-1:58)
5352. 4/7/89 gor Odel, Jonas; Hebron, WAS; Hebron, WAS; gee 6038. (A:108)
5353. 5/20/95 mor Odel, Joseph, Junr., farmer; Christie's Manor, Lower Canada;
Canadian and Nova Scotia Refugees' Pat., CLI; co-mors
4187, 6836; mee 5111.   (A:159)
5354. 9/28/01 mee Odell, Benajah; Queensbury, WAS. See 3021.
5355. 7/16/01 mor Ogden, David A. (w. Rebecca); City of N.Y.; ---, CLI;
co-mors 5360, 5364; mee 1639. Five contracts this
date involving these persons.   (B:43)
5356. 1/28/83 gor Ogden, Jonathan; Tomhanock, ALB; Provincial Pat., CHA;
gee 3221.   (B-1:124)
5357. 4/14/88 gor Ogden, Jonathan; Westfield, WAS; Provincial Pat., WAS;
gee 958.   (D:245)
5358. 3/9/90 mee Ogden, Jonathan; Westfield, WAS. See 5255.
5359. 9/20/97 mee Ogden, Jonathan; Charlton, SAR. See 1108.
5360. 7/16/01 mor Ogden, Martha. See 5364.
5361. 9/21/01 mee Ogden, Matthias; Argyle, WAS. See 2460.
5362. 9/26/01 mor Ogden, Matthias; Argyle, WAS; Kingsbury, WAS; mee 6868.
(D:143)
5363. 10/1/01 mor Ogden, Obediah; Queensbury, WAS; Queensbury, WAS; mee 3282.
(D:105)
5364. 7/16/01 mor Ogden, Thomas L. (w. Martha); City of N.Y. See 5355.
5365. 9/21/01 mor Olcott, Anna. See 5366.
5366. 9/21/01 mor Olcott, Thomas (w. Anna); ---, WAS; Granville, WAS;
mee 1693.   (D:91)
5367. 6/4/92 mee Olivie, Lorant; Champlain, CLI. See 205.
5368. 2/26/96 gee Ollcutt, Oliver; Cambridge, WAS. See 7135.
5369. 4/21/89 gee Olmstead, Aaron; ---, ---; ---, WAS; mee 838. (A:144)
5370. 9/4/95 gee Olmstead, Ebenezer; Bradford, ORA, VT. See 5855.
5371. 9/5/95 mor Olmsted, Ebenezer; Bradford, ORA, VT; Peru, CLI; mee 5856.
(A:162)
5372. 3/7/00 mee Olmsted, Ebenezer; Bradford, ORA, VT. See 189.
5373. 9/15/94 gee Omstead, Jedediah; ---, ---. See 2012.
5374. 1/1/95 gee Omstead, Jedediah; Hampton, WAS. See 1284.

5375. 1/1/95 gor Omstead, Jedediah; Hampton, WAS. See 8814 and 8815.
5376. 1/4/95 gor Omstead, Jedediah; Hampton, WAS. See 8816.
5377. 1/5/95 gor Omstead, Jedediah; Hampton, WAS. See 8817.
<u>5378.</u> 5/14/96 mor Orcutt, Erastus, yeoman; Cambridge, WAS; <u>Cambridge, WAS</u>; mee 3304. (B:45)
<u>5379.</u> 10/15/96 gor Orcutt, Erastus (w. Rachel), carpenter; Cambridge, WAS; <u>Cambridge, WAS</u>; gee 8358. (F:156)
<u>5380.</u> 8/17/95 gor Orcutt, Oliver (w. Philenda), farmer; Cambridge, WAS; <u>Cambridge, WAS</u>; gee 8357. (F:288)
5381. 8/17/95 gee Orcutt, Philenda. See 5380.
5382. 10/15/96 gor Orcutt, Rachel. See 5379.
5383. 8/13/95 gee Orcutt, William, blacksmith; Hartford, WAS. See 995.
<u>5384.</u> 5/12/98 gor Orcutt, William, blacksmith; Hartford, WAS; <u>Hartford, WAS</u>; gee 963. (D:3)
<u>5385.</u> 9/20/93 mor Ormsby, Joseph, yeoman; Plattsburgh, CLI; <u>Plattsburgh, CLI</u>; mee 5852. (A:112)
5386. 6/1/91 gee Orsburn, Alexander; Bridport, ADD, VT. See 6450.
<u>5387.</u> 3/17/01 mor Orton, Solomon; ---, ---; <u>land "west of the River Boquet"</u>, <u>ESS</u>; mee 3385. (A:65)
5388. 6/26/99 mee Osborn, David, Junr.; Kingsbury, WAS. See 2644.
<u>5389.</u> 8/25/00 mor Osborn, David, Junr., merchant; Kingsbury, WAS; <u>Kingsbury, WAS</u>; co-mees 7106, 7226. The co-mortgagees are executors of the will of "Platt Smith late of Dutchess County, deceased". (D:12)
<u>5390.</u> 3/15/00 mor Osborn, Joseph; Granville, WAS; <u>Granville, WAS</u>; mee 4138. (C:216)
5391. 11/3/01 mee Osbourn, David, Junr.; ---, ---. See 1356.
5392. 11/1/98 mee Osbourn, David, Junr., merchant; Kingsbury, WAS. See 3064.
<u>5393.</u> 12/23/99 gor Osgood, Aaron (w. Sarah); Westfield, WAS; <u>Westfield, WAS</u>; gee 575. (D:405)
5394. 10/14/89 gee Osgood, Aron; Kingsbury, WAS. See 3173.
<u>5395.</u> 9/3/99 mor Osgood, Caleb; Westfield, WAS; <u>Westfield, WAS</u>; mee 8184. (C:216)
<u>5396.</u> 11/12/00 mor Osgood, Levi, farmer; Westfield, WAS; <u>Westfield, WAS</u>; mee 3171. (D:17)
5397. 12/23/99 gor Osgood, Sarah. See 5393.
5398. 6/2/87 gee Osgood, Thomas; ---, ---. See 7055.
<u>5399.</u> 11/13/86 mor Ostrander, Henry; Plattsburgh, CLI; <u>Plattsburgh, CLI</u>; mee 6430. (A:23)
5400. 11/17/89 gee Ostrander, Henry; Plattsburgh, CLI. See 8767.
5401. 6/29/01 mee Ostrander, Henry; Plattsburgh, CLI. See 7423.
5402. 2/24/98 mee Ostrom, John; Duanesburgh, ALB. See 42.
5403. 9/1/95 gor Oswald, George; Cambridge, WAS. See 5411.
5404. 4/6/93 gee Oswald, George, Junr., farmer; Salem, WAS. See 2393.
5405. 4/6/93 mor Oswald, George, Junr., farmer; Salem, WAS. See 5409.
5406. 7/27/96 mor Oswald, Jennet. See 5412.
5407. 11/24/97 mor Oswald, Jennet. See 5413.
5408. 4/6/93 gee Oswald, Thomas, farmer; Salem, WAS. See 2393.
<u>5409.</u> 4/6/93 mor Oswald, Thomas, farmer; Salem, WAS; <u>Cambridge, WAS</u>; co-mor 5405; mee 2400. (A:416)
<u>5410.</u> 3/5/95 gor Oswald, Thomas; Cambridge, WAS; <u>Cambridge, WAS</u>; gee 6736. (C-2:211)
<u>5411.</u> 9/1/95 gor Oswald, Thomas; Cambridge, WAS; <u>Cambridge, WAS</u>.; co-gor 5403; gee 2174. (C-2:98)
<u>5412.</u> 7/27/96 mor Oswald, Thomas (w. Jennet), yeoman; Cambridge, WAS; <u>Cambridge, WAS</u>; mee 2411. (B:307)
<u>5413.</u> 11/24/97 mor Oswald, Thomas (w. Jennet), farmer; Cambridge, WAS; <u>Cambridge, WAS</u>; mee 2414. (B:227)
<u>5414.</u> 12/17/93 mor Otis, Richard, yeoman; ---, WAS; <u>Argyle, WAS</u>; co-mees 1183, 8036. (A:460)
<u>5415.</u> 12/17/93 mor Otis, William, yeoman; ---, WAS; <u>Argyle, WAS</u>; co-mees 1183, 8037. (A:463)
5416. 7/1/00 mor Owen, Charles; ---, ---. See 5419. Two contracts this date involving these persons.
<u>5417.</u> 5/1/00 mor Owen, Daniel, farmer; Chester, WAS; <u>Chester, WAS</u>; mee 7772. (D:215)

5418.	7/1/00	mor	Owen, Keziah; ---, ---; ---, ESS; mee 5572. (A:27)
5419.	7/1/00	mor	Owen, Leonard; ---, ---; ---, ESS; co-mor 5416; mee 5572.

Two contracts this date involving these persons.
(A:23), (A:30)

5420.	7/1/00	mor	Owen, Thadius; ---, ---; ---, ESS; mee 5572. (A:34)
5421.	11/25/01	mor	Page, Benjamin; Chateaugay, CLI; Old Military Township #7 (Chateaugay), CLI; mee 327. (B:60)
5422.	7/1/00	mor	Paige, Jonathan; ---, ---; ---, ESS; mee 5572. (A:50)
5423.	7/1/00	mor	Pain, Benjamin; ---, ---. See 4830.
5424.	5/21/95	mor	Pain, Peter, farmer; Willsborough, CLI; Willsborough, CLI; mee 2797. (A:190)
5425.	11/26/85	gor	Paine, Brinton; ---, DUT; Black Creek, WAS; gee 6405. (A:57)
5426.	8/6/90	mor	Paine, Daniel, Junr. (w. ---); ---, WAS. See 5429.
5427.	8/6/90	mor	Paine, Mary. See 5429.
5428.	8/6/90	mor	Paine, Moses (w. ---); ---, WAS. See 5429.
5429.	8/6/90	mor	Paine, Reuben (w. Mary); ---, WAS; Warren Pat., WAS; co-mors 5046, 5426, 5428; mee 4528. (B:80)
5430.	11/12/92	gee	Pairpoint, Thomas; Hebron, WAS. See 6972.
5431.	10/2/02	mor	Palmer, Ezekiel; ---, ---; Chesterfield, ESS; mee 760. (A:91)
5432.	9/20/01	mor	Palmer, Larah (perhaps Sarah?). See 5435.
5433.	7/1/00	mor	Palmer, Micah; ---, ---; ---, ESS; mee 5572. (A:53)
5434.	9/21/96	mor	Palmer, Nathaniel, farmer; Granville, WAS; Granville, WAS; mee 3764. (B:129)
5435.	9/21/01	mor	Palmer, Nathaniel (w. Larah or Sarah); ---, WAS; Granville, WAS; mee 1692. (D:95)
5436.	3/26/96	mor	Palmer, Samuel; Stanford, DUT; ---, WAS; mee 7022. (B:172)
5437.	7/1/00	mor	Palmer, Uriah; ---, ---; ---, ESS; mee 5572. (A:56)
5438.	7/1/00	mor	Pangborn, Joseph; ---, ---; ---, ESS; mee 5572. (A:74)
5439.	6/13/74	gor	Panton, Francis (w. Jane); City of N.Y.; Artillery Pat., CHA; gee 3495. (A:4)
5440.	5/6/75	gor	Panton, Francis (w. Jane); City of N.Y.; Artillery Pat., CHA; gee 3528. (A:19)
5441.	6/13/74	gor	Panton, Jane. See 5439.
5442.	5/6/75	gor	Panton, Jane. See 5440.
5443.	4/13/99	mee	Parce, John, farmer; Hartford, WAS. See 6613.
5444.	5/1/00	mor	Parce, Perry, farmer; Chester, WAS; Chester, WAS; mee 7772. (D:226)
5445.	2/15/01	mee	Pardner, Reserved; Bateman(?), DUT. See 2542.
5446.	5/17/02	mor	Parker, Andrew; Granville, WAS; Granville, WAS; mee 4157. (D:165)
5447.	5/13/00	mor	Parker, Benjamin (w. Speedy), farmer; Granville, WAS; Granville, WAS; mee 1541. (C:140)
5448.	3/12/93	gee	Parker, Eliphalet, farmer; Granville, WAS. See 946.
5449.	5/30/93	mor	Parker, Eliphalet, farmer; ---, WAS. See 5474.
5450.	1/12/99	mor	Parker, Eliphalet; Granville, WAS; Granville, WAS; mee 4134. (C:248)
5451.	9/3/99	gor	Parker, Eliphalet; Granville, WAS. See 5470.
5452.	6/20/01	gor	Parker, Eliphalet; Granville, WAS. See 5476.
5453.	5/30/01	mor	Parker, Eliphalet, Junr.; Granville, WAS; Granville, WAS; mee 4146. (D:84)
5454.	6/7/99	mor	Parker, George; ---, ---; Willsborough, ESS; mee 3228. (A:89)
5455.	7/19/93	gee	Parker, John; Plattsburgh, CLI. See 5982.
5456.	5/13/96	gee	Parker, John; Plattsburgh, CLI. See 7734.
5457.	5/30/96	mor	Parker, John, clothier; Plattsburgh, CLI; Canadian and Nova Scotia Refugees' Pat., CLI; mee 7732. (A:226)
5458.	8/20/96	gor	Parker, John; Plattsburgh, CLI; Champlain, CLI; gee 3817. (A:478)
5459.	8/20/96	gor	Parker, John (w. Lodeme), clothier; Plattsburgh, CLI; Champlain, CLI (in the Canadian and Nova Scotia Refugees' Patent); gee 5137. (B:16)
5460.	8/1/97	mee	Parker, John; Plattsburgh, CLI. See 1355.
5461.	7/17/98	gee	Parker, John; Willsborough, CLI. See 3736.
5462.	7/31/98	mor	Parker, John; Plattsburgh, CLI; Canadian and Nova Scotia Refugees' Pat., CLI; mee 5117. (A:331)
5463.	8/22/98	gor	Parker, John; Plattsburgh, CLI; Canadian and Nova Scotia Refugees' Pat., CLI; co-gees 6486, 6513. (B:194)

5464. 8/20/96 gor Parker, Lodeme. See 5459.
5465. 7/1/97 gee Parker, Lodeme; Plattsburgh, CLI. See 7404.
5466. 1/3/97 gor Parker, Lydia. See 5480.
5467. 2/8/98 mor Parker, Lydia. See 5478.
5468. 3/12/93 gee Parker, Michael, farmer; Granville, WAS. See 946.
5469. 5/30/93 mor Parker, Michael, farmer; ---, WAS. See 5474.
5470. 9/3/99 gor Parker, Michael; Granville, WAS; <u>Granville, WAS</u>; co-gors
          1651, 5451, 5475, 8726; gee 7583.   (F:90)
5471. 6/20/01 gor Parker, Michael; Granville, WAS. See 5476.
5472. 2/15/02 mor Parker, Michael; Granville, WAS; <u>Granville, WAS</u>; mee 4152.
                                                      (D:139)
5473. 3/12/93 gee Parker, Nathaniel, farmer; Granville, WAS. See 946.
5474. 5/30/93 mor Parker, Nathaniel, farmer; ---, WAS; <u>Granville, WAS</u>;
          co-mors 1650, 2666, 5449, 5469, 8729; mee 947. (A:414)
5475. 9/3/99 gor Parker, Nathaniel; Granville, WAS. See 5470.
5476. 6/20/01 gor Parker, Nathaniel; Granville, WAS; <u>Granville, WAS</u>; co-gors
          1652, 5452, 5471, 8730; gee 5331.   (E:333)
5477. 6/5/02 mor Parker, Peter; Granville, WAS; <u>Granville, WAS</u>; mee 4158.
                                                      (D:194)
5478. 2/8/98 mor Parker, Reuben (w. Lydia), farmer; Hartford, WAS; <u>Hartford,
          WAS</u>; mee 1483.   (B:312)
5479. 5/2/96 gee Parker, Richard, tanner; Argyle, WAS. See 2100a.
5480. 1/3/97 gor Parker, Richard (w. Lydia); Argyle, WAS; <u>Donald Campbell's
          Pat., WAS</u>; gee 7848.   (F:279)
5481. 5/13/00 mor Parker, Speedy. See 5447.
5482. 3/17/98 gee Parmeley, Ira; Cambridge, WAS. See 8404.
5483. 5/19/00 gee Parmeley, Ira; Cambridge, WAS. See 8434.
5484. 12/25/97 gee Parrish, John; Hebron, WAS. See 5235.
5485. 9/3/92 mor Parson, Eli; ---, WAS; <u>Westfield, WAS</u>; co-mor 1562; mee 7234.
                                                      (A:389)
5486. 7/8/97 mor Parsons, Asenith. See 5493.
5487. 3/23/93 mor Parsons, Charles; Plattsburgh, CLI; <u>Plattsburgh, CLI</u>;
          mee 5818.   (A:110)
5488. 10/28/95 mor Parsons, Charles; Plattsburgh, CLI; <u>Plattsburgh, CLI</u>; mee
          5737.   (A:166)
5489. 10/29/95 gee Parsons, Charles; Plattsburgh, CLI. See 5738 and 7436.
5490. 9/16/02 mee Parsons, Charles, Junr.; Plattsburgh, CLI. See 1334.
5491. 7/26/98 mee Parsons, James; City of N.Y. See 8699.
5492. 12/2/99 mee Parsons, James, merchant; City of N.Y. See 1857.
5493. 7/8/97 mor Parsons, John (w. Asenith); farmer; Granville, WAS;<u>Granville,WAS</u>
          co-mees 78, 2939, 2956. Co-mortgagees are "executors
          ... of the will of James Grant late of Pawling (DUT)
          ... deceased".   (B:201)
5494. 7/26/98 mee Parsons, John; City of N.Y. See 8699.
5494a. 7/26/98 mee Parsons, Samuel; City of N.Y. See 8699.
5495. 12/2/99 mee Parsons, Samuel, merchant; City of N.Y. See 1857.
5496 and 5497. Data repositioned.
5498. 10/28/97 gee Patchen, Zebulon, farmer; Hoosick, REN. See 2120. Three
          contracts this date involving these persons.
5499. 3/12/84 gor Paterson, Jane. See 5501.
5500. 3/10/84 gee Paterson, Joseph; Cornwall, ORA. See 872.
5501. 3/12/84 gor Paterson, Joseph (w. Jane), yeoman; Cornwall Precinct, ORA;
          Argyle, CHA; gee 873.   (B-2:55)
5502. 9/5/96 mor Paterson, Robert; ---, ---. See 5503.
5503. 9/5/96 mor Paterson, William; ---, ---; <u>Kingsbury, WAS</u>; co-mor 5502;
          mee 5167.   (B:86)
5504. 12/11/90 mor Patrick, John; Hebron, WAS; <u>Hebron, WAS</u>; co-mor 7034;
          mee 7460.   (A:261)
5505. 12/13/90 mor Patrick, John; Hebron, WAS; <u>Hebron, WAS</u>; co-mor 3044;
          mee 1063.   (A:267)
5506. 12/23/01 gor Patrick, John (w. Sarah Ann), merchant; City of N.Y.;
          <u>Whitehall, WAS</u>; co-gees 2315, 2660. (F:152)
5507. 12/23/01 gor Patrick, Sarah Ann. See 5506.
5508. 12/11/90 gee Patrik, John; ---, ---. See 7459.
5509. 2/11/96 gee Patten(?), Edward; Argyle, WAS. See 6692.
5510. 4/12/96 mor Patterson, Catharine. See 5512 and 5513. (two contracts)

5511. 2/26/96 mor Patterson, David, farmer; Salem, WAS; Salem, WAS; mee 2128.
(C:246)
5512. 4/12/96 mor Patterson, John (w. Catherine); Lansingburgh, REN; Part of
the Indian Purchase in the counties of WAS and MON;
co-mees 3896, 3897. (A:187)
5513. 4/12/96 mor Patterson, John (w. Catharine); Lansinburgh, REN; Indian
Purchase (Edward Jessup Pat.), WAS; co-mors 1585, 3128,
mee 3898. (B:41)
5514. 3/12/84 mor Patterson, Joseph; Cornwall, ORA; Argyle, CHA; mee 869. (A:34)
5515. 2/26/96 mor Patterson, Levi, farmer; Salem, WAS; Salem, WAS; mee 2128.
(C:245)
5516. 12/15/94 gor Patterson, Robert; Hartford, WAS; Hartford, WAS; gee 3320.
(C-2:102)
5517. 6/12/95 gee Patterson, Robert, yeoman; Cambridge, WAS. See 4960.
5518. 6/12/95 mor Patterson, Robert, yeoman; Cambridge, WAS; Cambridge, WAS;
mee 4961. (A:552)
5519. 10/15/01 mee Pattison, Robert, yeoman; Argyle, WAS. See 3621.
5520. 9/4/02 mee Payn, Benjamin; ---, ---. See 3027.
5521. 1/29/93 gee Payn, Joseph; Brookfield, CLI. See 5524.
5522. 1/29/93 gor Payn, Massey. See 5524.
5523. 10/16/89 mor Payn, Peter; Willsborough, CLI; Willsborough, CLI; mee 6440.
(A:31)
5524. 1/29/93 gor Payn, Peter, Junr. (w. Massey); Brookfield, CLI; Willsborough,
CLI; gee 5521. (A:365)
5525. 4/25/96 mor Payne, Daniel, farmer; Argyle, WAS. See 5529.
5526. 4/25/96 mor Payne, Isaac B., farmer; Argyle, WAS. See 5529.
5527. 2/13/94 mee Payne, James W., gentleman; City of N.Y. See 154.
5528. 4/25/96 mor Payne, Nathan, farmer; Argyle, WAS. See 5529.
5529. 4/25/96 mor Payne, Noah, Junr., farmer; Argyle, WAS; Argyle, WAS;
co-mors 5525, 5526, 5528, 5530, 5531; mee 4077. (B:23)
5530. 4/25/96 mor Payne, Samuel, farmer; Argyle, WAS. See 5529.
5531. 4/25/96 mor Payne, Stephen, farmer; Argyle, WAS. See 5529.
5532. 9/3/00 gee Peabody, Adriel, attorney; Plattsburgh, CLI. See 5655.
5533. 4/1/96 mee Pearce, David; Cambridge, WAS. See 6696.
5534. 6/1/98 mee Pearce, David; Cambridge, WAS. See 2326.
5535. 6/20/98 gor Pearce, David (w. Elizabeth); Cambridge, WAS. See 1720.
5536. 12/1/99 mee Pearce, David; Cambridge, WAS. See 2333.
5537. 6/20/98 gor Pearce, Elizabeth. See 5535.
5538. 2/8/98 mor Pearce, John, farmer; Hartford, WAS; Hartford, WAS; mee 1483.
(B:311)
5539. 2/22/98 mee Pearce, John, farmer; Hartford, WAS. See 1004, 1985, 6697.
5540. 3/12/98 mee Pearsall, Thomas, merchant; City of N.Y. See 7542.
5541. 1/24/92 mee Pearse, David; Cambridge, WAS. See 2054.
5542. 2/27/96 mor Pearsee, Jonathan, Junr.; City of N.Y. See 4109.
5543. 7/9/94 gee Pearson, George, merchant; Albany, ALB. See 6518.
5544. 4/20/92 gor Peck, Beaulah. See 5546.
5545. 9/28/84 gee Peck, John; Black Creek Dist., WAS. See 7050.
5546. 4/20/92 gor Peck, John (w. Beaulah), yeoman; Hebron, WAS; Hebron, WAS;
gee 8740. (B-2:73)
5547. 4/6/98 mor Peck, John, farmer; Hartford, WAS; Hartford, WAS; mee 1490.
(B:313)
5548. 5/20/91 gee Peck, Peter; Queensbury, WAS. See 8698.
5549. 6/2/92 gee Peck, Peter; Queensbury, WAS. See 3624.
5550. 2/21/93 gee Peck, Peter; Queensbury, WAS. See 8809.
5551. 8/8/96 gor Peebles, Abigail. See 5554.
5552. 12/1/00 mee Peebles, Gerrit; Argyle, WAS. See 3933.
5553. 12/23/01 mee Peebles, Gerrit, merchant; Argyle, WAS. See 5036.
5554. 8/8/96 gor Peebles, Hugh (w. Abigail); Halfmoon, SAR. See 7640.
5555. 1/2/98 mee Peebles, Hugh; ---, SAR. See 6645 and 6646.
5556. 10/27/98 gee Peebles, Hugh, merchant; Half Moon, SAR. See 4533.
5557. 2/14/00 mee Peebles, Hugh; ---, ---. See 2197.
5558. 2/14/00 mee Peebles, Hugh; ---, SAR. See 2198.
5559. 11/1/00 mee Peebles, Hugh; ---, SAR. See 5199.
5560. 6/9/89 mor Peerin, Thomas; Granville, WAS; Granville, WAS; mee 836.
(A:163)

5561. 3/3/93　　gor　Peet, Benjamin, yeoman; Cambridge, WAS; "Patent of Aquasicoke",
　　　　　　　　　　　　WAS; gee 3606.　　　　　　　　　　　　　　(D:115)
5562. 1/20/96　mor　Peet, Josiah; Easton, WAS; Easton, WAS; mee 7214. (B:49)
5563. 6/10/01　gor　Peirce, Caty. See 5565.
5564. 1/24/92　mor　Peirce, David; ---, ---; Walloomsack Pat., WAS; co-mees
　　　　　　　　　　　　1367, 4176, 4177. Co-mortgagees are all "executors of
　　　　　　　　　　　　John Livingston of the County of Saraghtoga". (A:317)
5565. 6/10/01　gor　Peirce, William (w. Caty), farmer; Argyle, WAS; ---, WAS
　　　　　　　　　　　　gee 3711.　　　　　　　　　　　　　　　　(E:337)
5566. 3/12/98　mee　Pell, Elijah, merchant; City of N.Y. See 7542.
5567. 12/1/97　gee　Pelley, Jonathan, yeoman; Whitehall, WAS. See 3989.
5568. 9/29/96　mor　Pennel, Robert, farmer; Salem, WAS; Salem, WAS; mee 2130.
　　　　　　　　　　　　　　　　　　　　　　　　　　　　　　(C:247)
5569. 2/10/80　gee　Pennel, Robert H.; White Creek, CHA. See 2023.
5570. 5/26/01　mor　Pennell, Robert, innkeeper; Salem, WAS; Salem, WAS;
　　　　　　　　　　　　co-mees 4670, 8863. Co-mortgagees are executors of the
　　　　　　　　　　　　estate of John Adams, dec'd.　　　　　　(D:47b)
5571. 5/1/00　　mee　"People of the State of New York". See 2456.
5572. 7/1/00　　mee　"People of the State of New York". See 60, 191, 381, 1456,
　　　　　　　　　　　　1516, 1612, 1829, 2017, 2020, 2085, 2345, 2627, 2970,
　　　　　　　　　　　　3315, 4253 (two contracts), 4830, 5418, 5419 (two contracts),
　　　　　　　　　　　　5420, 5422, 5433, 5437, 5438, 6207, 7001, 7033, 7828,
　　　　　　　　　　　　7833, 8194, 8657, 8660, 8715.
5573. 9/23/00　mor　Percy, Ephraim, farmer; Florida, MON; Old Military Township
　　　　　　　　　　　　#7 (Chateaugay), CLI; co-mees 281, 322.　　(B:4)
5574. 5/2/96　　gee　Perigo, Robert; ---, WAS. See 1185.
5575. 11/1/92　gee　Perine, John; Cambridge, WAS. See 2392.
5576. 3/3/94　　gee　Perine, John; Cambridge, WAS. See 2395.
5577. 2/20/98　mor　Perkins, Mary. See 5578 and 5579.
5578. 2/20/98　mor　Perkins, Moses (w. Mary), farmer; ---, ---; ---, WAS;
　　　　　　　　　　　　mee 5969.　　　　　　　　　　　　　　　(C:85)
5579. 2/20/98　mor　Perkins, Moses (w. Mary), farmer; Hampton, WAS; Hampton,
　　　　　　　　　　　　WAS; mee 5969.　　　　　　　　　　　　(C:243)
　　　　　　　　　　　　Perrigo. See also Corrigo.
5580. 5/2/96　　gor　Perrigo, Anna. See 5582.
5580a. 5/2/96　gor　Perrigo, Anna. See 5583. (two contracts)
5580b. 5/2/96　gor　Perrigo, Anna. See 5583a. (ten contracts)
5580c. 12/12/96 gor　Perrigo, Anna. See 5587.
5580d. 6/15/99　gor　Perrigo, Anna. See 5589.
5581. 5/2/96　　gor　Perrigo, Nancy (Anna, perhaps?). See 5583a. (Contracts
　　　　　　　　　　　　F:36, F:45, and F:47 have the wife of Robert Perrigo,
　　　　　　　　　　　　Junr., listed as "Nancy". All others have her listed "Anna".)
5581a. 5/2/96　gor　Perrigo, Nancy. See 5583b. (two contracts)
5582. 5/2/96　　gor　Perrigo, Robert, Junr. (w. Anna), gentleman; Argyle, WAS.
　　　　　　　　　　　　See 2099.
5583. 5/2/96　　gor　Perrigo, Robert, Junr. (w. Anna), gentleman; Argyle, WAS.
　　　　　　　　　　　　See 2100. (two contracts)
5583a. 5/2/96　gor　Perrigo, Robert, Junr. (w. Anna); Argyle, WAS. See 2100a.
　　　　　　　　　　　　See the parenthetical notes in 5581 above. (13 contracts)
5583b. 5/2/96　gor　Perrigo, Robert, Junr. (w. Nancy), gentleman; Argyle, WAS.
　　　　　　　　　　　　See 2100b. (two contracts)
5584. 5/2/96　　mee　Perrigo, Robert, Junr.; Argyle, WAS. See 411, 748, 3303,
　　　　　　　　　　　　3312, 3893, 6372, 6512, 7597, 8745.
5585. 5/2/96　　mor　Perrigo, Robert, Junr.; ---, WAS. See 2102. (three contracts)
5586. 5/3/96　　mee　Perrigo, Robert, Junr.; Argyle, WAS. See 1416.
5587. 12/12/96 gor　Perrigo, Robert, Junr. (w. Anna); Argyle, WAS. See 2104.
5588. 5/2/99　　mee　Perrigo, Robert, Junr., gentleman; Argyle, WAS. See 1417.
5589. 6/15/99　gor　Perrigo, Robert, Junr. (w. Anna); Argyle, WAS. See 2106.
5590. 12/30/91 mor　Perry, Aaron, yeoman; Cambridge, WAS; Van Curler Pat., WAS;
　　　　　　　　　　　　co-mor 5606; mee 2675.　　　　　　　　(A:409)
5591. 6/13/96　gor　Perry, Almy. See 5600.
5592. 9/22/00　gor　Perry, Amia. See 5601. (two contracts)
5593. 5/28/00　mor　Perry, Daniel, Junr.; Rutland, RUT, VT; Mooers Pat., CLI;
　　　　　　　　　　　　mee 1173.　　　　　　　　　　　　　　　(A:435)
5594. 3/1/94　　mee　Perry, Elnathan; Hebron, WAS. See 5303.
5595. 4/11/94　mor　Perry, Israel B. (w. Serentha). See 5602.

136

5596. 5/23/98 mor Perry, Israel Breaton; Cambridge, WAS; Cambridge, WAS; mee 4411. (C:294)
5597. 5/24/98 gee Perry, Israel Breaten; Cambridge, WAS. See 4414.
5598. 12/3/02 mor Perry, James; ---, ---; ---, ESS; co-mor 5603; mee 921. (A:94)
5599. 5/9/96 gee Perry, Jeremiah, yeoman; Cambridge, WAS. See 6150.
5600. 6/13/96 gor Perry, Jeremiah (w. Almy), yeoman; Cambridge, WAS; Cambridge, WAS; gee 1982. (E:357)
5601. 9/22/00 gor Perry, Jeremiah (w. Amia), gentleman; Cambridge, WAS; Cambridge, WAS; gee 1517. Two contracts this date involving these persons. (E:29), (E:31)
5602. 4/11/94 mor Perry, John (w. Sarah); ---, ---; Cambridge, WAS; co-mors 5595, 5605; mee 7362. (A:537)
5603. 12/3/02 mor Perry, Nathan; ---, ---. See 5598.
5604. 4/11/94 mor Perry, Sarah. See 5602.
5605. 4/11/94 mor Perry, Serentha. See 5595.
5606. 12/30/91 mor Perry, William, yeoman; Cambridge, WAS. See 5590.
5607. 5/16/91 gee Peters, Joseph, blacksmith; Cambridge, WAS. See 3975.
5608. 5/17/91 gee Peters, Joseph, blacksmith; Cambridge, WAS. See 3976.
5609. 10/25/91 --- Peterson, Ann; Argyle, WAS. See 4201 and 5618.
5610. 12/23/85 gee Peterson, John; Argyle, WAS. See 4203.
5611. 10/25/91 --- Peterson, John. Husband of Mary in 5615.
5612. 11/3/97 gor Peterson, John (w. Mary), farmer; Argyle, WAS; Argyle, WAS; gee 4322. (C-2:262)
5613. 10/7/00 gor Peterson, John (w. Mary); Argyle, WAS; Argyle, WAS; gee 3568. (E:55)
5614. 10/19/01 mor Peterson, Joseph; Argyle, WAS. See 5620.
5615. 10/25/91 --- Peterson, Mary; Argyle, WAS. See 4201.
5616. 11/3/97 gor Peterson, Mary. See 5612.
5617. 10/7/00 gor Peterson, Mary. See 5613.
5618. 10/25/91 --- Peterson, Nathan. Husband of Ann in 5609.
5619. 2/9/96 mor Peterson, Nathen; Argyle, WAS; Argyle, WAS; co-mees 4646, 6763, 6822, 8102. Co-mortgagees are "executors of John Morin Scott, Esq., deceased". (B:97)
5620. 10/19/01 mor Peterson, Robert; Argyle, WAS; Hebron, WAS; co-mor 5614; mee 3123. (D:100)
5621. 7/26/89 gee Pettet, Paschal. See 5622.
5622. 7/26/89 gor Pettet, Simon, "a refugee from Canada", gentleman; land granted (in Clinton County) to Pettet "by the Legislature of the State of New York"; gee 5621. (A:106)
5623. 3/6/93 gee Pettis, Joseph; Kingsbury, WAS. See 4482.
5624. 10/21/91 gee Pettis, Mathew, yeoman; Argyle, WAS. See 7084.
5625. 11/10/91 mor Pettis, Mathew, farmer; Argyle, WAS; Argyle, WAS; mee 7669. (A:317)
5626. 2/30/94 gor Pettis, Matthew; Argyle, WAS; ---, WAS; gee 5628. (E:282)
5627. 7/2/95 gor Pettis, Stephen; Kingsbury, WAS; Kingsbury, WAS; gee 2082. (B-2:477)
5628. 2/30/94 gee Pettis, William M., yeoman; Argyle, WAS. See 5626.
5629. 3/3/89 gor Pettit, Jabez; Plattsburgh, CLI; Plattsburgh, CLI; gee 5263. (A:48)
5630. 10/2/92 gee Pettit, Micajah, merchant; Kingsbury, WAS. See 2446.
5631. 1/11/97 mee Pettit, Micajah, merchant; Kingsbury, WAS. See 1667.
5632. 1/22/01 gee Pettit, Micajah; Kingsbury, WAS. See 2031.
5633. 8/29/97 gee Pettit, Micajah, Esq.; Kingsbury, WAS. See 2449.
5634. 3/12/98 mee Pettit, Micajah, Esq.; Kingsbury, WAS. See 2430.
5635. 5/26/85 gee Pettite, John; ---, ---. See 7055.
5636. 3/22/99 gee Pettys, John, yeoman; Easton, WAS. See 1043.
5637. 11/13/95 mor Pettys, Joseph, farmer; Easton, WAS; Saratoga Pat., WAS; mee 3668. (B:6)
5638. 1/18/94 mor Phelps, David, farmer; Plattsburgh, CLI; Plattsburgh, CLI; mee 5820. (A:116)
5639. 7/9/98 gor Phelps, David; Plattsburgh, CLI; Plattsburgh, CLI; gee 5083. (B:227)
5640. 3/20/80 gee Phelps, Eli, yeoman; Cambridge, WAS. See 8337.
5641. 11/8/97 mor Phelps, Eli; Cambridge, WAS; Cambridge, WAS; mee 5032. (B:223)
5642. 6/24/99 gor Phelps, Eli (w. Rachel), farmer; Cambridge, WAS; Cambridge, WAS; gee 1845. (D:150)

137

5643. 7/24/02 mor Phelps, Isaac; Granville, WAS; Granville, WAS; mee 4163.
(E:12)
5644. 7/1/02 mor Phelps, John; Westfield, WAS; Westfield, WAS; co-mees
7107, 7230. Co-mortgagees are executors of the estate of
Platt Smith "late of the County of Dutchess, deceased".
(E:32)
5645. 6/24/99 gor Phelps, Rachel. See 5642.
5646. 12/15/89 gee Phetteplace, John, ship carpenter; Westfield Dist., WAS.
See 3179.
5647. 9/28/96 mor Philips, Alman; Peru, CLI; Peru, CLI; mee 5862. (A:196)
5648. 2/20/98 mor Philips, Ruth. See 5649. (two contracts)
5649. 2/20/98 mor Philips, Welcome (w. Ruth), farmer; Hampton, WAS; Hampton,
WAS; mee 5969. Two contracts this date involving these
persons. (B:314), (C:243)
5650. 1/2/02 mor Philley, Lovisa. See 5651.
5651. 1/2/02 mor Philley, Roswell (w. Lovisa), bloomer (sic); Granville, WAS;
Whitehall, WAS; mee 21. (D:124)
5652. 9/21/98 gor Phillips, Alman; Peru, CLI; Peru, CLI; gee 8423. (B:272)
5653. 11/3/01 mee Phillips, Alman; ---, ---. See 2875.
5654. 9/22/96 mor Philmore, Eliphalet; Granville, WAS; Granville, WAS;
mee 3760. (B:115)
5655. 9/3/00 gor Picard, John; Champlain, CLI; Canadian and Nova Scotia
Refugees' Pat., CLI; co-gees 2089, 5532. (B:248)
5656. 4/1/96 mee Pierce, David; Cambridge, WAS. See 1779.
5657. 6/6/99 gor Pierce, David (w. Elizabeth); Cambridge, WAS; James Grant
Pat., WAS; gee 2327. (D:368)
5658. 5/21/99 mor Pierce, David Stone; Bolton, WAS; Bolton, WAS; mee 3440.
(C:248)
5659. 6/6/99 gor Pierce, Elizabeth. See 5657.
5660. 5/2/96 gee Pierce, William; Pittstown, REN. See 1187. (two contracts)
5661. 4/25/93 mor Piper, Judah; Charlotte, CHI, VT. See 982.
5662. 9/23/82 gor Pirkins, Gideon; Granville, CHA; ---, CHA; gee 5054. (B:80)
5663. 3/6/98 mor Pitcher, Lymon; Queensbury, WAS; Queensbury, WAS; mee 3314.
(C:241)
5664. 5/21/01 mor Pitcher, Nathaniel, farmer; Kingsbury, WAS; Kingsbury, WAS;
mee 2524. (D:56)
5665. 6/28/92 gor Pittotte, Simeon, "late a Canadian refugee"; ---, ---;
Canadian and Nova Scotia Refugees' Pat., CLI; gee 5108.
(A:355)
5666. 12/10/99 mee Pitts, Levi; Queensbury, WAS. See 380.
5667. 1/26/02 mee Place, Jeremiah, yeoman; Argyle, WAS. See 1152.
5668. 10/16/92 mee Platt, Charity. See 5803.
5669. 1/2/96 gor Platt, Charity. See 5822. (two contracts)
5670. 1/2/96 mor Platt, Charity. See 5807.
5671. 2/8/85 gee Platt, Charles, gentleman; ---, ---. See 5887.
5672. 8/6/85 gee Platt, Charles; Plattsburgh, WAS. See 5889.
5673. 3/14/87 gee Platt, Charles; ---, ---. See 5911.
5674. 7/17/87 gee Platt, Charles; Plattsburgh, WAS. See 5722.
5675. 11/7/87 gee Platt, Charles; Plattsburgh, WAS. See 126.
5676. 12/8/88 gee Platt, Charles; Plattsburgh, CLI. See 7309.
5677. 11/13/90 gee Platt, Charles; Plattsburgh, CLI. See 6449.
5678. 10/1/91 mor Platt, Charles; Plattsburgh, CLI; Plattsburgh, CLI; mee 8070.
(A:68)
5679. 10/11/91 mee Platt, Charles; Plattsburgh, CLI. See 2963.
5680. 6/29/92 gor Platt, Charles; Plattsburgh, CLI; Plattsburgh, CLI; gee
4460. (A:282)
5681. 2/25/96 gee Platt, Charles, gentleman, "son of ... Zephaniah (Platt)";
---, DUT. See 5935.
5682. 3/16/96 --- Platt, Charles; Poughkeepsie, DUT. See 290.
5683. 4/16/00 gee Platt, Charles; Plattsburgh, CLI. See 5763.
5684. 7/20/02 mee Platt, Charles; Plattsburgh, CLI. See 7725.
5685. 8/14/87 gee Platt, Charles, Esq.; Plattsburgh, WAS. See 5918.
5686. 2/18/89 gee Platt, Charles, Esq.; ---, CLI. See 5926.
5687. 12/19/89 gee Platt, Charles, Esq.; Plattsburgh, CLI. See 5142.
5688. 11/14/97 gee Platt, Charles, Junr., gentleman; Plattsburgh, CLI. See 3902.
5689. 4/6/96 gee Platt, Charles L., gentleman; ---, DUT. See 293.

5690. 2/8/97 gee Platt, Charles L.; Plattsburgh, CLI. See 5939.
5691. 11/3/97 mee Platt, Charles L., gentleman; ---, CLI. See 2722 and 6960.
5692. 2/27/98 mee Platt, Charles L.; Plattsburgh, CLI. See 3214.
5693. 3/1/98 mee Platt, Charles L., gentleman; ---, CLI. See 110 (three
           contracts) and 3593 (one contract).
5694. 3/16/98 mee Platt, Charles L.; Plattsburgh, CLI. See 3772.
5695. 4/14/98 mee Platt, Charles L.; Plattsburgh, CLI. See 5318.
5696. 6/22/98 gor Platt, Charles L.; Plattsburgh, CLI; Township #6 (Clinton),
           CLI; co-gors 271, 291, 313, 1527, 3884, 5713, 5751, 5872,
           7563, 8757; gee 999.   (B:145)
5697. 6/22/98 gor Platt, Charles L.; Plattsburgh, CLI; ---, CLI; co-gors
           291, 2200, 3371, 7117, 7178, 7563, 7566, 8076, 8101;
           gee 1345.   (B:148)
5698. 6/22/98 gor Platt, Charles L.; Plattsburgh, CLI; Old Military Township
           #7 (Chateaugay), CLI; co-gors 291, 2200, 3371, 7117,
           7178, 7563, 7566, 8076, 8101; gee 7708.   (B:150)
5699. 6/23/98 mee Platt, Charles L.; Plattsburgh, CLI. See 1000, 1346, 7709.
5700. 7/9/98 mee Platt, Charles L.; Plattsburgh, CLI. See 3712, 3715.
5701. 8/3/98 mee Platt, Charles L.; Plattsburgh, CLI. See 5753.
5702. 8/8/98 mee Platt, Charles L.; Plattsburgh, CLI. See 3594.
5703. 8/24/98 mee Platt, Charles L.; Plattsburgh, CLI. See 3901, 7421.
5704. 3/4/00 mor Platt, Charles L.; Whitestown, ONE; Plattsburgh, CLI;
           mee 7572.   (A:410)
5705. 8/14/99 gee Platt, Charles Z.; Whitestown, ONE. See 3694.
5706. 8/14/99 gor Platt, Charles Z.; Whitestown, ONE; Saratoga Pat., WAS;
           gee 3693.   (D:182)
5707. 2/4/01 mee Platt, George W.; Chateaugay, CLI. See 7485.
5708. 10/25/02 gor Platt, George W.; Chateaugay, CLI; Chateaugay, CLI;
           gee 5785.   (B:372)
5709. 8/9/02 mee Platt, Hiram; Cambridge, WAS. See 6022.
5710. 1/16/02 gor Platt, Isaac S.; Plattsburgh, CLI; Plattsburgh, CLI;
           gee 5795.   (B:316)
5711. 2/4/96 --- Platt, Jonas; ---, HER. See 5857.
5712. 2/24/96 mor Platt, Jonas; ---, HER. See 8754.
5713. 6/22/98 gor Platt, Jonas; ---, HER. See 5969.
5714. 8/15/01 --- Platt, Jonas; Whitestown, ONE; Chateaugay, CLI. Jonas,
           this date, appoints Nathaniel L. Platt as his attorney
           for the sale of the above lands in Chateaugay. (B:283)
5715. 8/15/01 gor Platt, Jonas; Whitestown, ONE; Chateaugay, CLI; gee 5790.
                                                          (B:307)
5716. 8/1/01 gee Platt, Levi; Peru, CLI. See 5946.
5717. 2/8/85 gee Platt, Nathaniel, gentleman; ---, ---. See 5887.
5718. 7/11/85 gor Platt, Nathaniel, gentleman; Charlotte Precinct, DUT.
           See 5833.
5719. 3/3/87 gee Platt, Nathaniel, yeoman; Washington Precinct, DUT.
           See 5908.
5720. 3/14/87 gee Platt, Nathaniel; ---, ---. See 5911.
5721. 3/23/87 gor Platt, Nathaniel, yeoman; Washington Precinct, DUT;
           Cumberland Head (Plattsburgh), WAS; gee 6249.(Cli. Co. A:144)
5722. 7/17/87 gor Platt, Nathaniel; ---, DUT; Plattsburgh, WAS; gee 5674.
                                                          (Clinton Co. A:251)
5723. 10/15/90 gor Platt, Nathaniel (w. Phebe); ---, CLI; Cumberland Head
           (Plattsburgh), CLI; gee 6253.   (A:166)
5724. 5/26/91 gor Platt, Nathaniel; Plattsburgh, CLI; Plattsburgh, CLI;
           gee 3745.   (A:193)
5725. 5/27/91 mee Platt, Nathaniel; Plattsburgh, CLI. See 3747.
5726. 7/19/91 mee Platt, Nathaniel; Plattsburgh, CLI. See 2457.
5727. 10/6/91 gor Platt, Nathaniel, gentleman; Plattsburgh, CLI; Plattsburgh,
           CLI; gee 544.   (A:211)
5728. 6/26/92 mee Platt, Nathaniel; Poughkeepsie, DUT. See 5847.
5729. 10/4/92 mee Platt, Nathaniel; Plattsburgh, CLI. See 539.
5730. 10/15/92 mee Platt, Nathaniel; Plattsburgh, CLI. See 3586.
5731. 5/10/93 mee Platt, Nathaniel, gentleman; Plattsburgh, CLI. See 2594.
5732. 2/20/95 gor Platt, Nathaniel; Plattsburgh, CLI; Zephaniah Platt's Pat.,
           CLI; gee 7170.   (A:495)

5733. 4/1/95 gor Platt, Nathaniel; Plattsburgh, CLI; "Great Location", CLI;
gee 4252. (A:357)
5734. 4/3/95 gor Platt, Nathaniel; Plattsburgh, CLI; Mallory's Bush, CLI;
gee 7312. (A:368)
5735. 4/11/95 gor Platt, Nathaniel; Plattsburgh, CLI; Peru, CLI; gee 2994.
(A:386)
5736. 7/9/95 gor Platt, Nathaniel; Plattsburgh, CLI; Plattsburgh, CLI;
gee 2346. (B:358)
5737. 10/28/95 mee Platt, Nathaniel; Plattsburgh, CLI. See 5488.
5738. 10/29/95 gor Platt, Nathaniel; Plattsburgh, CLI; Plattsburgh, CLI;
gee 5489. (A:389)
5739. 11/10/95 gor Platt, Nathaniel; Plattsburgh, CLI; Mallory's Bush, CLI;
gee 4828. (B:233)
5740. 11/27/95 mee Platt, Nathaniel; ---, CLI. See 990.
5741. 12/9/95 gee Platt, Nathaniel; Plattsburgh, CLI. See 7000.
5742. 12/18/95 gee Platt, Nathaniel; Plattsburgh, CLI. See 3202.
5743. 1/4/96 mee Platt, Nathaniel; Plattsburgh, CLI. See 1061, 2064.
5744. 2/4/96 --- Platt, Nathaniel; ---, CLI. See 5857.
5745. 2/17/96 gor Platt, Nathaniel; Plattsburgh, CLI; Plattsburgh, CLI;
co-gees 6455 and 7171. (A:413)
5746. 2/24/96 gee Platt, Nathaniel; ---, CLI. See 4804.
5747. 2/24/96 mor Platt, Nathaniel; ---, CLI. See 8754.
5748. 4/19/97 gee Platt, Nathaniel; Plattsburgh, CLI. See 2966.
5749. 6/6/98 mee Platt, Nathaniel; Plattsburgh, CLI. See 7422.
5750. 6/7/98 --- Platt, Nathaniel; Plattsburgh, CLI. See 3238.
5751. 6/22/98 gor Platt, Nathaniel; ---, CLI. See 5696.
5752. 7/3/98 mee Platt, Nathaniel; Plattsburgh, CLI. See 1237.
5753. 8/3/98 mor Platt, Nathaniel; Plattsburgh, CLI; Old Military Township
#7 (Chateaugay), CLI; mee 5701. (A:344)
5754. 10/25/98 mee Platt, Nathaniel; Plattsburgh, CLI. See 7385.
5755. 3/20/99 mee Platt, Nathaniel; Plattsburgh, CLI. See 7384.
5756. 4/21/99 mee Platt, Nathaniel; Plattsburgh, CLI. See 5983.
5757. 7/18/99 gor Platt, Nathaniel; Plattsburgh, CLI; Willsborough, ESS;
gee 2596. (A:28)
5758. 10/7/99 mee Platt, Nathaniel; Plattsburgh, CLI. See 1449.
5759. 12/28/99 mee Platt, Nathaniel; Plattsburgh, CLI. See 5813.
5760. 1/24/00 mee Platt, Nathaniel; Plattsburgh, CLI. See 3696.
5761. 2/28/00 gor Platt, Nathaniel; Plattsburgh, CLI; Chateaugay, CLI;
co-gors 5814 and 8760; gee 7225. (B:255)
5762. 4/7/00 gor Platt, Nathaniel; Plattsburgh, CLI; Plattsburgh, CLI;
gee 5786. (B:225)
5763. 4/16/00 gor Platt, Nathaniel; Plattsburgh, CLI; Plattsburgh Pat., CLI;
gee 5683. (B:266)
5764. 6/2/00 mee Platt, Nathaniel; ---, ---. See 3108.
5765. 8/18/00 mee Platt, Nathaniel; Plattsburgh, CLI. See 6549.
5766. 3/13/01 mee Platt, Nathaniel; Plattsburgh, CLI. See 5004 and 7724.
5767. 4/24/01 mee Platt, Nathaniel; Plattsburgh, CLI. See 6091.
5768. 5/29/01 mee Platt, Nathaniel; ---, ---. See 149.
5769. 8/1/01 mor Platt, Nathaniel; Plattsburgh, CLI; Plattsburgh, CLI;
mee 8169. (B:40)
5770. 8/5/01 mee Platt, Nathaniel; Plattsburgh, CLI. See 6551.
5771. 8/6/01 mee Platt, Nathaniel; Plattsburgh, CLI. See 2705.
5772. 9/8/01 mee Platt, Nathaniel; Plattsburgh, CLI. See 4874.
5773. 9/8/01 mee Platt, Nathaniel; Plattsburgh, CLI. See 3643.
5774. 10/6/01 mee Platt, Nathaniel; Plattsburgh, CLI. See 4275.
5775. 11/10/01 mee Platt, Nathaniel; Plattsburgh, CLI. See 3697.
5776. 11/14/01 mee Platt, Nathaniel; CLI. See 7383.
5777. 3/20/02 mee Platt, Nathaniel; ---, ---. See 1915.
5778. 5/4/02 mee Platt, Nathaniel; Plattsburgh, CLI. See 7306.
5779. 10/8/02 gor Platt, Nathaniel; Plattsburgh, CLI; Plattsburgh, CLI;
(land for a "highway for the People of the State of
New York"); co-gees 5951: Plattsburgh, town of:
supervisor, town clerk, overseers of the poor, and
Commissioners of Highways. (B:370)
5780. 8/1/87 mee Platt, Nathaniel, Esq.; ---, DUT. See 5980.
5781. 12/3/88 mee Platt, Nathaniel, Esq.; Poughkeepsie, DUT. See 2455.

5782. 10/31/89 gor Platt, Nathaniel, Esq; Plattsburgh, CLI; Cumberland Head
(Plattsburgh), CLI; gee 6197. (A:114)
5783. 11/3/89 gor Platt, Nathaniel, Esq.; Plattsburgh, CLI; Plattsburgh, CLI;
gee 5264. (A:117)
5784. 8/20/01 gee Platt, Nathaniel, Esq.; Plattsburgh, CLI. See 5948.
5785. 10/25/02 gee Platt, Nathaniel, Junr.; Plattsburgh, cLI. See 5708.
5786. 4/7/00 gee Platt, Nathaniel L.; Plattsburgh, CLI. See 5762.
5787. 12/17/00 gee Platt, Nathaniel L.; Plattsburgh, CLI. See 323.
5788. 8/1/01 gee Platt, Nathaniel L.; Plattsburgh, CLI. See 5947.
5789. 8/15/01 --- Platt, Nathaniel L.; Plattsburgh, cLI. See 5714.
5790. 8/15/01 gee Platt, Nathaniel L.; Plattsburgh, CLI. See 5715.
5791. 8/27/01 gee Platt, Nathaniel L.; Plattsburgh, CLI. See 377.
5792. 12/14/01 gee Platt, Nathaniel L.; Plattsburgh, cLI. See 5831.
5793. 12/17/01 gee Platt, Nathaniel L.; Plattsburgh, CLI. See 979.
5794. 12/17/01 gor Platt, Nathaniel L.; Plattsburgh, CLI; Plattsburgh, CLI;
gee 978. (B:348)
5795. 1/16/02 gee Platt, Nathaniel L.; Plattsburgh, CLI. See 5710.
5796. 2/2/02 mee Platt, Nathaniel L.; Plattsburgh, CLI. See 3104.
5797. 10/15/90 gor Platt, Phebe. See 5723.
5798. 12/8/89 gor Platt, Richard, gentleman; ---, ---. See 3443.
5799. 3/1/90 gor Platt, Richard, Esq.; City of N.Y. See 3448.
5800. 3/12/91 gor Platt, Richard, Esq.; ---, ---. See 3445.
5801. 5/18/92 gor Platt, Richard, Esq.; ---, ---. See 3446.
5802. 1/31/87 gee Platt, Theodorus; Plattsburgh, WAS. See 5903.
5803. 10/16/92 gor Platt, Theodorus, Esq.; (w. Charity); Plattsburgh, CLI;
Plattsburgh, CLI; gee 2425. (A:275)
5804. 10/18/92 gee Platt, Theodorus; Plattsburgh, CLI. See 5932.
5805. 11/8/92 mee Platt, Theodorus; Plattsburgh, cLI. See 7430.
5806. 1/1/96 gee Platt, Theodorus; ---, CLI. See 4529.
5807. 1/2/96 mor Platt, Theodorus (w. Charity); Old Military Township #6
(Clinton), CLI; mee 4800. (A:170)
5808. 2/8/97 gee Platt, Theodorus; Plattsburgh, CLI. See 5939.
5809. 4/11/98 mee Platt, Theodorus; Plattsburgh, CLI. See 3829, 3832.
5810. 5/21/98 gor Platt, Theodorus; Plattsburgh, CLI; Old Military Townships
6 and 7 (Clinton and Chateaugay), CLI; gee 7220. (B:151)
5811. 7/3/98 mee Platt, Theodorus; Plattsburgh, cLI. See 1237.
5812. 4/21/99 mee Platt, Theodorus; Plattsburgh, CLI. See 5983.
5813. 12/28/99 gor Platt, Theodorus; Plattsburgh, CLI; Zephaniah Platt's Pat.,
CLI; co-gees 5759, 5877. (B:303)
5814. 2/28/00 gor Platt, Theodorus; Plattsburgh, CLI. See 5761.
5815. 7/7/02 gee Platt, Theodorus; ---, ---. See 7869.
5816. 10/16/92 gee Platt, Theodorus, Esq.; Plattsburgh, CLI. See 2426.
5817. 10/23/92 mee Platt, Theodorus, Esq.; Plattsburgh, CLI. See 6287.
5818. 3/23/93 mee Platt, Theodorus, Esq.; Plattsburgh, CLI. See 5487.
5819. 5/4/93 gee Platt, Theodorus, Esq.; Plattsburgh, CLI. See 6635.
5820. 1/18/94 mee Platt, Theodorus, Esq.; Plattsburgh, CLI. See 5638.
5821. 3/22/94 gee Platt, Theodorus, Esq.; Plattsburgh, CLI. See 6636.
5822. 1/2/96 gor Platt, Theodorus, Esq. (w. Charity); Plattsburgh, cLI;
"land apart for the military", CLI; co-gees 259, 301
(A:465); also co-gees 6847 and 8078 (A:470).
5823. 2/7/97 gor Platt, Theodorus, Esq; Plattsburgh, cLI; ---, CLI;
gee 5867. (A:552)
5824. 10/26/97 gor Platt, Theodorus, Esq.; Plattsburgh, CLI; ---, CLI;
co-gors 333, 6850a, 8081a; gee 267. (B:88)
5825. 10/26/97 gor Platt, Theodorus, Esq.; Plattsburgh, cLI; ---, CLI;
co-gors 268, 309; co-gees 6849, 8080. (B:91)
5826. 11/14/97 gee Platt, Theodorus, Esq.; Plattsburgh, CLI. See 3902.
5827. 11/23/97 gor Platt, Theodorus, Esq.; Plattsburgh, CLI; Military Pat.,
CLI (in town of Chateaugay); gee 7115. (B:100)
5828. 11/24/97 mee Platt, Theodorus, Esq.; Plattsburgh, CLI. See 7116.
5829. 9/1/98 gor Platt, Theodorus, Esq.; Plattsburgh, CLI; Plattsburgh, CLI;
gee 977 (B:346); gee 2534 (B:242). (two contracts)
5830. 8/13/91 gee Platt, William Pitt, "son of Zephaniah Platt"; Poughkeepsie,
DUT. See 5927.
5831. 12/14/01 gor Platt, William Pitt; Plattsburgh, CLI; Plattsburgh, CLI;
gee 5792. (B:310)

141

5832.   Data repositioned.

<u>5833.</u>   7/11/85   gor   Platt, Zephaniah, gentleman; Poughkeepsie Precinct, DUT;
                                <u>---</u>, WAS; co-gor 5718; gee 6260.   (Clinton Co. A:162)
5834.   8/20/85   mee   Platt, Zephaniah; Poughkeepsie, DUT.   See 597.
5835.   9/7/86   mee   Platt, Zephaniah.   See 112.
<u>5836.</u>   3/16/87   gor   Platt, Zephaniah; Poughkeepsie, DUT; <u>Plattsburgh, WAS</u>;
                                gee 635.   (Clinton Co. A:33)
5837.   8/16/87   mee   Platt, Zephaniah.   See 6299.
<u>5838.</u>   3/20/88   gor   Platt, Zephaniah; ---, DUT; <u>Plattsburgh, CLI</u>; gee 5219. (A:514)
5839.   6/4/88   mee   Platt, Zephaniah.   See 594, 6301, 6560.
5839a. 6/10/88   mee   Platt, Zephaniah.   See 5077.
<u>5840.</u>   9/2/88   gor   Platt, Zephaniah; ---, DUT; <u>Zephaniah Platt's Pat.</u>, <u>CLI</u>;
                                gee 7181.   (A:497)
5841.   9/7/89   gee   Platt, Zephaniah; Poughkeepsie, DUT.   See 8765.
<u>5842.</u>   3/11/90   gor   Platt, Zephaniah; ---, DUT; <u>Zephaniah Platt's Pat.</u>, <u>CLI</u>;
                                gee 7183.   (A:446)
<u>5843.</u>   9/19/90   gor   Platt, Zephaniah; Poughkeepsie, DUT; <u>Totten and Crossfield</u>
                                <u>Purchase, CLI</u>; gee 6251.   (A:159)
5844.   10/12/90   mee   Platt, Zephaniah.   See 2322 and 7435.
5845.   10/5/91   mee   Platt, Zephaniah.   See 127.
5846.   2/9/92   mee   Platt, Zephaniah.   See 3831.
<u>5847.</u>   6/26/92   mor   Platt, Zephaniah; Poughkeepsie, DUT; <u>---</u>, CLI; mee 5728. (A:80)
<u>5848.</u>   10/3/92   mee   Platt, Zephaniah.   See 538.
<u>5849.</u>   10/10/92   gor   Platt, Zephaniah; Poughkeepsie, DUT; <u>Plattsburgh, CLI</u>;
                                gee 8362.   (A:327)
5850.   10/10/92   mee   Platt, Zephaniah.   See 8363, 8366.
5851.   10/15/92   mee   Platt, Zephaniah.   See 1864, 3586, 7310.
5852.   9/20/93   mee   Platt, Zephaniah.   See 2996, 5385.
5853.   5/15/94   gee   Platt, Zephaniah; Poughkeepsie, DUT.   See 6451.
5854.   9/27/94   mee   Platt, Zephaniah.   See 1520.
<u>5855.</u>   9/4/95   gor   Platt, Zephaniah; Poughkeepsie, DUT; <u>Peru, CLI</u>; gee 5370.
                                                                            (B:261)
5856.   9/5/95   mee   Platt, Zephaniah.   See 5371.
<u>5857.</u>   2/4/96   ---   Platt, Zephaniah; ---, DUT.; co-persons 260, 287, 302, 1525,
                                3879, 5711, 5744, 7559, 8752. This date these ten persons
                                jointly appoint Charles Platt of Poughkeepsie (DUT) to be
                                their attorney to sell their lands in Clinton County.
                                                                            (A:441)
5858.   2/24/96   mor   Platt, Zephaniah; ---, DUT.   See 8754.
5859.   3/1/96   mee   Platt, Zephaniah.   See 619.
5860.   9/7/96   mee   Platt, Zephaniah.   See 7905.
5861.   9/27/96   mee   Platt, Zephaniah.   See 2152.
5862.   9/28/96   mee   Platt, Zephaniah.   See 1521, 5647.
5863.   10/3/96   gee   Platt, Zephaniah; ---, DUT; See 2000.
<u>5864.</u>   10/3/96   gor   Platt, Zephaniah; Poughkeepsie, DUT; <u>Willsborough, CLI</u>;
                                gee 2095.   (B:158)
5865.   10/3/96   mee   Platt, Zephaniah.   See 1916, 2096, 8033.
5866.   1/17/97   mee   Platt, Zephaniah.   See 7994, 7995.
5867.   2/7/97   gee   Platt, Zephaniah; Poughkeepsie, DUT.   See 5823.
5868.   4/1/97   mee   Platt, Zephaniah.   See 615.
5869.   12/5/97   mee   Platt, Zephaniah.   See 7119.
5870.   3/3/98   mee   Platt, Zephaniah.   See 2461.
5871.   3/7/98   mee   Platt, Zephaniah.   See 1091.
5872.   6/22/98   gor   Platt, Zephaniah; ---, DUT.   See 5696.
<u>5873.</u>   9/3/98   gor   Platt, Zephaniah; Poughkeepsie, DUT; <u>Peru, CLI</u>; gee 196.
                                                                            (B:206)
5874.   9/4/98   mee   Platt, Zephaniah.   See 197
5875.   11/21/99   mee   Platt, Zephaniah.   See 4054, 6206.
5876.   12/6/99   mee   Platt, Zephaniah; Plattsburgh, CLI.   See 3887.
5877.   12/28/99   gee   Platt, Zephaniah; Plattsburgh, CLI.   See 5813.
5878.   5/15/00   mee   Platt, Zephaniah; Plattsburgh, CLI.   See 5290.
5879.   8/10/00   mee   Platt, Zephaniah.   See 2737.
5880.   9/10/00   mee   Platt, Zephaniah.   See 8717.
5881.   9/20/00   mee   Platt, Zephaniah.   See 2537.
5882.   10/17/00   mee   Platt, Zephaniah.   See 4544.

5883. 2/18/01 mee Platt, Zephaniah; Plattsburgh, CLI. See 3290.
5884. 6/29/01 mee Platt, Zephaniah; Plattsburgh, CLI. See 7504.
5885. 9/4/01 gor Platt, Zephaniah; Plattsburgh, CLI; Peru, CLI; co-gees
542, 548.   (B:280)
5886. 9/16/02 gor Platt, Zephaniah; Plattsburgh, CLI; Plattsburgh, CLI;
gee 383.   (B:368)
5887. 2/8/85 gor Platt, Zephaniah, Esq.; ---, ---; Plattsburgh, WAS;
co-gees 34, 4083, 5278, 5671, 5717, 6244, 6429, 7108,
7166, 7602, 7876.   (Clinton Co. A:539)
5888. 7/12/85 gor Platt, Zephaniah, Esq.; Poughkeepsie, DUT; Plattsburgh, WAS;
gee 4458.   (Clinton Co. A:256)
5889. 8/6/85 gor Platt, Zephaniah, Esq.; Poughkeepsie, DUT; Plattsburgh, WAS;
gee 5672.   (Clinton Co. A:235)
5890. 8/17/85 mee Platt, Zephaniah, Esq.; "of Plattsburgh of Poughkeepsie" (sic),
DUT. See 237.
5891. 8/20/85 gor Platt, Zephaniah, Esq.; Poughkeepsie, DUT; Plattsburgh, WAS;
gee 623.   (Clinton Co. B:341)
5892. 9/27/85 gor Platt, Zephaniah, Esq.; Poughkeepsie, DUT; Plattsburgh, WAS;
gee 8762.   (Clinton Co. A:1)
5893. 12/30/85 gee Platt, Zephaniah, Esq.; ---, ---. See 7055.
5894. 7/10/86 mee Platt, Zephaniah, Esq.; Poughkeepsie, DUT. See 6360.
5895. 7/29/86 gor Platt, Zephaniah, Esq.; Poughkeepsie, DUT; Plattsburgh, WAS;
gee 2421.   (Clinton Co. A:272)
5896. 9/6/86 gor Platt, Zephaniah, Esq.; Poughkeepsie, DUT; Plattsburgh, WAS;
gee 111.   (Clinton Co. A:5)
5897. 9/25/86 gor Platt, Zephaniah, Esq.; Poughkeepsie, DUT; Plattsburgh, WAS;
co-gees 7686, 7688.   (Clinton Co. A:12)
5898. 9/27/86 mee Platt, Zephaniah, Esq.; Poughkeepsie, DUT. See 2431.
5899. 9/27/86 mee Platt, Zephaniah, Esq.; Poughkeepsie, DUT. See 7689.
5900. 11/18/86 mee Platt, Zephaniah, Esq.; Poughkeepsie, DUT. See 1349.
5901. 1/25/87 gor Platt, Zephaniah, Esq.; Poughkeepsie, DUT; land "about
ten miles north of Crown Point", WAS; gee 6245.(Cli. Co. A:153)
5902. 1/25/87 gor Platt, Zephaniah, Esq.; Poughkeepsie, DUT; Plattsburgh, WAS;
gee 7109. Three contracts this date involving these
persons. (Clinton Co. A:97, 99, 101)
5903. 1/31/87 gor Platt, Zephaniah, Esq.; Poughkeepsie, DUT; Plattsburgh, WAS
(several parcels); gee 5802.   (Clinton Co. A:14)
5904. 2/1/87 gor Platt, Zephaniah, Esq.; Poughkeepsie, DUT; Plattsburgh, WAS;
gee 8170.   (Clinton Co. B:72)
5905. 2/22/87 gor Platt, Zephaniah, Esq.; Poughkeepsie, DUT; Plattsburgh, WAS;
gee 7179.   (Clinton Co. A:448)
5906. 3/2/87 gor Platt, Zephaniah, Esq.; Poughkeepsie, DUT; Plattsburgh, WAS;
(ten parcels); gee 6246   (Clinton Co. A:146)
5907. 3/2/87 gor Platt, Zephaniah, Esq.; Poughkeepsie, DUT; Plattsburgh, WAS;
gee 7523.   (Clinton Co. B:238)
5908. 3/3/87 gor Platt, Zephaniah, Esq.; Poughkeepsie, DUT; Cumberland Head
(Plattsburgh), WAS; gee 5719.   (Clinton Co. A:142)
5909. 3/9/87 gor Platt, Zephaniah, Esq.; Poughkeepsie, DUT; Plattsburgh, WAS;
gee 7143.   (Clinton Co. A:457)
5910. 3/14/87 gor Platt, Zephaniah, Esq.; Poughkeepsie, DUT; land "adjoining
the township of Plattsburgh", WAS; gee 7180.
(Clinton Co. A:451)
5911. 3/14/87 gor Platt, Zephaniah, Esq.; Poughkeepsie, DUT; Plattsburgh, WAS;
co-gees 2610, 4084, 5673, 5720, 6247, 6431, 7167, 7603,
7742, 7877, 8763.   (Clinton Co. A:542)
5912. 3/14/87 gor Platt, Zephaniah, Esq.; Poughkeepsie, DUT; Plattsburgh, WAS;
gee 8171.   (Clinton Co. B:71)
5913. 3/15/87 gor Platt, Zephaniah, Esq.; Poughkeepsie, DUT; ---, WAS;
gee 6248. (two contracts)   (Clinton Co. A:150, 157)
5914. 3/16/87 gor Platt, Zephaniah, Esq.; Poughkeepsie, DUT; Plattsburgh, WAS;
gee 633.   (Clinton Co. A:31)
5915. 4/11/87 gor Platt, Zephaniah, Esq.; Poughkeepsie, DUT; ---, WAS;
gee 7110.   (Clinton Co. A:103)
5916. 7/20/87 mee Platt, Zephaniah, Esq.; Poughkeepsie, DUT. See 8162.
5917. 7/25/87 gor Platt, Zephaniah, Esq.; Poughkeepsie, DUT; Plattsburgh, WAS;
gee 3570.   (Clinton Co. A:120)

5918. 8/4/87 gor Platt, Zephaniah, Esq.; Poughkeepsie, DUT; <u>Plattsburgh, WAS</u>;
                (several parcels); gee 5685.   (Clinton Co. A:228)
<u>5919.</u> 8/8/87 gor Platt, Zephaniah, Esq.; Poughkeepsie, DUT; <u>land "on the</u>
                <u>great river Sable"</u>, WAS; gee 1976 (Cli. Co. A:9);
                gee 2347 (Cli, Co. A:203). (two contracts)
<u>5920.</u> 8/8/87 gor Platt, Zephaniah, Esq.; Poughkeepsie, DUT; <u>---</u>, WAS;
                gee 4880 (Cli. Co. A:25); co-gees 2318, 2320 (Cli. Co.
                A:23). (two contracts)
<u>5921.</u> 8/14/87 gor Platt, Zephaniah, Esq.; Poughkeepsie, DUT; <u>Plattsburgh, WAS</u>;
                gee 5269.   (Clinton Co. A:110)
5922. 8/16/87 mee Platt, Zephaniah, Esq.; Poughkeepsie, DUT. See 5188 and 5976.
<u>5923.</u> 4/14/88 gor Platt, Zephaniah, Esq.; ---, DUT; <u>Philip Skene's Pat.</u>, CLI;
                gee 66.   (A:196)
<u>5924.</u> 6/2/88 gor Platt, Zephaniah, Esq; Poughkeepsie, DUT; <u>Plattsburgh, CLI</u>;
                gee 6559.   (A:7)
<u>5925.</u> 6/11/88 gor Platt, Zephaniah, Esq.; Poughkeepsie, DUT; <u>land "on the great</u>
                <u>river Sable"</u>, CLI; gee 2047.   (A:3)
<u>5926.</u> 2/18/89 gor Platt, Zephaniah, Esq.; Poughkeepsie, DUT; <u>Platt Tract</u>, CLI;
                gee 5686.   (A:231)
<u>5927.</u> 8/13/91 gor Platt, Zephaniah, Esq.; Poughkeepsie, DUT; <u>Plattsburgh, CLI</u>;
                gee 5830.   (A:233)
<u>5928.</u> 9/27/91 gor Platt, Zephaniah, Esq.; Poughkeepsie, DUT; <u>Plattsburgh, CLI</u>;
                gee 2371.   (A:210)
<u>5929.</u> 2/8/92 gor Platt, Zephaniah, Esq; ---, DUT; <u>Plattsburgh, CLI</u>; gee 3830.
                              (A:258)
<u>5930.</u> 10/16/92 gor Platt, Zephaniah, Esq.; ---, DUT; <u>Plattsburgh, CLI</u>; gee 3846.
                              (A:283)
5931. 10/17/92 gee Platt, Zephaniah, Esq.; Poughkeepsie, DUT. See 6633.
<u>5932.</u> 10/18/92 gor Platt, Zephaniah, Esq.; Poughkeepsie, DUT; <u>Plattsburgh, CLI</u>;
                gee 5804.   (A:304)
<u>5933.</u> 9/7/93 gor Platt, Zephaniah, Esq.; Poughkeepsie, DUT; <u>Peru, CLI</u>;
                gee 1518.   (A:317)
5934. 9/20/93 gee Platt, Zephaniah, Esq.; ---, DUT. See 8364.
<u>5935.</u> 2/25/96 gor Platt, Zephaniah; ---, DUT; <u>land "apart for the military"</u>, CLI;
                gee 5681.   (A:432)
<u>5936.</u> 10/3/96 gor Platt, Zephaniah, Esq.; Poughkeepsie, DUT; <u>Willsborough, CLI</u>;
                co-gees 6740, 6744.   (B:62)
5937. 11/8/96 gee Platt, Zephaniah, Esq.; Poughkeepsie, DUT. See 5080.
5938. 2/7/97 gee Platt, Zephaniah, Esq.; Poughkeepsie, DUT. See 7186.
<u>5939.</u> 2/8/97 gor Platt, Zephaniah, Esq.; Poughkeepsie, DUT; <u>Plattsburgh, CLI</u>;
                gee 5690 (B:1), 5808 (A:555), 7174 (B:5). (three contracts)
5940. 11/14/97 gee Platt, Zephaniah, Esq.; Poughkeepsie, DUT. See 3902.
5941. 3/3/98 mee Platt, Zephaniah, Esq.; Poughkeepsie, DUT. See 2462.
<u>5942.</u> 9/10/98 gor Platt, Zephaniah, Esq.; Poughkeepsie, DUT; <u>Plattsburgh, CLI</u>;
                co-gees 7488, 7490.   (B:322)
5943. 5/29/00 mee Platt, Zephaniah, Esq.; Plattsburgh, CLI. See 2361.
5944. 6/27/01 mee Platt, Zephaniah, Esq.; Plattsburgh, CLI. See 8761.
<u>5945.</u> 6/29/01 gor Platt, Zephaniah, Esq.; Plattsburgh, CLI; <u>land "between</u>
                <u>Beekman's and Dean's" Pats.</u>, CLI; gee 7503. (B:290)
<u>5946.</u> 8/1/01 gor Platt, Zephaniah, Esq.; Plattsburgh, CLI; <u>Chateaugay, CLI</u>;
                gee 5716.   (B:291)
<u>5947.</u> 8/1/01 gor Platt, Zephaniah, Esq.; Plattsburgh, CLI; <u>Plattsburgh, CLI</u>;
                gee 5788.   (B:304)
<u>5948.</u> 8/20/01 gor Platt, Zephaniah, Esq.; Plattsburgh, CLI; <u>Peru, CLI</u>;
                gee 5784.   (B:294)
5949. 12/3/01 mee Platt, Zephaniah, Esq.; Plattsburgh, CLI. See 1241.
5950. 12/23/01 mee Platt, Zephaniah, Esq.; Plattsburgh, CLI. See 574.
5951. 10/8/02 gee Plattsburgh, Town of; "supervisor, town clerk, overseers of
                the poor, and commissioners of Highways". See 5779.
<u>5952.</u> 3/13/95 mor Plumley, Alexander; Hartford, WAS; <u>Hartford, WAS</u>; mee 4782.
                              (A:536)
5953. 12/30/94 gee Plumly, Alexander, nailer; Hartford, WAS. See 1098.
5954. 9/20/92 gee Pollock, Carlile, merchant; City of N.Y. See 4273.
5955. 11/30/92 gee Pollock, Carlile, merchant; City of N.Y. See 4419.
5956. 8/1/93 mee Pollock, Carlile, merchant; City of N.Y. See 624.
<u>5957.</u> 8/30/93 gor Pollock, Carlile (w. Sophia), merchant, City of N.Y.;
                Hampton, WAS; gee 598.   (B-2:303)

5958. 8/31/93 mee Pollock, Carlile, merchant; City of N.Y. See 687.
5959. 9/2/93 mee Pollock, Carlile, merchant; City of N.Y. See 3599.
5960. 10/25/94 mee Pollock, Carlile, merchant; City of N.Y. See 2625.
5961. 11/21/94 gor Pollock, Carlile (w. Sophia), merchant; City of N.Y.;
Hampton, WAS; gee 5191.   (C-2:292)
5962. 11/21/94 mee Pollock, Carlile, merchant; City of N.Y. See 5165, 5192.
5963. 11/22/94 mee Pollock, Carlile, merchant; City of N.Y. See 5163.
5964. 11/28/94 mee Pollock, Carlile, merchant; City of N.Y. See 8317.
5965. 11/29/94 mee Pollock, Carlile, merchant; City of N.Y. See 1466, 7349.
5966. 12/2/94 mee Pollock, Carlile, merchant; City of N.Y. See 8385.
5967. 12/3/94 mee Pollock, Carlile, merchant; City of N.Y. See 2385.
5968. 3/7/97 gor Pollock, Carlile (w. Sophia), merchant; City of N.Y.;
Hampton, WAS; gee 5193.   (C-2:307)
5969. 2/20/98 mee Pollock, Carlile, merchant; City of N.Y. See 5578, 5579,
5649 (two contracts), 6648.
5970. 3/12/99 mee Pollock, Carlile, merchant; City of N.Y. See 733.
5971. 4/5/92 gee Pollock, George, merchant; City of N.Y. See 3855.
5972. 7/19/99 gee Pollock, George, merchant; City of N.Y. See 4534.
5973. 8/30/93 gor Pollock, Sophia. See 5957.
5974. 11/21/94 gor Pollock, Sophia. See 5961.
5975. 3/7/97 gor Pollock, Sophia. See 5968.
5976. 8/16/87 mor Pomeroy, Abner; Plattsburgh, WAS; Plattsburgh, WAS;
mee 5922.   (Clinton Co. A:6)
5977. 2/21/01 mor Pomeroy, Abner; Plattsburgh, CLI; Plattsburgh, CLI;
mee 5098.   (B:11)
5978. 8/25/02 gee Pomeroy, Abner; Plattsburgh, CLI. See 4848.
5979. 8/25/02 gee Pomeroy, Abner, Junr.; Plattsburgh, CLI. See 4848.
5980. 8/1/87 mor Pomeroy, Silas; Plattsburgh, WAS; Plattsburgh, WAS;
mee 5780.   (Clinton Co. A:21)
5981. 4/29/91 mor Pomeroy, Silas, farmer; Plattsburgh, CLI; Beekmantown, CLI;
mee 579.   (A:74)
5982. 7/19/93 gor Pomeroy, Silas; Plattsburgh, CLI; Zephaniah Platt's Pat., CLI;
gee 5455.   (A:325)
5983. 4/21/99 mor Pomeroy, Silas; Chateaugay, CLI; Old Military Township #7
(Chateaugay), CLI; co-mees 5756, 5812, 8759. (A:394)
5984. 9/9/01 mee Pomeroy, Silas; Chateaugay, CLI. See 1410.
5985. 7/15/00 mor Pomroy, Silas; Chateaugay, CLI; Chateaugay, CLI; mee 2153.
(B:73)
5986. 7/15/01 gor Pomroy, Silas; Chateaugay, CLI; Chateaugay, CLI; gee 2154.(B:345)
5987. 5/13/01 gor Pond, Jared; Ferrisburgh, ADD, VT. See 6416.
5988. 6/22/01 gor Pond, Jarid; Panton, ADD, VT. See 6417.
5989. 5/13/01 gor Pond, Mary; Ferrisburgh, ADD, VT. See 6416.
5990. 6/22/01 gor Pond, Mary; Panton, ADD, VT. See 6417.
5991. 7/10/99 mor Poole, Thomas, farmer; Salem, WAS; Salem, WAS; mee 4362. (C:249)
5992. 4/13/86 gor Pope, Henry; ---, WAS; Willsborough, WAS; co-gor 6488;
gee 7386.   (Clinton Co. A:50)
5993. 3/22/90 gor Porter, Benjamin; Crown Point, CLI; Crown Point, CLI;
gee 4186.   (A:128)
5994. 3/3/00 gee Porter, Stephen, farmer; Westfield, WAS. See 2930.
5995. 3/25/00 gee Porter, Stephen, farmer; Westfield, WAS. See 8220.
5996. 5/21/00 mor Porter, Stephen, farmer; Westfield, WAS; Westfield, WAS;
mee 8800.   (C:251)
5997. 7/20/93 gee Porter, William; Hebron, WAS. See 8742.
5998. 5/25/96 mee Porter(?), William; Hebron, WAS. See 4258.
5999. 7/21/97 mee Porter, William, merchant; Hebron, WAS. See 4259.
6000. 3/16/98 gee Porter, William, gentleman; ---, WAS. See 7265.
6001. 3/16/98 mor Porter, William, gentleman; ---, WAS; Blundell Pat., WAS;
mee 7266.   (C:242)
6002. 4/13/98 gee Porter, William, yeoman; Hebron, WAS. See 6956.
6003. 7/7/98 gee Porter, William, merchant; Hebron, WAS. See 3542.
6004. 11/2/98 gee Porter, William, gentleman; Hebron, WAS. See 8601.
6005. 4/16/00 gor Porter, William, merchant; Hebron, WAS; Hebron, WAS;
gee 3556.   (D:410)
6006. 7/18/99 mee Post, Henry, merchant; City of N.Y. See 4493.
6007. 5/23/87 gor Potan, Mathew, innholder; Albany, ALB; land in "Point Bush,
west side of Lake Champlain", WAS; co-gees 1180, 8496.(A:53)

145

6008. 7/6/93 mee Potter, Allen; Easton, WAS. See 953.
6009. 9/25/02 gor Potter, Allen; Argyle, WAS; Saratoga Pat., WAS; gee 6569.
    (F:275)
6010. 4/10/02 mor Potter, Chrystopher, "late of Argyle", WAS; Granville, WAS;
    mee 726. (D:157)
6011. 1/13/02 mor Potter, Cornelius; Easton, WAS; Saratoga Pat., WAS; co-mees
    500, 658. (D:142)
6012. 8/30/94 mee Potter, Ephraim, Mr.; Argyle, WAS. See 2604.
6013. 2/14/00 mor Powel, Ahitabel. See 6014.
6014. 2/14/00 mor Powel, Ebenezer (w. Ahitabel); Argyle, WAS. See 2198.
6015. 9/5/81 gee Powers, Avery; Granville, CHA. See 8543.
6016. 7/1/85 gee Powers, William; ---, ---. See 7055.
6017. 10/4/92 gee Pratt, Abraham; Cambridge, WAS. See 800.
6018. 10/27/92 gee Pratt, Abraham; Cambridge, WAS. See 2757.
6019. 2/1/96 gee Pratt, Abraham, yeoman; Cambridge, WAS. See 6152.
6020. 8/9/02 mor Pratt, Darius; Cambridge, WAS. See 6022.
6021. 8/9/02 mor Pratt, John; Cambridge, WAS. See 6022.
6022. 8/9/02 mor Pratt, Mary; Cambridge, WAS; Cambridge, WAS; co-mors 6020
    and 6021; mee 5709. Mortgagors are identified as "Mary
    Pratt, Darius Pratt, and John Pratt both of Cambridge."
    Perhaps Mary is wife of Darius. (E:17)
6023. 11/19/00 mor Pratt, Micah; Cambridge, WAS; Cambridge, WAS; mee 7227. (C:141)
6024. 5/2/96 mor Pratt, Reuben; Argyle, WAS; Argyle, WAS; mee 6070. (B:62)
6025. 7/3/92 gee Pratt, Samuel, farmer; Westfield, WAS. See 4448.
6026. 10/7/89 mor Pray, Nehemiah; Pawling, DUT; Willsborough, CLI; mee 6438.
    (A:32)
6027. 10/7/89 mor Pray, Simon; Pawling, DUT; Willsborough, CLI; mee 6438. (A:29)
6028. 10/17/89 gee Pray, Thomas; Pawling, DUT. See 6441.
6029. 10/17/89 mor Pray, Thomas; Pawling, DUT; Willsborough, CLI; mee 6442. (A:35)
6030. 8/24/90 mee Preston, Hannah, Mrs.; Cambridge, WAS. See 854.
6031. 1/18/90 mee Prevost, Augustine James Frederick, attorney; City of N.Y.
    See 1831, 8212, 8307.
6032. 1/18/90 mee Prevost, Augustine James Frederick, attorney; City of N.Y.
    See 8211.
6033. 1/19/90 mee Prevost, Augustine James Frederick, attorney; City of N.Y.
    See 23, 8210, 8213, 8309.
6034. 1/18/90 gor Prevost, Augustus James Frederick, attorney; City of N.Y.;
    Greenfield, WAS; gee 3839. (C-2:172)
6035. 1/19/90 mee Prevost, Augustus Frederick, attorney; City of N.Y. See 5161.
6036. 8/24/92 mor Price, John, farmer; ---, WAS; Glen Pat., WAS; mee 2863.
    (A:362)
6037. 6/21/00 mor Pride, Reuben, gentleman; Cambridge, WAS; Cambridge, WAS;
    mee 8360. (C:141)
6038. 4/7/89 gee Prince, Jacob; Cambridge, ALB. See 5352.
6039. 9/20/90 mee Prince, Job; Cambridge, WAS. See 5349.
6040. 2/18/86 gee Pringle, John; ---, ALB. See 851.
6041. 3/7/99 gee Prior, Edmond, merchant; City of N.Y. See 6284.
6042. 10/16/93 gee Prior, Edmund; City of N.Y. See 5345.
6043. 7/--/94 gee Prior, Edmund, merchant; City of N.Y. See 5346.
6044. 6/4/96 gor Prior, Edmund (w. Mary), merchant; City of N.Y.; Hoosick Pat.,
    WAS; gee 7217. (D:98)
6045. 7/18/99 mee Prior, Edmund, merchant; City of N.Y. See 4493.
6046. 1/12/00 gor Prior, Edmund (w. Mary); City of N.Y.; Clinton, CLI;
    gee 6302. (Mortgage Book B:15)
6047. 6/16/00 gor Prior, Edmund, merchant; City of N.Y.; Granville, WAS;
    co-gor 3279 (both grantors are trustees for the creditors
    of Joseph Jenks); gee 706. (D:452)
6048. 6/29/01 gor Prior, Edmund (w, Mary), merchant; City of N.Y.; Robert Earl
    Pat.(?), CLI; gee 863. (B:296)
6049. 12/12/01 gor Prior, Edmund (w. Mary), merchant; City of N.Y.; Champlain,
    CLI; gee 864. (B:299)
6050. 6/4/96 gor Prior, Mary. See 6044.
6051. 1/12/00 gor Prior, Mary. See 6046.
6052. 6/29/01 gor Prior, Mary. See 6048.
6053. 12/12/01 gor Prior, Mary. See 6049.
6054. 4/2/85 gor Pritcher, Nathaniel, yeoman; Kingsbury, WAS. See 4610.

6055. 5/24/94 mee Proctor, Thomas, Esq.; Philadelphia, ---, PA. See 4834.
6056. 5/22/99 gee Prollo, James L.; Cambridge, WAS. See 7635.
6057. 10/10/96 gee Proser, Benjamin; Easton, WAS. See 667.
6058. 10/3/92 gor Proudfit, Andrew, Dr. (w. Mary); Hebron, WAS; Whitehall, WAS; gee 6065.   (B-2:32)
6059. 7/7/96 mee Proudfit, Andrew, physician; Argyle, WAS. See 6181.
6060. 5/11/99 mee Proudfit, Andrew, physician; Argyle, WAS. See 3875.
6061. 1/4/00 mee Proudfit, Andrew, physician; Argyle, WAS. See 4028.
6062. 4/8/00 mee Proudfit, Andrew; Argyle, WAS. See 4189.
6063. 1/13/01 mee Proudfit, Andrew, physician; Argyle, WAS. See 7305.
6064. 9/25/01 gee Proudfit, Andrew. See 4571.
6065. 10/3/92 gee Proudfit, James, the Rev.; Salem, WAS. See 6058.
6066. 6/13/94 gee Proudfit, James; Salem, WAS. See 2685.
6067. 4/2/95 gee Proudfit. James, clerk; Salem, WAS. See 2699.
6068. 6/23/95 gor Proudfit, James, the Rev. (w, Mary); Salem, WAS; Whitehall, WAS; gee 389.   (B-2:458)
6069. 6/23/95 mee Proudfit, James, the Rev.; Salem, WAS. See 390.
6070. 5/2/96 mee Proudfit, James; Salem, WAS. See 6024.
6071. 10/3/92 gor Proudfit, Mary. See 6058.
6072. 6/23/95 gor Proudfit, Mary. See 6068.
6073. 8/15/86 gor Proudfitt, Andrew, "practitioner of physick"; Hebron, WAS; Salem, WAS; gee 6558.   (C-1:28)
6074. --/--/87 gee Proudfitt, Andrew; ---, ---. See 7055.
6075. 5/11/90 mor Proudfitt, Andrew, Doctor; ---, WAS; Black Creek Dist, WAS; mee 2884.   (A:213)
6076. 6/22/92 gee Proudfitt, Andrew, trustee of the First Presbyterian Congregation, Hebron, WAS. See 4207.
6076a. 3/3/84 --- Proudfoot, James, the Rev. (Presbyterian Church minister). See 1437.
6077. 3/20/98 gee Prouty, James; Salem, WAS. See 6079.
6078. 3/20/98 mor Prouty, James; Salem, WAS; Salem, WAS; mee 6080. (C:240)
6079. 3/20/98 gor Prouty, Richard (w. Susanna); Salem, WAS; Salem, WAS; gee 6077.   (C-2:280)
6080. 3/20/98 mee Prouty, Richard; Salem, WAS. See 6078.
6081. 12/15/98 mee Prouty, Richard; Salem, WAS. See 6082.
6082. 12/15/98 mor Prouty, Richard, Junr.; Salem, WAS; Salem, WAS; mee 6081.   (C:240)
6083. 3/20/98 gor Prouty, Susanna. See 6079.
6084. 1/17/90 mee Provost, Augustine James Frederick, attorney; City of N.Y. See 3838.
6085. 1/18/90 gor Provost, Augustine James Frederick, attorney; City of N.Y.; Greenfield, WAS; gee 5190.   (C-2:305)
6086. 1/18/90 mee Provost, Augustine James Frederick, attorney; City of N.Y. See 5169.
6087. 1/19/90 mee Provost, Augustine James Frederick, attorney; City of N.Y. See 5162 and 5184.
6088. 5/2/96 mor Pruyn, John F., gentleman; Albany, ALB; Donald Campbell's Pat., WAS; mee 1189.   (B:68)
6089. 3/3/92 mee Pruyne, Jacob J.; Albany, ALB. See 8144.
6090. 5/2/96 mor Pruyne, John F., gentleman; Albany, ALB; Donald Campbell's Pat., WAS; mee 8040.   (B:54)
6091. 4/24/01 mor Pulcifur, John; Plattsburgh, CLI; Plattsburgh, CLI; mee 5767.   (B:29)
6092. 6/1/02 mee Pulman, Jonathan, innkeeper; Cambridge, WAS. See 7918.
6093. 5/1/00 mor Punderson, John, farmer; Chester, WAS; Chester, WAS; mee 7772.   (D:218)
6094. 7/4/82 gee Purkins, Gideon; Granville, CHA. See 3386.
6095. 12/22/77 mor Putney, Gideon; ---, ---; Granville, WAS; mee 2372. (A:133)
6096. 3/11/00 mor Qua, Jane. See 6099.
6097. 12/9/93 gee Qua, John, yeoman; Hebron, WAS. See 8677.
6098. 1/24/94 gee Qua, John, yeoman; Hebron, WAS. See 6133.
6099. 3/11/00 mor Qua, John (w. Jane), yeoman; Hebron, WAS; Hebron, WAS; mee 2734.   (D:190)
6100. 1/18/02 mee Qua, John, Junr.; Hebron, WAS. See 144.
6101. 1/22/02 mee Qua, John, Senr., yeoman; Hebron, WAS. See 3052.
6102. 11/16/99 gor Qua, Margaret. See 6106.

6103.	12/2/99	mor	Qua, Margaret. See 6107.
6104.	1/1/88	gee	Qua, Robert, tailor; Hebron, WAS. See 6123.
<u>6105.</u>	8/31/99	mor	Qua, Robert, innkeeper; Hebron, WAS; <u>Hebron, WAS</u>;

6103. 12/2/99 mor Qua, Margaret. See 6107.
6104. 1/1/88 gee Qua, Robert, tailor; Hebron, WAS. See 6123.
<u>6105.</u> 8/31/99 mor Qua, Robert, innkeeper; Hebron, WAS; <u>Hebron, WAS</u>;
        mee 2897.   (C:248)
<u>6106.</u> 11/16/99 gor Qua, Robert (w. Margaret), tailor; Hebron, WAS; <u>Hebron, WAS</u>;
        gee 2668.   (E:184)
<u>6107.</u> 12/2/99 mor Qua, Robert (w. Margaret), yeoman; Hebron, WAS; <u>Hebron, WAS</u>;
        mee 8113.   (C:250)
6108. 7/4/92 gor Quackenbos, Catharine. See 6117.
6109. 10/8/01 gor Quackenbos, Catherine. See 6118.
6110. 5/8/75 gor Quackenbos, Cornelia. See 6119.
6111. 1/1/88 gor Quackenbos, Garret; City of N.Y. See 6123.
6112. 2/27/88 gor Quackenbos, Garret, gentleman; City of N.Y. See 6124.
6113. 1/13/96 gee Quackenbos, Garrit, farmer; Hebron, WAS. See 6224.
6114. 1/15/96 gee Quackenbos, Garrit, farmer; Hebron, WAS. See 6141.
6115. 9/24/71 gee Quackenbos, Johannis, baker; City of N.Y. See 6226.
6116. 5/8/75 gor Quackenbos, John, baker; City of N.Y. See 6120 and 6126.
<u>6117.</u> 7/4/92 gor Quackenbos, John (w. Catharine), baker; City of N.Y.;
        <u>Waghquampeguus(sic), WAS</u>; gee 1980.   (F:141)
<u>6118.</u> 10/8/01 gor Quackenbos, John (w. Catharine), gentleman' City of N.Y.;
        <u>Cambridge, WAS</u>; gee 6155.   (F:181)
6119. 5/8/75 gor Quackenbos, John (w. Cornelia), scepper (skipper?);
        Albany, ALB. See 6120.
6120. 5/8/75 gor Quackenbos, Nicholas, baker; City of N.Y.; <u>---, CHA</u>;
        co-gors 6110, 6116, 6119, 6122; gee 6125. (E:114)
6121. 5/8/75 gor Quackenbos, Nicholas, baker; City of N.Y. See 6126.
6122. 5/8/75 gor Quackenbos, Peter, baker; City of N.Y. See 6120 and 6126.
        (two contracts)
<u>6123.</u> 1/1/88 gor Quackenbos, Sophia, widow; City of N.Y.; <u>Hebron, WAS</u>;
        co-gors 974, 976, 6111; gee 6104. Sophia Q. (6123),
        Garret Q. (6111) and Sophia Brinkerhoff, "late Sophia
        Quackenbos",(976) are "the surviving executors of
        Walter Quackenbos, baker, deceased".   (E:191)
<u>6124.</u> 2/27/88 gor Quackenbos, Sophia, widow; City of N.Y.; <u>Waghquampequas (sic),</u>
        <u>ALB</u> (sic); co-gors 966, 970, 6112; gee 8445. (WAS Co. E:134)
6125. 5/8/75 gee Quackenbos, Walter, baker; Albany, ALB. See 6120.
<u>6126.</u> 5/8/75 gor Quackenbos, Walter, baker, City of N.Y. (sic); land "between
        <u>Cambridge and Hoosick", ALB</u> (sic); co-gors 6116, 6121,
        6122; co-gees 7028, 7029.   (Washington Co. E:297)
6127. 1/1/88 --- Quackenbos, Walter, dec'd. See 6123.
6128. 11/13/97 gor Quackenboss, Catherine. See 6140.
6129. 1/15/96 gor Quackenboss, Cornelia. See 6141.
6130. 11/12/96 gor Quackenboss, Cornelia. See 6142.
<u>6131.</u> 2/9/93 gor Quackenboss, Garret, gentleman; Hebron, WAS; <u>Hebron, WAS</u>;
        gee 4306.   (E:206)
6132. 11/20/90 gor Quackenboss, Gerrit, gentleman; Hebron, WAS. See 6146.
<u>6133.</u> 1/24/94 gor Quackenboss, Gerrit, gentleman; Hebron, WAS; <u>Hebron, WAS</u>;
        gee 2212 (B-2:134); gee 6098 (B-2:137). (two contracts)
<u>6134.</u> 2/16/96 gor Quackenboss, Gerrit (w. Mary); Hebron, WAS; <u>Cambridge, WAS</u>;
        gee 3585.   (D:26)
<u>6135.</u> 2/16/96 gor Quackenboss, Gerrit (w. Mary), gentleman; Hebron, WAS;
        <u>land "between Cambridge and Hoosick" Pats., WAS</u>;
        gee 8446.   (E:139)
6136. 7/11/86 gee Quackenboss, Henry; ---, ---. See 7055.
<u>6137.</u> 2/25/95 gor Quackenboss, Henry, Esq.; "Water Fleet" (Watervliet, ALB?),
        ---, --; <u>Salem, WAS</u>; gee 4753.(See 6141 for Watervliet)(D:427)
6138. 1/16/76 gee Quackenboss, John, baker; City of N.Y. See 859.
6139. 9/22/96 mee Quackenboss, John; City of N.Y. See 967.
<u>6140.</u> 11/13/97 gor Quackenboss, John (w. Catherine), gentleman; City of N.Y.;
        <u>Hebron, WAS</u>; gee 4954.   (E:397)
<u>6141.</u> 1/15/96 gor Quackenboss, John P. (w. Cornelia), shopkeeper; Watervliet,
        ALB; <u>Cambridge, WAS</u>; gee 6114.   (E:122)
<u>6142.</u> 11/12/96 gor Quackenboss, John P. (w. Cornelia), merchant; Watervliet,
        ALB; <u>Anagushanecook</u> (sic), WAS; gee 4381. (C-2:106)
6143. 4/6/98 mee Quackenboss, John P., merchant; Albany, ALB. See 485.
6144. 2/16/96 gor Quackenboss, Mary. See 6134 and 6135. (two contracts)

148

6145. 2/6/88 mor Quackenboss, Sophia, "widow of Garret Quackenboss, gentleman, and surviving executor of Walter Quackenboss, baker, late of the City of New York, deceased"; ---, ---; Hebron, WAS; co-mors 965, 969; mee 3293. The three mortgagors are executors of the estate of Garret Quackenboss, dec'd.(A:276)
6146. 11/20/90 gor Quackenboss, Sophia, "widow ... of Walter Quackenboss late of the City of New York", dec'd.; ---, ---; land "east side of Hudson's River", WAS; co-gors 972, 973, 6132; co-gees 1812, 3522. Grantors are all executors of the estate of Walter Quackenboss, dec'd.   (B-2:193)
6147. 11/20/90 gor Quackenboss, Sophia, the younger. See 973.
6148. 11/20/90 --- Quackenboss, Walter, dec'd. See 6145 and 6146.
6149. 8/6/93 gor Quackenbush, Catharine. See 6159.
6150. 5/9/96 gor Quackenbush, Garret (w. Mary), gentleman; Hebron, WAS; Cambridge, WAS; gee 5599.   (E:355)
6151. 3/10/02 gee Quackenbush, Garret, gentleman; Hebron, WAS. See 8674.
6152. 2/1/96 gor Quackenbush, Garrit (w. Mary); Hebron, WAS; Cambridge, WAS; gee 6019 (F:7); gee 6915 (C-2:294). (two contracts)
6153. 5/9/96 gor Quackenbush, Garrit (w. Mary), gentleman; Hebron, WAS; Cambridge, WAS; gee 8447.   (E:141)
6154. 11/4/00 --- Quackenbush, Gerrit, See 6164.
6155. 10/8/01 gee Quackenbush, Gerrit, farmer; Hebron, WAS. See 6118.
6156. 11/12/01 gor Quackenbush, Gerrit (w. Mary), yeoman; Hebron, WAS; Cambridge, WAS; gee 6913.   (F:9)
6157. 7/31/70 gee Quackenbush, Johannes, baker; City of N.Y. See 7989.
6158. 9/24/71 gor Quackenbush, Johannes (w. Margaret), baker; City of N.Y.; Cambridge Pat., ALB; gee 6225.   (WAS Co. E:107)
6159. 8/6/93 gor Quackenbush, John (w. Catharine), baker; City of N.Y.; Hebron, WAS; gee 975.   (B-2:100)
6160. 9/24/71 gor Quackenbush, Margaret. See 6158.
6161. 2/1/96 gor Quackenbush, Mary. See 6152. (two contracts)
6162. Data repositioned.
6163. 5/9/96 gor Quackenbush, Mary. See 6150 and 6153. (two contracts)
6164. 11/4/00 gee Quackenbush, Mary, wife of Gerrit Quackenbush; Hebron, WAS. See 8303.
6165. 11/12/01 gor Quackenbush, Mary. See 6156.
6166. 11/28/93 mee Quackenbush, Nicholas; Watervliet, ALB. See 4074.
6167. 1/20/97 gor Quackenbush, Nicholas, gentleman; Watervliet, ALB; Cambridge, WAS; gee 206.   (D:296)
6168. 1/7/01 mee Quackenbush, Nicholas; Watervliet, ALB. See 4070.
6169. 12/19/93 mee Quackenbush, Nicholas N., Esq.; Albany, ALB. See 2921.
6170. 6/1/90 gee Quick, Andrew; Nine Partners, DUT. See 6447.
6171. 6/22/99 mor Race, Andrew (w. Anna); Salem, WAS; Salem, WAS; mee 4933.   (C:212)
6172. 6/22/99 mor Race, Anna. See 6171.
6173. 3/5/99 gor Raleigh, Mary. See 6174 and 6176. (two contracts)
6174. 3/5/99 gor Raleigh, Walter (w. Mary); Cambridge, WAS; Cambridge, WAS; gee 2621.   (D:371)
6175. 3/5/99 gee Raleigh, Walter, Esq.; Cambridge, WAS. See 2622.
6176. 3/5/99 gor Raleigh, Walter, Esq. (w. Mary); Cambridge, WAS; Cambridge, WAS; gee 2621.   (D:373)
6177. 9/3/01 mee Raleigh, Walter, Esq.; Cambridge, WAS. See 1838.
6178. 5/1/02 mor Randal, Joseph, farmer; Chester, WAS; Chester, WAS; mee 7775.   (D:196)
6179. 11/29/99 mor Randle, John (w. Sarah), yeoman; Hebron, WAS; Hebron, WAS; mee 8109. The mortgagee is "the only surviving executor of the estate of John Morin Scott, Esq., deceased". (C:234)
6180. 11/29/99 mor Randle, Sarah. See 6179.
6181. 7/7/96 mor Randles, Andrew; Hebron, WAS; Hebron, WAS; co-mor 6187; mee 6059.   (B:85)
6182. 11/25/97 gor Randles, Andrew (w. Helena), yeoman; Hebron, WAS; Hebron, WAS; gee 6189.   (D:440)
6183. 5/10/98 gor Randles, Andrew, yeoman; Hebron, WAS; ---, WAS; co-gor 6185; gee 8331.   (E:385)
6184. 6/30/98 gor Randles, Andrew (w. Elenor); Hebron, WAS; Hebron, WAS; gee 2274.   (F:204)
6185. 5/10/98 gor Randles, Elenor. See 6183.

6186. 6/30/98 gor Randles, Elenor. See 6184.
6187. 7/7/96 mor Randles, Helena; Hebron, WAS. See 6181.
6188. 11/25/97 gee Randles, Helena. See 6182.
6189. 11/25/97 gee Randles, Hugh, yeoman; Hebron, WAS. See 6182.
6190. 11/29/91 gee Randles, Phebe, widow; Hebron, WAS. See 6803.
6191. 11/29/91 mor Randles, Phebe, widow; Hebron, WAS; Hebron, WAS; mee 2350.
                                                                 (C:231)
6192. 11/29/91 mor Randles, William, yeoman; Hebron, WAS; Hebron, WAS;
                   mee 2350.   (C:232)
6193. 10/16/01 mor Ranken, Daniel (w. Nancey), weaver; Argyle, WAS; Argyle Pat.,
                   WAS; mee 8444.   (E:6)
6194. 10/16/01 mor Ranken, Nancey. See 6193.
6195. 4/13/93 gor Rankin, Mathew, farmer; Westfield, WAS; Westfield, WAS;
                  gee 3956.   (B-2:405)
6196. 4/15/01 mor Ransom, Elisha, Esq.; Champlain, CLI; Champlain, CLI;
                  mee 5100.   (B:25)
6197. 10/31/89 gee Ransom, John, innholder; Plattsburgh, CLI. See 5782.
6198. 11/3/97 --- Ransom, Lewis; Cumberland Head (Plattsburgh), CLI.
                  See 4847.
6199. 4/10/99 mor Ransom, Lewis; Plattsburgh, CLI; ---, CLI; co-mees 6864
                  and 8096.   (A:439)
6200. 7/7/02 gee Ransom, Lewis; ---, ---. See 7869.
6201. --/--/87 --- Rapalier, John (forfeiture of his land). See 6670.
6202. 11/9/01 mor Rathbun, Giddeon; Arlington, BEN, VT; Granville, WAS;
                  mee 3900.   (D:113)
6203. 3/10/79 gee Rattoone, John; Perth Amboy, ---, NJ. See 7730.
6204. 3/13/87 gee Rattoone, John; Perth Amboy, ---, NJ; Argyle, WAS; gee 8424.
6205. 3/14/87 mee Rattoone, John; ---, ---. See 8425.   /   (A:45)
6206. 11/21/99 mor Rawson, Simeon; ---, ---; Crown Point, ESS; mee 5875. (A:6)
6207. 7/1/00 mor Ray, Daniel; ---, ---; ---, ESS; mee 5572.   (A:36)
6208. 9/15/00 mee Ray, Gilbert, yeoman; Hebron, WAS. See 2997.
6209. 10/13/01 mor Raymond, William; Granville, WAS. See 3826.
6210. 10/1/01 gee Raymond, William, Junr., merchant; Granville, WAS. See 4148.
6211. 10/28/01 gee Rea, John, blacksmith; Cambridge, WAS. See 1645.
6212. 10/28/01 mor Rea, John, blacksmith; Hebron, WAS; Hebron, WAS; mee 1646.
                                                                 (D:113)
6213. 5/5/90 mor Reab, George; ---, ALB; Salem, WAS; mee 4909.   (A:212)
6214. 9/10/90 gor Reab, George, merchant; ---, REN; Salem, WAS; gee 3153.
                                                                 (A:457)
6215. 9/10/90 mee Reab, George, merchant; Albany, ALB. See 3154.
6216. 9/10/90 mor Reab, George; ---, ALB; Salem, WAS (a record of a mortgage
                  discharge); mee 4908.   (A:216)
6217. 1/14/65 gor Read, Duncan, gentleman; City of N.Y.; Argyle, ALB;
                  co-gors 1209, 2774, 4689, 5011a; gee 1203.(WAS Co. C-2:14)
6218. Data repositioned.
6219. 1/15/65 gor Read, Duncan, gentleman; City of N.Y.; Argyle, ALB;
                  co-gors 1210, 2776, 4690, 5012; gee 1204 (C-2:17),
     (Deed bks., WAS Co.) gee 2766 (A:436), gee 2779 (A:539), gee 6219 (C-2:117),
                  gee 6906 (A:38), gee 7623 (A:288). (six contracts)
6220. 10/22/65 gor Read, Duncan, gentleman; City of N.Y.; Argyle, ALB;
                  co-gors 1217, 2778, 4692, 5014; gee 4579. (WAS Co. A:492)
6221. 12/21/68 gor Read, Lawrence, merchant; City of N.Y. See 8418.
6222. 10/7/94 gee Read, William; ---, ---. See 8583.
6223. 1/13/96 gor Reade, Catharine. See 6224.
6224. 1/13/96 gor Reade, John (w. Catharine), gentleman; Poughkeepsie, DUT;
                  Cambridge, WAS; gee 6113.   (E:124)
6225. 9/24/71 gee Reade, Joseph, attorney; City of N.Y. See 6158.
6226. 9/24/71 gor Reade, Joseph, Esq., attorney; City of N.Y.; Cambridge Pat.,
                  ALB; gee 6115.   (Washington Co. E:102)
6227. 6/20/90 gor Red, Roger, farmer; Argyle, WAS; Argyle, WAS; gee 4740.
                                                                 (C-2:177)
6228. 7/4/97 mor Reed, Abraham (w. Thankful); Granville, WAS; Granville, WAS;
                  co-mees 74, 2935, 2948.   (B:209)
6229. 10/31/00 mor Reed, Abraham, Junr.; Granville, WAS; Whitehall, WAS;
                  co-mees 354 and 8173. Co-mortgagees are overseers of
                  the poor, Granville.   (D:34b)

                                   150

6230. 11/19/91 gor Reed, Daniel, yeoman; Hebron, WAS; Hebron, WAS; gee 7505.
                                                                        (C-1:102)
6231. Data repositioned.
6232. 3/21/65 gor Reed, Duncan, gentleman; City of N.Y.; Argyle, ALB; co-gors
                                    1216, 2777, 4691, 5013; gee 6901. (Washington Co. C-2:110)
6233. 4/7/00 mor Reed, Elijah; Plattsburgh, CLI. See 6234.
6234. 4/7/00 mor Reed, Ephraim; Plattsburgh, CLI; Plattsburgh, CLI; mee 5091.
                                                             (A:425)
6235. 7/4/97 mor Reed, Kitchell (w. Mary), farmer; Granville, WAS; Granville,
                             WAS; co-mees 74, 2935, 2948.   (B:205)
6236. 7/4/97 mor Reed, Mary. See 6235.
6237. 4/15/91 mee Reed, Roger; Argyle, WAS. See 6898.
6238. 3/10/02 mor Reed, Simeon, Junr.; Pawlet, RUT, VT; Old Military Township
                             #7 (Chateaugay), CLI; mee 286.   (B:68)
6239. 7/14/97 mor Reed, Thankful. See 6228.
6240. 7/8/85 mee Reed, William; ---, ---. See 1364.
6241. 5/1/94 mee Reeve, John; ---, ---. See 7867.
6242. 5/27/00 gor Reeve, John; ---, ---. See 55.
6243. 5/24/02 --- Reeve, John; Montgomery, SOM, NJ; ---, CLI. Reeve, this
                             date, appoints John Addams as his attorney for the sale of
                             the above Clinton County lands.   (B:325)
6244. 2/8/85 gee Reeve, Simon R., gentleman; ---, ---. See 5887.
6245. 1/25/87 gee Reeve, Simon R.; ---, ---, NJ. See 5901.
6246. 3/2/87 gee Reeve, Simon R., gentleman; Tewkesbury, HUN, NJ. See 5906.
6247. 3/14/87 gee Reeve, Simon R.; ---, ---. See 5911.
6248. 3/15/87 gee Reeve, Simon R.; Tewkesbury, HUN, NJ. See 5913. (two contracts)
6249. 3/23/87 gee Reeve, Simon R.; Tewkesbury, HUN, NJ. See 5721.
6250. 4/2/87 gee Reeve, Simon R.; Tewkesbury, HUN, NJ. See 6432.
6251. 9/9/90 gee Reeve, Simon R.; ---, HUN, NJ. See 5843.
6252. 10/14/90 gee Reeve, Simon R.; ---, HUN, NJ. See 7759, 8327. (two contracts)
6253. 10/15/90 gee Reeve, Simon R.; ---, HUN, NJ. See 5723.
6254. 9/16/91 mee Reeve, Simon R.; ---, ---. See 108.
6255. 10/11/92 gor Reeve, Simon R.; ---, ---, NJ; Plattsburgh, CLI; co-gor
                             510; gee 90 (A:292); gee 2067 (A:318). (two contracts)
6256. 10/12/92 gor Reeve, Simon R.; Tewkesbury, HUN, NJ; Plattsburgh, CLI;
                             gee 106.   (A:269)
6257. 10/12/92 mee Reeve, Simon R.; ---, ---, NJ. See 91, 256, 2068.
6258. 5/1/94 --- Reeve, Simon R., deceased; ---, ---, NJ. See 7867.
6259. 5/27/00 --- Reeve, Simon R., dec'd.; ---, ---, NJ. See 55.
6260. 7/11/85 gee Reeves, Simon R., gentleman; ---, HUN, NJ. See 5833.
6261. 10/13/90 gor Reeves, Simon R.; ---, HUN, NJ; Plattsburgh, CLI; gee
                             244 (A:424); gee 2177 (A:168). (two contracts)
6262. 10/14/90 gor Reeves, Simon R., gentleman; ---, HUN, NJ; Plattsburgh, CLI;
                             gee 122 (A:173); gee 7865 (A:175). (two contracts)
6263. 10/14/90 mee Reeves, Simon R.; ---, HUN, NJ. See 105, 2179, 7866.
6264. 10/15/90 mee Reeves, Simon R.; ---, ---, NJ. See 241.
6265. 10/16/90 mee Reeves, Simon R.; ---, HUN, NJ. See 3212, 3994, 4459.
6266. 8/5/91 --- Reeves, Simon R.; ---, HUN, NJ. This date Reeves is
                             appointed by Samuel Bayard (508) to serve as his attorney
                             in the sale of his Clinton County lands.
6267. 12/28/90 mor Reid, Daniel; Hebron, WAS; Hebron, WAS; mee 1073. (A:270)
6268. 8/31/73 mee Reid, John, Colonel; ---, ---. See 4526.
6269. 12/27/98 gee Reid, John; ---, ---. See 6275.
6270. 10/30/01 gee Reid, John; ---, ---. See 4572.
6271. 9/25/01 gor Reid, Patrick, gentleman; ---, FRE, MD. See 4571.
6272. 10/30/01 gor Reid, Patrick, gentleman; ---, FRE, MD. See 4572.
6273. 4/2/86 gee Reid, William; ---, WAS. See 6746.
6274. 4/26/86 gee Reid, William; ---, WAS. See 4822.
6275. 12/27/98 gor Reid, William; Argyle, WAS; Argyle, WAS; gee 6269. (F:261)
6276. 7/28/96 gor Reid, William, Esq.; Argyle, WAS; Argyle, WAS; gee 4720.
                                                         (C-2:170)
6277. 12/27/98 gee Reid, William, Junr.; ---, ---. See 6278.
6278. 12/27/98 gor Reid, William, Senr., Esq.; Argyle, WAS; Argyle, WAS;
                             gee 6277.   (F:262)
6279. 11/9/98 mor Rexford, Daniel (w. Hannah); Hartford, WAS; Hartford, WAS;
                             mee 1495.   (C:259)

6280.	11/9/98	mor	Rexford, Hannah. See 6279.
			Rey. See also Wray.
6281.	5/5/85	gee	Rey, George; Albany, ALB. See 8282.
6282.	11/9/92	mor	Reyley, John, yeoman; Troy, REN; Jessup Pat., WAS;
			co-mor 1461; mee 8043. (A:398)
6283.	1/30/99	gee	Reynolds, Abraham; Willsborough, CLI. See 2691.
6284.	3/7/99	gor	Reynolds, Asa (w. Hannah), gentleman; Granville, WAS;
			Granville, WAS; co-gees 3059, 6041. (D:453)
6285.	4/10/00	mor	Reynolds, Asa; Granville, WAS; Granville, WAS; mee 6354.
			(C:238)
6286.	10/15/90	mor	Reynolds, Benjamin; ---, CLI; Plattsburgh, CLI; mee 43. (A:61)
6287.	10/23/92	mor	Reynolds, Benjamin; Plattsburgh, cLI; Plattsburgh, CLI;
			mee 5817. (A:93)
6288.	7/27/02	mor	Reynolds, Benjamin; Chateaugay, CLI; Chateaugay, CLI;
			mee 330. (B:79)
6289.	6/23/00	gee	Reynolds, Elijah; Easton, WAS. See 1783.
6290.	3/18/99	mor	Reynolds, Gilbert; Peru, cLI; Old Military Township #7
			(Chateaugay), CLI; co-mees 277, 336. (A:415)
6291.	3/7/99	gor	Reynolds, Hannah. See 6284.
6292.	5/21/91	gee	Reynolds, Hugh, yeoman; Hebron, WAS. See 7461.
6293.	10/29/94	mee	Reynolds, Israel, cooper, Peru, CLI. See 8330.
6294.	9/14/95	mee	Reynolds, Israel; Peru, CLI. See 7518.
6295.	10/12/02	mor	Reynolds, James; ---, ---; Willsborough, ESS; mee 6502. (A:92)
6296.	10/12/02	mor	Reynolds, Jared; ---, ---; Willsborough, ESS; mee 6502. (A:93)
6297.	5/2/96	gee	Reynolds, John, farmer; Petersburgh, REN. See 2100a.
6298.	5/10/99	gee	Reynolds, Joseph; Argyle, WAS. See 1708.
6299.	8/16/87	mor	Reynolds, Lucias; Plattsburgh, WAS; Plattsburgh, WAS;
			mee 5837. (Clinton Co. A:11)
6300.	7/1/00	mor	Reynolds, Newell; ---, ---. See 2020.
6301.	6/4/88	mor	Reynolds, Reuben; Plattsburgh, CLI; Plattsburgh, CLI;
			mee 5839. (A:13)
6302.	1/12/00	gee	Rhinelander, Jacob; City of N.Y. See 6046.
6303.	2/17/00	gee	Rice, Asa; Cambridge, WAS. See 7907.
6304.	6/5/84	gee	Rice, David; New Perth, CHA. See 1438.
6305.	2/21/93	gee	Rice, David, yeoman; Salem, WAS. See 1760.
6306.	2/23/93	gor	Rice, David; Salem, WAS; Salem, WAS; gee 7729. (B-2:35)
6307.	9/13/96	mor	Rice, Seth; Whiting, ADD, VT; Platt Rogers' Pat., WAS;
			mee 7745. (A:355)
6308.	7/5/88	gee	Rich, Amos; Westfield, WAS. See 2241.
6309.	2/28/98	gee	Rich, Elijah; ---, ---; Crown Point, CLI; mee 7749. (A:14)
6310.	7/5/88	gee	Rich, James; Westfield, WAS. See 2241.
6311.	5/20/99	gee	Rich, John; Cambridge, WAS. See 6601.
6312.	5/20/99	gor	Rich, John (w. Susanna); Cambridge, WAS; Cambridge, WAS;
			gee 1978. (D:110)
6313.	5/20/99	mor	Rich, John; Cambridge, WAS; Cambridge, WAS; mee 6602. (C:264)
6314.	8/10/01	mor	Rich, John, farmer; Cambridge, WAS; Cambridge, WAS; mee 3267.
			(D:79)
6315.	9/21/93	mor	Rich, Nathaniel, yeoman; ---, ADD, VT; ---, WAS and CLI
			mee 1182 (two contracts). (WAS Co. A:123, 453)
6316.	5/20/99	gor	Rich, Susanna. See 6312.
6317.	12/24/98	gee	Rich, Thadeus; Cambridge, WAS. See 6599.
6318.	8/26/93	gee	Richardson, Benjamin; Whitehall, WAS. See 3598.
6319.	6/15/97	gor	Richardson, Benjamin; Manlius, ONO; Peru, CLI; co-gees
			531, 8215. (B:58)
6320.	6/15/97	mee	Richardson, Benjamin; Manlius, ONO. See 616.
6321.	1/16/96	---	Richardson, Bille(?). See 3847.
6322.	2/10/00	mor	Richardson, Billy (w. Tryphena); Granville, WAS; Granville,
			WAS; mee 720. (C:237)
6323.	2/14/00	gor	Richardson, Daniel (w. Polly); Whitehall, WAS; Whitehall,
			WAS; gee 3345. (D:360)
6324.	2/14/00	gor	Richardson, Polly. See 6323.
6325.	1/16/96	gee	Richardson, Tryphena; Granville, WAS. See 3847.
6326.	2/10/00	mor	Richardson, Tryphena. See 6322.
6327.	6/11/99	mor	Rider, Phebe. See 6328.
6328.	6/11/99	mor	Rider, Zerah (w. Phebe); Salem, WAS; Cambridge, WAS; mee 1867.
			(C:229)

6329. 9/25/01 gee Rigg, Edward. See 4571.
Right. See also Wright.
6330. 5/2/96 gee Right, Elijah. See 2100a.
6331. 5/2/96 gee Right, Laughlin. See 2100a.
6332. 12/24/95 mee Rising, Josiah, yeoman; ———, WAS. See 1950.
6333. 5/20/95 gor Roach, Rachel, "a child of Moses Bartlet, deceased";
Salem, WAS; Salem, WAS; gee 472.   (D:238)
6334. 6/8/84 gee Roach, Thomas; City of N.Y. See 4097.
6335. 6/10/84 mor Roach, Thomas, merchant; City of N.Y.; Skenesborough, WAS;
mee 4091.   (Deed Book B-1:110)
6336. 7/28/87 gor Roach, Thomas, merchant; City of N.Y.; Skenesborough(?), WAS;
gee 3713.   (B-2:211)
6337. 3/22/88 gor Roach, Thomas, City of N.Y.; Skenesborough(?), WAS;
gee 4420.   (B-2:215)
6338. 6/12/00 mor Roads, Hester. See 6339.
6339. 6/12/00 mor Roads, John (w. Hester); Cambridge, WAS; Cambridge, WAS;
mee 2330.   (C:238)
6340. 5/21/84 gee Robards, William, yeoman; Queensbury, WAS. See 861. (two
contracts)
6341. 8/11/96 gee Robards, William, yeoman; Queensbury, WAS. See 2636.
6342. 7/19/00 gee Robards, William; Queensbury, WAS. See 1952.
6343. 3/10/99 mor Robarts, David; Clarendon, RUT, VT; Champlain, CLI;
mee 361.   (B:82)
6344. 4/15/02 gor Robbins, Artemus (w. Eve), physician; Argyle, WAS; Argyle,
WAS; gee 8347.   (F:290)
6345. 4/21/02 mor Robbins, Artemus, physician; Argyle, WAS; Argyle, WAS;
mee 8348.   (E:1)
6346. 4/15/02 gor Robbins, Eve. See 6344.
6347. 8/2/83 gee Robbins, Levi; Hartford, ———, CT. See 8230.
6348. 8/2/83 gee Robbins, Wait; Hartford, ———, CT. See 8230.
6349. 5/10/97 mor Roberds, Phebe. See 6350.
6350. 5/10/97 mor Roberds, William (w. Phebe); Queensbury, WAS; Queensbury,
WAS; co-mees 3281, 6838, 8746.   (B:224)
6351. 10/30/01 gee Roberson, William; ———, ———. See 4572.
6352. 3/1/98 gee Roberts, Benjamin, farmer; ———, CLI. See 6852.
6353. 3/2/98 gor Roberts, Benjamin, farmer; ———, CLI; Old Military Township
#7 (Chateaugay), CLI; co-mees 6854, 8085.   (A:266)
6354. 4/10/00 mee Roberts, Daniel; Granville, WAS. See 6285.
6355. 3/10/99 mor Roberts, David; Clarendon, RUT, VT; Champlain, CLI; mee 361a.
(B:67)
6356. 1/31/98 gor Roberts, Elizabeth. See 6365.
6357. 8/7/98 mor Roberts, Ethan; ———, CLI; Old Military Township #7
(Chateaugay), CLI; co-mees 273, 315.   (A:348)
6358. 12/8/98 mee Roberts, John; Plattsburgh, CLI. See 1359.
6359. 2/28/01 mee Roberts, John; Plattsburgh, CLI. See 7526.
6360. 7/10/86 mor Roberts, Peter; ———, ———; Plattsburgh, WAS; mee 5894.
(Deed Book B-1:244)
6361. 5/3/88 mor Roberts, William; ———, ———; Argyle, WAS; co-mor 1274;
mee 7657.   (A:84)
6362. 10/7/94 gee Roberts, William; ———, ———. See 8583.
6363. 6/27/97 gee Roberts, William; Troy, REN. See 1275.
6364. 6/27/97 mee Roberts, William; ———, ———. See 1276.
6365. 1/31/98 gor Roberts, William (w. Elizabeth), Troy, REN; Argyle, WAS;
gee 4944.   (C-2:239)
6366. 5/3/80 gee Roberts, William, Junr., farmer; ———, ALB. See 7648.
6367. 5/26/74 gor Robertson, Alexander (w. Mary), merchant; City of N.Y.;
Argyle, WAS; gee 6716.   (B-1:214)
6368. 7/12/93 gor Robertson, Andrew, weaver; Salem, WAS; Salem, WAS;
gee 3663.   (B-2:275)
6369. 2/25/83 gor Robertson, Archibald; Cambridge, WAS; Cambridge, WAS;
gee 6467.   (D:307)
6370. 6/22/91 gor Robertson, Archibald; ———, ———. See 8450.
6371. 9/14/99 gor Robertson, Archibald, farmer; Cambridge, WAS; Cambridge,
WAS; gee 2614.   (D:226)
6372. 5/2/96 mor Robertson, Francis, farmer; Argyle, WAS; Donald Campbell's
Pat., WAS; co-mees 1290, 2101, 2217, 5584.   (C:230)

153

6373. 12/29/98 gee Robertson, James, merchant; Montreal, Canada. See 163.
6374. 5/25/99 gee Robertson, John; Cambridge, WAS. See 7636.
6375. 5/26/74 gor Robertson, Mary. See 6367.
6376. 6/15/92 mor Robertson, Mary. See 6381.
6377. 3/11/96 gee Robertson, Patrick, joiner; Cambridge, WAS. See 4385.
6378. 6/30/96 gee Robertson, Robert; Argyle, WAS. See 8046.
6379. 10/30/01 gee Robertson, Robert; ---, ---. See 4572.
6380. 6/14/92 gee Robertson, William, yeoman; Argyle, WAS. See 6755.
6381. 6/15/92 mor Robertson, William (w. Mary), yeoman; Argyle, WAS; Argyle, WAS; mee 6781.   (A:379)
6382. 5/27/00 mor Robinson, Aulise. See 6387.
6383. 7/7/91 gee Robinson, Edmond, farmer; Easton, WAS. See 779.
6384. 7/7/91 mee Robinson, Edward, farmer; Easton, WAS. See 7487.
6385. 7/7/91 gee Robinson, Elihu, farmer; Easton, WAS. See 779.
6386. 7/7/91 mor Robinson, Elihu, farmer; Easton, WAS. See 7487.
6387. 5/27/00 mor Robinson, James (w. Aulise); Argyle, WAS; Argyle, WAS; mee 4078.   (C:239)
6388. 4/29/00 mor Robinson, Stephen, yeoman; Hebron, WAS; Hebron, WAS; mee 6846.   (C:235)
6389. 10/15/91 gee Robison, John, merchant; Albany, ALB. See 6519.
6390. 10/12/93 mor Roblee, Cloe. See 6392.
6391. 10/12/93 gee Roblee, Thomas; Granville, WAS. See 4789.
6392. 10/12/93 mor Roblee, Thomas (w. Cloe); Granville, WAS. See 3787.
6393. 5/12/02 gor Roblee, Thomas, yeoman; Granville, WAS. See 3778.
6394. 9/2/95 gee Rock, John, farmer; Argyle, WAS. See 2548.
6395. 8/1/01 gee Roe(?), John, blacksmith; "at present of Cambridge". See 3289.
6396. 4/16/93 gor Roe, Phillips; ---, SUF; Zephaniah Platt's Pat., CLI; gee 6403.   (A:407)
6397. 12/3/89 --- Rogers, ---(?); City of N.Y. See 155.
6398. 5/13/01 gor Rogers, Ananias; Ferrisburgh, ADD, VT. See 6416.
6399. 6/22/01 gor Rogers, Ananias; Ferrisburgh, ADD, VT. See 6417.
6400. 10/19/01 mee Rogers, Ananias; ---, ---. See 150.
6401. 2/13/02 mee Rogers, Ananias; ---, ---. See 2634 and 4545.
6402. 12/3/89 gee Rogers, Charles Platt; City of N.Y. See 4053.
6403. 4/16/93 gor Rogers, Charles Platt; ---, DUT. See 6396.
6404. 10/23/95 mee Rogers, Charles Platt; ---, CLI. See 634.
6405. 11/26/85 gee Rogers, Clark; Hancock, BER, MA. See 5425.
6406. 11/5/90 gor Rogers, Clark; Hancock, BER, MA; Hebron, WAS; gee 6427 (A:179); gee 6463 (A:179). (two contracts)
6407. 11/6/90 gor Rogers, Clark, yeoman; Hancock, BER, MA; Hebron, WAS; gee 6408.   (C-1:63)
6408. 11/6/90 gee Rogers, Clark, Junr., "son of Clark Rogers"; ---, ---. See 6407.
6409. 11/30/90 gor Rogers, Clark, Junr.; Hebron, WAS; Hebron, WAS; gee 3010.   (A:218)
6410. 8/17/99 mor Rogers, Dorothy. See 6428.
6411. 8/13/02 gee Rogers, Dudley; Cambridge, WAS. See 2835.
6412. 8/13/02 mor Rogers, Dudley; Cambridge, WAS; Salem, WAS; mee 2836. (E:10)
6413. 4/27/92 mee Rogers, Elnathan, joiner; Champlain, CLI. See 4295.
6414. 4/29/95 mee Rogers, Elnathan; Champlain, CLI. See 805.
6415. 4/18/01 mee Rogers, Henry, merchant; City of N.Y. See 7494.
6416. 5/13/01 gor Rogers, Ida; Ferrisburgh, ADD, VT; ---, CLI; co-gors 3109, 3111, 5987, 5989, 6398, 6418, 6421, 6456, 6461, 6464; co-gees 540, 547.   (B:275)
6417. 6/22/01 gor Rogers, Ida; Ferrisburgh, ADD, VT; Elizabethtown, ESS; co-gors 3110, 3112, 5988, 5990, 6399, 6419, 6422, 6457, 6462, 6465; gee 17   (A:66)
6418. 5/13/01 gor Rogers, Ida, Junr.; Ferrisburgh, ADD, VT. See 6416.
6419. 6/22/01 gor Rogers, Ida, Junr.; Ferrisburgh, ADD, VT. See 6417.
6420. lacking mor Rogers, Jacob, administrator of the estate of Platt Rogers, dec'd.; ---, ---; ---, ESS; mee 855.   (A:63)
6421. 5/13/01 gor Rogers, Jacob; Ferrisburgh, ADD, VT. See 6416.
6422. 6/22/01 gor Rogers, Jacob; Ferrisburgh, ADD, VT. See 6417.
6423. 10/19/01 mee Rogers, Jacob; ---, ---. See 150.
6424. 2/7/02 mee Rogers, Jacob; ---, ---. See 7684.

6425. 2/13/02 mee Rogers, Jacob; ---, ---. See 2634 and 4545.
6426. 3/20/99 gee Rogers, James, farmer; Salem, WAS. See 6881.
6427. 11/5/90 gee Rogers, Joshua, son of Clark Rogers; Hebron, WAS. See 6406.
6428. 8/17/99 mor Rogers, Nathan (w. Dorothy), farmer; Easton, WAS; Cambridge
                     Pat., WAS; mee 4037.   (C:236)
6429. 2/8/85   gee Rogers, Platt, gentleman; ---, ---. See 5887.
6430. 11/13/86 mee Rogers, Platt; Rumbout Precinct; DUT. See 5399.
6431. 3/14/87 gee Rogers, Platt; ---, ---. See 5911.
6432. 4/2/87   gor Rogers, Platt; Rumbout Precinct, DUT; land "near Split
                     Rock", WAS; gee 6250. (Split Rock is on the Boquet
                     River, south of present-day Elizabethtown, ESS).
                                                        (Clinton Co. A:155)
6433. 7/11/87 mee Rogers, Platt; Rumbout Precinct, DUT. See 153.
6434. --/--/89 mee Rogers, Platt; Fishkill, DUT. See 6938.
6435. 4/2/89   gor Rogers, Platt; Rumbout Precinct, DUT; Platt Rogers Pat., CLI;
                     gee 7182.   (A:453)
6436. 10/6/89 mee Rogers, Platt; Fishkill, DUT. See 6944.
6437. 10/7/89 gor Rogers, Platt; Fishkill, DUT; Willsborough, CLI; gee 6937.
                                                                     (A:190)
6438. 10/7/89 mee Rogers, Platt; Fishkill Dist., DUT. See 5317, 6026, 6027.
6439. 10/14/89 gor Rogers, Platt; Fishkill, DUT; Willsborough, CLI; gee 2016.
                                                                     (A:320)
6440. 10/16/89 mee Rogers, Platt; Fishkill, DUT. See 2707 and 5523.
6441. 10/17/89 gor Rogers, Platt; Fishkill, DUT; Willsborough, CLI; gee 6028
                     (A:524); gee 6922 (A:188). (two contracts)
6442. 10/17/89 mee Rogers, Platt; Fishkill, DUT. See 2015, 2018, 6029, 6923,
                     6924.
6443. 11/6/89 gor Rogers, Platt; Fishkill, DUT; ---, CLI; gee 3493. (A:123)
6444. 11/6/89 gor Rogers, Platt; Fishkill, DUT; Willsborough, CLI; gee 6920.
                                                                     (A:116)
6445. 11/6/89 mee Rogers, Platt; Fishkill, DUT. See 6921.
6446. 11/7/89 gor Rogers, Platt; Fishkill, DUT; Plattsburgh, CLI; gee 8766.
                                                                     (A:337)
6447. 6/1/90   gor Rogers, Platt; Fishkill, DUT; Willsborough, CLI; gee 6170.
                                                                     (A:297)
6448. 10/9/90 gor Rogers, Platt; Fishkill, DUT; Willsborough, CLI; gee 8270.
                                                                     (A:213)
6449. 11/13/90 gor Rogers, Platt; Fishkill, DUT; Plattsburgh, CLI; gee 5677.
                                                                     (A:242)
6450. 6/1/91   gor Rogers, Platt; Fishkill, DUT; Willsborough, CLI; gee 85
                     (A:372); gee 630 (A:253); gee 3223 (A:286); gee 5386
                     (A:216). (four contracts)
6451. 5/15/94 gor Rogers, Platt; Fishkill, DUT; Willsborough, CLI; gee 5853.
                                                                     (A:333)
6452. 12/1/95 gor Rogers, Platt; Fishkill, DUT; Crown Point Dist; CLI;
                     gee 1918.   (A:480)
6453. 1/1/96   gor Rogers, Platt; Ferrisburgh, ADD, VT (sic); Crown Point Dist.,
                     CLI; gee 3502.   (B:301)
6454. 1/1/96   gor Rogers, Platt; Fishkill, DUT (sic); Crown Point Dist., CLI;
                     gee 4296.   (B:182)
6455. 2/17/96 gee Rogers, Platt; ---, DUT. See 5745.
6456. 5/13/01 gor Rogers, Platt; Ferrisburgh, ADD, VT. See 6416.
6457. 6/22/01 gor Rogers, Platt; Ferrisburgh, ADD, VT. See 6417.
6458. lacking --- Rogers, Platt, dec'd. See 6420.
6459. 2/21/00 mor Rogers, Rachel. See 6460.
6460. 2/21/00 mor Rogers, Samuel (w. Rachel); Cambridge, WAS; Cambridge, WAS;
                     mee 2328.   (C:234)
6461. 5/13/01 gor Rogers, Syche; Ferrisburgh, ADD, VT. See 6416.
6462. 6/22/01 gor Rogers, Syche; Ferrisburgh, ADD, VT. See 6417.
6463. 11/5/90 gee Rogers, Thomas, son of Clark Rogers; Hebron, WAS. See 6406.
6464. 5/13/01 gor Rogers, Thomas; Ferrisburgh, ADD, VT. See 6416.
6465. 6/22/01 gor Rogers, Thomas; Ferrisburgh, ADD, VT. See 6417.
6466. 2/13/83 gee Rogers, William; New Perth, CHA. See 1434.
6467. 2/25/83 gee Rollo, James; Cambridge, WAS. See 6369.
6468. 10/1/85 gee Rollo, James, yeoman; Cambridge, WAS. See 6994.
6469. 1/22/00 gee Rollo, James; Cambridge, WAS. See 4510.

6470. 5/5/01 mee Rollo, James; Cambridge, WAS. See 1159.
6471. 5/13/00 mor Rood, Asa (w. Elizabeth); Granville, WAS; <u>Granville, WAS</u>;
mee 1541. (C:235)
6472. 5/13/00 mor Rood, Elizabeth. See 6471.
6473. 5/15/02 mor Rood, Robert; Granville, WAS; <u>Granville, WAS</u>; mee 4156
(D:166)
6474. 6/24/67 gee Roosevelt, James, merchant; City of N.Y. See 1202.
6475. 12/12/98 mee Roosevelt, James C., gentleman; City of N.Y. See 7390 and
7391. (two contracts)
6476. 11/29/00 mee Roosevelt, James C., gentleman; "late of the City of New
York but now of Jamaica, Long Island". See 7392.
6477. 12/10/95 gee Root, Lucretia, "wife of Solomon Root, yeoman"; Hebron, WAS.
See 8383.
6478. 12/10/95 --- Root, Solomon. See 6477.
6479. 5/3/97 mor Root, William, yeoman; Hebron, WAS; <u>Hebron, WAS</u>; mee 8598.
(B:161)
6480. 7/2/92 gee Rose, Elisha, farmer; Westfield, WAS. See 4446.
6481. 5/11/95 mor Rose, Elisha; Hartford, WAS; <u>Hartford, WAS</u>; mee 4894. (A:547)
6482. 2/8/98 mor Rose, Elisha (w. Marcy), farmer; Hartford, WAS; <u>Hartford,</u>
WAS; mee 1483. (B:321)
6483. 2/8/98 mor Rose, Marcy. See 6482.
6484. 6/7/93 gor Rosevelt, Isaac, "executor of the ... will ... of James
Rosevelt late of the City of New York, deceased"; City
of N.Y.; <u>Argyle, WAS</u>; co-gors 1065, 1067, 1069, 1076,
1847, 1848; gee 8258. (B-2:61)
6485. 6/7/93 --- Rosevelt, James, dec'd. See 6484.
6486. 8/22/98 gee Rosier, George, merchant; City of N.Y. See 5463.
6487. 4/30/89 gor Ross, Artemas; Schaghticoke, ALB; <u>Queensbury, WAS</u>; gee 899.
(B-2:220)
6488. 4/13/86 gor Ross, Daniel; ---, WAS. See 5992.
6489. 3/20/87 gor Ross, Daniel (w. Elizabeth), farmer; Willsborough, WAS;
<u>Willsborough, WAS</u>; gee 2593. (A:69)
6490. 3/17/97 gor Ross, Daniel; Willsborough, CLI; <u>Willsborough, CLI</u>;
gee 2536. (B:84)
6491. 9/7/98 mee Ross, Daniel; Willsborough, CLI. See 3244.
6492. 11/21/98 mee Ross, Daniel; Willsborough, CLI. See 3227.
6493. 4/10/99 gor Ross, Daniel; Willsborough, ESS; <u>Willsborough, ESS</u>; gee
6919. (A:39)
6494. 7/2/99 mee Ross, Daniel; ---, ---. See 2578 and 8718.
6495. 2/23/01 mee Ross, Daniel; ---, ---. See 2539.
6496. 5/12/01 mee Ross, Daniel; ---, ---. See 1704.
6497. 5/30/01 mee Ross, Daniel; ---, ---. See 1899.
6498. 9/30/01 mee Ross, Daniel; ---, ---. See 7382.
6499. 2/12/02 mee Ross, Daniel; ---, ---. See 1902.
6500. 4/1/02 mee Ross, Daniel; ---, ---. See 3804.
6501. 8/25/02 mee Ross, Daniel; ---, ---. See 1097.
6502. 10/12/02 mee Ross, Daniel; ---, ---. See 6295 and 6296.
6503. 1/--/96 gor Ross, Daniel, Esq., "high sheriff of the County of Clinton";
---, ---; <u>Plattsburgh, CLI</u> (sheriff's sale); gee 8768.
(A:435)
6504. 10/3/96 gor Ross, Daniel, Esq., sheriff of Clinton County; ---, ---;
<u>Peru, CLI</u> (sheriff's sale); gee 5120. (B:31)
6505. 10/16/97 gor Ross, Daniel, Esq.; Willsborough, CLI; <u>Willsborough, CLI</u>;
gee 6932. (A:68)
6506. 5/23/98 gee Ross, Daniel, Esq.; ---, CLI. See 7629.
6507. 5/23/98 mor Ross, Daniel, Esq.; ---, CLI; <u>---, CLI</u>; co-mor 3384; mee 7630.
(A:301)
6508. 7/3/99 gor Ross, Daniel, Esq.; Willsborough, ESS; <u>Willsborough, ESS</u>;
gee 2595. (A:26)
6509. 3/23/01 gee Ross, Daniel, Esq. See 3391.
6510. 5/26/88 gee Ross, Daniel, Junr., gentleman; Willsborough, CLI. See
1869.
6511. 3/20/87 gor Ross, Elizabeth. See 6489.
6512. 5/2/96 mor Ross, Samuel, yeoman; Petersburgh, REN; <u>Argyle, WAS</u>;
co-mees 1290, 2101, 2228, 5584. (C:230)
6513. 8/22/98 gee Roulet, John Sigirmund, merchant; City of N.Y. See 5463.

6514. 1/--/91 gor Rous, Jaque (w. Therese); ---, CLI; Canadian and Nova Scotia Refugees' Pat., CLI; gee 5312. (A:260)
6514a. 1/--/91 gor Rous, Therese. See 6514.
6515. 1/11/94 mor Rouse, Jacob (w. Levina), farmer; Argyle, WAS; Argyle, WAS; mee 2656. (A:468)
6516. 11/8/93 mor Rouse, James, farmer; ---, WAS; ---, WAS; mee 7208. (A:458)
6517. 11/18/93 mor Rouse, James; ---, WAS; ---, WAS; mee 1255. (A:457)
6518. 7/9/94 gor Rouse, Jaque (w. Therese), gentleman; ---, CLI; Canadian and Nova Scotia Refugees' Pat., CLI; co-gees 1184 and 5543. (A:349)
6519. 10/15/91 gor Rouse, Jaque (w. Therese); Albany, ALB; Canadian and Nova Scotia Refugees' Pat., CLI; gee 6389. (A:218)
6520. 11/7/91 gor Rouse, Jaque (w. Therise), "a Canadian refugee"; ---, CLI; Canadian and Nova Scotia Refugees' Pat., CLI; gee 5313. (A:222)
6521. 11/7/91 gor Rouse, Jaque (w. Therise); ---, ---; "bounty lands granted originally by the (N.Y.) legislature to John Baptiste Martin as a Canadian refugee"(lands in Clinton Co.); gee 5313. (A:224)
6522. 5/20/89 gee Rouse, Jaques; Champlain, CLI. See 2417.
6523. 5/30/89 gee Rouse, Jaques; Champlain, CLI. See 2418 and 2892.
6524. 12/1/01 gee Rouse, Joseph, tailor; Easton, WAS. See 7401.
6525. 1/11/94 mor Rouse, Levina. See 6515.
6526. 5/1/94 mor Rouse, Simon; ---, WAS; Westfield, WAS; mee 1256. (A:484)
6527. Data repositioned.
6528. 7/9/94 gor Rouse, Therese. See 6518.
6529. 10/15/91 gor Rouse, Therese. See 6519.
6530. 11/7/91 gor Rouse, Therise. See 6520 and 6521.
6531. 6/4/85 gee Rowan, James; ---, ---. See 7055.
6532. 6/17/85 gee Rowan, James; New Perth, WAS. See 8283. (two contracts)
6533. 4/2/88 gee Rowan, James, blacksmith; Salem, WAS. See 4262.
6534. 4/30/93 gee Rowan, James, blacksmith; Salem, WAS. See 1220.
6535. 6/26/94 gee Rowan, James; Hebron, WAS. See 7791.
6536. 4/29/01 gee Rowan, James; Salem, WAS. See 8539.
6537. 3/19/95 mor Rowan, James, Junr., farmer; Hebron, WAS; Hebron, WAS mee 2451. (A:538)
6538. 7/29/74 gor Rowan, John, freeholder; New Perth, CHA. See 176.
6539. 11/1/79 gee Rowan, John; New Perth, CHA. See 1429.
6540. 9/10/96 gee Rowan, John; ---, ---. See 6622.
6541. 6/6/94 gor Rowan, Mary. See 6543.
6542. 6/6/94 gor Rowan, Stephen; Salem, WAS; Salem, WAS; gee 3155. (B-2:201)
6543. 6/6/94 gor Rowan, Stephen (w. Mary), yeoman; Salem, WAS; Salem, WAS gee 3155. (Mary's signature is dated 7/16/94) (B-2:219)
6544. 6/26/94 gee Rowan, Stephen, yeoman; Salem, WAS. See 2515.
6545. 5/2/01 mor Rowe, Asa (w. Oladine); ---, ---; ---, ESS; co-mees 7407 and 8304. (A:67)
6546. 5/2/01 mor Rowe, Oladine. See 6545.
6547. 2/2/02 gee Rowley, Silvester; Granville, WAS. See 7915.
6548. 9/17/99 mor Rowlison, Rial; Canaan, ---, CT; Plattsburgh, CLI; mee 7601. (A:428)
6549. 8/18/00 mor Rowlison, John; Plattsburgh, CLI; Plattsburgh, CLI; mee 5765. (A:444)
6550. 8/19/00 mor Rowlson, John; Plattsburgh, CLI; Plattsburgh, CLI; mee 1450. (B:2)
6551. 8/5/01 mor Rowlson, John; Plattsburgh, CLI; Plattsburgh, CLI; mee 5770. (B:54)
6552. 9/16/99 gee Rowlson, Rial, farmer; Canaan, ---, CT. See 7600.
6553. 7/28/00 gor Rows, James, "alias Jaque",(w. Therese); Champlain, CLI; Champlain, CLI; gee 3078. (B:252)
6554. 7/29/00 mee Rows, James, "alias Jaque"; Champlain, CLI. See 3079.
6555. 7/28/00 gor Rows, Jaque. See 6553.
6556. 7/29/00 mee Rows, Jaque. See 6554.
6557. 7/28/00 gor Rows, Therese. See 6553.
6558. 8/15/86 gee Rude, Dan; Salem, WAS. See 6073.
6559. 6/2/88 gee Ruger, Gideon, blacksmith; Plattsburgh, CLI. See 5924.
6560. 6/4/88 mor Ruger, Gideon, blacksmith; Plattsburgh, CLI; Plattsburgh, CLI; mee 5839. (A:14)

157

6561.	9/7/69	gor	Rugg, Joseph; ---, ---. See 7955.
6562.	4/20/73	gor	Rugg, Joseph; ---, ---. See 7957.
6563.	6/28/92	gee	Ruggles, Denison, yeoman; Salem, WAS. See 2344.
6564.	5/28/01	gee	Russel, Barnabas; Bedford, BRI, MA. See 2469.
6565.	2/6/02	gee	Russel, Barnabas; New Bedford, BRI, MA. See 2472.
6566.	6/1/02	gee	Russel, Newton, farmer; Willsborough, ESS. See 2408.
6567.	7/4/01	mor	Russell, Anna. See 6568.
<u>6568.</u>	7/4/01	mor	Russell, Barnabas (w. Anna), farmer; Easton, WAS; <u>Easton,</u> <u>WAS</u>; mee 2470. (D:73b)
6569.	9/25/02	gee	Russell, Barnabas; Easton, WAS. See 6009.
6570.	--/--/67	gee	Russell, Ebenezer; ---, ---. See 7055.
6571.	10/31/98	mee	Russell, Ebenezer; Salem, WAS. See 8712.
6572.	10/7/01	---	Russell, Ebenezer. See 5291.
6573.	6/9/83	gee	Russell, Ebenezer, Esq.; White Creek, CHA. See 4431.
<u>6574.</u>	6/27/92	gor	Russell, Ebenezer, Esq.; Salem, WAS; <u>Salem, WAS</u>; gee 6593. (A:477)
6575.	6/30/92	gor	Russell, Ebenezer, Esq.; Salem, WAS. See 4445.
6576.	7/2/92	gor	Russell, Ebenezer, Esq.; Salem, WAS. See 4447. (three contracts)
6577.	7/3/92	gor	Russell, Ebenezer, Esq.; Salem, WAS. See 4448.
6578.	8/14/92	gor	Russell, Ebenezer, Esq.; Salem, WAS. See 4450. (two contracts)
6579.	7/17/92	mee	Russell, Ebenezer, the Honorable; ---, ---. See 447.
6580.	7/18/92	mee	Russell, Ebenezer, the Honorable; ---, ---. See 1657.
6581.	7/31/92	mee	Russell, Ebenezer, the Honorable; ---, ---. See 1616.
<u>6582.</u>	1/18/00	mor	Russell, Humphrey (w. Sylvia), yeoman; Cambridge, WAS; <u>Cambridge, WAS</u>; co-mees 3418, 3425. (C:234)
6583.	10/7/94	gee	Russell, Jeremiah; ---, ---. See 8583.
6584.	10/4/96	gee	Russell, Jeremiah; Fairfield, WAS. See 8593.
6585.	3/16/92	gee	Russell, Jeremiah, Esq.; ---, WAS. See 7670.
<u>6586.</u>	3/16/92	mor	Russell, Jeremiah, Esq.; ---, WAS; <u>Beekman Pat., WAS</u>; mee 7671. (A:324)
6587.	5/1/99	gee	Russell, Jeremiah, Esq.; Westfield, WAS. See 803.
6588.	8/21/00	gee	Russell, Jeremiah, Esq.; Fairfield, WAS. See 8603.
<u>6589.</u>	3/8/98	mor	Russell, John; Salem, WAS; <u>Hebron, WAS</u>; mee 6703. (B:319)
<u>6590.</u>	3/8/98	mor	Russell, John; Salem, WAS; <u>Salem, WAS</u>; mee 6703. (B:320)
<u>6591.</u>	3/26/98	mor	Russell, John; Salem, WAS; <u>Salem, WAS</u>; gee 7513. (C-2:275)
6592.	1/18/00	mor	Russell, Sylvia. See 6582.
6593.	6/27/92	gee	Russell, William, son of Ebenezer Russell, Esq.; Salem, WAS. See 6574.
6594.	5/28/98	mee	Russell, William; Cambridge, WAS. See 8137.
<u>6595.</u>	8/13/97	mor	Rust, Amaziah; Cambidge, WAS; <u>Cambridge Pat., WAS</u>; mee 600. (B:214)
<u>6596.</u>	10/20/01	mor	Rutherford, Aaron, farmer; Argyle, WAS; <u>Argyle, WAS</u>; mee 4591. (D:107)
<u>6597.</u>	6/26/90	mor	Rutty(?), Zebulon; Cambridge, ALB; <u>land "east side of</u> <u>Hudson's river", WAS</u>; mee 8840. (A:482)
6598.	5/28/98	gee	Ryan, John, farmer; ---, ---, NY. See 8005.
<u>6599.</u>	12/24/98	gor	Ryan, John (w. Patience); Hoosick, REN; <u>Cambridge, WAS</u>; gee 6317. (D:105)
<u>6600.</u>	12/24/98	gor	Ryan, John (w. Patience); ---, WAS; <u>Cambridge, WAS</u>; co-gees 8161, 8163. (D:108)
<u>6601.</u>	5/20/99	gor	Ryan, John (w. Patience); Hoosick, REN; <u>Cambridge, WAS</u>; gee 6311. (D:107)
6602.	5/20/99	mee	Ryan, John; Hoosick, REN. See 6313.
6603.	12/24/98	gor	Ryan, Patience. See 6599 and 6600. (two contracts)
6604.	5/20/99	gor	Ryan, Patience. See 6601.
6605.	7/1/84	gor	Ryckman, William, executor of the estate of Henry Franklin, "late of the City of New York", dec'd., merchant; ---, ---; <u>Kingsbury, WAS</u>; gee 2203. (B-1:177)
6606.	5/15/00	mee	Ryon, John, yeoman; Hoosick, REN. See 8353.
<u>6607.</u>	1/22/00	mor	Sabin, Isaac; Peru, CLI; <u>Peru, CLI</u>; mee 1973. (B:5)
<u>6608.</u>	8/6/93	mor	Sacket, Augustus, attorney; City of N.Y.; <u>Indian Purchase,</u> <u>WAS and MON</u>; mee 2591. (WAS Co. A:436)
<u>6609.</u>	1/23/96	mor	Sacket, Augustus (w. Minerva); City of N.Y.; <u>Indian Purchase,</u> <u>CLI</u>; mee 3812. (A:174)
6610.	1/23/96	mor	Sacket, Minerva. See 6609.

6611. 1/22/96 mor Sackett, Augustus (w. Minerva); City of N.Y.; Indian
Purchase, CLI; mee 4231.   (A:173)
6612. 1/22/96 mor Sackett, Augustus (w. Minerva); City of N.Y.; ---, CLI;
mee 4080.   (A:186)
6613. 4/13/99 mor Sackett, Elijah, farmer; Hartford, WAS; Hartford, WAS;
mee 5443.   (C:262)
6614. 1/22/96 mor Sackett, Minerva. See 6611 and 6612. (two contracts)
6615. 9/10/96 mor Safford, Anna. See 6622.
6616. 4/7/00 mee Safford, Benjamin, farmer; Argyle, WAS. See 4384.
6617. 10/10/92 gee Safford, David, Junr.; Cambridge, WAS. See 2391.
6618. 6/11/93 mor Safford, David, Junr., farmer; Cambeidge, WAS; Cambridge,
WAS; mee 2673.   (A:415)
6619. 5/16/97 gee Safford, John; Canterbury, WIN, CT. See 2602.
6620. 5/4/95 mor Safford, Samuel; Salem, WAS; Salem, WAS; mee 4425. (C:233)
6621. 9/10/96 gee Safford, Samuel; Salem, WAS. See 2984.
6622. 9/10/96 mor Safford, Samuel (w. Anna); Salem, WAS; Salem, WAS; co-mees
2985, 6540, 7843. Co-mortgagees are all "executors of
the ... will of Joseph Tomb, late of Salem ..., physician,
deceased".   (B:91)
6623. 3/22/94 gor Sailly, Marie Ann. See 6636.
6624. 9/26/92 gee Sailly, Peter; Plattsburgh, CLI. See 2424.
6625. 1/3/93 mee Sailly, Peter; Plattsburgh, CLI. See 7763.
6626. 3/6/95 mor Sailly, Peter, merchant; ---, CLI; Plattsburgh, CLI;
mee 2176.   (A:151)
6627. 9/4/97 mor Sailly, Peter; Plattsburgh, CLI; Plattsburgh, CLI;
mee 2652.   (A:247)
6628. 2/2/00 mee Sailly, Peter, merchant; Plattsburgh, CLI. See 3138.
6629. 8/2/02 gor Sailly, Peter; Plattsburgh, CLI; Plattsburgh, CLI; gee 1126.
(B:354)
6630. 6/18/89 gee Sailly, Peter, Esq.; Plattsburgh, CLI. See 2429. (A:82)
6631. 7/7/91 gee Sailly, Peter, Esq.; Plattsburgh, CLI. See 2420.
6632. 9/20/91 mee Sailly, Peter, Esq.; Plattsburgh, CLI. See 255 and 7431.
6633. 10/17/92 gor Sailly, Peter, Esq.; Plattsburgh, CLI; ---, CLI; co-gors
5197, 8659; gee 5931.   (A:279)
6634. 3/5/93 mee Sailly, Peter, Esq.; Plattsburgh, CLI. See 7764.
6635. 5/4/93 gor Sailly, Peter, Esq.; Plattsburgh, CLI; ---, CLI; gee 5819.
(A:306)
6636. 3/22/94 gor Sailly, Peter, Esq. (w. Marie Ann); Plattsburgh, CLI;
Plattsburgh, CLI; gee 5821.   (A:329)
6637. 4/8/00 gee Sailly, Peter, Esq.; Plattsburgh, CLI. See 2493.
6638. 11/14/88 gee St. John, Ezra; Saratoga, ALB. See 4236.
6639. 5/2/96 gee Sampson, Levi, farmer; Argyle, WAS. See 2100a.
6640. 7/21/02 mor Sampson, Oliver; Granville, WAS; Granville, WAS; mee 4162.
(E:13)
6641. 1/2/98 mor Sanders, Hannah. See 6642.
6642. 1/2/98 mor Sanders, John (w. Hannah). See 6645.
6643. 1/2/98 mor Sanders, Lucy. See 6646.
6644. 1/2/98 mor Sanders, Martha. See 6645.
6645. 1/2/98 mor Sanders, Peter (w. Martha); Argyle, WAS; Argyle, WAS;
co-mors 6641, 6642; co-mees 770, 782, 787, 5555. (C:237)
6646. 1/2/98 mor Sanders, William (w. Lucy); Argyle, WAS; Argyle, WAS;
co-mees 770, 782, 791, 5555.   (C:236)
6647. 2/20/98 mor Sandford, Lydia. See 6648.
6648. 2/20/98 mor Sandford, Newton (w. Lydia), farmer; Hampton, WAS; Hampton,
WAS; mee 5969.   (C:253)
6649. 11/5/98 mor Sanford, David; Queensbury, WAS; Queensbury, WAS; mee 2523.
(C:258)
6650. 2/23/01 mor Sanford, Simeon, yeoman; Granville, WAS; ---, WAS; co-mees
5240, 8176.   (D:60b)
6651. 7/28/89 mor Santoir, Jacob; Willsborough, CLI; Willsborough, CLI;
mee 3492.   (A:40)
6652. 2/11/92 mor Santure, Jacob, yeoman; Willsborough, CLI; Judd Pat., CLI;
mee 49.   (A:89)
6653. 1/8/93 gee Sargent, Isaac; Westfield, WAS. See 4397.
6654. 3/5/96 gee Sargent, Isaac; Westfield, WAS. See 3432.
6655. 11/7/96 gee Sargent, Isaac; Westfield, WAS. See 1029.

6656.	12/9/96	gor	Sargent, Isaac; Westfield, WAS; Westfield, WAS; gee 254.
			(C-2:207)
6657.	7/1/97	gee	Sargent, Isaac; Westfield, WAS. See 7695.
6658.	10/1/01	mor	Saunders, Augustus; Queensbury, WAS; Queensbury, WAS;
			mee 3282. (D:104)
6659.	9/25/99	gee	Savage, David; Hartford, WAS. See 5088.
6660.	9/25/99	mor	Savage, David; Hartford, WAS; Champlain, CLI; mee 5089.
			(A:400)
6661.	4/12/00	gee	Savage, David, shoemaker; Champlain, CLI. See 5145.
6662.	8/11/01	gee	Savage, David, shoemaker; Champlain, CLI. See 1844.
6663.	4/1/02	gee	Savage, David; Champlain, CLI. See 986.
6664.	6/7/02	gee	Savage, David, farmer; Champlain, CLI. See 3382.
6665.	4/22/76	gor	Savage, Edward; New Perth, CHA; New Perth, CHA; gee 4771.
			(C-1:47)
6666.	5/18/79	gee	Savage, Edward; New Perth, CHA. See 4699.
6667.	1/1/85	gor	Savage, Edward; New Perth, WAS; New Perth, WAS; gee 2670.
			(B-1:148)
6668.	7/1/85	gee	Savage, Edward; ---, ---. See 7055.
6669.	7/8/85	mee	Savage, Edward; ---, ---. See 1364.
6670.	-/-/87	gee	Savage, Edward; ---, ---. See 6201.
6671.	4/26/90	gor	Savage, Edward; ---, ---; ---, WAS; gee 4715. (A:159)
6672.	6/18/92	gor	Savage, Edward; ---, ---. ---, WAS; gee 4717. (C-1:83)
6673.	4/19/94	mee	Savage, Edward; Salem, WAS. See 3428.
6674.	5/13/96	mee	Savage, Edward; Salem, WAS. See 3979, 8256, 8831.
6675.	3/1/90	gee	Savage, Edward, Esq.; Salem, WAS. See 3448.
6676.	6/8/91	gor	Savage, Edward, Esq.; Salem, WAS. See 8572.
6677.	12/29/96	mee	Savage, Edward, Esq.; Salem, WAS. See 2266.
6678.	10/17/97	mee	Savage, Edward, Esq.; Salem, WAS. See 3946.
6679.	11/19/83	gee	Savage, Jacob; ---, CHA. See 8546.
6680.	4/20/76	gee	Savage, James; New Perth, CHA. See 3785.
6681.	9/10/83	gee	Savage, James; White Creek, CHA. See 4398.
6682.	12/31/83	gee	Savage, James, Junr.; New Perth, CHA. See 6684.
6683.	-/-/70	gee	Savage, John, Capt.; "New Perth on White Creek", ALB.
			See 1792.
6684.	12/31/83	gor	Savage, John, Senr.; New Perth, CHA; ---, CHA; gee 6682.
			(A:122)
6685.	2/11/96	gor	Savage, Martha. See 6692.
6686.	2/8/98	mor	Savage, Mary. See 6688.
6687.	8/23/94	gor	Savage, Phebe. See 6690.
6688.	2/8/98	mor	Savage, Reuben (w. Mary), farmer; Hartford, WAS; Hartford,
			WAS; mee 1483. (B:322)
6689.	11/5/87	mor	Savage, Rogers, yeoman; ---, WAS; Argyle, WAS; mee 5187.
			(A:66)
6690.	8/23/94	gor	Savage, Rogers (w. Phebe); Argyle, WAS; Argyle, WAS;
			gee 228. (C-2:235)
6691.	2/15/91	gor	Savage, Thomas More; City of N.Y. See 2729.
6692.	2/11/96	gor	Savage, William (w. Martha); Kingsbury, WAS; Kingsbury, WAS;
			gee 5509. (C-2:157)
6693.	4/2/95	mor	Savidge, David; ---, WAS. See 6694.
6694.	4/2/95	mor	Savidge, William; ---, WAS; Kingsbury, WAS; co-mor 6693;
			mee 648. (B:19)
6695.	11/5/87	gee	Savige, Rogers; Argyle, WAS. See 5186.
6696.	4/1/96	mor	Sawin, George; Cambridge, WAS; Cambridge, WAS; mee 5533.
			(C:257)
6697.	2/22/98	mor	Sawyer, John, "yeoman or merchant"; Hartford, WAS;
			Hartford, WAS; mee 5539. (C:254)
6698.	7/27/89	gee	Sawyer, Joseph; Charlotte, CHI, VT. See 3481.
6699.	7/27/89	mor	Sawyer, Joseph; Charlotte, CHI, VT; Willsborough, CLI;
			mee 3490. (A:22)
6700.	6/1/84	gee	Sawyer, Moses; Granville, WAS. See 8514.
6701.	6/1/84	gor	Sawyer, Moses; Granville, WAS; Granville, WAS; gee 8410.
			(B-1:121)
6702.	12/2/89	gee	Schamp, George; Salem, WAS. See 8570.
6703.	3/8/98	mee	Schamp, George; Salem, WAS. See 6589 and 6590.
6704.	3/10/85	mor	Schaw, Daniel (w. Sarah); City of N.Y.; Argyle, WAS; mee 4611.
			(A:72)
6705.	3/10/85	mor	Schaw, Sarah. See 6704.

6706. 10/23/95 gor Schermerhorn, Barnardus Freeman; Schenectady, ALB;
                    Quashicook, WAS; gee 1380.   (E:34)
6707. 11/8/91 gor Schermerhorn, Jacob; Schenectady, ALB; ---, WAS; gee 3217.
                                                                  (B-2:359)
6708. 11/9/91 mee Schermerhorn, Jacob; Schenectady, ALB. See 3220.
6709. 1/4/98   gor Schermerhorn, Jacob, farmer; Schenectady, ALB; Cambridge,
                    Dist., WAS; gee 6895.   (D:283)
6710. 8/15/98 mee Schermerhorn, Jacob; Schenectady, ALB. See 3605.
6711. 6/17/94 gor Schermerhorn, Jeremiah (w. Nancy), gentleman; Schenectady,
                    ALB; Cambridge, WAS; gee 421.   (E:293)
6712. 6/17/94 gor Schermerhorn, Nancy. See 6711.
6713. 4/22/84 gor Schermerhorn, Ryer; Schenectady, ALB; land "along the
                    Batten Kill", WAS; gee 3955.   (F:65)
6714. 12/30/93 gor Schneider, George, "late of the City of New York, ... a
                    reduced subaltern officer but now of Gleidsburg ...
                    Germany", gentleman; Cockroft Pat., WAS; gee 1987.
                                                                  (B-2:255)
6715. 1/24/94 gor Schneider, George, gentleman; "Gleiberg, Germany"; Cockroft
                    Pat., WAS; gee 1988.   (B-2:257)
6716. 5/26/74 gee Schult, Casparus, farmer; Manor of Livingston, ALB. See 6367.
6717. 3/7/85   gee Schult, Casparus, farmer; ---, ALB. See 6723.
6718. 5/7/85   gee Schult, Casparus, farmer; ---, ALB. See 4000.
6719. 3/12/98 gor Schump, George, saddler; Salem, WAS; Salem, WAS; co-gees
                    7541, 7543.   (E:315)
6720. 9/23/85 --- Schuyler, Adonia. See 6734.
6721. 3/7/85   gor Schuyler, Ann, "heir of Elizabeth Campbell late of the
                    City of New York, deceased". See 6723.
6722. 9/23/85 gor Schuyler, Arent I. (w. Swan); New Barbadoes Neck, BER, NJ;
                    Hoosick Pat., ALB; gee 8032.   (C-2:8)
6723. 3/7/85   gor Schuyler, Cathalina, "heir of Elizabeth Campbell late of the
                    City of New York, deceased"; ---, ---; Argyle, WAS;
                    co-gor 6721; gee 6717.   (B-1:204)
6724. 4/26/68 gor Schuyler, Catherine. See 6730.
6725. 4/26/68 gor Schuyler, Cortlandt, Capt; Albany, ALB. See 6730.
6726. 9/23/85 --- Schuyler, Gertrude. See 6734.
6727. 9/29/85 gor Schuyler, John (w. Mary); Bardoes Neck, BER, NJ; Hoosick
                    Pat., ALB (sic); gee 569.   (WAS Co. B-2:519)
6728. 7/5/02   gor Schuyler, Lena. See 6733.
6729. 9/25/85 gor Schuyler, Mary. See 6727.
6730. 4/26/68 gor Schuyler, Philip, Esq. (w. Catharine); Albany, ALB; Saratoga,
                    ALB; co-gors 1511, 1512, 6725; co-gees 560, 572.
                                                      (WAS Co. B-2:289)
6731. 4/10/90 gor Schuyler, Philip, Esq.; Albany, ALB; Plattsburgh, CLI;
                    gee 4183.   (B:50)
6732. 7/5/93   gor Schuyler, Philip, the Honorable, Esq.; Albany, ALB; land
                    "between Ticonderoga and Crown Point", CLI; co-gees
                    1933, 1935, 5307. Co-grantees are all "children, heirs,
                    and devisers of Samuel Deall late of the City of New
                    York, merchant, deceased".   (A:415)
6733. 7/5/02   gor Schuyler, Stephen T. (w. Lena), gentleman, Troy, REN; John
                    Schuyler, Junior's Pat., WAS; gee 7260.   (F:272)
6734. 9/23/85 gor Schuyler, Swan(?), "daughter of Adonia Schuyler and Gertrude
                    his wife". See 6722.
6735. 4/1/02   mor Scot, Abraham (w. Prudence), farmer; Hebron, WAS; Hebron, WAS;
                    mee 5229.   (E:35)
6736. 3/5/95   gee Scot, Benjamin; Cambridge, WAS. See 5410.
6737. 6/15/92 gor Scot, Helena, widow of John Morin Scot, dec'd.; ---, ---;
                    Hebron, WAS; co-gors 4623, 4640, 6817; gee 4386. (A:322)
6738. 6/15/92 gor Scot, John Morin, Esq., dec'd. See 6737.
6739. 4/1/02   mor Scot, Prudence. See 6735.
6740. 10/3/96 gee Scott, Aaron; Willsborough, CLI. See 5936.
6741. 9/3/02   gee Scott, Aaron; Cornwall, ADD, VT. See 8225.
6742. 9/3/02   mor Scott, Aaron; ---, ---; Willsborough, ESS; mee 8226. (A:88)
6743. 10/20/00 gee Scott, Asahel M.; Cambridge, WAS. See 140.
6744. 10/3/96 gee Scott, Ebor; Willsborough, CLI. See 5936.
6745. 12/14/80 mee Scott, Helena; ---, ---. See 3572.

6746. 4/2/86 gor Scott, Helena, "widow and executor of the estate of John
Morin Scott"; City of N.Y.; Argyle, WAS; co-gors 4613,
4630, 6805; gee 6273.   (A:136)
6747. 6/7/86 mee Scott, Helena; ---, ---. See 4953.
6748. 12/14/87 mee Scott, Helena; ---, ---. See 7191.
6749. 5/8/89 mee Scott, Helena. See 3648.
6750. 6/6/89 mee Scott, Helena; ---, ---. See 682.
6751. 6/25/89 gor Scott, Helena; ---, ---; Hebron, WAS; co-gors 4618, 4635,
6814; gee 2517. Grantors are all heirs of "the Hon.
John Morine Scott, Esq.", dec'd.   (A:302)
6752. 10/7/90 mee Scott, Helena; ---, ---. See 1365.
6753. 5/3/91 mee Scott, Helena, widow of John Morine Scott, dec'd.; ---, ---.
See 3547.
6754. 5/28/92 gor Scott, Helena, widow of John Morin Scott; City of N.Y.;
Hebron, WAS; co-gors 4621, 4638, 6815; gee 3704. (A:305)
6755. 6/14/92 gor Scott, Helena, widow of John Morin Scott, Esq., dec'd.;
City of N.Y.; Argyle, WAS; co-gors 4622, 4639, 6816;
gee 6380. Grantors are all executors of the estate of
John Morin Scott, Esq., dec'd.   (C-1:69)
6756. 6/15/92 gor Scott, Helena, widow of John Morin Scott, Esq., dec'd.;
---, ---; Hebron, WAS; co-gors 4623, 4640, 6817; gee 2514.
"Grantors are all executors of John Morin Scott, Esq., dec'd."
(C-1:71)
6757. 5/8/93 gor Scott, Helena, widow of John Morin Scott, Esq., dec'd.;
City of N.Y.; Argyle, WAS; co-gors 4641, 6818, 8103;
co-gees 2855, 4701, 7619, 8021.   Grantors are all
"executors of the late John Morin Scott", dec'd. (B-2:299)
6758. 5/8/93 mee Scott, Helena; ---, ---. See 7620.
6759. 7/2/94 gor Scott, Helena; City of N.Y.; Hebron, WAS; co-gors 4643, 6819;
gee 2647. Grantors are all executors of the estate of
John Morin Scott, Esq., dec'd.   (B-2:226)
6760. 7/2/94 mee Scott, Helena; City of N.Y. See 2648.
6761. 6/13/95 gor Scott, Helena, widow of John Morin Scott, dec'd.; City of N.Y.
See 6820.
6762. 2/9/96 gor Scott, Helena, "now Helena Myers"; City of N.Y. See 6821.
6763. 2/9/96 mee Scott, Helena, "now Helena Myers"; City of N.Y. See 2273,
4500, and 5619. (three contracts)
6764. 6/18/96 gor Scott, Helena, "now Helena Myers"; City of N.Y.; Hebron, WAS;
co-gors ("by their attorney Alexander Webster, Esq.")
4648, 6828, 8107; gee 2671. Grantors are all executors
of the estate of John Morin Scott, Esq., dec'd. (F:124)
6765. 7/8/97 mee Scott, Helena, widow of John Morin Scott, dec'd.; City of N.Y.
See 8015.
6766. 11/28/98 mee Scott, Helena, widow of John Morin Scott, Esq., dec;d;
City of N.Y. See 8643.
6767. 12/1/99 --- Scott, Helena, dec'd., "late Helena Myer"). See 8111.
6768. 2/18/02 --- Scott, Helena, dec'd, "late Helena Myer"). See 8117.
6769. 7/1/85 gee Scott, John; ---, ---. See 7055.
6770. 7/1/85 mor Scott, John; ---, ---; Skenesborough, WAS; mee 8555.
(Deed Book B-1:226)
6771. 4/14/75 mee Scott, John Morin, attorney; City of N.Y. See 3429.
6772. 4/2/86 --- Scott, John Morin, dec'd. See 6746.
6773. 6/7/86 --- Scott, John Morin, dec'd. See 4953.
6774. 12/14/87 mee Scott, John Morin, dec'd.; City of N.Y. ("executors" of his
estate are the "mortgagee"). See 7188.
6774a. 6/6/89 --- Scott, John Morin, dec'd. See 2349a.
6775. 5/28/92 --- Scott, John Morin, dec'd. See 6754.
6776. 12/23/95 mee Scott, John Morin, dec'd, "executors of". See 8320.
6777. 12/14/87 mee Scott, John Morin, Esq., dec'd, "executors of". See 7136.
6778. 11/29/91 --- Scott, John Morin, Esq., dec'd. See 6191.
6779. 6/14/92 --- Scott, John Morin, Esq., dec'd. See 6755.
6780. 6/15/92 --- Scott, John Morin, Esq., dec'd.; ---, ---. See 6756.
6781. 6/15/92 mee Scott, John Morin, Esq., dec'd., executors of the estate of.
See 6381.
6782. 7/5/92 mee Scott, John Morin, Esq., dec'd., executors of the estate of.
See 7308.

6783. 7/2/94 --- Scott, John Morin, Esq., dec'd.; ---, ---. See 2648, 6759.
6784. 6/13/95 --- Scott, John Morin, Esq., dec'd. See 6820.
6785. 2/9/96 --- Scott, John Morin, Esq., dec'd. See 2273, 4500, 5619, 6821.
6786. 6/18/96 --- Scott, John Morin, Esq., dec'd. See 6764.
6787. 12/13/96 --- Scott, John Morin, Esq., dec'd. See 2351.
6788. 12/18/96 --- Scott, John Morin, Esq., dec'd.; City of N.Y. See 6810.
6789. 2/1/97 --- Scott, John Morin, Esq., dec'd. See 8276.
6790. 11/28/98 --- Scott, John Morin, Esq., dec'd. See 8643.
6791. 11/29/99 --- Scott, John Morin, Esq., dec'd. See 6179 and 8110.
6792. 12/1/99 --- Scott, John Morin, Esq., dec'd. See 8111.
6793. 12/2/99 --- Scott, John Morin, Esq., dec'd. See 6107 and 8112.
6794. 12/10/99 --- Scott, John Morin, Esq., dec'd. See 8114.
6795. 12/18/99 --- Scott, John Morin, Esq., dec'd. See 8115.
6796. 12/28/99 --- Scott, John Morin, Esq., dec'd. See 5323.
6797. 2/18/02 --- Scott, John Morin, Esq., dec'd. See 8117.
6798. 12/14/87 --- Scott, John Morine, dec'd.; ---, ---. See 7191.
6799. 10/7/90 --- Scott, John Morine, The Hon., dec'd.; ---, ---. See 1365.
6800. 5/3/91 --- Scott, John Morine, dec'd.; ---, ---. See 3547.
6801. 12/22/91 --- Scott, John Morine, dec'd.; ---, ---. See 3548.
6802. 6/25/89 --- Scott, John Morine, Esq., dec'd. See 6751.
6803. 11/29/91 gor Scott, John Morine, Esq., dec'd., executors of (not named);
---, ---; Hebron, WAS; gee 6190.   (B-2:91)
6804. 7/8/97 --- Scott, John Morine, Esq., dec'd. See 8015.
6805. 4/2/86 gor Scott, Lewis A.; City of N.Y. See 6746.
6806. 6/7/86 mee Scott, Lewis A.; ---, ---. See 4953.
6807. 12/14/87 mee Scott, Lewis A.; ---, ---. See 7191.
6808. 5/8/93 mee Scott, Lewis A.; ---, ---. See 7620.
6809. 7/2/94 mee Scott, Lewis A.; City of N.Y. See 2648.
6810. 12/18/96 gor Scott, Lewis A.; ---, ---; Hebron, WAS; co-gors 5253, 8108;
gee 3096. Grantors are all executors of the estate of
John Morin Scott, Esq., dec'd.   (F:127)
6811. 12/14/80 mee Scott, Lewis A., Esq.; ---, ---. See 3572.
6812. 5/8/89 mee Scott, Lewis A., Esq. See 3648.
6813. 6/6/89 mee Scott, Lewis A., Esq. See 682.
6814. 6/25/89 gor Scott, Lewis A., Esq. See 6751.
6815. 5/28/92 gor Scott, Lewis A., Esq.; City of N.Y. See 6754.
6816. 6/14/92 gor Scott, Lewis A., Esq.; City of N.Y. See 6755.
6817. 6/15/92 gor Scott, Lewis A., Esq.; City of N.Y. See 6737 and 6756.
6818. 5/8/93 gor Scott, Lewis A., Esq.; City of N.Y. See 6757.
6819. 7/2/94 gor Scott, Lewis A., Esq.; City of N.Y. See 6759.
6820. 6/13/95 gor Scott, Lewis A., Esq.; City of N.Y.; Hebron, WAS; co-gors
6761, 8104 ; gee 7714. Grantors are all executors of the
estate of John Morin Scott, Esq., dec'd.   (D:214)
6821. 2/9/96 gor Scott, Lewis A., Esq.; City of N.Y.; Argyle, WAS; co-gors
4645, 6762, 8105; gee 4499. Grantors are all executors
of the estate of John Morin Scott, Esq., dec'd. (C-2:298)
6822. 2/9/96 mee Scott, Lewis A., Esq.; City of N.Y. See 2273, 4500, 5619.
6823. 7/8/97 mee Scott, Lewis A., Esq.; City of N.Y. See 8015.
6824. 11/28/98 mee Scott, Lewis A., Esq.; City of N.Y. See 8643.
6825. Data repositioned.
6826. 10/7/90 mee Scott, Lewis Allair, Esq.; ---, ---. See 1365.
6827. 5/3/91 mee Scott, Lewis Allair, Esq.; ---, ---. See 3547.
6828. 6/18/96 gor Scott, Lewis Allair, Esq.; City of N.Y. See 6764.
6829. 12/1/99 --- Scott, Lewis Allaire, Esq., dec'd. See 8111.
6830. 2/18/02 --- Scott, Lewis Allaire, Esq., dec'd. See 8117.
6831. Data repositioned.
6832. 3/22/91 mor Scott, Mathew, merchant; Hillsdale, COL; Whitehall, WAS;
mee 8523.   (A:297)
6833. 9/10/75 gor Scott, Matthew; Hillsdale, COL; Whitehall, WAS; gee 7498.
(C-2:85)
6834. 9/22/96 gee Scott, Paul, blacksmith; Granville, WAS. See 3765.
6835. 9/23/96 mor Scott, Paul; Granville, WAS; Granville, WAS; mee 3767. (B:113)
6836. 5/20/95 mor Scriver, Frederick, farmer; Christie's Manor, Lower Canada.
See 5353.
6837. 8/10/87 mor Seaman, Walter; Bedford, WES; Indian Purchase, WAS; mee 8254.
(A:65)

6838. 5/10/97 mee Seaman, Willet; City of N.Y. See 6350.
6839. 4/15/01 gee Seamans, Stephen; ---, ---. See 2132.
6840. 7/1/85 mor Searl, Gedon; Skenesborough, WAS; Skenesborough, WAS;
                mee 8555.   (Deed Book B-1;224)
6841. 7/1/85 mor Searl, Gideon, Junr.; ---, ---; Skenesborough, WAS;
                mee 8555.   (Deed Book B-1;228)
6842. 9/4/97 mor Searls, Abigail, seamstress; Salem, WAS; Salem, WAS;
                mee 3655.   (C;210)
6843. 7/1/85 gee Searls, Gideon; ---, ---. See 7055.
6844. 7/1/85 gee Searls, Gideon, Junr.; ---, ---. See 7055.
6845. 1/25/86 gee Sears, Stephen; ---, LIT, CT. See 8234.
6846. 4/29/00 mee Sebor, Jacob, merchant; City of N.Y. See 6388.
6847. 1/2/96 gee Sebring, Isaac, merchant; City of N.Y. See 5822.
6848. 6/24/97 --- Sebring, Isaac, merchant; City of N.Y.; ---, CLI; co-persons
                265 and 8079. These three persons, this date, appoint
                William Bailey to be their attorney for the division of
                their jointly-held lands in Clinton County.   (B;86)
6849. 10/26/97 gee Sebring, Isaac, merchant; City of N.Y. See 5825.
6850. 10/26/97 gor Sebring, Isaac, merchant; City of N.Y. See 334.
6850a. 10/26/97 gor Sebring, Isaac, merchant; City of N.Y. See 5824.
6851. 11/24/97 --- Sebring, Isaac, merchant; City of N.Y.; Old Military
                Townships 6 and 7 (Clinton and Chateaugay), CLI; co-person
                8082. These two persons this date appoint William Bailey,
                Esq. of Plattsburgh (CLI) as their attorney to sell the
                above lands.   (B;118)
6852. 3/1/98 gor Sebring, Isaac, merchant; City of N.Y.; James Caldwell Pat.,
                CLI; co-gor 8083; gee 6352.   (B;112)
6853. 3/1/98 mee Sebring, Isaac, merchant; City of N.Y. See 4108.
6854. 3/2/98 mee Sebring, Isaac, merchant; City of N.Y. See 621, 1342, 6353.
6855. 3/3/98 mee Sebring, Isaac, merchant; City of N.Y. See 5233.
6856. 6/7/98 gee Sebring, Isaac, merchant; City of N.Y. See 7570.
6857. 6/8/98 mor Sebring, Isaac (w. Jane), merchant; City of N.Y.; ---, CLI;
                co-mors 8073, 8089; mee 7571. Two contracts this date
                involving these persons.   (A;305), (A;306)
6858. 8/7/98 mee Sebring, Isaac; City of N.Y. See 3067.
6859. 8/15/98 gor Sebring, Isaac, merchant; City of N.Y.; Old Military Township
                #7 (Chateaugay), CLI; co-gor 8091; gee 3068.   (B;257)
6860. 8/16/98 mee Sebring, Isaac; City of N.Y. See 2279, 3069, 7493.
6861. 10/20/98 mee Sebring, Isaac; ---, ---. See 3252.
6862. 11/17/98 mee Sebring, Isaac; ---, ---. See 2091.
6863. 12/22/98 mee Sebring, Isaac, merchant; City of N.Y. See 3215.
6864. 4/10/99 mee Sebring, Isaac; City of N.Y. See 6199.
6865. 5/16/01 mee Sebring, Isaac, merchant; City of N.Y. See 688.
6866. 12/-/01 mee Sebring, Isaac; City of N.Y. See 898.
6867. 6/8/98 mor Sebring, Jane. See 6857. (two contracts)
6868. 9/26/01 mee Seelye, Benjamin; Kingsbury, WAS. See 5362.
6869. 10/14/95 mor Seelye, Lewis (w. Desire); Kingsbury, WAS; Kingsbury, WAS;
                mee 3008.   (A;608)
6870. 1/29/78 gor Seley, Abel; New Fairfield, FAI, CT; Queensbury, CHA;
                co-gors 6871, 6872, 6873, 8834, 8835; gee 6874. (C-1;40)
6871. 1/29/78 gor Seley, Benjamin; New Milford, LIT, CT. See 6870.
6872. 1/29/78 gor Seley, Bradley; New Fairfield, FAI, CT. See 6870.
6873. 1/29/78 gor Seley, Nathaniel; New Fairfield, FAI, CT. See 6870.
6874. 1/29/74 gee Seley, Nehemiah; Queensbury, CHA. See 6870.
6875. 3/20/99 gor Selfridge, Edward (w. Elizabeth); Hebron, WAS. See 6881.
6876. 3/20/99 gor Selfridge, Elizabeth. See 6875.
6877. 3/20/99 gor Selfridge, Mary. See 6881.
6878. 11/21/91 gee Selfridge, William, yeoman; Cambridge, WAS. See 4559.
6879. 11/24/91 mor Selfridge, William, yeoman; Cambridge, WAS; Hebron, WAS;
                mee 4560.   (A;309)
6880. 8/3/96 mor Selfridge, William, yeoman; Hebron, WAS; Hebron, WAS;
                mee 8591.   (B;76)
6881. 3/20/99 gor Selfridge, William (w. Mary); Hebron, WAS; Hebron, WAS;
                co-gors 6875, 6876; gee 6426.   (D;347)
6882. 5/19/98 gor Service, Elizabeth, "widow of William Kinlock, late of
                Boston (MA), mariner, deceased. See 6883.

164

6883. 5/19/98 gor Service, Robert (w. Elizabeth); Finnsbury Square, London,
England; Argyle, WAS; gee 3916.   (E:6)
6884. 6/1/98 mee Service, Thomas, merchant; City of N.Y. See 3931.
6885. 12/8/02 mee Service, Thomas, merchant; City of N.Y. See 7481.
6886. 11/24/02 mee Service, Thomas, merchant; City of N.Y. See 4604.
6887. 12/22/02 mee Service, Thomas, merchant; City of N.Y. See 3932.
6888. 4/2/91 mee Seton, William, merchant; City of N.Y. See 4215.
6889. 7/26/93 gor Seton, William, merchant; City of N.Y.; William Cockroft
Pat., WAS; gee 7632. Grantor is executor of the estate
of Peter Middleton, physician, "late of the City of New
York, deceased".   (F:159)
6890. 5/31/96 gor Seton, William, "executor of the estate of Peter Middleton
late of the City of New York, deceased"; ---, ---;
Scotch Pat., WAS; gee 4321.   (C-2:264)
6891. 11/23/97 gor Seton, William, exec. of the est. of Peter Middleton, dec'd.;
City of N.Y.; Argyle Pat., WAS; gee 7484.   (D:225)
6892. 7/3/95 gor Seton, William, Esq., exec. of the est. of Peter Middleton
late of the City of N.Y., dec'd.; City of N.Y.; Provincial
Pat., WAS; gee 1171.   (B-2:453)
6893. 11/17/84 gee Shadforth, Thomas, grandfather of "Miss Anne Gilliland";
Janesborough, WAS. See 2786.
6894. 7/10/90 mor Shapley, Richard; Hebron, WAS; Hebron, WAS; mee 1072. (A:266)
6895. 1/4/98 gee Sharp, Cornelious; Cambridge, WAS. See 6709.
6896. 2/9/96 gee Sharpe, Cornelius; Cambridge, WAS. See 7997.
6897. 9/6/96 gee Shaver, George; Peru, CLI. See 537.
6898. 4/15/91 mor Shaw, Alexander; ---, ---; Argyle, WAS; mee 6237. (A:293)
6899. 6/24/67 gee Shaw, David, merchant; City of N.Y. See 1202.
6900. 5/10/91 --- Shaw, Devid, merchant; ---, ---. See 2124.
6901. 3/21/65 gee Shaw, Duncan, ropemaker; City of N.Y. See 6232.
6902. 8/5/93 gee Shaw, Duncan; ---, WAS. See 8821.
6903. 6/7/99 gee Shaw, James, yeoman; Argyle, WAS. See 4946.
6904. 6/7/99 mor Shaw, James, yeoman; Argyle, WAS; Argyle, WAS; mee 4947.
                                                     (C:229)
6905. 9/6/99 gor Shaw, James, merchant; Argyle, WAS; Argyle, WAS; gee 1272.
                                                     (E:70)
6906. 1/15/65 gee Shaw, John, Junr., "son of Neal Shaw ropemaker in New York".
See 6219.
6907. 3/13/89 gee Shaw, Joseph; ---, WAS. See 125.
6908. 1/15/65 --- Shaw, Neal. See 6906.
6909. 6/5/92 gee Shaw, William; ---, ---, RI. See 8001.
6910. 3/15/99 mor Shearer, James; Cambridge, WAS; Cambridge, WAS; co-mees
4382, 8862. Mortgagees are executors of the estate of
"John Adams late of Cambridge, deceased".   (C:263)
6911. 6/16/98 mor Shearman, Christopher; ---, WAS; Hartford, WAS; mee 935.
                                                     (C:255)
6912. 10/28/97 gor Shearman, Ebenezer (w. Mercy), yeoman; Cambridge Dist.,
WAS; Cambridge Dist., WAS; gee 167.   (D:66)
6913. 11/12/01 gee Shearman, Joseph, yeoman; Cambridge, WAS. See 6156.
6914. 10/28/97 gor Shearman, Mercy. See 6912.
6915. 2/1/96 gee Shearman, Oliver, house carpenter; Cambridge, WAS. See 6152.
6916. 2/10/02 mee Shearman, Roland; ---, ---. See 2760.
6917. 1/4/94 gee Shearman, Stephen; Cambridge, WAS. See 4416.
6918. 10/14/89 gee Shelden, Daniel; Willsborough, CLI. See 6927.
6919. 4/10/99 gee Shelden, Daniel; Willsborough, ESS. See 6493.
6920. 11/6/89 gee Shelden, Edmond; Willsborough, CLI. See 6444.
6921. 11/6/89 mor Shelden, Edmond; Willsborough, CLI; Willsborough, CLI;
mee 6445.   (A:36)
6922. 10/17/89 gee Shelden, Isaac; Pawling, DUT. See 6441.
6923. 10/17/89 mor Shelden, Isaac; Pawling, DUT; Willsborough, CLI; mee 6442.
                                                     (A:33)
6924. 10/17/89 mor Shelden, Isaac, Junr.; Pawling, DUT; Willsborough, CLI;
mee 6442.   (A:34)
6925. 12/19/82 gee Shelden, John, yeoman; Cambridge, ALB. See 891.
6926. 6/18/83 gor Shelden, John, yeoman; Cambridge, ALB; Kingsbury, CHA;
co-gees 8502, 8507.   (B-2:507)

6927. 10/14/89 gor Shelden, Joseph, yeoman; Willsborough, CLI; Willsborough,
                          CLI; gee 6918.   (A:112)
6928. 8/10/97 gee Shelden, Joseph; Willsborough, CLI. See 3473.
6929. 8/11/97 gor Shelden, Joseph (w. Ruth); Willsborough, CLI; Willsborough,
                          CLI; gee 3465.   (A:16)
6930. 7/17/98 gee Shelden, Joseph; Willsborough, CLI. See 3474.
6931. 7/18/98 gor Shelden, Joseph (w. Ruth); Willsborough, CLI; Willsborough,
                          CLI; gee 3611 (A:18); gee 3614 (A:19). (two contracts)
6932. 10/16/97 gee Shelden, Luther; Pawling, DUT. See 6505.
6933. 7/6/88 mor Shelden, Reuben; ---, ---; Granville, WAS; mee 2380. (A:138)
6934. 8/11/97 gor Shelden, Ruth. See 6929.
6935. 7/18/98 gor Shelden, Ruth. See 6931. (two contracts)
6936. 5/14/98 gee Shelden, Samuel; Argyle, WAS. See 7358.
6937. 10/7/89 gee Shelden, Winter; Clinton, DUT. See 6437.
6938. --/--/89 mor Shelden, Winton; Clinton, DUT; Willsborough, CLI; mee 6434.
                                                                     (A:27)
6939. 8/19/97 gor Sheldon, John; Rupert, BEN, VT; Peru, CLI; gee 6943. (B:167)
6940. 1/20/84 gee Sheldon, Joseph, gentleman; Dover, DUT. See 2785.
6941. 7/4/96 gee Sheldon, Samuel, farmer; Easton, WAS. See 4010.
6942. 4/27/01 mee Sheldon, Samuel; Easton, WAS. See 8481.
6943. 8/19/97 gee Sheldon, Thaddeus; Peru, CLI. See 6939.
6944. 10/6/89 mor Sheldon, Timothy; Clinton, DUT; Willsborough, CLI; mee 6436.
                                                                     (A:27)
6945. 3/13/98 mor Shelly, Aaron (w. Lorana); ---, WAS; Hartford, WAS; mee 928.
                                                                     (C:255)
6946. 8/22/99 gor Shelly, Aaron (w. Lorany), yeoman; Hartford, WAS; Hartford,
                          WAS; gee 8368.   (E:239)
6947. 12/6/00 gor Shelly, Aaron (w. Lorany), farmer; Hartford, WAS; Hartford,
                          WAS; gee 3300.   (E:65)
6948. 5/5/01 mee Shelly, Alexander, Senr.; Cambridge, WAS. See 1159.
6949. 3/13/98 mor Shelly, Lorana. See 6945.
6950. 8/22/99 gor Shelly, Lorany. See 6946.
6951. 12/6/00 gor Shelly, Lorany. See 6947.
6952. 4/13/98 gor Shepard, Anna. See 6956.
6953. 10/28/97 mor Shepard, Edward, yeoman; Hebron, WAS; Hebron, WAS; mee
                          8600.   (B:221)
6954. 7/25/92 mor Shepard, John, Junr., yeoman; Hebron, WAS; Hebron, WAS;
                          mee 6984.   (A:381)
6955. 5/3/97 mor Shepard, John, Junr., yeoman; Hebron, WAS; Hebron, WAS;
                          mee 8598.   (B:165)
6956. 4/13/98 gor Shepard, John, Junr. (w. Anna), yeoman; Hebron, WAS;
                          Hebron, WAS; gee 6002.   (D:191)
6957. 9/17/96 gor Shepard, Silas; Hebron, WAS; Hebron, WAS; gee 4255. (C-2:227)
6958. 5/3/97 mor Shepard, Silas, yeoman; Hebron, WAS; Hebron, WAS; mee 8598.
                                                                     (B:162)
6959. 2/15/02 gor Shepard, Zebulon R.; Granville, WAS; Granville, WAS;
                          gee 3404.   (F:185)
6960. 11/3/97 mor Sheperd, Jonathan, farmer; ---, RUT, VT; Canadian and Nova
                          Scotia Refugees' Township #7 (Chateaugay), CLI; co-mor
                          6961; mee 5691.   (A:240)
6961. 11/3/97 mor Sheperd, Ralph, farmer; ---, CHI, VT. See 6960.
6962. 5/3/97 mor Shepheard, Edward, yeoman; Hebron, WAS; Hebron, WAS; mee
                          8598.   (B:167)
6963. 5/3/97 mor Shepheard, Turner, yeoman; Hebron, WAS; Hebron, WAS;
                          mee 8598.   (B:164)
6964. 12/10/90 gee Shepherd, Bohan, farmer; Hebron, WAS. See 6970.
6965. 12/10/90 mee Shepherd, Bohan; Hebron, WAS. See 6971.
6966. 12/10/90 gee Shepherd, Edward, farmer; Hebron, WAS. See 6970.
6967. 12/10/90 mee Shepherd, Edward; Hebron, WAS. See 6971.
6968. 7/22/90 gee Shepherd, John; Hebron, WAS. See 6986.
6969. 7/22/90 mor Shepherd, John; Hebron, WAS; Sheriff's Pat. "in Hebron",
                          WAS; mee 6977.   (A:246)
6970. 12/10/90 gor Shepherd, John, farmer; Hebron, WAS; Hebron, WAS; co-gees
                          6964, 6966.   (A:171)
6971. 12/10/90 mor Shepherd, John; Hebron, WAS; personal property?; co-mees
                          6965, 6967.   (A:263)

166

6972. 11/12/92 gor Shepherd, John, Junr.; ---, ---; Hebron, WAS; gee 5430.
(B-2:535)
6973. 7/22/90 mor Shepherd, Silas; Hebron, WAS; Hebron, WAS; mee 6976. (A:230)
6974. 8/16/92 mor Shepherd, Silas, yeoman; Hebron, WAS; Hebron, WAS; mee
6985.
(A:382)
6975. 8/24/90 mor Shepherd, William; Hebron, WAS; Hebron, WAS; mee 6979.
(A:249)
6976. 7/22/90 mee Shereiff, William, Colonel; ---, ---. See 6973.
6977. 7/22/90 mee Shereiff, William, Colonel; "Kingdom of Great Britain".
See 6969.
6978. 8/24/90 mee Shereiff, William, Colonel; ---, ---. See 1905, 3512,
7189, 7573, 8177, 8494.
6979. 8/24/90 mee Shereiff, William, Colonel; "Kingdom of Great Britain".
See 6975.
6980. 9/2/90 mee Shereiff, William, Colonel; "Kingdom of Great Britain".
See 611.
6981. 9/30/90 mee Shereiff, William, Colonel; "Kingdom of Great Britain".
See 1394 and 2738.
6982. 7/15/91 mee Shereiff, William, Colonel; ---, ---. See 2094.
6983. 7/15/91 mee Shereiff, William, Colonel; "Kingdom of Great Britain".
See 5027.
6984. 7/25/92 mee Shereiff, William, Colonel; "Kingdom of Great Britain".
See 6954.
6985. 8/16/92 mee Shereiff, William, Colonel; "Kingdom of Great Britain".
See 6974.
6986. 7/22/90 gor Shereiff, William, Colonel, Esq., gentleman; ---, ---;
Hebron, WAS; gee 6968.
(A:258)
6987. 9/2/90 gor Shereiff, William, Colonel, Esq.; ---, ---; Shereiff's
Pat., WAS; gee 612.
(B-2:496)
6988. 12/13/91 mor Sherer, William, farmer; Hebron, WAS; Hebron, WAS;
mee 8294.
(A:369)
6989. 7/22/92 mee Sheriff, William, Colonel; "Kingdom of Great Britain".
See 3504.
6990. 6/7/92 mee Sheriff, William, Esq.; "Kingdom of Great Britain".
See 2703.
6991. 11/18/01 gee Sheril, Recompence; Easthampton, SUF. See 7003.
6992. 6/-/98 mor Sherman, Abraham (w. Amy); ---, WAS; Hartford, WAS;
mee 934.
(C:256)
6993. 6/-/98 mor Sherman, Amy. See 6992.
6994. 10/1/85 gor Sherman, Fortunatus; Cambridge, WAS; Cambridge, WAS;
gee 6468.
(D:402)
6995. 6/22/91 gor Sherman, Fortunatus; ---, ---. See 8450.
6996. 7/14/01 mee Sherman, Josiah; ---, ---. See 2087.
6997. 8/24/90 mee Sherriff, William, Colonel; "Kingdom of Great Britain".
see 5053 and 7320.
6998. 8/24/90 gor Sherriff, William, Colonel, Esq.; ---, ---; Hebron, WAS;
gee 1904.
(A:398)
6999. 9/2/90 gor Sherriff, William, Colonel, Esq.; ---, ---; Hebron, WAS;
gee 612.
(C-2:321)
7000. 12/9/95 gor Sherry, Seth; Plattsburgh, CLI; Plattsburgh, CLI;
gee 5741.
(A:397)
7001. 7/1/00 mor Sherry, Seth; ---, ---; ---, ESS; mee 5572. (A:59)
7002. 9/8/01 gor Sherry, Seth; Plattsburgh, CLI; Jay, ESS; gee 4055. (A:64)
7003. 11/18/01 gor Sherry, Seth; Plattsburgh, CLI; Jay, ESS; gee 6991. (A:62)
7004. 6/1/85 gee Sherwood, Abiel; ---, ---. See 7055.
7005. 3/5/89 gor Sherwood, Adial; Argyle, WAS; Kingsbury Pat., WAS; gee 7017.
(B-2:23)
7006. 6/7/86 gee Sherwood, Adiel, farmer; ---, WAS. See 1513.
7007. 8/26/86 gee Sherwood, Adiel, farmer; ---, WAS. See 7149.
7008. 9/6/89 gor Sherwood, Adiel; Argyle, WAS; Artillery Pat., WAS; gee 2931.
(A:295)
7009. 9/21/96 mee Sherwood, Adiel; ---, ---. See 884.
7010. 4/4/92 gor Sherwood, Adiel, Esq.; Argyle, WAS; ---, WAS; gee 3788.
(B-2:348)
7011. 6/4/92 gor Sherwood, Adiel, Esq.; Fort Edward, WAS; Artillery Pat.,
WAS; gee 8218.
(A:341)

7012. 2/12/95 gor Sherwood, Adiel, Esq.; Argyle, WAS; Artillery Pat., WAS; gee 8219.
(B-2:345)
7013. 2/10/96 gor Sherwood, Adiel, Esq. (w. Sarah); Argyle, WAS; Fort Edward
Pat., WAS; gee 7773.
(B-2:525)
7014. 2/10/96 gor Sherwood, Sarah. See 7013.
7015. 11/19/87 gee Sherwood, Seth; Kingsbury, WAS. See 737.
7016. 8/29/88 gee Sherwood, Seth, Capt.; Kingsbury, WAS. See 2236.
7017. 3/5/89 gee Sherwood, Seth; Argyle, WAS. See 7005.
7018. 7/20/92 gee Sherwood, Seth; Kingsbury, WAS. See 1219.
7019. 1/20/95 gor Sherwood, Seth (w. Susanna); Kingsbury, WAS; Kingsbury Pat.,
WAS; gee 1524. Two contracts this date involving these
persons.   (C-2:176) and (C-2:190)
7020. 4/6/97 gor Sherwood, Seth; Scipio, ONO; Tuttle Pat., WAS; co-gees
661, 663.   (D:13)
7021. 3/24/91 gor Sherwood, Seth, Esq.; Kingsbury, WAS; Kingsbury, WAS;
gee 5213.   (A:292)
7022. 3/26/96 mee Sherwood, Seymour; Stanford, DUT. See 5436.
7023. 1/20/95 gor Sherwood, Susanna. See 7019. (two contracts)
7024. 1/10/92 gor Shever(?), John; Livingston Manor, COL. See 3923.
7025. 6/4/94 gee Shiland, John, Junr., farmer; Cambridge, WAS. See 3699.
7026. 5/2/96 gee Shineer, Elijah; Argyle, WAS. See 2100b.
7027. 3/1/87 gee Shingham, Joseph; ---, ---. See 7055.
7028. 5/8/75 gee Shippen, Cornelia. See 7029.
7029. 5/8/75 gee Shippen, John Peter Quackenbos (w. Cornelia); Albany, ALB.
See 6126.
7030. 10/14/92 mor Shondler, Andrew, tailor; Cambridge, WAS; Cambridge, WAS;
mee 8853.   (A:387)
7031. 10/9/95 gor Shondler, Andrew; Cambridge, WAS; Cambridge, WAS; gee 530.
(D:153)
7032. 10/10/95 mee Shondler, Andrew, Cambridge, WAS. See 678 and 1093.
7033. 7/1/00 mor Shove, Minor; ---, ---; ---, ESS; co-mor 5050; mee 5572
(A:18)
7034. 12/11/90 mor Shumerg(?), Asa; Hebron, WAS. See 5504.
7035. 8/1/93 gor Shummway, Asa, yeoman; Hebron, WAS; Hebron, WAS; gee 7462.
(B-2:87)
7036. 4/4/89 mee Sill, Richard, Esq.; ---, ---. See 7932.
7037. 2/8/98 mor Sill, Zechariah, blacksmith; Hartford, WAS; Hartford, WAS;
mee 1483.   (B:323)
7038. 10/11/96 mor Simmons, Ebenezer, farmer; Granville, WAS; Granville, WAS;
mee 3769.   (B:121)
7039. 10/7/95 mor Simmons, John; Westfield, WAS; Westfield, WAS; mee 7232.
(A:609)
7040. 7/4/00 gee Simmons, Stephen, yeoman; Kingsbury, WAS. See 4901.
7041. 1/16/99 gor Simpson, Alexander; Salem, WAS; Salem, WAS; gee 7042.
Two contracts this date involving these persons.
(D:122), (D:124)
7042. 1/16/99 gee Simpson, Alexander, Junr.; Salem, WAS. See 7041.(two contracts)
7043. 12/30/89 gee Simpson, Andrew, yeoman; Salem, WAS. See 4779.
7044. 11/23/02 mor Simpson, David; Cambridge, WAS; Cambridge, WAS; co-mees
1618, 1619, 4672, 8864.   (E:34)
7045. 7/24/02 mor Simpson, John; "Caldwell Park, south end of Lake George",
WAS; Caldwell Park, south end of Lake George, WAS;
mee 1195.   (E:15)
7046. 8/26/97 gee Simpson, Robert, brewer; Cambridge, WAS. See 3308.
(two contracts)
7047. 6/26/92 gor Simpson, Alexander; Salem, WAS; Salem, WAS; gee 7048.
(C-1:92)
7048. 6/26/92 gee Simpson, Andrew, farmer; Salem, WAS. See 7047.
7049. 6/26/93 mor Simson, Andrew, yeoman; Salem, WAS; Salem, WAS; mee 4738.
(A:422)
7050. 9/28/84 gor Sintott, Bernard, gentleman; Branford, ---, CT; Black Creek
Dist., WAS; gee 5545.   (A:263)
7051. 12/29/00 gee Skeels, Joseph; Champlain, CLI. See 827.
7052. 6/7/99 gee Skeels, William, yeoman; Whitehall, WAS. See 3795.
7053. 7/20/87 --- Skeen, ---. See 100.
7054. 1784-87 --- Skeen, Andrew P. (forfeiture of his lands in Washington Co.)
Forfeiture jointly with that of the principal forfeiter,
7055.

7055. 1784-87 --- Skeen, Philip (forfeiture of his lands in Washington Co.;
see also 7054); ---, ---; Skenesborough, WAS; gees
30, 31, 32, 151, 463, 689, 690, 762, 1055, 1135, 1136,
1137, 1141, 1144, 2233, 2234, 2242, 2365, 2629, 2637,
2638, 2643, 2645, 2711, 2852, 3024, 3025, 3175, 3191,
3207, 3337, 3342, 3607, 3749, 3793, 3803, 4256, 4315,
4316, 4317, 4399, 4441, 4517, 4606, 4844, 4877, 4988,
5060, 5315, 5398, 5635, 5893, 6016, 6074, 6136, 6531,
6570, 6668, 6769, 6843, 6844, 7004, 7027, 7374, 7500,
7502, 7530, 7532, 7534, 7554, 7555, 7668, 7703, 7706,
7711, 7735, 7861, 7910, 8147, 8149, 8150, 8491, 8516,
8518, 8519, 8520, 8547, 8554, 8654, 8785 (90 contracts)
(Brief filings on end pages of Deed Book A)

7056. 7/22/72 mor Skene, Philip, Major; Skenesborough, CHA; Skenesborough, CHA;
mee 7307.   (A:13)
7057. 5/5/85 --- Skenes, Andrew P.; ---, ---. See 8282.
7058. 5/5/85 --- Skenes, Philip. See 8282.
7059. 7/8/90 gee Skinner, Calvin; Cambridge, WAS. See 7279.
7060. 2/1/96 gee Skinner, Calvin; Cambridge, WAS. See 7801.
7061. 6/15/99 gor Skinner, Elizabeth. See 7065.
7062. 12/5/93 mor Skinner, Israel; ---, ---, NY. See 7064.
7063. 6/15/99 --- Skinner, Israel, dec'd. See 7065 and 7066.
7064. 12/5/93 mor Skinner, John; ---, ---, NY; Cambridge, WAS; co-mors
7062, 7068; mee 1771.   (A:448)
7065. 6/15/99 gor Skinner, John (w. Elizabeth), yeoman; Cambridge, WAS;
Cambridge, WAS; co-gors 7066, 7069; gee 4558. The four
grantors, together with Israel Skinner "now deceased",
formerly jointly held a mortgage here.   (D:165)
7066. 6/15/99 gor Skinner, Lovisa, "widow of Israel Skinner, deceased, and
now wife of Timothy Skinner". See 7063 and 7069.
7067. 1/2/02 mee Skinner, Reuben; Granville, WAS. See 5207.
7068. 12/5/93 mor Skinner, Timothy; ---, ---, NY. See 7064.
7069. 6/15/99 gor Skinner, Timothy (w. Lovisa), yeoman; Cambridge, WAS.
See 7065.

7070. 2/13/98 gee Sloan, James; Westfield, WAS. See 7195.
7071. 3/15/98 mor Sloan, James; Westfield, WAS; Westfield, WAS; mee 8796.
(C:256)
7072. 8/20/93 gor Sloan, Sarah, "farmer"; ---, ---. See 7073.
7073. 8/20/93 gor Sloan, William, farmer; Westfield, WAS; co-gor 7072;
co-gees 2909, 2920.   (D:155)

7074. 10/10/01 mor Slocum, Elisabeth. See 7077.
7075. 2/21/00 mee Slocum, Matthew; Cambridge, WAS. See 4795.
7076. 9/2/94 mor Slocum, Paul, farmer; Cambridge, WAS; Saratoga Pat., WAS;
mee 536.   (B:57)
7077. 10/10/01 mor Slocum, Paul (w. Elisabeth), husbandman; Hartford, WAS;
Hartford, WAS; mee 4967.   (D:114)

7078. 4/18/83 gee Small, James; Cambridge Dist., ALB. See 1764.
7079. 11/4/93 gee Small, James, farmer; Cambridge, WAS. See 8422.
7080. 2/13/98 gor Smith, Abigail. See 7195.
7081. 6/25/93 mor Smith, Allen, farmer; Plattsburgh, CLI; Plattsburgh, CLI;
mee 7524.   (A:104)
7082. 6/11/01 mor Smith, Amos (w. Olive), farmer; Hebron, WAS; Hebron, WAS;
mee 5228.   (D:70b)
7083. 5/17/00 gor Smith, Anne. See 7118.
7084. 10/21/91 gor Smith, Anny, "relict of Daniel Smith late of Argyle", dec'd;
---, ---; Argyle, WAS; co-gors (all "heirs unto the
said Daniel") 7090, 7092, 7093, 7096, 7137, 7251;
gee 5624.   (B-2:11)
7085. 2/9/92 gee Smith, Aron; Hebron, WAS. See 3698.
7086. 12/11/82 gor Smith, Baronitt; ---, CHA; ---, CHA; gee 7102. (C-1:60)
7087. 6/27/00 mor Smith, Benjamin; ---, ---; Elizabethtown, ESS; mee 5168.
(A:11)
7088. 11/15/87 gee Smith, Calvin; Hebron, WAS. See 7157.
7089. 8/16/96 mee Smith, Calvin; Hebron, WAS. See 1776.
7090. 10/21/91 gor Smith, Catherine; Argyle, WAS. See 7084.
7091. 4/22/96 mor Smith, Danford, Esq. (w. Presilla); Cambridge, WAS;
Cambridge, WAS; mee 8849.   (B:148)

169

7092. 10/21/91 gor Smith, Daniel. See 7084.
7092a. 10/21/91 --- Smith, Daniel, dec'd. See 7084.
7093. 10/21/91 gor Smith, Duncan; Argyle, WAS. See 7084.
7094. 4/16/02 mor Smith, Eleazer, Junr., farmer; Granville, WAS; Granville, WAS; mee 712. (D:189)
7095. 4/27/98 mor Smith, Elijah, blacksmith; ---, ---. See 2262.
7096. 10/21/91 gor Smith, Elizabeth. See 7084.
7097. 5/1/98 gor Smith, Elizabeth; ---, ---; De Forest Pat., WAS; co-gor 1979; gee 8302. Grantors are executors of the estate of Thomas Smith, Esq., dec'd., who was the last surviving heir of the Honorable William Smith "formerly of the City of New York" also deceased. (F:130)
7098. 8/5/02 mor Smith, Ephraim; Champlain, CLI; ---, CLI; mee 7792. (B:75)
7099. 7/22/01 gor Smith, Harriet; ---, ---. See 7134.
7100. 9/4/96 gor Smith, Harriot; Lower Canada. See 7133. (two contracts)
7101. 11/2/97 mee Smith, Henry P.; Salem, WAS. See 4811.
7102. 12/11/82 gee Smith, Henry Prusia; ---, CHA. See 7086.
7103. 6/2/85 mee Smith, Henry Prusia; ---, ---. See 1465.
7104. 4/8/96 mee Smith, Henry Prusia; Salem, WAS. See 1581.
7105. 12/24/98 mee Smith, Isaac; ---, ---. See 5062.
7106. 8/25/00 mee Smith, Isaac; ---, ---. See 5389.
7107. 7/1/02 mee Smith, Isaac; ---, ---. See 5644.
7108. 2/8/85 gee Smith, Israel, gentleman; ---, ---. See 5887.
7109. 1/25/87 gee Smith, Israel, merchant; Poughkeepsie, DUT. See 5902. (three contracts)
7110. 4/11/87 gee Smith, Israel, merchant; Poughkeepsie, DUT. See 5915.
7111. 4/25/93 --- Smith, Israel, dec'd. See 7168.
7112. 9/10/93 --- Smith, Israel, dec'd. See 3906.
7113. 3/16/96 --- Smith, Jacob; ---, DUT. See 290.
7114. 3/16/96 mor Smith, Jacob; ---, DUT. See 289.
7115. 11/23/97 gee Smith, Jacob; "Chateauguay", CLI. See 5827.
7116. 11/24/97 mor Smith, Jacob; Chateaugay, CLI; Old Military Township #7 (Chateaugay), CLI; mee 5828. (A:239)
7117. 6/22/98 gor Smith, Jacob; ---, DUT; See 5697 and 5698. (two contracts)
7118. 5/17/00 gor Smith, James (w. Anne); Easton, WAS; Saratoga Pat., WAS; gee 8010. (E:39)
7119. 12/5/97 mor Smith, James Scott, Esq. (w. Mary); Poughkeepsie, DUT; ---, CLI; co-mees 298, 5869. (A:248)
7120. 12/5/97 mor Smith, James Scott, Esq. (w. Mary); Poughkeepsie, DUT; Military Tract, CLI; mee 299. (A:251)
7121. 6/23/98 mor Smith, James Scott, Esq.; Poughkeepsie, DUT; Old Military Township #3 (Black Brook), CLI; mee 1477. (A:391)
7122. 3/16/98 gor Smith, Jane. See 7265.
7123. 1/24/89 gor Smith, Janet. See 7293.
7124. 7/8/90 gor Smith, Janet. See 7279.
7125. 7/27/90 gor Smith, Janet. See 7294.
7126. 4/28/91 gor Smith, Janet. See 7296.
7127. 5/31/94 gor Smith, Janet; ---, ---. See 7299.
7128. 8/20/94 gor Smith, Janet. See 7300 and 7301. (two contracts)
7129. 6/15/95 gor Smith, Janet, widow; Quebec, Lower Canada "but at present of the City of New York" (heir under the will of Elizabeth Livingston, dec'd.) Saratoga Pat., WAS; co-gors 174, 177, 4227, 4238, 4240, 4242, 4247, 4824, 4827; gee 2547. (C-2:257)
7130. 2/5/96 gor Smith, Janet; Lower Canada; ---, WAS; co-gors 7160, 7281; gee 5239. (C-2:56)
7131. 2/25/96 gor Smith, Janet; Lower Canada; ---, WAS; co-gors 7161, 7282; gee 423 (C-2:68), 7439 (C-2:60), 7442 (C-2:62), 8805 (C-2:35). (four contracts)
7132. 2/26/96 gor Smith, Janet; Lower Canada; ---, WAS; co-gors 7162, 7283; gee 7987. (F:154)
7133. 9/4/96 gor Smith, Janet; Lower Canada; Cambridge Pat., WAS; co-gors 7100, 7163, 7284; gee 3006 (C-2:87), 3132 (C-2:122) (two contracts)
7134. 7/22/01 gor Smith, Janet; ---, ---; Cambridge, WAS; co-gors 7099, 7165, 7286; gee 5126. Grantors are all executors of the will of "William Smith deceased in the Province of Lower Canada". (E:403)

7135. 2/26/96 gor Smith, Jannet; Lower Canada; ---, WAS; co-gors 7162, 7283;
gee 5368.   (C-2:64)
7136. 12/14/87 mor Smith, Jedediah, yeoman; Hebron, WAS; Hebron, WAS; mee
6777.   (A:372)
7137. 10/21/91 gor Smith, John; Argyle, WAS. See 7084.
7138. 5/3/97 gor Smith, John (w. Margaret); ---, ---. See 7807.
7139. 5/4/97 gor Smith, John; ---, ---. See 7810.
7140. 5/4/97 mee Smith, John; ---, ---. See 8248.
7141. 7/28/98 gee Smith, John; Argyle, WAS. See 3917.
7142. 7/13/73 mee Smith, John, Esq.; ---, ---. See 3796.
7143. 3/9/87 gor Smith, John, Esq.; ---, SUF. See 5909.
7144. 8/4/73 mee Smith, John W.; ---, ---. See 2669.
7145. 1/2/65 gee Smith, Joseph, merchant; Birmingham, Great Britain.
See 4832.
7146. 12/21/68 gee Smith, Joseph, merchant; Birmingham, England. See 8418.
7147. 6/25/85 gor Smith, Joseph; Birmingham, Kingdom of Great Britain;
Kingsbury, WAS; gee 1590.   (C-1:55)
7148. 8/5/86 gor Smith, Joseph; Birmingham, Kingdom of Great Britain;
Kingsbury, WAS; gee 1591.   (C-1:54)
7149. 8/26/86 gor Smith, Joseph, merchant; Birmingham, Great Britain;
Kingsbury, WAS; gee 7007.   (A:342)
7150. 8/28/86 gor Smith, Joseph; Birmingham, Kingdom of Great Britain;
Kingsbury, WAS; gee 5208.   (C-1:43)
7151. 11/16/99 gor Smith, Joshua (w. Sibil); Hampton, WAS; Hampton, WAS;
gee 763.   (E:57)
7152. 2/5/98 gor Smith, Lemuel; ---, WAS; Saratoga Pat., WAS; co-gees
2555, 8011.   (E:61)
7153. 2/5/98 mor Smith, Lemuel; ---, WAS; Saratoga Pat., WAS; co-mees
2556, 8012.   (C:85)
7154. 5/1/97 mor Smith, Margaret. See 7176.
7155. 5/3/97 gor Smith, Margaret. See 7138.
7156. 3/7/87 gee Smith, Marten; Pawlet, RUT, VT. See 7263.
7157. 11/15/87 gor Smith, Martin; Pawlet, RUT, VT; Hebron Dist., WAS; gee 7088.
(A:60)
7158. 5/31/94 gor Smith, Mary; ---, ---. See 7299.
7159. 8/20/94 gor Smith, Mary. See 7300 and 7301. (two contracts)
7160. 2/5/96 gor Smith, Mary; Lower Canada. See 7130.
7161. 2/25/96 gor Smith, Mary; Province of Lower Canada. See 7131. (four
contracts)
7162. 2/26/96 gor Smith, Mary; Lower Canada. See 7132 and 7135. (two contracts)
7163. 9/4/96 gor Smith, Mary; Lower Canada. See 7133. (two contracts)
7164. 12/5/97 mor Smith, Mary. See 7119 and 7120. (two contracts)
7165. 7/22/01 gor Smith, Mary; ---, ---. See 7134.
7166. 2/8/85 gee Smith, Melancton, gentleman; ---, ---. See 5887.
7167. 3/14/87 gee Smith, Melancton; ---, ---. See 5911.
7168. 4/25/93 gor Smith, Melancton; ---, ---; Plattsburgh. CLI; co-gors
3210 and 3877 (these two and Melancton are "surviving
executors of the estate of Israel Smith",dec'd.) as well
as 1475 and 7599 (these two are executors of the estate
of Peter Tappen, dec'd.); gee 3904.   (A:315)
7169. 9/10/93 mee Smith, Melancton; ---, ---. See 3906.
7170. 2/20/95 gee Smith, Melancton, merchant; City of N.Y. See 5732.
7171. 2/17/96 gee Smith, Melancton; City of N.Y. See 5745.
7172. 3/16/96 --- Smith, Melancton; City of N.Y. See 290.
7173. 3/16/96 mor Smith, Melancton; City of N.Y. See 289.
7174. 2/8/97 gee Smith, Melancton; City of N.Y. See 5939.
7175. 2/10/97 gor Smith, Melancton; City of N.Y.; Plattsburgh. CLI; gee 3911.
(B:66)
7176. 5/1/97 mor Smith, Melancton (w. Margaret), merchant; City of N.Y.
Zephaniah Platt's Pat., CLI; mee 3883.   (A:231)
7177. 11/14/97 gee Smith, Melancton; City of N.Y. See 3902.
7178. 6/22/98 gor Smith, Melancton; City of N.Y. See 5697 and 5698. (two
contracts)
7179. 2/22/87 gee Smith, Melancton, Esq.; City of N.Y. See 5905.
7180. 3/14/87 gee Smith, Melancton, Esq.; City of N.Y. See 5910.
7181. 9/2/88 gee Smith, Melancton, Esq.; City of N.Y. See 5840.

7182. 4/2/89 gee Smith, Melancton, Esq.; City of N.Y. See 6435.
7183. 3/11/90 gee Smith, Melancton, Esq.; City of N.Y. See 5842.
7184. 5/2/93 gee Smith, Melancton, Esq.; City of N.Y. See 7744.
7185. 2/6/97 gee Smith, Melancton, Esq.; City of N.Y. See 4087.
7186. 2/7/97 gor Smith, Melancton, Esq.; City of N.Y.; Plattsburgh, CLI;
                gee 5938.   (A:549)
7187. 3/14/97 mee Smith, Melancton, Esq.; City of N.Y. See 3909.
7188. 12/14/87 mor Smith, Mosier, yeoman; Hebron, WAS; Hebron, WAS; mee 6774.
                                                                (A:370)
7189. 8/24/90 mor Smith, Nahum; Hebron, WAS; Shereiff's Pat in Hebron, WAS;
                mee 6978.   (A:225)
7190. 7/7/91 gor Smith, Nahum; Hebron, WAS; Hebron, WAS; co-gees 1903, 1906.
                                                                (A:408)
7191. 12/14/87 mor Smith, Nathan; Hebron, WAS; Hebron, WAS; co-mees 4615,
                4632, 6748, 6807. The co-mortgagees are all executors
                of the estate of John Morine Scott, dec'd.   (A:287)
7192. 11/23/01 gee Smith, Nathaniel; "now or late of Pawlet in Vermont".
                See 2590.
7193. 6/11/01 mor Smith, Olive. See 7082.
7194. 1/24/95 mor Smith, Oliver; Westfield, WAS; Westfield, WAS; mee 1236.
                                                                (C:254)
7195. 2/13/98 gor Smith, Oliver (w. Abigail); Westfield, WAS; Westfield, WAS;
                gee 7070.   (C-2:240)
7196. 5/27/00 gor Smith, Orton; Bristol, England; Kingsbury, WAS; gee 376.
                                                                (E:152)
7197. 6/28/00 gor Smith, Orton; Bristol, England; Kingsbury, WAS; gee 8378
                (E:157); gee 8707 (E:154). (two contracts)
7198. 7/7/96 mor Smith, Patrick; Sorella, Canada; Bayard Pat., WAS; mee 7611.
                                                                (D:82)
7199. 9/17/99 mor Smith, Patrick; ---, WAS; Fort Edward Pat., WAS; mee 804.
                                                                (C:233)
7200. 9/1/92 gee Smith, Phebe; City of N.Y. See 7204.
7201. 10/5/90 gee Smith, Philip, physician; Easton, ALB. See 3180.
7202. 10/25/90 gee Smith, Philip, physician; Easton, ALB. See 3181.
7203. 8/8/92 gee Smith, Philip; ---, WAS. See 5204.
7204. 9/1/92 gee Smith, Philip (w. Phebe), physician; Westfield, WAS. See 3182.
7205. 11/23/92 gee Smith, Philip, physician; ---, WAS. See 4485.
7206. 6/11/93 mee Smith, Philip, Dr.; Easton, WAS. See 659.
7207. 7/27/93 gee Smith, Philip, physician; Easton, WAS. See 3183.
7208. 11/8/93 mee Smith, Philip, physician; ---, WAS. See 6516.
7209. 12/24/93 gee Smith, Philip, physician; ---, WAS. See 4971.
7210. 11/20/94 gee Smith, Philip, physician; ---, WAS. See 491.
7211. 10/7/95 gee Smith, Philip, physician; ---, WAS. See 3438.
7212. 10/7/95 mee Smith, Philip, physician; Easton, WAS. See 2336.
7213. 11/4/95 mee Smith, Philip; Easton, WAS. See 8071.
7214. 1/20/96 mee Smith, Philip, Mr.; Easton, WAS. See 5562.
7215. 4/2/96 gor Smith, Philip, physician; ---, WAS; Hitchcock Pat., WAS.
                gee 8205.   (E:246)
7216. 4/2/96 mee Smith, Philip, physician; ---, WAS. See 8206.
7217. 6/4/96 gee Smith, Philip; Cambridge, WAS. See 6044.
7218. 11/17/97 mee Smith, Philip; Cambridge, WAS. See 3354.
7219. 3/31/98 gee Smith, Philip; ---, WAS. See 8820.
7220. 5/21/98 gee Smith, Philip; Cambridge, WAS. See 5810.
7221. 9/12/98 mee Smith, Philip; Cambridge, WAS. See 3662.
7222. 12/24/98 mee Smith, Philip; ---, ---. See 5062.
7223. 10/3/99 mee Smith, Philip; Cambridge, WAS. See 1331.
7224. 11/21/99 gee Smith, Philip; ---, WAS. See 7873.
7225. 2/28/00 gee Smith, Philip; Cambridge, WAS. See 5761.
7226. 8/25/00 mee Smith, Philip; ---, ---. See 5389.
7227. 11/19/00 mee Smith, Philip; Cambridge, WAS. See 6023.
7228. 6/28/02 gor Smith, Philip; Cambridge, WAS; Bolton, WAS; gee 8826. (F:284)
7229. 6/28/02 mee Smith, Philip; Cambridge, WAS. See 5310 and 8827.
7230. 7/1/02 mee Smith, Philip; ---, ---. See 5644.
7231. 7/15/02 mee Smith, Philip; Cambridge, WAS. See 2554.
7232. 10/7/95 mee Smith, Philip, Esq.; Easton, WAS. See 7039.
7233. 11/6/98 gor Smith, Philip, Esq., sheriff; ---, WAS; Cockroft Pat, WAS;
                (sheriff's sale); gee 1400.   (D:249)

7234.   9/3/92   mee   Smith, Phillip; Easton, WAS.   See 148, 1893, 5485.
7235.   10/27/92 mee   Smith, Phillip, Dr.; Easton, WAS.   See 529.
7236.   2/13/98   mee   Smith, Phillip; ---, WAS.   See 2352.
7237.   9/3/92   mor   Smith, Phillip, Junr.; ---, WAS.   See 148.
7238.   11/5/94   gee   Smith, Platt; "Ninetown"(?), DUT.   See 1675.
7239.   11/1/96   mee   Smith, Platt, merchant; ---, DUT.   See 7868.
7240.   12/24/98 ---   Smith, Platt, dec'd.   See 5062.
7241.   6/26/99   ---   Smith, Platt, dec'd.   See 2644.
7242.   8/25/00   ---   Smith, Platt, dec'd.; ---, DUT.   See 5389.
7243.   7/1/02   ---   Smith, Platt, dec'd.   See 5644.
7244.   4/22/96   mor   Smith, Presilla.   See 7091.
7245.   2/5/90   mor   Smith, Reuben; Argyle, WAS; personal property?; mee 4868.
                                                                       (A:211)
7246.   5/21/99   mor   Smith, Reuben; Bolton, WAS; Bolton, WAS; mee 3440. (C:228)
7247.   2/19/96   gee   Smith, Robert; Watervliet, ALB.   See 765.
7248.   2/20/96   gee   Smith, Robert; Watervliet, ALB.   See 4123.
7249.   5/13/96   gee   Smith, Robert; Troy, REN.   See 1230.
7250.   5/8/02   gee   Smith, Ruluff; Whitehall, WAS.   See 5022.
7251.   10/21/91 gor   Smith, Samuel; Argyle, WAS.   See 7084.
7252.   4/22/96   gee   Smith, Sanford, Esq.; Cambridge, WAS.   See 8848.
7253.   11/16/99 gor   Smith, Sibil.   See 7151.
7254.   4/25/95   gee   Smith, Simeon; Westhaven, RUT, VT.   See 683.
7255.   11/24/95 gee   Smith, Simeon; Westhaven, RUT, VT.   See 8244.
7256.   2/26/96   mor   Smith, Simeon, farmer; Salem, WAS; Salem, WAS; mee 2128.
                                                                       (C:260)
7257.   5/2/96   gee   Smith, Solomon; ---, WAS.   See 1186.
7258.   5/2/96   mor   Smith, Solomon; ---, WAS; Donald Campbell's Pat., WAS;
                          mee 8040.   (B:53)
7259.   8/12/96   gee   Smith, Solomon, merchant; Argyle, WAS.   See 7653.
7260.   7/5/02   gee   Smith, Solomon, gentleman; Argyle, WAS.   See 6733.
7261.   3/30/95   gee   Smith, Solomon, Esq.; Argyle, WAS.   See 3012.
7262.   6/11/83   gee   Smith, Stephen; Rupert, BEN, VT.   See 7482.
7263.   3/7/87   gor   Smith, Stephen; Rupert, BEN, VT; Black Creek Dist., WAS;
                          gee 7156.   (A:59)
7264.   8/4/73   moc   Smith, Thomas; ---, ---.   See 2669.
7265.   3/16/98   gor   Smith, Thomas (w. Jane), merchant; City of N.Y.; Blundell
                          Pat., WAS; gee 6000.   (D:187)
7266.   3/16/98   mee   Smith, Thomas, merchant; City of N.Y.   See 6001.
7267.   8/11/98   mee   Smith, Thomas; Brook Haven, SUF.   See 7883.
7268.   1/1/00   gee   Smith, Thomas; ---, WAS.   See 4920.
7269.   1/2/00   mor   Smith, Thomas; Argyle, WAS.   See 68.
7270.   7/13/73   gor   Smith, Thomas, Esq.; ---, ---.   See 3796.
7271.   9/12/74   gor   Smith, Thomas, Esq.; City of N.Y.; ---, CHA; gee 4310.
                                                                       (B-1:100)
7272.   2/2/88   gor   Smith, Thomas, Esq., "one of the executors ... in the will
                          of William Smith, Esquire, deceased"; City of N.Y.;
                          Schermerhorn Pat., WAS; gee 8850.   (B-2:28)
7273.   2/2/90   gor   Smith, Thomas, Esq.; City of N.Y.; Schermerhorn Pat., WAS;
                          gee 420.   (C-2:70)
7274.   4/1/90   mee   Smith, Thomas, Esq.; City of N.Y..   See 4329.
7275.   5/22/90   mee   Smith, Thomas, Esq.; City of N.Y.   See 2512.
7276.   10/6/90   mee   Smith, Thomas, Esq.; ---, ---.   See 2741.
7277.   5/1/98   ---   Smith, Thomas, Esq.. dec'd.; ---, ---.   See 7097.
7278.   8/4/73   mee   Smith, William; ---, ---.   See 2669.
7279.   7/8/90   gor   Smith, William (w. Janet); Province of Quebec, Canada;
                          Cambridge, WAS; gee 7059.   (D:128)
7280.   8/20/94   ---   Smith, William, dec'd.   See 7300.   (two contracts)
7281.   2/5/96   gor   Smith, William; Lower Canada.   See 7130.
7282.   2/25/96   gor   Smith, William; Lower Canada.   See 7131. (four contracts)
7283.   2/26/96   gor   Smith, William; Lower Canada.   See 7132 and 7135.   (two
                          contracts)
7284.   9/4/96   gor   Smith, William; Lower Canada.   See 7133.
7285.   5/1/98   ---   Smith, William, the Honorable, dec'd.; City of N.Y.   See 7097.
7286.   7/22/01   gor   Smith, William; ---, ---.   See 7134.
7287.   7/22/01   ---   Smith, William, dec'd.; Lower Canada.   See 7134.
7288.   5/1/02   mor   Smith, William, farmer; Chester, WAS; Chester, WAS; mee 7775.
                                                                       (D:198)

7289. 7/13/73 --- Smith, William, Esq., dec'd.; ---, ---. See 3796.
7290. 8/4/73   --- Smith, William, Esq., dec'd.; ---, ---. See 2669.
7291. 12/28/81 gee Smith, William, Esq., yeoman. See 8279.
7292. 2/2/88   --- Smith, William, Esq., dec'd. See 7272.
<u>7293.</u> 1/24/89 gor Smith, William, Esq. (w. Janet), by his attornies William
                          Smith, Junr and Daniel McCormick, gentlemen, of the
                          City of New York; Province of Canada; <u>Cambridge, ALB</u>;
                          co-gees 7795, 7800.   (WAS Co. E:351)
<u>7294.</u> 7/27/90 gor Smith, William, Esq. (w. Janet); Province of Quebec,
                          Canada; <u>Cambridge, ALB</u>; gee 3397.   (WAS Co. D:68)
<u>7295.</u> 10/1/90 gor Smith, William, Esq., Chief Justice of the Province of
                          Quebec, Canada; <u>Cambridge, ALB</u>; gee 2850. (WAS Co. B-2:436)
<u>7296.</u> 4/28/91 gor Smith, William, Esq. (w. Janet), Chief Justice of the
                          Province of Quebec; <u>Cambridge, WAS</u>; gee 2269. (D:80)
7297. 7/6/92   mee Smith, William, the Honorable, Chief Justice of the
                          Province of Quebec. See 7368.
7298. 5/31/94 --- Smith, William, dec'd. See 7299.
<u>7299.</u> 5/31/94 gor Smith, William, Esq.; Lower Canada; <u>Cambridge, WAS</u>; co-gors
                          7127, 7158; gee 2664. Grantors are all executors of the
                          estate of William Smith, Esq., "late chief justice of the
                          Province of Quebec, deceased".   (C-2:296)
<u>7300.</u> 8/20/94 --- Smith, William, Esq., Province of Lower Canada; <u>Cambridge,</u>
                          <u>WAS</u>; co-gors 7128, 7159; gee 2651. Grantors are both
                          "executors of the will of William Smith, late chief
                          justice of the Province of Quebec", dec'd. (C-2:54)
<u>7301.</u> 8/20/94 gor Smith, William, Esq.; Lower Canada; <u>Cambridge, WAS</u>; co-gors
                          7128, 7159. (Grantors are all "executors of the will of
                          William Smith", dec'd.); gee 2650.   (C-2:58)
7302. 1/24/89 --- Smith, William, Junr.; City of N.Y. See 7293.
<u>7303.</u> 7/30/01 mor Smyth, Patrick; "Lorel Parish", Lower Canada; <u>---, WAS</u>;
                          co-mees 802, 7612.   (D:83)
7304. 1/13/01 mor Snider, Experience. See 7305.
<u>7305.</u> 1/13/01 mor Snider, Moses (w. Experience); Argyle, WAS; <u>Argyle, WAS</u>;
                          mee 6063.   (D:3)
<u>7306.</u> 5/4/02   mor Snow, Aaron; Champlain, CLI; <u>Plattsburgh, CLI</u>; mee 5778.
                                                                  (B:70)
7307. 7/22/72 mee Society of the Hospital; City of N.Y. See 7056.
<u>7308.</u> 7/5/92   mor Sole(?), Cornelius, yeoman; Cambridge, WAS; <u>Hebron, WAS</u>;
                          co-mor 8333; mee 6782.   (A:373)
<u>7309.</u> 12/8/88 gor Soper, Moses; Plattsburgh, CLI; <u>land "in the Gift Lot"</u>,
                          <u>CLI</u>; gee 5676.   (A:240)
<u>7310.</u> 10/15/92 mor Soper, Moses; Plattsburgh, CLI; <u>Plattsburgh, CLI</u>; mee 5851.
                                                                  (A:88)
7311. 7/7/86   gee Sorrall, James; ---, ---. See 2618.
7312. 4/3/95   gee Southmayd, John William; Mallory's Bush, CLI. See 5734.
7313. 9/7/69   gor Southwick, Benjamin; ---, ---. See 7955.
7314. 4/20/73 gor Southwick, Benjamin; ---, ---. See 7957.
7315. 12/29/91 gee Southwick, Elisha; ---, ---. See 4878.
<u>7316.</u> 2/25/00 mor Southwick, George; Queensbury, WAS; <u>Queensbury, WAS</u>;
                          mee 7989.   (D:15a)
7317. 9/7/69   gor Southwick, Samuel; ---, ---. See 7955.
7318. 4/20/73 gor Southwick, Samuel; ---, ---. See 7957.
7319. 12/29/91 gee Sowle, Tibbits; ---, ---. See 4878.
<u>7320.</u> 8/24/90 mor Spalding, Leonard; Hebron, WAS; <u>Hebron, WAS</u>; mee 6997.
                                                                  (A:274)
7321. 7/17/93 --- Sparham, Ann. See 7325.
7322. 5/5/96   gor Sparham, Ann Ulrica, "daughter of Adolphus Benzell". See
                          7326. (two contracts)
7323. 5/20/85 mor Sparham, Anna Ulrica. See 7324.
<u>7324.</u> 5/20/85 mor Sparham, Thomas (w. Anna Ulrica); ---, ---; <u>land "to the</u>
                          <u>southward of Crown Point"</u>, WAS; mee 3261.   (A:76)
<u>7325.</u> 7/17/93 --- Sparham, Thomas; Kingston, Middle Dist., Upper Canada
                          (in conjunction with "Ann Sparham of the same place").
                          This date these two persons appoint Abel Spencer, Esq.
                          of Clarendon(?), RUT, VT to serve as their attorney in
                          the sale of their <u>lands south of Crown Point, CLI</u>. (A:532)

7326.	5/5/96	gor	Sparham, Thomas (w. Ann Ulrica); Upper Canada; Benzell's Pat., (Crown Point), CLI; gee 2868 (A:528); gee 2869 (A:530). Two contracts this date involving these persons.
7327.	2/20/01	mor	Sparks, Abigail. See 7329.
7328.	2/20/01	gee	Sparks, Henry; ---, WAS. See 936.
7329.	2/20/01	mor	Sparks, Henry (w. Abigail); ---, WAS; Hartford, WAS; mee 937. (D:21b)
7330.	7/17/93	---	Spencer, Abel, Esq. See 7325.
7331.	2/23/86	gee	Spencer, Alpheus; Artillery Pat., WAS. See 3193.
7332.	3/1/86	mor	Spencer, Alpheus; ---, ---; ---, WAS; mee 3194. (Deed Book B-1:237)
7333.	2/4/95	gor	Spencer, Alpheus (w. Hepzibah); Westfield, WAS; Westfield, WAS; gee 1028. (B-2:419)
7334.	2/7/95	gor	Spencer, Alpheus (w. Hepzibah); Westfield, WAS; Westfield, WAS; gee 3431 (B-2:417); gee 4452 (C-2:309). (two contracts)
7335.	2/26/95	gor	Spencer, Alpheus (w. Hepzibah); Westfield, WAS; Westfield, WAS; gee 888. (B-2:415)
7336.	6/11/73	mor	Spencer, Benjamin; Durham, CHA; Durham, CHA; mee 3072. (A:1)
7337.	2/26/95	gee	Spencer, Hepzibah. See 7335.
7338.	2/4/95	gor	Spencer, Hepzibah. See 7333.
7339.	2/7/95	gor	Spencer, Hepzibah. See 7334. (two contracts)
7340.	9/10/92	mor	Spencer, Jeremiah, farmer; Granville, WAS. See 4114.
7341.	7/3/93	gee	Spencer, Jeremiah; Milton, SAR. See 4115.
7342.	10/21/93	gee	Spencer, Jeremiah, farmer; Granville, WAS. See 4116.
7343.	2/15/96	gor	Spencer, Jeremiah, farmer; Granville, WAS; Granville, WAS; gee 3623. (C-2:89)
7344.	9/21/01	mor	Spenser, Jeremiah (w. Lydia); ---, WAS; Granville, WAS; mee 1693. (D:97)
7345.	9/21/01	mor	Spenser, Lydia. See 7344.
7346.	12/4/93	mor	Speyer, John, merchant; City of N.Y.; Old Military Township #5 (Dannemora), CLI; co-mees 4168, 4170. (A:119)
7347.	6/3/97	mor	Spicer, Jeremiah (w. Rhoda), farmer; Granville, WAS; Granville, WAS; co-mees 72, 2933, 2944. Co-mortgagees are all "executors of the will of James Grant late of Pawling" (DUT), dec'd. (B:199)
7348.	6/3/97	mor	Spicer, Rhoda. See 7347.
7349.	11/29/94	mor	Spoor, Nicholas (w. Zilpha), farmer; Hampton, WAS; Hampton, WAS; mee 5965. (A:517)
7350.	11/29/94	mor	Spoor, Zilpha. See 7349.
7351.	10/1/96	mor	Sprague, Abraham; Granville, WAS; Granville, WAS; mee 3768. (B:110)
7352.	3/15/84	gor	Sprague, David; Cambridge, WAS; Kingsbury, CHA; gee 2520. (C-1:19)
7353.	9/6/90	gor	Sprague, David; Cambridge, WAS; Cambridge Pat., WAS; gee 2848. (B-2:448)
7354.	6/22/91	gor	Sprague, David; ---, ---. See 8450.
7355.	10/26/91	gor	Sprague, David; Cambridge, WAS; Cambridge, WAS; gee 3080. (C-2:142)
7356.	5/2/96	gee	Sprague, David; Balltown, SAR. See 1186 and 2100a.
7357.	5/2/96	mor	Sprague, David; Balltown, SAR; Donald Campbell's Pat, WAS; mee 1189. (B:69)
7358.	5/14/98	gor	Sprague, David (w. Peace); Argyle, WAS; Argyle, WAS; gee 6936. (D:50)
7359.	1/14/02	mee	Sprague, David; ---, ---. See 8421.
7360.	6/2/93	mee	Sprague, David, Esq.; Cambridge, WAS. See 409.
7361.	4/1/94	mee	Sprague, David, Esq.; Cambridge, WAS. See 2681.
7362.	4/11/94	mee	Sprague, David, Esq.; Saratoga, SAR. See 5602.
7363.	5/2/96	gee	Sprague, David, Esq.; Argyle, WAS. See 2100a.
7364.	5/14/99	mor	Sprague, David, Esq.; Argyle, WAS; Argyle, WAS; mee 1402. (C:223)
7365.	10/20/01	mor	Sprague, David, Esq.; Argyle, WAS; Argyle, WAS; mee 4591. (D:110)
7366.	5/14/98	gor	Sprague, Peace. See 7358.
7367.	1/7/91	gor	Sprauge (sic), David; Cambridge Dist., ALB; Cambridge Dist., ALB; gee 1769. (A:320)

7368. 7/6/92 mor Sprauge (sic), David, yeoman; ---, WAS; Cambridge Pat., WAS; mee 7297. (A:393)
7369. 4/1/94 gor Sprauge (sic), David, Esq. (w. Peace); Cambridge, WAS; Cambridge Pat., WAS; co-gees 2693, 2696. (B-2:239)
7370. 4/1/94 gor Sprauge, Peace. See 7369.
7371. 7/20/87 gor Spring, John; Granville, WAS; Granville, WAS; gee 3751. (A:51)
7372. 11/1/86 gor Spring, Nathaniel; Granville, WAS; Granville, WAS; gee 3753. (A:52)
7373. 2/26/96 mor Spring, Daniel, cordwainer; Salem, WAS; Salem, WAS; mee 2128. (C:261)
7374. 5/25/85 gee Squire, Josiah; ---, ---. See 7055.
7375. 5/26/85 mor Squire, Josiah; Skenesborough, WAS; Skenesborough, WAS (lands forfeited by Philip and Andrew P. Skeene); co-mees 4297, 7605. (Deed Book B-1:158)
7376. 3/14/87 gee Stafford, Amos; Coventry, KEN, RI. See 2795.
7377. 6/11/88 gee Stafford, Amos; Willsborough, CLI. See 1871.
7377a. 6/11/88 gee Stafford, Benjamin; Willsborough, CLI. See 1883.
7378. 12/1/88 gee Stafford, Benjamin, yeoman; Willsborough, CLI. See 2807.
7379. 4/27/99 gee Stafford, Benjamin, farmer; Willsborough, ESS. See 2806.
7380. 10/29/00 mee Stafford, Benjamin; ---, ---. See 7497.
7381. 9/28/84 gee Stafford, David; Willsborough, WAS. See 2793.
7382. 9/30/01 mor Stafford, Job; ---, ---; Willsborough, ESS; mee 6498. (A:70)
7383. 11/14/01 mor Stafford, John; Peru, CLI; Peru, CLI; mee 5776. (B:57)
7384. 3/20/99 mor Stafford, Palmer; Peru, CLI; Peru, CLI; mee 5755. (B:1)
7385. 10/25/98 mor Stafford, Rowland; Plattsburgh, CLI; Plattsburgh, CLI; mee 5754. (A:421)
7386. 4/13/86 gee Stafford, Thomas; "late of Willsborough", WAS. See 5992.
7387. 6/24/93 gee Stafford, Thomas, farmer; Willsborough, CLI. See 2814.
7388. 12/12/98 mor Stagg, Catherine. See 7390.
7388a. 12/12/98 mor Stagg, Catherine. See 7391.
7389. 11/29/00 mor Stagg, Catherine. See 7392.
7390. 12/12/98 mor Stagg, Thomas (w. Catherine), merchant; City of N.Y.; Palmer's Purchase, WAS; co-mors 3822, 3823; mee 6475. (C:230)
7391. 12/12/98 mor Stagg, Thomas (w. Catherine), merchant; City of N.Y.; Roberts Pat., WAS; co-mors 3822, 3823; mee 6475. (C:231)
7392. 11/29/00 mor Stagg, Thomas (w. Catherine), merchant; City of N.Y.; Roberts Pat., WAS; mee 6476. (C:211)
7393. 12/10/98 gee Standish, Daniel, yeoman; Cambridge, WAS. See 3834.
7394. 9/11/66 gor Standish, David, Esq., "Captain Lieutenant in his Majesty's Royal Train of Artillery"; ---, ---; land "east side of Hudson's River", ALB; gee 8779. (B-2:157)
7395. 7/5/98 mor Standish, Lois. See 7396.
7396. 7/5/98 mor Standish, Samuel (w. Lois); ---, ---; ---, WAS; co-mees 80, 2941, 2959. (C:253)
7397. 2/8/98 mor Stanton, Amos (w. Sarah), farmer; Hartford, WAS; Hartford, WAS; mee 1483. (B:324)
7398. 2/8/98 mor Stanton, Ssrah. See 7397.
7399. 12/29/91 gee Staples, Abraham; ---, ---. See 4878.
7400. 10/7/99 mor Starbuck, Benjamin; Easton, WAS; Easton, WAS; co-mor 7402; mee 8747. (C:234)
7401. 12/1/01 gor Starbuck, Benjamin, carpenter; Easton, WAS; Easton, WAS; gee 6524. (F:149)
7402. 10/7/99 mor Starbuck, Charles; Easton, WAS. See 7400.
7403. 5/1/00 mor Starbuck, James, farmer; Chester, WAS; Chester, WAS; mee 7772. (D:212)
7404. 7/1/97 gor Starks, Stephen; Peru, CLI; Zephaniah Paltt's Pat., CLI; gee 5465. (B:110)
7405. 12/26/01 mor Starks, Stephen, Chateaugay, CLI; Chateaugay, CLI; mee 622.
7406. 7/1/00 mee State of New York. See 5572. (B:51)
7407. 5/2/01 mee Steel, Helena, wife of Capt. John Steel "of Salem" (presumably Salem, WAS). See 6545.
7408. 12/20/92 --- Steel, Jane. See 7419.
7409. 12/20/92 --- Steel, Jane (the younger). See 7419.
7410. 7/29/87 gee Steel, John, carpenter; New Perth, WAS. See 1442.

176

7411. 12/20/92 --- Steel, John. See 7419.
7412. 5/2/01 --- Steel, John, Capt.; "of Salem" (presumably Salem, WAS).
                 See 7407.
7413. 7/4/97 mor Steel, Jonathan (w. Sarahan), farmer; Granville, WAS;
                 Granville, WAS; co-mees 74, 2935, 2948. Co-mortgagees
                 are all "executors ... of the ... will of James Grant
                 late of Pawling" (DUT), dec'd.   (B:196)
7414. 8/13/92 gee Steel, Joshua. See 7418.
7415. 12/20/92 mor Steel, Joshua; Salem, WAS; Salem(?), WAS; mee 7419. (A:444)
7416. 12/20/92 --- Steel, Mary. See 7419.
7417. 7/4/97 mor Steel, Sarahan. See 7413.
7418. 8/13/92 gor Steel, Thomas; Salem, WAS; Salem, WAS; gee 7414. (B-2:112)
7419. 12/20/92 mee Steel, Thomas, Mr.; Salem, WAS. This document mentions
                 Thomas' wife Jane, his daughters Jane and Mary, his
                 daughter Elizabeth McNeiss, and his son John. See 7415.
7420. 4/5/02 mor Steele, Ezekiel; Champlain, CLI; Champlain, CLI; mee 5103.
                                                                   (B:74)
7421. 8/24/98 mor Stephens, Elijah; Chateaugay, CLI; Old Military Township #7
                 (Chateaugay), CLI; mee 5703.   (A:346)
7422. 6/6/98 mor Stephens, Ephraim; Plattsburgh, CLI; ---, CLI; co-mees
                 5082, 5749.   (A:312)
7423. 6/29/01 mor Stephens, Ephraim; Plattsburgh, CLI; Plattsburgh, CLI;
                 mee 5401.   (B:71)
7424. 9/19/99 gor Stephens, Matthew (w. Rebecca); Cambridge, WAS; Cambridge
                 Pat., WAS; gee 4281.   (D:288)
7425. 9/19/99 mee Stephens, Matthew; Cambridge, WAS. See 4282.
7426. 9/19/99 gor Stephens, Rebecca. See 7424.
7427. 6/7/88 gor Stephenson, Amasa, farmer; Plattsburgh, CLI. See 7433.
7428. 5/18/90 gee Stephenson, Amasa, farmer; Plattsburgh, CLI. See 1350.
7429. 10/12/90 mor Stephenson, Amasa; Plattsburgh, CLI. See 7435.
7430. 11/8/92 mor Stephenson, Amasa; Plattsburgh, CLI; Plattsburgh, CLI;
                 mee 5805.   (A:96)
7431. 9/20/91 mor Stephenson, James; Plattsburgh, CLI; Plattsburgh, CLI;
                 mee 6632.   (A:66)
7432. 9/29/92 gor Stephenson, James; Kent, LIT, CT; Plattsburgh, CLI;
                 gee 7760.   (A:294)
7433. 6/7/88 gor Stephenson, John, farmer; Plattsburgh, CLI; Plattsburgh, CLI;
                 co-gor 7427; gee 5104.   (A:20)
7434. 5/18/90 gee Stephenson, John, farmer; Plattsburgh, CLI. See 1350.
7435. 10/12/90 mor Stephenson, John; Plattsburgh, CLI; Plattsburgh, CLI; co-mor
                 7429; mee 5844.   (A:52)
7436. 10/29/95 gor Stephenson, John; Plattsburgh, CLI; Plattsburgh, CLI;
                 gee 5489.   (A:391)
7437. 1/13/00 mee Stevens, Hannah; Cambridge, WAS. See 7443.
7438. 1/13/00 mor Stevens, Martha. See 7443.
7439. 2/25/96 gee Stevens, Mathew; Cambridge, WAS. See 7131.
7440. 10/7/99 mor Stevens, Simon; Salem, WAS; Campton, WAS; co-mor 7441;
                 mee 4057.   (C:164)
7441. 10/7/99 mor Stevens, Theodorus; Salem, WAS. See 7440.
7442. 2/25/96 gee Stevens, Thomas; Cambridge, WAS. See 7131.
7443. 1/13/00 mor Stevens, Thomas (w, Martha); Cambridge, WAS; Cambridge, WAS;
                 mee 7437.   (D:65)
7444. 7/1/02 mor Stevenson, Andrew; Westfield, WAS; Artillery Pat., WAS;
                 mee 4194.   (E:18)
7445. 12/20/94 gor Stevenson, Elizabeth. See 7448.
7446. 4/20/95 gee Stevenson, James, physician; Cambridge, WAS. See 2034.
7447. 6/2/00 gee Stevenson, John, merchant; Argyle, WAS. See 1749.
7448. 12/20/94 gor Stevenson, Peter (w. Elizabeth), weaver; Argyle, WAS;
                 Argyle, WAS; gee 7850.   (B-2:349)
7449. 10/30/94 gee Stevenson, Samuel, farmer; Salem, WAS. See 2918.
7450. 5/5/01 mee Stevenson, William; Cambridge, WAS. See 1159.
7451. 2/4/84 gee Steveson, Andrew; Kingsbury, CHA. See 4567.
7452. 12/15/91 gor Steward, Samuel, farmer; Westfield, WAS; Westfield, WAS;
                 gee 3325.   (C-2:198)
7453. 12/5/86 gee Steward, William, yeoman; Saratoga, ALB. See 2553.
7454. 10/27/98 gee Steward, William, farmer; Easton, WAS. See 2549.

7455. 2/27/86 gor Stewart, Alexander, yeoman; New Perth Dist., WAS; White
                  Creek or New Perth Dist., WAS; gee 2834.   (F:250)
7456. 5/28/96 gee Stewart, Alexander; Thurman, WAS. See 7776.
7457. 1/26/91 gor Stewart, Archibald (w. Jane); Salem, WAS. See 1403.
7458. 9/8/81 gee Stewart, David; White Creek, CHA. See 8278.
7459. 12/11/90 gor Stewart, David, yeoman; Hebron, WAS; Hebron, WAS; co-gees
                  3043, 5508.   (A:325)
7460. 12/11/90 mee Stewart, David; Hebron, WAS. See 5504.
7461. 5/21/91 gor Stewart, David, yeoman; Hebron, WAS; Hebron, WAS; gee 6292.
                                                                   (A:215)
7462. 8/1/93 gee Stewart, David, yeoman; Hebron, WAS. See 7035.
7463. 5/18/99 gor Stewart, David, yeoman; Hebron, WAS; Hebron, WAS; gee 2903.
                                                                   (D:208)
7464. 8/20/86 gor Stewart, James; Salem(?), WAS; Hebron, WAS; gee 2021. (A:201)
7465. 12/12/91 mee Stewart, James, Capt.; ---, ---. See 3649.
7466. 1/26/91 gor Stewart, Jane; Salem, WAS. See 1403.
7467. 4/2/85 gee Stewart, John, cordwainer; Kingsbury, WAS. See 4610.
7468. 3/7/89 gor Stewart, John; Granville, WAS; Morrison(?) Pat., WAS;
                  gee 1606.   (D:351)
7469. 10/19/92 gee Stewart, John; Hebron, TOL, CT. See 8339.
7470. 6/26/98 mor Stewart, Joseph (w. Rosanna); Cambridge, WAS; Hartford, WAS;
                  mee 1493.   (C:252)
7471. 4/26/02 mor Stewart, Joseph, Esq. (w. Rosanna); Cambridge, WAS; Hartford,
                  WAS; mee 4167.   (D:169)
7472. 7/2/92 gee Stewart, Oliver, farmer; Westfield, WAS. See 4446.
7473. 10/7/99 gor Stewart, Oliver, yeoman; Hartford, WAS; Hartford, WAS;
                  gee 8459.   (D:309)
7474. 10/7/99 mee Stewart, Oliver, yeoman; Hartford, WAS. See 8460.
7475. 10/11/91 gee Stewart, Robert, yeoman; Salem, WAS. See 4336.
7476. 10/12/91 mor Stewart, Robert, yeoman; Salem, WAS; Salem, WAS; mee 4337.
                                                                   (A:294)
7477. 6/26/98 mor Stewart, Rosanna. See 7470.
7478. 4/26/02 mor Stewart, Rosanna. See 7471.
7479. 5/10/80 gee Stewart, Samuel; New Perth, CHA. See 2078.
7480. 10/24/85 gor Stewart, Samuel; New Perth, WAS; New Perth, WAS; gee 4467.
                                                                   (C-1:42)
7481. 12/8/02 mor Stewart, Samuel (w. Thomasin); ---, ---; Argyle, WAS;
                  mee 6885.   (E:39)
7482. 6/11/83 gor Stewart, Samuel, Senr. (w. Allis); New Perth, CHA; Black
                  Creek, CHA; gee 7262.   (B:72)
7483. 12/8/02 mor Stewart, Thomasin. See 7481.
7484. 11/23/97 gee Stewart, Walter, farmer; Argyle, WAS. See 6891.
7485. 2/4/01 mor Stewart, William; South Hero, CHI, VT; Chateaugay, CLI;
                  mee 5707.   (B:20)
7486. 7/7/91 gee Stickland, Ebenezer, farmer; Easton, WAS. See 779.
7487. 7/7/91 mor Stickland, Ebenezer, farmer; Easton, WAS; Saratoga Pat, WAS;
                  co-mors 653, 6384, 6386; mee 780.   (A:292)
7488. 9/10/98 gee Stickle, Edward; Plattsburgh, CLI. See 5942.
7489. 5/1/02 gor Stickle, Edward; Plattsburgh, CLI; Plattsburgh, CLI;
                  gee 5143.   (B:324)
7490. 9/10/98 gee Stickle, Jacob; Plattsburgh, CLI. See 5942.
7491. 4/28/02 gor Stickles, Edward; Plattsburgh, CLI; Plattsburgh, CLI;
                  gee 7492.   (B:318)
7492. 4/28/02 gee Stickles, Jacob; Plattsburgh, CLI. See 7491.
7493. 8/16/98 mor Stiles, Avery; ---, CLI; Old Military Township #7 (Chateaugay),
                  CLI; co-mees 6860, 8092.   (A:336)
7494. 4/18/01 mor Stillwell, Jeremiah (w. Margrit); Troy, REN; Cambridge, WAS;
                  co-mees 3819, 6415.   (D:35b)
7495. 4/18/01 mor Stillwell, Margrit. See 7494.
7496. 10/21/97 mor Stillwell, Barnet; Willsborough, CLI; Willsborough, CLI;
                  mee 2803.   (A:244)
7497. 10/29/00 mor Stillwell, Barnet; ---, ---; land "east bank of River Boquet",
                  ESS; mee 7380.   (A:38)
7498. 9/10/75 gee Stockwell, Levi; Whitehall, WAS. See 6833.
7499. 3/10/91 gor Stockwell, Levi; Whitehall, WAS; Whitehall, WAS; gee 2543.
                                                                   (B-2:203)

7500. 12/15/84 gee Stockwell, Levy; ---, ---. See 7055.
7501. 6/8/85 mor Stockwell, Levy; Skenesborough, WAS; Skenesborough, WAS;
mee 8553.   (Deed Book B-1:164)
7502. 11/17/85 gee Stockwell, Levy; ---, ---. See 7055.
7503. 6/29/01 gee Stockwell, Paul; Shoreham, ADD, VT. See 5945.
7504. 6/29/01 mor Stockwell, Paul; Shoreham, ADD, VT; Champlain, CLI; mee 5884.
(B:33)
7505. 11/19/91 gee Stodard, Reuben; ---, ---. See 6230.
7506. 2/19/96 mor Stoddard, Isaac (w. Mercy); Cambridge, WAS; Hoosick Pat.,
WAS; mee 567.   (B:19)
7507. 2/20/96 gee Stoddard, Isaac; Cambridge, WAS. See 568.
7508. 2/19/96 gee Stoddard, Mercy. See 7506.
7509. 3/9/98 gee Stodderd, Gerusha. See 7510.
7510. 3/9/98 mor Stodderd, Reuben (w. Gerusha), farmer; Hartford, WAS;
Hartford, WAS; mee 1488.   (C:252)
7511. 5/1/79 gee Stone, Aaron, yeoman; Greenwich, HAM, MA. See 7517.
7512. 9/12/-- gee Stone, Abner; New Perth, CHA. See 1424.
7513. 3/26/98 gee Stone, Abner; Salem, WAS. See 6591.
7514. 3/6/01 gee Stone, Abner; Salem, WAS; Salem, WAS; mee 4334. (D:23b)
7515. 1/24/00 gee Stone, Abner, Esq.; Salem, WAS. See 7949.
7516. 4/8/00 gee Stone, Abner, Esq.; Salem, WAS. See 8462.
7517. 5/1/79 gor Stone, Alexander, gentleman; Williamstown, BER, MA; New Perth,
CHA; gee 7511.   (C-1;36)
7518. 9/14/95 mor Stone, Eli; Jericho, CHI, VT; Peru, CLI; mee 6294. (A:167)
7519. 3/8/75 mor Stone, Nathan; Windsor, CUM, NY (now Windsor, Vermont);
Rutland, CHA, NY (this land probably in the area of present-
day Rutland County, Vermont since NY and NH, before the
Revolutionary War, issued land grants in the territory
which would become Vermont); mee 1557. The mortgagee was
New York's lieutenant governor, 1761-76.   (A:57)
7520. 9/8/00 mee Storm, Thomas; ---, ---. See 4986, 4987, and 8367.
7521. 12/3/00 mee Storm, Thomas; ---, ---. See 8732.
7522. 12/23/00 mee Storm, Thomas; ---, ---. See 1921 and 2736.
7523. 3/2/87 gee Storm, Thomas, Esq.; City of N.Y. See 5907.
7524. 6/25/93 mee Storm, Thomas, Esq.; City of N.Y. See 7081 and 7904.
7525. 7/1/00 mee Storrs, Joseph; ---, ---. See 381.
7526. 2/28/01 mor Storry, John, innkeeper; Plattsburgh, CLI; Plattsburgh, CLI;
co-mees 4356, 6359.   (B:21)
7527. 12/1/00 mor Story, John, yeoman; Kingsbury, WAS; Kingsbury, WAS; mee
4212.   (D:6)
7528. 5/5/01 mor Stout, Mary. See 7529. (two contracts)
7529. 5/5/01 mor Stout, William (w. Mary); Argyle, WAS; Argyle, WAS; mee 4473
(D:39b); mee 4496 (D:38b). (two contracts)
7530. 6/8/85 gee Stow, Seth; ---, ---. See 7055.
7531. 6/8/85 mor Stow, Seth; Skenesborough, WAS; Skenesborough, WAS; mee 8552.
(Deed Book B-1:163)
7532. 7/1/85 gee Stow, Simeon; ---, ---. See 7055.
7533. 7/2/85 mor Stow, Simeon; Skenesborough, WAS; Skenesborough, WAS; mee
8557.   (A:36)
7534. 6/2/87 gee Stow, Simeon; ---, ---. See 7055.
7535. 2/11/01 gee Stow, Timothy, merchant; Albany, ALB. See 1192.
7536. 2/11/01 mor Stow, Timothy, merchant; Thurman, WAS; land "west side of
Lake George, WAS; mee 1193.   (D:14)
7537. 2/28/00 mor Stower, Asa, physician; Queensbury, WAS; Queensbury, WAS;
mee 7899.   (D:15)
7538. 11/3/01 mee Stower, Asa; ---, ---. See 1356.
7539. 2/10/84 gor Streben (see also Strevel), Johannes; "Livingston Manner",
---, --- (presumably Livingston Manor, COL); Argyle, CHA;
gee 3935. See 7546 and 7551.   (B-1:194)
7540. 3/12/98 mor Streeter, Adah. See 7544.
7541. 3/12/98 gee Streeter, John, saddler; Salem, WAS. See 6719.
7542. 3/12/98 mor Streeter, John (w. Rebecca), saddler; Salem, WAS; Salem,
WAS; co-mors 7540, 7544; co-mees 5540, 5566.   (B:326)
7543. 3/12/98 gee Streeter, Joshua, saddler; Salem, WAS. See 6719.
7544. 3/12/98 mor Streeter, Joshua (w. Adah), saddler; Salem, WAS. See 7542.
7545. 3/12/98 mor Streeter, Rebecca. See 7542.

179

7546. 8/10/84 gee Strevel, John; "Livingston Manner", ---, --. See 3938.
See also 7539 and 7551.
7547. 11/3/02 mee Stringham, James S.; City of N.Y. See 8542.
7548. 11/3/02 mee Stringham, John B.; City of N.Y. See 8542.
7549. 11/3/02 mee Stringham, Joseph; City of N.Y. See 8542.
7550. 6/1/99 mee Stringham, Thomas; Clinton, DUT. See 379.
7551. 5/4/84? gee Strivil, Johannes; ---, ---. See 3744. See also 7539 and
7546.
7552. 11/18/00 mor Stuart, Ambrose, blacksmith; Cambridge, WAS; ---, WAS;
co-mees 3741, 3757. (D:25)
7553. 5/8/66 gor Stuart, George, "a disbanded Soldier having served ...
during the late War and last belonging to the Seventy
Eighth Regiment of Foot"; ---, ---; land "east side of
Hudson's River", ALB; gee 4820. (A:12)
7554. 12/15/84 gee Sturdevant, Consider; ---, ---. See 7055.
7555. 3/12/85 gee Sturdevant, Consider; ---, ---. See 7055.
7556. 7/21/92 gee Sturdevant, Perez; Kingsbury, WAS. See 5209.
7557. 12/2/99 gor Sturtevant, Freelove. See 7558.
7558. 12/2/99 gor Sturtevant, Perez (w. Freelove); Kingsbury, WAS; Kingsbury,
WAS; gee 8374. (D:383)
7559. 2/4/96 --- Sutherland, Solomon; ---, DUT. See 5857.
7560. 2/24/96 mor Sutherland, Solomon; ---, DUT. See 8754.
7561. 3/16/96 --- Sutherland, Solomon; ---, DUT. See 290.
7562. 3/16/96 mor Sutherland, Solomon; ---, DUT. See 289.
7563. 6/22/98 gor Sutherland, Solomon; ---, DUT. See 5696, 5697, and 5698.
(three contracts)
7564. 3/16/96 --- Suydam, Samuel; City of N.Y. See 290.
7565. 3/16/96 mor Suydam, Samuel; City of N.Y. See 289.
7566. 6/22/98 gor Suydam, Samuel; City of N.Y. See 5697 and 5698. (two contracts)
7567. 11/9/91 mor Swain, John, yeoman; Easton, WAS; Easton, WAS; mee 7568. (A:434)
7568. 11/9/91 mee Swain, Uriah, mariner; "Island of Nantuckett,"---, --. See 7567.
7569. 6/4/98 gor Swartwout, Bernardus, merchant; City of N.Y.; Old Military
Township #6 (Clinton), CLI; co-gees 270, 311. (B:138)
7570. 6/7/98 gor Swartwout, Bernardus, merchant; City of N.Y.; Old Military
Township #6 (Clinton), CLI; co-gees 6856, 8088. (B:141)
7571. 6/8/98 mee Swartwout, Bernardus, merchant; City of N.Y. See 312 and
6857.
7572. 3/4/00 mee Swartwout, Bernardus, Junr.; City of N.Y. See 5704.
7573. 8/24/90 mor Sweet, Ezra; Hebron, WAS; Shereiff's Pat. in Hebron, WAS;
mee 6978. (A:227)
7574. 7/10/90 mor Sweet, John; Hebron, WAS; Hebron, WAS; mee 1072. (A:237)
7575. 7/5/97 mor Syks, Noah (w. Sybbyl), blacksmith; Granville, WAS; Granville,
WAS; co-mees 75, 2936, 2950. Co-mortgagees are all
"executors of the ... will of James Grant late of Pawling",
(DUT), dec'd. (B:197)
7576. 7/5/97 mor Syks, Sybbyl. See 7575.
7577. 4/8/89 gee Taber, John; Cambridge(?), WAS. See 8318.
7578. 7/8/89 gor Taber, John, house carpenter; Cambridge Dist., ALB; Hoosick
Pat., ALB (sic); gee 113. (WAS Co. D:161)
7579. 2/20/96 gor Taber, John (w. Penelopa), carpenter; Greenfield, SAR;
Hoosick Pat., WAS; gee 1981. (F:138)
7580. 12/21/99 mor Taber, Lewis, yeoman; Easton, WAS; Saratoga Pat., WAS;
mee 8055. (C:175)
7581. 2/20/96 gor Taber, Penelopa. See 7579.
7582. 5/1/02 mor Tabor, Abraham, farmer; Chester, WAS; Chester, WAS; mee 7775.
(D:209)
7583. 9/3/99 gee Tailer, Medad; Granville, WAS. See 5470.
7584. 6/28/82 gee Takel, James, yeoman; New Perth, CHA. See 4875.
7585. 6/23/90 mee Tallman, Isaac, merchant; Pawling, DUT. See 81.
7586. 6/23/90 mee Tallman, Isaac I., merchant; Pawling, DUT. See 81.
7587. 4/8/90 mor Tallman, Isaac I., Esq.; ---, DUT; Plattsburgh, CLI; mee 2312.
(A:51)
7588. 6/23/90 mee Tallman, Peter, merchant; Pawling, DUT. See 81.
7589. 4/13/01 mee Tanner, John; Granville, WAS. See 224.
7590. 3/21/94 gee Tanner, Joseph; Granville, WAS. See 1928.
7591. 7/6/88 gee Tanner, Joshua; Granville, WAS. See 2378.

7592.	7/6/88	mor	Tanner, Joshua; Granville, WAS; <u>Granville, WAS</u>; mee 2379.
			(A:126)
7593.	3/16/89	gee	Tanner, Joshua; Granville, WAS. See 829.
7594.	3/16/89	mor	Tanner, Joshua; Granville, WAS; <u>Granville, WAS</u>; mee 837.
			(A:141)
7595.	3/12/95	gor	Tanner, Joshua (w. Lois), yeoman; Granville, WAS; <u>Granville,</u>
			<u>WAS</u>; gee 1263. (C-2:278)
7596.	3/12/95	gor	Tanner, Lois. See 7595.
7597.	5/2/96	mor	Tanner, Thomas, farmer; Argyle, WAS; <u>Argyle, WAS</u>; co-mees
			1290, 2101, 2217, 5584. (C:270)
7598.	4/25/93	---	Tappan, Peter, dec'd. See 7168.
7599.	4/25/93	gor	Tappen, Elizabeth; ---, ---. See 7168.
7600.	9/16/99	gor	Tappen, Elizabeth; Poughkeepsie, DUT; <u>Plattsburgh, CLI</u>;
			co-gor 1476; gee 6552. Both of the grantors are
			executors of the estate of Peter Tappen "late of
			Poughkeepsie, Esquire", dec'd. (B:221)
7601.	9/17/99	mee	Tappen, Elizabeth; Poughkeepsie, DUT. See 6548.
7602.	2/8/85	gee	Tappen, Peter, gentleman; ---, ---. See 5887.
7603.	3/14/87	gee	Tappen, Peter; ---, ---. See 5911.
7604.	4/20/93	gor	Tayler, Alexander, farmer; Argyle, WAS; <u>Argyle, WAS</u>;
			co-gor 7607; gee 7613. (B-2:70)
7605.	5/26/85	mee	Tayler, John; ---, ---. See 7375.
7606.	11/24/85	mee	Tayler, John; Albany, ALB. See 4684.
7607.	4/20/93	gor	Tayler, John; Argyle, WAS. See 7604.
7608.	12/24/94	mee	Tayler, John, "attorney for Archibald Brown of the City of
			Glascow ..., Scotland, druggist". See 2409.
7609.	2/17/01	mee	Tayler, John; Albany, ALB. See 5096.
7610.	1/24/92	mee	Tayler, John, Esq.; Albany, ALB. See 3828.
7611.	7/7/96	mee	Tayler, John, Esq.; Albany, ALB. See 7198.
7612.	7/30/01	mee	Tayler, John, Esq.; Albany, ALB. See 7303.
7613.	4/20/93	gee	Tayler, John, Senr., weaver; Argyle, WAS. See 7604.
7614.	4/22/94	gee	Tayler, Joseph, yeoman; Argyle, WAS. See 4586.
7615.	11/20/95	gee	Tayler, Joseph; Argyle, WAS. See 8067.
7616.	11/20/95	mor	Tayler, Joseph; Argyle, WAS; <u>Argyle, WAS</u>; mee 8068. (B:3)
7617.	1/--/96	gor	Tayler, Joseph; Argyle, WAS; <u>Argyle, WAS</u>; gee 2302. (B-2:531)
7618.	10/8/89	gor	Tayler, Stephen; Willsborough, CLI; <u>James McBride Pat., CLI</u>;
			gee 4798. (A:107)
7619.	5/8/93	gee	Taylor, Alexander; Argyle, WAS. See 6757.
7620.	5/8/93	mor	Taylor, Alexander, yeoman; Argyle, WAS; <u>Argyle, WAS</u>;
			co-mors 2856, 4702, 8014; co-mees 4642, 6758, 6808.
			Co-mortgagees are all executors of the estate of **John**
			Morine Scott, Esq., dec'd. (A:442)
7621.	3/12/96	mee	Taylor, Benjamin; City of N.Y. See 948.
7622.	12/16/99	mor	Taylor, Dorcas, spinster; Hebron, WAS; <u>Argyle, WAS</u>; co-mees
			4048, 4050. (C:174)
7623.	1/15/65	gee	Taylor, Duncan, farmer; ---, ORA. See 6219.
7624.	5/29/97	mor	Taylor, Elizabeth. See 7647.
7625.	7/4/96	mee	Taylor, John, merchant; City of N.Y. See 4005.
7626.	6/1/98	mee	Taylor, John, merchant; City of N.Y. See 204.
7627.	7/14/01	mee	Taylor, John, yeoman; ---, REN. See 1931.
7628.	8/27/94	gee	Taylor, John, Esq.; Albany, ALB. See 2815.
7629.	5/23/98	gor	Taylor, John, Esq.; Albany, ALB; <u>---, CLI</u>; co-gees 3383,
			6506. (ESS Co. A:11)
7630.	5/23/98	mee	Taylor, John, Esq.; Albany, ALB. See 6507, 7630.
7631.	8/18/00	mee	Taylor, John, Esq.; Albany, ALB. See 8511.
7632.	7/26/93	gee	Taylor, Joseph, farmer; ---, WAS. See 6889.
7633.	4/24/94	mor	Taylor, Joseph, yeoman; Argyle, WAS; <u>Argyle, WAS</u>; mee 4598.
			(A:479)
7634.	5/9/99	gee	Taylor, Joseph, farmer; Argyle, WAS. See 4082.
7635.	5/22/99	gor	Taylor, Joseph, farmer; Argyle, WAS; <u>Argyle, WAS</u>; gee 6056.
			(D:114)
7636.	5/25/99	gor	Taylor, Joseph; Argyle, WAS; <u>Argyle, WAS</u>; gee 6374. (D:134)
7637.	4/13/02	mor	Taylor, Joseph (w. Lydia), farmer; Hartford, WAS; <u>Hartford,</u>
			<u>WAS</u>; mee 4166. (D:158)
7638.	4/13/02	mor	Taylor, Lydia. See 7637.
7639.	8/8/96	gor	Taylor, Mary. See 7640.

7640. 8/8/96 gor Taylor, Maylon, Esq. (w. Mary); ---, ---; Whitehall, WAS;
　　　　　　　　　co-gors 5551, 5554; gee 2885.　　　　　　　(D:319)
7641. 12/12/01 gor Taylor, Medad; Granville, WAS; Granville, WAS; gee 3968.
　　　　　　　　　　　　　　　　　　　　　　　　　　　　　　　(F:96)
7642. 1/31/98 mor Taylor, Nathan, farmer; Hartford, WAS; Hartford, WAS;
　　　　　　　　　mee 1481.　　　　　　　　　　　　　　　　(B:329)
7643. 9/19/86 gee Taylor, Prince; ---, ---. See 4058.
7644. 7/2/89 gee Taylor, Prince; ---, CLI. See 1016.
7645. 6/10/69 gor Taylor, William; Coventry, WIN, CT; Turner Pat., ALB;
　　　　　　　　　gee 4261.　　　　　　　　　　　(WAS Co. B:145)
7646. 5/21/93 gee Taylor, William; Cambridge, WAS. See 2263.
7647. 5/29/97 mor Taylor, William (w. Elizabeth); Cambridge, WAS; Cambridge,
　　　　　　　　　WAS; mee 2164.　　　　　　　　　　　　　(B:175)
7648. 5/3/80 gor Tearse, Peter B.; ---, WAS; Argyle, WAS; co-gees 1273,
　　　　　　　　　6366.　　　　　　　　　　　　　　　　　　(A:188)
7649. 4/15/88 gor Tearse, Peter B., Esq.; Argyle, WAS; Argyle, WAS; gee 4659.
　　　　　　　　　　　　　　　　　　　　　　　　　　　　　　(A:368)
7650. 1/18/93 gor Tearse, Peter B., Esq., sheriff of Washington County;
　　　　　　　　　---, ---; Hebron, WAS (sheriff's sale); gee 8035. (B-2:80)
7651. 8/6/93 mor Tearse, Peter B., Esq.; Argyle, WAS; Argyle, WAS; mee 8528.
　　　　　　　　　　　　　　　　　　　　　　　　　　　　　　(A:430)
7652. 8/12/96 gor Teebles, Abby. See 7653.
7653. 8/12/96 gor Teebles, Hugh (w. Abby); Half Moon, SAR; John Schuyler
　　　　　　　　　Junior's Pat., WAS; gee 7259.　　　　　　(C-2:130)
7654. 12/9/01 mee Tefft, David; Argyle, WAS. See 3056.
7655. 7/10/87? mor Teirce, Mary. See 7656.
7656. 7/10/87? mor Teirce, Peter B. (w. Mary); ---, ---; Argyle, WAS; mee 1208.
　　　　　　　　　　　　　　　　　　　　　　　　　　　　　　(A:44)
7657. 5/3/88 mee Teirce, Peter B., Esq.; ---, ---. See 1274 and 6361.
7658. 5/29/90 gor Teirce, Peter B., Esq., sheriff of Washington County; ---,
　　　　　　　　　---; Granville, WAS (sheriff's sale); co-gees 2052, 8251.
　　　　　　　　　　　　　　　　　　　　　　　　　　　　　　(A:159)
7659. 7/13/99 gee Telfaire, George; Argyle, WAS. See 2723.
7660. 10/28/85 gor Ten Broeck, Abraham, Esq.; Albany, ALB; Walloomsack Pat., WAS;
　　　　　　　　　gee 3441.　　　　　　　　　　　　　　　　(D:5)
7661. 11/3/86 gor Ten Broeck, Abraham, Esq.; Albany, ALB; Walloomsack Pat., WAS;
　　　　　　　　　co-gees 8187, 8714.　　　　　　　　　　　(D:256)
7662. 8/10/90 gor Ten Broeck, Abraham, Esq.; Albany, ALB; Plattsburgh(?), CLI;
　　　　　　　　　co-gees 199, 201.　　　　　　　　　　　　(A:171)
7663. 8/11/90 mee Ten Broeck, Abraham, Esq.; Albany, ALB. See 202.
7664. 4/28/92 gor Ten Broeck, Abraham, Esq.; Albany, ALB; Zephaniah Platt's
　　　　　　　　　Pat., CLI; gee 5179.　　　　　　　　　　　(A:302)
7665. 4/28/92 mee Ten Broeck, Abraham, Esq.; Albany, ALB. See 5180.
7666. 6/24/88 mor Teney, Solomon, yeoman; Simsbury, ---, CT; Whitehall, WAS;
　　　　　　　　　co-mor 7667; mee 4318.　　　　　　　　　　(A:80)
7667. 6/24/88 mor Teney, Stephen, yeoman; Simsbury, ---, CT. See 7666.
7668. 3/6/87 gor Ten Eyck, Abraham; ---, ---. See 7055.
7669. 11/10/91 mee Ten Eyck, Abraham, merchant; Albany, ALB. See 5625.
7670. 3/16/92 gor Ten Eyck, Abraham, gentleman; Albany, ALB; Jessup's Pat.,
　　　　　　　　　WAS; gee 6585.　　　　　　　　　　　　　(B-2:152)
7671. 3/16/92 mee Ten Eyck, Abraham, gantleman; Albany, ALB. See 6586.
7672. 8/15/93 mee Ten Eyck, Abraham; Albany, ALB. See 1908.
7673. 2/1/94 mee Ten Eyck, Elcie. See 7677.
7674. 7/6/99 mee Ten Eyck, Harmanus, merchant; Albany, ALB. See 8483.
7675. 5/20/00 mee Ten Eyck, Harmanus, merchant; Albany, ALB. See 680 and 8484.
7676. 2/20/01 mee Ten Eyck, Harmanus, merchant; Albany, ALB. See 495.
7677. 2/1/94 mee Ten Eyck, Myndert S. (w. Elcie); ---, ---. See 1038.
7678. 6/29/01 mor Terrell, Joseph; Champlain, CLI; Champlain, CLI; mee 5101.
7679. 6/1/92 gee Terril, Amos; Hebron, WAS. See 8741.　　　　　/ (B:36)
7680. 1/7/99 gee Terry, Shubel; Easton, WAS. See 3242.
7681. 7/2/92 gor Teryl, Samuel, farmer; Hebron, WAS. See 3122.
7682. 6/9/98 mor Tews, William, farmer; Hartford, WAS; Hartford, WAS; mee 1492.
　　　　　　　　　　　　　　　　　　　　　　　　　　　　　　(B:332)
7683. 2/13/00 gee Thacker, Townsend; Willsborough, ESS. See 2633.
7684. 2/7/02 mor Thacker, Townsend; ---, ---; James Judd's Pat., ESS; mee 6424.
　　　　　　　　　　　　　　　　　　　　　　　　　　　　　　(A:95)

7685. 10/5/98 mor Thayer, Israel; ---, CLI; Old Military Township #7
(Chateaugay), CLI; co-mees 274, 316. (A:362)
7686. 9/25/86 gee Thew, Garret, gentleman; Haverstraw Precinct, ORA. See 5897.
7687. 9/27/86 mor Thew, Garret; Haverstraw Precinct, ORA. See 7689.
7688. 9/25/86 gee Thew, Gilbert, gentleman; Haverstraw Precinct, ORA. See 5897.
7689. 9/27/86 mor Thew, Gilbert, gentleman; Haverstraw Precinct, ORA;
Plattsburgh, WAS; co-mor 7687; mee 5899. (A:3)
7690. 1/7/89 gor Thew, Gilbert, farmer; Plattsburgh, CLI; Plattsburgh, CLI
(several parcels); gee 5270. (A:44)
7691. 1/7/89 mee Thew, Gilbert; Plattsburgh, CLI. See 5271.
7692. 4/17/90 mor Thew, Gilbert; Plattsburgh, CLI; Plattsburgh, CLI; mee 5273.
(A:45)
7693. 4/11/97 mee Thomas, Caleb, blacksmith; Champlain, CLI. See 2889.
7694. 11/16/85 gee Thomas, David, yeoman; ---, WAS. See 4403.
7695. 7/1/97 gor Thomas, David, gentleman; Salem, WAS; Westfield, WAS;
gee 6657. (C-2:208)
7696. 5/1/98 mee Thomas, David; Salem, WAS. See 2397.
7697. 6/4/98 mee Thomas, David; Salem, WAS. See 1315.
7698. 2/11/00 mee Thomas, David, "the Elder"; Cambridge, WAS. See 8197.
7699. 12/28/89 gee Thomas, David, Esq.; Salem, WAS. See 8571.
7700. 6/20/96 gee Thomas, David, Esq.; Salem, WAS. See 8406.
7701. 9/22/96 gee Thomas, David, Esq.; Salem, WAS. See 7951.
7702. 10/5/96 gee Thomas, David, Esq.; Salem, WAS. See 7952.
7703. 12/15/84 gee Thomas, Ephraim; ---, ---. See 7055.
7704. 3/20/94 gee Thomas, Gardiner; Argyle, WAS. See 1398.
7705. 9/7/69 gor Thomas, George; ---, ---. See 7955.
7706. 12/10/84 gee Thomas, John; ---, ---. See 7055.
7707. 1/11/94 mee Thomas, Joseph; Cambridge, WAS. See 3287.
7708. 6/22/98 gee Thomas, Joseph; Hartford, WAS. See 5698.
7709. 6/23/98 mor Thomas, Joseph; Hartford, WAS; Old Military Township #7
(Chateaugay), CLI; mee 5699. (A:317)
7710. 12/26/91 gor Thomas, Robert (w. Sarah); Saratoga, SAR; land "east side of
Hudson's River", WAS; gee 3062. (A:256)
7711. 12/10/84 gee Thomas, Samuel; ---, ---. See 7055.
7712. 12/26/91 gor Thomas, Sarah. See 7710.
7713. 6/22/93 gee Thomas, Seth, house carpenter; Cambridge, WAS. See 97.
7714. 6/13/95 gee Thomas, William; Hebron, WAS. See 6820.
7715. 5/30/01 gee Thomas, William, yeoman; Hebron, WAS. See 8666.
7716. 2/26/96 mor Thompson, Alexander; Salem, WAS; Salem, WAS; mee 2128. (C:269)
7717. 12/20/96 mor Thompson, Hannah; Hebron, WAS. See 7720.
7718. 7/5/93 mee Thompson, Israel, Esq.; Pittstown, REN. See 2300.
7719. 2/16/87 gor Thompson, James; Salem, WAS; Salem, WAS; gee 5172. (A:142)
7720. 12/20/96 mor Thompson, James; Hebron, WAS; Hebron, WAS; co-mors 2978,
2988, 7717; mee 1268. (B:157)
7721. 5/25/96 mor Thompson, Jesse(?), farmer; Granville, WAS; Granville, WAS;
mee 3848. (B:74)
7722. 9/29/02 mee Thompson, Nathan; Argyle, WAS. See 1784.
7723. 2/15/91 gor Thompson, Robert; City of N.Y. See 2729.
7724. 3/13/01 mor Thompson, Sebe; Plattsburgh, CLI; Plattsburgh, CLI; mee 5766.
(B:27)
7725. 7/20/02 mor Thompson, Sebo(?); Plattsburgh, CLI; Plattsburgh, CLI;
mee 5684. (B:81)
7726. 5/22/00 gee Thompson, William, Junr.; Salem, WAS. See 605.
7727. 4/20/73 gor Thomson, George; ---, ---. See 7957.
7728. 3/10/79 gor Thomson, Hannah. See 7730.
7729. 2/23/93 gee Thomson, James; Brookfield, WOR, MA. See 6306.
7730. 3/10/79 gor Thomson, John (w. Hannah); Perth Amboy, ---, NJ; Argyle,
WAS; gee 6203. (A:47)
7731. 12/9/83 gee Thomson, William; New Perth, CHA. See 1393.
7732. 5/30/96 mee Thomson, William; Goshen, ORA. See 5457.
7733. 4/5/92 gee Thomson, William, Esq.; Goshen, ORA. See 4016.
7734. 5/13/96 gor Thomson, William, Esq.; Goshen, ORA; Canadian and Nova Scotia
Refugees' Pat., CLI; gee 5456. (A:519)
7735. 3/12/85 gee Thomson, Willis; ---, ---. See 7055.
7736. 9/21/01 mor Thorn, Martha. See 7738.
7737. 6/26/01 mee Thorn, Stephen; Granville, WAS. See 5332.

183

<u>7738.</u>	9/21/01	mor	Thorn, Stephen (w. Martha); ---, WAS; <u>Granville, WAS</u>; mee 1694. (D:93)
7739.	10/6/01	gee	Thorn, Stephen; Granville, WAS. See 708.
7740.	12/12/01	mee	Thorn, Stephen; Granville, WAS. See 3969.
7741.	12/17/01	mee	Thorn, Stephen; Granville, WAS. See 2019.
7742.	3/14/87	gee	Thorn, William; ---, ---. See 5911.
<u>7743.</u>	6/27/92	gor	Thorn, William, gentleman; Washington, DUT; <u>land "west side of the great River Ausable"</u>, CLI; gee 545. (A:412)
<u>7744.</u>	5/2/93	gor	Thorn, William, yeoman; Washington, DUT; <u>Zephaniah Platt's Pat.</u>, CLI; gee 7184. (A:455)
7745.	9/13/96	mee	Thorn, William; ---, DUT. See 6307.
<u>7746.</u>	10/3/96	gor	Thorn, William; ---, DUT; <u>Willsborough, CLI</u>; gee 3257. (B:60)
7747.	10/3/96	mee	Thorn, William; ---, DUT. See 3258.
7748.	2/22/98	mee	Thorn, William; ---, DUT. See 3841.
7749.	2/28/98	mee	Thorn, William; ---, ---. See 6309.
7750.	2/28/98	mor	Thorn, William; ---, DUT. See 4251.
7751.	4/9/00	mee	Thorne, Daniel, merchant; City of N.Y. See 1826.
7752.	4/9/00	mee	Thorne, William, merchant; City of N.Y. See 1826.
<u>7753.</u>	10/15/00	mor	Thurber, Cromwell; Champlain, CLI; <u>Champlain, CLI</u>; mee 1702. (B:8)
<u>7754.</u>	2/20/01	mor	Thurber, Eddy; Champlain, CLI; <u>Champlain, CLI</u>; mee 5097. (B:10)
<u>7755.</u>	11/20/93	gor	Thurber, Edward; Stillwater, SAR; <u>Mark Graves Pat., CLI</u>; gee 7758. (B:230)
7756.	7/15/99	gee	Thurber, Edward, Junr.; Champlain, CLI. See 7757.
<u>7757.</u>	7/15/99	gor	Thurber, Edward, Senr.; Champlain, CLI; <u>Champlain, CLI</u>; gee 7756. (B:228)
7758.	11/20/93	gee	Thurber, John; Stillwater, SAR. See 7755.
<u>7759.</u>	10/14/90	mor	Thurber, Joseph; ---, CLI; <u>Plattsburgh, CLI</u>; mee 6252. (A:57)
7760.	9/29/92	gee	Thurber, Joseph; Plattsburgh, CLI. See 7432.
<u>7761.</u>	4/10/94	gor	Thurber, Joseph; Plattsburgh, CLI; <u>Plattsburgh, CLI</u>; gee 242.
7761a.	3/28/01	mee	Thurbur, Eddy; Champlain, CLI. See 1895. / (A:353)
7762.	10/18/93	gee	Thurbur, Edward; Stillwater, SAR. See 5129.
<u>7763.</u>	1/3/93	mor	Thurbur, Joseph; Plattsburgh, CLI; <u>Plattsburgh, CLI</u>; mee 6625. (A:98)
<u>7764.</u>	3/5/93	mor	Thurbur, Keley; Plattsburgh, CLI; <u>Plattsburgh, CLI</u>; mee 6634. (A:102)
7765.	5/28/96	gor	Thurman, Catharine. See 7776.
<u>7766.</u>	2/1/96	gor	Thurman, John, merchant; City of N.Y.; <u>Thurman, WAS</u>; gee 4471 (C-2:282); gee 4498 (C-2:281); gee 4656 (F:168). (three contracts)
<u>7767.</u>	2/5/96	gor	Thurman, John, merchant; City of N.Y.; <u>Thurman, WAS</u>; gee 561. (C-2:192)
<u>7768.</u>	8/29/96	gor	Thurman, John, merchant; City of N.Y.; <u>Thurman, WAS</u>; co-gor 7777; gee 3894. (C-2:150)
7769.	1/26/98	mee	Thurman, John; Thurman, WAS. See 7996.
<u>7770.</u>	3/2/99	gor	Thurman, John, merchant; Thurman, WAS; <u>Thurman, WAS</u>; co-gor 7778; gee 1917. (E:263)
7771.	4/24/99	mee	Thurman, John; Thurman, WAS. See 3583.
7772.	5/1/00	mee	Thurman, John, Esq.; Thurman, WAS. See 375, 386 (3 contracts), 435, 905 (2 contracts), 906, 907 (2 contracts), 1258 (2 contracts), 1861, 1862, 1863 (2 contracts), 2257 (2 contracts), 2306, 2635, 2962, 2973, 3524 (2 contracts), 4363, 4972, 4973, 4976 (2 contracts), 4978 (2 contracts), 4979, 4980, 5202, 5417, 5444, 6093, 7403, 8156. A total of 39 contracts this date.
7773.	2/10/96	gee	Thurman, John, Esq.; City of N.Y. See 7013.
7774.	12/31/99	mee	Thurman, John, Esq.; Thurman, WAS. See 3582.
7775.	5/1/02	mee	Thurman, John, Esq.; Thurman, WAS. See 1896, 2258, 2467, 2580 (2 contracts), 3213, 4119, 4981, 5055, 5200, 6178, 7288, 7582, 8490. A total of 14 contracts this date.
<u>7776.</u>	5/28/96	gor	Thurman, Richardson (w. Catharine); Thurman, WAS; <u>Thurman, WAS</u>; gee 7456. (C-2:328)
7777.	8/29/96	gor	Thurman, Richardson; Thurman, WAS. See 7768.
7778.	3/2/99	gor	Thurman, Richardson, yeoman; Thurman, WAS. See 7770.
<u>7779.</u>	9/26/00	mor	Tibbits, Benjamin; Queensbury, WAS; <u>Queensbury, WAS</u>; mee 2511. (E:3)

184

7780. 4/19/02 mee Tibbits, Benjamin; Troy, REN. See 1558.
7781. 7/7/02 mee Tibbits, Benjamin; Troy, REN. See 4941.
7782. 4/19/02 mee Tibbits, George; Troy, REN. See 1558.
7783. 7/7/02 mee Tibbits, George; Troy, REN. See 4941.
7784. 4/13/99 gee Tibbitts, Benjamin, merchant; Troy, REN. See 3717.
7785. 4/13/99 gee Tibbitts, George, merchant; Troy, REN. See 3717.
7786. 6/1/02 mor Tifft, James, yeoman; Easton, WAS. See 4524.
7787. 11/28/95 mor Tifft, John, farmer; Easton, WAS; Saratoga Pat., WAS;
                    mee 3669.   (B:13)
7788. 6/3/88 gee Tifft, Pardon, yeoman; Argyle, WAS. See 1235.
7789. 10/7/94 gee Tifft, Stanton; ---, ---. See 8583.
7790. 9/1/95 gee Tifft, William, gentleman; Easton, WAS. See 781.
7791. 6/26/94 gor Tilford, George; Hebron, WAS; Hebron, WAS; gee 6535. (B-2:365)
7792. 8/5/02 mee Tillotson, Thomas, Esq.; ---, ---, NY. See 7098.
7793. 2/1/96 gor Tilton, Bathiah. See 7801.
7794. 3/11/99 gor Tilton, Bethiah. See 7802.
7795. 1/24/89 gee Tilton, Ebenezer; Cambridge, ALB. See 7293.
7796. 2/1/96 gor Tilton, Ebenezer (w. Hepzabah); Cambridge, WAS. See 7801.
7797. 3/11/99 gor Tilton, Ebenezer (w. Hepzabah); Cambridge, WAS. See 7802.
7798. 2/1/96 gor Tilton, Hepzabah. See 7796.
7799. 3/11/99 gor Tilton, Hepzabah. See 7802.
7800. 1/24/89 gee Tilton, John; Cambridge, ALB. See 7293.
7801. 2/1/96 gor Tilton, John (w. Bathiah); Cambridge, WAS; Cambridge Pat.,
                    WAS; co-gors 7796, 7798; gee 7060.   (D:126)
7802. 3/11/99 gor Tilton, John (w. Bethiah); Cambridge, WAS; Cambridge, WAS;
                    co-gors 7797, 7799; gee 4966.   (D:354)
7803. 5/3/97 gor Tinkee, Coonrad; ---, ---. See 7807.
7804. 5/4/97 mee Tinkee, Coonrad; ---, ---. See 8248.
7805. 5/4/97 gor Tinkee, Coonrod; ---, ---. See 7810/
7806. 5/3/97 gor Tinkee, Hannah. See 7807.
7807. 5/3/97 gor Tinkee, Henry (w. Hannah); ---, ---; Argyle, WAS; co-gors
                    3943, 3947, 7138, 7155, 7803, 7809, 7812; gee 8247.
                                                                (C-2:203)
7808. 5/4/97 gee Tinkee, Henry; Argyle, WAS. See 7810.
7809. 5/3/97 gor Tinkee, John; ---, ---. See 7807.
7810. 5/4/97 gor Tinkee, John; ---, ---; Argyle, WAS; co-gors 3929, 7139,
                    7805, 7813; gee 7808. All grantors and the grantee are
                    "children" of Thomas Henry Tinkee, dec'd.   (C-2:197)
7811. 5/4/97 mee Tinkee, John; ---, ---. See 8248.
7812. 5/3/97 gor Tinkee, Lanah; ---, ---. See 7807.
7813. 5/4/97 gor Tinkee, Lanah. See 7810.
7814. 5/4/97 mee Tinkee, Lanah; ---, ---. See 8248.
7815. 5/4/97 --- Tinkey, Thomas Henry, dec'd. See 7810.
7816. 6/9/74 gee Tinkey, Hendrick; ---, ORA. See 4796.
7817. 5/9/01 mee Tinkey, Henry, farmer; Argyle, WAS. See 4888.
7818. 11/16/01 mor Tinkey, Henry, farmer; Argyle, WAS; Argyle, WAS; mee 4593.
                                                                (D:119)
7819. 5/10/95 gor Titus, Ebenezer, yeoman; Springfield, OTS; Salem, WAS;
                    gee 7824.   (C-2:140)
7820. 7/22/94 gor Titus, James, yeoman; Springfield, OTS; Salem, WAS; gee 7823.
                                                                (C-2:141)
7821. 8/20/92 gee Titus, Robert; Salem, WAS. See 7827.
7822. 2/5/93 gee Titus, Robert, yeoman; Salem, WAS. See 7825.
7823. 7/22/94 gee Titus, Robert, yeoman; Salem, WAS. See 7820.
7824. 5/10/95 gee Titus, Robert, yeoman; Salem, WAS. See 7819.
7825. 2/5/93 gor Titus, Samuel, yeoman; Salem, WAS; Salem, WAS; gee 7822.
                                                                (B-2:49)
7826. 10/30/72 gee Titus, Timothy; New Perth, CHA. See 3557.
7827. 8/20/92 gor Titus, Timothy, yeoman; Salem, WAS; Salem, WAS; gee 7821.
                                                                (B-2:47)
7828. 7/1/00 mor Tobey, Jesse; ---, ---; ---, ESS; mee 5572.   (A:52)
7829. 12/29/91 gee Tobias, John; ---, ---. See 4878.
7830. 9/17/94 gee Tobias, John; ---, WAS. See 2428.
7831. 9/7/96 gor Tobias, John; Cambridge, WAS; Plattsburgh, CLI; gee 8770.
                                                                (A:501)
7832. 9/8/96 mee Tobias, John; ---, WAS. See 8771.

185

7833.	7/1/00	mor	Toby, Jesse; ---, ---. ---, ESS; mee 5572. (A:73)
7834.	3/5/92	gor	Todd, Jeane. See 7837.
7835.	3/5/92	gee	Todd, John; Cambridge, WAS. See 8842.
7836.	3/5/92	gor	Todd, John; Cambridge, WAS; Cambridge, WAS; gee 2065. (A:514)
7837.	3/5/92	gor	Todd, John (w. Jeane); Cambridge, WAS; Cambridge Pat., WAS; gee 2065. (B-2:95)
7838.	8/20/93	gee	Todd, John; Argyle, WAS. See 4983.
7839.	9/6/94	gee	Todd, John, farmer; Argyle, WAS. See 2529.
7840.	3/15/97	gor	Tollibois, Jaque, gentleman; "late a Lieutenant in the Regiment commanded by James Livingston"; Parish of Grand Stours(?), Lower Canada; Champlain, CLI (in the Canadian and Nova Scotia Refugees' Pat.); gee 4017. (B:20)
7841.	12/6/91	gee	Tomb(?), James, farmer; Salem, WAS. See 2506.
7842.	7/16/92	gee	Tomb, James, farmer; Salem, WAS. See 7844.
7843.	9/10/96	mee	Tomb, James; ---, ---. See 6622.
7844.	7/16/92	gor	Tomb, Joseph (w. Lettice), physician; Salem, WAS; Salem, WAS; gee 7842. (C-2:86)
7845.	9/10/96	---	Tomb, Joseph, dec'd.; Salem, WAS. See 6622.
7846.	7/16/92	gor	Tomb, Lettice. See 7844.
7847.	3/3/84	gee	Tombly (?), Joseph; ---, ---. See 1437.
7848.	1/3/97	gee	Tompson, Nathan; Argyle, WAS. See 5480.
7849.	7/6/96	gor	Torrey, John, house carpenter; City of N.Y. See 4487.
7850.	12/20/94	gee	Touhey(?), Henry, farmer; Argyle, WAS. See 7448.
7851.	3/4/96	gor	Town, Eunice. See 7852.
7852.	3/4/96	gor	Town, Francis (w. Eunice), carpenter; Hebron, WAS; Hebron, WAS; gee 8664. (C-2:193)
7853.	9/4/98	mor	Town, William; Granville, WAS; Granville, WAS; mee 4133. (C:267)
7854.	1/15/98	mee	Towner, Samuel; ---, ---. See 3430.
7855.	7/1/85	mor	Towns(?), Isaac; Skenesborough, WAS; Skenesborough, WAS; mee 8555. (A:35)
7856.	6/7/98	mor	Townsend, Amasa, Junr. (w. Sarah), yeoman; Hartford, WAS; Hartford, WAS; mee 365. (C:16)
7857.	6/7/98	mor	Townsend, Sarah. See 7856.
7858.	2/12/98	mor	Townson, Calvin; Hartford, WAS; Hartford, WAS; mee 1485. (B:328)
7859.	7/29/91	mor	Townsown (sic), Amasa (w. Sarah); Westfield, WAS. See 4104.
7860.	7/29/91	mor	Townsown (sic), Sarah. See 7859.
7861.	7/1/85	gee	Tozer, Elishama; ---, ---. See 7055.
7862.	3/6/86	mor	Tozor, Elishema; Skenesborough, WAS; Skenesborough, WAS; mee 3195. (Deed Book B:236)
7863.	7/6/88	mor	Tracy, Theophilus; ---, ---; Granville, WAS; mee 2380. (A:140)
7864.	7/1/88	gee	Tracy, Theophilus, Junr., yeoman; Granville, WAS. See 2382.
7865.	10/14/90	gee	Travis, Abraham; Plattsburgh, CLI. See 6262.
7866.	10/14/90	mor	Travis, Abraham; Plattsburgh, cLI; Cumberland Head (Plattsburgh), CLI; mee 6263. (A:54)
7867.	5/1/94	mor	Travis, Abraham; Plattsburgh, CLI; Cumberland Head (Plattsburgh), CLI; co-mees 54, 6241. Co-mortgagees are executors of the estate of Simon R. Reeve "late of New Jersey", dec'd. Co-mortgagees are acting in trust for the legatees of the estate of S.R.R. above (legatees not named). (A:128)
7868.	11/1/96	mor	Travis, Abraham, yeoman; ---, CLI; Cumberland Head (Plattsburgh), CLI; mee 7239. (A:214)
7869.	7/7/02	gor	Travis, Abraham (w. Sylvia), carpenter; Plattsburgh, CLI; Plattsburgh, CLI; co-gees 556, 1974, 5813, 6200. Co-grantees are all supervisors of the County of Clinton. (B:364)
7870.	7/7/02	gor	Travis, Sylvia. See 7869.
7871.	8/24/93	mee	Treadwell, Nathaniel Hazard. See 3905.
7872.	5/1/90	mor	Treadwell, Thomas, Esq.; Smithtown, SUF; ---, CLI; mee 7923. (A:46)
7873.	11/21/99	gor	Treadwell, Thomas, Esq.; ---, CLI; Plattsburgh, CLI; gee 7224. (A:216)
7874.	9/3/00	mor	Treat, John; Hartford, WAS; Westfield, WAS; mee 2009. (C:176)
7875.	8/13/91	gee	Tredwell, Nathaniel; Plattsburgh, cLI. See 7880.
7876.	2/8/85	gee	Tredwell, Thomas, gentleman; ---, ---. See 5887.

7877. 3/14/87 gee Tredwell, Thomas; ---, ---. See 5911.
7878. 4/30/90 gee Tredwell, Thomas; Smithtown, SUF. See 4962.
7879. 8/1/95 gee Tredwell, Thomas; Plattsburgh, CLI. See 8266.
7880. 8/13/91 gor Tredwell, Thomas, Esq.; Huntington, SUF; Plattsburgh, CLI;
       gee 7875. (A:201)
7881. 8/23/92 gor Tredwell, Thomas, Esq.; Huntington, SUF; land "north side
       of river Saranac", CLI; gee 3903. (A:308)
7882. 11/6/93 mee Tredwell, Thomas, Esq.; Huntington, SUF. See 5299.
7883. 8/11/98 mor Tredwell, Thomas, Esq.; Plattsburgh, CLI; Plattsburgh, CLI;
       mee 7267. (A:359)
7884. 9/20/73 gor Trickett, Margaret. See 7885.
7885. 9/20/73 gor Trickett, Thomas (w. Margaret), "late Quarter Master of
       his Majesty's forty-fourth Regiment of Foot"; Chambly,
       Dist. of Montreal, Quebec; land "on waters from Wood
       Creek running into Lake Champlain (Whitehall area?), WAS;
       co-gees 3034, 4243. (A:15)
7886. 2/26/00 mor Trimble, Alexander, one of the heirs of George Trimble,
       dec'd.; Crown Point, ESS; ---, CLI; co-mees 3411, 3640,
       3960, 7892, 7894, 7895, 7897. (A:427)
7887. 10/24/93 mor Trimble, George, merchant; Ticonderoga, CLI; land "between
       Ticonderoga and Crown Point", CLI; co-mees 505, 506, 3463,
       4246. (A:125)
7888. 2/26/00 --- Trimble, George, dec'd. See 7886.
7889. 4/1/96 mee Trimble, George, Esq.; Crown Point, CLI. See 8179.
7890. 11/3/96 mee Trimble, George, Esq.; Crown Point, CLI. See 1027.
7891. 11/9/01 --- Trimble, George, Esq., dec'd; ---, CLI. See 3412.
7892. 2/26/00 mee Trimble, John; Crown Point, ESS. See 7886.
7893. 1/9/01 gor Trimble, John; Crown Point, ESS; Allen Campbell's Pat., ESS;
       co-gees 5215, 5216. (A:23)
7894. 2/26/00 mee Trimble, Sarah. See 7886.
7895. 2/26/00 mee Trimble, Timothy; ---, ORA. See 7886.
7896. 11/9/01 --- Trimble, Timothy; ---, ORA. See 3412.
7897. 2/26/00 mee Trimble, William; ---, ORA. See 7886.
7898. 2/25/00 mee Tripp, James; Queensbury, WAS. See 7316.
7899. 2/28/00 mee Tripp, James, yeoman; Queensbury, WAS. See 7537.
7900. 11/5/98 mor Tripp, Jonathan; Queensbury, WAS; Queensbury, WAS; mee 2523.
       (C:268)
7901. 9/28/01 mee Tripp, Jonathan; Queensbury, WAS. See 3021.
7902. 4/8/00 gee Tripp, Robert; Champlain, CLI. See 5092.
7903. 7/7/86 gee Trivin(?), James; ---, ---. See 2618.
7904. 6/25/93 mor Truesdell, Ichabod, carpenter; Plattsburgh, CLI; Plattsburgh,
       CLI; mee 7524. (A:103)
7905. 9/7/96 mor Truesdill, Ichabod; Plattsburgh, CLI; Plattsburgh, CLI;
       mee 5860. (A:195)
7906. 4/15/96 mor Trull(?), Willard (w. -?-); Cambridge, WAS; Cambridge, WAS;
       mee 4018. (B:154)
7907. 2/17/00 mor Trull, William; Cambridge, WAS; Bane Pat., WAS; mee 6303.
       (D:22b)
7908. 10/14/96 gee Trustees of the Episcopal Church in Salem (trustees not
       named). See 695.
7909. 11/18/95 gor Trustees of the First Presbyterian Congregation; New Perth,
       WAS; Salem, WAS; gee 7950. Trustees' signature: "Alex-
       ander McNish Trustee Clark" (sic). "Clark" may be "clerk"?
7910. 6/1/85 gee Tubbs, Zebulon; ---, ---. See 7055. / C-2:78)
7911. 1/12/97 gor Tubbs, Zebulon, yeoman; Whitehall, WAS; Whitehall, WAS;
       co-gees 3708, 3709. (C-2:114)
7912. 1/14/97 mee Tubbs, Zebulon, yeoman; Whitehall, WAS. See 3710.
7913. 1/15/02 gee Tucker, Daniel; Granville, WAS. See 408.
7914. 1/22/02 mor Tucker, Daniel; Granville, WAS; Granville, WAS; mee 4151.
       (D:140)
7915. 2/2/02 gor Tucker, Daniel; Granville, WAS; ---, WAS; gee 6547. (F:121)
7916. 5/8/98 gee Tucker, Joshua, farmer; Argyle, WAS. See 8419.
7917. 5/9/98 mor Tucker, Joshua; Argyle, WAS; Argyle, WAS; mee 8420. (C:270)
7918. 6/1/02 mor Tucker, Joshua; Argyle, WAS; Argyle, WAS; mee 6092. (D:231)
7919. 12/17/93 mor Tucker, Loeth, yeoman; ---, WAS; Argyle, WAS; co-mees 1183,
       8036. (A:459)

187

7920. 12/10/94 gee Tuman, William; Philadelphia, ---, PA. See 909.
7921. 1/3/86 mor Tupper(?), Reuben; ---, ---; Artillery Pat., WAS; mee 3192.
                                                    (Deed Book B:234)
7922. 2/23/86 gee Tupper, Ruben; --- WAS. See 3193.
7923. 5/1/90 mee Turnbull, George, Esq.; City of N.Y. See 7872.
7924. 3/5/83 gee Turner, Abraham, farmer; "Whitely, HAM, MA (presumably
                    Whately). See 8613.
7925. 6/24/95 gor Turner, Abraham, yeoman; Salem, WAS; Salem, WAS; gee 4997.
                                                    (C-2:31)
7926. 6/24/95 mee Turner, Abraham, yeoman; Salem, WAS. See 4998.
7927. 6/30/95 gor Turner, Abraham, yeoman; Salem, WAS; Salem, WAS; gee 4999.
                                                    (C-2:29)
7928. 3/12/83 gee Turner, Abraham, Junr.; New Perth, CHA. See 8620.
7929. 8/4/83 gor Turner, Abraham, Junr., farmer; New Perth, CHA; New Perth,
                    CHA; gee 5160.   (B-1:136)
7930. 4/10/87 gee Turner, Abraham, Junr. See 7935.
7931. 11/25/87 gor Turner, Abraham, Junr., farmer; Salem, WAS; Salem, WAS;
                    gee 7936.   (A:381)
7932. 4/4/89 mor Turner, Abraham, Junr.; ---, ---; Salem, WAS; mee 7036.
                                                    (A:132)
7933. 9/14/89 gor Turner, Abraham, Junr., yeoman; Salem, WAS; Salem, WAS;
                    gee 4996.   (A:433)
7934. 3/21/86 gee Turner, Abraham, Senr.; Salem, WAS. See 8290.
7935. 4/10/87 gor Turner, Abraham, Senr.; Salem, WAS; ---, WAS; gee 7930.
                                                    (A:125)
7936. 11/25/87 gee Turner, Abraham, Senr.; ---, ---. See 7931.
7937. 4/21/88 gor Turner, Abraham, Senr.; Salem, WAS; ---, WAS; gee 4995.
                                                    (A:105)
7938. 9/7/69 gor Turner, Alexander; ---, ---. See 7955.
7939. 9/7/69 --- Turner, Alexander, dec'd. See 7955.
7940. 2/10/73 gee Turner, Alexander; White Creek, CHA. See 7956.
7941. 4/20/73 --- Turner, Alexander, dec'd.; ---, ---. See 7957.
7942. 11/7/73 gor Turner, Alexander; White Creek, CHA; Turner Pat., CHA;
                    gee 8688.   (B-1:16)
7943. 4/20/73 gor Turner, Alexander, Junr.; ---, ---. See 7957.
7944. 1/24/86 gee Turner, Alexander, Junr.; New Perth, WAS. See 8286.
7945. 5/8/92 gor Turner, Alexander, Junr.; yeoman; Salem, WAS; Salem, WAS;
                    gee 7960.   (A:415)
7946. 11/26/94 gor Turner, Alexander, Senr. (w. Sarah), yeoman; Salem, WAS;
                    Whitehall, WAS; co-gors 7954, 7958. 8310, 8316; co-gees
                    4009, 8585.   (B-2:442)
7947. 4/12/97 gee Turner, Alexander, Senr., Esq; Salem, WAS. See 7953.
7948. 6/8/97 gee Turner, Alexander, Esq.; Salem, WAS. See 1620.
7949. 1/24/00 gor Turner, Alexander, Senr. (w. Sarah); Salem, WAS; Salem, WAS;
                    gee 7515.   (E:15)
7950. 11/18/95 gee Turner, Alexander, J., Major; New Perth, WAS. See 7909.
7951. 9/22/96 gor Turner, Alexander J. (w. Sarah); Salem, WAS; Salem, WAS;
                    gee 7701.   (C-2:80)
7952. 10/5/96 gor Turner, Alexander J. (w. Sarah); Salem, WAS; Salem, WAS;
                    gee 7702.   (C-2:82)
7953. 4/12/97 gor Turner, Alexander J., Esq. (w. Sarah); Salem, WAS; Salem,
                    WAS; gee 7947.   (C-2:203)
7954. 11/26/94 gor Turner, Eleanor. See 7958.
7955. 9/7/69 gor Turner, James, "heir at law to his father Alexander Turner,
                    deceased"; ---, ---; land "East side of Hudson's River",
                    ALB; co-gors 387, 814, 816, 1623, 1631, 1791, 1824,
                    2267, 2974, 3129, 3774, 3913, 4287, 4289, 4404, 4461,
                    4855, 6561, 7313, 7317, 7705, 7939, 8437; gee 1790.
                                                    (A:118)
7956. 2/10/73 gor Turner, James; White Creek, CHA; ---, CHA; gee 7940. (C-2:99)
7957. 4/20/73 gor Turner, James, "heir at law to his father Alexander Turner,
                    deceased"; land "east side of Hudson's river, CHA; co-gors
                    388, 815, 817, 1624, 1632, 1775, 1822, 2268, 2975, 3130,
                    3776, 3914, 4286, 4290, 4294, 4405, 4462, 4464, 4856,
                    6562, 7314, 7318, 7727, 7943; co-gees 4454, 4455, 4456.
                                                    (B-1:55)

188

7958. 11/26/94 gor Turner, James (w. Eleanor); Whitehall, WAS. See 7946.
7959. 5/13/00 mor Turner, Olive. See 7962.
7960. 5/8/92 gee Turner, Reuben, farmer; Salem, WAS. See 7945.
7961. 3/23/98 mor Turner, Roger; Granville, WAS; Granville, WAS; mee 4131.
The mortgagee is administrator of the estate of Abel
Gumstock, dec'd. "in behalf of the widow and heirs ..."
(C:265)
7962. 5/13/00 mor Turner, Roger (w. Olive), farmer; Granville, WAS; Granville,
WAS; mee 1541. (C:175)
7963. 8/5/01 mor Turner, Roger; Granville, WAS; Granville, WAS; mee 4147.
(D:85)
7964. 11/26/94 gor Turner, Sarah. See 7946.
7965. 9/22/96 gor Turner, Sarah. See 7951.
7966. 10/5/96 gor Turner, Sarah. See 7952.
7967. 4/12/97 gor Turner, Sarah. See 7953.
7968. 1/24/00 gor Turner, Sarah. See 7949.
7969. 11/30/96 mor Tuslin, Benjamin (w. Sarah), farmer; Cambridge, WAS; land
"East side of Hudson's River", WAS; co-mees 69, 2932, 2942.
Co-mortgagees are "executors to the ... will ... of James
Grant, deceased". (B:136)
7970. 11/30/96 mor Tuslin, Sarah. See 7969.
7971. 12/2/88 gee Tuthill, Richard; Salem, WAS. See 4750.
7972. 1/3/91 gor Tuthill, Richard, cordwainer; Salem, WAS; Salem, WAS;
gee 4752 (D:424); gee 5001 (A:391). (two contracts)
7973. 7/1/85 mor Tylor, Benijah; Skenesborough, WAS; Skenesborough, WAS;
mee 8555. (A:38)
7974. 7/20/93 mor Tyon(?), Michael, farmer; Champlain, CLI; Champlain, CLI;
mee 5135. (A:109)
7975. 7/2/92 gee Tyril, Amos, farmer; Hebron, WAS. See 3122.
7976. 5/9/01 mee Underhill, Augustus; Hartford, WAS. See 8155.
7977. 7/10/93 mee Underhill, Townsend, merchant; City of N.Y. See 5343.
7978. 9/1/98 mor Upham, Hildah. See 7979.
7979. 9/1/98 mor Upham, Joseph P. (w. Hildah); Granville, WAS; Granville,
WAS; mee 3851. (C:266)
7980. 7/6/97 mor Utter, Amos (w. Hannah), farmer; Granville, WAS; Granville,
WAS; co-mees 76, 2937, 2952. Co-mortgagees are executors
of the will of James Grant of Pawling (DUT), dec'd. (B:198)
7981. 7/6/97 mor Utter, Hannah. See 7980.
7982. 2/8/98 mor Utter, Joanna. See 7983.
7983. 2/8/98 mor Utter, John (w. Joanna), farmer; Hartford, WAS; Hartford,
WAS; mee 1483. (B:333)
7984. 7/6/99 gee Vail, Edward; Danby, RUT, VT See 128.
7985. 2/4/00 gee Vail, Edward, Esq.; Danby, ---, VT. See 3066.
7986. 11/29/00 gee Valentine, Daniel, farmer; Cambridge, WAS. See 1787.
7987. 2/26/96 gee Valentine, Joseph; Cambridge, WAS. See 7132.
7988. 11/11/73 mor Valentine, Thomas, surveyor of lands, City of N.Y.;
Fincastle, CHA ("on east side of Lake Champlain" -
probably in Vermont); mee 396. (A:9)
7989. 7/31/70 gor Van Antwerp, Wilhelmus, mariner; Albany, ALB, Cambridge, ALB;
gee 6157. (E:98)
7990. 5/21/95 mee Van Benschooten, Jacob; ---, ---. See 3459.
7991. 5/21/95 mee Van Benschooten, Mathew; ---, ---. See 3459.
7992. 5/21/95 mee Van Benschooten, Peter; ---, ---. See 3459.
7993. 1/1/97 mor Van Benthuysen, Barent; Clinton, DUT; land "part of the
Indian Purchase", CLI; mee 4086. (A:208)
7994. 1/17/97 mor Van Benthuysen, Barent; Clinton, DUT; ---, CLI; co-mor 3461;
mee 5866. (A:209)
7995. 1/17/97 mor Van Benthuysen, Barent; Clinton, DUT; Platt's Pat., CLI;
mee 5866. (B:241)
7996. 1/26/98 mor Van Benthuysen, Garrit, yeoman; Rhinebeck, DUT; land "on
Schroon Lake in the counties of Clinton and Washington";
mee 7769. (C:22)
7997. 2/9/96 gor Van Bomel, Christoffel (w. Sarah), farmer; "Broad Alben",
MON; Cambridge, WAS; gee 6896. (D:286)
7998. 2/9/96 gor Van Bomel, Sarah. See 7997.
7999. 7/1/00 mee Van Bunschooten, Matthew; Fishkill, DUT; See 8774.

189

8000. 11/24/91 mee Van Buren, Gerrit; Easton, WAS. See 4292.
8001. 6/5/92 gor Van Buskirk, Martin, "as attorney for Johannes Ackerson
                    of Cambridge", WAS; Cambridge, WAS; Cambridge, WAS;
                    co-gee 1050, 6909.   (C-2:52)
8002. 12/5/84 gor Van Cortland, Augustus(w. Catharine); "Lower Yonker", WES;
                    Hoosick Pat., ALB; gee 117.   (Washington Co. C-2:48)
8003. 12/5/84 gor Van Cortland, Catharine. See 8002.
8004. 5/18/93 mee Van Cortland, Frederick; Yonkers, WES. See 8025.
8005. 5/28/98 gor Van Cortlandt, Frederick, gentleman; ---, WES; Hoosick Pat.,
                    WAS; gee 6598.   (D:456)
8006. 1/16/97 gor Van Curler, Aaron; Cambridge, WAS; land "east of Hudsons
                    River", WAS; gee 143.   (D:7)
8007. 1/5/96 gor V. Denbergh; Argyle, WAS; Argyle, WAS; co-gor 4705; gee
                    2303.   (B-2:530)
8008. 6/26/76 gee Vandenbergh, Cathrine. See 8009.
8009. 6/26/76 gee Vandenbergh, Cornelius (w. Cathrine); Saratoga Pat., ALB.
                    See 1993.
8010. 5/17/00 gee Vandenbergh, Gerrett C.; Easton, WAS. See 7118.
8011. 2/5/98 gee Vandenbergh, Gerrit C.; ---, ---, NY. See 7152.
8012. 2/5/98 mee Vandenbergh, Gerrit C.; ---, WAS. See 7153.
8013. 11/4/00 gor Vandenbergh, Gerrit I.; ---, ---. See 2557.
8014. 5/8/93 mor Vandenbergh, John, yeoman; Argyle, WAS. See 7620.
8015. 7/8/97 mor Van Denbergh, John, merchant; Argyle, WAS; Argyle, WAS;
                    co-mees 4649, 6765, 6823. Co-mortgagees are "executors
                    of John Morine Scott", dec'd.   (B:250)
8016. 12/4/99 gor Vandenbergh, John; Half Moon, SAR; Argyle, WAS; co-gor 8017;
                    gee 902.   (D:272)
8017. 12/4/99 gor Vandenbergh, John, Junr.; Half Moon, SAR. See 8016.
8018. 9/27/94 gee Vandenbergh, Killian, farmer; Argyle, WAS. See 2563.
8019. 9/27/94 gor Vandenbergh, Killian, farmer; Argyle, WAS; Saratoga Pat,
                    WAS; gee 2546.   (B-2:314)
8020. 5/4/95 gor Van Den Bergh, Killian, farmer; Argyle, WAS; Argyle, WAS;
                    co-gees 3972, 3996.   (B-2:480)
8021. 5/8/93 gee Vanderberick, John; Argyle, WAS. See 6757.
8022. 3/14/98 mor Vandusee, James (w. Nabby), carpenter; Hartford, WAS;
                    Hartford, WAS; mee 1489.   (B:334)
8023. 3/14/98 mor Vandusee, Nabby. See 8022.
8024. 10/19/02 mor Van Duzee, James; Hartford, WAS; Granville, WAS; mee 714.
                                          (E:23)
8025. 5/18/93 mor Van Hassel, Abraham (w. Hannah); Cambridge, WAS; Hoosick
                    Pat., WAS; mee 8004.   (A:407)
8026. 5/18/93 mor Van Hassel, Hannah. See 8025.
8027. 7/30/93 mee Van Horn, Augustus, merchant; City of N.Y. See 2185.
8028. 7/5/91 mee Van Horne, Ann Margaret. See 8031.
8029. 9/28/92 mee Van Horne, Garret, merchant; City of N.Y. See 2562.
8030. 9/7/92 gor Van Horne, Garrett, merchant; City of N.Y.; Saratoga Pat.,
                    WAS; gee 2561.   (B-2:1)
8031. 7/5/91 gor Van Horne, Garrit (w. Ann Margaret), merchant; City of N.Y.;
                    "Easttown", Saratoga Pat., WAS; gee 2340.   (A:232)
8032. 9/23/85 gee Van Ness, Philip; Cambridge, WAS. See 6722.
8033. 10/3/96 mor Van Ornum, Jacob; Willsborough, CLI; Willsborough, CLI;
                    mee 5865.   (A:202)
8034. 5/2/96 gor V. Rensselaer, Jeremiah, gentleman; Albany, ALB. See 1186.
                    (three contracts)
8035. 1/18/93 gee Van Rensselaer, Jeremiah, gentleman; Albany, ALB. See 7650.
8036. 12/17/93 mee Van Rensselaer, Jeremiah; ---, ---. See 5414 and 7919.
8037. 12/17/93 mee Van Rensselaer, Jeremiah; Albany, ALB. See 2726, 5415,
                    and 8321. (three contracts)
8038. 8/5/94 gee Van Rensselaer, Jeremiah; Albany, ALB. See 2092.
8039. 5/2/96 gor Van Rensselaer, Jeremiah, gentleman; Albany, ALB. See 1185.
8039a. 5/2/96 gor Van Rensselaer, Jeremiah, gentleman; Albany, ALB. See 1187.
                    (two contracts)
8040. 5/2/96 mee Van Rensselaer, Jeremiah; Albany, ALB. See 6090 and 7258.
8041. 6/27/97 gor Van Rensselaer, Jeremiah, gentleman; Albany, ALB; Argyle, WAS;
                    co-gor 1191; gee 3307.   (C-2:213)
8042. 7/16/98 mee Van Rensselaer, Jeremiah, citizen; Albany, ALB. See 1726.

8043. 11/9/92 mee Van Rensselaer, Jeremiah, Esq.; Albany, ALB. See 6282.
8044. Data repositioned.
8045. 5/2/96 mee Van Rensselaer, Jeremiah, Esq.; Albany, ALB. See 2102
and 4919.
8046. 6/30/96 gor Van Rensselaer, Jeremiah Caldwell; Albany, ALB; ---, WAS;
co-gors 1177, 1190; gee 6378.   (D:52)
8047. 6/27/93 mor Van Rensselaer, John; Troy, REN; land "nine miles (north?)
from Crown Point", CLI; mee 4799.   (A:105)
8048. 5/21/99 mee Van Rensselaer, John; Troy, REN. See 4492.
8049. 2/1/94 mee Van Rensselaer, Killian R. (w. Margreta); ---, ---. See 1038.
8050. 2/1/94 mee Van Rensselaer, Margreta. See 8049.
8051. 11/6/92 mee Van Rensselaer, Philip S.; Albany, ALB. See 5065.
8052. 10/31/99 gor Van Schaick, Evert D. B., gentleman; ---, WAS. See 8054.
8053. 6/15/95 gee Van Schaick, Garrit T., merchant; Easton, WAS. See 1992.
8054. 10/31/99 gor Van Schaick, Hendrick, gentleman; ---, WAS; Easton, WAS;
co-gor 8052; gee 3995.   (E:200)
8055. 12/21/99 mee Van Schaick, Hendrick, gentleman; Easton, WAS. See 7580.
8056. 11/9/02 mee Van Schaick, Hendrick, farmer; Easton, WAS. See 952.
8057. 12/6/97 mee Van Solingen, Henry Moore, physician; City of N.Y. See 2725.
8058. 4/13/91 gee Van Tuyl, Abraham; Cambridge, WAS. See 24.
8059. 4/16/91 gee Van Tuyle, Abraham; Argyle, WAS. See 1325.
8060. 6/5/00 gee Van Tuyle, Abraham; Cambridge, WAS. See 5183.
8061. 5/20/90 gee Van Valkenburgh, Levi; Granville, WAS. See 2250.
8062. 11/20/95 gor Van Vleck, Ann. See 8067.
8063. 4/12/92 gor Van Vleck, Henry, dec'd.; City of N.Y. See 8065.
8064. 10/27/92 --- Van Vleck, Henry, dec'd.; City of N.Y. See 8066.
8065. 4/12/92 gor Van Vleck, Isaac, "acting executor of the ... will of Henry
Van Vleck, late of the City of New York", dec'd.; City of
N.Y.; Argyle, WAS; gee 4494.   (B-2:7)
8066. 10/27/92 mee Van Vleck, Isaac, "the only active executor of the ... will
... of Henry Van Vleck", merchant, deceased. See 4497.
8067. 11/20/95 gor Van Vleck, Isaac (w. Ann); City of N.Y.; Argyle, WAS; gee
7615.   (B-2:499)
8068. 11/20/95 mee Van Vleck, Isaac; City of N.Y. See 7616.
8069. 5/25/98 mee Van Wagenen, Gerrit H., merchant; City of N.Y. See 968.
8070. 10/1/91 mee Van Wagenen, Hubert, gentleman; City of N.Y. See 5678.
8071. 11/4/95 mor Van Warner, Jacob; Westfield, WAS; Westfield, WAS; mee 7213.
8072. 6/8/98 mee Van Wyck, Hannah. See 8089.   (B:18)
8073. 6/8/98 mor Van Wyck, Hannah. See 8089.
8074. 3/16/96 --- Van Wyck, Isaac; ---, DUT. See 290.
8075. 3/16/96 mor Van Wyck, Isaac; ---, DUT. See 289.
8076. 6/22/98 gor Van Wyck, Isaac; ---, DUT. See 5697 and 5698 (two contracts)
8077. 10/12/01 mee Van Wyck, Isaac, Esq.; Fishkill, DUT. See 5261.
8078. 1/2/96 gee Van Wyck, Theodorus, merchant; City of N.Y. See 5822.
8079. 6/24/97 --- Van Wyck, Theodorus, merchant; City of N.Y. See 6848.
8080. 10/26/97 gee Van Wyck, Theodorus, merchant; City of N.Y. See 5825.
8081. 10/26/97 gor Van Wyck, Theodorus, merchant; City of N.Y. See 334.
8081a. 10/26/97 gor Van Wyck, Theodorus, merchant; City of N.Y. See 5824.
8082. 11/24/97 --- Van Wyck, Theodorus, merchant; City of N.Y. See 6851.
8083. 3/1/98 gor Van Wyck, Theodorus, merchant; City of N.Y. See 6852.
8084. 3/1/98 mee Van Wyck, Theodorus, merchant; City of N.Y. See 4108.
8085. 3/2/98 mee Van Wyck, Theodorus; ---, ---. See 6353.
8086. 3/2/98 mee Van Wyck, Theodorus, merchant; City of N.Y. See 621 and 1342.
8087. 3/3/98 mee Van Wyck, Theodorus, merchant; City of N.Y. See 5233.
8088. 6/7/98 gee Van Wyck, Theodorus, merchant; City of N.Y. See 7570.
8089. 6/8/98 mor Van Wyck, Theodorus (w. Hannah), merchant; City of N.Y.
See 6857. (two contracts)
8090. 8/7/98 mee Van Wyck, Theodorus; City of N.Y. See 3067.
8091. 8/15/98 gor Van Wyck, Theodorus, merchant; City of N.Y. See 6859.
8092. 8/16/98 mee Van Wyck, Theodorus; City of N.Y. See 2279, 3069, and 7493.
8093. 10/20/98 mee Van Wyck, Theodorus; City of N.Y. See 3252.
8094. 11/17/98 mee Van Wyck, Theodorus; City of N.Y. See 2091.
8095. 12/22/98 mee Van Wyck, Theodorus, merchant; City of N.Y. See 3215.
8096. 4/10/99 mee Van Wyck, Theodorus; City of N.Y. See 6199.
8097. 5/16/01 mee Van Wyck, Theodorus, merchant; City of N.Y. See 688.
8098. 12/-/01 mee Van Wyck, Theodorus; City of N.Y. See 898.

8099. 3/16/96 --- Van Wyck, William; City of N.Y. See 290.
8100. 3/16/96 mor Van Wyck, William; City of N.Y. See 289.
8101. 6/22/98 gor Van Wyck, William; City of N.Y. See 5697 and 5698.
8102. 2/9/96 mee Varick, Richard; ---, ---. See 5619.
8103. 5/8/93 gor Varick, Richard, Esq.; City of N.Y. See 6757.
8104. 6/13/95 gor Varick, Richard, Esq.; City of N.Y. See 6820.
8105. 2/9/96 gor Varick, Richard, Esq.; City of N.Y. See 6821.
8106. 2/9/96 mee Varick, Richard, Esq.; City of N.Y. See 4500.
8107. 6/18/96 gor Varick, Richard, Esq.; City of N.Y. See 6764.
8108. 12/18/96 gor Varick, Richard, Esq.; ---, ---. See 6810.
8109. 11/29/99 mee Varick, Richard, Esq.; City of N.Y. See 6179.
8110. 11/29/99 mee Varick, Richard, Esq., "surviving executor of the estate of
              John Morin Scott, Esq., late of the City of New York",
              dec'd. See 2772.
8111. 12/1/99 gor Varick, Richard, Esq., "survivor of Lewis Allaire Scott late
              of the same city (N.Y.C.), Esquire, deceased and of Mary
              McKnight deceased ... and of Helena Scott (late Helena
              Myer) of the same city, deceased, the executors named in
              the last will of John Morin Scott, Esq., deceased"; City
              of N.Y.; Hebron, WAS; gee 8637.   (E:286)
8112. 12/2/99 mee Varick, Richard, Esq., "sole surviving executor of the
              estate of John Morin Scott, Esq.", dec'd. See 3706 and
              8665.
8113. 12/2/99 mee Varick, Richard, Esq.; City of N.Y. See 6107.
8114. 12/10/99 mee Varick, Richard, Esq., "the only surviving executor of the
              estate of John Morin Scott, Esq.", dec'd.; City of N.Y.
              See 2821.
8115. 12/18/99 mee Varick, Richard, Esq.; City of N.Y. See 3097.
8116. 12/28/99 mee Varick, Richard, Esq.; City of N.Y. See 5323.
8117. 2/18/02 gor Varick, Richard, Esq.; City of N.Y.; Argyle, WAS; gee 8672.
                                                            (F:175)
8118. 2/22/02 mee Varick, Richard, Esq.; City of N.Y. See 8673.
8119. 2/9/96 mee Varick, Richard, Esq.; City of N.Y. See 2273.
8120. 6/14/92 gor Vastenous, Louis, "a Canadian Refugee"; ---, ---.; Canadian
              and Nova Scotia Refugees' Pat., CLI; gee 5107. (A:394)
8121. 5/14/95 gee Vaughan, Benjamin; New Fairfield, ---, CT. See 849. (two
              contracts)
8122. 11/23/01 gee Vaughan, Benjamin, farmer; Willsborough, ESS. See 3738.
8123. 11/23/01 mor Vaughan, Benjamin; ---, ---; Willsborough, ESS; See 3737.
                                                            (A:76)
8124. 9/1/02 mor Vaughan, Jonathan; Hartford, WAS; Hartford, WAS; co-mor 216;
              mee 1113.   (E:19)
8125. 5/14/95 mor Vaughn, Benjamin; New Fairfield, ---, CT; Willsborough, CLI;
              mee 850.   (A:163)
8126. 9/23/88 mor Verley, Michael; Champlain, CLI; Champlain, CLI; mee 8764.
                                                            (A:18)
8127. 5/19/95 mee Vernor, James, merchant; Albany, ALB. See 8129.
8128. 12/13/96 mee Vernor, James, merchant; Albany, ALB. See 3529.
8129. 5/19/95 mor Vernor, John, Junr.; Kingsbury, WAS; Kingsbury, WAS; co-mees
              3339, 8127.   (A:549)
8130. 7/6/91 gee Vial, John, yeoman; Willsborough, CLI. See 46.
8131. 7/5/91 mor Viall, Abraham; Willsborough, CLI; Judd Pat., CLI; mee 45.
                                                            (A:73)
8132. 7/6/91 gee Viall, Abraham, yeoman; Willsborough, ESS. See 46.
8133. 7/6/91 mor Viall, John; Plattsburgh, CLI; Judd Pat., CLI; mee 47. (A:70)
8134. 9/6/00 gor Viall, John (w. Mary); Willsborough, ESS; Willsborough, ESS;
              gee 8136.   (A:34)
8135. 9/6/00 gor Viall, Mary. See 8134.
8136. 9/6/00 gee Viall, Phillip; Willsborough, ESS. See 8134.
8137. 5/28/98 mor Videto, James; Cambridge, WAS; James Bean Pat., WAS; mee
              6594.   (C:7)
8138. 6/26/01 mor Viele, Caty. See 8141.
8139. 3/3/92 mor Viele, Elizabeth. See 8144.
8140. 5/19/96 gor Viele, Elizabeth. See 8142.
8141. 6/26/01 mor Viele, Jacob L. (w. Caty); Cambridge, WAS; Hoosick, Pat., WAS; mee
              mee 2678.   (D:66)

8142. 5/19/96 gor Viele, Peter (w. Elizabeth); Cambridge, WAS; Cambridge, WAS;
          co-gees 3030 and 3032. (C-2:104)
8143. 4/3/97 gee Viele, Peter; ---, WAS. See 3033.
8144. 3/3/92 mor Viele, Peter H. (w. Elizabeth), farmer; Faiagsskoak (sic),
          WAS; Faiagsskoak, WAS; mee 6089. (A:323)
8145. 1/5/88 mee Vincent, Sarah; City of N.Y. See 4607.
8146. 7/22/91 mee Vincent, Sarah, spinster; City of N.Y. See 4608.
8147. 12/10/84 gee Vine, Ebenezer; ---, ---. See 7055.
8148. 4/23/01 mee Vine, Ebenezer; Whitehall, WAS. See 5267.
8149. 12/30/85 gee Vine, Robert; ---, ---. See 7055.
8150. 12/10/84 gee Vine, Solomon; ---, ---. See 7055.
8151. 4/24/02 gee Volentine, Daniel; Cambridge, WAS. See 8154.
8152. 8/19/96 gor Volentine, Esther. See 8153.
8153. 8/19/96 gor Volentine, Joseph (w. Esther), farmer; Cambridge, WAS;
          Cambridge, WAS; gee 1279. (E:162)
8154. 4/24/02 gor Volentine, Joseph; Cambridge, WAS; Cambridge, WAS; gee 8151.
          (F:252)
8155. 5/9/01 mor Vorce, Ebenezer; Kingsbury, WAS; Hartford, WAS; co-mor
          5292; mee 1005 (D:40b); mee 7976 (D:41b). (two contracts)
8156. 5/1/00 mor Vowers, Jonathan, farmer; Chester, WAS; Chester, WAS;
          mee 7772. (D:223)
8157. 5/23/97 mee Vrooman, Adam; ---, "Schoharry County". See 3451.
8158. 7/4/00 mee Vrooman, Adam; Middleburgh, SCHO. See 1338.
8159. 9/16/01 mee Vrooman, Adam; Middleburgh, SCHO. See 1324.
8160. 6/2/01 mee Wager, Philip, farmer; Claverack, COL. See 3519.
8161. 12/24/98 gee Wait, Ezra; Cambridge, WAS. See 6600.
8162. 7/20/87 mor Wait, John; Plattsburgh, WAS; Plattsburgh, WAS; mee 5916.
          (A:5)
8163. 12/24/98 gee Wait, Lara; Cambridge, WAS. See 6600.
8164. 8/15/98 mor Waite, Benjamin; Hartford, WAS; Hartford, WAS; co-mees
          5005, 5006. (B:346, small print)
8165. 9/22/96 mor Waite, Joseph, yeoman; Granville, WAS; Granville, WAS;
          mee 3766. (B:116)
8166. 12/4/82 gee Waite, William; Hoosick Dist., ALB. See 8335.
8167. 5/23/01 mee Waite, William, yeoman; Cambridge, WAS. See 1594.
8168. 4/19/00 gee Waldo, Daniel; Hebron, WAS. See 4260.
8169. 8/1/01 mee Walker, Benjamin; City of N.Y. See 5769.
8170. 2/1/87 gee Walker, Benjamin, Esq.; City of N.Y. See 5904.
8171. 3/14/87 gee Walker, Benjamin, Esq.; City of N.Y. See 5912.
8172. 4/3/00 mee Walker, Ebenezer; ---, ---. See 1344.
8173. 10/31/00 mee Walker, Ebenezer; ---, ---. See 6229.
8174. 11/7/00 mee Walker, Ebenezer; ---, ---. See 3141.
8175. 1/16/01 mee Walker, Ebenezer; ---, ---. See 1923.
8176. 2/23/01 mee Walker, Ebenezer, yeoman; Granville, WAS. See 6650.
8177. 8/24/90 mor Walker, Isaac; Hebron, WAS; Shereiff's Pat., WAS; mee 6978.
          (A:221)
8178. 8/9/91 gee Walker, Josiah, yeoman; Hebron, WAS. See 4064.
8179. 4/1/96 mor Walker, Robert; Crown Point, CLI; ---, CLI; mee 7889. (A:182)
8180. 6/12/90 gee Wallace, Benjamin, merchant; City of N.Y. See 2891.
8181. 10/17/94 gee Wallace, John; Pawlet, RUT, VT. See 2158.
8182. 6/30/98 gor Wallace, John; Westfield, WAS; Westfield(?), WAS; gee 3503.
          (F:113)
8183. 8/6/98 gor Wallacem John; Westfield, WAS; Westfield, WAS; gee 4181.
          (F:111)
8184. 9/3/99 mee Wallace, John; Westfield, WAS. See 5395.
8185. 4/2/00 mee Waller, Charity. See 8186.
8186. 4/2/00 mor Waller, Joseph (w. Charity), yeoman; Hartford, WAS; Hartford,
          WAS; mee 1754. (C:189)
8187. 11/3/86 gee Wallis, Benjamin, yeoman; ---, ALB. See 7661.
8188. 2/8/98 mor Wallor, Charity. See 8189.
8189. 2/8/98 mor Wallor, Samuel (w. Charity), farmer; Hartford, WAS; Hartford,
          WAS; mee 1483. (B:345)
8190. 9/2/01 gee Walsh, Murty, yeoman; Cambridge, WAS. See 2833 and 2998.
8191. 10/30/65 gor Walton, Abraham, merchant; City of N.Y.; land "East side of
          Hudsons River, ALB; gee 8778. (B-2:163)
8192. 4/6/95 mee Walton, Abraham; City of N.Y. See 1955.

8193. 1/10/86 gee Ward, Benjamin; Black Creek Dist., WAS. See 1507.
8194. 7/1/00 mor Ward, David; ---, ---; ---, ESS; co-mors 172, 840; mee 5572.
                                                                    (A:58)
8195. 1/1/88 gee Ward, Elihu, yeoman; Hebron, WAS. See 8634.
8196. 12/31/94 gee Ward, Elihu; Cambridge, WAS (Elihu is "sun" of Obadiah).
                   See 8202.
8197. 2/11/00 gor Ward, Elihu (w. Zeborah); Cambridge, WAS; Cambridge, WAS;
                   gee 7698.   (D:343)
8198. 12/10/89 gee Ward, Humphrey; Hebron, WAS. See 1246.
8199. 10/15/89 mor Ward, John, farmer; Plattsburgh, CLI; Beekmantown, CLI;
                   mee 584.   (A:41)
8200. 2/26/96 mor Ward, Nahum, farmer; Salem, WAS; Salem, WAS; mee 2128.
                   Two contracts this date involving these persons.
                                                          (C:8) and (C:9)
8201. 4/6/83 gee Ward, Obadiah; Cambridge, WAS. See 3301.
8202. 12/31/94 gor Ward, Obadiah; Cambridge, WAS; Cambridge, WAS; gee 8196.
                                                               (D:341)
8203. 12/24/01 mor Ward, Zadock; ---, ---; Jay, ESS; mee 186. (A:75)
8204. 2/11/00 gor Ward, Zeborah. See 8197.
8205. 4/2/96 gee Ware, James; ---, WAS. See 7215.
8206. 4/2/96 mor Ware, James; ---, WAS; Hitchcock Pat., WAS; mee 7216. (B:48)
8207. 7/26/02 mor Ware, James, Esq.; Bolton, WAS; land "west side of Lake
                   George", WAS; co-mees 1179, 1196.   (E:15)
8208. 9/13/99 gee Warner, John; Easton, WAS. See 8356.
8209. 2/13/00 mor Warner, Zebulon; ---, ---; Willsborough, ESS; mee 5178.
                                                               (A:10)
8210. 1/19/90 mor Warren, Asa; Hampton, WAS; ---, WAS; mee 6033. (A:200)
8211. 1/18/90 mor Warren, Caleb; Hampton, WAS; Hampton, WAS; mee 6032. See
                   also 2623.   (A:329)
8212. 1/18/90 mor Warren, Caleb; Hampton, WAS; land "west line of Poultney", ---,
                   VT; mee 6031.   (A:208)
8213. 1/19/90 mor Warren, Gideon, Esq.; Hampton, WAS; land "west line of
                   Poultney", ---, VT; mee 6033.   (A:201)
8214. 5/28/00 mor Warren, Lyman; Rutland, RUT, VT; Mooers Pat., CLI; mee 1170.
                                                               (A:434)
8215. 6/15/97 gee Warren, Moses; Peru, CLI. See 6319.
8216. 6/15/97 mor Warren, Moses; Peru, CLI. See 616.
8217. 7/1/00 mor Warrin, Nathan; ---, ---. See 4830.
8218. 6/4/92 gee Washburn, Hope; Westfield, WAS. See 7011.
8219. 2/12/95 gee Washburn, Hope; Westfield, WAS. See 7012.
8220. 3/25/00 gor Washburn, Hope (w. Tabatha), farmer; Westfield, WAS;
                   Westfield, WAS; gee 5995.   (D:394)
8221. 2/26/96 mor Washburn, Philip, farmer; Salem, WAS; Salem, WAS; mee 2128.
                                                               (C:10)
8222. 3/25/00 gor Washburn, Tabatha. See 8220.
8223. 4/3/01 mor Waste, Bezaleel, farmer; Bolton, WAS; ---, WAS; mee 2299.
                                                               (D:162)
8224. 4/3/01 mor Waste, Bezaleel, Junr., farmer; Bolton, WAS; James Caldwell
                   Pat., WAS; mee 2299.   (D:80)
8225. 9/3/02 gor Waterbury, Silvanus; Willsborough, ESS; Willsborough, ESS;
                   gee 6741.   (A:61)
8226. 9/3/02 mee Waterbury, Silvanus; ---, ---. See 6742.
8227. 6/7/99 mor Waterbury, Sylvanus; ---, ---; Willsborough, ESS; mee 3228.
                                                               (A:5)
8228. 8/1/87 gor Waterhouse, Abraham; Saybrook, MID, CT; land "three miles
                   east of south Bay", WAS; gee 8239.   (A:48)
8229. 5/12/83 gor Waterhouse, Samuel, yeoman; Pawlet, RUT, VT; Skene's Pat.,
                   CHA; gee 3629.   (C-1:25)
8230. 8/2/83 gor Waterhouse, Samuel; New Haven, CHA; New Haven, CHA; co-gees
                   6347, 6348.   (B-1:167)
8231. 10/2/84 gor Waterhouse, Samuel, yeoman; East Bay, WAS; Skene's Pat., WAS;
                   gee 3157.   (C-1:57)
8232. 11/30/84 gor Waterhouse, Samuel, yeoman; East Bay, WAS; ---, WAS; gee 1832.
                                                               (C-1:49)
8233. 6/15/85 gor Waterhouse, Samuel, yeoman; East Bay, WAS; Skene's Pat., WAS;
                   gee 1455.   (C-1:61)

8234. 1/25/86 gor Waterhouse, Samuel; East Bay, WAS; ---, WAS; gee 6845.
(B-2:18)
8235. 3/2/86 gor Waterhouse, Samuel; East Bay, WAS; ---, WAS; gee 3915. (A:255)
8236. 10/30/86 gor Waterhouse, Samuel; Hampton, WAS; Skene's Pat., WAS;
gee 1280. (C-1:51)
8237. 5/31/92 gor Waterhouse, Samuel; ---, WAS; Cambridge Pat., WAS; gee 2781.
(A:285)
8238. 1/31/93 mor Waterhouse, Samuel, yeoman; Hampton, WAS; Hampton, WAS;
mee 1353. (A:403)
8239. 8/1/87 gee Waterhouse, Samuel, Junr.; Hampton, WAS. See 8228.
8240. 9/17/88 gor Waterhouse, Samuel, Junr.; Hampton, WAS; Skene's Pat., WAS;
gee 3159. (A:110)
8241. 9/15/94 gee Waterhouse, Samuel, Junr.; ---, ---. See 2012.
8242. 1/1/95 gee Waterhouse, Samuel, Junr.; Hampton, WAS. See 8814.
8243. 1/1/95 gor Waterhouse, Samuel, Junr.; Hampton, WAS. See 1284 and 8815.
(two contracts)
8244. 11/24/95 gor Waterhouse, Samuel, Junr.; Hampton, WAS; Hampton, WAS; gee
7255. (D:388)
8245. 11/10/98 gee Waterman, Anson; Addison, ADD, VT. See 1058.
8246. 3/6/01 mor Waterman, Anson; Plattsburgh, CLI; Plattsburgh, CLI;
mee 324. (B:28)
8247. 5/3/97 gee Waters, Elisha; Argyle, WAS. See 7807.
8248. 5/4/97 mor Waters, Elisha (w. Ziba); Argyle, WAS; Argyle, WAS; co-mees
3948, 7140, 7804, 7811, 7814. (B:179)
8249. 4/27/98 mee Waters, Elisha, farmer; Argyle, WAS. See 2262.
8250. 5/4/97 mor Waters, Ziba. See 8248.
8251. 5/29/90 gee Watkins, Henry; Granville, WAS. See 7658.
8252. 10/11/84 gor Watson, Jacob, merchant; City of N.Y.; land "west bank of
Hudson's River", WAS; gee 819. (F:23)
8253. 10/12/84 mee Watson, Jacob, merchant; City of N.Y. See 820.
8254. 8/10/87 mee Watson, Jacob; City of N.Y. See 6837.
8255. 5/7/95 mee Watson, Jacob, merchant; City of N.Y. See 821.
8256. 5/13/96 mor Watson, John, yeoman; Cambridge, WAS; Cambridge, WAS; co-mees
6674, 8859. (B:37)
8257. 5/4/97 gor Watson, John, yeoman; Cambridge, WAS; Cambridge, WAS;
gee 8861. (E:217)
8258. 6/7/93 gee Watson, Mathew, tailor; City of N.Y. See 6484.
8259. 6/10/93 gor Watson, Mathew, tailor; City of N.Y.; Argyle, WAS; gee 1077.
(B-2:66)
8260. 9/7/74 mee Watts, John, Esq.; City of N.Y. See 2142.
8261. 11/12/89 gor Way, Asa; Argyle, WAS; Kingsbury, WAS; gee 5043. (B-2:59)
8262. 11/12/00 mor Weatherby, William, farmer; Kingsbury, WAS; Westfield, WAS;
mee 3171. (D:16)
8263. 2/28/86 gee Webb, David; New Perth, WAS. See 8288.
8264. 10/15/89 mor Webb, Isaac; Plattsburgh, CLI; Beekman, CLI; mee 592. (A:42)
8265. 1/15/90 mor Webb. Isaac, farmer; Plattsburgh, CLI; Beekman, CLI; mee 593.
(A:43)
8266. 8/1/95 gor Webb, Isaac; Charlotte, ---, VT; William Beekman Pat., CLI;
gee 7879. (A:388)
8267. 7/9/01 gor Webb, John P. (w. Ruth), schoolmaster; Easton, WAS; Easton,
WAS; gee 521. (F:235)
8268. 7/3/92 gee Webb, Leonard, farmer; Salem, WAS. See 4780.
8269. 7/9/01 gee Webb, Ruth. See 8267.
8270. 10/9/90 gee Webber, William; Willsborough, CLI. See 6448.
8271. 11/10/96 gor Weber, William; ---, ---; Brookfield Pat., CLI; gee 3499. (B:54)
8272. 9/7/74 mor Webster, Alexander; New Perth, CHA; Kemp Pat., CHA; mee 3868.
(A:19)
8273. 3/15/86 mee Webster, Alexander; ---, ---. See 4376.
8274. 7/1/88 --- Webster, Alexander, Esq.; Hebron, WAS. See 2382.
8275. 5/3/90 gor Webster, Alexander; Hebron, WAS; De Forest Pat., WAS; gee 2518.
(A:303)
8276. 2/1/97 gor Webster, Alexander, attorney for the executors of the estate
of "the late John Morin Scott, Esquire", dec'd.; Hebron,
WAS; Hebron, WAS; gee 8638. (C-2:311)
8277. 5/4/76 gor Webster, Alexander, Esq.; New Perth, CHA; land "northward of
New Perth", WAS; gee 4626. (B-2:503)

8278.   9/8/81   gor   Webster, Alexander, Esq., commissioner of forfeitures;
                        ---, ---; ---, WAS (sold under attainder through "treason"
                        of John Tabor Kemp, Esq.; ---, WAS; co-gor 3545; gee 7458.
                                                                    (C-1:84)
8279.   12/28/81 gor   Webster, Alexander, Esq., commissioner of forfeitures;
                        ---, ---; Black Creek, CHA (attainder of John Tabor Kemp?)
                        co-gor 3546; gee 7291.   (B:74)
8280.   11/21/82 gor   Webster, Alexander, Esq., commissioner of forfeiture along
                        with #3539; ---, ---; Black Creek, CHA (attainder of -?-);
                        co-gor 3539; gee 4735.   (A:405)
8281.   12/23/84 gor   Webster, Alexander, Esq., "attorney for the Hon. James Duane,
                        Esq. of the City of New York"; ---, ---; Hampton, WAS;
                        gee 649.   (C-1:62)
8282.   5/5/85   gor   Webster, Alexander, Esq., commissioner of forfeitures;
                        ---, ---; Artillery Pat., WAS (attainder of Philip and
                        Andrew P. Skenes); gee 6281.   (B-2:262)
8283.   6/17/85   gor   Webster, Alexander, Esq.. commissioner of forfeitures; ---,
                        ---; New Perth, WAS (attainder of Oliver De Laney, Esq.);
                        gee 6532. (two contracts)   (A:401), (B-2:485)
8284.   6/24/85   gor   Webster, Alexander, Esq., commissioner of forfeitures; ---,
                        ---; New Perth, WAS (attainder of Oliver Delaney, Esq.);
                        gee 4751.   (D:428)
8285.   7/1/85   gor   Webster, Alexander, Esq., commissioner of forfeitures; ---,
                        ---; New Perth, WAS (attainder of Oliver Delancey, Esq.,
                        "late of the City of New York"); gee 173.   (F:207)
8286.   1/24/86   gor   Webster, Alexander, Esq., commissioner of forfeitures; ---,
                        ---; New Perth, WAS (attainder of Oliver De Laney, Esq.)
                        gee 7944.   (A:340)
8287.   2/6/86   gor   Webster, Alexander, Esq., commissioner of forfeitures; ---,
                        ---; New Perth, WAS (attainder of Oliver De Lancey of the
                        City of N.Y.); gee 5171.   (A:143)
8288.   2/28/86   gor   Webster, Alexander, Esq., commissioner of forfeitures; ---,
                        ---; New Perth, WAS (attainder of Oliver De Laney of the
                        City of N.Y.); gee 8263.   (A:432)
8289.   3/14/86   gor   Webster, Alexander, Esq., commissioner of forfeitures; ---,
                        ---; Salem, WAS (attainder of Oliver De Lancey, Esq.,
                        "late of the City of New York"); gee 3324. (C-1:39)
8290.   3/21/86   gor   Webster, Alexander, Esq., commissioner of forfeitures; ---,
                        ---; Salem, WAS (attainder of Oliver De Laney, Esq.);
                        gee 7934.   (A:379)
8291.   10/26/90 gor   Webster, Alexander, Esq.; Hebron, WAS; De Forest Pat., WAS;
                        gee 2742.   (C-1:75)
8292.   4/21/91   gor   Webster, Alexander, Esq.; Hebron, WAS; ---, WAS; gee 4330.
                                                                    (E:256)
8293.   7/15/91   gee   Webster, Alexander, Esq.; ---, WAS. See 1074.
8294.   12/13/91 mee   Webster, Alexander, Esq.; Hebron, WAS. See 6988.
8295.   12/23/91 mee   Webster, Alexander, Esq.; Hebron, WAS. See 4387 and 4388.
8296.   7/4/92   mee   Webster, Alexander, Esq.; ---, ---. See 3782.
8297.   6/18/96   ---   Webster, Alexander, Esq. See 6764.
8298.   11/3/96   mee   Webster, Alexander; Hebron, WAS. See 3160.
8299.   1/23/97   gor   Webster, Alexander, Esq.; ---, ---; Hampton, WAS; co-gor
                        8313; gee 1750.   (D:204)
8300.   1/23/97   mee   Webster, Alexander, Esq.; ---, ---. See 1281.
8301.   7/5/97   mee   Webster, Alexander, Esq.; Hebron, WAS(?). See 4501.
8302.   5/1/98   gee   Webster, Alexander, Esq.; ---, WAS. See 7097.
8303.   11/4/00   gor   Webster, Alexander, Esq.; Hebron, WAS; De Forest Pat., WAS;
                        gee 6164.   (F:133)
8304.   5/2/01   mee   Webster, Alexander, Senr.; ---, ---. See 6545.
8305.   1/4/95   gee   Webster, Alexander, Senr., Esq.; Hebron, WAS. See 8816.
8306.   9/20/87   gee   Webster, Alexander, 3rd, yeoman; Black Creek Dist., WAS.
                        See 8479.
8307.   1/18/90   mor   Webster, Ashbil; Hampton, WAS; land "west line of Poultney",
                        ---, VT; mee 6031.   (A:204)
8308.   11/28/94 mor   Webster, Elizabeth. See 8317.
8309.   1/19/90   mor   Webster, Elizur, Junr.; Hampton, WAS; ---, WAS; mee 6033.
                                                                    (A:184)

8310. 11/26/94 gor Webster, George (w. Janet); Hebron, WAS. See 7946.
8311. 1/4/95 gee Webster, George, surveyor; Hebron, WAS. See 8816.
8312. 11/3/96 mee Webster, George; Hebron, WAS. See 3160.
8313. 1/23/97 gor Webster, George, surveyor; Hebron, WAS. See 8299.
8314. 1/23/97 gor Webster, George, surveyor; Hebron, WAS. See 1281.
8315. 7/5/97 mee Webster, George, surveyor; Hebron, WAS. See 4501.
8316. 11/26/94 gor Webster, Janet. See 8310.
8317. 11/28/94 mor Webster, Obadiah (w. Elizabeth), farmer; Hampton, WAS;
     Hampton, WAS; mee 5964. (A:519)
8318. 4/8/89 gor Weed, Noah; Cambridge, WAS; ---, WAS; gee 7577. (C-2:219)
8319. 5/5/94 gor Weed, William, weaver; Argyle, WAS; Argyle, WAS; gee 2278.
     (B-2:346)
8320. 12/23/95 mor Weer, David, yeoman; Argyle, WAS; Hebron, WAS; mee 6776.
     (B:98)
8321. 12/17/93 mor Weir, David, yeoman; ---, WAS; Argyle, WAS; co-mees 1183,
     8037. (A:462)
8322. 2/12/76 gee Weir, John, yeoman; Cambridge, ALB. See 4044.
8323. 2/16/02 gee Weir, John; Cambridge, WAS. See 881.
8324. 2/17/02 gee Weir, John; Cambridge, WAS. See 8326.
8325. 2/16/02 gee Weir, Thomas; Cambridge, WAS. See 881.
8326. 2/17/02 mor Weir, Thomas; Cambridge, WAS; Wilson's Pat., WAS; co-mor
     8324; mee 882. (E:22)
8327. 10/14/90 mor Wells, Benjamin; Plattsburgh, CLI; Plattsburgh, CLI;
     mee 6252. (A:56)
8328. 8/15/93 mor Wells, Benjamin, farmer; Cambridge, WAS; Saratoga Pat., WAS;
     mee 5020. (A:486)
8329. 10/16/94 gee Wells, Benjamin, yeoman; Hebron, WAS. See 1568.
8330. 10/29/94 mor Wells, Benjamin, carpenter; Peru, CLI; Peru, CLI; mee 6293.
     (A:145)
8331. 5/10/98 gee Wells, Benjamin, tailor; Hebron, WAS. See 6183.
8332. 6/6/00 mor Wells, Benjamin; Peru, CLI; Peru, CLI; mee 1975. (A:438)
8333. 7/5/92 mor Wells, Caleb, yeoman; Cambridge, WAS. See 7308.
8334. 10/7/94 gee Wells, Daniel; ---, ---. See 8583.
8335. 12/4/82 gor Wells, Edmund; Cambridge, ALB; Cambridge, ALB; gee 8166.
     (E:340)
8336. 6/22/91 gor Wells, Edmund; ---, ---. See 8450.
8337. 3/20/80 gor Wells, Edmund, Esq.; Cambridge, ALB; Cambridge, WAS(?);
     gee 5640. (D:136)
8338. 11/24/82 gor Wells, Edmund, Esq.; Cambridge, WAS; Cambridge, WAS;
     gee 1695. (E:222)
8339. 10/19/92 gor Wells, Edmund, Esq.; Cambridge, WAS; Cambridge, WAS;
     gee 7469. (D:178)
8340. 6/13/94 gor Wells, Edmund, Esq.; Cambridge, WAS; Cambridge, WAS;
     gee 4666, 4859. (D:300)
8341. 6/23/97 gor Wells, Elisha; Plattsburgh, CLI; Plattsburgh, CLI; co-gor
     392; gee 1633. (Mort. Book A:436)
8342. 6/23/97 mor Wells, Elisha; Plattsburgh, CLI; Plattsburgh, CLI; co-mor
     393; mee 1634a. (A:226)
8343. 3/5/98 mor Wells, Elisha; Plattsburgh, CLI; Plattsburgh Pat., CLI;
     mee 50. (A:309)
8344. 8/7/01 gee Wells, James, merchant; Argyle, WAS. See 5338.
8345. 11/12/01 mor Wells, James, merchant; Argyle, WAS; Argyle, WAS; mee 565.
     (D:160)
8346. 11/24/01 gee Wells, James, merchant; Argyle, WAS. See 571.
8347. 4/15/02 gee Wells, James, merchant; Argyle, WAS. See 6344.
8348. 4/21/02 mee Wells, James, merchant; Argyle, WAS. See 6345.
8349. 11/15/00 mee Wells, Jonathan; Queensbury, WAS. See 492.
8350. 12/19/01 mor Wells, Joseph; Plattsburgh, CLI; Plattsburgh, CLI; mee 1958.
     (B:50)
8351. 1/7/96 mor Wells, Joshua, farmer; ---, HER; Jessup's Purchase, WAS;
     mee 5336. (C:188)
8352. 12/31/92 gee Wells, Lemuel, gentleman; City of N.Y. See 2809.
8353. 5/15/00 mor Wells, William A., yeoman; Cambridge, WAS; Hoosick Pat.,
     WAS; mee 6606. (C:118)
8354. 6/22/91 gor Welsh, John; ---, ---. See 8450.
8355. 7/29/74 gee Welsh, Joseph, heckler(?); New Perth, CHA. See 176.

8356. 9/13/99 gor Wendell, Abraham E.; Easton, WAS; Easton, WAS; gee 8208. (E:18)
8357. 8/17/95 gee Wendell, Cornelius, gentleman; Cambridge, WAS. See 5380.
8358. 10/15/96 gee Wendell, Cornelius, gentleman; Cambridge, WAS. See 5379.
8359. 5/6/96 gee Wendell, Gerrit, attorney; Cambridge, WAS. See 3275.
8360. 6/21/00 mee Wendell, Gerrit, Esq.; Cambridge, WAS. See 6037.
8361. 7/6/88 mor West, Levi; Granville, WAS; Granville, WAS; mee 2379. (A:116)
8362. 10/10/92 gee West, Samuel; Plattsburgh, CLI. See 5849.
8363. 10/10/92 mor West, Samuel; Plattsburgh, CLI; Plattsburgh, CLI; mee 5850.
(A:86)
8364. 9/20/93 gor West, Samuel, yeoman; Peru, CLI; "Bell's Location", CLI;
co-gees 1519, 5934.   (A:313)
8365. 10/18/96 mor West, William B.; ---, WAS. See 1087.
8366. 10/10/92 mor West, William Barber; Plattsburgh, CLI; Plattsburgh, CLI;
mee 5850.   (A:87)
8367. 9/8/00 mor Westcock, Zeba; ---, ---; Elizabethtown, ESS; mee 7520. (A:46)
8368. 8/22/99 gee Westion, John, yeoman; Cambridge, WAS. See 6946.
8369. 1/14/98 gee Weston, Roswell; ---, ---. See 2168.
8370. 1/17/98 mor Weston, Roswell; ---, ---; Kingsbury, WAS; mee 2169. (C:187)
8371. 8/10/99 gee Weston, Roswell; Kingsbury, WAS. See 4957.
8372. 10/8/99 gee Weston, Roswell, gentleman; Kingsbury, WAS. See 5214.
8373. 4/28/01 gee Weston, Roswell; Kingsbury, WAS. See 8627.
8374. 12/2/99 gee Weston, Roswell, Esq.; Kingsbury, WAS. See 7558.
8375. 10/7/00 gee Weston, Roswell, Esq.; Sandy Hill (probably in Kingsbury),
WAS. See 2540.
8376. 3/9/86 mor Westover, Nathaniel; ---, ---; Skenesborough, WAS; mee 3196.
(Deed Book B:237)
8377. 2/9/01 gor Wetherbee, John, Junr.; Kingsbury, WAS; Kingsbury, WAS;
gee 8379.   (E:155)
8378. 6/28/00 gee Wetherbee, Richard; Kingsbury, WAS. See 7197.
8379. 2/9/01 gee Wetherbee, Richard; Kingsbury, WAS. See 8377.
8380. 9/2/00 mor Whallon, Reuben, tailor; Argyle, WAS; Argyle, WAS; mee 4410.
(C:188)
8381. 11/6/93 gee Wheadon, David, Junr.; Hebron, WAS. See 3505.
8382. 10/3/94 gee Wheadon, Denison; Hebron, WAS. See 4205.
8383. 12/10/95 gor Wheadon, Denison, yeoman; Hebron, WAS; Hebron, WAS; co-gees
6477, 6478.   (B-2:524)
8384. 12/2/94 mor Wheat, Isabella. See 8385.
8385. 12/2/94 mor Wheat, Samuel (w. Isabella), farmer; Hampton, WAS; Hampton,
WAS; mee 5966.   (A:513)
8386. 5/13/85 gee Whedon, Daniel, farmer; Black Creek Dist., WAS. See 1911.
8387. 4/15/82 gor Wheeler, Ephraim; White Creek, CHA; White Creek, CHA;
gee 646.   (A:31)
8388. 10/10/86 gor Wheeler, Ephraim, farmer; Salem, WAS; Salem, WAS; co-gees
1384, 1388, 2206.   (A:313)
8389. 2/23/01 mee Wheeler, Melancthon; Whitehall, WAS. See 2081.
8390. 5/25/01 mee Wheeler, Melancthon; Whitehall, WAS. See 2359.
8391. 1/10/85 gor Whelor, Ephraim; White Creek, WAS; White Creek, WAS; gee 638.
(C-1:16)
8392. 5/21/91 gor Whipple, Freelove. See 8395.
8393. 9/3/01 mor Whipple, Israel (w. Mercy), farmer; Cambridge, WAS; Cambridge,
WAS; mee 1837.   (D:88b)
8394. 3/27/02 mor Whipple, Israel (w. Mercy), yeoman; Cambridge, WAS; Cambridge,
WAS; mee 4003.   (E:6)
8395. 5/21/91 gor Whipple, Job, Esq. (w. Freelove); Argyle, WAS; ---, WAS;
co-gees 2283, 2528.   (B-2:373)
8396. 9/3/01 mor Whipple, Mercy. See 8393.
8397. 3/27/02 mor Whipple, Mercy. See 8394.
8398. 4/1/01 mor Whipple, Michael; Cambridge, WAS; Cambridge, WAS; mee 1834.
(D:36b)
8399. 9/21/01 mor Whitcomb, Scotter(?); ---, WAS; Granville, WAS; mee 1693.
(D:95)
8400. 12/15/95 gor Whitcomb, Scottoway; Granville, WAS; Granville, WAS; co-gees
3608, 8487.   (B-2:522)
8401. 11/4/93 gor White, Alexander (w. Lydia); Cambridge, WAS. See 8422.
8402. 4/10/92 gee White, Andrew; Cambridge, WAS. See 515.
8403. 1/31/93 gee White, Andrew; Cambridge, WAS. See 3302.

8404. 3/17/98 gor White, Andrew; Cambridge, WAS; <u>Cambridge, WAS</u>; gee 5482.
                                                                    (E:3)
8405. 5/19/00 --- White, Andrew. See 8434.
8406. 6/20/96 gor White, Andrew, Esq., sheriff; ---, WAS; <u>Argyle, WAS</u>;
                   (sheriff's sale); gee 7700.   (C-2:83)
8407. 1/11/94 mor White, Daniel; Granville, WAS; <u>Granville, WAS</u>; mee 4126.
                                                                    (A:452)
8408. 2/25/97 mor White, Daniel; Granville, WAS; <u>Granville, WAS</u>; mee 4165.
                                                                    (B:149)
8409. 8/21/98 mor White, Daniel; Granville, WAS; <u>Granville, WAS</u>; mee 4132.
                                                                    (C:272)
8410. 6/1/84 gee White, Daniel H.; East Haddam, ---, CT. See 6701.
8411. 4/30/93 gee White, Elijah, gentleman; Granville, WAS. See 5334.
8412. 6/22/95 gor White, Elijah (w. Elizabeth); Granville, WAS; <u>Granville,</u>
                   <u>WAS</u>; gee 3620.   (D:267)
8413. 7/21/97 mor White, Elijah (w. Elizabeth), gentleman; Granville, WAS;
                   <u>Granville, WAS</u>; co-mees 79, 2940, 2957. Mortgagees are
                   all executors of the estate of James Grant "late of
                   Pawling" (DUT), dec'd.   (C:114)
8414. 3/9/98 gor White, Elijah (w. Elizabeth); Granville, WAS; <u>Granville,</u>
                   <u>WAS</u>; gee 3619.   (D:262)
8415. 6/22/95 gor White, Elizabeth. See 8412.
8416. 7/21/97 mor White, Elizabeth. See 8413.
8417. 3/9/98 gor White, Elizabeth. See 8414.
8418. 12/21/68 gor White, Henry, merchant; City of N.Y.; <u>Kingsbury, ALB</u>;
                   co-gors 1995, 6221; gee 7146. Grantors are all "assignees
                   appointed to the estate of Isaac Man, late of the City of
                   New York", merchant.   (Washington Co. C-2:334)
8419. 5/8/98 gor White, Ichabod (w. Rhoda); Argyle, WAS; <u>Argyle, WAS</u>;
                   gee 7916.   (F:221)
8420. 5/9/98 mee White, Ichabod; Argyle, WAS. See 7917.
8421. 1/14/02 mor White, Ichabod (w. Rhoda); Argyle, WAS; <u>Argyle, WAS</u>;
                   mee 7359.   (D:150)
8422. 11/4/93 gor White, James (w. Mary); Cambridge, WAS; <u>Cambridge, WAS</u>;
                   co-gors 8401, 8432; gee 7079.   (B-2:384)
8423. 9/21/98 gee White, James; Colrain, ---, MA. See 5652.
8424. 3/13/87 gee White, John; Hebron, WAS. See 6204.
8425. 3/14/87 mor White, John; Hebron, WAS; <u>Argyle, WAS</u>; mee 6205. (A:43)
8426. 3/14/89 mor White, John; Whitehall, WAS; <u>Whitehall, WAS</u>; mee 8567.
                                                                    (A:172)
8427. 1/1/94 gee White, John; Argyle, WAS. See 3949.
8428. 2/20/98 gee White, John; Argyle, WAS. See 8441.
8429. 8/8/99 gee White, John, merchant; Argyle, WAS. See 3925.
8430. 11/20/00 gee White, John, farmer; Argyle, WAS. See 4350.
8431. 9/25/01 gee White, John. See 4571.
8432. 11/4/93 gor White, Lydia. See 8401.
8433. 11/4/93 gor White, Mary. See 8422.
8434. 5/19/00 gor White, Rebekah, "wife of Andrew White"; Cambridge, WAS;
                   <u>Cambridge, WAS</u>; gee 5483.   (E:5)
8435. 5/8/98 gor White, Rhoda. See 8419.
8436. 1/14/02 mor White, Rhoda. See 8421.
8437. 9/7/69 gor White, Thomas. See 7955.
8438. 9/23/00 gee White, Thomas; Peru, CLI. See 2316.
8439. 9/24/00 mor White, Thomas; Peru, CLI; <u>Peru, CLI</u>; mee 2317.   (B:72)
8440. 1/1/94 gee White, Walter; Argyle, WAS. See 3949.
8441. 2/20/98 gor White, Walter; Argyle, WAS; <u>Argyle, WAS</u>; gee 8428. (D:276)
8442. 11/20/00 gor White, Walter; Argyle, WAS. See 4351.
8443. 5/11/01 gor White, Walter; Argyle, WAS; <u>Argyle Pat., WAS</u>; gee 2040.
                                                                    (E:323)
8444. 10/16/01 mee White, Walter; Argyle, WAS. See 6193.
8445. 2/27/88 gee Whiteside, John, farmer; Cambridge Dist., ALB. See 6124.
8446. 2/16/96 gee Whiteside, John, yeoman; Cambridge, WAS. See 6135.
8447. 5/9/96 gee Whiteside, John, yeoman; Cambridge, WAS. See 6153.
8448. 11/22/69 gee Whiteside, Phineas, yeoman; Cambridge, ALB. See 1551.
8449. 11/24/69 gee Whiteside, Phineas, yeoman; Cambridge, ALB. See 1552.

8450. 6/22/91 gor Whiteside, Phineas; ---, ---; Cambridge, WAS; co-gors 203, 601, 2069, 4392, 6370, 6995, 7354, 8336, 8354, 8838; gee 2162. (B-2:110)
8451. 3/9/98 mor Whitford, Anna. See 8452.
8452. 3/9/98 mor Whitford, Ezekiel (w. Anna), farmer; Hartford, WAS; Hartford, WAS; mee 1488. (B:346)
8453. 4/11/96 mor Whitiker, Seth, farmer; Stephentown, REN; Saratoga Pat., WAS; mee 3683. (B:30)
8454. 2/28/01 mor Whitlock, Samuel; Granville, WAS; Granville, WAS; mee 3516. (D:37b)
8455. 10/24/91 mor Whitney, Cornelius, 2nd; Granville, WAS; Granville, WAS; mee 1641. (A:295)
8456. 10/11/96 mor Whitney, Cornelius, farmer; Granville, WAS; Granville, WAS; mee 3769. (B:126)
8457. 5/13/00 mor Whitney, Cornelius (w. Sarah Church); Granville, WAS; Granville, WAS; mee 1541. (C:185)
8458. 5/15/02 mor Whitney, Cornelius; Granville, WAS; Granville, WAS; mee 1456. (D:166)
8459. 10/7/99 gee Whitney, David, yeoman; Hartford, WAS. See 7473.
8460. 10/7/99 mor Whitney, David, yeoman; Hartford, WAS; Hartford, WAS; mee 7474. (C:116)
8461. 6/6/99 mor Whitney, Henry, silversmith; Salem, WAS; Salem, WAS; mee 3527. The mortgagee is "sole executor and heiress of St. John Honeywood, Esq., late of Salem, deceased". (C:114)
8462. 4/8/00 gor Whitney, Henry, silversmith; Salem, WAS; Salem, WAS; gee 7516. (E:13)
8463. 9/21/01 mor Whitney, Joanna. See 8467.
8464. 7/6/88 mor Whitney, John; Granville, WAS; Granville, WAS; mee 2381. (A:110)
8465. 7/6/88 mor Whitney, Joshua; ---, ---; Granville, WAS; mee 2379. (A:88)
8466. 4/22/89 mor Whitney, Joshua; Granville, WAS; Granville, WAS; mee 835. (A:168)
8467. 9/21/01 mor Whitney, Joshua (w. Joanna); ---, WAS; Granville, WAS; mee 1694. (D:94)
8468. 7/6/88 gee Whitney, Joshua, Junr., yeoman; Granville, WAS. See 2378.
8469. 7/6/88 mor Whitney, Joshua, Junr.; Granville, WAS; Granville, WAS; mee 2379. (A:109)
8470. 5/13/00 mor Whitney, Sarah Church. See 8457.
8471. 9/7/91 mee Whorter, John; Granville, WAS. See 8723.
8472. 6/30/97 mee Whorter, John; Granville, WAS. See 1031.
8473. 4/26/96 mee Whorter, John, Esq.; Granville, WAS. See 2403.
8474. 6/2/97 gee Whorter, John, Esq.; Granville, WAS. See 8648.
8475. 6/30/97 gor Whorter, John, Esq.; Granville, WAS; Granville, WAS; gee 1030. (F:186)
8476. 7/27/97 gee Whorter, John, Esq.; Granville, WAS. See 2363.
8477. 3/5/98 mor Whorter, John, Esq.; Granville, WAS; Granville, WAS; mee 3571. (B:268)
8478. 1/16/87 gee Whorter, Samuel; Hebron, WAS. See 5351.
8479. 9/20/87 gor Whyte, John, yeoman; Black Creek Dist., WAS; Black Creek Dist., WAS; gee 8306. (F:86)
8480. 4/8/88 gor Whyte, John; Hebron, WAS; Hebron, WAS; gee 4654. (A:354)
8481. 4/27/01 mor Wicker, Lemuel; Easton, WAS; Easton, WAS; mee 6942. (D:58)
8482. 4/7/96 mor Wilbur, Job, carpenter; Easton, WAS; Saratoga, WAS; mee 3678. (B:29)
8483. 7/6/99 mor Wilbur, Joseph (w. Mary), farmer; Easton, WAS; Saratoga Pat., WAS; co-mees 776, 796, 7674. (C:115)
8484. 5/20/00 mor Wilbur, Joseph (w. Mary), farmer; Easton, WAS; Saratoga Pat., WAS; co-mees 777, 797, 7675. (C:186)
8485. 7/6/99 mor Wilbur, Mary. See 8483.
8486. 5/20/00 mor Wilbur, Mary. See 8484.
8487. 12/15/95 gee Wilcox, Ephraim; Lee, BER, MA. See 8400.
8488. 2/4/97 gor Wilcox, Jared, farmer; Hebron, WAS; Hebron, WAS; gee 943. (C-2:331)
8489. 5/3/97 mor Wilcox, Jared, yeoman; Hebron, WAS; Hebron, WAS; mee 8598. (B:163)

8490. 5/1/02 mor Wilcox, Roger, farmer; Chester, WAS; Chester, WAS; mee 7775.
(D:214)
8491. 6/2/87 gee Wildo, Solomon; ---, ---. See 7055.
8492. 12/7/87 mor Wildo, Solomon; Whitehall, WAS; Whitehall, WAS; mee 8564.
(A:171)
8493. 6/23/96 gee Willard, Elias, physician; Stillwater, SAR. See 4213.
8494. 8/24/90 mor Willcox, Jared; Hebron, WAS; Shereiff's Pat. in Hebron, WAS;
mee 6978. (A:224)
8495. 2/4/94 mor Willcox, Robert, farmer; ---, WAS; Walloomsack Pat., WAS;
mee 1959. (A:455)
8496. 5/23/87 gee Willett, Edward; Albany, ALB. See 6007.
8497. 4/13/97 gor Willett, Marinus; City of N.Y.; Peru, CLI; gee 180. (B:37)
8498. 4/13/97 mee Willett, Marinus; City of N.Y.. See 181. (two contracts)
8499. 1/2/98 gor Willett, Marinus, Esq.; City of N.Y.; Peru, CLI; gee 182.
(B:165)
8500. 1/3/98 mee Willett, Marinus, Esq.; City of N.Y. See 183.
8501. 11/3/97 mor Willey, Jabez, farmer; ---, HAR, CT. See 2722.
8502. 6/18/83 gee Williams, Darling; Cambridge, WAS. See 6926.
8503. 4/12/01 mee Williams, Darling; Kingsbury, WAS. See 1835.
8504. 11/4/01 gor Williams, George, farmer; Salem, WAS; Salem, WAS; gee 8607.
(E:442)
8505. 6/26/97 gee Williams, Gershom; Cambridge, WAS. See 3581.
8506. 3/9/02 mee Williams, Gershom; Cambridge, WAS. See 3984.
8507. 6/18/83 gee Williams, Isaac; Cambridge, ALB. See 6926.
8508. 4/12/01 mee Williams, Isaac; Kingsbury, WAS. See 1835.
8509. 9/5/81 gee Williams, Jabez; ---, CHA. See 8543.
8510. 11/27/94 gee Williams, Jacob; Canaan, LIT, CT. See 5052.
8511. 8/18/00 mor Williams, Jesse; Champlain, CLI; Canadian and Nova Scotia
Refugees' Pat., CLI.; mee 7631. (A:442)
8512. 2/19/02 mor Williams, Jesse; Champlain, CLI; Champlain, CLI; mee 5102.
(B:70)
8513. 5/1/82 gor Williams, John; New Perth, CHA; Granville, CHA; co-gor 4426;
gee 1655. (C-1:9)
8514. 6/1/84 gor Williams, John; White Creek, WAS; Morrison Pat., WAS; co-gor
4439; gee 6700. (B:127)
8515. 7/13/84 gor Williams, John; White Creek, WAS; Granville, WAS; co-gor
4440; gee 352. (A:411)
8516. 12/10/84 gee Williams, John. See 7055.
8517. 1/6/85 gor Williams, John; White Creek, WAS; White Creek, WAS; gee 1689.
(A:166)
8518. 6/4/85 gee Williams, John; ---, ---. See 7055.
8518a. 7/6/86 gee Williams, John; ---, WAS. See 3197.
8519. 6/2/87 gee Williams, John; ---, ---. See 7055.
8520. 11/15/87 gee Williams, John; ---, ---. See 7055.
8521. Data repositioned.
8522. 8/3/90 mee Williams, John, General; ---, ---. See 3922.
8523. 3/22/91 mee Williams, John; Salem, WAS. See 6832.
8524. 3/30/92 gee Williams, John; ---, ---. See 2125.
8525. 6/29/92 gee Williams, John; Salem, WAS. See 3311.
8526. 7/24/92 mee Williams, John; Salem, WAS. See 3162.
8527. 7/1/93 gor Williams, John; Salem, WAS; Salem, WAS; gee 1313. (B-2:233)
8528. 8/6/93 mee Williams, John; Salem, WAS. See 7651.
8529. 10/7/94 gee Williams, John; ---, ---. See 8583.
8530. 10/22/94 gor Williams, John; Salem, WAS; Salem, WAS; gee 3656. (B-2:278)
8531. 12/17/94 gee Williams, John; Salem, WAS. See 4265.
8532. 6/1/96 gor Williams, John; Salem, WAS; Salem, WAS; gee 4943. (D:11)
8533. 6/25/96 gor Williams, John; Salem, WAS; Westfield, WAS; gee 1642. (C-2:205)
8534. 6/25/96 mee Williams, John; Salem, WAS. See 3912.
8535. 8/24/96 mee Williams, John; Salem, WAS. See 245.
8536. 11/21/96 mee Williams, John, General; Salem, WAS. See 563.
8537. 4/4/99 mee Williams, John; Salem, WAS. See 4219.
8538. 4/11/00 gor Williams, John; Salem, WAS; Whitehall, WAS; gee 1814. (D:377)
8539. 4/29/01 gor Williams, John; Salem, WAS; Salem, WAS; gee 6536. (F:265)
8540. 5/2/01 gor Williams, John; Salem, WAS; Whitehall, WAS; gee 3022. (E:439)
8541. 1/25/02 mee Williams, John; Salem, WAS. See 2249.

8542. 11/3/02 mor Williams, John; Salem, WAS; <u>Whitehall, WAS</u>; co-mees 7547,
　　　　　　　　 7548, 7549.　　　　　　　　　　　　　　　　　　(E:28)
8543. 9/5/81 gor Williams, John, Dr.; ---, ---; <u>Granville, CHA</u>; co-gor 4436;
　　　　　　　　 gees 212 (B-1:35), 751 (B-1:36), 2893 (B-1:39), 3343
　　　　　　　　 (B-1:30), 3344 (B-1:29), 4434 (B-1:35), 6015 (B-1:33),
　　　　　　　　 8509 (B-1:38), 8609 (B-1:32). (nine contracts)
8544. 11/19/81 gor Williams, John, Doctor; ---, CHA; <u>Granville, CHA</u>; co-gor
　　　　　　　　 4437; gee 752.　　　　　　　　　　　　　　　　　(E:248)
8545. 11/19/83 gor Williams, John, Dr.; ---, CHA; <u>Granville, CHA</u>; co-gor 4438;
　　　　　　　　 gee 3161.　　　　　　　　　　　　　　　　　　(B-1:184)
8546. 11/19/83 gor Williams, John, Doctor; ---, CHA; <u>---, CHA</u>; co-gor 4427;
　　　　　　　　 gee 6679.　　　　　　　　　　　　　　　　　　(A:236)
8547. 1/-/85 gee Williams, John, Dr.; ---, ---. See 7055.
8548. 5/25/85 mee Williams, John, Dr.; White Creek, WAS. See 1056.
8549. 5/28/85 mee Williams, John, Dr.; White Creek, WAS. See 462, 3750.
　　　　　　　　 (two contracts)
8550. 6/1/85 mee Williams, John, Dr.; ---, ---. See 5061.
8551. 6/4/85 mee Williams, John, Dr.; ---, ---. See 761.
8552. 6/8/85 mee Williams, John, Dr.; ---, ---. See 7531.
8553. 6/8/85 mee Williams, John, Dr.; New Perth, WAS. See 7501.
8554. 7/1/85 gee Williams, John, Dr.; ---, ---. See 7055.
8555. 7/1/85 mee Williams, John, Dr.; ---, ---. See 2853, 6770, 6840, 6841,
　　　　　　　　 7855, 7973.
8556. 7/2/85 mee Williams, John, Dr.; ---, ---. See 3350.
8557. 7/2/85 mee Williams, John, Dr.; ---, CHA. See 7533.
8558. 10/7/85 mee Williams, John, Dr.; ---, ---. See 2630 and 2639.
8559. 7/6/86 mee Williams, John, Dr.; ---, ---. See 3198.
8560. 8/16/86 gor Williams, John, Dr.; ---, WAS; <u>Granville, WAS</u>; co-gor 4428;
　　　　　　　　 gee 3452.　　　　　　　　　　　　　　　　　　(C-1:12)
8561. 9/1/86 gor Williams, John, Dr.; Salem, WAS; <u>Whitehall, WAS</u>; gee 1138.
　　　　　　　　　　　　　　　　　　　　　　　　　　　　　　(C-1:45)
8562. 9/1/86 mee Williams, John, Dr.; ---, ---. See 1139.
8563. 12/6/87 mee Williams, John, Dr.; ---, ---. See 152.
8564. 12/7/87 mee Williams, John, Dr.; ---, ---. See 33 and 8492.
8565. 1/2/88 mee Williams, John, Dr.; ---, ---. See 2728.
8566. 2/5/89 mee Williams, John, Dr. See 3178.
8567. 3/14/89 mee Williams, John, Dr. See 8426.
8568. 5/29/90 gor Williams, John, Dr.; Salem, WAS; <u>Whitehall, WAS</u>; gee 1821.
　　　　　　　　　　　　　　　　　　　　　　　　　　　　　　(A:429)
8569. 3/7/85 gor Williams, John, Esq.; New Perth, WAS; <u>New Perth Dist., WAS</u>;
　　　　　　　　 gee 3335.　　　　　　　　　　　　　　　　　　(C-1:25)
8570. 12/2/89 gor Williams, John, Esq.; Salem, WAS; <u>Salem, WAS</u>; gee 6702.
　　　　　　　　　　　　　　　　　　　　　　　　　　　　　　(C-2:154)
8571. 12/28/89 gor Williams, John, Esq.; Salem, WAS; <u>Salem, WAS</u>; gee 7699.
　　　　　　　　　　　　　　　　　　　　　　　　　　　　　　(B-2:486)
8572. 6/8/91 gor Williams, John, Esq.; Salem, WAS; <u>Whitehall, WAS</u>; co-gor
　　　　　　　　 6676; gee 3988.　　　　　　　　　　　　　　　(C-2:256)
8573. 7/15/91 gee Williams, John, Esq.; ---, WAS. See 1074.
8574. 4/3/92 mor Williams, John, Esq.; Salem, WAS; <u>Salem, WAS</u>; mee 2121. (A:325)
8575. 7/3/92 gor Williams, John, Esq.; Salem, WAS; <u>Salem, WAS</u>; gee 603. (A:410)
8576. 7/5/92 mee Williams, John, Esq.; ---, ---. See 3530.
8577. 12/28/92 gee Williams, John, Esq.; ---, WAS. See 4076.
8578. 1/9/93 gee Williams, John, Esq.; Salem, WAS. See 3101.
8579. 5/10/93 mee Williams, John, Esq.; ---, ---. See 754.
8580. 7/15/93 mee Williams, John, Esq.; Salem, WAS. See 2396.
8581. 8/16/94 gor Williams, John, Esq.; Salem, WAS; <u>Salem, WAS</u>; gee 2983.
　　　　　　　　　　　　　　　　　　　　　　　　　　　　　　(B-2:269)
8582. 10/3/94 gor Williams, John, Esq.; Salem, WAS; <u>Salem, WAS</u>; gee 3653.
　　　　　　　　　　　　　　　　　　　　　　　　　　　　　　(B-2:279)
8583. 10/7/94 gor Williams, John, Esq.; Salem, WAS; <u>Salem, WAS</u> (land sold
　　　　　　　　 "for a courthouse and gaol"); co-gees 1140, 1597, 2624,
　　　　　　　　 4127, 4257, 4359, 4893, 6222, 6362, 6583, 7789, 8334,
　　　　　　　　 8529, 8790. Co-grantees are all supervisors of the
　　　　　　　　 County of Washington.　　　　　　　　　　　　　(B-2:273)
8584. 10/22/94 gor Williams, John, Esq.; Salem, WAS; <u>---, WAS</u>; gee 3654.
　　　　　　　　　　　　　　　　　　　　　　　　　　　　　　(B-2:280)

8585. 11/26/94 gee Williams, John, Esq.; Salem, WAS. See 7946.
8586. 12/30/94 mee Williams, John, Esq.; Salem, WAS. See 4777.
8587. 11/7/95 gor Williams, John, Esq. (w. Susannah); Salem, WAS; Salem, WAS;
                   gee 758.   (C-2:66)
8588. 11/15/95 mee Williams, John, Esq.; Salem, WAS. See 8625.
8589. 6/23/96 gor Williams, John, Esq. (w. Susannah); Salem, WAS; Grant Pat.,
                   WAS; gee 422.   (C-2:15)
8590. 6/25/96 mee Williams, John, Esq.; Salem, WAS. See 1643.
8591. 8/3/96 mee Williams, John, Esq.; Salem, WAS. See 6880.
8592. 8/19/96 mee Williams, John, Esq.. Salem, WAS. See 2497.
8593. 10/4/96 gor Williams, John, Esq.; Salem, WAS; Fairfield, WAS; gee 6584.
                                                                  (C-2:191)
8594. 10/21/96 mor Williams, John, Esq. (w. Susannah); Salem, WAS; Hebron, WAS;
                   co-mees 3187, 4248.   (B:109)
8595. 10/24/96 mee Williams, John, Esq.; Salem, WAS. See 885.
8596. 11/15/96 gor Williams, John, Esq.; Salem, WAS; Salem, WAS; gee 1815.
                                                                  (C-2:158)
8597. 4/12/97 gor Williams, John, Esq.; Salem, WAS; Salem, WAS; gee 4755.
                                                                  (D:426)
8598. 5/3/97 mee Williams, John, Esq.; Salem, WAS. See 1161, 3540, 3664,
                   6479, 6955, 6958, 6962, 6963, and 8489.
8599. 10/7/97 gor Williams. John, Esq.; Salem, WAS; Hebron, WAS; co-gees
                   3541, 3554a.   (F:5)
8600. 10/28/97 mee Williams, John, Esq.; Salem, WAS. See 6953.
8601. 11/2/98 gor Williams, John, Esq.; Salem, WAS; Hebron, WAS; gee 6004.
                                                                  (F:3)
8602. 4/26/99 mee Williams, John, Esq.; Salem, WAS. See 2976.
8603. 8/21/00 gor Williams, John, Esq.; Salem, WAS; Fairfield, WAS; gee 6588.
                                                                  (E:35)
8604. 5/28/01 gee Williams, John, Esq.; Salem, WAS. See 4682.
8605. 5/28/01 mee Williams, John, Esq.; Salem, WAS. See 4687.
8606. 9/21/01 mor Williams, John, Esq.; ---, WAS; Granville, WAS; mee 1694.
                                                                  (D:144)
8607. 11/4/01 gee Williams, John, Junr., gentleman; Salem, WAS. See 8504.
8608. 6/9/00 gee Williams, Joseph, farmer; Easton, WAS. See 1547.
8609. 9/5/81 gee Williams, Lemuel; Granville, CHA. See 8543.
8610. 2/15/96 gor Williams, Lemuel, yeoman; Granville, WAS; Granville, WAS;
                   gee 8619.   (C-2:92)
8611. 9/22/96 mor Williams, Lemuel; Granville, WAS; ---, WAS; mee 3766. (B:111)
8612. 6/4/98 mor Williams, Lemuel; Granville, WAS; Granville, WAS; co-mor
                   8616; co-mees 705, 719, 3514.   (B:343 small print)
8613. 3/5/83 gor Williams, Lewis; New Perth, CHA; New Perth, CHA; gee 7924.
                                                                  (A:198)
8614. 5/1/71 gee Williams, Lodowick, tailor; ---, ---. See 1423.
8615. 12/15/97 gor Williams, Mary. See 8621.
8616. 6/14/98 mor Williams, Silvester; Granville, WAS. See 8612.
8617. 11/7/95 gor Williams, Susannah. See 8587.
8618. 6/23/96 gor Williams, Susannah. See 8589.
8619. 2/15/96 gee Williams, Sylvester; Granville, WAS. See 8610.
8620. 3/12/83 gor Williams, Thomas, farmer; New Perth, CHA; New Perth, CHA;
                   gee 7928.   (B-1:133)
8621. 12/15/97 gor Williams, Thomas (w. Mary), farmer; Saratoga, SAR; Argyle,
                   WAS; co-gees 3997, 3999.   (D:335)
8622. 4/27/87 mee Williams, Timothy; Lansingburgh, ALB. See 3040.
8623. 1/31/67 gor Williamson, John, Esq., "Capt. Lieutenant in the Royal
                   Regiment of Artillery"; ---, ---; land "east side of
                   Hudson's River", ALB; gee 8780.   (B-2:167)
8624. 9/30/67 gor Williamson, John, "Captain Lieutenant in the Royal Regiment
                   of Artillery"; ---, ---; land "east side of Hudson's
                   River", ALB; gee 8781.   (B-2:173)
8625. 11/15/95 mor Willoughby, Ebenezer, gentleman; Kingsbury, WAS; Kingsbury,
                   WAS; mee 8588.   (B:21)
8626. 6/15/99 mee Willoughby, Ebenezer; Kingsbury, WAS. See 822.
8627. 4/28/01 gor Willoughby, Ebenezer (w. Hannah); Kingsbury, WAS; Kingsbury,
                   WAS; gee 8373.   (E:266)
8628. 4/28/01 gor Willoughby, Hannah. See 8627.

8629. 6/23/97 gee Wills, Elisha; Plattsburgh, CLI. See 1634.
8630. 7/10/90 mor Wills, Peter; Hebron, WAS; Hebron, WAS; mee 1072. (A:234)
8631. 7/10/90 mor Willson, Amos, yeoman; Hebron, WAS; Hebron, WAS; mee 1072.
(A:241)
8632. 6/2/97 gor Willson, Amos, farmer; Waston, WAS. See 8648.
8633. 10/8/91 gor Willson, Daniel, Westfield, WAS; Westfield, WAS; gee 8653.
(A:225)
8634. 1/1/88 gor Willson, Gile, Capt.; Hebron, WAS; Hebron, WAS; gee 8195
(A:395); gee 8652 (A:396). (two contracts)
8635. 2/1/97 gee Willson, Gile, Major; Hebron, WAS. See 4209.
8636. 6/1/98 mor Willson, Ruth), farmer, Hebron, WAS; Hartford, WAS; mee 1491.
(B:342, small pront)
8637. 12/1/99 gee Willson, Gile, yeoman; Hebron, WAS. See 8111.
8638. 2/1/97 gee Willson, Guile; Hebron, WAS. See 8276.
8639. 11/1/72 gee Willson, James, farmer; New Perth, CHA. See 1425.
8640. 4/20/80 gee Willson, John; New Perth, CHA. See 8651.
8641. 5/14/93 mor Willson, John; Cambridge, WAS; Cambridge, WAS; mee 1663.
(A:411)
8642. 1/27/94 gor Willson, John (w. Nancy), farmer; Cambridge, WAS; Cambridge,
WAS; gee 5305. (B-2:308)
8643. 11/28/98 mor Willson, John, yeoman; Hebron, WAS; Hebron, WAS; co-mees
4650, 6766, 6824. Co-mortgagees are all executors of the
estate of John Morin Scott, Esq., dec'd. (C:115)
8644. 5/14/99 mor Willson, John, farmer; Argyle, WAS; Argyle, WAS; mee 3000.
(C:11)
8645. 1/15/02 gor Willson, John, yeoman; Colrain, HAM, MA; Easton, WAS; gee
164. (F:62)
8646. 1/27/94 gor Willson, Nancy. See 8642.
8647. 4/29/85 gee Willson, Nathan; "late from Greenwich", HAM, MA. See 1033.
8648. 6/2/97 gor Willson, Reuben, farmer; Easton, WAS; Granville, WAS; co-gor
8632; gee 8471. (C-2:184)
8649. 10/26/92 gor Willson, Robert; Hebron, WAS; Hebron, WAS; gee 3117. (B-2:93)
8650. 6/1/98 mor Willson, Ruth. See 8636.
8651. 4/20/80 gor Willson, Samuel; New Perth, CHA; ---, CHA; gee 8640. (B-1:12)
8652. 1/1/88 gee Willson, Samuel, yeoman; Hebron, WAS. See 8634.
8653. 10/8/91 gee Willson, Samuel D.; Westfield, WAS. See 8633.
8654. 10/6/85 gee Willson, Thomas; ---, ---. See 7055.
8655. 3/20/93 mor Wilsie, Thomas; Christie's Manor, Lower Canada. See 8656.
8656. 3/20/93 mor Wilsie, William, Junr.; Christie's Manor, Lower, Canada;
Champlain, CLI; co-mor 8655; mee 3659. (A:101)
8657. 7/1/00 mor Wilson, Cyrus; ---, ---; ---, ESS; mee 5572. (A:26)
8658. 6/29/90 mor Wilson, Daniel; ---, ---; Westfield, WAS; mee 3189. (A:218)
8659. 10/17/92 gor Wilson, David; cordwainer; Plattsburgh, CLI. See 6633.
8660. 7/1/00 mor Wilson, Elias; ---, ---; ---, ESS; mee 5572. (A:19)
8661. 1/1/87 gor Wilson, George, yeoman; Cambridge Dist., WAS; Cambridge
Dist., WAS; gee 3145. (B-2:468)
8662. 1/31/86 gee Wilson, Gile; Black Creek Dist., WAS. See 1505.
8663. 8/14/86 gor Wilson, Gile; Black Creek Dist., WAS; Kempe"s Pat., WAS;
gee 8668. (C-1:18)
8664. 3/4/96 gee Wilson, Gile, gentleman; Hebron, WAS. See 7852.
8665. 12/2/99 mor Wilson, Gile (w. Ruth), yeoman; Hebron, WAS; Hebron, WAS;
mee 8112. (C:117)
8666. 5/30/01 gor Wilson, Guile (w. Ruth), yeoman; Hebron, WAS; Hebron, WAS;
gee 7715. (E:289)
8667. 2/1/75 gor Wilson, James; New Perth, CHA; ---, CHA; gee 8689. (B-1:11)
8668. 8/14/86 gee Wilson, James; Black Creek, WAS. See 8663.
8669. 5/1/00 mor Wilson, James (w. Susannah), merchant; Argyle, WAS; Hebron,
WAS; mee 3050. (C:117)
8670. 10/13/00 gor Wilson, James (w. Susannah), merchant; Hebron, WAS; Argyle,
WAS; gee 4221. (E:345)
8671. 10/13/00 mee Wilson, James, merchant; Hebron, WAS. See 4222.
8672. 2/18/02 gee Wilson, James, Esq.; Hebron, WAS. See 8117.
8673. 2/22/02 mor Wilson, James, Esq. (w. Susannah); Hebron, WAS; Argyle,
WAS; mee 8118. (D:148)
8674. 3/10/02 gor Wilson, James, Esq. (w. Susannah); Hebron, WAS; Argyle,
WAS; gee 6151. (F:179)

8675. 3/30/74 gee Wilson, John, farmer; ---, CHA. See 8685.
8676. 6/28/74 gor Wilson, John; ---, ALB. See 2731.
8677. 12/9/93 gor Wilson, John, yeoman; Hebron, WAS; Hebron, WAS; gee 6097.
　　　　　　　　　　　　　　　　　　　　　　　　　　　　　(B-2:139)
8678. 1/19/96 gee Wilson, John, yeoman; Cambridge, WAS. See 8679.
8679. 1/19/96 gor Wilson, John (w. Mary), yeoman; Hebron, WAS; Argyle, WAS;
　　　　　　　　　gee 1743 (C-2:261); gee 8678 (C-2:260). (two contracts)
8680. 5/17/99 mee Wilson, John; Hebron, WAS. See 4453.
8681. 1/19/96 gor Wilson, Mary. See 8679. (two contracts)
8682. 12/12/95 mor Wilson, Patrick, yeoman; "late of Salem", WAS; Hebron, WAS;
　　　　　　　　　mee 1502.　　　　　　　　　　　　　　　　　　(B:4)
8683. 7/10/90 gee Wilson, Peter, yeoman; ---, WAS. See 1071.
8684. 12/16/73 gor Wilson, Robert, farmer; ---, CHA; ---, CHA; co-gor 3115;
　　　　　　　　　gee 3536.　　　　　　　　　　　　　　　　　　(E:273)
8685. 3/30/74 gor Wilson, Robert, farmer; ---, CHA; land "East side of Hudson's
　　　　　　　　　River", CHA; co-gor 3116; gee 8675.　　　　(B-2:204)
8686. 12/2/99 mor Wilson, Ruth. See 8665.
8687. 5/30/01 gor Wilson, Ruth. See 8666.
8688. 11/7/73 gee Wilson, Samuel; White Creek, CHA. See 7942.
8689. 2/1/75 gee Wilson, Samuel; New Perth, CHA. See 8667.
8690. 11/29/91 gor Wilson, Samuel D.; Westfield, WAS; Westfield, WAS; gee 4433.
　　　　　　　　　　　　　　　　　　　　　　　　　　　　　(B-2:310)
8691. 5/1/00 mor Wilson, Susannah. See 8669.
8692. 10/13/00 gor Wilson, Susannah. See 8670.
8693. 2/22/02 mor Wilson, Susannah. See 8673.
8694. 3/10/02 gor Wilson, Susannah. See 8674.
8695. 9/1/94 gor Wilson, Thomas, yeoman; Whitehall, WAS; Whitehall, WAS;
　　　　　　　　　gee 5076.　　　　　　　　　　　　　　　　　(B-2:242)
8696. 6/17/80 gor Wing, Abraham, yeoman; Queensbury, CHA; Queensbury, CHA;
　　　　　　　　　gee 1036.　　　　　　　　　　　　　　　　　(A:371)
8697. 2/10/89 mor Wing, Abraham; Queensbury, WAS; Dist. of Saratoga, ALB (sic)
　　　　　　　　　mee 847.　　　　　　　　　　　Washington Co. A:130)
8698. 5/20/91 gor Wing, Abraham; Queensbury, WAS; Queensbury, WAS; gee 5548.
　　　　　　　　　　　　　　　　　　　　　　　　　　　　　(A:301)
8699. 7/26/98 mor Wing, Benjamin (w. Thankful); Queensbury, WAS; Queensbury,
　　　　　　　　　WAS; co-mees 865, 1535, 1536, 1537, 3102, 3966, 3970,
　　　　　　　　　5491, 5494, 5494a.　　　　　　　　　　　　　(C:271)
8700. 10/19/02 mor Wing, Benjamin, farmer; Queensbury, WAS; Queensbury, WAS;
　　　　　　　　　mee 8802.　　　　　　　　　　　　　　　　　(E:25)
8701. 7/26/98 mor Wing, Thankful. See 8699.
8702. 12/5/99 mor Winnegar, Samuel; Westfield, WAS; ---, WAS; co-mor 2384;
　　　　　　　　　mee 2007.　　　　　　　　　　　　　　　　　(C:116)
8703. 11/2/96 mor Winslow, John; Dartmouth, BRI, MA; Cambridge, WAS; mee 2066.
　　　　　　　　　　　　　　　　　　　　　　　　　　　　　(B:151)
8704. 9/6/96 gee Winter, Charles; Peru, CLI. See 537.
8705. 7/16/94 gor Witbeck, Lina. See 8706.
8706. 7/16/94 gor Witbeck, Thomas L., Esq., (w. Lina); Watervliet, ALB;
　　　　　　　　　Willsborough, CLI; gee 2817.　　　　　　　(A:5)
8707. 6/28/00 gee Witherbee, John, Junr; Kingsbury, WAS. See 7197.
8708. 5/2/98 gor Withey, Ephraim (w. Sarah), farmer; Hebron, WAS; Hebron, WAS;
　　　　　　　　　gee 3534.　　　　　　　　　　　　　　　　　(D:30)
8709. 5/2/98 gor Withey, Sarah. See 8708.
8710. 7/10/90 gee Withy, Ephraim; Hebron, WAS. See 1071.
8711. 7/10/90 mor Withy, Ephraim; Hebron, WAS; Hebron, WAS; mee 1072. (A:257)
8712. 10/31/98 mor Wood, Amos, yeoman; Hartford, WAS; Hartford, WAS; co-mees
　　　　　　　　　4430, 6571.　　　　　　　　　　　　　　　　(C:273)
8713. 8/26/84 gor Wood, Esek; Cambridge Dist., ALB; Hoosick Pat., ALB (sic)
　　　　　　　　　gee 2180.　　　　　　　　　　　　(WAS Co. D:177)
8714. 11/3/86 gee Wood, John, yeoman; ---, ALB. See 7661.
8715. 7/1/00 mor Wood, Jonas; ---, ---; ---, ESS; mee 5572.　　(A:29)
8716. 12/1/98 gee Wood, Jonathan; ---, WAS. See 940.
8717. 9/10/00 mor Wood, Jonathan; ---, ---; Willsborough, ESS; mee 5880. (A:61)
8718. 7/2/99 mor Wood, Levi; ---, ---; Willsborough, ESS; mee 6494. (A:43)
8719. 6/21/97 gee Wood, Nathaniel, Junr., yeoman; Nobletown, COL. See 3807.
8720. 6/22/97 mor Wood, Nathaniel, Junr., yeoman; Nobletown, COL; Whitehall,
　　　　　　　　　WAS; mee 3808.　　　　　　　　　　　　　　(B:189)

8721. 12/29/91 gee Wood, Walter; ---, ---. See 4878.
8722. 5/9/86 gee Woodall, Jonas; Hebron Dist., WAS. See 4785.
8723. 9/7/91 mor Woodard, Archabald, farmer; Hebron, WAS; Hebron, WAS;
      mee 8471. (A:298)
8724. 6/11/01 mor Woodard, Elizabeth. See 8725.
8725. 6/11/01 mor Woodard, Joseph (w. Elizabeth), farmer; Hebron, WAS; Hebron,
      WAS; mee 5228. (D:71b)
8726. 9/3/99 gor Woodroughf, Joseph; Granville, WAS. See 5470.
8727. 11/9/96 gee Woodruff, Appleton; Elizabethtown, CLI. See 5284.
8728. 3/12/93 gee Woodruff, Joseph, farmer; Granville, WAS. See 946.
8729. 5/30/93 mor Woodruff, Joseph, farmer; ---, WAS. See 5474.
8730. 6/20/01 gor Woodruff, Joseph; Granville, WAS. See 5476.
8731. 5/1/02 gee Woodruff, Roger Hooker; Willsborough, ESS. See 5289.
8732. 12/3/00 mor Woodruff, Timothy; ---, ---; Elizabethtown, ESS; mee 7521.
      (A:47)
8733. 1/30/00 mor Woodward, Jesse (w. Ruth); Cambridge, WAS; Cambridge, WAS;
      mee 4038. (C:186)
8734. 6/30/00 mee Woodward, Joseph, yeoman; Hebron, WAS. See 2569 and 2571.
8735. 6/1/92 gor Woodward, Lydia. See 8741. (three contracts)
8736. 7/20/93 gor Woodward, Lydia. See 8742.
8737. 6/1/92 gor Woodward, Polly. See 8739. (three contracts)
8738. 1/30/00 mor Woodward, Ruth. See 8733.
8739. 6/1/92 gor Woodward, Theophilus (w. Polly); Fairhaven, RUT, VT. See
      8741. (three contracts)
8740. 4/20/92 gee Woodward, William, gentleman; Hebron, WAS. See 5546.
8741. 6/1/92 gor Woodward, William (w. Lydia); Hebron, WAS; Hebron, WAS;
      co-gors 8737, 8739; gee 1910 (A:421); gee 3121 (A:423);
      gee 7679 (A:449). (three contracts)
8742. 7/20/93 gor Woodward, William (w. Lydia); Hebron, WAS; Hebron, WAS;
      gee 5997. (B-2:246)
8743. 6/13/91 gee Woodwards, Theophilus; Hebron, WAS. See 4674.
8744. 6/13/91 gee Woodwards, William; Hebron, WAS. See 4674.
8745. 5/2/96 mor Woodworth, Eleazer, farmer; Argyle, WAS; Argyle, WAS;
      co-mees 1292, 2101, 2228, 5584. (C:12)
8746. 5/10/97 mee Wooley, Joseph; Nine Partners, DUT. See 6350.
8747. 10/7/99 mee Woolley, William; Easton, WAS. See 7400.
8748. 9/7/89 gor Woolsey, Alida. See 8765.
8749. 2/29/96 gor Woolsey, Alida. See 8755.
8750. 7/10/96 gor Woolsey, Alida. See 8769.
8751. 1/16/97 gor Woolsey, Alida. See 8772.
8752. 2/4/96 --- Woolsey, Melancthon L.; ---, CLI. See 5857.
8753. 2/24/96 gee Woolsey, Melancthon L.; ---, CLI. See 4804.
8754. 2/24/96 mor Woolsey, Melancthon L.; ---, ---; Old Military Township #6
      (Clinton), CLI; co-mors 261, 288, 303, 1526, 3880, 5712,
      5747, 5858, 7560; mee 4801. (A:176)
8755. 2/29/96 gor Woolsey, Melancthon L. (w. Alida); Plattsburgh, CLI;
      Plattsburgh, CLI; gee 5025. (B:43)
8756. 4/19/97 gee Woolsey, Melancthon L.; Plattsburgh, CLI. See 2966.
8757. 6/22/98 gor Woolsey, Melancthon L.; ---, CLI. See 5696.
8758. 7/3/98 mee Woolsey, Melancthon L.; Plattsburgh, CLI. See 1237.
8759. 4/21/99 mee Woolsey, Melancthon L.; Plattsburgh, CLI. See 5983.
8760. 2/28/00 gor Woolsey, Melancthon L.; Plattsburgh, CLI. See 5761.
8761. 6/27/01 mor Woolsey, Melancthon L.; Plattsburgh, CLI; Plattsburgh, CLI;
      mee 5944. (B:35)
8762. 9/27/85 gee Woolsey, Melancthon Lloyd; Plattsburgh, WAS. See 5892.
8763. 3/14/87 gee Woolsey, Melancthon Lloyd; ---, ---. See 5911.
8764. 9/23/88 mee Woolsey, Melancthon Lloyd; Plattsburgh, CLI. See 8126.
8765. 9/7/89 gor Woolsey, Melancthon Lloyd, Esq. (w. Alida); Plattsburgh, CLI;
      Plattsburgh, CLI; gee 5841. (A:299)
8766. 11/7/89 gee Woolsey, Melancthon Lloyd; Plattsburgh, CLI. See 6446.
8767. 11/17/89 gor Woolsey, Melancthon Lloyd; Plattsburgh, CLI; Plattsburgh, CLI;
      gee 5400. (A:340)
8768. 1/-/96 gee Woolsey, Melancthon Lloyd; Plattsburgh, CLI. See 6503.
8769. 7/10/96 gor Woolsey, Melancthon Lloyd (w. Alida); Plattsburgh, CLI;
      Plattsburgh, CLI; gee 5026. (B:42)
8770. 9/7/96 gee Woolsey, Melancthon Lloyd; Plattsburgh, CLI. See 7831.

8771. 9/8/96 mor Woolsey, Melancthon Lloyd; Plattsburgh, CLI; Cumberland
 Head (Plattsburgh), CLI; mee 7832.   (A:193)
8772. 1/16/97 gor Woolsey, Melancthon Lloyd (w. Alida); Plattsburgh, CLI;
 Plattsburgh, CLI; geo 3106.   (B:40)
8773. 4/9/94 mor Woolsey, Melancthon Lloyd, Esq.; Plattsburgh, CLI;
 Plattsburgh, CLI; mee 2532.   (A:124)
8774. 7/1/00 mor Woolsey, Melancthon Lloyd, Esq.; Plattsburgh, CLI;
 Plattsburgh, CLI; mee 7999.   (A:442)
8775. 6/19/98 gor Worth, Edmund (w. Hannah), yeoman; Easton, WAS; Saratoga
 Pat., WAS; gee 3003.   (C-2:346)
8776. 12/20/99 gor Worth, Edmund; Easton, WAS; Easton, WAS; co-gor 2609a;
 gee 1044.   (E:165)
8777. 6/19/98 gor Worth, Hannah. See 8775.
 Wray. See also Rey.
8778. 10/30/65 gee Wray, George, gentleman; Albany, ALB. See 8191.
8779. 9/11/66 gee Wray, George,"clerk of the stores to his Majesty's Royal
 Train of Artillery". See 7394.
8780. 1/31/67 gee Wray, George, "clerk of Stores to the Royal Artillery".
 See 8623.
8781. 9/30/67 gee Wray, George, "clerk of the stores to the Royal Artillery".
 See 8624.
8782. 9/15/68 gee Wray, George, "clerk of his Majesty's Ordinance"; gentleman;
 Albany, ALB. See 1914.
8783. 6/5/71 gee Wray, George. "Clerk of Stores to the Royal Artillery".
 ---, ---. See 890.
8784. 5/5/85 gee Wray, George. Probably "George Rey" posted under this date
 is the same person as "George Wray" identified in entries
 8778 through 8802 inclusive.
8785. 5/28/85 gee Wray, George; ---, ---. See 7055.
8786. 11/16/85 gee Wray, George; ---, ---. See 4403.
8787. 8/11/86 mor Wray, George, gentleman; Albany, Alb; land "near Fort Ann",
 WAS; mee 1052.   (A:62)
8788. 3/28/92 gee Wray, George, gentleman; Westfield, WAS. See 2764.
8789. 6/22/93 gee Wray, George, gentleman; Albany, ALB. See 1053.
8790. 10/7/94 gee Wray, George; ---, ---. See 8583.
8791. 4/9/98 mee Wray, George, gentleman; Westfield, WAS. See 4102.
8792. 9/19/98 mee Wray, George; Westfield, WAS. See 1598.
8793. 12/1/98 mee Wray, George; Westfield, WAS. See 2657.
8794. 7/15/99 gee Wray, George; ---, WAS. See 2771.
8795. 7/21/94 gor Wray, George, Esq.; Westfield, WAS; Westfield, WAS; gee 8803.
                                                       (B-2:271)
8796. 3/15/98 mee Wray, George, Esq.; Westfield, WAS. See 7071.
8797. 5/11/98 mee Wray, George, Esq.; Westfield, WAS. See 3254.
8798. 5/22/98 mee Wray, George, Esq.; Westfield, WAS. See 3026.
8799. 11/12/98 mee Wray, George, Esq.; Westfield, WAS. See 1761 and 2929.
8800. 5/21/00 mee Wray, George, Esq.; Westfield, WAS. See 5996.
8801. 6/16/00 mee Wray, George, Esq.; Westfield, WAS. See 2432.
8802. 10/19/02 mee Wray, George, Esq.; Westfield, WAS. See 8700.
8803. 7/21/94 gee Wray, John, yeoman; Westfield, WAS. See 8795.
8804. Data repositioned.
 Wright. See also Right.
8805. 2/25/96 gee Wright, Abraham; Cambridge, WAS. See 7131.
8806. 7/3/97 gor Wright, Abraham (w. Phebe); Cambridge, WAS; Cambridge, WAS;
 gee 5201.   (F:223)
8807. 7/22/97 mor Wright, Abraham; Cambridge, WAS; Queensbury, WAS; mee 71.
                                                       (B:211)
8808. 11/18/99 gee Wright, Abraham; Queensbury, WAS. See 2502.
8809. 2/21/93 gor Wright, Ebenezer; New Haven, ADD, VT; ---, WAS; co-gor 8825;
 gee 5550.   (B-2:99)
8810. 6/27/98 gee Wright, Elijah, blacksmith; Argyle, WAS. See 2906.
8811 8812. 9/15/94 gee Wright, Enoch; ---, ---. See 2012.
8813. 1/1/95 gee Wright, Enoch; Whitehall, WAS. See 1284.
8814. 1/1/95 gor Wright, Enoch; Whitehall, WAS; ---, WAS; co-gors 1106,
 1285, 1371, 5375; gee 8242.   (B-2:322)
8815. 1/1/95 gor Wright, Enoch; Whitehall, WAS; ---, WAS; co-gors 1106,
 1371, 5375, 8243; gee 1283.   (B-2:325)
8811 - - - Data repositioned.

8816. 1/4/95 gor Wright, Enoch (w. Tryphana); Whitehall, WAS; Hampton and
                   Whitehall, WAS; co-gors 1368, 1372, 5376; co-gees
                   8305, 8311.   (B-2:482)
8817. 1/5/95 gor Wright, Enoch; Whitehall, WAS; ---, WAS; co-gor 5377;
                   gee 1373.   (B-2:329)
8818. 4/2/00 mee Wright, Isaac; ---, ---. See 2084.
8819. 4/30/01 gee Wright, Isaac; ---, ---. See 2086.
8820. 3/31/98 gor Wright, Jacob, farmer; "now or late of ... Washington
                   County"; Crosfield's Purchase, WAS; gee 7219. (D:96)
8821. 8/5/93 gor Wright, James; ---, WAS; Argyle, WAS; gee 6902. (C-2:94)
8822. 4/10/99 mee Wright, John; New Castle, WES. See 1953.
8823. 5/20/00 mee Wright, John; New Castle, WES. See 1946.
8824. 7/3/97 gor Wright, Phebe. See 8806.
8825. 2/21/93 gor Wright, Rachel; New Haven, ADD, VT. See 8809.
8826. 6/28/02 gee Wright, Thomas M.; Bolton, WAS. See 7228.
8827. 6/28/02 mor Wright, Thomas M.; Bolton, WAS; Bolton, WAS; mee 7229. (E:30)
8828. 1/4/95 gor Wright, Tryphana. See 8816.
8829. 2/25/96 mor Wyer, Robert, farmer, Salem, WAS; Salem, WAS; mee 2127. (C:12)
8830. 2/5/95 gor Wyman, Baldwin, yeoman; Cambridge, WAS. See 4380.
8831. 5/13/96 mor Wyman, Baldwin; Cambridge, WAS; Cambridge, WAS; co-mees
                   6674, 8859.   (B:39)
8832. 12/10/91 mor Wyman, Benjamin; Salem, WAS; Salem, WAS; mee 487. (A:390)
8833. 12/13/91 gee Wyman, Benjamin; Salem, WAS. See 488. (two contracts)
8834. 1/29/78 gor Yates, Deborough. See 8835.
8835. 1/29/78 gor Yates, Paul (w. Deborough); New Milford, LIT, CT. See 6870.
8836. 12/5/88 gee Younglove, Aaron, yeoman; Cambridge Dist., WAS. See 8851.
8837. 4/5/99 mee Younglove, Aaron, Cambridge, WAS. See 3148.
8838. 6/22/91 gor Younglove, John; ---, ---. See 8450.
8839. 4/1/95 gor Younglove. John (w. Martha); Cambridge, WAS; Cambridge Pat.,
                   WAS, gee 1125.   (B-2:544)
8840. 6/26/90 mee Younglove, John, Esq.; Cambridge, ALB. See 6597.
8841. 9/25/90 gor Younglove, John, Esq.; Cambridge, WAS; Cambridge, WAS;
                   gee 2849.   (B-2:501)
8842. 3/5/92 gor Younglove, John, Esq.; Cambridge, WAS; Cambridge, WAS;
                   gee 7835.   (B-2:402)
8843. 5/2/93 gor Younglove, John, Esq.; Cambridge, WAS; Cambridge, WAS;
                   gee 5125.   (E:401)
8844. 12/30/94 gee Younglove, John, Esq.; Cambridge, WAS. See 5257.
8845. 7/4/95 gor Younglove, John, Esq. (w. Martha); Cambridge, WAS; Cambridge,
                   WAS; gee 1545.   (B-2:541)
8846. 2/26/96 mee Younglove, John, Esq.; Cambridge, WAS. See 3579.
8847. 4/1/96 gee Younglove, John, Esq.; Cambridge, WAS. See 3580.
8848. 4/22/96 gor Younglove, John, Esq. (w. Martha); Cambridge, WAS;
                   Cambridge, WAS; gee 7252.   (B-2:537)
8849. 4/22/96 mee Younglove, John, Esq.; Cambridge, WAS. See 7091.
8850. 2/2/88 gee Younglove, Joseph, farmer; ---, ALB. See 7272.
8851. 12/5/88 gor Younglove, Joseph, yeoman; Cambridge Dist., WAS; Cambridge
                   Dist., WAS; gee 8836.   (B-2:12)
8852. 10/12/90 gor Younglove, Joseph, gentleman; ---, ---; Cambridge, WAS;
                   gee 3263.   (A:349)
8853. 10/14/92 mee Younglove, Joseph; Cambridge, WAS. See 7030.
8854. 11/29/92 mee Younglove, Joseph; Cambridge, WAS. See 3264.
8855. 4/26/94 mor Younglove, Joseph, farmer; Cambridge, WAS; Cambridge, WAS;
                   mee 397.   (A:474)
8856. 6/2/94 mee Younglove, Joseph; Cambridge, WAS. See 2155.
8857. 6/13/94 gee Younglove, Joseph; Cambridge, WAS. See 4042.
8858. 7/10/94 gee Younglove, Joseph, yeoman; Cambridge, WAS. See 4657.
8859. 5/13/96 mee Younglove, Joseph; Cambridge, WAS. See 3979, 8256, 8831.
8860. 2/13/97 gor Younglove, Joseph, yeoman; Cambridge Dist., WAS; Cambridge
                   Dist., WAS; gee 1452.   (C-2:209)
8861. 5/4/97 gee Younglove, Joseph; Cambridge, WAS. See 8257.
8862. 3/15/99 mee Younglove, Joseph; Cambridge, WAS. See 6910.
8863. 5/26/01 gee Younglove, Joseph; ---, ---. See 5570.
8864. 11/23/02 mee Younglove, Joseph; Cambridge, WAS. See 7044.
8865. 5/1/96 gor Younglove, Lidia. See 8866.
8866. 5/1/96 gor Younglove, Lucas (w. Lidia); Cambridge, WAS; Cambridge Pat.,
                   WAS; gee 1.   (C-2:174)

8867. 5/1/96   mee Younglove, Lucas; Cambridge, WAS. See 2.
8868. 4/1/95   gor Younglove, Martha. See 8839.
8869. 7/4/95   gor Younglove, Martha. See 8845.
8870. 4/22/96   gor Younglove, Martha. See 8848.
8871. 7/10/90   mor Youngs, William; Hebron, WAS; Hebron, WAS; mee 1072. (A:233)

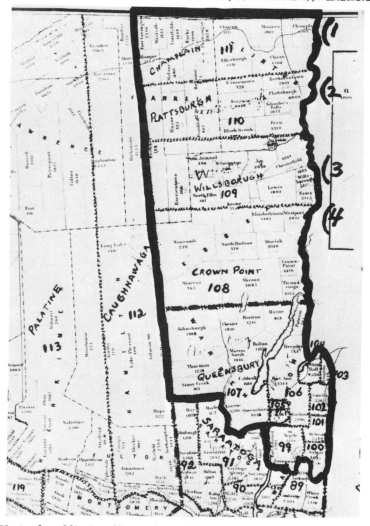

99. Argyle	102. Granville	105. Kingsbury	108. Crown Point	111. Champlain
100. Salem	103. Hampton	106. Westfield	109. Willsborough	
101. Hebron	104. Whitehall	107. Queensbury	110. Plattsburgh	

The small print notations reflect the towns and their populations as of 1855. Other than the formation of Altona, Brighton, Santa Clara, and Waverly, 1857-88, the town boundaries of 1855 have remained relatively fixed. For a large print delineation of the towns of today see Rand McNally's Commercial Atlas and Marketing Guide.

The regions denoted above as 1, 2, 3, and 4 are discussed in Appendix B. Source of map segment: Julia Boyer-Reinstein's Souvenir Map, 1957 (State Archives, Albany) delineating the 120 towns of New York as defined by the state legislature, 7 March 1788.

APPENDIX A

FORMATION AND POPULATION OF NORTHEASTERN NEW YORK TOWNS PRIOR TO 1803

Dates of formation of the twenty-five towns organized in northeastern New York prior to 1803 (present-day counties here posted):

Argyle, Washington --- Patent, 3/13/1764; town, 3/23/1786.
Bolton, Warren ------- Town (from Thurman), 3/25/1799.
Cambridge, Washington- Patent, 7/21/1761; town, 3/7/1788.
Champlain, Clinton --- Town, 3/7/1788 (Chateaugay from Champlain, 3/15/1799).
Chateaugay, Franklin - Town (from Champlain), 3/15/1799.
Chester, Warren ------ Town (from Thurman), 3/25/1799.
Chesterfield, Essex -- Town (from Willsborough), 2/20/1802.
Crown Point, Essex --- Town, 3/23/1786 (Elizabethtown from Crown Point, 2/12/98).
Easton, Washington --- Town (from Saratoga and Stillwater), 3/3/1789. Originally
            a part of Saratoga Patent.
Elizabethtown, Essex - Town (from Crown Point), 2/12/1798.
Fairfield, Warren ---- Town (from Queensbury), 4/10/1792. Name changed to
            Luzerne, 4/6/1808.
Granville, Washington- Town, 3/23/1786.
Hampton, Washington -- Town, 3/3/1786.
Hartford, Washington - Town (from Westfield), 3/12/1793. Name changed to Fort
            Ann, 4/6/1808.
Hebron, Washington --- Town, 3/23/1786.
Jay, Essex ----------- Town (from Willsborough), 1/16/1798.
Kingsbury, Washington- Patent, 5/18/1762; town, 3/23/1786.
Peru, Clinton -------- Town (from Plattsburgh and Willsborough), 12/28/1792.
Plattsburgh, Clinton - Town, 4/4/1785 (part of Peru from Plattsburgh, 12/28/1792).
Queensbury, Warren --- Patent, 5/20/1762; town, 3/13/1786 (Fairfield from
            Queensbury, 4/10/1792).
Salem, Washington ---- Patent, 8/7/1764; town, 3/23/1786.
Thurman, Warren ------ Town, 4/10/1792 (Bolton and Chester from Thurman, 3/25/99).
Westfield, Washington- Town, 3/23/1786. Name changed to Fort Ann, 4/6/1808.
Whitehall, Washington- Patent (in the name Skenesborough), 3/31/1765; town (in
            the name Whitehall), 3/23/1786.
Willsborough, Essex -- Town (from Crown Point), 3/7/1788 (part of Peru from
            Willsborough, 12/28/1792; all of Jay, 1/16/1798; and
            all of Chesterfield, 2/20/1802).

Population of the thirteen towns of northeastern New York in 1790:

Clinton County	pop.	Washington County	pop.
(This county in 1790 was more than twice the size of Washington.)		Queensbury ----------------	1080
		Argyle ---------------------	2341
		Granville ------------------	2240
		Hampton --------------------	463
Champlain ---------------	578	Hebron ---------------------	1703
Plattsburgh -------------	458	Kingsbury ------------------	1120
pop. sub-total- 1036		Salem ----------------------	2186
Crown Point -------------	203	Westfield ------------------	2103
Willsborough ------------	375	Whitehall ------------------	797
pop. sub-total- 573		pop. sub-total- 12953	
Totals	1614		14033

In 1790 Champlain and Plattsburgh together covered the approximate area of present-day Clinton and Franklin counties combined. Similarly, Crown Point and Willsborough then blanketed present-day Essex County. Queensbury alone spanned present-day Warren County. The remaining eight towns of the region together covered present-day Washington County.

February 7, 1791 Cambridge and Easton, with 1790 populations of 4996 and 2359 respectively, were annexed to Washington County from Albany County.

Population of the twenty-four towns of northeastern New York in 1800:

Clinton County	pop.	Essex County	pop.	Washington County	pop.
				Bolton -----------	959
				Chester ----------	508
				Queensbury -------	1435
				Thurman ----------	1332
				sub-total- 4234	
				Argyle -----------	4597
				Cambridge --------	6187
				Easton -----------	3069
				Fairfield --------	591
				Granville --------	3175
				Hampton ----------	700
				Hartford ---------	2108
Chateaugay -----	443	Crown Point -	941	Hebron -----------	2528
				Kingsbury --------	1651
Champlain ------	1169	Elizabethtown	899	Salem ------------	2861
Peru -----------	1347	Jay ---------	601	Westfield --------	2502
Plattsburgh ----	1400	Willsborough	1716	Whitehall --------	1604
sub-total 3916				sub-total 31573	
Totals	4359		4157		35807

In 1800 Chateaugay covered the approximate area of present-day Franklin County.
Champlain, Peru, and Plattsburgh then blanketed present-day Clinton County.
Essex County's boundaries have remained relatively fixed from the date of their
original determination in 1799 through the present. Bolton, Chester, Queensbury,
and Thurman in 1800 together spanned all of present-day Warren County. The
twelve towns above listed in sequence Argyle through Whitehall in 1800 covered
all of present-day Washington County.

Numbers of deeds and mortgage agreements filed by counties in northeastern
New York, 1772 through 1802 inclusive:

Counties and time intervals	Numbers of deeds filed	Numbers of mortgages filed	Totals
Charlotte/Washington (1772-1802)	1410	1176	2586
Clinton (1788-1802) ------------	402	422	824
Essex (1799-1802) --------------	45	95	140
Totals	1857	1693	3550

Names, residence places, and dates of appointment of the clerks of Washington
County prior to 1803:

Patrick Smith of Argyle, 8 September 1773

Ebenezer Clarke of Salem, 8 May 1777

John McCrea of Salem, 16 April 1785

St. John Honeywood of Salem, 24 February 1797

Gerrit L. Wendell of Cambridge, 9 October 1798

Prior to 1788 there were scattered settlers in the areas of
present-day Chateaugay and Chazy. Any of these persons who then wished
to file their deeds had to anticipate a round-trip of between 300 and
400 miles. From Crown Point northward (see the X for this community
on the map segment of page 4) there then were no roads worthy of the
name. Crown Point lay 120 miles south of Chateaugay.

The National Climatic Center in its annual report for New York, 1980,
lists 101 days between "freezes" that year for Chazy compared to 116
for Salem and 196 for Riverhead. The N.C. C. (Climates of the States,
2:697, 9) reports: "A durable snow cover generally begins to develop in

212

the ... northern lowlands (of New York) by late November and remains ...
until various times in April.... The Adirondack region (primarily in
Essex County) records from 35 to 45 days with below zero temperatures in
normal to severe winters with a somewhat fewer number ... occurring near
Lake Champlain."

Effective 7 March 1788, upon the establshment of Clinton County,
maximum travel distances for would-be record filers were appreciably
reduced. Now the residents of southern Clinton County had only to
travel 150 miles round trip to file their records in Plattsburgh.
Residents of northern Washington County (the present north portion of
Warren County) had only to travel 160 miles round trip to file their
records in the Salem-Cambridge area.

INCOMPLETENESS IN DEED FILINGS IN NORTHEASTERN NEW YORK PRIOR TO 1803

A deed-to-mortgage comparison

Washington County was formed 12 March 1772. **Patrick Smith of Argyle** assumed his duties as **county clerk 8 September 1773.** The first deed was county-filed 30 June 1774. By this date eleven mortgages had been filed, the first just twenty-three days after clerk Smith's appointment. As reported in Appendix A, both Clinton and Essex counties in their formative years recorded more mortgages than deeds. This pattern was evidenced also in Washington County where 44 mortgages and 31 deeds were filed between 1772 and 1788.

In data gathering for Part 2 it was observed that throughout the time span 1772 through 1802, the deeds were generally filed several months or years after the dates of their signings. This time lag between date of signing and date of filing was more pronounced in the earlier years of note although there were still appreciable lags as late as 1802. Entry 4354 in Part 2 reflects a deed signing year of 1764. For this contract the county file shows a recording year of 1798. The corresponding dates pertaining to entries 6225 and 6126 are 1771 versus 1801 and 1775 versus 1801 respectively.

No delays comparable to those above were observed for any of the mortgage filings. Presumably the new land owners, once they had pocketed their deeds, felt relatively secure. In contrast the money-lenders, financially unsatisfied at the outset, were eager to file or to have their agents file their mortgage agreements.

Appendix A reveals that by the end of 1802 a total of 1857 deeds and 1693 mortgages had been filed in northeastern New York. This represents an excess of less than 10% in deed filings compared to mortgage filings. Based on the lag-time postings above pertaining to deed recordings and on information yet to be here disclosed it is suggested that in northeastern New York, 1772 through 1802, the number of deed signings exceeded the number of mortgage signings far beyond the 10% level.

A deed-to-assessment-list comparison

David Kendall Martin in "A 1798 United States Assessment List for Northern New York State" (N.Y. Genealogical and Biographical Record 113: 93-102; 152-60; 231-8 (1982)) reconstructs the 1798 assessment lists for the three towns of Champlain, Peru, and Plattsburgh. He states that no other town lists related to the 1798 tax are known to have survived for New York. In his postings he distinguishes between landowners and tenants. At time of assessment the former, without exception, must have been deed holders in their own names or in those of their fathers or grandfathers.

The lists which here follow result from a comparison of Mr. Martin's list with that found in Part 2 of this report.

Champlain landowners whose names appear uniquely on the assessment list of 1798:
(None of the full names or surnames here posted is found, Champlain-related,
in Part 2 of this report; persons whose names are here preceded by an
asterisk are individuals whose full names or surnames do not appear at all
in Part 2)

* Adrian (or Adullin), Peabody
* Adullin (or Adrian), Peabody
* Amlin, Charles
  Antil, Edward, heirs of
* Ashman, William
* Ashmun, Samuel
  Badlam, William
  Beeman, Nathan
* Bender, Joseph
* Boudet, James
  Boulangy, Julian
    (see entry 609 of Part 1)
  Boulangy, Noel
* Bouran, Widow
  Boyd, Kelly
  Cable, John
  Cantine, Peter
* Chandenet, Francois
* Chandonet, Margaret
  Chin, Edward
  Colvin, Jeremiah
  Cooper, Charles D.
* Corp, Joseph
  Dean, James
* Dottre, Willard
* Dumas (or Durnan), Eneas
* Durnan (or Dumas), Eneas
  Eddy, Robert
  Fitch, Jabez
  Freeman, Constant
* Fry, ---, heirs of
  Gregory, Seth
  Hamtramuk, John
  Hatfield, Moses
  Ingles, George
* Jauney, John
  Kellogg, Eliphalet, Junr.
  Kirby, ---
* Labelle, Eneas
* La Fortune, Joseph
  Lansing, Abraham G.
* Le Dame, Antoine
* Lefamboise, Jean B.
* Lefromboise, Jaque
  Le Roy, James
  Le Roy, Simon
  Lewis, William, Junr.
  Lewis, William, Senr.
* Lizotte, Louis
* Longchamp, Louise, heirs of
* Longchamp, Patience
* Lusier, Jean B., Senr.
* Lusier, Jean Bapste, Junr.
* Marvin (or Mervin), Jared
* Mervin (or Marvin), Jared
  Mitchell, Andrew

* Palen, Gilbert
* Paulent, Aimable
* Paulent, Antoine
  Pearsee, Jonathan
  Pearson, ---
  Pearson, George
* Pryx, Asline
    (see entries 205 & 234 in Part 2)
* Pryx, Asline, Junr.
    (see entries 205 & 234 in Part 2)
* Reuben, Allen
* Reuben, Isaac
* Robege, Peter
* Robye, Peter
* Runnels, Gilbert
* Seaburn, ---
* Seaburn, Benjamin
* Shattuck, William
  Squier, Ezra
* Stoughton, Samuel
  Taylor, John
  Torey, William
* Traversee, Joseph
* Traversee, Joseph, Junr.
  Tremble, George, heirs of
  Trembly, Bruno
* Troop, Josiah
  Trumble, Levy
* Vanderhyder, Jacob
  Van Wyck, ---
  Van Wyck, Thomas
  Wait, John
  Watson, Alkanah
  Watson, Jacob
* Wellsey, William
  Willet, Samuel
* Willey, Jabez
* Wit, ---

Total number of persons identified above - 90

Total number of persons "starred" above - 49

From the 1800 census report for Champlain:
total population - - - - - - 1612
approx. number of "contract-eligible males" 386
  (definition of term and method of
determining "contract-eligible males"
furnished in note, page 218).
By 1800 the Champlain of 1798 had been
split into Champlain and Chateaugay.
The two figures immediately above reflect
the totals for these two towns combined.

Peru landowners whose names appear uniquely on the assessment list of 1798:
(None of the full names or surnames here posted is found, Peru-related,
in Part 2 of this report; persons whose names are here preceded by an
asterisk are individuals whose full names or surnames do not appear at all
in Part 2)

Baker, Ebenezer
Baker, Isaac
Banker, William
Barker, Isaac
Barker, Nicholas
Barnes, Joseph
Bates, Zadoc
Beach, Joseph
* Bean, James
Bigalow, Ephraim
Boardman, William
Bowne, Benjamin
Bragg, Benjamin
Bragg, Elihu
Briggs, Elihu
Brown, Samuel
Brown, Solomon
Buck, Israel
Bull, Norman
* Clyd, William
Cole, Isaac
Day, Amos
Day, David
* De Bar, Andres
Dickson, Moses
Douglass, Asa
Douglass, John
Earl, Benjamin
* Edmond, P. & Co.
* Eeells, Simeon
* Eells, Waterman
Eights, Abram
Everest, Joseph
Everest, Joseph, Junr.
Everitt, Edward
Everitt, George
* Evers, James W.
Finch, Isaac
Finch, Isaac, Junr.
Finch, James
* Fulton, William
George, David
* Gilson, D.
* Gorges, David
* Gridley, Nathaniel
* Gridley, Noah
Griffeth, Jonathan
* Hackston, Jeremiah
* Hallock, Edward
* Hallock, Peter
Hamilton, Patric
Hawley, Samuel
* Heart, Philip
* Hendy, Barzilla
Hills, Bela
Hitchcock, ---
Hobart, John S.
Hobart, Noah
* Humedieu, Ezra L.

Jackson, Daniel
Jackson, Samuel
Jackson, Theophilus
* Jakax, Joseph J.
* Jakers, Joseph
* Lavvanway, Joseph
Leavingston, Gilbert
Lewis, William
* Lowing, William
Moasley, John
Moon, Robert
* Nicholas, Elezer
Norton, Rufus
* Ondlay, Major
Orsburn, David
Orsburn, John
Palmer, Edward, Junr.
Palmer, Edward, Senr.
Palmer, Ezekiel
Palmer, Uriah
* Parkis, Daniel
Prier, Edmund & Co.
Raymond, John
* Ricketson, Abednego
* Ryley, Lawrence
Sanders, Oliver
Simmons, Caleb
Skeels, Truman
Stantton, John
Stewart, Peter
Taylor, John
Taylor, Samuel
Taylor, William
Thorn, William
Torry, Josiah
Warner, Lupton
Waterman, ---
Waterman, Uriah
* Weatherwax, David
* Weatherwax, Martin
* Weldon, Benjamin
Weston, James
Whitcomb, Robert
Williams, John
Wood, ---
* Wrangham, William
Wright, Isaac

Total number of persons identified above - 106

Total number of persons "starred" above - 31

From the 1800 census report for Peru:
total population - - - - - - 1347
approx. number of "contract-eligible males" 276
(definition of term and method of
determining "contract-eligible males"
furnished in note, page 218).

Plattsburgh landowners whose names appear uniquely on the assessment list of 1798:
(None of the full names or surnames here posted is found, Plattsburgh-related,
in Part 2 of this report; persons whose names are here preceded by an
asterisk are individuals whose full names or surnames do not appear at all
in Part 2)

Bayard, Nicholas
* Boyer, Richard
Brewer, William
Bulliss, Germond
Carter, William
Chase, Enoch
* Chittenden, Nathaniel
Collins, Charles
Coon, Joseph
Corbin, Moses
Corbin, Moses, Junr.
* Corkle, Robert
Culver, Francis
Culver, John
Deen, ---
De Long, Peter
* Domeny, Henry
* Dominy, Hervey
* Dominy, John
Douglass, Thomas
* Favies, Luis
Green, Joseph
Hamilton, John
Hammond, Benjamin
Hammond, Daniel
Hammond, James
* Hare, David
* Hare, Michael
Hazen, Moses
* Horlston, George
Hubbard, Ezekiel
* Hurlbut, Zacheus
Jones, Daniel, Junr.
Jones, Roswell
Jones, Russell
* Klenkert, John
Leek, Benjamin

McCarter, William
McIntyer, Richard
McIntyre, Stephen
* Mack, Jacob
Mane, James
Marsh, George
Mason, Andy
* Munn, Arad
Newton, Simon
* Nicholas, Caleb
* Purdy, Henry
Rice, Solomon
Road, Rogers
Robertson, John
Rock, Francis Lee
* Scribner, Jonathan
* Shooey, Seth
* Sperry, Seth
Stevenson, Amasa
Stevenson, John
* Stratton, John
Turner, Ezra
Vaughn, Benjamin
* Weeks, Jacob
* Winchel, Martin

Total number of persons identified above - 62

Total number of persons "starred" above - 22

From the 1800 census report for Plattsburgh:
total population - - - - - - 1400
approx. number of "contract-eligible males" 296
(definition of term and method of
determining "contract-eligible males"
furnished in note below)

These postings of pages 216 through 218, drawn from 1798 assessment lists
for three northeastern New York towns, identify approximately 250 landowners
whose deeds were apparently not county filed within the time span 1772 through 1802.

Note: "Contract-eligible males" are free white males age 21 or older. They
may be identified in approximate numbers for any town of reference on either
of the first two federal census reports thus:

For 1800 - the number of free white males age 26 or older added to one-half
the number age 16 through 25

For 1790 - the number of fwm's age 21 or older in 1800 (see above) divided
by the number of fwm's age 16 or older in 1800 multiplied by
the number of fwm's age 16 or older in 1790.

A paired-towns comparison, New York versus Vermont

In 1790 (see map page 210 with its Vermont-area numbers 1–4) the four
Vermont towns of Alburgh, South Hero, Shelburne, and Panton abutted on Champlain,
Plattsburgh, Willsborough, and Crown Point respectively. As revealed in the
table below each pair of abutting towns (Willsborough and Shelburne, for example)
reflected at this time essentially matching population figures. On this table
the series of question marks for the number of deeds and mortgages filed by
towns in New York result from the use of loose terminology for land locations
on the documents and from this state's practice of _county_ filing. In Vermont
where the land records have always been filed in the _town_ clerk's office there
is no problem in determining the community where a land parcel lies.

Since New York has always filed by counties the county of location of early-
day lands that have been filed can be readily determined. Between 1 January 1790
and 1 March 1799 the cumulative territory of the four New York towns of reference
above blanketed all of what was then Clinton County. Between the latter date
and 31 December 1800 this same territory covered all lands in Clinton and in
newly-formed Essex counties. Through these coincidences the final two summary
lines of the table below are posted devoid of question marks. In order to
obtain population figures as of 1800 for the territory originally covered by the
four New York towns of reference these adjustments had to be made:

For Champlain of 1790 – Champlain and Chateaugay, 1800
For Plattsburgh of 1790 – Plattsburgh and Peru, 1800
For Willsborough, 1790 – Willsborough and Jay, 1800
For Crown Point, 1790 – Crown Point and Elizabethtown, 1800.

A PAIRED-TOWN COMPARISON OF LAND RECORD FILINGS, NEW YORK VERSUS VERMONT, 1790–1800

Town and state	pop. 1790	pop. 1800	Increase in pop. 1790–1800	Number of deeds filed 1790–1800	Number of morts. filed 1790–1800	Number of deeds and morts. filed 1790–1800
Champlain, NY –	578	1612	1034	?	?	?
Alburgh, VT ---	446	750	304	185	24	209
Plattsburgh, NY	458	2747	2289	?	?	?
South Hero, VT-	537	678	141	734	2	736
Willsborough, NY	375	2317	1942	?	?	?
Shelburne, VT --	387	723	336	271	0	271
Crown Point, NY-	203	1840	1637	?	?	?
Panton, VT -----	220	363	143	254	0	254
FOUR TOWNS, NY –	1614	8516	6902	299	388	687
FOUR TOWNS, VT –	1590	2514	924	1444	26	1470

Cumulatively in 1790 the four towns of Vermont and the four towns of New
York had matching population totals (1590 versus 1614). Between 1790 and 1800
New York's towns of reference increased in population at a rate more than seven
times that of Vermont. Yet within this time span Vermont's clerks filed five
times as many deeds as did their counterparts in New York (Panton's records
unavailable, 1786–92). Reasons for this deed-related difference or for the
even sharper mortgage-related difference have not been here sought.

Deverick, Nicholas, 9
Ditmars, Johannes, 12
Dodd, Morris, 10
Dole, James, 8
Dougherty, Jeremiah, 8
Dougherty, John, 8
Duane, Cornelius, 6
Dubois, Peter, 6
Dunbar, George, 6
Duncan, James, 11
Duperoon, Philip, 6
Duwey, Ebenezer, 5
Duyckinck, Christopher, 12
Eaton, Thomas, 7
Ecuyer, Simeon, 7
Egberts, Thomas, 10
Elliot, Benjamin, 8
Elliott, Hamilton, 8
Ellsworth, Verdine, 6
Embury, Peter, 7
Embury, Philip, 7
Emott, James, 6
Euler, George, 9
Everitt, Thomas, 12
Faesch, George, 7
Fairchild, Jesse, 10
Fairlie, Joseph, 9
Farlow, Charles, 9
Feris, William, 12
Figg, Daniel, 9
Filer, Samuel, 5
Fink, Alexander, 9
Finney, John, 9
Fonda, Adam, 10
Fonda, Douwe, 10
Fonda, Jelles, 10
Fonda, John, 10 (2 refs.)
Fonda, Yelles, 10
Forbes, Alex, 12
Ford, Samuel, 9
Ford, Thomas, 8
Ford, William, 6
Forman, William, 6
Foster, Manuel, 8
Foy, John, 7
Frazier, Thomas, 8
Friend, William, 10
Friswell, John, 11 (2 refs.)
Frost, Thomas, 6
Gardiner, John, 10
Gardinier, Jacob, 10
Gardner, Jacob, 10
Garland, Peter, 9
Gelliet, John, 5
Gibson, Barne, 9
Gibson, James, 9
Gilbert, Samuel, 5
Gilbert, Samuel, Jr., 5
Gilbert, Thomas, 5
Gillaspie, Neil, 6
Gillespie, Thomas, 9
Gillilan, John, 10
Glazier, Beamsly, 6
Godwin, John, 6

Godwin, William, 6
Goelet, Peter, 12
Goldthwaite, Joseph, 11
Graham, Patrick, 9
Grant, James, 7
Grant, Robert, 11
Grant, William, 7
Graves, Jedediah, 8
Gulse, William, 11
Hales, George, 9
Hales, John, 9
Hall, Jacob, 8 (2 refs.)
Halling, John, 9
Hammersly, Thomas, 12
Hansen, Hendrick, 10
Hansen, Peter, N., 10
Hansen, Richard, 10
Hargrave, Robert, 12
Harris, Gerreych, 9
Hasborne, Thomas, 9
Haswell, Edward, 9
Hay, A. Hawkes, 12
Hess, Johannes, 6
Hickler, Philip, 7
Hicks, Whitehead, 6
Hitchcock, Isaac, 6
Hitchcock, John, 6
Hitchcock, Jonathan, 6
Hitchcock, William, 9
Hodge, John, 8
Hoffman, Valentine, 9
Holland, George, 9
Holland, Thomas, 12
Hooper, John, 8
Horsefield, Israel, 12
Hosford, Obadiah, 5
House, Eliphalet, 5
Howard, John, 8
Howell, Crismus, 7
Hughs, Peter, 8
Human, John, 9
Hun, William, 6
Hungerford, Samuel, 8
Hungerford, Thomas, 8
Hunter, David, 8 (2 refs.)
Hutchinson, Jonathan, 5
Ingham, Daniel, 5
Jackson, Hugh, 10
Jessup, Ebenezer, 8 (2 refs.), 10 (2 refs.)
Jessup, Edward, 8 (2 refs.), 10 (2 refs.)
Jessup, Joseph, Jr., 8 (2 refs.), 10
Johnson, David, 6
Johnson, William, 8 (2 refs.)
Jones, Benjamin, 12
Jones, Elias, 12
Jones, Ezekiel, 5
Jones, Joel, 5
Jones, Jonathan, 8 (2 refs.)
Jones, Samuel, 5, 6
Jones, Thomas, 6
Joyce, Edward, 12
Kane, John, 9
Keen, John, 10
Keffler, Francis, 12

Vander Heyden, Jacob, 5
Vanderveer, Cornelius, 12
Vanderveer, Jacobus, 12
Van Deusen, Matthew, 11
Van Dyck, Rudolphus, 12
Van Orden, Andrew, 11
Van Rensselaer, Henry K., 11
Van Rensselaer, Jeremiah, 11
Van Rensselaer, Philip, 11
Van Rensselaer, Stephen, 5
Van Veghten, Anthony, 11
Van Zandt, Tobias, 6
Veder, Abraham, 10
Veder, Volckert, 10
Voorhees, Adrian, 12
Voorhees, John, Jr., 11
Vredenburgh, John, 12
Vrooman, Hendrick, 10
Vrooman, Hendrick, Jr., 10
Vrooman, John Hendrick, 10
Waldron, Samuel, 12
Wallace, Robert, 11
Walton, Joseph, 7
Wanser, Abraham, 8
Wanser, Anthony, 8
Warner, John, 6
Warton, John, 11
Weathers, Richard, 10
Weaver, Daniel, 9
Webb, William, 6
Weeks, Jonathan, 8
Wells, Edmund, 5
Wells, Joseph, 5
Wells, Thomas, 5
Wells, William, 9
Wemp, Barent B., 10
Wemp, Hendrick, 10
White, Alexander, 6
White, Philip, 8
Widdershine, Daniel, 9
Wildman, Benjamin, 6
Williams, Charles, 5
Williamson, John, 7
Wilson, George, 7
Wilson, James, 7
Wilson, John, 7 (2 refs.)
Wilson, Samuel, 7
Wilson, William, 7
Winne, Levinius, 5
Winterton, William, 5
Wood, Timothy, 10, 11
Woods, John, 6
Wool, Jeremiah, 6
Woort, Cornelius Van Sante, 8
Wright, Abiel, 6
Wright, Ephraim, 5
Wright, Job, 10
Wright, Kent, 6
Yates, Robert, 11
Yeoman, Joseph, 9
Young, Moses, 9
Zimmerman, Henry, 9